Datsun 280ZX Automotive Repair Manual

Rik Paul
and John H Haynes Member of the Guild of Motoring Writers

Models covered:
1979 thru 1983
Datsun 280ZX; GL, Deluxe and Turbo models; 2-seater and 2 + 2,
with 2.8 liter in-line six-cylinder engine

ISBN 1 85010 124 8

ABCDE

Printed in England   *(4N2 — 563)*

Haynes Publishing Group
Sparkford Nr Yeovil
Somerset BA22 7JJ England

Haynes Publications, Inc
861 Lawrence Drive
Newbury Park
California 91320 USA

Acknowledgements

Thanks are due to the Nissan Motor Company for their assistance with technical information and supply of certain illustrations.

The Champion Spark Plug Company supplied the illustrations showing the various spark plug conditions. The bodywork repair photographs used in this manual were provided by Lloyd's Industries Limited who supply 'Turtle Wax', 'Dupli-Color Holts', and other Holts range products.

About this manual

Its purpose

The purpose of this manual is to help you get the best value from your vehicle. It can do so in several ways. It can help you decide what work must be done even if you choose to get it done by a dealer service department or a repair shop; it provides information and procedures for routine maintenance and servicing; and it offers diagnostic and repair procedures to follow when trouble occurs.

It is hoped that you will use the manual to tackle the work yourself. For many simpler jobs, doing it yourself may be quicker than arranging an appointment to get the vehicle into a shop and making the trips to leave it and pick it up. More importantly, a lot of money can be saved by avoiding the expense the shop must pass on to you to cover its labor and overhead costs. An added benefit is the sense of satisfaction and accomplishment that you feel after having done the job yourself.

Using the manual

The manual is divided into Chapters. Each Chapter is divided into numbered Sections, which are headed in bold type between horizontal lines. Each Section consists of consecutively numbered paragraphs.

The two types of illustrations used (figures and photographs) are referenced by a number preceding their captions. Figure reference numbers denote Chapter and numerical sequence in the Chapter; i.e. Fig. 12.4 means Chapter 12, figure number 4. Figure captions are followed by a Section number which ties the figure to a specific portion of the text. All photographs apply to the Chapter in which they appear, and the reference number pinpoints the pertinent Section and paragraph.

Procedures, once described in the text, are not normally repeated. When it is necessary to refer to another Chapter, the reference will be given as Chapter and Section number; i.e. Chapter 1/16. Cross references given without use of the word 'Chapter' apply to Sections and/or paragraphs in the same Chapter. For example, 'see Section 8' means in the same Chapter.

Reference to the left or right of the vehicle is based on the assumption that one is sitting in the driver's seat facing forward.

Even though extreme care has been taken during the preparation of this manual, neither the publisher nor the author can accept responsibility for any errors in, or omissions from, the information given.

Introduction to the Datsun 280ZX

The Datsun 280ZX was introduced in 1979, and is a highly redesigned, upgraded version of the popular Z series cars. While the Z cars were originally designed as sports cars, the ZX series is intended to fit a more luxurious grand touring image.

In 1981, a turbocharged version was released which uses an exhaust gas powered turbine to force more fuel/air mixture into the cylinders for additional power.

All ZX cars utilize an in-line, overhead-cam six-cylinder engine with a computer-controlled electronic fuel injection system, and are available with either a 5-speed manual transmission or a 3-speed automatic transmission. (1979 models are also available with a 4-speed manual transmission, while the 1981 Turbo ZX is only available with automatic transmission.)

Two body styles are available; the 2-seater version and the roomier, slightly longer 2 + 2 (4-seater) version. Either version can be obtained in the GL (Grand Luxury) styling/convenience package. Up to 1981, a more economical Deluxe package was also offered with the 2-seater version.

Further information on the 280ZX's various systems and components, as well as complete specifications, can be found in the appropriate individual Chapters.

Contents

Datsun 280ZX 2-seater GL

Datsun 280ZX Turbo
2+2 coupé

Buying parts and vehicle identification numbers

Buying spare parts

Spare parts are available from many sources, which generally fall into one of two categories – authorized dealer parts departments and independent retail auto parts stores. Our advice concerning spare parts is as follows:

Authorized dealer parts department: This is the best source for parts which are peculiar to your vehicle and not generally available elsewhere (i.e. major engine parts, transmission parts, trim pieces, etc). It is also the only place you should buy parts if your vehicle is still under warranty, as non-factory parts may invalidate the warranty. To be sure of obtaining the correct parts, have your vehicle's engine and chassis numbers available and, if possible, take the old parts along for positive identification.

Retail auto parts stores: Good auto parts stores will stock frequently needed components which wear out relatively fast (i.e.

clutch components, exhaust systems, brake parts, tune-up parts, etc). These stores often supply new or reconditioned parts on an exchange basis, which can save a considerable amount of money. Discount auto stores are often very good places to buy materials and parts needed for general vehicle maintenance (i.e. oil, grease, filters, spark plugs, belts, touch-up paint; bulbs. etc). They also usually sell tools and general accessories, have convenient hours, charge lower prices, and can often be found not far from your home.

Vehicle identification numbers

Regardless from which source parts are obtained, it is essential to provide correct information concerning the vehicle model and year of manufacture plus the engine serial number and the vehicle identification number (VIN). The accompanying illustrations show where these important numbers can be found.

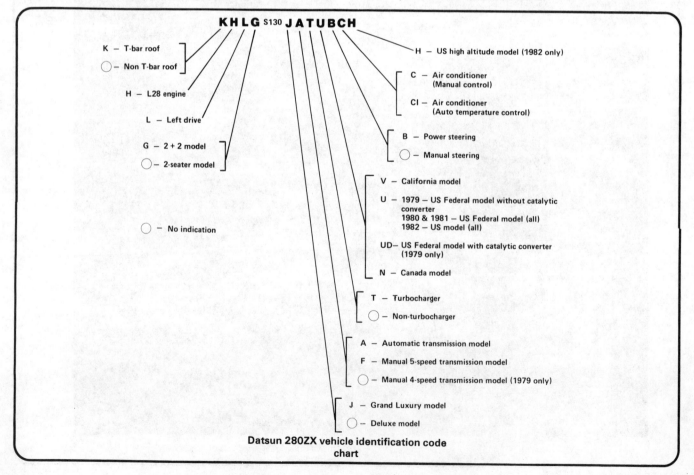

Datsun 280ZX vehicle identification code chart

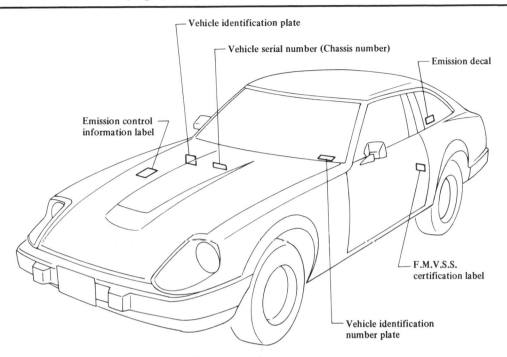

Locations of various information plates and labels on the 280ZX

Vehicle identification number (VIN):
    This very important identification number is located on a plate attached to the left top of the dashboard and can be easily seen while looking through the windshield from the outside of the car (photo). The VIN also appears on the Vehicle Certificate of Title and Registration. It gives such valuable information as where and when the vehicle was manufactured, the model year and the body style.

Vehicle identification plate:
    This plate, which is attached to the right side of the firewall in the engine compartment contains the car type, engine capacity, maximum horsepower, wheel-base, engine type and car chassis serial number.

Vehicle serial number:
    The vehicle chassis serial number, in addition to being found on the vehicle identification plate, is also stamped on the firewall adjacent to the identification plate.

Engine serial number:
    The engine serial number is stamped on the right side of the cylinder block, directly below the two middle spark plugs and above the engine oil dipstick.

Manual transmission serial number:
    The serial number for the manual transmission is stamped onto the top of the transmission's clutch housing.

Automatic transmission serial number:
    The serial number for the automatic transmission is located on the right side of the transmission case.

Color code label:
    A sticker with the color code of the car's paint is located on the top right side of the radiator support. This number is useful for matching the color and type of paint for repair work.

Emission control information label:
    This label is located on the right underside of the hood. Information contained on this label includes the types of emissions systems used on the car and basic tune-up specs.

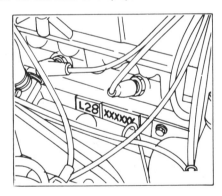

Location of the engine serial number

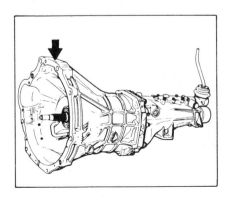

Location of manual transmission serial number (arrow)

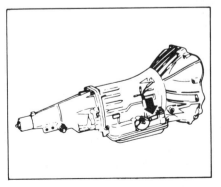

Location of the automatic transmission serial number (arrow)

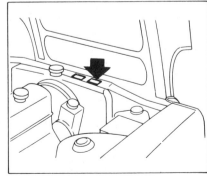

Location of the color code label on the radiator support (arrow)

Maintenance techniques, tools and working facilities

Basic maintenance techniques

There are a number of techniques involved in maintenance and repair that will be referred to throughout this manual. Application of these techniques will enable the home mechanic to be more efficient, better organized and capable of performing the various tasks properly, which will ensure that the repair job is thorough and complete.

Fasteners

Fasteners, basically, are nuts, bolts, studs and screws used to hold two or more parts together. There are a few things to keep in mind when working with fasteners. Almost all of them use a locking device of some type; either a lock washer, locknut, locking tab or thread adhesive. All threaded fasteners should be clean and straight, with undamaged threads and undamaged corners on the hex head where the wrench fits. Develop the habit of replacing damaged nuts and bolts with new ones. Special locknuts with nylon or fiber inserts can only be used once. If they are removed, they lose their locking ability and must be replaced with new ones.

Rusted nuts and bolts should be treated with a penetrating fluid to ease removal and prevent breakage. Some mechanics use turpentine in a spout-type oil can, which works quite well. After applying the rust penetrant, let it "work" for a few minutes before trying to loosen the nut or bolt. Badly rusted fasteners may have to be chiseled or sawed off or removed with a special nut breaker, available at tool stores.

If a bolt or stud breaks off in an assembly, it can be drilled and removed with a special tool commonly available for this purpose. Most automotive machine shops can perform this task, as well as other repair procedures (such as repair of threaded holes that have been stripped out).

Flat washers and lock washers, when removed from an assembly, should always be replaced exactly as removed. Replace damaged washers with new ones. Always use a flat washer between a lock washer and any soft metal surface (such as aluminum), thin sheet metal or plastic.

Fastener sizes

For a number of reasons, automobile manufacturers are making wider and wider use of metric fasteners. Therefore, it is important to be able to tell the difference between standard (sometimes called U.S., English or SAE) and metric hardware, since thay cannot be interchanged.

All bolts, whether standard or metric, are sized according to diameter, thread pitch and length. For example, a standard $\frac{1}{2}$ – 13 x 1 bolt is $\frac{1}{2}$ inch in diameter, has 13 threads per inch and is 1 inch long. An M12 – 1.75 x 25 metric bolt is 12 mm in diameter, has a thread pitch of 1.75 mm (the distance between threads) and is 25 mm long. The two bolts are nearly identical, and easily confused, but they are not interchangeable.

In addition to the differences in diameter, thread pitch and length, metric and standard bolts can also be distinguished by examining the bolt heads. To begin with, the distance across the flats on a standard bolt head is measured in inches, while the same dimension on a metric bolt is measured in millimeters (the same is true for nuts). As a result, a standard wrench should not be used on a metric bolt and a metric wrench should not be used on a standard bolt. Also, standard bolts have slashes radiating out from the center of the head to denote the grade or strength of the bolt (which is an indication of the amount of torque that can be applied to it). The greater the number of slashes, the greater the strength of the bolt (grades 0 through 5 are commonly used on automobiles). Metric bolts have a property class (grade) number, rather than a slash, molded into their heads to indicate bolt strength. In this case, the higher the number the stronger the bolt (property class numbers 8.8, 9.8 and 10.9 are commonly used on automobiles).

Strength markings can also be used to distinguish standard hex nuts from metric hex nuts. Standard nuts have dots stamped into one side, while metric nuts are marked with a number. The greater the number of dots, or the higher the number, the greater the strength of the nut.

Metric studs are also marked on their ends according to property class (grade). Larger studs are numbered (the same as metric bolts), while smaller studs carry a geometric code to denote grade.

It should be noted that many fasteners, especially Grades 0 through 2, have no distinguishing marks on them. When such is the case, the only way to determine whether it is standard or metric is to measure the thread pitch or compare it to a known fastener of the same size.

Since fasteners of the same size (both standard and metric) may have different strength ratings, be sure to reinstall any bolts, studs or nuts removed from your vehicle in their original locations. Also, when replacing a fastener with a new one, make sure that the new one has a strength rating equal to or greater than the original.

Tightening sequences and procedures

Most threaded fasteners should be tightened to a specific torque value (torque is basically a twisting force). Over-tightening the fastener can weaken it and lead to eventual breakage, while under-tightening can cause it to eventually come loose. Bolts, screws and studs, depending on the materials they are made of and their thread diameters, have specific torque values (many of which are noted in the Specifications Section at the beginning of each Chapter). Be sure to follow the torque recommendations closely. For fasteners not assigned a specific torque, a general torque value chart is presented here as a guide. As was previously mentioned, the size and grade of a fastener determine the amount of torque that can safely be applied to it. The figures listed here are approximate for Grade 2 and Grade 3 fasteners (higher grades can tolerate higher torque values).

Metric thread sizes

	ft-lb	Nm
M-6	6 to 9	9 to 12
M-8	14 to 21	19 to 28
M-10	28 to 40	38 to 54
M-12	50 to 71	68 to 96
M-14	80 to 140	109 to 154

Pipe thread sizes

	ft-lb	Nm
$\frac{1}{8}$	5 to 8	7 to 10
$\frac{1}{4}$	12 to 18	17 to 24
$\frac{3}{8}$	22 to 33	30 to 44
$\frac{1}{2}$	25 to 35	34 to 47

U.S. thread sizes

	ft-lb	Nm
$\frac{1}{4}$ - 20	6 to 9	9 to 12
$\frac{5}{16}$ - 18	12 to 18	17 to 24
$\frac{5}{16}$ - 24	14 to 20	19 to 27
$\frac{3}{8}$ - 16	22 to 32	30 to 43
$\frac{3}{8}$ - 24	27 to 38	37 to 51
$\frac{7}{16}$ - 14	40 to 55	55 to 74
$\frac{7}{16}$ - 20	40 to 60	55 to 81
$\frac{1}{2}$ - 13	55 to 80	75 to 108

Fasteners laid out in a pattern (i.e. cylinder head bolts, oil pan bolts, differential cover bolts, etc.) must be loosened and tightened in a definite sequence to avoid warping the component. Initially, the bolts or nuts should be assembled finger-tight only. Next, they should be tightened one full turn each, in a criss-cross or diagonal pattern. After each one has been tightened one full turn, return to the first one and tighten them all one half turn, following the same pattern. Finally, tighten each of them one-quarter turn at a time until they all have been tightened to the proper torque value. To loosen and remove them the procedure would be reversed.

Component disassembly

Component disassembly should be done with care and purpose to help ensure that the parts go back together properly. Always keep track of the sequence in which parts are removed. Make note of special characteristics or markings on parts that can be installed more than one way (such as a grooved thrust washer on a shaft). It is a good idea to lay the disassembled parts out on a clean surface in the order that they were removed. It may also be helpful to make simple sketches or take instant photos of components before removal.

When removing fasteners from an assembly, keep track of their locations. Sometimes threading a bolt back in a part, or putting the washers and nut back on a stud, can prevent mixups later. If nuts and bolts cannot be returned to their original locations, they should be kept in a compartment box or a series of small boxes. A cupcake or muffin tin is ideal for this purpose, since each cavity can hold the bolts and nuts from a particular area (i.e. oil pan bolts, valve cover bolts, engine mount bolts, etc.). A pan of this type is especially helpful when working on assemblies with very small parts (such as the carburetor, alternator, valve train or interior dash and trim pieces). The cavities can be marked with paint or tape to identify the contents.

Whenever wiring looms, harnesses or connectors are separated, it's a good idea to identify them with numbered pieces of masking tape so that they can be easily reconnected.

Gasket sealing surfaces

Throughout any vehicle, gaskets are used to seal the mating surfaces between two parts and keep lubricants, fluids, vacuum or pressure contained in an assembly.

Many times these gaskets are coated with a liquid or paste-type gasket sealing compound before assembly. Age, heat and pressure can sometimes cause the two parts to stick together so tightly that they are very difficult to separate. Often the assembly can be loosened by striking it with a soft-faced hammer near the mating surfaces. A regular hammer can be used if a block of wood is placed between the hammer and the part. Do not hammer on cast parts or parts that could be easily damaged. With any particularly stubborn part, always recheck to see that every fastener has been removed.

Avoid using a screwdriver or bar to pry apart an assembly, as they can easily mar the gasket sealing surfaces of the parts (which must remain smooth). If prying is absolutely necessary, use an old broom handle, but keep in mind that extra clean-up will be necessary if the wood splinters.

After the parts are separated, the old gasket must be carefully scraped off and the gasket surfaces cleaned. Stubborn gasket material can be soaked with rust penetrant or treated with a special chemical to soften it so that it can be easily scraped off. A scraper can be fashioned from a piece of copper tubing by flattening and sharpening one end. Copper is recommended because it is usually softer than the surfaces to be scraped, which reduces the chance of gouging the part. Some gaskets can be removed with a wire brush, but regardless of the method used, the 1 mating surfaces must be left clean and smooth. If for some reason the gasket surface is gouged, then a gasket sealer thick enough to fill scratches will have to be used upon reassembly of the components. For most applications, a non-drying (or semi-drying) gasket sealer should be used.

Hose removal tips

Caution: *If equipped with air conditioning, do not ever disconnect any of the a/c hoses without first de-pressurizing the system.*

Hose removal precautions closely parallel gasket removal precautions. Avoid scratching or gouging the surface that the hose mates against or the connection may leak. This is especially true for radiator hoses. Because of various chemical reactions, the rubber in hoses can bond itself to the metal spigot that the hose fits over. To remove a hose, first loosen the hose clamps that secure it to the spigot. Then, with slip joint pliers, grab the hose at the clamp and rotate it around the spigot. Work it back and forth until it is completely free, then pull it off (silicone or other lubricants will ease removal if they can be applied between the hose and the spigot). Apply the same lubricant to the inside of the hose and the outside of the spigot to simplify installation.

If a hose clamp is broken or damaged, do not re-use it. Do not re-use hoses that are cracked, split or torn.

Tools

A selection of good tools is a basic requirement for anyone who plans to maintain and repair his or her own vehicle. For the owner who has few tools, if any, the initial investment might seem high, but when compared to the spiraling costs of professional auto maintenance and repair, it is a wise one.

To help the owner decide which tools are needed to perform the tasks detailed in this manual, the following tool lists are offered: *Maintenance and minor repair, Repair and overhaul* and *Special*. The newcomer to practical mechanics should start off with the *Maintenance and minor repair* tool kit, which is adequate for the simpler jobs performed on a vehicle. Then, as his confidence and experience grow, he can tackle more difficult tasks, buying additional tools as they are needed. Eventually the basic kit will be expanded into the *Repair and overhaul* tool set. Over a period of time, the experienced do-it-yourselfer will assemble a tool set complete enough for most repair and overhaul procedures and will add tools from the *Special* category when he feels the expense is justified by the frequency of use.

Maintenance and minor repair tool kit

The tools in this list should be considered the minimum for performance of routine maintenance, servicing and minor repair work. We recommend the purchase of combination wrenches (box end and open end combined in one wrench); while more expensive than open-ended ones, they offer the advantages of both types of wrench.

Combination wrench set ($\frac{1}{4}$ in to 1 in or 6 mm to 19 mm)
Adjustable wrench – 8 in
Spark plug wrench (with rubber insert)
Spark plug gap adjusting tool
Feeler gauge set
Brake bleeder wrench
Standard screwdriver ($\frac{5}{16}$ in x 6 in)
Phillips screwdriver (No. 2 x 6 in)
Combination pliers – 6 in
Hacksaw and assortment of blades
Tire pressure gauge
Grease gun
Oil can
Fine emery cloth
Wire brush
Battery post and cable cleaning tool
Oil filter wrench
Funnel (medium size)
Safety goggles
Jackstands (2)
Drain pan

Note: If basic tune-ups are going to be a part of routine maintenance, it will be necessary to purchase a good quality stroboscopic timing light and a combination tachometer/dwell meter. Although they are included in the list of Special tools, they are mentioned here because they are absolutely necessary for tuning most vehicles properly.

Repair and overhaul tool set

These tools are essential for anyone who plans to perform major repairs and are in addition to those in the Maintenance and minor repair tool kit. Included is a comprehensive set of sockets which, though expensive, will be found invaluable because of their versatility (especially when various extensions and drives are available). We recommend the $\frac{1}{2}$ in drive over the $\frac{3}{8}$ in drive. Although the larger drive is bulky and more expensive, it has the capability of accepting a very wide range of large sockets (ideally, the mechanic would have a $\frac{3}{8}$ in drive set and a $\frac{1}{2}$ in drive set).

Socket set(s)
Reversible ratchet
Extension – 10 in
Universal joint
Torque wrench (same size drive as sockets)
Ball pein hammer – 8 oz
Soft-faced hammer (plastic/rubber)
Standard screwdriver ($\frac{1}{4}$ in x 6 in)
Standard screwdriver (stubby – $\frac{5}{16}$ in)
Phillips screwdriver (No. 3 x 8 in)
Phillips screwdriver (stubby – No. 2)

Pliers – vise grip
Pliers – lineman's
Pliers – needle nose
Pliers – snap-ring (internal and external)
Cold chisel – $\frac{1}{2}$ in
Scriber
Scraper (made from flattened copper tubing)
Center punch
Pin punches ($\frac{1}{16}$, $\frac{1}{8}$, $\frac{3}{16}$ in)
Steel rule/straight edge – 12 in
Allen wrench set ($\frac{1}{8}$ to $\frac{3}{8}$ in or 4 mm to 10 mm)
A selection of files
Wire brush (large)
Jackstands (second set)
Jack (scissor or hydraulic type)

Note: Another tool which is often useful is an electric drill motor with a chuck capacity of $\frac{3}{8}$ in (and a set of good quality drill bits).

Special tools

The tools in this list include those which are not used regularly, are expensive to buy, or which need to be used in accordance with their manufacturer's instructions. Unless these tools will be used frequently, it is not very economical to purchase many of them. A consideration would be to split the cost and use between yourself and a friend or friends. In addition, most of these tools can be obtained from a tool rental shop on a temporary basis.

This list contains only those tools and instruments widely available to the public, and not those special tools produced by vehicle manufacturers for distribution to dealer service departments. Occasionally, references to the manufacturer's special tools are included in the text of this manual. Generally, an alternative method of doing the job without the special tool is offered. However, sometimes there is no alternative to their use. Where this is the case, and the tool cannot be purchased or borrowed, the work should be turned over to the dealer, a repair shop or an automotive machine shop.

Valve spring compressor
Piston ring groove cleaning tool
Piston ring compressor
Piston ring installation tool
Cylinder compression gauge
Cylinder ridge reamer
Cylinder surfacing hone
Cylinder bore gauge
Micrometer(s) and/or dial calipers
Hydraulic lifter removal tool
Balljoint separator
Universal-type puller
Impact screwdriver
Dial indicator set
Stroboscopic timing light (inductive pickup)
Hand-operated vacuum/pressure pump
Tachometer/dwell meter
Universal electrical multi-meter
Cable hoist
Brake spring removal and installation tools
Floor jack

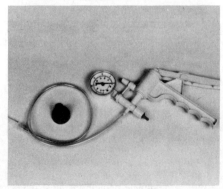

Vacuum tester

Dial gauge set

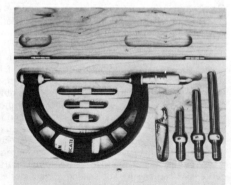

Micrometer set

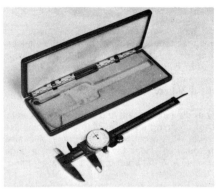

Dial caliper

Cylinder bore gauge

Piston ring compressor

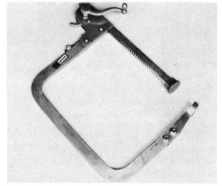

Valve spring compressor

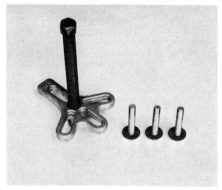

Universal hub puller

Piston ring groove cleaner

Cylinder ridge reamer

Piston ring expander

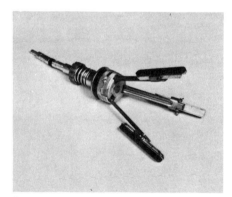

Cylinder surfacing hone

Buying tools

For the do-it-yourselfer who is just starting to get involved in vehicle maintenance and repair, there are a couple of options available when purchasing tools. If maintenance and minor repair is the extent of the work to be done, the purchase of individual tools is satisfactory. If, on the other hand, extensive work is planned, it would be a good idea to purchase a modest tool set from one of the large retail chain stores. A set can usually be bought at a substantial savings over the individual tool prices (and they often come with a tool box). As additional tools are needed, add-on sets, individual tools and a larger tool box can be purchased to expand the tool selection. Building a tool set gradually allows the cost of the tools to be spread over a longer period of time and gives the mechanic the freedom to choose only those tools that will actually be used.

Tool stores will often be the only source of some of the special tools that are needed, but regardless of where tools are bought, try to avoid cheap ones (especially when buying screwdrivers and sockets) because they won't last very long. The expense involved in replacing cheap tools will eventually be greater than the initial cost of quality tools.

Care and maintenance of tools

Good tools are expensive, so it makes sense to treat them with respect. Keep them in a clean and usable condition and store them properly when not in use. Always wipe off any dirt, grease or metal chips before putting them away. Never leave tools lying around in the work area. Upon completion of a job, always check closely under the hood for tools that may have been left there (so they don't get lost during a test drive).

Some tools, such as screwdrivers, pliers, wrenches and sockets, can be hung on a panel mounted on the garage or workshop wall, while others should be kept in a tool box or tray. Measuring instruments, gauges, meters, etc. must be carefully stored where they cannot be damaged by weather or impact from other tools.

When tools are used with care and stored properly, they will last a very long time. Even with the best of care, tools will wear out if used frequently. When a tool is damaged or worn out, replace it; subsequent jobs will be safer and more enjoyable if you do.

Working facilities

Not to be overlooked when discussing tools is the workshop. If anything more than routine maintenance is to be carried out, some sort of suitable work area is essential.

It is understood, and appreciated, that many home mechanics do not have a good workshop or garage available, and end up removing an engine or doing major repairs outside (it is recommended that the overhaul or repair be completed under the cover of a roof).

A clean, flat workbench or table of suitable working height is an absolute necessity. The workshop should be equipped with a vise that has a jaw opening of at least four inches.

As mentioned previously, some clean, dry storage space is also required for tools, as well as the lubricants, fluids, cleaning solvents, etc. which soon become necessary.

Sometimes waste oil and fluids, drained from the engine or transmission during normal maintenance or repairs, present a disposal problem. To avoid pouring oil on the ground or into the sewage system, simply pour the used fluids into large containers, seal them with caps and deliver them to a local recycling center or disposal facility. Plastic jugs (such as old anti-freeze containers) are ideal for this purpose.

Always keep a supply of old newspapers and clean rags available. Old towels are excellent for mopping up spills. Many mechanics use rolls of paper towels for most work because they are readily available and disposable. To keep the area under the vehicle clean, a large cardboard box can be cut open and flattened to protect the garage or shop floor.

Whenever working over a painted surface (such as when leaning over a fender to service something under the hood), always cover it with an old blanket or bedspread to protect the finish. Vinyl covered pads, made especially for this purpose, are available at auto parts stores.

Automotive chemicals and lubricants

A number of automotive chemicals and lubricants are available for use in vehicle maintenance and repair. They represent a wide variety of products ranging from cleaning solvents and degreasers to lubricants and protective sprays for rubber, plastic and vinyl.

Contact point/spark plug cleaner is a solvent used to clean oily film and dirt from points, grime from electrical connectors and oil deposits from spark plugs. It is oil free and leaves no residue. It can also be used to remove gum and varnish from carburetor jets and other orifices.

Carburetor cleaner is similar to contact point/spark plug cleaner but it is a stronger solvent and may leave a slight oily residue. It is not recommended for cleaning electrical components or connections.

Brake system cleaner is used to remove grease or brake fluid from brake system components (where clean surfaces are absolutely necessary and petroleum-based solvents cannot be used); it also leaves no residue.

Silicone based lubricants are used to protect rubber parts such as hoses, weatherstripping and grommets, and are used as lubricants for hinges and locks.

Multi-purpose grease is an all purpose lubricant used whenever grease is more practical than a liquid lubricant such as oil. Some multi-purpose grease is colored white and specially formulated to be more resistant to water than ordinary grease.

Bearing grease/wheel bearing grease is a heavy grease used where increased loads and friction are encountered (i.e. wheel bearings, universal joints, etc.).

High temperature wheel bearing grease is designed to withstand the extreme temperatures encountered by wheel bearings in disc brake equipped vehicles. It usually contains molybdenum disulfide, which is a 'dry' type lubricant.

Gear oil (sometimes called gear lube) is a specially designed oil used in differentials, manual transmissions and manual gearboxes, as well as other areas where high friction, high temperature lubrication is required. It is available in a number of viscosities (weights) for various applications.

Motor oil, of course, is the lubricant specially formulated for use in the engine. It normally contains a wide variety of additives to prevent corrosion and reduce foaming and wear. Motor oil comes in various weights (viscosity ratings) of from 5 to 80. The recommended weight of the oil depends on the seasonal temperature and the demands on the engine. Light oil is used in cold climates and under light load conditions; heavy oil is used in hot climates and where high loads are encountered. Multi-viscosity oils are designed to have characteristics of both light and heavy oils and are available in a number of weights from 5W-20 to 20W-50.

Oil additives range from viscosity index improvers to slick chemical treatments that purportedly reduce friction. It should be noted that most oil manufacturers caution against using additives with their oils.

Gas additives perform several functions, depending on their chemical makeup. They usually contain solvents that help dissolve gum and varnish that build up on carburetor and intake parts. They also serve to break down carbon deposits that form on the inside surfaces of the combustion chambers. Some additives contain upper cylinder lubricants for valves and piston rings.

Brake fluid is a specially formulated hydraulic fluid that can withstand the heat and pressure encountered in brake systems. Care must be taken that this fluid does not come in contact with painted surfaces or plastics. An opened container should always be resealed to prevent contamination by water or dirt.

Undercoating is a petroleum-based tar-like substance that is designed to protect metal surfaces on the under-side of a vehicle from corrosion. It also acts as a sound deadening agent by insulating the bottom of the vehicle.

Weatherstrip cement is used to bond weatherstripping around doors, windows and trunk lids. It is sometimes used to attach trim pieces as well.

Degreasers are heavy duty solvents used to remove grease and grime that accumulate on engine and chassis components. They can be sprayed or brushed on and, depending on the type, are rinsed with either water or solvent.

Solvents are used alone or in combination with degreasers to clean parts and assemblies during repair and overhaul. The home mechanic should use only solvents that are non-flammable and that do not produce irritating fumes.

Gasket sealing compounds may be used in conjunction with gaskets, to improve their sealing capabilities, or alone, to seal metal-to-metal joints. Many gasket sealers can withstand extreme heat, some are impervious to gasoline and lubricants, while others are capable of filling and sealing large cavities. Depending on the intended use, gasket sealers either dry hard or stay relatively soft and pliable. They are usually applied by hand, with a brush, or are sprayed on the gasket sealing surfaces.

Thread cement is an adhesive locking compound that prevents threaded fasteners from loosening because of vibration. It is available in a variety of types for different applications.

Moisture dispersants are usually sprays that can be used to dry out electrical components such as the distributor, fuse block and wiring connectors. Some types can also be used as treatment for rubber and as a lubricant for hinges, cables and locks.

Waxes and polishes are used to help protect painted and plated surfaces from the weather. Different types of paint may require the use of different types of wax or polish. Some polishes utilize a chemical or abrasive cleaner to help remove the top layer of oxidized (dull) paint in older vehicles. In recent years, many non-wax polishes (that contain a wide variety of chemicals such as polymers and silicones) have been introduced. These non-wax polishes are usually easier to apply and last longer than conventional waxes and polishes.

Jacking and towing

Jacking

The jack supplied with the car should be used only for changing a wheel due to a flat or for raising the car enough to allow jackstands to be placed under the car to support its weight. Under no circumstances should repair work be done under the car while it is supported by this jack, nor should the engine be started or run while this jack is being used.

The 280ZX comes equipped with a scissors-type jack, which is designed to lift one corner of the car by being used at the points shown in the accompanying illustration.

The car should be on level ground with the transmission in Park (automatic) or Reverse (manual). The parking brake should be firmly set. Blocking the front and rear of the wheel on the same side as the one being lifted will further prevent the car from rolling.

Remove the jack from the trunk and assemble it. Place the jack under the appropriate jacking point, turn it clockwise and slowly raise it so that it engages in the notch formed in the rocker panel. The base of the jack should still be sitting flat on the ground.

Operate the jack with a slow, smooth motion, and be attentive to any shifting in the weight of the car.

Raise the vehicle just enough so either the wheel and tire to be changed just clears the ground, or so jackstands can be placed into position under the car. If jackstands are being used, they should be placed under the body at the points shown in the accompanying figures. Then, rotate the jack lever counterclockwise to lower it until the weight of the car is off the jack. **Note:** *If both sides cannot be inserted at one time, place one into position and lower the car. The other corner of the car will have to be raised in order to insert the other stand.*

To remove the jackstands, the jack must be used once more to lift the vehicle so the stands can be removed from under the car. Then the car can be lowered to the ground and the jack removed.

When using a garage jack to lift one end of the car, it should be placed under the differential carrier in order to lift the rear, and under the front suspension crossmember to lift the front.

Towing

The car can be towed while rolling on its own wheels, providing that the transmission, axles, steering system and power train are in good condition. If any of these components are damaged, a dolly must be used.

Safety is a major consideration when towing, and all applicable state and local laws should be obeyed. A safety chain system must be used for all towing. (Conventional sling-type equipment is not recommended for towing from the front).

Towing equipment should be securely attached to the main structural members of the car and not to the bumper or brackets. Tow hooks are provided on both the front and rear of the car for this purpose. These can also be used in emergency situations, such as pulling the car from mud, snow, a ditch, etc. Do not apply force to these hooks in a sideward direction.

While towing, the parking brake should be fully released and the transmission should be in Neutral. The steering must be unlocked (ignition switch in the Off position). Remember that power steering and power brakes will not work with the engine off.

An automatic transmission model should not be towed with the front wheels raised at a speed greater than 20 mph (30 kph), or further than 20 miles (30 km). A manual transmission model can be towed at speeds up to 50 mph (80 kph) and a distance of 50 miles (80 km). If the speed or distance must be greater, then the driveshaft should be removed to prevent damage to the transmission.

When towing with the rear wheels raised, the steering wheel should be secured in the straight-ahead position with rope or other suitable means. Do not place the ignition switch in the Lock position, as this will damage the lock mechanism.

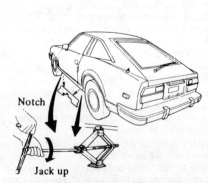

The scissors-type jack supplied with the 280ZX should be securely engaged in one of the rocker panel notches during use

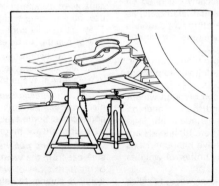

Correct positioning of jackstands for supporting the rear of the car

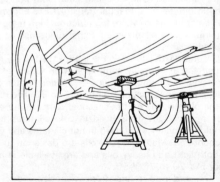

Correct positioning of jackstands for supporting the front of the car

Safety first!

Regardless of how enthusiastic you may be about getting on with the job at hand, take the time to ensure that your safety is not jeopardized. A moment's lack of attention can result in an accident, as can failure to observe certain simple safety precautions. The possibility of an accident will always exist, and the following points should not be considered a comprehensive list of all dangers. Rather, they are intended to make you aware of the risks and to encourage a safety conscious approach to all work you carry out on your vehicle.

Essential DOs and DON'Ts

DON'T rely on a jack when working under the vehicle. Always use approved jackstands to support the weight of the vehicle and place them under the recommended lift or support points.

DON'T attempt to loosen extremely tight fasteners (i.e. wheel lug nuts) while the vehicle is on a jack — it may fall.

DON'T start the engine without first making sure that the transmission is in Neutral (or Park where applicable) and the parking brake is set.

DON'T remove the radiator cap from a hot cooling system — let it cool or cover it with a cloth and release the pressure gradually.

DON'T attempt to drain the engine oil until you are sure it has cooled to the point that it will not burn you.

DON'T touch any part of the engine or exhaust system until it has cooled sufficiently to avoid burns.

DON'T siphon toxic liquids such as gasoline, antifreeze and brake fluid by mouth, or allow them to remain on your skin.

DON'T inhale brake lining dust — it is potentially hazardous (see *Asbestos* below)

DON'T allow spilled oil or grease to remain on the floor — wipe it up before someone slips on it.

DON'T use loose fitting wrenches or other tools which may slip and cause injury.

DON'T push on wrenches when loosening or tightening nuts or bolts. Always try to pull the wrench toward you. If the situation calls for pushing the wrench away, push with an open hand to avoid scraped knuckles if the wrench should slip.

DON'T attempt to lift a heavy component alone — get someone to help you.

DON'T rush or take unsafe shortcuts to finish a job.

DON'T allow children or animals in or around the vehicle while you are working on it.

DO wear eye protection when using power tools such as a drill, sander, bench grinder, etc. and when working under a vehicle.

DO keep loose clothing and long hair well out of the way of moving parts.

DO make sure that any hoist used has a safe working load rating adequate for the job.

DO get someone to check on you periodically when working alone on a vehicle.

DO carry out work in a logical sequence and make sure that everything is correctly assembled and tightened.

DO keep chemicals and fluids tightly capped and out of the reach of children and pets.

DO remember that your vehicle's safety affects that of yourself and others. If in doubt on any point, get professional advice.

Asbestos

Certain friction, insulating, sealing, and other products — such as brake linings, brake bands, clutch linings, torque converters, gaskets, etc. — contain asbestos. *Extreme care must be taken to avoid inhalation of dust from such products since it is hazardous to health.* If in doubt, assume that they *do* contain asbestos.

Fire

Remember at all times that gasoline is highly flammable. Never smoke or have any kind of open flame around when working on a vehicle. But the risk does not end there. A spark caused by an electrical short circuit, by two metal surfaces contacting each other, or even by static electricity built up in your body under certain conditions, can ignite gasoline vapors, which in a confined space are highly explosive. Do not, under any circumstances, use gasoline for cleaning parts. Use an approved safety solvent.

Always disconnect the battery ground (–) cable *at the battery* before working on any part of the fuel system or electrical system. Never risk spilling fuel on a hot engine or exhaust component.

It is strongly recommended that a fire extinguisher suitable for use on fuel and electrical fires be kept handy in the garage or workshop at all times. Never try to extinguish a fuel or electrical fire with water.

Fumes

Certain fumes are highly toxic and can quickly cause unconsciousness and even death if inhaled to any extent. Gasoline vapor falls into this category, as do the vapors from some cleaning solvents. Any draining or pouring of such volatile fluids should be done in a well ventilated area.

When using cleaning fluids and solvents, read the instructions on the container carefully. Never use materials from unmarked containers.

Never run the engine in an enclosed space, such as a garage. Exhaust fumes contain carbon monoxide, which is extremely poisonous. If you need to run the engine, always do so in the open air, or at least have the rear of the vehicle outside the work area.

If you are fortunate enough to have the use of an inspection pit, never drain or pour gasoline and never run the engine while the vehicle is over the pit. The fumes, being heavier than air, will concentrate in the pit with possibly lethal results.

The battery

Never create a spark or allow a bare light bulb near the battery. The battery normally gives off a certain amount of hydrogen gas, which is highly explosive.

Always disconnect the battery ground (–) cable *at the battery* before working on the fuel or electrical systems.

If possible, loosen the filler caps or cover when charging the battery from an external source. Do not charge at an excessive rate or the battery may burst.

Take care when adding water and when carrying a battery. The electrolyte, even when diluted, is very corrosive and should not be allowed to contact clothing or skin.

Always wear eye protection when cleaning the battery to prevent the caustic deposits from entering your eyes.

Household current

When using an electric power tool, inspection light, etc., which operates on household current, always make sure that the tool is correctly connected to its plug and that, where necessary, it is properly grounded. Do not use such items in damp conditions and, again, do not create a spark or apply excessive heat in the vicinity of fuel or fuel vapor.

Secondary ignition system voltage

A severe electric shock can result from touching certain parts of the ignition system (such as the spark plug wires) when the engine is running or being cranked, particularly if components are damp or the insulation is defective. In the case of an electronic ignition system, the secondary system voltage is much higher and could prove fatal.

Troubleshooting

Contents

This section provides an easy-reference guide to the more common faults which may occur during the operation of your Datsun. These faults and their probable causes are grouped under their respective systems e.g. Engine, Cooling System, etc., and also refer to the Chapter and/or Section which deals with the problem.

Remember that successful troubleshooting is not a mysterious 'black art' practiced only by professional mechanics, it's simply the result of a bit of knowledge combined with an intelligent, systematic approach to the problem. Always work by a process of elimination starting with the simplest solution and working through to the most complex — and never overlook the obvious. Even the most thorough and organized motorists have been known to forget to fill the gas tank or have left the car lights on overnight, so don't assume that you are above such oversights.

Finally, always get clear in your mind why a fault has occurred and take steps to ensure that it doesn't happen again. If the electrical system fails owing to a poor connection, check all other connections in the system to make sure that they don't fail as well; if a particular fuse continues to blow, find out why — don't just go on replacing fuses. Remember, failure of a small component can often be indicative of potential failure or incorrect functioning of a more important component or system.

Engine and performance

1   Engine will not rotate when attempting to start

1   Battery terminal connections loose or corroded. Check the cable terminals at the battery; tighten or clean corrosion as necessary.
2   Battery discharged or faulty. If the cable connectors are clean and tight on the battery posts, turn the key to the On position and switch on the headlights and/or windshield wipers. If these fail to function, the battery is discharged.
3   Automatic transmission not fully engaged in Park (P) or Neutral (N).
4   Broken, loose or disconnected wiring in the starting circuit. Inspect all wiring and connectors at the battery, starter solenoid and ignition switch (on steering column).
5   Starter motor pinion jammed on flywheel ring gear. If manual transmission, place gearshift in gear and rock the car to manually turn the engine. Remove starter (Chapter 5) and inspect pinion and flywheel (Chapter 2) at earliest convenience.
6   Starter solenoid faulty (Chapter 5).
7   Starter motor faulty (Chapter 5).
8   Ignition switch faulty (Chapter 10).

2   Engine rotates but will not start

1   Fuel tank empty.
2   Battery discharged (engine rotates slowly). Check the operation of electrical components as described in previous Section.
3   Battery terminal connections loose or corroded. See previous Section.
4   Fuel not reaching injectors. Check for clogged fuel filter or lines, or defective fuel pump. Also make sure the tank vent lines are not clogged. (Chapter 4).
5   EFI or ECCS system not operating properly. Check the relay, control unit, exhaust gas sensor and wiring harness for loose connections or damage (Chapter 4).
6   Faulty distributor components. Check the cap and rotor (Chapter 1.
7   Low cylinder compression (test compression as described in Chapter 1).
8   Valve clearances not properly adjusted (Chapter 1).
9   Water in fuel. Drain and fill with new fuel.
10   Defective cylinder head temperature sensor (Chapter 4).
11   Air leak. Check intake manifold, engine oil dipstick, oil cap, PCV valve and air flow meter hoses.
12   Excessive moisture on, or damage to ignition components (Chapter 5).
13   Worn, faulty or incorrectly adjusted spark plugs (Chapter 1).

14   Broken, loose or disconnected wiring in the starting circuit (see previous Section).
15   Distributor loose, thus changing ignition timing. Turn the distributor body as necessary to start the engine, then set ignition timing as soon as possible (Chapter 1).
16   Broken, loose or disconnected wires at the ignition coil, or faulty coil (Chapter 5).

3   Starter motor operates without rotating engine

1   Starter pinion sticking. Remove the starter (Chapter 5) and inspect.
2   Starter pinion or engine flywheel teeth worn or broken. Remove the inspection cover on the left side of the engine and inspect.

4   Engine hard to start when cold

1   Battery discharged or low. Check as described in Section 1.
2   Fuel not reaching the injector system. Check the fuel filter, lines and fuel pump (Chapter 4).
3   Faulty EFI or ECCS system (Chapter 4).

5   Engine hard to start when hot

1   Air filter in need of replacement.
2   Fuel not reaching EFI or ECCS system (see Section 4). Check particularly for a vapor lock situation, brought about by clogged fuel tank vent lines.

6   Starter motor noisy or excessively rough in engagement

1   Pinion or flywheel gear teeth worn or broken. Remove the inspection cover on the left side of the engine and inspect.
2   Starter motor retaining bolts loose or missing.

7   Engine starts but stops immediately

1   Loose or faulty electrical connections at distributor, coil or generator.
2   Vacuum leak at the gasket surfaces of the intake manifold. Check that all mounting bolts are tightened to specifications and all vacuum hoses connected to the manifold are positioned properly and are in good condition.
3   Fuel not reaching injectors (see Section 4).
4   EFI or ECCS system not working properly. Check the relay, control unit, injectors and air regulator (Chapter 4).

8   Engine 'lopes' while idling or idles erratically

1   Vacuum leakage. Check mounting bolts at the intake manifold for tightness. Check that all vacuum hoses are connected and are in good condition. Use a stethoscope or a length of fuel line hose held against your ear to listen for vacuum leaks while the engine is running. A hissing sound will be heard. A soapy water solution will also detect leaks. Check the intake manifold gasket surfaces.
2   Leaking EGR valve or plugged PCV valve (see Chapter 6).
3   Air cleaner clogged and in need of replacement (Chapter 1).
4   Fuel pump not delivering sufficient fuel (Section 4).
5   Leaking head gasket. If this is suspected, perform a cylinder compression check (Chapter 1).
6   Timing chain or gears worn and in need of renewal (Chapter 2).
7   Camshaft lobes worn, necessitating the removal of the camshaft for inspection (Chapter 2).
8   Valve clearances out of adjustment (Chapter 1).
9   Ignition timing out of adjustment (Chapter 1).
10   Ignition system not operating properly (Chapter 5).
11   EFI or ECCS system not operating properly (Chapter 4).
12   Damaged exhaust gas sensor (Chapter 1).

9 Engine misses at idle speed

1   Spark plugs faulty or not gapped properly (Chapter 1).
2   Faulty spark plug wires (Chapter 1).
3   Excessive moisture and/or damage on distributor components (Chapter 1).
4   Shorts in ignition, coil or spark plug wires.
5   Sticking or faulty emissions systems (see Chapter 6).
6   Clogged fuel filter and/or foreign matter in fuel. Remove the fuel filter (Chapter 1) and inspect.
7   Vacuum leaks at intake manifold or at hose connections. Check as described in Section 8.
8   Incorrect idle speed (Chapter 1) or idle mixture (Chapter 4).
9   Incorrect ignition timing (Chapter 1).
10 Uneven or low cylinder compression. Remove plugs and use compression tester as per manufacturer's instructions (Chapter 1).

10 Excessively high idle speed

1   Defective air regulator (Chapter 4).
2   Throttle valve opened excessively at idle (Chapter 4).
3   Idle speed incorrectly adjusted (Chapter 1).
4   Defective Vacuum Control Valve (VCV) (Chapter 6).
5   Valve clearances incorrectly adjusted (Chapter 1).

11 Battery will not hold a charge

1   Alternator drivebelt defective or not adjusted properly (Chapter 1).
2   Battery terminals loose or corroded (Chapter 1).
3   Alternator not charging properly (Chapter 5).
4   Loose, broken or faulty wiring in the charging circuit (Chapter 5).
5   Short in vehicle circuitry causing a continual drain on battery (Chapter 10).
6   Battery defective internally.
7   Faulty regulator (Chapter 5).

12 Ignition light fails to go out

1   Fault in alternator or charging circuit (Chapter 5).
2   Alternator drivebelt defective or not properly adjusted (Chapter 1).

13 Ignition light fails to come on when key is turned

1   Ignition light bulb faulty (Chapter 10).
2   Alternator faulty (Chapter 5).
3   Fault in the printed circuit, dash wiring or bulb holder (Chapter 10).

14 Engine misses throughout driving speed range

1   Fuel filter clogged and/or impurities in the fuel system. Check fuel filter (Chapter 1) or clean system (Chapter 4).
2   Faulty or incorrectly gapped spark plugs (Chapter 1).
3   Incorrectly set ignition timing (Chapter 1).
4   Cracked distributor cap, disconnected distributor wires, or damage to the distributor components (Chapter 1).
5   Leaking spark plug wires (Chapter 1).
6   Emissions system components faulty (Chapter 6).
7   Low or uneven cylinder compression pressures. Remove spark plugs and test compression with gauge (Chapter 1).
8   Weak or faulty ignition coil (Chapter 5).
9   Weak or faulty ignition system (Chapter 5).
10 Vacuum leaks at intake manifold or vacuum hoses (see Section 8).
11 Loose EFI or ECCS harness connections (Chapter 4).
12 Leaky EGR valve (Chapter 6).
13 Defective EFI or ECCS control unit (Chapter 4).

15 Hesitation or stumble on acceleration

1   Ignition timing incorrectly set (Chapter 1).

2   Ignition system not operating properly (Chapter 5).
3   Air flow meter not operating properly. Check for smooth movement of the flap (Chapter 4).
4   Intake air leakage. Check at the PCV valve, VC valve, engine oil dipstick, oil cap, intake manifold and air flow meter hoses (refer to Section 8).
5   Mixture ratio feedback system not operating properly (Chapter 6).
6   Low fuel pressure. Check for proper operation of the fuel pump, and for blockage in the fuel filter and lines (Chapter 4).
7   EFI or ECCS system not operating correctly (Chapter 4).

16 Engine stalls

1   Idle speed incorrectly set (Chapter 1).
2   Fuel filter clogged and/or water and impurities in the fuel system (Chapter 1).
3   EFI or ECCS system not operating properly (Chapter 4).
4   Distributor components damp, or damage to distributor cap, rotor etc. (Chapter 1).
5   Emissions system components faulty (Chapter 6).
6   Faulty or incorrectly gapped spark plugs. (Chapter 1). Also check spark plug wires (Chapter 1).
7   Vacuum leak at the intake manifold or vacuum hoses. Check as described in Section 8.
8   Valve lash incorrectly set (Chapter 1).
9   Defective exhaust gas sensor (Chapter 1).

17 Engine lacks power

1   Incorrect ignition timing (Chapter 1).
2   Excessive play in distributor shaft. At the same time check for faulty distributor cap, wires, etc. (Chapter 1).
3   Faulty or incorrectly gapped spark plugs (Chapter 1).
4   Air cleaner needs replacing (Chapter 1).
5   Weak coil or condensor (Chapter 5).
6   Faulty coil (Chapter 5).
7   Brakes binding (Chapters 1 and 9).
8   Automatic transmission fluid level incorrect, causing slippage (Chapter 1).
9   Manual transmission clutch slipping (Chapter 8).
10 Fuel filter clogged and/or impurities in the fuel system (Chapters 1 and 4).
11 EGR system not functioning properly (Chapter 6).
12 Use of sub-standard fuel. Fill tank with proper octane fuel.
13 Low or uneven cylinder compression pressures. Test with compression tester, which will also detect leaking valves and/or blown head gasket (Chapter 1).
14 EFI or ECCS system not operating properly. Check for seized injector, loose harness connectors, defective throttle valve switch, defective air flow meter, or if the throttle valve is not opening all the way (Chapter 4).
15 Intake air leak. Check around the intake manifold, the engine oil dipstick, oil cap, air intake air flow meter hoses, and PCV valve (refer to Section 8).

18 Engine backfires

1   EGR system not functioning properly (Chapter 6).
2   Ignition timing incorrect (Chapter 1).
3   EFI or ECCS system not operating properly (Chapter 4).
4   Mixture ratio feedback system not operating properly (Chapter 6).
5   Vacuum leak (refer to Section 8).
6   Valve clearances not correctly adjusted (Chapter 1).
7   Damaged valve springs or sticking valves (Chapter 2).
8   Intake air leak (see Section 15).

19 Engine surges while holding accelerator steady

1   Air flow meter not functioning properly. Check for smooth movement of the flap (Chapter 4).
2   Intake air leak (see previous Section).
3   Fuel pump not working properly (Chapter 4).

4   Mixture ratio feedback system not operating properly (Chapter 6).
5   EFI or ECCS system not operating properly (Chapter 4).

20 Pinging or knocking engine sounds on hard acceleration or uphill

1   Incorrect grade of fuel. Fill tank with fuel of the proper octane rating.
2   Ignition timing incorrect (Chapter 1).
3   Carbon build-up in combustion chambers. Remove cylinder head and have chambers cleaned (Chapter 2).
4   Improper spark plugs (Chapter 1).

21 Engine diesels (continues to run) after switching off

1   Idle speed too fast (Chapter 1).
2   Ignition timing incorrectly adjusted (Chapter 1).
3   Incorrect heat range of spark plugs (Chapter 1).
4   Intake air leak (see Section 15).
5   Carbon build-up in combustion chamber. Remove the cylinder head and have chambers cleaned (Chapter 2).
6   Valves sticking (Chapter 2).
7   Damaged cylinder head temperature sensor (Chapter 4).
8   Valve clearance incorrectly adjusted (Chapter 1).
9   EGR system not operating properly (Chapter 6).
10 EFI system not operating properly. Check the control unit, the air flow meter and for loose harness connections (Chapter 4).
11 Check for causes of overheating (Section 27).

22 Low oil pressure

1   Improper grade of oil.
2   Oil pump regulator valve not operating properly (Chapter 2).
3   Oil pump worn or damaged (Chapter 2).
4   Engine overheating (refer to Section 28).
5   Clogged oil filter (Chapter 1).
6   Clogged oil strainer (Chapter 2).
7   Oil pressure gauge not working properly (Chapter 2).

23 Excessive oil consumption

1   Loose oil drain plug.
2   Loose or damaged oil pan gasket (Chapter 2).
3   Loose or damaged timing chain cover gasket (Chapter 2).
4   Front or rear crankshaft oil seal leaking (Chapter 2).
5   Loose or damaged rocker cover gasket (Chapter 2).
6   Oil filter not tightened all the way (Chapter 1).
7   Loose or damaged oil pressure switch (Chapter 2).
8   Pistons and cylinders excessively worn (Chapter 2).
9   Pistons rings not positioned correctly on pistons (Chapter 2).
10 Worn or damaged piston rings (Chapter 2).
11 Intake and/or exhaust valve oil seals in need of replacement (Chapter 2).
12 Worn valve stems. Valves in need of replacement (Chapter 2).

24 Excessive fuel consumption (see also insufficient power)

1   Dirty or clogged air filter element (Chapter 1).
2   Incorrectly set ignition timing (Chapter 1).
3   Incorrectly set idle speed (Chapter 1).
4   Low tire pressure or incorrect tire size (Chapter 11).
5   Fuel leakage. Check all connections, lines and components in the fuel system (Chapter 4).
6   EFI or ECCS system not operating properly (Chapter 4).

25 Fuel odor

1   Fuel leakage. Check all connections, lines and components of the fuel system (Chapter 4).
2   Fuel tank overfilled. Fill only to automatic shut-off.

3   Charcoal canister filter in Evaporative Emissions Control system in need of replacement (Chapter 6).
4   Vapor leaks from Evaporative Emissions Control system lines (Chapter 6).

26 Miscellaneous engine noises

1   *A strong dull noise that becomes more rapid as the engine accelerates* indicates worn or damaged crankshaft bearings or an unevenly worn crankshaft. To pinpoint the troublespot, remove the spark plug wire from one plug at a time and crank the engine over. If the noise stops, the cylinder with the removed plug wire indicates the problem area. Replace the bearing and/or service or replace the crankshaft (Chapter 2).
2   *A similar (yet slightly higher pitched) noise* to the crankshaft knocking described in the previous paragraph, that becomes more rapid as the engine accelerates, indicates worn or damaged connecting rod bearings (Chapter 2). The procedure for locating the problem cylinder is the same as described in paragraph 1.
3   *An overlapping metallic noise that increases in intensity as the engine speed increases, yet diminishes as the engine warms up* indicates abnormal piston and cylinder wear (Chapter 2). To locate the problem cylinder, use the procedure described in paragraph 1.
4   *A rapid clicking noise that becomes faster as the engine accelerates* indicates a worn piston pin or piston pin hole. This sound will happen each time the piston hits the highest and lowest points of its stroke (Chapter 2). The procedure for locating the problem piston is described in paragraph 1.
5   *A metallic noise coming from the water pump* indicates worn or damaged water pump bearings or pump. Replace the water pump with a new one (Chapter 3).
6   *A rapid tapping sound or clicking sound that becomes faster as the engine speed increases* indicates "valve tapping" or improperly adjusted valve clearances. This can be identified by holding one end of a plastic hose to your ear and placing the other end at different spots along the length of the rocker cover. The point where the sound is loudest indicates the problem valve. Adjust the valve clearance (Chapter 1).
7   *A steady metallic rattling or rapping sound coming from the area of the timing chain cover* indicates a worn, damaged or out-of-adjustment timing chain. Service or replace the chain and related components (Chapter 2).

Engine cooling system

27 Overheating

1   Insufficient coolant in system (Chapter 1).
2   Fan belt defective or not adjusted properly (Chapter 1).
3   Radiator core blocked or radiator grille dirty and restricted (Chapter 3).
4   Thermostat faulty (Chapter 3).
5   Fan not functioning properly (Chapter 3).
6   Radiator cap not maintaining proper pressure. Have cap pressure tested by gas station or repair shop.
7   Ignition timing incorrect (Chapter 1).
8   Defective water pump (Chapter 3).
9   Improper grade of engine oil.
10 Inaccurate temperature gauge (Chapter 10).

28 Overcooling

1   Thermostat faulty (Chapter 3).
2   Inaccurate temperature gauge (Chapter 10).

29 External coolant leakage

1   Deteriorated or damaged hoses. Loose clamps at hose connections (Chapter 1).
2   Water pump seals defective. If this is the case, water will drip from the 'weep' hole in the water pump body (Chapter 3).
3   Leakage from radiator core or header tank. This will require the

radiator to be professionally repaired (see Chapter 3 for removal procedures).
4   Engine drain plugs or water jacket freeze plugs leaking (see Chapters 1 and 2).
5   Leak from water temperature gauge connections (Chapter 2).
6   Leak from damaged gaskets or small cracks (Chapter 2).
7   Damaged head gasket. This can be verified by checking the condition of the engine oil as noted in Section 30.

30 Internal coolant leakage

Note: *Internal coolant leaks can usually be detected by examining the oil. Check the dipstick and inside of valve cover for water deposits and an oil consistency like that of a milkshake.*
1   Faulty cylinder head gasket. Have the system pressure-tested professionally or remove the cylinder head (Chapter 2) and inspect.
2   Cracked cylinder bore or cylinder head. Dismantle engine and inspect (Chapter 2).
3   Loose cylinder head bolts (tighten as described in Chapter 2).

31 Abnormal loss

1   Overfilling system (Chapter 1).
2   Coolant boiling away due to overheating (see causes in Section 15).
3   Internal or external leakage (see Sections 22 and 23).
4   Faulty radiator cap. Have the cap pressure-tested.

32 Poor coolant circulation

1   Inoperative water pump. A quick test is to pinch the top radiator hose closed with your hand while the engine is idling, then let loose. You should feel a surge of coolant if the pump is working properly (Chapter 3).
2   Restriction in cooling system. Drain, flush and refill the system (Chapter 1). If it appears necessary, remove the radiator (Chapter 3) and have it reverse-flushed or professionally cleaned.
3   Loose water pump drivebelt (Chapter 3).
4   Thermostat sticking (Chapter 3).
5   Insufficient coolant (Chapter 1).

33 Corrosion

1   Excessive impurities in the water. Soft, clean water is recommended. Distilled or rainwater is satisfactory.
2   Insufficient antifreeze solution. (Refer to Chapter 1 or 3 for the proper ratio of water to antifreeze).
3   Infrequent flushing and draining of system. Regular flushing of the cooling system should be carried out at the specified intervals as described in *Routine maintenance schedule (Chapter 1)*.

Clutch
Note: *All service information on the clutch is contained in Chapter 8, unless otherwise noted.*

34 Fails to release (pedal pressed to the floor – shift lever does not move freely in and out of Reverse)

1   Clutch face wet with oil. Remove clutch disc and inspect.
2   Clutch disc warped, bent or excessively damaged.
3   Diaphragm spring fatigued. Remove clutch cover/pressure plate assembly and inspect.
4   Leakage of fluid from clutch hydraulic system. Inspect master cylinder, operating cylinder and connecting lines.
5   Air in clutch hydraulic system. Bleed the system.
6   Insufficient pedal stroke. Check and adjust as necessary.
7   Piston cup in operating cylinder deformed or damaged.
8   Lack of grease on pilot bushing.

35 Clutch slips (engine speed increases with no increase in road speed)

1   Worn or oil soaked clutch disc facing.
2   Clutch disc not seated in. It may take 30 or 40 normal starts for a new disc to seat.
3   Diaphragm spring weak or damaged. Remove clutch cover/pressure plate assembly and inspect.
4   Flywheel warped (Chapter 2).
5   Debris in master cylinder preventing the piston from returning to its normal position.
6   Clutch hydraulic line damaged.

36 Grabbing (chattering) on take-up

1   Oil on clutch disc facings. Remove disc and inspect. Correct any leakage source.
2   Worn or loose engine or transmission mounts. These units may move slightly when clutch is released. Inspect mounts and bolts.
3   Worn splines on clutch gear. Remove clutch components and inspect.
4   Warped pressure plate or flywheel. Remove clutch components and inspect.
5   Diaphragm spring fatigued. Remove clutch cover/pressure plate assembly and inspect.
6   Clutch disc facing hardened or warped.
7   Clutch disc rivets loose.

37 Squeal or rumble with clutch fully engaged (pedal released)

1   Improper pedal adjustment. Adjust pedal free play.
2   Release bearing binding on transmission bearing retainer. Remove clutch components and check bearing. Remove any burrs or nicks, clean and relubricate before reinstallation.
3   Pilot bushing worn or damaged.
4   Clutch disc rivets loose.
5   Clutch disc cracked.
6   Fatigued clutch disc torsion springs. Replace clutch disc.

38 Squeal or rumble with clutch fully disengaged (pedal depressed)

1   Worn, faulty or broken release bearing.
2   Worn or broken pressure plate diaphragm finger.

39 Clutch pedal stays on floor when disengaged

1   Bind in linkage or release bearing. Inspect linkage or remove clutch components as necessary.
2   Linkage springs being over-extended. Adjust linkage for proper lash. Make sure proper pedal stop (bumper) is installed.

Manual transmission
Note: *All service information on the manual transmission is contained within Chapter 7, unless otherwise noted.*

40 Noisy in Neutral with engine running

1   Input shaft bearing worn.
2   Damaged main drive gear bearing.
3   Insufficient transmission oil (Chapter 1).
4   Transmission oil in poor condition. Drain and fill with proper grade oil. Check old oil for water or debris (Chapter 1).
5   Noise can be caused by variations in engine torque. Change the idle speed and see if noise disappears.

41 Noisy in all gears

1 Either of the above causes, and/or:
2 Worn or damaged output gear bearings or shaft.

42 Noisy in one particular gear

1 Worn, damaged or chipped gear teeth for that particular gear.
2 Worn or damaged synchronizer for that particular gear.

43 Slips out of gear

1 Transmission loose on clutch housing.
2 Stiff shift lever seal.
3 Shift linkage binding.
4 Broken or loose input gear bearing retainer.
5 Dirt between clutch lever and engine housing.
6 Worn linkage.
7 Damaged or worn check balls, fork rod ball grooves or check springs.
8 Worn mainshaft or countershaft bearings.
9 Loose engine mounts (Chapter 2).
10 Excessive gear end play.
11 Wear in synchronizer units.

44 Fluid leakage

1 Excessive amount of lubricant in transmission (see Chapter 1 for correct checking procedures). Drain lubricant as required.
2 Side cover loose or gasket damaged.
3 Rear oil seal or speedometer oil seal in need of replacement.
4 To pinpoint a leak, first remove all built-up dirt and grime from around the transmission. Degreasing agents and/or steam cleaning will achieve this. With the underside clean, drive the car at low speeds so the air flow will not blow the leak far from its source. Raise the car and determine where the leak is coming from.

45 Difficulty in engaging gears

1 Clutch not releasing fully.
2 Loose or damaged shift linkage. Make a thorough inspection, replacing parts as necessary.
3 Insufficient transmission oil (Chapter 1).
4 Transmission oil in poor condition. Drain and fill with proper grade of oil. Check oil for water or debris (Chapter 1).
5 Worn or damaged striking rod.
6 Sticking or jamming gears.

46 Noise occurs while shifting gears

1 Check for proper operation of the clutch (Chapter 8).
2 Faulty synchromesh assemblies. Measure baulk ring-to-gear clearance. Also, check for wear or damage to baulk rings or any parts of the synchromesh assemblies.

Automatic transmission

Note: *Due to the complexity of the automatic transmission, it is difficult for the home mechanic to properly diagnose and service this component. For problems other than the following, the vehicle should be taken to a reputable mechanic.*

47 Fluid leakage

1 Automatic transmission fluid is a deep red color, and fluid leaks should not be confused with engine oil which can easily be blown by air flow to the transmission.
2 To pinpoint a leak, first remove all built-up dirt and grime from around the transmission. Degreasing agents and/or steam cleaning

will achieve this. With the underside clean, drive the car at low speeds so the air flow will not blow the leak from its source. Raise the car and determine where the leak is coming from. Common areas of leakage are:
   a)   Fluid pan: tighten mounting bolts and/or replace pan gasket as necessary (Chapter 1).
   b)   Rear extension: tighten bolts and/or replace oil seal as necessary (Chapter 8).
   c)   Filler pipe: replace the rubber oil seal where pipe enters transmission case.
   d)   Transmission oil lines: tighten connectors where lines enter transmission case and/or replace lines.
   e)   Vent pipe: transmission over-filled and/or water in fluid (see checking procedures, Chapter 1).
   f)   Speedometer connector: replace the O-ring where speedometer cable enters transmission case.

48 General shift mechanism problems

1 Section 2 in Chapter 7 deals with checking and adjusting the shift linkage on automatic transmissions. Common problems which may be attributed to maladjusted linkage are:
   a)   Engine starting in gears other than P (Park) or N (Neutral).
   b)   Indicator on quadrant pointing to a gear other than the one actually being used.
   c)   Vehicle will not hold firm when in P (Park) position.

49 Transmission will not downshift with accelerator pedal pressed to the floor

Section 4 in Chapter 7 deals with adjusting the kickdown switch to enable the transmission to downshift properly.

50 Engine will start in gears other than P (Park) or N (Neutral)

Section 3 in Chapter 7 deals with adjusting the neutral start switch used with automatic transmissions.

51 Transmission slips, shifts rough, is noisy or has no drive in forward or reverse gears

1 There are many probable causes for the above problems, but the home mechanic should concern himself only with one possibility; fluid level.
2 Before taking the vehicle to a specialist, check the level and condition of the fluid as described in Chapter 1. Correct fluid level as necessary or change the fluid and filter if needed. If problem persists, have a professional diagnose the probable cause.

Driveshaft

52 Leakage of fluid at front of driveshaft

1 Defective transmission rear oil seal. See Chapter 7 for replacing procedures. While this is done, check the splined yoke for burrs or a rough condition which may be damaging the seal. If found, these can be dressed with crocus cloth or a fine dressing stone.

53 Knock or clunk when transmission is under initial load (just after transmission is put into gear)

1 Loose or disconnected rear suspension components. Check all mounting bolts and bushings (Chapters 1 and 11).
2 Loose driveshaft bolts. Inspect all bolts and nuts and tighten to torque specifications (Chapter 8).
3 Worn or damaged universal joint bearings. Replace driveshaft (Chapter 8).
4 Worn sleeve yoke and mainshaft spline (Chapter 8).

54 Metallic grating sound consistent with road speed

Pronounced wear in the universal joint bearings. Replace driveshaft (Chapter 8).

55 Vibration

Note: *Before it can be assumed that the driveshaft is at fault, make sure the tires are perfectly balanced and perform the following test.*
1   Install a tachometer inside the car to monitor engine speed as the car is driven. Drive the car and note the engine speed at which the vibration (roughness) is most pronounced. Now shift the transmission to a different gear and bring the engine speed to the same point.
2   If the vibration occurs at the same engine speed (rpm) regardless of which gear the transmission is in, the driveshaft is NOT at fault since the driveshaft speed varies.
3   If the vibration decreases or is eliminated when the transmission is in a different gear at the same engine speed, refer to the following probable causes.
4   Bent or dented driveshaft. Inspect and replace as necessary (Chapter 8).
5   Undercoating or built-up dirt, etc. on the driveshaft. Clean the shaft thoroughly and test.
6   Worn universal joint bearings. Replace the driveshaft (Chapter 8).
7   Driveshaft and/or companion flange out of balance. Check for missing weights on the shaft. Remove driveshaft (Chapter 8) and reinstall 180° from original position. Retest. Have driveshaft professionally balanced if problem persists.
8   Loose installation of the driveshaft (Chapter 8).
9   Worn transmission rear bushing (Chapter 7).

56 Scraping noise

Check that the dust cover on the sleeve yoke is not rubbing on the transmission rear extension (Chapter 8).

Differential and rear driveaxles

57 Instability while driving

1   Worn driveaxle ball spline (Chapter 8).
2   Damaged differential mounting insulator (Chapter 8).

58 Noise – same when in drive as when vehicle is coasting

1   Road noise. No corrective procedures available.
2   Tire noise. Inspect tires and tire pressures (Chapter 1).
3   Wheel bearings loose, worn or damaged (Chapter 1).
4   Insufficient differential oil (Chapter 1).
5   Defective differential (Chapter 8).
6   Lack of rear driveaxle grease (Chapter 8).
7   Incorrect endplay adjustment of rear axle stub (Chapter 8).
8   Worn spline portion of rear axle stub (Chapter 8).
9   Loose driveaxle connecting bolts (Chapter 8).
10 Damaged or deformed differential mounting insulator or mounting plate rubber (Chapter 8).
11 Defective universal joints in rear driveaxles.

59 Knocking sound during starting or gear shifting

Defective or incorrectly adjusted differential (Chapter 8).

60 Noise only while turning

Defective differential (Chapter 8).

61 Vibration

See probable causes under 'Driveshaft'. Proceed under the guidelines listed for the driveshaft. If the problem persists, check the rear wheel bearings by raising the rear of the car and spinning the wheels by hand. Listen for evidence of rough (noisy) bearings. Remove and inspect (Chapter 8).

62 Oil leakage

1   Damaged pinion or side oil seals on differential (Chapter 8).
2   Damaged rear driveaxle dust (Chapter 8).
3   Differential cover leaking. Tighten mounting bolts or replace the gasket as required (Chapter 8).
4   Loose filler or drain plug on differential (Chapter 1).
5   Damaged rear axle stub grease seal (Chapter 8).
6   Clogged or damaged breather on diferential (Chapter 8).

Brakes
Note: *Before assuming a brake problem exists, check: that the tires are in good condition and are inflated properly (Chapter 1); the front end alignment is correct (Chapter 11); and that the vehicle is not loaded with weight in an unequal manner. All service procedures for the braking system are described in Chapter 9, unless otherwise noted.*

63 Vehicle pulls to one side under braking

1   Defective, damaged or oil-contaminated disc pad on one side. Inspect as described in Chapter 1. Refer to Chapter 9 if replacement is required.
2   Excessive wear of brake pad material or disc on one side. Inspect and correct as necessary.
3   Loose or disconnected front suspension components. Inspect and tighten all bolts to specifications (Chapter 1).
4   Defective caliper assembly. Remove caliper and inspect for stuck piston or damage.
5   Disc pad-to-rotor adjustment needed. Inspect automatic adjusting mechanism for proper operation.
6   Scored or out-of-round rotor.
7   Loose caliper mounting.
8   Incorrect adjustment of wheel bearings.

64 Noise (high-pitched squeak)

1   Front brake pads worn out. This noise comes from the wear sensor rubbing against the disc. Replace pads with new ones immediately.
2   Glazed or contaminated pads.
3   Dirty or scored rotor.
4   Bent support plate.

65 Excessive brake pedal travel

1   Partial brake system failure. Inspect entire system (Chapter 1) and correct as required.
2   Insufficient fluid in master cylinder. Check (Chapter 1) and add fluid and bleed system if necessary.
3   Air in system. Bleed system.
4   Excessive lateral play of discs.
5   Brakes out of adjustment. Inspect the operation of the automatic adjusters.
6   Defective check valve. Replace valve and bleed system.

66 Brake pedal feels spongy when depressed

1   Air in hydraulic lines. Bleed the brake system.
2   Faulty flexible hoses. Inspect all system hoses and lines. Replace parts as necessary.
3   Master cylinder mountings insecure. Inspect master cylinder bolts (nuts) and torque-tighten to specifications.

4 Master cylinder faulty.
5 Incorrect pad-to-rotor clearance. Check operation of automatic adjusters.
6 Defective check valve. Replace valve and bleed system.
7 Clogged reservoir cap vent hole.
8 Deformed rubber brake lines.
9 Soft or swollen caliper seals.
10 Poor quality brake fluid. Bleed entire system and fill with new approved fluid.

67 Excessive effort required to stop vehicle

1 Power brake booster not operating properly.
2 Excessively worn pads. Inspect and replace if necessary.
3 One or more caliper pistons seized or sticking. Inspect and rebuild as required.
4 Brake pads contaminated with oil or grease. Inspect and replace as required.
5 New pads installed and not yet 'bedded in'. It will take a while for the new material to seat against the rotor.
6 Worn or damaged master cylinder or caliper assemblies. Check particularly for frozen pistons.
7 Also see causes listed under Section 66.

68 Pedal travels to floor with little resistance

Little or no fluid in the master cylinder reservoir caused by: leaking caliper piston(s); loose, damaged or disconnected brake lines. Inspect entire system and correct as necessary.

69 Brake pedal pulsates during brake application

1 Wheel bearings not adjusted properly or in need of replacement (Chapter 1).
2 Caliper not sliding properly due to improper installation or obstructions. Remove and inspect.
3 Rotor not within specifications. Remove the rotor and check for excessive lateral run-out and parallelism. Have the rotor professionally machined or replace it with a new one. Also check that all rotors are the same thickness.

70 Brakes drag (indicated by sluggish engine performance or wheels being very hot after driving)

1 Output rod adjustment too long at the brake pedal.
2 Obstructed master cylinder compensator. Disassemble master cylinder and clean.
3 Master cylinder piston seized in bore. Overhaul master cylinder.
4 Caliper assembly in need of overhaul.
5 Brake pads need replacing.
6 Piston cups in master cylinder or caliper assembly deformed. Overhaul master cylinder.
7 Rotor not within specs (Section 69).
8 Parking brake assembly will not release.
9 Clogged brake lines.
10 Wheel bearings out of adjustment (Chapter 8).
11 Brake pedal height improperly adjusted.

71 Rear brakes lock up under light brake application (indicated by a skidding effect)

1 Tire pressures too high.
2 Tires excessively worn (Chapter 11).
3 Defective NP valve.

72 Rear brakes lock up under heavy brake application (indicated by a skidding effect)

1 Tire pressures too high.
2 Tires excessively worn (Chapter 11).

3 Front brake pads contaminated with oil, mud or water. Clean or replace the pads.
4 Front brake pads excessively worn.
5 Poor front braking effect caused by defective master cylinder or caliper assembly.

Suspension and steering
Note: All service procedures for the suspension and steering systems are described in Chapter 11, unless otherwise noted.

73 Car pulls to one side

1 Tire pressures uneven (Chapter 1).
2 Defective tire (Chapter 1).
3 Excessive wear in suspension or steering components (Chapter 1).
4 Front end in need of alignment.
5 Front brakes dragging. Inspect braking system as described in Section 70.
6 Wheel bearings improperly adjusted (Chapter 4).
7 Wheel lug nuts not tight.

74 Shimmy, shake or vibration

1 Tire or wheel out of balance or out of round. Have professionally balanced.
2 Loose, worn or out of adjustment wheel bearings (Chapter 1).
3 Shock absorbers and/or suspension components worn or damaged.
4 Wheel lug nuts not tight.
5 Incorrect tire pressures.
6 Excessively worn or damaged tire.
7 Loosely mounted steering gear housing.
8 Steering gear improperly adjusted.
9 Loose, worn or damaged steering components.

75 Excessive pitching and/or rolling around corners or during braking

1 Defective shock absorbers. replace as a set.
2 Broken or weak coil springs and/or suspension components.
3 Worn or damaged stabilizer bar or bushings.
4 Worn or damaged rear suspension arm or bushings.

76 Wandering or general instability

1 Improper tire pressures.
2 Worn or damaged transverse link or tension rod bushings.
3 Incorrect front end alignment.
4 Worn or damaged steering linkage or transverse link.
5 Improperly adjusted steering gear.
6 Out of balance wheels.
7 Loose wheel lug nuts.
8 Worn or damaged rear suspension arm bushings, suspension member insulator or differential mounting insulator.
9 Worn rear shock absorbers.
10 Fatigued or damaged rear coil springs.

77 Excessively stiff steering

1 Lack of lubricant in power steering fluid reservoir (Chapter 1).
2 Incorrect tire pressures (Chapter 1).
3 Lack of lubrication at balljoints (Chapter 1).
4 Front end out of alignment.
5 Steering gear out of adjustment or lacking lubrication.
6 Improperly adjusted wheel bearings.
7 Defective strut assembly mounting bearing.
8 Air in power steering fluid. Bleed system.
9 Tire pressures too low.
10 Worn or damaged balljoints.

11 Worn or damaged steering linkage.
12 See also Section 79.

78 Excessive play in steering

1 Loose wheel bearings (Chapter 1).
2 Excessive wear in suspension or steering components (Chapter 1).
3 Steering gear improperly adjusted.
4 Incorrect front end alignment.

79 Lack of power assistance (with power steering systems)

1 Steering pump drivebelt faulty or not adjusted properly (Chapter 1).
2 Fluid level low (Chapter 1).
3 Hoses or pipes restricting the flow. Inspect and replace parts as necessary.
4 Air in power steering system. Bleed system.
5 Defective power steering pump.

80 Steering wheel fails to return to straight-ahead position

1 Incorrect front end alignment.
2 Tire pressures too low.
3 Steering gears improperly engaged.
4 Steering column out of alignment.
5 Worn or damaged balljoint.
6 Worn or damaged steering linkage.
7 Improperly lubricated idler arm.
8 Insufficient oil in steering gear.
9 Lack of fluid in power steering pump.

81 Steering effort not the same in both directions (power system)

1 Fluid leakage from steering gear.
2 Clogged fluid passage in steering gear.

82 Noisy power steering pump

1 Insufficient oil in pump.
2 Clogged hoses or oil filter in pump.
3 Loose pulley.
4 Improperly adjusted drivebelt (Chapter 1).
5 Defective pump.

83 Miscellaneous noises

1 Improper tire pressures.
2 Insufficiently lubricated balljoint or steering linkage.
3 Loose or worn steering gear, steering linkage or suspension components.
4 Defective shock absorber.
5 Defective wheel bearing.
6 Worn or damaged transverse link or tension rod bushing.
7 Damaged coil spring.
8 Loose wheel lug nuts.
9 Worn or damaged rear suspension arm bushings.
10 Worn or damaged rear shock absorber mounting bushing.
11 Incorrect rear axle end play adjustment.
12 See also causes of noises at the driveshaft and differential.

84 Excessive tire wear (not specific to one area)

1 Incorrect tire pressures.
2 Tires out of balance. Have professionally balanced.
3 Wheels damaged. Inspect and replace as necessary.
4 Suspension or steering components excessively worn (Chapter 1).

85 Excessive tire wear on outside edge

1 Inflation pressures not correct.
2 Excessive speed on turns.
3 Front-end alignment incorrect (excessive toe-in). Have professionally aligned.
4 Suspension arm bent or twisted.

86 Excessive tire wear on inside edge

1 Inflation pressures incorrect.
2 Front-end alignment incorrect (toe-out). Have professionally aligned.
3 Loose or damaged steering components (Chapter 1).

87 Tire tread worn in one place

1 Tires out of balance. Balance tires professionally.
2 Damaged or buckled wheel. Inspect and replace if necessary.
3 Defective tire.

Chapter 1 Tune-up and routine maintenance

Contents

Specifications

Note: *Additional specifications and torque figures can be found in each individual Chapter.*

Quick-reference capacities

	US	Liters	Imperial
Engine oil			
With oil filter	$4\frac{3}{4}$ qt	4.5	4 qt
Without oil filter	$4\frac{1}{4}$ qt	4.0	$3\frac{1}{2}$ qt
Fuel tank	$21\frac{1}{8}$ gal	80	$17\frac{5}{8}$ gal
Engine coolant			
With reservoir	$11\frac{1}{8}$ qt	10.5	$9\frac{1}{4}$ qt
Without reservoir	$10\frac{1}{4}$ qt	9.7	$8\frac{1}{2}$ qt
Transmission			
Manual	$4\frac{1}{4}$ pt	2.0	$3\frac{1}{2}$ pt
Automatic	$5\frac{7}{8}$ qt	5.5	$4\frac{7}{8}$ qt
Power steering system			
1979	$1\frac{1}{2}$ qt	1.4	$1\frac{1}{4}$ qt
1980 thru 1982	$1\frac{1}{8}$ qt	1.1	1 qt
Differential			
R200 type	$2\frac{3}{4}$ pt	1.3	$2\frac{1}{4}$ pt
R180 type	$2\frac{1}{8}$ pt	1.0	$1\frac{3}{4}$ pt
Windshield washer tank			
1979 and 1980	3 qt	2.8	$2\frac{1}{2}$ qt
1981 and 1982	$3\frac{1}{8}$ qt	3.0	$2\frac{5}{8}$ qt
Headlight cleaner tank	$2\frac{1}{8}$ qt	2.0	$1\frac{3}{4}$ qt

Recommended fluids and lubricants

Engine oil*		
−30°F to 20°F		SAE 5W-20
		SAE 5W-30
0°F to 60°F		SAE 10W
		SAE 5W-30

20°F to 100°F ....

SAE 10W-30
SAE 10W-40
SAE 20W
SAE 10W-30
SAE 10W-40
SAE 20W-40
SAE 20W-50

*All engine lubricants should be labeled API SE

Automatic transmission fluid ....

DEXRON type

Manual transmission oil ....

API GL-4 SAE 140W (above 50°F)
SAE 90W (between 30° and 100°F)
SAE 85W (between 10° and 85°F)
SAE 80W-90 (below 100°F)
SAE 80W (below 85°F)
SAE 75W (below 50°F)

Steering gear oil .... API GL-4 (refer to manual transmission oil for correct weight)
Differential oil .... API GL-5 (refer to manual transmission oil for correct weight)
Power steering fluid .... DEXRON type
Brake fluid .... DOT 3
Clutch fluid .... DOT 3 brake fluid
Coolant .... Mixture of good quality ethylene glycol based antifreeze and water, in at least a 50/50 ratio (but not to exceed 70/30 ratio of antifreeze to water)

Windshield washer solvent .... Good quality solvent intended for this use (in freezing temperatures, a windshield washer antifreeze/solvent should be used with water to prevent the system from freezing)

Parking brake cables .... Chassis grease
Chassis lubrication .... Chassis grease
Hood and door hinges .... Engine oil
Hood latch assembly
  Pivots and spring anchor .... Engine oil
  Release pawl .... Chassis grease
Key lock cylinders .... Spray lubricant

Engine — general

Spark plugs

	1979	1980 and 1981	1982
US models	B6ES-11	BP6ES-11	BPR6ES-11
Canada (and optional for US models)	BT6ES-11	BPR6ES-11	BPR6ES-11

Spark plug gap .... 0.039 to 0.043 in (1.0 to 1.1 mm)
Valve clearance
  Intake (nos. 2, 3, 5, 8,10 and 11 in Fig. 1.29)
    Hot .... 0.010 in (0.25 mm)
    Cold .... 0.007 in (0.17 mm)
  Exhaust (nos. 1, 4, 6, 7, 9 and 12 in Fig. 1.29)
    Hot .... 0.012 in (0.30 mm)
    Cold .... 0.009 in (0.24 mm)

Ignition timing and idle speed
1979
Manual transmission
  US Federal models with catalytic converter .... 10° BTDC at 700 rpm
  All others .... 10° BTDC at 800 rpm
Automatic transmission .... 10° BTDC at 700 rpm
1980 (all)*
10 ± 2° BTDC at 700 ± 100 rpm
1981
Non-turbo** .... 8 ± 2° BTDC at 700 ± 100 rpm
Canada non-turbo .... 10 ± 2° BTDC at 700 ± 100 rpm
Turbo .... 20 ± 3° BTDC at 650 ± 50 rpm
1982
Non-turbo (all)** .... 8 ± 2° BTDC at 700 ± 100 rpm
Turbo
  Manual transmission .... 20 ± 3° BTDC at 700 ± 50 rpm
  Automatic transmission .... 20 ± 3° BTDC at 650 ± 50 rpm

*US Federal models only: Ignition timing should be checked with the distributor vacuum advance hose disconnected and plugged.
**Ignition timing should be checked with the distributor vacuum advance hose disconnected and plugged.

Idle mixture (CO%) adjustment
1979
US Federal models with catalytic converter and all
  California models .... 0.5% or lower
US Federal models without catalytic converter and all
  Canada models .... 1.0% or lower
1980
California .... Preset
US Federal .... 1.0% ± 0.8%
Canada .... 5.0 ± 1.0%

1981

All US and Turbo .... Preset

Canada .... 5.0 ± 1.0%

1982 (all) .... Preset

Cylinder compression pressure

    Normal pressure

        Non-turbo .... 171 psi (12.0 kg/cm²)

        Turbo .... 142 psi (10.0 kg/cm²)

    Minimum pressure

        Non-turbo .... 128 psi (9.0 kg/cm²)

        Turbo .... 100 psi (7.0 kg/cm²)

Chassis and body – general

Clutch pedal

    Height .... 8 in (203 mm)

    Free play .... 0.04 to 0.20 in (1 to 5 mm)

Brake pedal

    Height

        Manual transmission .... $7\frac{1}{4}$ in (184 mm)

        Automatic transmission .... $7\frac{5}{8}$ in (193 mm)

    Free play .... 0.04 to 0.20 in (1 to 5 mm)

    Depressed height

        Manual transmission .... Over $3\frac{1}{8}$ in (80 mm)

        Automatic transmission .... Over $3\frac{1}{2}$ in (90 mm)

Brake pad wear limit .... 0.08 in (2 mm)

Rotor thickness wear limit

    Front .... 0.709 in (18.0 mm)

    Rear .... 0.339 in (8.6 mm)

Parking brake adjustment

    Number of notches .... 4 to 6

    Lever stroke (measured at center of handle) .... $3\frac{3}{8}$ to $4\frac{1}{4}$ in (86 to 109 mm)

Tire pressures (all, including spare) (measured with tires cold) .... 28 psi

Front end alignment

    Camber .... −35' to 55'

    Caster .... 4° 10' to 5° 40'

    Toe-in .... 1 to 3 mm (0.04 to 0.12 in) or 6' to 16'

Front wheel turning angle

    Power steering

        Inside .... 32° to 36°

        Outside .... $24\frac{1}{2}$° to $28\frac{1}{2}$°

    Manual steering

        Inside .... $33\frac{1}{2}$° to $37\frac{1}{2}$°

        Outside .... 29° to 33°

Torque specifications

	ft-lb	m-kg
Spark plugs	12	1.7
Oil pan drain plug	18	2.5
Pivot locknut	40	5.5
Manual transmission drain plug	22	3.0
Manual transmission filler plug	22	3.0
Differential drain plug	36	7.0
Differential filler plug	36	7.0
Wheel lug nuts	65	9.0

1 Introduction

This Chapter was designed to help the home mechanic maintain his (or her) car for peak performance, economy, safety and longevity.

On the following pages you will find a maintenance schedule along with Sections which deal specifically with each item on the schedule. Included are visual checks, adjustments and item replacements. Location of the various components mentioned can be aided by referring to the engine compartment and other overall photos included.

Servicing your car using the time/mileage maintenance schedule and the sequenced Sections will give you a planned program of maintenance. Keep in mind that it is a full plan, and maintaining only a few items at the specified intervals will not give you the same results.

You will find as you service your car that many of the procedures can, and should, be grouped together due to the nature of the job at hand. Examples of this are as follows:

If the car is fully raised for a chassis lubrication, for example, this is the ideal time for the following checks: manual transmission fluid, differential fluid, exhaust system, suspension, steering and the fuel system.

If the tires and wheels are removed, as during a routine tire rotation, go ahead and check the brakes and wheel bearings at the same time.

If you must borrow or rent a torque wrench, you will do best to service the spark plugs, repack (or replace) the wheel bearings and check any other critical bolts for proper torque all in the same day to save time and money.

The first step of this or any maintenance plan is to prepare yourself before the actual work begins. Read through the appropriate Sections for all work that is to be performed before you begin. Gather together all necessary parts and tools. If it appears you could have a problem during a particular job, don't hesitate to ask advice from your local parts man or dealer service department.

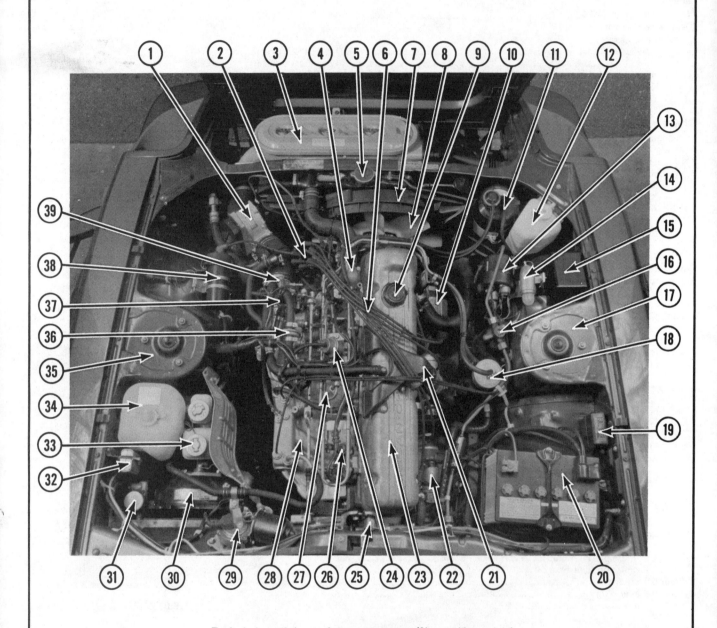

Typical view of the engine compartment (Non-turbo models)

1 Air flow meter	11 Charcoal canister	20 Battery	30 Brake booster
2 Distributor	12 Coolant reservoir	21 Auxiliary cooling fan	31 Clutch master cylinder
3 Air cleaner	13 A/C vacuum tank	22 Starter motor	32 Dropping resistor
4 Thermostat housing	14 Engine compartment light	23 Rocker arm cover	33 Brake master cylinder
5 Radiator cap	15 Relay box	24 Pressure regulator	34 Windshield washer tank
6 Spark plug wires	16 A/C receiver drier and	25 Hood latch	35 Left shock well
7 Fan shroud	sight glass	26 Injector	36 Air regulator
8 Fan	17 Right shock well	27 Fuel pipe assembly	37 Cold start valve
9 Engine oil filler cap	18 Fuel filter	28 Intake manifold	38 Ignition coil
10 Alternator	19 Fusible link compartment	29 Wiper motor	39 Throttle chamber

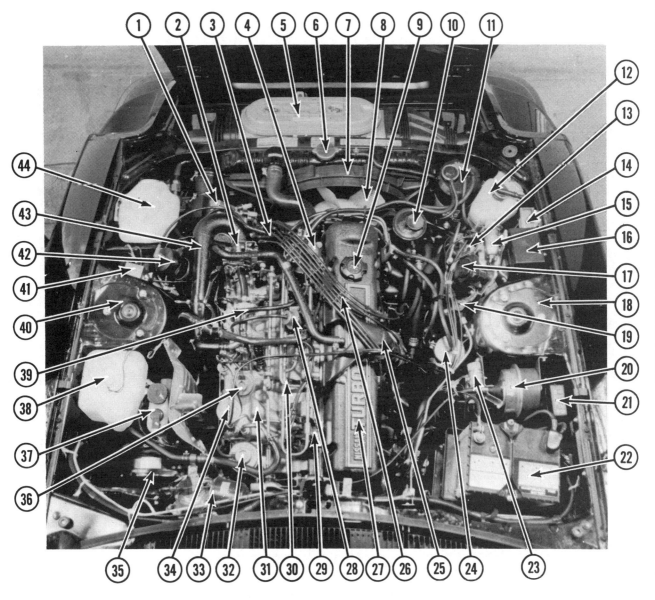

Typical view of the engine compartment (Turbo models)

1 Air flow meter	17 ASCD vacuum pump	32 EGR valve
2 Throttle chamber	18 Right shock well	33 Wiper motor
3 Distributor	19 A/C receiver drier and	34 Turbocharger emergency
4 Thermostat housing	sight glass	relief valve
5 Air cleaner	20 Automatic speed control	35 Brake booster
6 Radiator cap	device actuator	36 AAC valve
7 Fan shroud	21 Fusible link compartment	37 Brake master cylinder
8 Fan	22 Battery	38 Windshield washer tank
9 Engine oil filler cap	23 ASCD servo valve	39 Air regulator
10 Power steering pump	24 Fuel filter	40 Left shock well
and reservoir	25 Auxiliary cooling fan	41 Turbocharging system
11 Charcoal canister	26 Spark plug wires	boost sensor
12 Coolant reservoir	27 Rocker arm cover	42 Ignition coil
13 A/C vacuum tank	28 Pressure regulator	43 Air inlet pipe
14 Headlamp sensor	29 Injector	44 Headlight cleaner tank
15 Engine compartment light	30 Fuel pipe assembly	
16 Relay box	31 Intake manifold	

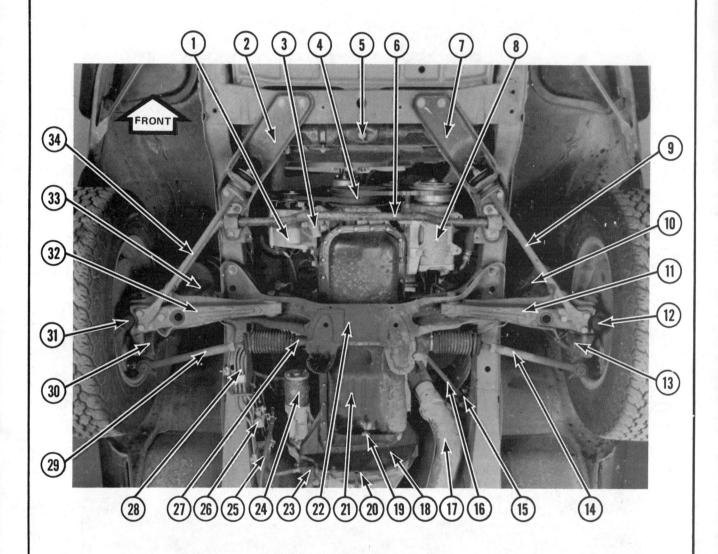

Typical view of the engine compartment underside (w/rack and pinion)

1 Alternator	13 Left steering knuckle	25 Parking brake cable
2 Right tension rod bracket	14 Left tie-rod (side rod)	26 Neutral pressure (NP) valve
3 Oil pump	15 Steering column rubber	27 Rack-and-pinion unit
4 Crankshaft pulley	coupling	28 Fuel lines
5 Radiator drain plug	16 Lower joint shaft	29 Right tie-rod (side rod)
6 Front stabilizer bar	17 Front exhaust pipe	30 Right steering knuckle
7 Left tension rod bracket	18 Rear plate	31 Right balljoint
8 A/C compressor	19 Engine oil drain plug	32 Right transverse link
9 Left tension rod	20 Transmission	33 Right spring and strut
10 Left spring and strut	21 Oil pan	assembly
assembly	22 Crossmember	34 Right tension rod
11 Left transverse link	23 Clutch operating cylinder	
12 Left balljoint	24 Starter motor	

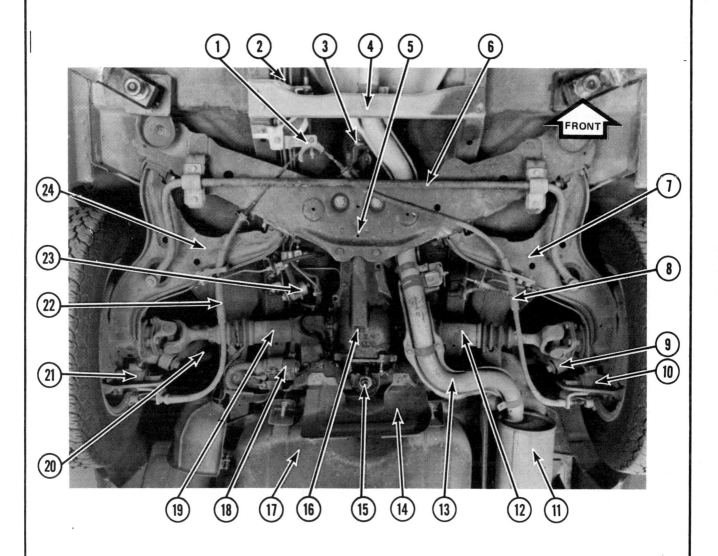

Typical view of rear underside of car

1 Parking brake equalizer
2 Fuel lines
3 Driveshaft
4 Rear crossmember
5 Suspension member
6 Rear stabilizer bar
7 Left suspension arm
8 Rear parking brake cable
9 Left rear shock absorber

10 Left rear brake caliper
11 Muffler
12 Left drive axle
13 Intermediate exhaust pipe
14 Fuel tank protector
15 Differential rear mounting
    insulator
16 Differential

17 Fuel tank
18 Fuel pump
19 Right drive axle
20 Right rear shock absorber
21 Right rear brake caliper
22 Rear parking brake cable
23 Fuel damper
24 Right suspension arm

2   Routine maintenance intervals

Note: *The pre-drive inspection outlined in the owner's manual covers checks and maintenance that should be carried out on a daily or pre-drive basis. It is condensed and included here to remind you of its importance. Always perform the pre-drive inspection at every maintenance interval (in addition to the procedures listed).*

Before driving
Check the engine oil level (Sec 4)
Check the engine coolant level (Sec 4)
Check the tires and tire pressures (Sec 5)
Check the automatic transmission fluid level (Sec 4)
Check the windshield washer fluid level (Sec 4)
Check the power steering fluid level, if equipped (Sec 4)

At the first 1000 miles
Check the drivebelts (Sec 12)
Check the intake and exhaust valve adjustments (Sec 19)
Check and adjust the idle speed (Sec 15)
Check and adjust the mixture ratio (where applicable) (Sec 17)
Inspect the steering gearbox or rack and pinion (Sec 32)
Inspect the suspension system (Sec 32)
Inspect the driveshaft (Sec 34)

Every 3750 miles
Change the engine oil and filter (Turbo models) (Sec 8)

Every 7500 miles or 6 months – whichever comes first
Change the engine oil and filter (Sec 8)
Check all fluid levels (Sec 4)

Every 15 000 miles or 12 months – whichever comes first
Check the drivebelts (Sec 12)
Check the intake and exhaust valve adjustments (Sec 19)
Check the idle speed (Sec 15)
Check the mixture ratio (where applicable) (Sec 17)
Check and adjust the ignition timing (Sec 16)
Replace the PCV valve (Sec 22)
Inspect the brakes (Sec 30)
Check the steering and suspension components (Sec 32)
Lubricate the chassis components (Sec 29)
Check the fuel system components (Sec 35)
Check the exhaust system (Sec 33)
Check the driveshaft (Sec 34)
Rotate the tires (Sec 5)
Lubricate the body components (Sec 29)
Check the clutch pedal adjustments (Sec 26)
Check the parking brake adjustment (Sec 27)
Check and adjust the throttle linkage (Sec 25)
Change the automatic transmission fluid if the car is driven under abnormal conditions (Sec 38)
Inspect the cooling system (Sec 24)
Check the manual transmission oil (Sec 4)
Check the differential oil (Sec 4)
Check the brake pedal adjustments (Sec 31)

Every 30 000 miles or 24 months – whichever comes first
Replace the air cleaner filter (Sec 13)
Check the vapor lines (should be done by Datsun dealer)
Inspect and service the cooling system (Sec 24)
Replace the spark plugs (Sec 10)
Check the spark plug wires (Sec 11)
Check the exhaust gas sensor (where applicable) (Sec 37)
Replace the air induction valve filter (where applicable) (Sec 23)
Inspect the brake booster vacuum hoses and check valve (Sec 30)
Check the front wheel bearings (Sec 28)
Change differential gear oil if a trailer is frequently towed (Sec 40)
Replace the charcoal canister (EEC) filter (Sec 36)
Service the catalytic converter (Sec 33)
Change the automatic transmission fluid (Sec 38)
Replace the fuel filter (Sec 21)
Inspect the fuel tank vacuum relief valve (Sec 35)
Change the manual transmission oil (Sec 39)
Inspect the air-conditioning system (should be done by dealer)

3   Tune-up – general information

The term "Tune-up" is loosely used for any general operation that puts the engine back in its proper running condition. A tune-up is not a specific operation, but rather a combination of individual operations, such as replacing the spark plugs, adjusting the idle speed, setting the ignition timing, etc.

If, from the time the car is new, the routine maintenance schedule (Section 2) is followed closely and frequent checks are made of fluid levels and high wear items, as suggested throughout this manual, the engine will be kept in relatively good running condition and the need for additional tune-ups will be minimized.

More likely than not, however, there will be times when the engine is running poorly due to lack of regular maintenance. This is even more likely if a used car is bought which has not received regular and frequent maintenance checks. In such cases an engine tune-up will be needed outside of the regular routine maintenance intervals.

The following series of operations are those most often needed to bring a generally poor running engine back into a proper state of tune.

Minor tune-up
Clean, inspect and test battery (Sec 9)
Check all engine fluids (Sec 4)
Test cylinder compression (Sec 18)
Check and adjust drivebelts (Sec 12)
Replace spark plugs (Sec 10)
Inspect distributor cap and rotor (Sec 14)
Inspect spark plug and coil wires (Sec 11)
Replace air filter (Sec 13)
Check and adjust idle speed (Sec 15)
Check and adjust ignition timing (Sec 16)
Check and adjust mixture ratio (Sec 17)
Replace fuel filter (Sec 21)
Replace air induction valve filter (where applicable) (Sec 23)
Replace PCV valve (Sec 22)
Adjust valve clearances (Sec 19)
Check and service cooling system (Sec 24)

Major tune-up (the above operations combined with those listed below)
Check vacuum advance system (Chapter 6, Spark Timing Control System)
Check EGR system (Chapter 6)
Test alternator and voltage regulator (Chapter 5)
Test ignition system (Chapter 5)
Test charging system (Chapter 5)
Check fuel system (Sec 35 and Chapter 4)

4   Fluid levels check

1   There are a number of components on a vehicle which rely on the use of fluids to perform their job. Through the normal operation of the car, these fluids are used up and must be replenished before damage occurs. See *Recommended Lubricants* for the specific fluid to be used when adding is required. When checking fluid levels, it is important that the car is on a level surface.

Engine oil
2   The engine oil level is checked with a dipstick which is located at the right side of the engine block. This dipstick travels through a tube and into the oil pan at the bottom of the engine (Fig. 1.1).
3   The oil level should be checked preferably before the car has been driven, or about 15 minutes after the engine has been shut off. If the oil is checked immediately after driving the car, some of the oil will remain in the upper engine components, thus giving an inaccurate reading on the dipstick.
4   Pull the dipstick from its tube and wipe all the oil from the end with a clean rag. Insert the clean dipstick all the way back into the oil pan and pull it out again. Observe the oil at the end of the dipstick. At its highest point, the level should be between the L and H marks.
5   It takes approximately one quart of oil to raise the level from the L mark to the H mark on the dipstick. Do not allow the level to drop below the L mark, as this may cause engine damage due to oil starvation. On the other hand, do not overfill the engine by adding oil

above the H mark, as this may result in oil-fouled spark plugs, oil leaks or oil seal failures.

6 Oil is added to the engine after removing a twist-off cap located on the rocker arm cover. An oil can spout or funnel will reduce spills as the oil is poured in.

7 Checking the oil level can also be a step toward preventative maintenance. If you find the oil level dropping abnormally, this is an indication of oil leakage or internal engine wear which should be corrected. If there are water droplets in the oil, or it is milky-looking, this also indicates component failure, and the engine should be checked immediately. The condition of the oil can also be checked along with the level. With the dipstick removed from the engine, take your thumb and index finger and wipe the oil up the dipstick, looking for small dirt particles or engine filings which will cling to the dipstick. This is an indication that the oil should be drained and fresh oil added (Section 7).

Engine coolant

Caution: *Do not allow antifreeze to come in contact with your skin or painted surfaces of the car. Flush contacted areas immediately with plenty of water.*

8 Most vehicles are equipped with a pressurized coolant recovery system which makes coolant level checks very easy. A white coolant reservoir is connected by a hose to the radiator cap. As the engine heats up during operation, coolant is forced from the radiator, through the connecting tube and into the reservoir. As the engine cools, this coolant is automatically drawn back into the radiator to keep the level correct.

9 On models with a coolant reservoir, the coolant level should be checked when the engine is hot. Merely observe the level of fluid in the reservoir, which should be between the Max and Min marks on the side of the reservoir. On models without a reservoir tank, the engine should be cold because the radiator cap must be removed.

10 Under no circumstances should the radiator cap be removed while the system is hot, as escaping steam could cause serious injury. Wait until the engine has completely cooled, then wrap a thick cloth around the cap and turn it to its first stop. If any steam escapes from the cap, allow the engine to cool further. Then remove the cap and check the level in the radiator. It should be about 1 inch below the bottom of the filler neck (A in Fig. 1.2).

11 If only a small amount of coolant is required to bring the system up to the proper level, regular water can be used. However, to maintain the proper antifreeze/water mixture in the system, both should be mixed together to replenish a low level. High-quality antifreeze offering protection to −20°F should be mixed with water in the proportion specified on the container.

12 On models with a coolant reservoir coolant should be added to the reservoir after removing the cap at the top of the reservoir. On models without a coolant reservoir, fill the radiator to the proper level. Then run the engine for a few minutes with the radiator cap off. If the coolant level drops, fill it again to the proper level.

13 As the coolant level is checked, observe the condition of the coolant. It should be relatively clear. If the fluid is brown or a rust color, this is an indication that the system should be drained, flushed and refilled.

14 If the cooling system requires repeated additions to keep the proper level, have the pressure radiator cap checked for proper sealing ability. Also check for leaks in the system (cracked hoses, loose hose connections, leaking gaskets, etc).

Windshield washer

15 The fluid for the windshield washer system is located in a plastic reservoir to the left of the brake master cylinder. The level inside the reservoir should be maintained near the top of the reservoir.

16 An approved washer solvent should be added through the plastic cap whenever replenishing is required. Do not use plain water alone in this system, especially in cold climates where the water could freeze.

Battery

Caution: *There are certain precautions to be taken when working on or near the battery: a) Never expose a battery to open flame or sparks which could ignite the hydrogen gas given off by the battery; b) Wear protective clothing and eye protection to reduce the possibility of the corrosive sulfuric acid solution inside the battery harming you (if the fluid is splashed or spilled, flush the contacted area immediately with plenty of water); c) Remove all metal jewelry which could contact the*

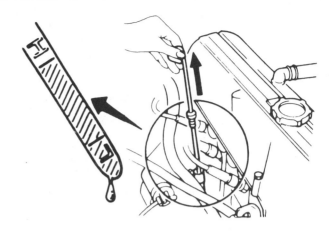

Fig. 1.1 The dipstick for the engine oil is located on the right side of the engine (Sec 4)

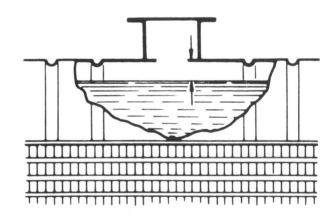

Fig. 1.2 On models not equipped with a coolant reservoir tank, the coolant level should be kept about 1 in below the bottom of the filler neck (Sec 4)

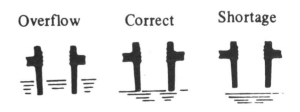

Fig. 1.3 The correct level for the battery electrolyte is just to the bottom of the filler hole rings (Sec 4)

positive terminal and another grounded metal source, thus causing a short circuit; d) Always keep batteries and battery acid out of the reach of children.

17 Vehicles equipped with maintenance-free batteries require no maintenance as the battery case is sealed and has no removal caps for adding water.

18 If equipped with a conventional battery, the caps on the top of the battery should be removed periodically to check for a low water level. This check will be more critical during the warm summer months.

19 Remove each of the caps and add distilled water to bring the level of each cell to the split ring in the filler opening.

20 At the same time the battery water level is checked, the overall condition of the battery and its related components should be inspected. If corrosion is found on the cable ends or battery terminals, remove the cables and clean away all corrosion using a baking soda/water solution or a wire brush cleaning tool designed for this purpose.

Brake master cylinder
Caution: *Be careful not to spill brake fluid on any painted surfaces of the car, as it can damage the paint finish. If spilled, wash immediately with plenty of water.*

21 The brake master cylinder is located on the left side of the engine compartment, and has two reservoirs or chambers each with its own cap.

22 To check the level of the brake fluid, simply note how high the fluid is in relation to the Max and Min marks on the side of each reservoir.

23 Some models are equipped with brake fluid warning lights in the dash which indicate when the brake fluid in the master cylinder is too low.

24 If the brake fluid is significantly below the Max mark, or if the brake fluid warning light comes on, additional fluid should be added to the reservoir.

25 Before removing the cap, use a rag to clean off all dirt, grease, etc. from around the cap area. If any foreign matter enters the master cylinder with the cap removed, blockage in the brake system lines can occur.

26 Remove the cap and lift it out of the reservoir.

27 Carefully pour the specified brake fluid into the master cylinder. Be sure the specified fluid is used, as mixing different types of brake fluid can cause damage to the system. See *Recommended lubricants* in the front of this Chapter or your owner's manual.

28 At this time the fluid and master cylinder can be inspected for contamination. Normally, the braking system will not need periodic draining and refilling, but if rust deposits, dirt particles or water droplets are seen in the fluid, the system should be drained and refilled with fresh fluid.

29 Reinstall the master cylinder cap. Make sure it is properly seated to prevent fluid leakage and/or system pressure loss.

30 The brake fluid in the master cylinder will drop slightly as the brake pads at each wheel wear down during normal operation. If the master cylinder requires repeated replenishing to keep it at the proper level, this is an indication of leakage in the brake system which should be corrected immediately. Check all brake lines and their connections, along with the booster (see Chapter 9 for more information).

31 If upon checking the master cylinder fluid level you discover that one or both reservoirs is below the Min mark or totally empty, the braking system should be bled (Chapter 9). When the fluid level gets low, air can enter the system and should be removed by bleeding the brakes.

Clutch fluid
Caution: *Be careful not to spill brake fluid on any painted surfaces of the car, as it can damage the paint finish. If spilled, wash immediately with plenty of water.*

32 To check the level of the fluid in the clutch master cylinder, simply note how high the fluid is in relation to the Max and Min marks on the side of the reservoir.

33 If the clutch fluid is significantly below the Max mark, additional fluid should be added to the reservoir.

34 Before removing the cap, use a rag to clean all dirt, grease, etc. from around the cap area. If any foreign matter enters the master cylinder with the cap removed, blockage in the clutch system lines can occur. Also make sure all painted surfaces around the master cylinder are covered, as the fluid will ruin paintwork.

Add to "MAX." level

Fig. 1.4 The brake master cylinder on 1982 models use a single reservoir which is divided into two chambers (Sec 4)

35 Remove the cap by twisting it counterclockwise, and lifting it off the reservoir.

36 Carefully pour the specified brake fluid into the master cylinder. Be sure the specified fluid is used, as mixing different types can cause damage to the system. See *Recommended lubricants* in the front of this Chapter or your owner's manual.

37 At this time the fluid and master cylinder can be inspected for contamination. Normally, the clutch system will not need periodic draining and refilling, but if rust deposits, dirt particles or water droplets are seen in the fluid, the system should be dismantled, drained and refilled with fresh fluid.

38 Reinstall the master cylinder cap. Make sure it is properly seated to prevent fluid leakage and/or system pressure loss.

39 If the master cylinder requires repeated replenishing to keep it at the proper level, this is an indication of leakage in the clutch system which should be corrected immediately. Check all clutch lines and their connections (see Chapter 8 for more information).

40 If upon checking the master cylinder fluid level you discover that the fluid is below the Min mark or totally empty, the clutch system should be bled (Chapter 8).

Manual transmission
41 Manual shift transmissions do not have a dipstick. The fluid level is checked by removing a plug in the side of the transmission case (photo). Locate this plug and use a rag to clean the plug and the area around it.

4.41 Locations of the manual transmission filler (upper) and drain (lower) plugs

42 With the vehicle components cold, remove the plug. If fluid immediately starts leaking out, thread the plug back into the transmission because the fluid level is alright. If there is no fluid leakage, completely remove the plug and place your little finger inside the hole. The fluid level should be just at the bottom of the plug hole.

43 If the transmission needs more fluid, use a syringe or small pump in the plug hole to fill the fluid up to the proper level.

44 Thread the plug back into the transmission and tighten it securely. Drive the car and check for leaks around the plug.

Automatic transmission

45 The fluid inside the transmission must be at normal operating temperature to get an accurate reading on the dipstick. This is done by driving the car for several miles, making frequent starts and stops to allow the transmission to shift through all gears.

46 Park the car on a level surface, place the selector lever in Park and leave the engine running at an idle.

47 Remove the transmission dipstick (located on the right side, near the rear of the engine) and wipe all the fluid from the end of the dipstick with a clean rag.

48 Push the dipstick back into the transmission until the cap seats firmly on the dipstick tube. Now remove the dipstick again and observe the fluid on the end. The highest point of fluid should be between the H mark and $\frac{1}{4}$ inch below the H mark.

49 If the fluid level is at or below the L mark on the dipstick, add sufficient fluid to raise the level to the H mark. Fluid should be added directly into the dipstick guide tube, using a funnel to prevent spills.

50 It is important that the transmission not be overfilled. Under no circumstances should the fluid level be above the H mark on the dipstick, as this could cause internal damage to the transmission. The best way to prevent overfilling is to add fluid a little at a time, driving the car and checking the level between additions.

51 Use only transmission fluid of the Dexron type as specified in *Recommended lubricants* at the front of this Chapter.

52 The condition of the fluid should also be checked along with the level (photo). If the fluid at the end of the dipstick is a dark reddish-brown color, or if the fluid has a 'burnt' smell, the transmission fluid should be changed. If you are in doubt about the condition of the fluid, purchase some new fluid and compare the two for color and smell.

Differential

53 Like the manual transmission the rear axle has an inspection and fill plug which must be removed to check the fluid level.

54 Remove the plug from the differential. Use your little finger to reach inside the rear axle housing to feel the level of the fluid. It should be at the bottom of the plug hole.

55 If this is not the case, add the proper lubricant to the rear axle carrier through the plug hole. A syringe, small funnel or pump can be used for this.

56 Tighten the plug securely and check for leaks after the first few miles of driving.

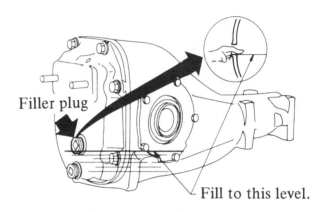

Filler plug

Fill to this level.

Fig. 1.6 The differential filler plug, used for checking the oil level, is the upper of the two plugs located in the rear cover (Sec 4)

Power steering

57 Unlike manual steering, the power steering system relies on fluid which may, over a period of time, require replenishing.

58 The reservoir for the power steering pump is mounted at the right front of the engine.

59 On 1979 through 1981 models the power steering fluid level can be checked either after the car has been driven, with the fluid at operating temperature, or with the engine and fluid cold. On 1982 models, the fluid should only be checked when cold. Either way, the front wheels should be pointed straight ahead.

60 With the engine shut off, use a rag to clean the reservoir cap and the areas around the cap. This will help to prevent foreign material from falling into the reservoir when the cap is removed.

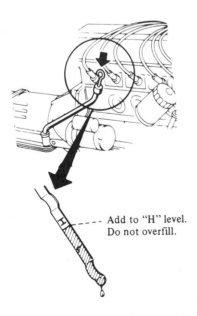

Add to "H" level.
Do not overfill.

Fig. 1.5 The dipstick for checking the automatic transmission fluid is located at the rear right side of the engine (Sec 4)

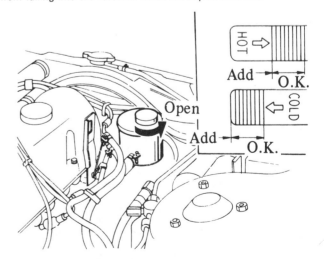

HOT
Add O.K.
Open
COLD
Add O.K.

Fig. 1.7 On 1979 through 1981 models, the power steering fluid can be checked either hot or cold and should be within the appropriate area on the dipstick (Sec 4)

61 Twist off the reservoir cap which has a built-in dipstick attached to it. Pull off the cap and clean the fluid at the bottom of the dipstick with a clean rag. Now reinstall the dipstick/cap assembly to get a fluid level reading. Remove the dipstick/cap and observe the fluid level. It should be within the 'hot' range marked on the dipstick if the fluid is hot, or within the 'cold' range if the fluid is cold. 1982 models only have one range on the dipstick.
62 If additional fluid is required, pour the specified lubricant directly into the reservoir using a funnel to prevent spills.
63 If the reservoir requires frequent fluid additions, all power steering hoses, hose connections, the power steering pump and the steering box or rack-and-pinion should be carefully checked for leaks.

5   Wheels and tires – inspection, maintenance and servicing

General information

All Datsuns are equipped with metric-sized fiberglass or steel belted radial tires. Use of other size or type of tires may affect the ride and handling of the car. Do not mix different types of tires such as radials and bias belted on the same car, as handling may be seriously affected.

It is recommended that tires be replaced in pairs on the same axle, but if only one tire is being replaced, be sure it is of the same size, structure and tread design as the other.

To achieve the maximum life of your tires they should be rotated on the car at 7500 miles and then again at 15 000 mile intervals, as outlined in the car's *Routine maintenance* schedule and detailed in this Section.

Tire and wheel balance is important to the overall handling, braking and performance of the car. Unbalanced wheels can adversely affect handling and ride characteristics as well as tire life. Whenever a tire is installed on a wheel, the tire and wheel should be balanced by a qualified shop with the proper equipment.

This car is equipped with a space-saver type spare tire which is designed to save space in the trunk as well as being easier to handle due to its lighter weight. It is designed for emergency use only and is stored in a deflated condition. Either an air pump or a canister of compressed air is supplied with the tire in order to inflate it. Following use, this tire can be deflated once more and stored for repeated uses. The compressed air canister, however, is only good for one use and must be replaced. Refer elsewhere in this Section for the proper procedure to use with this spare tire.

The compact spare tire and wheel are designed for use with each other only, and neither the tire nor the wheel should be coupled with other types or sizes of wheels and tires.

Because the compact spare is designed as a temporary replacement for an out-of-service standard wheel and tire, the compact spare should be used on the car only until the standard wheel and tire are repaired or replaced. Continuous use of the compact spare at speeds of over 50 mph (80 kph) is not recommended. In addition, the expected tread life of the compact spare is only about 3000 miles (4800 kilometers).

Caution: *Be sure to use lug nuts designed for steel wheels only with this spare.*

Inspection

1 Periodically inspecting the tires can not only prevent you from being stranded with a flat tire, but can also give you clues as to possible problems with the steering and suspension systems before major damage occurs.
2 Proper tire inflation adds miles to the lifespan of the tires, allows the car to achieve maximum miles-per-gallon figures, and helps the overall riding comfort of the car.
3 When inspecting the tire, first check the wear on the tread. Irregularities in the tread pattern (cupping, flat spots, more wear on one side than the other) can give a good indication of problems in the maintenance or adjustment of tires, suspension and front end components. The accompanying illustration gives some common examples of tire wear patterns and their usual causes. If a tire exhibits a wear pattern caused by incorrect front end alignment, refer to Section 16.
4 The tires should be replaced when the depth of the tread pattern is worn to a minimum of $\frac{1}{16}$-in (1.5 mm) or when the tire wear indicator becomes exposed. Correct tire pressures and driving techniques have an important influence on tire life. Heavy cornering, excessively rapid

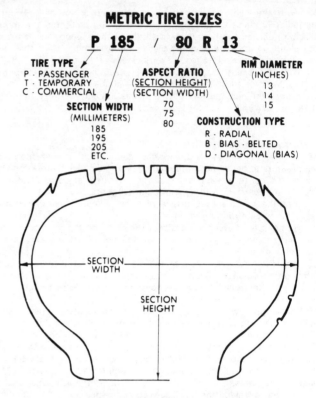

**Fig. 1.8 Code used for metric tire sizes
(Sec 5)**

acceleration and sharp braking increase tire wear. Extremely worn tires are not only very susceptible to going flat but are especially dangerous in wet weather conditions.
5 Also check the tread area for cuts or punctures. Many times a nail or tack will imbed itself into the tire tread and yet the tire will hold its air pressure for a short time. In most cases, a repair shop or gas station can repair the punctured tire.
6 It is also important to check the sidewalls of the tire, both inside and outside. Check for the rubber being deteriorated, cut or punctured. Also inspect the inboard side of the tire for signs of brake fluid leakage, which indicates that a thorough brake inspection is needed immediately (Section 30).
7 Because tire pressure has a substantial effect on handling and wear, the pressure in all tires should be checked at least once a month or before any extended trips and set to the correct pressure.
8 Incorrect tire pressures cannot be determined merely by looking at the tire. This is especially true for radial tires. A tire pressure gauge must be used. If you do not already have a reliable gauge, it is a good idea to purchase one and keep it in the glove box. Built-in pressure gauges at gas stations are often unreliable. If you are in doubt as to the accuracy of your gauge, many repair shops have 'master' pressure gauges which you can use for comparison purposes.
9 Always check tire inflation when the tires are cold. Cold, in this case, means that the car has not been driven more than one mile after sitting for three hours or more. It is normal for the pressure to increase 4 to 8 pounds or more when the tires are hot.
10 Unscrew the valve cap protruding from the wheel or hubcap and firmly press the gauge onto the valve stem. Observe the reading on the gauge and check this figure against the recommended tire pressure listed on the tire placard or in the Specifications at the beginning of this Chapter. This tire placard is usually found attached to the inside of the glove box door.
11 Check all tires and add air as necessary to bring all tires up to the recommended pressure levels. Be sure to reinstall the valve caps, which will keep dirt and moisture out of the valve stem mechanism.
12 Wheels must be replaced if they are bent, dented, leak air, have elongated bolt holes, are heavily rusted, ovaled, out of vertical symmetry or if the lug nuts won't stay tight. Wheel repairs that use welding or peening are not recommended, as this can weaken the metal.

Condition	Probable cause	Corrective action
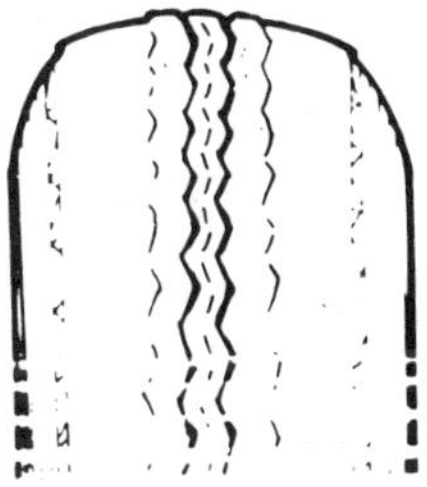 Shoulder wear	• Underinflation (both sides wear) • Incorrect wheel camber (one side wear) • Hard cornering • Lack of rotation	• Measure and adjust pressure. • Repair, or replace axle and suspension parts. • Reduce speed. • Rotate tires.
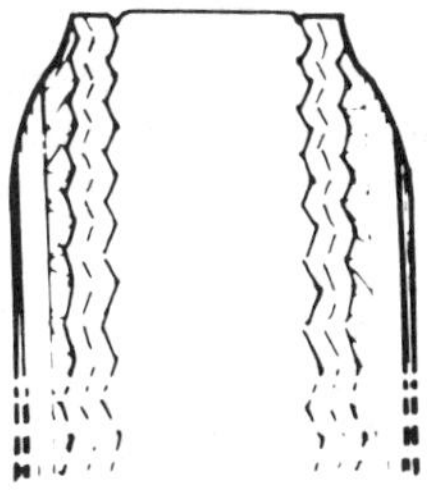 Center wear	• Overinflation • Lack of rotation	• Measure and adjust pressure. • Rotate tires.
Feathered edge 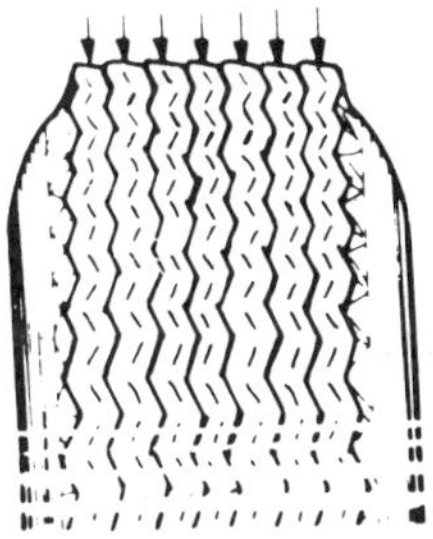 Toe-in or toe-out wear	• Incorrect toe	• Adjust toe-in.
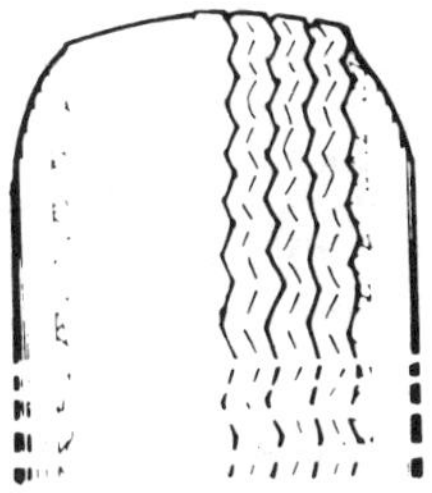 Uneven wear	• Incorrect camber or caster • Malfunctioning suspension • Unbalanced wheel • Out-of-round brake drum • Other mechanical conditions • Lack of rotation	• Repair, or replace axle and suspension parts. • Repair, replace or, if necessary, reinstall. • Balance or replace. • Correct or replace. • Correct or replace. • Rotate tires.

Fig. 1.9 The pattern of tire tread wear is indicative of various problems in the front end (Sec 5)

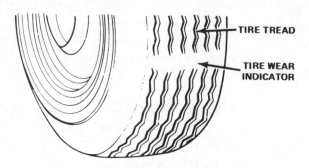

Fig. 1.10 Tire wear indicators are designed into the tread of the tires as a warning that they need replacing (Sec 5)

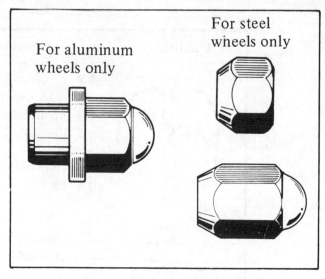

Fig. 1.11 Different wheel lugs are used for aluminum and steel wheels and should not be interchanged (Sec 5)

Wheel and tire replacement

13 With the car on a level surface, the parking brake on and the transmission in gear (manual transmissions should be in Reverse; automatic should be in Park) remove the hub cap, if equipped, and loosen, but do not remove, the wheel lug nuts.

14 Using a jack positioned in the proper location on the car (see *Jacking and towing* at the front of this manual), raise the car just enough so that the tire clears the ground surface.

15 Remove the lug nuts.

16 Remove the wheel and tire.

17 If a flat tire is being replaced, ensure that there's adequate ground clearance for the new inflated tire, then mount the wheel and tire on the wheel studs.

18 Apply a light coat of spray lubricant or light oil to the wheel stud threads and install the lug nuts. On steel wheels, be sure the cone-shaped end faces the wheel.

19 Lower the car until the tire contacts the ground and the wheel studs are centered in their wheel holes.

20 Tighten the lug nuts evenly in a cross-pattern, and torque to specs.

21 Lower the car completely and remove the jack.

22 Replace the hub cap, if so equipped.

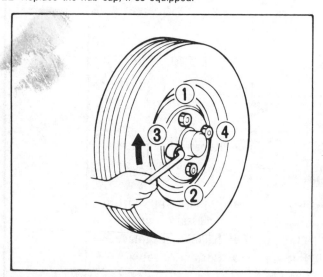

Fig. 1.12 The wheel lug nuts should be tightened in the diagonal pattern shown (Sec 5)

Spare tire mounting and dismounting

23 Remove the uninflated spare tire and the compressed air canister or air compressor from the rear compartment.

24 Jack up the car (referring to the *Jacking and towing* section in the front of this manual, if necessary) and remove the damaged tire.

25 Mount the still uninflated spare tire onto the axle and install the wheel lug nuts only finger tight. **Caution:** *Use only lug nuts designed for steel wheels to retain the spare tire to the axle.* On cars equipped with aluminum wheels, special lug nuts for this purpose are included in the car's tool kit.

Inflation with compressed air canister

Caution: *Prior to inflation, carefully read the directions and caution notes on both the air canister and spare tire.*

26 Position the spare tire so the tire valve is at the 6 o'clock position.

27 **Note:** *If the outside temperature is below 14°F, the air canister should be warmed up prior to operation. This can be done by placing the canister next to the windshield defroster for about 5 to 10 minutes.* Remove the valve cap from the spare tire, and position the air canister on the valve. Holding the canister tightly in place, depress the release button. You should be able to hear the gas entering the spare tire. **Caution:** *The metal parts of the canister become extremely cold during inflation and can cause frostbite, so adequate protection should be used to prevent contact.*

28 To be sure as much gas as possible enters the tire, hold the canister in position with the button depressed for an additional minute after the sound stops.

29 Following inflation, remove the canister from the tire valve and save it for later disposal. **Note:** *A new air canister should be bought promptly to be prepared for further emergencies.*

30 Replace the tire valve cap, lower the car to the ground, and fully tighten the wheel lug nuts in the sequence shown in Fig. 1.12. The spare tire is now ready to be driven on. **Note:** *In cold weather the tire may not appear fully inflated. In this case, drive slowly for the first mile or two until the tire temperature rises and the pressure increases.*

Spare tire inflation with air compressor

31 Remove the valve cap from the spare tire, and securely connect the air compressor hose to the valve.

32 Insert the air compressor power cord into the cigarette lighter socket. It will take about six minutes for the compressor to inflate the tire to the recommended pressure of 28 psi. **Note:** *Running the engine will increase the operation of the air compressor, but prior to doing this, the car should be lowered from the jack so the weight is on the spare tire.*

33 Once the tire is fully inflated, remove the power cord plug from the cigarette lighter socket. Check the tire for correct pressure with a pressure gauge and adjust it as necessary.

34 Disconnect the air compressor hose from the tire valve and replace the valve cap. Lower the car to the ground (if not already done) and fully tighten the wheel lug nuts.

Spare tire deflation

35 After dismounting the spare tire from the axle, the tire can be deflated by depressing the valve core button in the valve stem, or by removing the valve core with a valve core removing tool. **Note:** *Be careful not to inhale the escaping air from the tire.*

36 After the spare tire is deflated, flatten the tire to its original shape, replace the valve cap, and store it in the rear compartment.

Tire rotation

37 The tires should be rotated at the specified intervals and whenever uneven wear is noticed. Since the car will be raised and the tires removed anyway, this is a good time to check the brakes (Section 30) and/or repack the wheel bearings (Section 28). Read over these Sections if this is to be done at the same time.

38 The location for each tire in the rotation sequence depends on the type of tire used on your car. Tire type can be determined by reading the raised printing on the sidewall of the tire.

39 Radial tires, used on this car, tend to wear faster in the shoulder area than other tire designs. This is especially so for the front tires. Therefore, in order to obtain the maximum life from the tires, they should be rotated at 15 000 mile intervals, as shown in the *Routine maintenance* schedule.

40 Rotating the tires simply means that the rear tires are removed from the rear axle and remounted on the front axle. At the same time, the front tires are likewise transferred to the rear axle.

41 It is important with radial tires that the tires be kept on the same side of the car during rotation. For example, the right rear tire should be remounted in the right front position, while the right front tire is remounted in the right rear position. The same goes for the left side.

42 See the information at the front of this manual for the proper procedures to follow in raising the car and changing a tire; however, if the brakes are to be checked do not apply the parking brake as stated. Make sure the tires are blocked to prevent the car from rolling.

43 Preferably, the entire car should be raised at the same time. This can be done on a hoist or by jacking up each corner of the car and then lowering the car onto jackstands placed under the frame rails. Always use four jackstands and make sure the car is firmly supported all around.

44 After rotation, check and adjust the tire pressures as necessary and be sure to check wheel nut tightness.

6 Front end alignment

1 A front end alignment refers to the adjustments made to the front wheels so that they are in proper angular relationship to the suspension and the ground. Front wheels that are out of proper alignment not only affect steering control but also increase tire wear. On Datsuns, all of the front end adjustments (except toe-in) are preset at the factory and cannot be adjusted. If the camber, caster or steering axis (kingpin) inclination is found to be incorrect, this indicates wear of the related components.

2 Getting the proper front wheel alignment is a very tedious exacting process and one in which complicated and expensive machines are necessary to perform the job properly. Because of this, it is advisable

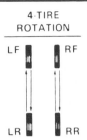

Fig. 1.13 Correct rotation sequence for radial tires (Sec 5)

to have a specialist with the proper equipment perform these tasks.

3 We will, however, use this space to give you a basic idea of what is involved with front end alignment so you can better understand the process and deal intelligently with shops which do this work.

4 *Toe-in* is the turning in of the front wheels. The purpose of a toe-in specification is to ensure parallel rolling of the front wheels. In a car with zero toe-in the distance between the front edges of the wheels will be the same as the distance between the rear edges of the wheels. The actual amount of toe-in is normally only a fraction of an inch. The 280ZX has a maximum static toe-in of 0 to 2 mm per wheel. Thus the distance between the front edges of the wheels should be a maximum of 4 mm less than the distance between the rear edges of the wheels when the car is standing. This is because even when the wheels are set to toe-in slightly when the vehicle is standing still, they tend to roll parallel on the road when the car is moving.

5 Toe-in is controlled by the adjustment of the tie-rod. Incorrect toe-in will cause the tires to wear improperly by making them 'scrub' against the road surface.

6 *Camber* is the tilting of the front wheels from the vertical when viewed from the front of the vehicle. When the wheels tilt outward at the top, the camber is said to be positive (+). When the wheels tilt inward at the top the camber is negative (–). The amount of tilt is measured in degrees from the vertical and this movement is called the camber angle. This angle affects the amount of tire tread which contacts the road and compensates for changes in the suspension geometry when the car is cornering or travelling over undulating surfaces.

7 *Caster* is the angle between the steering axis and a vertical line when viewed from each side of the car. Positive caster is when the steering axis is inclined rearward.

8 *Steering axis inclination* is the angle, when viewed from the front of the car, between the vertical and an imaginary line drawn between the upper and lower suspension arm pivots.

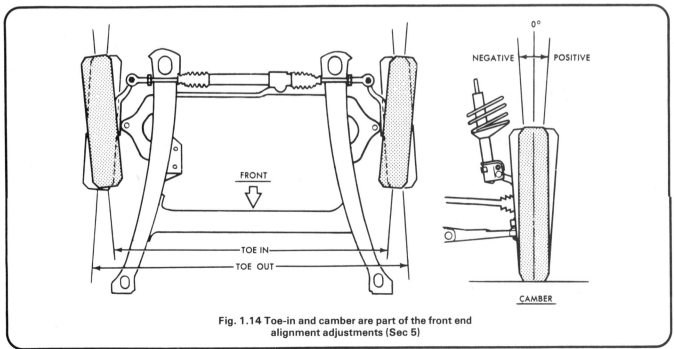

Fig. 1.14 Toe-in and camber are part of the front end alignment adjustments (Sec 5)

7 Wiper blade replacement

1 The wiper blade is removed by simply depressing the release tab at the end of the wiper arm, and pulling the blade out from the arm.
2 If it is necessary to remove the rubber element from the blade, compress and remove the locking clip from the bottom of the wiper blade (photo) and slide the element out.
3 If it is necessary to replace the wiper arm, remove the nut that secures the wiper arm to the linkage (photo), and lift off the arm.
4 When installing the wiper arm, be sure it is lined up with the other arm, and check for proper positioning on the shaft.

8 Engine oil and filter change

1 Frequent oil changes may be the best form of preventative maintenance available for the home mechanic. When engine oil gets old, it gets diluted and contaminated, which ultimately leads to premature parts wear.
2 Although some sources recommend oil filter changes every other oil change, we feel that the minimal cost of an oil filter and the relative ease with which it is installed dictate that a new filter be used whenever the oil is changed.
3 The tools necessary for a normal oil and filter change are: a wrench to fit the drain plug at the bottom of the oil pan; an oil filter wrench to remove the old filter; a container with at least a six quart capacity to drain the old oil into; and a funnel or oil can spout to help pour fresh oil into the engine.
4 In addition, you should have plenty of clean rags and newspapers handy to mop up any spills. Access to the underside of the car is greatly improved if the car can be lifted on a hoist, driven onto ramps or supported by jackstands. **Caution**: *Do not work under a car which is supported only by a bumper, hydraulic or scissors-type jack.*
5 If this is your first change on the car, it is a good idea to crawl underneath and familiarize yourself with the locations of the oil drain plug and the oil filter. Since the engine and exhaust components will be warm during the actual work, it is best to figure out any potential problems before the car and its accessories are hot.
6 Allow the car to warm up to normal operating temperature. If the new oil or any tools are needed, use this warm-up time to gather everything necessary for the job. The correct type of oil to buy for your application can be found in *Recommended lubricants* in the front of this Chapter.
7 With the engine oil warm (warm engine oil will drain better and more built-up sludge will be removed with the oil), raise the vehicle for access beneath. Make sure the car is firmly supported.
8 Move all necessary tools, rags and newspapers under the car. Position the drain pan under the drain plug. Keep in mind that the oil will initially flow from the pan with some force, so place the pan accordingly.
9 Being careful not to touch any of the hot exhaust pipe components, use the wrench to remove the drain plug near the bottom of the oil pan. Depending on how hot the oil has become, you may want to wear gloves while unscrewing the plug the final few turns.
10 Allow the old oil to drain into the pan. It may be necessary to move the pan farther under the engine as the oil flow reduces to a trickle.
11 After all the oil has drained, clean the drain plug thoroughly with a clean rag. Small metal filings may cling to this plug which could immediately contaminate your new oil (photo).
12 Clean the area around the drain plug opening and reinstall the drain plug. Tighten the plug securely with your wrench. If a torque wrench is available, the torque setting is 25 ft-lb.
13 Move the drain pan into position under the oil filter.
14 Now use the filter wrench to loosen the oil filter. Chain or metal band-type filter wrenches may distort the filter canister, but don't worry too much about this as the filter will be discarded anyway.
15 If the filter is on so tight it cannot be loosened, or is inaccessible with a filter wrench, as a last resort you can punch a metal bar or long screwdriver directly through the bottom of the canister and use this as a T-bar to turn the filter. If this must be done, be prepared for oil to spurt out of the canister as it is punctured.
6 Completely unscrew the old filter. Be careful, it is full of oil. Empty the old oil inside the filter into the drain pan.
17 Compare the old filter with the new one to make sure they are of the same type.

8.11 Metal particles attached to the engine drain plug are a sign of oil contamination and high internal engine wear

18 Use a clean rag to remove all oil, dirt and sludge from the area where the oil filter mounts to the engine. Check the old filter to make sure the rubber gasket is not stuck to the engine mounting surface. If this gasket is stuck to the engine (use a flashlight if necessary), remove it.
19 Open one of the cans of new oil and smear a light coat of this fresh oil onto the rubber gasket of the new oil filter.
20 Attach the new filter to the engine following the tightening directions printed on the filter canister or packing box. Most filter manufacturers recommend against using a filter wrench due to possible overtightening or damage to the canister.
21 Remove all tools, rags, etc. from under the car, being careful not to spill the oil in the drain pan. Lower the car off its support devices.
22 Move to the engine compartment and locate the oil filler cap on the rocker arm cover.
23 If an oil can spout is used, push the spout into the top of the oil can and pour the fresh oil through the filler opening. A funnel placed into the opening may also be used.
24 Pour about three quarts of fresh oil into the engine. Wait a few minutes to allow the oil to drain to the pan, then check the level on the oil dipstick (see Section 2 if necessary). If the oil level is at or near the lower L mark, start the engine and allow the new oil to circulate.
25 Run the engine for only about a minute and then shut it off. Immediately look under the car and check for leaks at the oil pan drain plug and around the oil filter. If either is leaking, tighten with a bit more force.
26 With the new oil circulated and the filter now completely full, recheck the level on the dipstick and add enough oil to bring the level to the H mark on the dipstick.
27 During the first few trips after an oil change, make a point to check for leaks, and also check the oil level.
28 The old oil drained from the engine cannot be reused in its present state and should be disposed of. Oil reclamation centers, auto repair shops and gas stations will normally accept the oil which can be refined and used again. After the oil has cooled, it can be drained into a suitable container (capped plastic jugs, topped bottles, milk cartons, etc.) for transport to one of these disposal sites.

9 Battery maintenance and servicing

General maintenance and testing

1 In models equipped with a conventional battery, the electrolyte level should be checked every week. Refer to Section 4.
2 If the car is equipped with a battery level warning light the fluid level should still be checked visually on a regular basis to make sure all cells are remaining even.
3 On some models a sealed maintenance-free battery is used. As opposed to conventional batteries, it has no vent plugs in the top, and is completely sealed except for a small vent hole. Because of its sealed

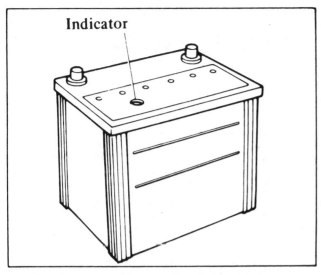

Fig. 1.15 The maintenance-free type battery has a built-in indicator on top to show the state of charge (Sec 9)

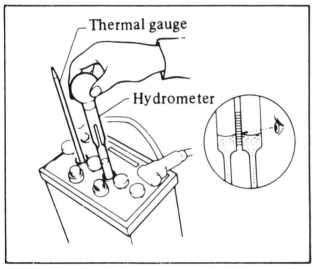

Fig 1.16 Using a hydrometer is the most accurate method of finding the specific gravity of the battery (Sec 9)

	ACTUAL SPECIFIC GRAVITY										
1.300	1.280	1.284	1.288	1.292	1.296	1.300	1.304	1.308	1.312	1.316	1.320
1.280	1.260	1.264	1.268	1.272	1.276	1.280	1.284	1.288	1.292	1.296	1.300
1.260	1.240	1.244	1.248	1.252	1.256	1.260	1.264	1.268	1.272	1.276	1.280
1.240	1.220	1.224	1.228	1.232	1.236	1.240	1.244	1.248	1.252	1.256	1.260
1.220	1.200	1.204	1.208	1.212	1.216	1.220	1.224	1.288	1.232	1.236	1.240
1.200	1.180	1.184	1.188	1.192	1.196	1.200	1.204	1.208	1.212	1.216	1.220
1.180	1.160	1.164	1.168	1.172	1.176	1.180	1.184	1.188	1.192	1.196	1.200
1.160	1.140	1.144	1.148	1.152	1.156	1.160	1.164	1.168	1.172	1.176	1.180
1.140	1.120	1.124	1.128	1.132	1.136	1.140	1.144	1.148	1.152	1.156	1,160
1.120	1.100	1.104	1.108	1.112	1.116	1.120	1.124	1.128	1.132	1.136	1.140
1.100	1.080	1.084	1.088	1.092	1.096	1.100	1.104	1.108	1.112	1.116	1.120
	−1°C	4°C	10°C	16°C	21°C	27°C	32°C	38°C	43°C	49°C	54°C
	30°F	40°F	50°F	60°F	70°F	80°F	90°F	100°F	110°F	120°F	130°F
	ELECTROLYTE TEMPERATURE										

(INDICATED SPECIFIC GRAVITY — left-hand vertical column label)

Fig. 1.17 Battery specific gravity temperature correction chart (Sec 9)

design this battery never needs water added, which greatly decreases the normal maintenance of it.

4 A temperature-compensated hydrometer is built into the top of maintenance-free batteries, which gives an indication of the electrolyte level and the battery's state of charge. If a blue indicator is seen in the indicator window on top of the battery, then the battery is properly charged. If the indicator is transparent, then the battery's charge is low and requires charging.

5 Periodically clean the top and sides of the battery, removing all dirt and moisture. This helps prevent corrosion and ensures that the battery does not become partially discharged by leakage through dampness and dirt.

6 Once every three months, remove the battery and inspect the battery securing bolts, the battery clamp plate, and battery leads for corrosion (white fluffy deposits on the metal which are brittle to touch). If any corrosion is found, clean off the deposits with an ammonia or baking soda solution. After cleaning, smear petroleum jelly on the battery terminals and lead connectors. Application of a zinc-base primer and/or underbody paint will help to prevent recurrence of corrosion on body panel metal.

7 The freezing point of electrolyte depends on its specific gravity. Since freezing can ruin a battery, it should be kept in a fully charged state to protect against freezing.

8 If topping-up a conventional battery becomes excessive and the case has been inspected for cracks that could cause leakage, but none are found, the battery is being over-charged and the alternator will have to be tested and if necessary serviced as described in Chapter 5.

9 If any doubt exists about the state of charge of a battery, a hydrometer should be used to test it by withdrawing a little electrolyte from each cell in turn.

10 The specific gravity of the electrolyte at the temperature of 80°F (26.7°C) will be approximately 1.270 for a fully charged battery. For every 10°F (5.5°C) that the electrolyte temperature is above that stated, add 0.04 to the specific gravity or subtract 0.04 if the temperature is below that stated.

11 A specific gravity reading of 1.240 with an electrolyte temperature of 80°F (26.7°C) indicates a half-charged battery.

12 Some of the common causes of battery failure are:

Accessories, especially headlights, left on overnight or for several hours.
Slow average driving speeds for short intervals.
The electrical load of the car being more than the alternator output. This is especially common when several high-draw accessories are being used simultaneously, such as radios/stereos, air conditioning, window defoggers, light systems, etc.
Charging system faults, such as electrical shorts, slipping belt, defective alternator or faulty voltage regulator.
Battery neglect, such as loose or corroded terminals or loose battery hold-down clamp.

Battery charging

13 In winter when heavy demand is placed upon the battery, such as when starting from cold, and much electrical equipment is continually in use, it's a good idea to occasionally have the battery fully charged from an external source.

14 When charging the battery the negative cable should be disconnected. Also the charger leads should be connected to the battery **before** the charger is plugged in or turned on. If the leads are connected to the battery terminals after the charger is on, a spark could occur which could ignite the battery gases.

15 The battery should be charged at a low rate of about 4 to 6 amps, and should be left on for at least a couple of hours. Alternatively, a trickle charger charging at the rate of 1.5 amps can be safely used overnight.

16 Special rapid 'boost' charges which are claimed to restore the power of the battery in one to two hours are most dangerous, as they can cause serious damage to the battery plates. This type of charge should only be used in a 'crisis' situation.

17 The battery should be left on the charger only until the specific gravity of the battery is brought up to a normal level (paragraphs 9 - 11). On maintenance-free batteries, continue to charge only until the blue indicator is seen in the indicator window. Do not overcharge the battery. **Note:** *Some 'automatic' battery chargers will automatically shut off after the battery is fully charged, making it unnecessary to keep a close watch on the state of charge.*

18 When disconnecting the charger, once again turn the charger off or unplug it **before** disconnecting the charger leads from the battery.

Emergency jump starting

Note: *When jump starting the battery, be sure that the voltage of the booster battery does not exceed 12 volts. Jumping from a higher voltage rating battery can cause damage to the electronic control unit and other electrical components.*

19 Apply the parking brake and place the transmission in Park if automatic, or Neutral if manual.
20 Remove any rings, watches, or other jewelry.
21 Do not allow any battery acid to contact eyes, skin, clothing or painted surfaces. Flush any contacted area immediately with water.
22 Hook up one end of the positive jumper cable to the positive terminal of the booster battery and the other end to the positive terminal of the discharged battery. Do not permit the vehicles to touch each other. Be sure that the positive jumper cable does not contact any metal part of either car, as this will create a short circuit.
23 Hook up one end of the negative jumper cable to the negative terminal of the booster battery and the other end to a solid engine ground at least 18 inches (450 mm) from the discharged battery. Do not connect the cable directly to the negative terminal of the dead battery.
24 Start the engine of the car that is providing the boost and turn off all electrical accessories.
25 Start the engine of the car with the discharged battery.
26 Reverse these directions exactly when removing the jumper cables. The negative cable must be removed from the engine that was jump-started first.

Battery removal and installation

27 The battery is located at the front right side of the engine compartment, and is held in place by a hold-down clamp across the top of the battery case.
28 As hydrogen gas is produced by the battery, keep open flames or lighted cigarettes away from the battery at all times.
29 Always keep the battery in the upright position. Any spilled electrolyte from the vent hole should be immediately flushed with large quantities of water. Wear eye protection when working with a battery to prevent serious eye damage from splashed fluid.
30 Always disconnect the negative (–) battery cable first, followed by the positive (+) cable.
31 If equipped with a battery fluid warning light, disconnect the wiring lead running to one of the battery vent caps.
32 Loosen the two clamp nuts until the hooked bottom ends of the clamp rods can be disengaged from the battery support bracket. Then lift off the entire clamp assembly.
33 Carefully lift the battery from its tray and out of the engine compartment.
34 Installation is a reverse of removal; however, make sure that the hold-down clamp is securely tightened. Do not over-tighten, however, as this may damage the battery case. The battery posts and cable ends should be cleaned prior to connection.

10 Spark plugs replacement

1 Properly functioning spark plugs are a necessity if the engine is to perform properly. At the intervals specified in the *Routine maintenance* schedule, the spark plugs should be replaced with new ones.
2 There are six spark plugs used in the L28E and L28ET engines, and they are located on the right side of the cylinder head.
3 In most cases the tools necessary for a spark plug replacement job are a plug wrench or spark plug socket which fits onto a ratchet wrench and a spark plug feeler gauge to check and adjust the spark plug gap. Special spark plug wire removal tools are also available for separating the wire boot from the spark plug.
4 The best policy to follow when replacing spark plugs is to purchase the new spark plugs beforehand, adjust them to the proper gap and then replace each plug one at a time.
5 When buying the new spark plugs it is important to replace the old plugs with new ones of the same heat range and type. A series of numbers and letters are stamped on the plug to help identify each variation. The correct type of plug for your Datsun engine can be found in the Specifications at the beginning of this Chapter, but should be

checked with the information found in the factory owner's manual. If differences exist between these sources, purchase the type specified by the factory.
6 With the new spark plugs at hand, allow the engine to thoroughly cool before attempting the removal. During this cooling time, each of the new spark plugs can be inspected for defects and the gap can be checked.
7 The spark plug gap is of considerable importance. If it is too large or too small the size of the spark and its efficiency will be seriously impaired. The gap is checked by inserting the proper thickness gauge between the electrodes at the tip of the plug. The gap between these electrodes should be the same as that given in the Specifications. The gauge wire or blade should just touch each of the electrodes. If the gap is incorrect, use the notched adjuster on the gauge to bend the curved side electrode slightly until the proper gap is achieved. The center electrode should never be bent as this may crack the insulation and cause plug failure, or worse.
8 Also, at this time check for cracks in the spark plug body, indicating the spark plug should be replaced with a new one. If the side electrode is not exactly over the center one, use the notched adjuster to align the two.
9 Cover the fenders of the car to prevent damage to exterior paint.
10 With the engine cool, remove the spark plug wire from one spark plug. Do this by grabbing the boot at the end of the wire, not the wire itself. Sometimes it is necessary to use a twisting motion while the

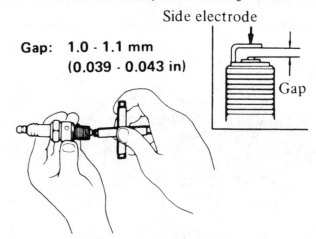

Gap: 1.0 - 1.1 mm (0.039 - 0.043 in)

Side electrode

Gap

Fig. 1.18 To adjust the gap of the spark plug, the side electrode is bent until it is the proper distance from the center electrode (Sec 10)

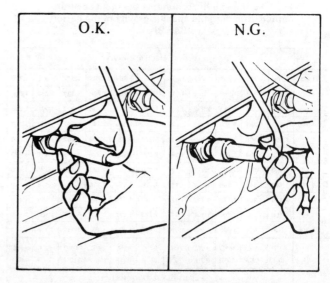

O.K.   N.G.

Fig. 1.19 When disconnecting the wires from the spark plugs, always pull the wire boot, not the wire itself (Sec 10)

boot and plug wire is pulled free. Using a plug wire removal tool is the easiest and safest method.

11 If compressed air is available, use this to blow any dirt or foreign material away from the spark plug area. A common bicycle pump will also work. The idea here is to eliminate the possibility of foreign material falling into the engine cylinder as the spark plug is replaced.

12 Now place the spark plug wrench or socket over the plug and remove it from the engine by turning in a counterclockwise motion.

13 The condition and appearance of the spark plugs will tell much about the condition and tune of the engine. If the insulator nose of the spark plug is clean and white with no deposits, this is indicative of a weak mixture, or too hot a plug (a hot plug transfers heat away from the electrode slowly – a cold plug transfers it away quickly).

14 If the tip and insulator nose is covered with hard, black-looking deposits, then this is indicative that the mixture is too rich. Should the plug be black and oily, then it is likely that the engine is fairly worn, as well as the mixture being too rich.

15 If the insulator nose is covered with light tan to greyish brown deposits, then the mixture is correct and it is likely that the engine is in good condition.

16 If there are any traces of long, brown, tapering stains on the outside of the white portion of the plug, then the plug will have to be replaced with a new one, as this shows that there is a faulty joint between the plug body and the insulator, and compression is being allowed to leak away.

17 Compare the spark plug with those shown on page 131 to get an indication of the overall running condition of the engine.

18 Insert one of the new plugs into the engine, tightening it as much as possible by hand. The spark plug should screw easily into the engine. If it doesn't, change the angle of the spark plug slightly, as chances are the threads are not matched (cross-threaded).

19 Firmly tighten the spark plug with the wrench or socket. It is best to use a torque wrench for this to assure that the plug is seated correctly. The correct torque figure is shown in the Specifications.

20 Before pushing the spark plug wire onto the end of the plug, inspect it following the procedures outlined in Section 10.

21 Install the plug wire to the new spark plug.

11 Spark plug wires check

1 The spark plug wires should be checked at the recommended intervals or whenever new spark plugs are installed.

2 The wires should be inspected one at a time to prevent mixing up the order which is essential for proper engine operation.

3 Disconnect the plug wire from the spark plug. A removal tool can be used for this, or you can grab the rubber boot, twist slightly and then pull the wire free. Do not pull on the wire itself, only on the rubber boot.

4 Inspect inside the boot for corrosion which will look like a white, crusty powder. Some models use a conductive white grease which should not be mistaken for corrosion.

5 Now push the wire and boot back onto the end of the spark plug. It should be a tight fit on the plug end. If not, remove the wire and use a pair of pliers to carefully crimp the metal connector inside the wire boot until the fit is secure.

6 Now using a clean rag, clean the wire its entire length. Remove all built-up dirt and grease. As this is done, inspect for burns, cracks or any other form of damage. Bend the wires in several places to ensure the conductive inside wire has not hardened.

7 Disconnect the wire at the distributor (again, pulling and twisting only on the rubber boot). Check for corrosion and a tight fit in the same manner as the spark plug end.

8 Reinstall the wire boot onto the top of the distributor.

9 Check the remaining spark plug wires in the same way, making sure they are securely fastened at the distributor and spark plug.

10 A visual check of the spark plug wires can also be made. In a darkened garage (make sure there is ventilation), start the engine and observe each plug wire. Be careful not to come into contact with any moving engine parts. If there is a break or fault in the wire, you will be able to see arcing or a small spark at the damaged area.

11 If it is decided the spark plug wires are in need of replacement, purchase a new set for your specific engine model. Wire sets can be purchased which are pre-cut to the proper size and with the rubber boots already installed. Remove and replace each wire individually to prevent mix-ups in the firing sequence.

12 Drivebelt check and adjustment

1 The drivebelts, or V-belts as they are sometimes called, at the front of the engine play an important role in the overall operation of the car and its components. Due to their function and material make-up, the belts are prone to failure after a period of time and should be inspected and adjusted periodically to prevent major engine damage.

2 The number of belts used on a particular car depends on the accessories installed. Drivebelts are used to turn: the alternator, power steering pump; water pump; fan; and air conditioning compressor (one belt is used to turn both the alternator and water pump/fan).

3 With the engine off, open the hood and locate the various belts at the front of the engine. Using your fingers (and a flashlight if necessary), move along the belts checking for cracks or separation. Also check for fraying and for glazing which gives the belt a shiny appearance. Both sides of the belts should be inspected, which means you will have to twist the belt to check the underside.

4 The tension of each belt is checked by pushing on the belt at a distance halfway between the pulleys. Push firmly with your thumb and see how much the belt moves downward (deflects). A rule of thumb, so to speak, is that if the distance (pulley center to pulley center) is between 7 inches and 11 inches the belt should deflect $\frac{1}{4}$ inch. If the belt is longer and travels between pulleys spaced 12 inches to 16 inches apart, the belt should deflect $\frac{1}{2}$ in.

5 If it is found necessary to adjust the belt tension of one of the belts, either to make it tighter or looser, refer to the appropriate procedure below.

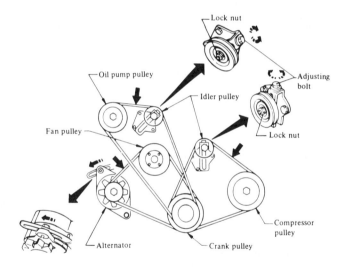

Fig. 1.20 Adjustment methods for the engine drivebelts (Sec 12)

Alternator/water pump belt

6 Loosen both the upper alternator adjusting bolt and the lower alternator mounting bolt.

7 Pivot the alternator either away from the engine or toward the engine until the proper belt tension is obtained. It may be necessary to use some sort of pry bar to move the alternator. If this is done to gain the proper leverage, be very careful not to damage either the alternator or the part pried against.

8 While holding the alternator in that position, retighten the two bolts. Then recheck the belt tension to make sure it is still correct.

Air conditioning compressor belt and power steering belt

9 Both of the belts that turn these components use idler pulleys to control the tension. There are two ways to adjust the tension, depending on the type of idler pulley used.

10 On one type, the idler pulley locknut, at the center of the pulley, must first be loosened. Then turn the idler pulley adjusting bolt either clockwise or counterclockwise, until the proper belt tension is obtained. Retighten the idler pulley locknut.

11 With the other type of idler pulley, the lock bolt is the bolt used to attach the pulley to its bracket. While holding the pulley with an open-

end wrench, loosen the lock bolt. Then, using either the open end wrench or a pry bar, move the idler pulley in the required direction to produce the correct belt tension. While holding it in this position, retighten the lock bolt.

12 With either pulley, after retightening the locknut or bolt, recheck the belt tension to make sure it is still correct.

13 Air filter replacement

1   At the specific intervals, the air filter should be replaced with a new one. A thorough program of preventive maintenance would also call for the filter to be inspected periodically between changes, especially if the car is often driven in dusty conditions.
2   The air filter is located inside the air cleaner housing at the front of the engine compartment, directly behind the radiator.
3   Remove the three wingnuts that hold the top plate to the air cleaner body and lift it off.
4   Lift the air filter out of the housing. If it is covered with dirt or soot, it should be replaced.
5   Wipe the inside of the air cleaner housing with a rag.
6   Place the old filter (if in good condition) or the new filter (if replacement is necessary) into the air cleaner housing.
7   Reinstall the top plate of the air cleaner and tighten the wing nuts.

14 Distributor check

1   Although the breakerless distributor used on this car requires much less maintenance than conventional distributors, periodic inspections should be performed at the intervals specified in the *Routine maintenance* schedule and whenever any work is performed on the distributor.
2   Remove the distributor cap by first disconnecting the ignition coil wire from the coil, and then unsnapping the spring clips that hold the cap to the distributor body.
3   Place the cap, with the spark plug and coil wires still attached, out of the way. Use a length of wire or tape to secure it, if necessary.
4   Remove the rotor, which is now visible at the top of the distributor shaft. The rotor simply pulls off the shaft. Place the rotor in a safe place where it cannot be damaged.
5   Visually inspect the various distributor components for any obvious signs of wear or damage. If dirt or oil has built up in the distributor, remove it by using a contact cleaner or other electrical parts solvent.
6   On Non-turbo models check the wire connections at the IC unit on the outside of the distributor body to make sure the connector is clean and tight. Also check the wires to make sure they are not cracked or broken.
7   Also on Non-turbo models, while the distributor cap is off, check the air gap as described in Chapter 5.
8   Before installing the rotor, inspect it for cracks or damage. Carefully check the condition of the metal contact at the top of the rotor for excessive burning or pitting. If in doubt as to its quality, replace it with a new one.
9   Before installing the distributor cap, inspect it for cracks or damage. Closely examine the contacts on the inside of the cap for excessive corrosion or damage (photo). Slight scoring is normal. Again, if in doubt as to the quality of the cap, replace it with a new one as described in Chapter 5.

15 Idle speed adjustment

1   Engine idle speed is the speed at which the engine operates when no accelerator pedal pressure is applied. This speed is critical to the performance of the engine itself, as well as many engine sub-systems.
2   A hand-held tachometer must be used when adjusting idle speed to get an accurate reading. The exact hook-up for these meters varies with the manufacturer, so follow the particular directions included.
3   Set the parking brake and block the wheels. Be sure the transmission is in Neutral (manual transmission) or Park (automatic transmission).
4   If equipped with an air conditioner, be sure it is turned off.
5   Start the engine and allow it to reach normal operating temperature.

14.9 If the distributor cap or rotor terminals are corroded or damaged, the cap should be replaced with a new one

6   Open the hood and run the engine at about 2000 rpm for about two minutes. Then allow it to idle again.
7   Race the engine two or three times and then allow it to idle again for about a minute.
8   If the car has an automatic transmission, have an assistant shift to Drive while keeping the brake pedal firmly depressed. If it has a manual transmission, it can remain in Neutral.
9   Now check the engine idle speed with the tachometer and compare it with the Specifications at the beginning of this Chapter.
10 If the idle speed is not correct, turn the idle speed adjusting screw (clockwise for slower, counterclockwise for faster) until the idle speed is correctly set (photo).
11 Automatic transmissions can now be shifted back to Park and the engine turned off.

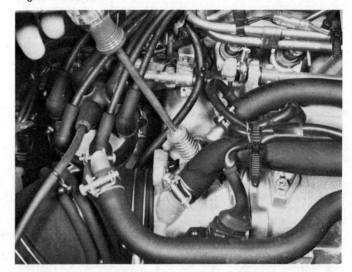

15.10 The idle adjusting screw is located on the top of the throttle chamber

16 Ignition timing

Note: *This procedure does not apply to Turbo models. For 1981 Turbo models refer to Step 17. For 1982 Turbo models see your dealer.*
1   The proper ignition timing setting for your car is printed on the tune-up decal located on the underside of the hood. It can also be found in the Specifications Section at the beginning of this Chapter. If there are any discrepancies between these specs, the tune-up decal should be given preference.

2   Locate the timing mark plate located alongside the crankshaft pulley (photo). The O mark is Top Dead Center (TDC). To locate which mark the notch in the pulley must line up with to achieve correct timing, count back from the O mark the number of degrees BTDC (Before Top Dead Center) as noted in Specifications. Normally, each mark on the timing plate equals 5 degrees. Thus if your vehicle specifications call for 6° BTDC, you should make a mark with fine paint or chalk just before the 5 mark on the timing plate.

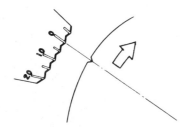

Fig. 1.21 Correct ignition timing is achieved when the notch in the crankshaft pulley lines up with the appropriate point on the timing plate (timing marks are spaced at 5° increments) (Sec 16)

3   Now locate the timing notch in the pulley and mark it with a dab of paint or chalk so it will be visible under the strobe light. To locate the notch it may be necessary to have an assistant temporarily turn the ignition off and on in short bursts to bring the notch into a position where it can be cleaned and marked. **Note:** *Stay clear of all moving engine components if the engine is turned in this manner.*
4   Connect a tachometer according to the manufacturer's instructions and
check that the idle speed is correct. Adjust, if necessary, as described in Section 15.
5   Allow the engine to reach normal operating temperature. Be sure the air conditioner, if equipped, is off. On appropriate models as noted in the Specifications, disconnect the distributor vacuum advance line from its canister and securely plug it.
6   With the ignition off, connect the pick-up lead of the timing light to the number one spark plug wire. This is the wire leading to the spark plug closest to the front of the car. Use either a jumper lead between the wire and plug or an inductive-type pick-up. Do not pierce the wire or attempt to insert a wire between the boot and the wire. Connect the timing light power leads according to the manufacturer's instructions.
7   Check that the wiring for the timing light is clear of all moving engine components, then start the engine.
8   Point the flashing timing light at the timing marks, again being careful not to come in contact with moving parts. The marks you made should appear stationary. If the marks are in alignment, the timing is correct. If the marks are not aligned, turn off the engine.
9   Loosen the adjusting screws at the base of the distributor (indicated by the long slots they are mated with) just until the distributor can be rotated.
10   Now start the engine and slowly rotate the distributor either left or right until the timing marks coincide.
11   Shut off the engine and tighten the distributor adjusting screws, being careful not to move the distributor.
12   Restart the engine and recheck the timing to make sure the marks are still in alignment.
13   Disconnect the timing light.
14   Race the engine two or three times and then allow it to run at idle. Recheck the idle speed with the tachometer. If it has changed from its correct setting, readjust it.
15   Drive the car and listen for 'pinging' noises. These will be most noticeable when the engine is hot and under load (climbing a hill, accelerating from a stop). If you hear engine pinging, the ignition timing is too far advanced (Before Top Dead Center). Reconnect the timing light and turn the distributor to move the mark 1° or 2° in the retard direction (counterclockwise). Road test the car again for proper operation.
16   To keep 'pinging' at a minimum, yet still allow you to operate the car at the specified timing setting, it is advisable to use gasoline of the same octane at all times. Switching fuel brands and octane levels can decrease performance and economy, and possibly damage the engine.
17   Although the ignition timing on 1981 Turbo models is controlled by the electronic control unit and normally needs no adjustment, it is

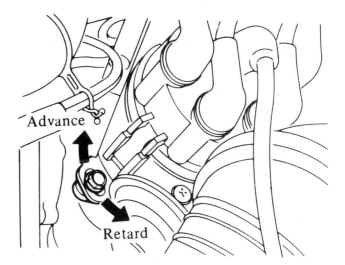

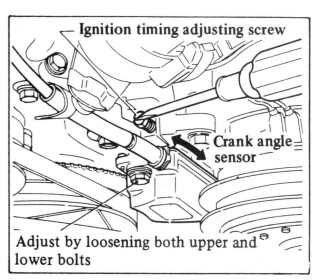

Fig. 1.22 Ignition timing is adjusted by swiveling the distributor slightly either clockwise or counterclockwise on standard models (above) or turning the crank angle sensor adjusting screw on 1981 Turbo models (below)

possible the timing can go wrong if the crank angle sensor becomes misaligned. The crank angle sensor is located at the front of the engine, alongside the crankshaft pulley.
18   In such an instance, the ignition timing can be adjusted by following the procedure described for standard models with the following exception:
19   Instead of adjusting the timing by loosening the distributor adjusting screws, the crank angle sensor mounting bolts should be loosened. The timing can then be adjusted by turning the adjusting screw at the top of the sensor. Once the timing is correctly adjusted, retighten the sensor mounting screws.
20   Following adjustment of the ignition timing, the radial adjustment of the crank angle sensor should be checked as described in Chapter 4.

17 Idle fuel/air ratio adjustment

Note: *The mixture ratio on certain models is preset at the factory, and cannot be readjusted. Check the Specifications of this Chapter for the specifics on each model. In order to adjust the mixture ratio on adjustable models, a CO% tester is needed, which is placed in the tailpipe of the car.*
1   On models equipped with air conditioning, the a/c compressor should be left off during the entire operation. Also the parking brake should be fully applied.

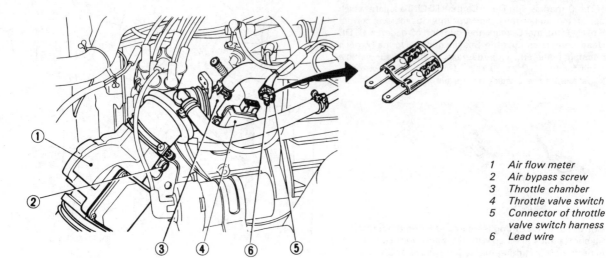

1 Air flow meter
2 Air bypass screw
3 Throttle chamber
4 Throttle valve switch
5 Connector of throttle
   valve switch harness
6 Lead wire

Fig. 1.23 The mixture ratio should be adjusted only under full enrichment, achieved by connecting the numbers 24 and 30 terminals of the throttle valve switch connector with a jumper wire (Sec 17)

1979 models

2 Start the engine and allow it to warm up to normal operating temperature.
3 Check the idle speed, using the procedure described in Section 15, and adjust it if necessary.
4 Check the ignition timing as described in Section 16 and adjust it if necessary.
5 If the car has an automatic transmission, have an assistant shift to Drive while keeping the brake pedal firmly depressed. If it has a manual transmission, it can remain in Neutral.
6 At this point check the CO% by inserting the probe of the CO% tester into the tailpipe at least 16 inches, and refer to the Specifications at the beginning of this Chapter for the proper setting. As soon as a reading is taken, shift automatic transmissions cars back to Neutral.
7 If the CO% reading does not match the Specifications, it must be adjusted, using the following procedure.
8 Turn the engine off and disconnect the wiring connector from the throttle valve switch.
9 Use a jumper wire with male terminals crimped or soldered to each end to connect the number 24 and 30 terminals of the throttle valve switch connector, as shown in Fig. 1.23.
10 Start the engine again, race it two or three times, and then allow it to idle for about a minute.
11 Remove the blind plug from the air by-pass screw on the air flow meter.
12 Have an assistant shift automatic transmission cars back to Drive with the brake applied, as before. Then turn the screw to adjust the CO% to the proper level for your altitude, as shown below (clockwise to make it richer; counterclockwise to make it leaner).

Altitude	CO% for US Federal models with catalytic converter	CO% for all other models
0 to 2000 ft (0 to 600 m)	5.1%	3.3%
2000 to 4000 ft (600 to 1200 m)	6.4%	4.7%
4000 to 6000 ft (1200 to 1800 m)	7.3%	5.7%
Over 6000 ft (1800 m)	8.3%	6.7%

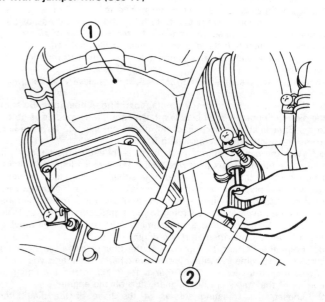

Fig. 1.24 The mixture ratio is adjusted by turning the air bypass screw on the air flow meter (Sec 17)

1 Air flow meter   2 Air bypass screw

13 When the proper CO% level has been obtained, turn the engine off (automatic transmission models should be shifted back to Neutral) and remove the jumper wire from the throttle valve switch connector. Reconnect the wire to the throttle valve switch.
14 Check the idle speed one more time, and adjust it if it has changed.
15 Check the CO% one more time to be sure it matches the levels listed in the Specifications at the beginning of this Chapter.

1980 and 1981 models

16 Start the engine and allow it to warm up to normal operating temperature.
17 Check the idle speed, using the procedure described in Section 15, and adjust it if necessary.
18 Turn the engine off and disconnect the wiring connector from the throttle valve switch.
19 Disconnect the charcoal canister purge hose from the intake manifold, and securely plug the manifold connector.

20 On 1980 US Federal models, disconnect the air induction hose where it connects with the metal pipe, and securely plug the pipe.

21 On appropriate models, as designated in the Specifications, disconnect the distributor vacuum advance hose from the vacuum canister and securely plug the hose.

22 Restart the engine and race it two or three times, then allow it to idle for about a minute.

23 Check the idle speed adjustment again, and readjust it if necessary.

24 Check the ignition timing as described in Section 16 and adjust it if necessary.

25 Use a jumper wire with male terminals crimped or soldered to each end to connect the number 24 and 30 terminals of the throttle valve switch connector.

26 Race the engine two or three times and then allow it to idle.

27 If the car has an automatic transmission, have an assistant shift to Drive (D) while keeping the brake pedal firmly depressed. If it has a manual transmission, it can remain in Neutral.

28 Check the CO% by inserting the probe of the CO% tester at least 16 inches into the tailpipe, and refer to the Specifications for the proper setting. **Note:** *For altitudes above 2000 feet (600 meters) refer to the CO% compensation chart below.*

Altitude	US models	Canada models
2000 to 4000 ft (600 to 1200 m)	2.4%	6.4%
4000 to 6000 ft (1200 to 1800 m)	3.5%	7.3%
Over 6000 ft (1800 m)	4.7%	8.3%

29 If the CO% does not match the Specifications, it must be adjusted by first removing the blind plug from the air bypass screw on the air flow meter, then adjusting the CO% to the proper level by turning the screw (clockwise to make it richer; counterclockwise to make it leaner).

30 Following adjustment, reinstall the plug over the air bypass screw, and then disconnect the jumper wire from the throttle valve switch connector.

31 To double check all settings, repeat the procedure described in paragraphs 22 through 30.

32 When all settings have been double checked, turn the engine off and reconnect the wiring connector to the throttle valve switch.

33 Unplug and reconnect the distributor vacuum advance hose, the canister purge hose and the air induction hose, as required.

34 Restart the engine and race it two or three times, and then allow it to idle.

35 Recheck the idle speed, and readjust it if necessary.

18 Cylinder compression testing

1 The purpose of testing the cylinder compression is to check the condition of the sealing components within the combustion chamber. Specifically, this test reveals excessive wear of the piston rings, cylinder walls or valves.

2 The only special tool needed for this test is a compression tester. These are available in two main types; one that screws into the spark plug hole, and a type that is simply held tightly in the spark plug hole. The screw-in types are usually more expensive, but are more accurate and easier to use.

3 Before beginning, check that the battery is fully charged and the engine oil is properly filled.

4 Start the engine and allow it to idle until it reaches normal operating temperature. Then turn it off.

5 Remove all six spark plugs from the cylinder head.

6 Disconnect the wiring connectors from all six injectors, and the wiring connector from the cold start valve.

7 Have an assistant depress the accelerator pedal all the way so the throttle valve is fully open.

8 Insert the compression tester into the first spark plug hole and have your assistant crank the engine over several times. Watch the gauge of the compression tester carefully and note the highest reading obtained.

9 Jot this reading down on a piece of paper. Then repeat the test on the other five cylinders.

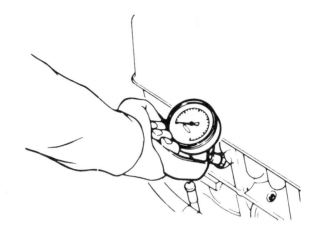

Fig. 1.25 Testing the cylinder compression with a compression gauge can pinpoint faulty rings or valves (Sec 18)

10 A compression reading of around 171 psi indicates that compression is normal. Readings slightly below this are acceptable as long as all cylinders are relatively even. No cylinder should have a reading less than 80% of the highest reading obtained.

11 If one or more cylinders are significantly lower than the others, or if readings of below 128 psi are obtained, then too much compression is being lost and servicing is required.

12 To help pinpoint the source of the problem, squirt a small amount of engine oil into the cylinder(s) giving the low readings, and retest the compression as before.

a) If the reading was higher after adding the oil, then the piston rings or cylinder walls are probably worn.

b) If the reading remained low, then the valves are either sticking or are not seating properly.

13 If cylinder compression is abnormally low in two adjacent cylinders, and adding oil does not help improve the compression, then the head gasket is probably damaged between these two cylinders. This could also be the cause for oil or water entering the combustion chamber.

14 If the compression tests show too much compression in the cylinders, then there could be excessive carbon build-up in the combustion chamber, which would also be a cause for hard starting when the engine is warm.

19 Valve clearance adjustment

1 Although the valves can be adjusted with the engine cold, it is better to adjust them with the engine hot. If they are adjusted cold, they should be rechecked once the engine has warmed up, and readjusted if necessary to conform to the hot engine specifications.

2 Start the engine and allow it to reach normal operating temperature. Then turn the engine off.

3 Remove the rocker arm cover as described in Chapter 2.

4 Rotate the camshaft so that the number one cam lobe points straight up. This can be done by using a ratchet wrench and socket on the crankshaft pulley bolt, at the front of the engine, and turning the crankshaft counterclockwise. Removing the spark plugs makes this easier. Another method is to use the ignition key to operate the starter in short bursts. If this is done the ignition coil wire should be disconnected from the distributor cap and grounded on the engine to prevent the engine from firing.

5 The valve clearance is measured by inserting the proper feeler gauge between the end of the cam lobe and the valve rocker. It should move with a slight drag when slid back and forth.

6 If the gap is either too large or too small, loosen the rocker pivot locknut and turn the rocker pivot to obtain the correct gap.

7 Once the gap has been set, hold the rocker pivot in position with the one wrench and retighten the rocker pivot locknut with another.

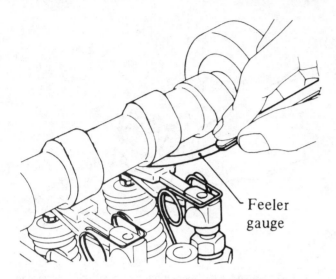

Fig. 1.26 Valve clearance is measured by inserting a feeler gauge between the cam lobe and the valve rocker (Sec 19)

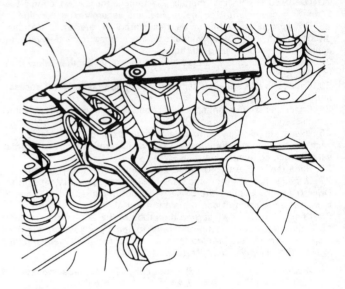

Fig. 1.27 Two wrenches should be used to adjust the valve clearance; one to loosen and tighten the locknut, and the other to turn or hold the rocker pivot (Sec 19)

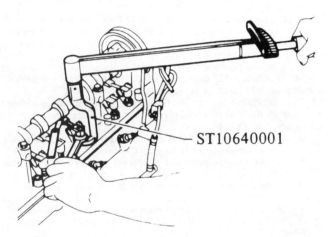

Fig. 1.28 Correct torquing of the rocker pivot locknut requires the use of a special adaptor such as the Datsun tool shown (Sec 19)

8   Recheck the valve clearance. Sometimes it will change slightly when the pivot locknut is tightened. If this is the case, readjust it until it is correct.
9   With the camshaft in this position, the number 1, 3, 7, 8, 9 and 11 valves can be adjusted using the procedure just described.
10 Now rotate the camshaft until the number one cam lobe is pointing straight down. In this position the number 2, 4, 5, 6, 10 and 12 valves can be adjusted in the same manner.
11 Tighten each pivot locknut with a special tool and torque to specifications.
12 After all valves have been adjusted, reinstall the rocker arm cover.

20 Fuel system pressure reduction

1979 models

1   Disconnect the negative battery cable.
2   Disconnect the wiring connector from the cold start valve.
3   Using two jumper wires, connect the cold start valve terminals to the terminals of the battery and allow them to remain connected for a few seconds. Take care not to touch the jumper wires together, as this will short circuit the battery.
4   Remove the jumper wires and reconnect the cold start valve wiring connector.
5   Reconnect the negative battery cable.

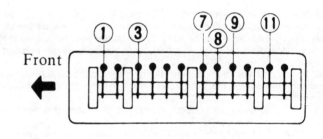

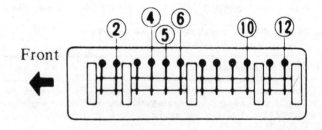

Fig. 1.29 With the number one cam lobe pointing up, the valves in the upper figure can be adjusted, while the valves in the lower figure can be adjusted when the number one cam lobe is pointing down (Sec 19)

1980 and 1981 Non-turbo models

6   Start the engine and allow it to idle.
7   Lift off the cover from the engine relay compartment.
8   With the engine still running, remove the fuel pump relay 2 (Fig. 1.31).
9   Wait for the engine to stall; then crank it over two or three more times.
10 Turn the ignition switch off, reinstall the fuel pump relay 2, and replace the relay compartment cover.

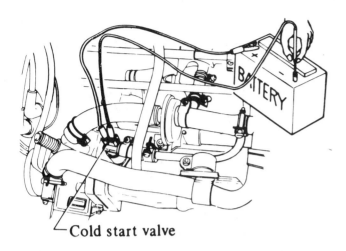

Fig. 1.30 On 1979 models, the fuel pressure is reduced by connecting the terminals of the cold start valve to the battery for a few seconds (Sec 20)

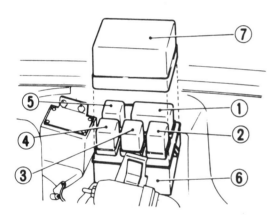

Fig. 1.31 The fuel pump relay two is located in the engine compartment relay box (Sec 20)

1	Fuel pump relay	5	Inhibitor relay
2	Lighting relay	6	Relay bracket
3	Bulb check relay	7	Relay bracket cover
4	Air conditioner relay		

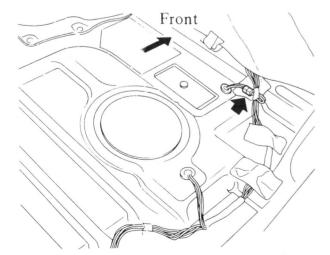

Fig. 1.32 On 1982 models, the wiring connector leading to the fuel pump must be disconnected to reduce the fuel pressure (Sec 20)

All 1982 and turbo models

11 Start the engine and allow it to idle.

12 With the engine still running, disconnect the wiring connector leading to the fuel pump (Fig. 1.32).

13 Wait for the engine to stall, then crank it over two or three more times.

14 Turn the ignition switch off, then reconnect the fuel pump wiring connector.

21 Fuel filter replacement

1 The fuel filter is a metal canister-like object attached by a bracket to the right shock well, and is specially designed for the high fuel pressures of the Datsun Electronic Fuel Injection system. Be sure to replace it with an equivalent fuel filter.

2 Before disconnecting the fuel lines from the filter, the pressure in the fuel system must be reduced to prevent dangerous spraying. For this procedure, refer to Section 20.

3 Disconnect both fuel lines from the fuel filter, and lift the filter out of its bracket.

4 When connecting the fuel lines to the new filter, use new hose clamps and position them so they are 3 mm ($\frac{1}{8}$ in) from the end of the hose.

22 PCV valve replacement

1 The PCV valve is located on the underside of the intake manifold. It is connected to a short rubber hose, which leads into the crankcase.

2 When purchasing a replacement PCV valve, make sure it is the proper type for your car.

3 Loosen the clamp that secures the hose to the PCV valve and disconnect the hose from the valve (photo).

22.3 The PCV valve (arrow) is located on the underside of the intake manifold

4 Unscrew the valve from the intake manifold.

5 Compare the old valve with the new one to make sure they are the same.

6 Screw the new valve into the manifold and connect the hose to it.

7 More information on the PCV system can be found in Chapter 6.

23 Air induction valve filter replacement

Note: *The air induction system is used only on 1980 US Federal models. The valve case and filter are located at the ignition coil.*

1 Disconnect the negative battery cable.

2 For clearance, remove the ignition coil. Refer to Chapter 5, if necessary.

3 Disconnect the rubber hoses from the valve case and lift it out.

4   Remove the screws that retain the valve case halves and separate the sections.
5   Lift out the old filter and install the new filter in its place.
6   The remainder of the procedure is the reverse of removal. When reinstalling the valve case, be sure the hoses are connected to the correct sides, so air will flow in the proper direction.

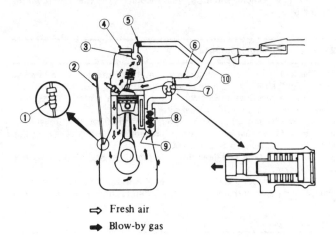

⇒   Fresh air
➡   Blow-by gas

Fig. 1.33 The PCV valve is located on the underside of the intake manifold (typical layout) (Sec 22)

1	Seal rubber	6	Throttle chamber
2	Oil level gauge	7	PCV valve
3	Baffle plate	8	Steel net
4	Oil filler cap	9	Baffle plate
5	Flame arrester	10	Air duct

24 Cooling system check and servicing

Checking
1   Many major engine failures can be attributed to a faulty cooling system. If equipped with an automatic transmission, the cooling system also plays an integral role in extending the life of the transmission.
2   The cooling system should be checked with the engine cold. Do this before the car is driven for the day or after it has been shut off for one or two hours.
3   Remove the radiator cap and thoroughly clean the cap (inside and out) with clean water. Also clean the filler neck on the radiator. All traces of corrosion should be removed.
4   Carefully check the upper and lower radiator hoses along with the smaller diameter heater hoses. Inspect their entire length, replacing any hose which is cracked, swollen or shows signs of deterioration. Cracks may become more apparent if the hose is squeezed.
5   Also check that all hose connections are tight. A leak in the cooling system will usually show up as white or rust-colored deposits on the areas adjoining the leak.
6   Use compressed air or a soft brush to remove bugs, leaves, etc, from the front of the radiator or air conditioning condensor. Be careful not to damage or cut yourself on the sharp cooling fins.
7   Finally, have the cap and system tested for proper pressure. If you do not have a pressure tester, most gas stations and repair shops will do this for a minimal charge.

Servicing
8   Periodically the cooling system should also be drained, flushed and refilled as per the *Routine maintenance* schedule. This is to replenish the antifreeze mixture and prevent rust and corrosion which can impair the performance of the cooling system and ultimately cause engine damage.
9   **CAUTION**: *As antifreeze is a poisonous solution, take care not to spill any of the cooling mixture on the vehicle's paint or your own skin. If this happens, rinse immediately with plenty of clear water. Also, it is advisable to consult your local authorities about the dumping of*

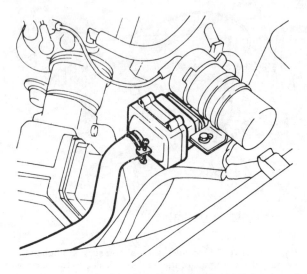

Fig. 1.34 The air induction valve case on 1980 US Federal models is located at the ignition coil (Sec 23)

Air cleaner side

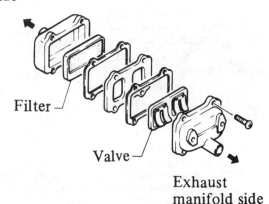

Filter

Valve

Exhaust manifold side

Fig. 1.35 Exploded view of the air induction valve case, showing location of filter and direction of reed valves (Sec 23)

antifreeze before draining the cooling system. In many areas reclamation centers have been set up to collect automobile oil and drained antifreeze/water mixtures rather than allowing these liquids to be added to the sewage and water facilities.
10 With the engine cold, remove the radiator pressure fill cap.
11 Move a large container under the radiator to catch the water/antifreeze mixture as it is drained.
12 Drain the radiator by opening the radiator drain valve, located in the center of the radiator's bottom. If this drain has excessive corrosion and cannot be turned easily, disconnect the lower radiator hose to allow the coolant to drain. Be careful that none of the solution is splashed on your skin or in your eyes.
13 If accessible, remove the cylinder block drain plug located at the left rear of the cylinder block. This will allow the coolant to drain from the engine itself.
14 If equipped disconnect the radiator overflow pipe and remove the reservoir. Flush it out with clean water.
15 Place a cold water hose (a common garden hose is fine) in the radiator filler neck at the top of the radiator and flush the system until the water runs clear at all drain points.
16 In severe cases of contamination or clogging of the radiator, remove it (see Chapter 3) and reverse-flush it. This involves simply inserting the cold pressure hose in the bottom radiator outlet to allow the clear water to run against the normal flow, draining through the

top. A radiator repair shop should be consulted if further cleaning or repair is necessary.

17 Where the coolant is regularly drained and the system refilled with the correct antifreeze/inhibitor mixture there should be no need to employ chemical cleaners or descalers.

18 To refill the system, reconnect the radiator hoses and install the drain plug securely in the engine. Special thread sealing tape (available at auto parts stores) should be used on the drain plug going into the engine block. Install the expansion reservoir and the overflow hose.

19 Fill the radiator to about an inch below the base of the filler neck. If equipped, add more coolant to the expansion reservoir so that it reaches the Min mark.

20 Run the engine until normal operating temperature is reached, and with the engine idling, add coolant up to the correct level (see Section 4), then install the radiator cap. Install the reservoir cap.

21 Always refill the system with a mixture of high-quality antifreeze and water in at least a 50/50 proportion. The antifreeze should not exceed a 70/30 ratio with the water, however.

22 Keep a close watch on the coolant level and the various cooling hoses during the first few miles or driving. Tighten the hose clamps and/or add more coolant mixture as necessary.

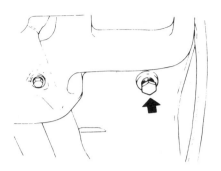

Fig. 1.36 The engine block drain plug is located at the left rear of the engine (Sec 24)

25 Accelerator linkage check and pedal adjustment

1 With the engine off, depress the accelerator pedal several times to make sure that the linkage is operating smoothly, without jamming or dragging. Also check that the pedal is returning to its original position when released.

2 Check the height of the accelerator pedal. It should be about $5\frac{1}{2}$ in (140 mm). If the height is not correct, loosen the locknut, and turn the pedal stopper bolt until the correct adjustment is obtained. Then retighten the locknut.

3 Have an assistant fully depress the accelerator pedal several times, and look into the throttle chamber to make sure the throttle valve is opening fully when the pedal is depressed and is closing fully when the pedal is released.

26 Clutch pedal adjustments

1 If equipped with a manual transmission, it is important to have the clutch pedal height and free play correctly adjusted. The height of the pedal is the distance it sits away from the floor (measurement H in Fig. 1.37) and the free play is the pedal slack or the distance the pedal can be depressed before it begins to have any effect on the clutch (measurement A in Fig. 1.37) Both of these measurements can be found in the Specifications of this Chapter. If these measurements are not as specified, the clutch pedal should be adjusted by using the following procedures.

2 First, ensure that the adjusting rod is correctly adjusted by measuring the distance between its ends (measurement L in Fig. 1.38). It should be $6\frac{3}{32}$ in (155 mm). If this distance is not correct, loosen the locknuts at each end of the center adjuster, and turn the adjuster until the correct adjustment is obtained. Then retighten the adjuster locknuts.

3 Now loosen the locknut and back off the pedal stopper or clutch switch (depending on model) so it is no longer touching the clutch pedal.

4 Loosen the pushrod locknut, and turn the pushrod until the distance between the top center of the pedal pad is $8\frac{1}{8}$ in (206 mm) from the floor panel. Then retighten the pushrod locknut. **Note:** *Be sure when making this adjustment that the pedal is not contacting the pedal stopper or clutch switch.*

5 Turn the pedal stopper or clutch switch in toward the pedal until the distance between the top center of the pedal pad and the floor panel is 8 in (203 mm). Then retighten the pedal stopper/clutch switch locknut. **Note:** *When making this adjustment, be sure that the pedal is not depressed more than $\frac{5}{32}$ in (4 mm) and that the pushrod is not pushed beyond its free play.*

6 Following adjustment of the pedal height, check that the pedal free play is between $\frac{1}{32}$ and $\frac{3}{16}$ in (1 to 5 mm). If it is not, readjust as in paragraph 2 until the free play is correct.

7 Following all adjustments, fully depress and release the pedal several times to ensure that the clutch linkage is operating smoothly and that there is no binding or squeaks.

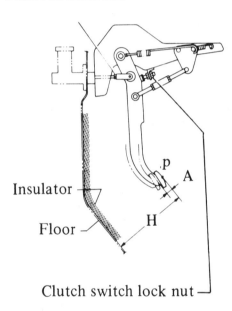

Push rod lock nut

Insulator

Floor

Clutch switch lock nut

Fig. 1.37 The clutch pedal should be periodically adjusted for correct height and free play (Sec 26)

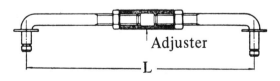

Adjuster

L

Fig. 1.38 The length (L) of the clutch pedal adjusting rod should be set at $6\frac{3}{32}$ in (155 mm) (Sec 26)

27 Parking brake adjustment

1   The parking brake does not need routine maintenance but the cable may stretch over a period of time necessitating adjustment. Also, the parking brake should be checked for proper adjustment whenever the rear brake cables have been disconnected.
2   While sitting in the driver's seat, pull up on the parking brake lever with heavy pulling force. When correctly adjusted the lever should move upward four to six ratchet clicks. The adjustment can be checked also by measuring the distance the lever moves upward. The proper adjustment is $3\frac{3}{8}$ to $1\frac{1}{4}$ in (86 to 109 mm), measured at the center of the handle. If the movement of the lever is shorter or longer than these specifications, the parking brake needs adjustment.
3   For clearance raise the rear of the car and support it on jackstands.
4   Loosen the locknut at the parking brake cable adjuster.
5   Turn the adjusting nut until the parking brake lever, when pulled, moves the proper distance.
6   Retighten the locknut.
7   Before lowering the car to the ground, check that both rear wheels turn freely with the parking brake released, and that there is no brake drag in either direction. Also be sure there is no slack in the rear parking brake cables when the lever is fully released.
8   Following adjustment, check that the parking brake warning light comes on after the lever has been pulled back one ratchet click, but goes off when the lever is fully released. If the warning light switch needs adjustment, remove the console box (Chapter 10), and bend the switch plate into position until the light operates as described.

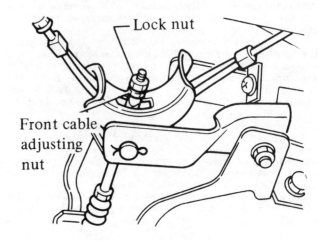

Fig. 1.39 Location of the parking brake cable adjusting nut (Sec 27)

28 Wheel bearings check

1   In most cases, the wheel bearings will not need servicing until the brake pads are changed. However, these bearings should be checked whenever the front wheels are raised for any reason.
2   With the vehicle securely supported on jackstands, spin the wheel and check for noise, rolling resistance or free play. Now grab the top of the tire with one hand and the bottom of the tire with the other. Move the tire in and out on the spindle. If it moves more than 0.005 in, the bearings should be checked, and replaced if necessary. Refer to Chapter 11 for the proper procedure.
3   Also, check for grease leakage from the front wheel bearing seals by first removing the wheel and tire, and inspecting the area around the bearing. Again, refer to Chapter 11 for replacement of the seals.

29 Chassis and body lubrication

1   A grease gun and a cartridge filled with the proper grease (see *Recommended lubricants)* are the only equipment necessary to lubricate the balljoints and tie-rods.
2   The balljoint grease fitting is located on the underside of each balljoint (photo), while the tie-rod fitting is located on the bottom of the joint between the tie-rod and the steering knuckle.
3   For easier access under the car, raise the vehicle with a jack and place jackstands under the frame. Make sure the car is firmly supported by the stands.
4   If grease nipples are not already installed in the greasing locations, the plugs will have to be removed and nipples screwed into place.
5   Before you do any greasing, force a little of the grease out of the nozzle to remove any dirt from the end of the gun. Wipe the nozzle clean with a rag.
6   Wipe the grease fitting nipple clean and push the nozzle firmly over the fitting nipple. Squeeze the trigger on the grease gun to force grease into the component. Both the balljoints and tie-rods should be lubricated until the rubber reservoir is firm to the touch. Do not pump too much grease into these fittings as this could rupture the reservoir. If the grease seeps out around the grease gun nozzle, the nipple is clogged or the nozzle is not fully seated around the fitting nipple. Resecure the gun nozzle to the fitting and try again. If necessary, replace the fitting.
7   Wipe any excess grease from the components and the grease fitting.
8   Next lower the front of the car, and raise the rear, again supported

29.2 Location of the balljoint (left) and tie-rod (right) grease fittings

by jackstands. Wipe any dirt or grease from around the grease plugs on the rear driveaxles. Then remove the plugs and install grease nipples in their place. Pump in grease as described above. **Note:** *If too much grease is added, it will leak from the dust seals, which could ruin the seals. Following greasing, remove the grease nipples once more and reinstall the plugs.*
9   While you are under the car, clean and lubricate the brake cable along with its cable guides and levers. This can be done by smearing some of the chassis grease onto the cable and its related parts with your fingers.
10   Lower the car to the ground for the remaining body lubrication process.
11   Open the hood and rear door and smear a little chassis grease on the respective latch mechanisms. Have an assistant pull the release knob from inside the car as you lubricate the cable at the latch.
12   Lubricate all the hinges (door, hood, trunk) with a few drops of light engine oil to keep them in proper working order.
13   Finally, the key lock cylinders can be lubricated with spray-on graphite, which is available at auto parts stores.

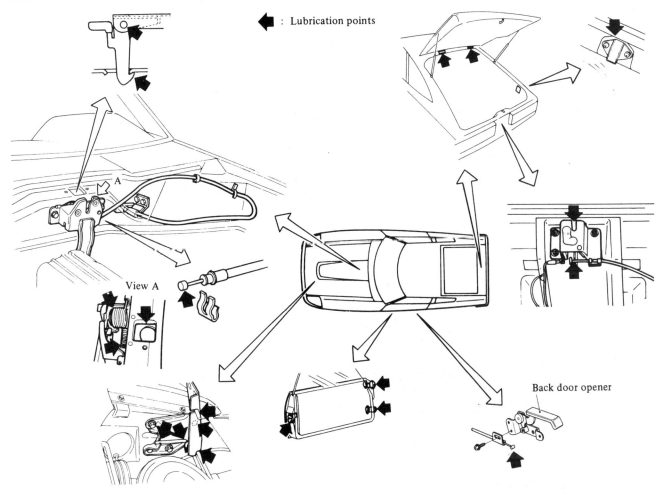

: Lubrication points

View A

Back door opener

Fig. 1.40 Lubrication points on the 280ZX body (Sec 29)

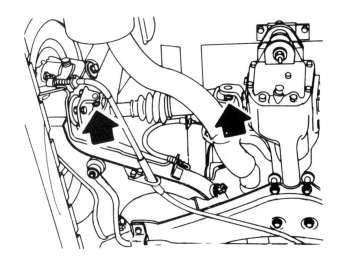

Fig. 1.41 Location of the lubrication plugs on the rear drive axles (Sec 29)

30 Brakes check

1   The brakes should be inspected every time the wheels are removed or whenever a fault is suspected. Indication of a potential braking system fault are: the car pulls to one side when brake pedal is depressed; noises coming from the brakes when they are applied; excessive brake pedal travel; pulsating pedal; and leakage of fluid, usually seen on the inside of the tire or wheel.

2   The thickness of the lining on the disc pads should be checked on a regular basis as damage can occur if the linings become excessively worn. All four pads on each axle (two on each wheel) should be replaced at the same time. Also, do not mix different types of replacement pads. All should be manufactured from the same material to give uniform performance.

3   To perform an inspection of the disc pad linings, first remove the wheel. Now visible is the disc brake caliper which contains the pads. There is an outer pad and an inner pad. Both can be seen through the inspection opening in the top of the caliper.

4   Measure the thickness of the lining material (see accompanying figure). If it is thinner than 2 mm (0.08 in), the pads should be replaced.

5   For a more thorough inspection, remove the pads as described in Chapter 9, and check that their surfaces are not glazed or deeply scored. If so, they should be replaced.

6   While checking the pad linings, also inspect the rotor surface for scoring or 'hot spots' indicated by small discolored blemishes. Light scoring is acceptable but if the damage is excessive the rotor should be resurfaced or replaced. The rotor should also be measured at several different points along its circumference with a micrometer to be sure it is not beyond its thickness wear limit (Specifications) (photo).

7   Before installing the wheels, check for any leakage around the brake hose connections leading to the caliper or damage (cracking, splitting, etc) to the brake hose. Replace the hose or fittings as necessary, referring to Chapter 9.

8   Finally, open the hood and check the hydraulic lines running from the master cylinder for any leakage. Also, check the vacuum lines running to the power brake booster to be sure they are not hardened or cracked, and are tight on their connections.

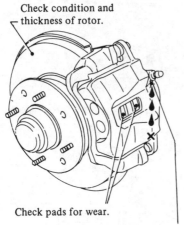

Check condition and thickness of rotor.

Check pads for wear.

Check caliper operation and inspect for leaks.

Fig. 1.42 The brake pad thickness can be easily checked by viewing through the inspection hole in the top of the caliper (Sec 30)

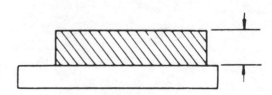

Fig. 1.43 Only the brake pad lining should be measured when checking the thickness of the brake pads (Sec 30)

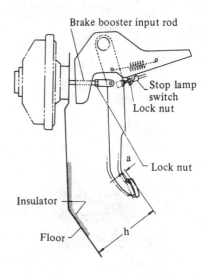

Brake booster input rod

Stop lamp switch

Lock nut

a — Lock nut

Insulator

Floor

h

Fig. 1.44 The brake pedal should be periodically inspected for correct height and free play (Sec 31)

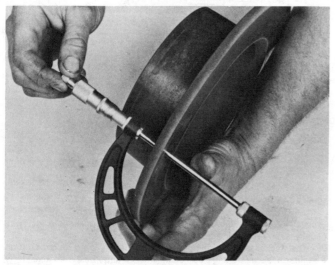

30.6 A micrometer should be used to check for uniformity in the thickness of the brake rotor

31 Brake pedal adjustments

1   The height of the brake pedal is the distance the pedal sits away from the floor. This distance should be between $7\frac{1}{8}$ and $7\frac{7}{8}$ in (181 and 187 mm) on manual transmission models, or $7\frac{1}{2}$ and $7\frac{3}{4}$ in (190 and 196 mm) on automatic transmission models. If the pedal height is not within this range, loosen the locknut on the stop lamp switch located in the bracket just forward of the brake pedal, and turn the switch in or out until the pedal height is correctly adjusted. Retighten the locknut.
2   The free play is the pedal slack, or the distance the pedal can be depressed before it begins to have any effect on brakes. This distance should be $\frac{1}{32}$ to $\frac{3}{16}$ in (1 to 5 mm). If it is not, loosen the locknut on the brake booster input rod, to which the brake pedal is attached. Turn the input rod until the free play is correctly adjusted, and then retighten the locknut.

32 Suspension and steering check

1   Whenever the front of the car is raised for service it is a good idea to visually check the suspension and steering components for wear.
2   Indications of a fault in these systems are: excessive play in the steering wheel before the front wheels react; excessive sway around

corners or body movement over rough roads, and binding at some point as the steering wheel is turned.
3   Before the car is raised for inspection, test the shock absorbers by pushing downwards to rock the car at each corner. If you push the car down and it does not come back to a level position within one or two bounces, the shocks are worn and need to be replaced. As this is done, check for squeaks and strange noises from the suspension components. Information on shock absorber and suspension components can be found in Chapter 11.
4   Now raise the front end of the car and support it firmly with jackstands. Because of the work to be done, make sure the car cannot fall from the stands.
5   Crawl under the car and check for loose bolts, broken or disconnected parts and deteriorated rubber bushings on all suspension and steering components. Look for grease or fluid leaking from around the steering gear assembly or rack-and-pinion. Check the power steering hoses and their connections for leaks.
6   The balljoint seals should, likewise, be checked at this time. After cleaning around the balljoints, inspect the seals for wear, cracking or damage, and replace if necessary as described in Chapter 11.
7   Grip the top and bottom of the wheel and try to rock it. It will not take any great effort to be able to feel any play in the wheel bearing. If this play is very noticeable it would be a good idea to adjust it right away as it could confuse further examinations. It is also possible that during this check, play may be discovered in the lower suspension balljoint (at the foot of the suspension strut). If this is the case the balljoint will need renewal.
8   Next grip each side of the wheel and try rocking it laterally. Steady pressure will, of course, turn the steering but an alternated back and

forward pressure will reveal any loose joint. If some play is felt it would be easier to get assistance from someone, so that while one person rocks the wheel from side to side, the other can look at the joints, bushes and connections in the steering linkage. On models equipped with a steering gear box there are eight places where the play may occur (Fig. 1.46). The two outer balljoints on the tie-rods are the most likely, followed by the two inner joints on the same rods, where they join to the center rod. Any play in these means renewal of the balljoint. Next are the two swivel bushes, one at each end of the center rod. Finally check the steering box Pitman arm balljoint and the one on the idler arm which supports the center rod on the side opposite the steering box. This unit is bolted to the side of the frame member and any play calls for renewal of the bushes.

9 To check the steering box, first make sure that the bolts holding the steering box to the side-frame member are tight. Then get another person to help examine the mechanism. One should look at, or get hold of, the Pitman arm at the bottom of the steering box while the other turns the steering wheel a little way from side-to-side. The amount of lost motion between the steering wheel and the Pitman arm indicates the degree of wear somewhere in the steering box mechanism. This check should be carried out with the wheels first of all in the straight-ahead position and then at nearly full lock on each side. If the play only occurs noticeably in the straight-ahead position then the wear is most probably in the worm and/or nut. If it occurs at all positions of the steering, then the wear is probably in the sector shaft bearing. Oil leaks from the unit are another indication of such wear. In either case the steering box will need removal for closer examination and repair.

10 On rack-and-pinion models, check for play at the outer ends of the tie-rods, or excessive play within the rack-and-pinion itself. Also check for grease leakage from the rack-and-pinion boots.

11 Following the inspection of the front, a similar inspection should be made of the rear suspension, again checking for loose bolts, damaged or disconnected parts and deteriorated rubber bushings.

◄ : Check tightening torque.

Fig. 1.45 Torque inspection points on the front suspension (Sec 32)

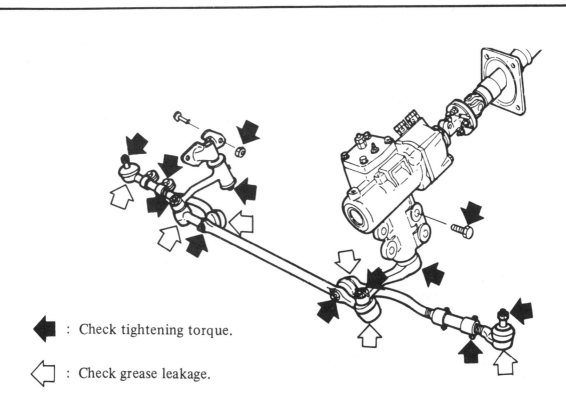

◄ : Check tightening torque.

◁ : Check grease leakage.

Fig. 1.46 Steering linkage inspection points for models equipped with a steering gear box (Sec 32)

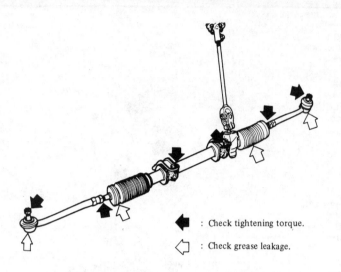

Fig. 1.47 Inspection points for models equipped with rack-and-pinion (Sec 32)

◀ : Check tightening torque.

◁ : Check grease leakage.

◀ : Check tightening torque.

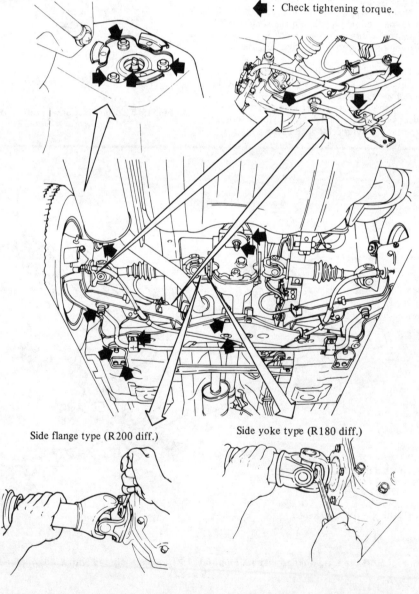

Side flange type (R200 diff.)　　Side yoke type (R180 diff.)

Fig. 1.48 Inspection points of the rear suspension and drive axles on standard models (Sec 32)

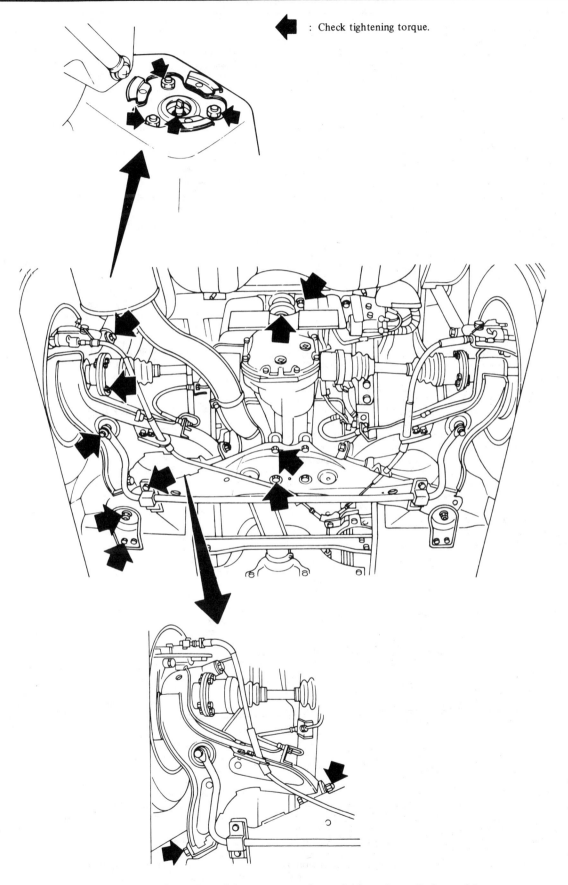

: Check tightening torque.

Fig. 1.49 Inspection points of the rear suspension and drive axles on Turbo models
(Sec 32)

33 Exhaust system check

1   With the exhaust system cold (at least three hours after being driven), check the complete exhaust system from its starting point at the engine to the end of the tailpipe. This is best done on a hoist where full access is available.
2   Check the pipes and their connections for signs of leakage and/or corrosion indicating a potential failure. Check that all brackets and hangers are in good condition and are tight.
3   At the same time, inspect the underside of the body for holes, corrosion, open seams, etc. which may allow exhaust gases to enter the trunk or passenger compartment. Seal all body openings with silicone or body putty.
4   Rattles and other driving noises can often be traced to the exhaust system, especially the mounts and hangers. Try to move the pipes, muffler and catalytic converter. If the components can come into contact with the body or driveline parts, secure the exhaust system with new mountings.
5   This is also an ideal time to check the running condition of the engine by inspecting the very end of the tailpipe. The exhaust deposits here are an indication of engine tune. If the pipe is black and sooty or bright white deposits are found here, the engine is in need of a thorough tune-up.

34 Drivetrain inspection

1   Raise the rear of the car and support it securely on jackstands. The transmission should be in Neutral.
2   Slide under the car and visually inspect the condition of the driveshaft. Look for any dents or cracks in the tubing. If any are found the driveshaft must be replaced (Chapter 8).
3   Check for any oil leakage at the front or rear of the driveshaft. Leakage where the driveshaft enters the transmission indicates a defective rear transmission seal. Leakage where the driveshaft enters the differential indicates a defective pinion seal. For these operations refer to Chapters 7 and 8 respectively.
4   While still under the car, have an assistant turn the rear wheel so the driveshaft will rotate. As it does, check that the universal joints are operating properly without binding, noise or looseness. Refer to Chapter 8 to correct any problems.
5   The universal joints can also be checked with the driveshaft motionless, by gripping your hands on either side of the joint and attempting to twist the joint. Any movement at all in the joint is a sign of considerable wear. Lifting up on the shaft will also indicate movement in the universal joints.
6   Finally check the driveshaft mounting bolts at both ends to make sure they are tight.
7   At the same time, check for looseness in the universal joints of the rear driveaxles in the same manner described above. Also check for grease or oil leakage from around the rear driveaxles by inspecting the rubber boots and both ends of each axle. Oil leakage at the differential junction indicates a defective side oil seal. Leakage at the wheel side indicates a defective rear axle grease seal, while leakage of the boots means a damaged rubber boot. Refer to Chapter 8 for servicing.

35 Fuel system check

There are certain precautions to take when inspecting or servicing the fuel system components. Work in a well ventilated area and do not allow open flames (cigarettes, appliance pilot lights, etc) near the work area. Mop up spills immediately and do not store fuel-soaked rags where they could ignite.
Caution: *The fuel system is under considerable pressure. Prior to disconnecting any fuel lines, the pressure in the system must be reduced. For this procedure refer to Section 20. Plug all disconnected fuel lines immediately after disconnection to prevent the tank from emptying itself.*
1   The fuel system is most easily checked with the car raised on a hoist where the components under the car are readily visible and accessible.
2   If the smell of gasoline is noticed while driving, or after the car has sat in the sun, the system should be thoroughly inspected immediately.
3   Remove the gas filler cap and check for damage, corrosion and a

proper sealing imprint on the gasket. Replace the cap with a new one if necessary.
4   With the car raised, inspect the gas tank and filler neck for punctures, cracks or any damage. The connection between the filler neck and the tank is especially critical. Somet imes a rubber filler neck will leak due to loose clamps or deteriorated rubber; problems a home mechanic can usually rectify.

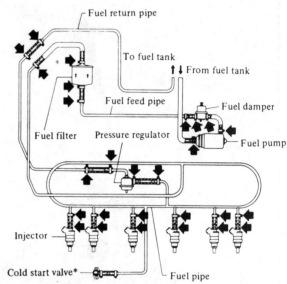

Fig. 1.50 When inspecting the fuel system, check carefully for leaks at the points where metal lines and rubber hoses join (Sec 35)

5   Do not under any circumstances try to repair a fuel tank yourself (except rubber components) unless you have considerable experience. A welding torch or any open flame can easily cause the fuel vapors to explode if the proper precautions are not taken.
6   Carefully check all rubber hoses and metal lines leading away from the fuel tank. Check for loose connections, deteriorated hose, crimped lines or damage of any kind. Follow these lines up to the front of the car, carefully inspecting them all the way. Repair or replace damaged sections as necessary.
7   If a fuel odor is still evident after the inspection, inspect the EEC system, as described in Chapter 6.
8   At this time the fuel tank vacuum relief valve should also be checked. The vacuum relief valve is integrated with the fuel check valve and is located to the right of the differential rear cover.

   a)   Disconnect the rubber hoses connecting the fuel check valve with the evaporation tubes (Fig. 1.51).
   b)   Remove the bolts retaining the check valve cover to the body, and lift off the valve and cover assembly. Then remove the check valve from the cover.
   c)   Wipe the valve housing clean, and then blow first a light amount of air into outlet C (Fig. 1.52), and then a heavier amount. No air should be felt passing through the valve when air is blown softly into the C port, but a heavier amount of air should open the diaphragm, allowing the entire amount of air to pass through. If this is not happening as described, the valve is defective and should be replaced.
   d)   Next, attempt to suck air through the C port. If you are not able to, the valve is normal. If you are able to suck air through the C port, the valve is defective and should be replaced.
   e)   Reinstallation of the valve and cover is the reverse of the removal procedure.

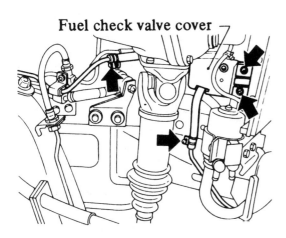

Fuel check valve cover

Fig. 1.51 Disconnection points for removing the fuel check valve and cover (Sec 35)

36 Evaporative Emissions Control (EEC) filter replacement

1   The function of the EEC system is to draw fuel vapors from the fuel tank, store them in a charcoal canister and then burn these fumes during normal engine operation.
2   The filter at the bottom of the charcoal canister should be replaced at the specified intervals. If, however, a fuel odor is detected, the canister, filter and system hoses should immediately be inspected for fault (Chapter 6).
3   To replace the filter, locate the canister at the front of the engine, on the left side of the radiator. It has three or four hoses running out of the top of it.
4   The canister is held to the body only by a strap, secured around the outside of the canister body. The canister is removed by simply releasing the strap and lifting it out.
5   Turn the canister upside-down and pull the old filter from the bottom of the canister.
6   Push the new filter into the bottom of the canister, making sure it is seated all the way around.
7   Place the canister back into position and secure the strap around it to hold it in position.
8   The EEC system is explained in more detail in Chapter 6.

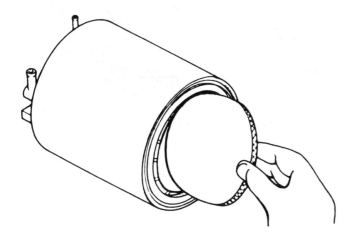

Fig. 1.53 The EEC filter is located at the bottom of the charcoal canister (Sec 36)

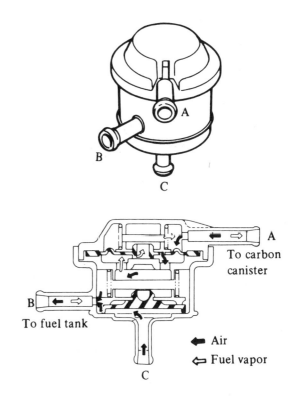

A
To carbon canister

B
To fuel tank

◀ Air
⇐ Fuel vapor

C

Fig. 1.52 Outlet identification and cross-sectional view of the fuel tank vacuum relief and check valve (Sec 35)

37 Exhaust gas sensor servicing

1   The exhaust gas sensor is a screw-in type sensor located in the exhaust manifold on 1980 Californian models, 1981 US and Turbo models, and all 1982 models. The sensor should be inspected at the intervals shown in the routine maintenance schedule, but need not be replaced unless found faulty.
2   Start the engine and allow it to warm up to its normal operating temperature.
3   Run the engine at about 2000 rpm for about two minutes.
4   With the engine still running, check to see if the inspection light on the bottom of the control unit is blinking on and off more than five times during a 10-second period. A mirror will have to be used to see the inspection light. The control unit is mounted on the left side firewall under the dash. Do NOT disconnect the wiring harness connector from the control unit.
5   If the control unit inspection light is operating as described, there is no problem. If not, the system should be checked out by a Datsun dealer.
6   If the exhaust gas sensor needs to be replaced, it may be difficult to remove when the engine is cold, so the operation is best done with the engine at operating temperature.
    a)   Remove the wiring connector from the sensor.
    b)   Apply a penetrating oil to the threads of the exhaust gas sensor and allow it to soak in for about 5 minutes.
    c)   Carefully unscrew the sensor and remove it. Be careful that you do not damage the threads in the exhaust manifold while removing the sensor.
    d)   Coat the threads of the new sensor completely with an anti-seize compound and install it.
    e)   Carefully torque the sensor to specifications.
    f)   Reconnect the wiring connector to the sensor.
7   Whether the exhaust gas sensor has been inspected and/or replaced or not, at 30 000 miles the exhaust gas sensor warning lamp will come on to indicate that the sensor should be inspected and serviced if necessary. Therefore, after inspecting the exhaust gas sensor, disconnect the warning lamp harness connector located under the right side of the instrument panel, so that it will not remain on (Fig. 1.54).

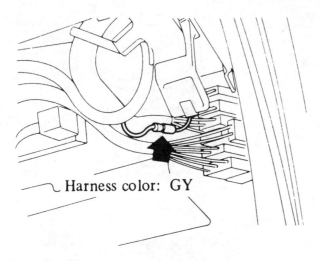

Fig. 1.54 Once the exhaust gas sensor warning light comes on, it can be turned off by disconnecting the wiring connector under the right side of the instrument panel (Sec 37)

38 Automatic transmission fluid change

1   At the specified time intervals, the transmission fluid should be changed. The routine maintenance chart calls for an automatic transmission fluid change only once every 30 000 miles. This interval should be shortened to every 15 000 miles if the car is normally driven under one or more of the following conditions: heavy city traffic; where the outside temperature normally reaches 90°F or higher; in very hilly or mountain areas; or if a trailer is frequently pulled.

2   Since there is no drain plug, the transmission oil pan must be removed from the bottom of the transmission to drain the fluid. Before doing any draining, purchase the specified transmission fluid (see *Recommended lubricants* in the front of this Chapter) and an oil pan gasket.

3   Other tools necessary for this job include: jackstands to support the vehicle in a raised position; wrench to remove the oil pan bolts; standard screwdriver; drain pan capable of holding at least 8 pints; newspapers and clean rags.

4   The fluid should be drained immediately after the car has been driven. This will remove any built-up sediment better than if the fluid were cold. Because of this, it may be wise to wear protective gloves (fluid temperature can exceed 350° in a hot transmission).

5   After the car has been driven to warm up the fluid, raise the vehicle and place it on jackstands for access underneath.

6   Move the necessary equipment under the car, being careful not to touch any of the hot exhaust components.

7   Place the drain pan under the transmission oil pan and remove the oil pan bolts along the rear and sides of the pan. Loosen, but do not remove, the bolts at the front of the pan.

8   Carefully pry the pan downward at the rear, allowing the hot fluid to drain into the drain pan. If necessary, use a screwdriver to break the gasket seal at the rear of the pan; however, do not damage the pan or transmission in the process.

9   Support the pan and remove the remaining bolts at the front of the pan. Lower the pan and drain the remaining fluid into the drain receptacle. As this is done, check the fluid for metal filings which may be an indication of internal failure.

10 Thoroughly clean the transmission oil pan with solvent. Inspect for metal filings or foreign matter. Dry with compressed air if available. It is important that all remaining gasket material be removed from the oil pan mounting flange. Use a gasket scraper or putty knife for this.

11 Apply a bead of gasket sealant around the oil pan mounting surface, with the sealant to the inside of the bolt holes. Press the new gasket into place on the pan, making sure all bolt holes line up.

12 Lift the pan up to the bottom of the transmission and install the mounting bolts. Tighten the bolts in a diagonal fashion, working around the pan. Using a torque wrench, tighten the bolts to specifications.

13 Lower the car off its jackstands.

14 Open the hood and remove the transmission fluid dipstick from its guide tube.

15 It is best to add a little fluid at a time, continually checking the level with the dipstick. Allow the fluid time to drain into the pan. Add fluid until the level just registers on the end of the dipstick. In most cases, a good starting point will be four to five pints added to the transmission through the filler tube (use a funnel to prevent spills).

16 With the selector lever in Park, apply the parking brake and start the engine without depressing the accelerator pedal (if possible). Do not race the engine at a high speed; run at slow idle only.

17 Depress the brake pedal and shift the transmission through each gear. Place the selector back into Park and check the level on the dipstick (with the engine still idling). Look under the car for leaks around the transmission oil pan mating surface.

18 Add more fluid through the dipstick tube until the level on the dipstick is $\frac{1}{4}$ inch below the lower mark on the dipstick. Do not allow the fluid level to go above this point, as the transmission would then be overfull, necessitating the removal of the pan to drain the excess fluid.

19 Push the dipstick firmly back into its tube and drive the car to reach normal operating temperature (15 miles of highway driving or its equivalent in the city). Park the car on a level surface and check the fluid level on the dipstick with the engine idling and the transmission in Park. The level should now be at the upper mark on the dipstick. If not, add more fluid as necessary to bring the level up to this point. Again, do not overfill.

39 Manual transmission oil change

1   Drive the car for a few miles to thoroughly warm up the transmission oil.

2   Move a drain pan (at least a five pint capacity), rags, nespapers and a $\frac{1}{2}$-in drive ratchet wrench with extension under the car.

3   With the drain pan and newspapers in position under the transmission, use the wrench and extension to loosen the drain plug located in the underside of the transmission case (photo).

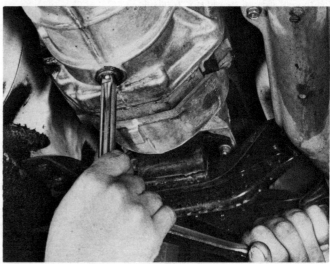

39.3 A $\frac{1}{2}$ in drive ratchet extension can be used to remove the manual transmission and differential drain plugs

4   Once loosened, carefully unscrew it with your fingers until you can remove it from the transmission. Allow all of the oil to drain into the pan. **Note:** *If the plug is still too hot to touch, use the wrench to remove it all the way, and simply allow it to drop into the pan.*

5   If the transmission is equipped with a magnetic drain plug, inspect it for bits of metal clinging to it. If there are, this is a sign of excessive internal wear of the transmission, indicating that the internal components of the transmission should be carefully inspected in the near future. If the transmission is not equipped with a magnetic drain plug, allow the oil in the pan too cool and then feel with your hands along the bottom of the drain pain for any metal bits.

6   Clean the drain plug off, then reinstall it in the transmission, torquing it to Specifications.
7   Now remove the transmission oil inspection plug located on the left side of the transmission case. Using a hand pump or syringe, fill the transmision with the correct amount and grade of oil (see Specifications), until the level is just at the bottom of the inspection plug hole.
8   Now reinstall the inspection plug, torquing it to specifications.

___

40 Differential oil change

1   Move a drain pan (at least five pint capacity), rags, newspapers and a $\frac{1}{2}$ in drive ratchet wrench with extension under the rear of the car.
2   With the drain pan under the differential, use the wrench and extension to loosen the differential drain plug. It is the lower of the two plugs in the rear of the differential.
3   Once loosened, carefully unscrew it with your fingers until you can remove it from the differential case.
4   Allow all of the oil to drain into the pan. Then replace the drain plug, torqueing it to Specifications.
5   Feel with your hands along the bottom of the drain pan for any metal bits that may have come out with the oil. If there are some, this is a sign of excessive internal wear of the differential, indicating that the internal components should be carefully inspected in the near future.
6   Now remove the differential inspection plug located above the drain plug. Using a hand pump, syringe or funnel fill the differential with the correct amount and grade of oil (see Specifications), until the level is just at the bottom of the inspection plug hole.
7   Now reinstall the inspection plug, torqueing it to specifications.

Chapter 2 Engine

Contents

Specifications

General

Engine model	
Non-turbo models	L28E
Turbo models	L28ET
Type	In-line six-cylinder with overhead cam
Firing order	1-5-3-6-2-4
Displacement	2753 cc
Compression ratio	
Non-turbo models	8.8 : 1
Turbo models	7.4 : 1
Bore and stroke	3.386 x 3.110 in (86.0 x 79.0 mm)

Cylinder head

Surface warp limit	0.004 in (0.1 mm)

Camshaft

Outer diameter of camshaft journal	1.8878 to 1.8883 in (47.949 to 47.962 mm)
End play	0.0031 to 0.0150 in (0.08 to 0.38 mm)
Cam lobe height	
1979 thru 1981 models (all)	1.5866 to 1.5886 in (40.30 to 40.35 mm)
1982 US models	
Intake	1.5728 to 1.5748 in (39.95 to 40.00 mm)
Exhaust	1.5866 to 1.5886 in (40.30 to 40.35 mm)
1982 Canada models (all)	1.5866 to 1.5886 in (40.30 to 40.35 mm)

Cam lobe wear limit	0.0059 in (0.15 mm)
Camshaft bend (total indicator reading at center journal)	0.0020 in (0.5 mm) max
Inner diameter of bearing	1.8898 to 1.8904 in (48.000 to 48.016 mm)
Journal-to-bearing clearance	
Standard	0.0015 to 0.0026 in (0.038 to 0.067 mm)
Maximum	0.004 in (0.1 mm)

Valves

Valve head diameter	
Intake	1.732 to 1.740 in (44.0 to 44.2 mm)
Exhaust	1.378 to 1.386 in (35.0 to 35.2 mm)
Valve length	
1979 and 1980 models	
Intake	4.52 to 4.54 in (114.9 to 115.2 mm)
Exhaust	4.56 to 4.57 in (115.7 to 116.0 mm)
1981 and 1982 models	
Intake	4.4409 to 4.4527 in (112.8 to 113.1 mm)
Exhaust	4.4724 to 4.4842 in (113.6 to 113.9 mm)
Valve stem diameter	
Intake	0.3136 to 0.3142 in (7.965 to 7.980 mm)
Exhaust	0.3128 to 0.3134 in (7.945 to 7.960 mm)
Valve face angle	45.5°
Valve head margin (wear limit)	0.020 in (0.5 mm)
Grinding of valve stem end limit	0.020 in (0.5 mm)
Valve spring free height	
Outer spring	1.9677 in (49.98 mm)
Inner spring	1.7657 in (44.85 mm)
Valve spring assembled height	
Outer spring	1.575 in @ 47 lb (40.0 mm @ 21.3 kg)
Inner spring	1.378 in @ 27.1 lb (35.0 mm @ 12.3 kg)
Out-of-square limit	
Outer spring	0.087 in (2.2 mm)
Inner spring	0.047 in (1.2 mm)
Valve guide diameter	
Outer	0.4733 to 0.4738 in (12.023 to 12.034 mm)
Inner	0.3150 to 0.3157 in (8.000 to 8.018 mm)
Valve stem-to-guide clearance	
Intake	0.0008 to 0.0021 in (0.020 to 0.053 mm)
Exhaust	0.0016 to 0.0029 in (0.040 to 0.073 mm)
Stem end deflection limit	0.008 in (0.2 mm)

Cylinder block

Surface warp limit	0.004 in (0.1 mm)
Inner diameter of cylinder bore	3.3858 to 3.3878 in (86.00 to 86.05 mm)
Cylinder bore out-of-round (standard)	0.0008 in (0.02 mm)
Cylinder bore taper (standard)	0.0008 in (0.02 mm)
Piston-to-cylinder clearance	0.0010 to 0.0018 in (0.025 to 0.045 mm)

Pistons

Diameter	
Standard size	
1979 and 1980 models	3.3852 to 3.3872 in (85.985 to 86.035 mm)
1981 and 1982 models	3.3844 to 3.3864 in (85.965 to 86.015 mm)
1st oversize	3.4041 to 3.4061 in (86.465 to 86.515 mm)
2nd oversize	3.4238 to 3.4258 in (86.965 to 87.015 mm)
Piston ring end gap	
Top ring	
Non-turbo models	0.0098 to 0.0157 in (0.25 to 0.40 mm)
Turbo models	0.0075 to 0.0130 in (0.19 to 0.33 mm)
Second ring	
1979 and 1980 models	0.0118 to 0.0197 in (0.30 to 0.50 mm)
1981 and 1982 models	0.0059 to 0.0118 in (0.15 to 0.30 mm)
Oil ring	0.0120 to 0.0354 in (0.30 to 0.90 mm)
Piston ring side clearance	
Top ring	0.0016 to 0.0029 in (0.040 to 0.073 mm)
Second ring	0.0012 to 0.0025 in (0.030 to 0.063 mm)
Oil ring	0.0009 to 0.0028 in (0.023 to 0.070 mm)

Connecting rod and bearing

Connecting rod big end play	0.008 to 0.012 in (0.2 to 0.3 mm)
Connecting rod bearing sizes	**Crankpin diameter**
Standard	1.9670 to 1.9675 in (49.961 to 49.974 mm)
0.0024 in (0.06 mm) Undersize	1.9646 to 1.9651 in (49.901 to 49.914 mm)
0.0047 in (0.12 mm) Undersize	1.9622 to 1.9628 in (49.841 to 49.854 mm)

0.0098 in (0.25 mm) Undersize	1.9571 to 1.9576 in (49.711 to 49.724 mm)
0.0197 in (0.51 mm) Undersize	1.9473 to 1.9478 in (49.461 to 49.474 mm)
0.0295 in (0.75 mm) Undersize	1.9374 to 1.9379 in (49.211 to 49.224 mm)
0.0394 in (1.00 mm) Undersize	1.9276 to 1.9281 in (48.961 to 48.974 mm)

Connecting rod bearing running clearance
- Standard ... 0.009 to 0.0026 in (0.024 to 0.066 mm)
- Maximum ... 0.0047 in (0.12 mm)

Crankshaft and main bearings

Crank journal diameter ... 2.1631 to 2.1636 in (54.942 to 54.955 mm)
Crankpin diameter ... 1.9670 to 1.9675 in (49.961 to 49.974 mm)

Journal and pin taper and out-of-round
- Standard ... less than 0.0004 in (0.01 mm)
- Maximum ... 0.0012 in (0.03 mm)

Crankshaft free end play
- Standard ... 0.0020 to 0.0071 in (0.05 to 0.18 mm)
- Maximum ... 0.012 in (0.3 mm)

Main bearing running clearance
- Standard ... 0.0008 to 0.0026 in (0.020 to 0.066 mm)
- Maximum ... 0.0047 in (0.12 mm)

Main bearing sizes

	Bearing thickness	Crank journal diameter
Standard	0.0717 to 0.0722 in (1.822 to 1.835 mm)	2.1631 to 2.1636 in (54.942 to 54.955 mm)
0.0098 in (0.25 mm) Undersize	0.0767 to 0.0772 in (1.947 to 1.960 mm)	2.1532 to 2.1537 in (54.692 to 54.705 mm)
0.0197 in (0.50 mm) Undersize	0.0816 to 0.0821 in (2.072 to 2.085 mm)	2.1434 to 2.1439 in (54.442 to 54.455 mm)
0.0295 in (0.75 mm) Undersize	0.0865 to 0.0870 in (2.197 to 2.210 mm)	2.1335 to 2.1341 in (54.192 to 54.205 mm)
0.0394 in (1.00 mm) Undersize	0.0914 to 0.0919 in (2.322 to 2.335 mm)	2.1237 to 2.1242 in (53.942 to 53.955 mm)

Flywheel maximum runout

Flywheel maximum runout ... 0.0059 in (0.15 mm)

Oil pump

Rotor tip clearance ... less than 0.0079 in (0.20 mm)
Outer rotor-to-body clearance ... less than 0.0197 in (0.50 mm)
Rotor side clearance ... less than 0.0024 in (0.06 mm)
Pump body side clearancee ... less than 0.0012 in (0.03 mm)

Torque specifications

	ft-lb	m-kg
Front cover bolts		
Small	5	0.7
Large	10	1.3
Chain guide bolts	6	0.8
Chain tensioner bolts	6	0.8
Water pump bolts		
Small	5	0.7
Large	10	1.3
Crankshaft pulley bolt	108	15.0
Intake manifold bolts and nut	15	1.9
Alternator bracket bolts	36	5.0
Alternator adjusting bolt	18	2.5
Engine mounting bracket bolts	25	3.5
Exhaust manifold bolts and nuts	14	1.9
EGR tube nut	29	3.0
A/C compressor bracket bolts	36	5.0
Cylinder head bolts	55	7.5
Camshaft sprocket bolt	102	14.0
Spark plugs	12	1.7
Main bearing cap bolts	36	5.0
Connecting rod big end nut	36	5.0
Oil pan bolts	6	0.8
Oil pan drain plug	18	2.5
Gusset-to-cylinder block bolts	22	3.0
Flywheel bolts	101	14.0
Clutch cover bolts	18	2.5
Torque converter bolts	32	4.5
Transmission-to-cylinder block bolts	38	5.2
Transmission-to-gusset bolts	37	5.2
Oil pump bolts	10	1.3
Engine support bracket-to-insulator	27	3.7
Exhaust manifold-to-exhaust pipe	16	2.3
Pivot locknuts	40	5.5
Rocker cover bolts	10	1.3
Pivot bushing bolts	72	10.0

1   General information

The L28E and L28ET (Turbo) engines used in the 280ZX are the six-cylinder in-line type, with valve operation by means of an overhead camshaft. Both engines are very similar in design, with any differences noted in the appropriate sections.

The cast iron cylinder block contains the six bores and acts as a rigid support for the seven bearing crankshaft. The machined cylinder bores are surrounded by water jackets to dissipate heat and control operating temperature.

Two valves per cylinder are mounted in the aluminum cylinder head and are actuated by a pivot type rocker arm in direct contact with the cam mechanism. Double springs are installed to each valve.

The camshaft is driven by a roller chain from the front of the crankshaft. Chain tension is controlled by a tensioner which is operated by oil and spring pressure. The rubber shoe type tensioner controls vibration and tension of the chain.

The pistons are of a special aluminum casting with struts to control thermal expansion. There are two compression and one oil control ring. The piston pin is a hollow steel shaft which is fully floating in the piston and a press fit in the connecting rod small-end. The pistons are attached to the crankshaft via forged steel connecting rods.

The distributor, which is mounted on the left-hand side of the cylinder block, is driven by a helical gear mounted on the front of the crankshaft. The oil pump, which is mounted low down on the right-hand side of the cylinder block, is on a common center-line to the distributor and is driven by the same helical gear.

The crankshaft, which is made of special forged steel, has internal oil passages to provide lubrication to the main and big-end bearings. Oil is delivered, via the filter and pressure relief valve, to the main oil gallery from which it passes to the main bearing journals and then to the connecting-rod bearing journals through drillings in the crankshaft. Oil spillage from the connecting rod big-ends, as well as a jet hole drilled through the connecting rod into the big-ends, provides splash lubrication for the pistons and connecting rod small ends. At the top of the engine, galleries drilled in the camshaft supports provide oil for the five bearings, while a pipe that runs along the length of the camshaft, delivers oil to each cam pad surface, to provide lubrication for the rocker arm and pivot. On Turbo models, oil is also passed through the turbocharger and engine oil cooler.

Whenever engine work is required, there are some basic steps which the home mechanic should perform before any work is begun. These preliminary steps will help prevent delays during the operation. They are as follows:

a) Read through the appropriate sections in this manual to get an understanding of the processes involved, tools necessary and replacement parts which will be needed

b) Contact your local Datsun dealer or automotive parts store to check on replacement parts availability and cost. In many cases, a decision must be made beforehand whether to simply remove the faulty component and replace it with a new or rebuilt unit or to overhaul the existing part

Caution: *If the vehicle is equipped with air conditioning, it is imperative that a qualified specialist depressurize the system if this is required to perform the necessary engine repair work. The home mechanic should never disconnect any of the air conditioning system while it is still pressurized, as this can cause serious personal injury as well as possibly damage the air-conditioning system. Ascertain if depressurization is necessary while the vehicle is still operational*

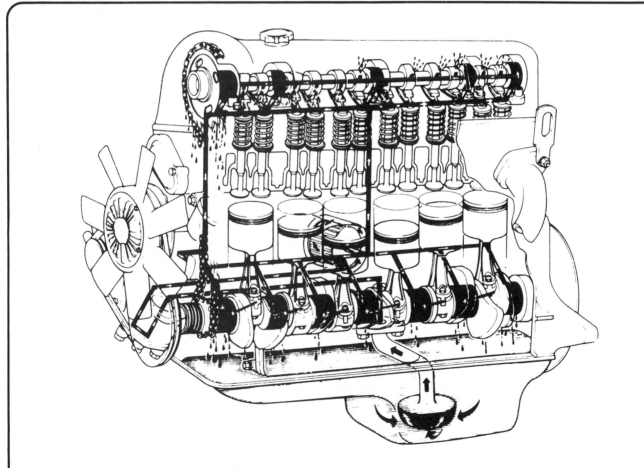

Fig. 2.1 Oil flow within the lubrication system (Sec 1)

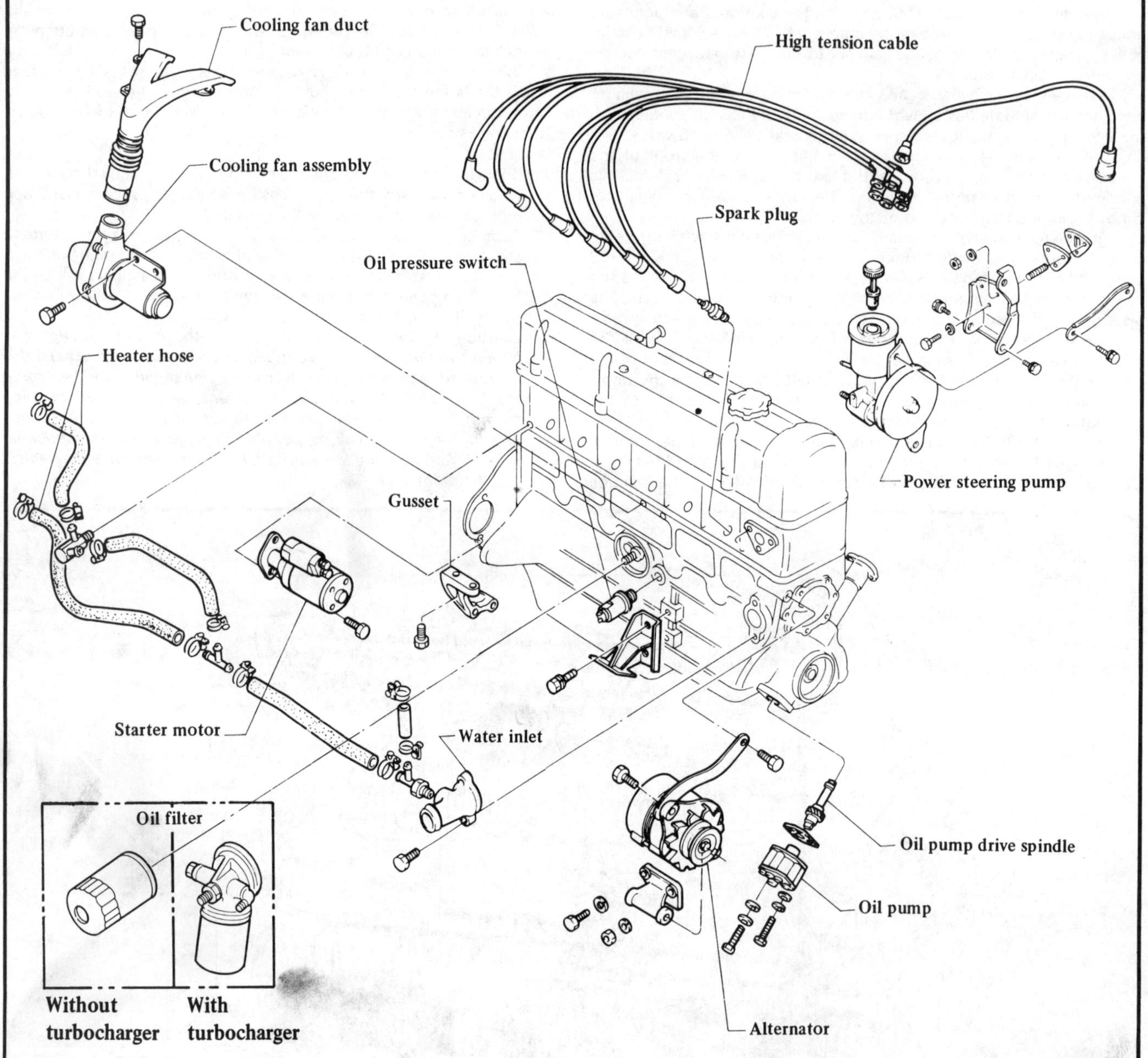

66

Cooling fan duct

Cooling fan assembly

Heater hose

Oil pressure switch

Gusset

Starter motor

Water inlet

Oil filter

Without turbocharger

With turbocharger

High tension cable

Spark plug

Power steering pump

Oil pump drive spindle

Oil pump

Alternator

Fig. 2.2 External components of the engine (right side)

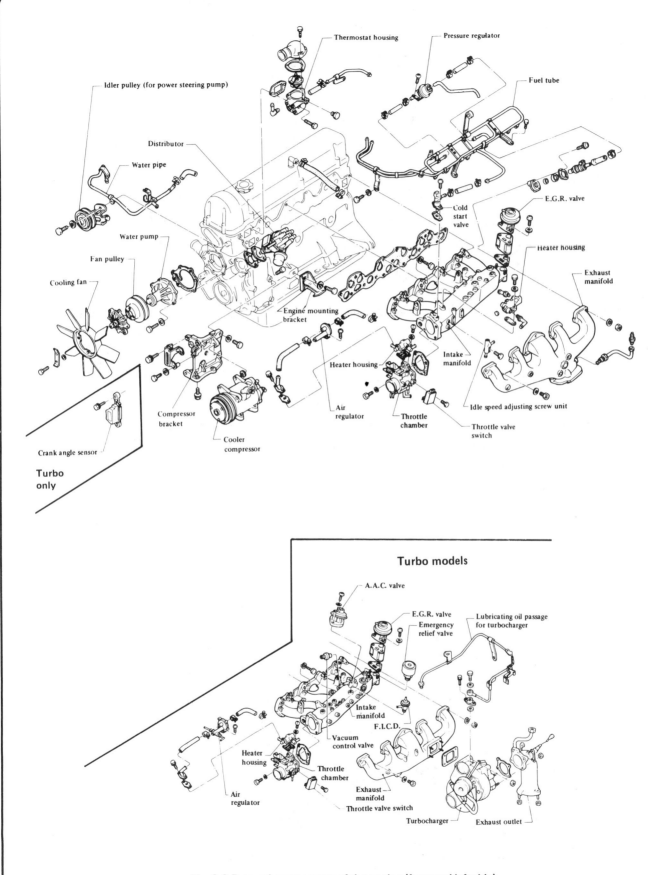

Fig. 2.3 External components of the engine (front and left side)

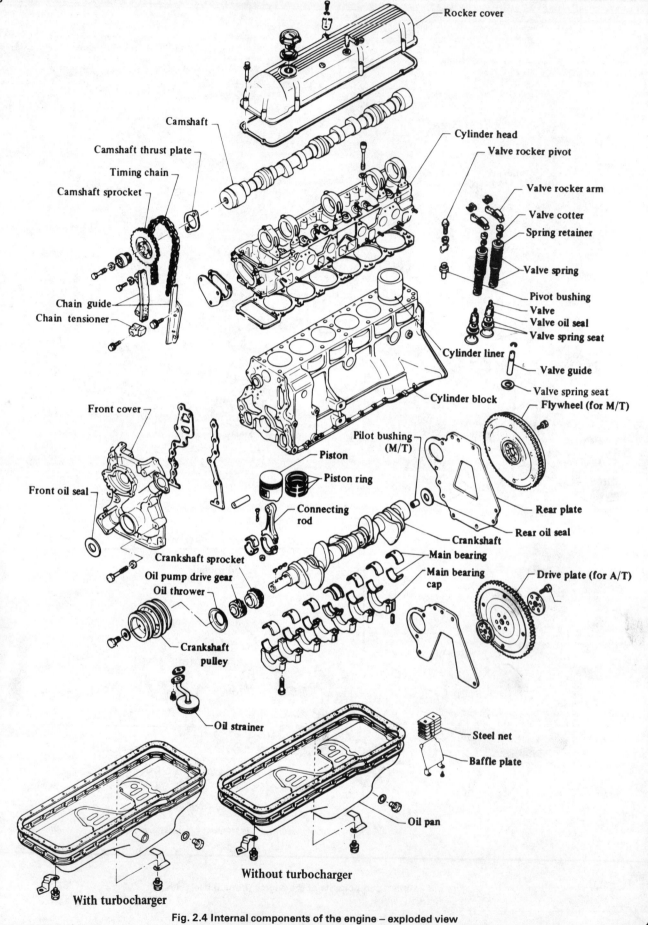

Fig. 2.4 Internal components of the engine – exploded view

2 Top Dead Center (TDC) positioning

1   Top Dead Center (TDC) is a reference to the position of a piston and is a critical part of many engine operations, including ignition timing, valve timing, valve clearance adjustment and the removal and installation of the distributor and oil pump.

2   When a piston is at TDC it is at the highest point of its stroke in the cylinder. Since each piston travels up and down twice for every time its spark fires, TDC generally refers to the piston at the top of its compression stroke, or the stroke on which the spark plug fires.

3   In order to bring a piston to its TDC position, the crankshaft must be turned. There are various methods of doing this (mentioned below). **Note:** *Prior to using any of these methods, the transmission should be shifted to the Neutral position and the ignition coil wire should be removed from the distributor cap and grounded on the engine to prevent the engine from firing.*

   a) The most accurate method is to use a ratchet wrench and socket on the crankshaft pulley bolt at the front of the engine to turn the crankshaft by hand. Normal engine rotation is in a clockwise direction. Prior to this, the spark plugs should be removed to make moving the pistons easier.

   b) An easier method is to use a remote self-starter switch hooked up to the starter motor to turn the engine. This is quick and the fine control of a self-starter switch allows you to bring the piston close to its TDC position. It can then be set precisely by using the wrench and socket as described above.

   c) If a self-starter switch is not available, the same basic method can be used by having an assistant in the driver's seat turn the ignition key to Start in short bursts in order to bring the piston close to its TDC position. Again, a ratchet wrench and socket then can be used to set the piston exactly.

4   Various methods can be used to tell when the piston is at its TDC position. Remember that the number 1 and 6, 2 and 5, and 3 and 4 pistons are at the top of their stroke at the same time. Therefore more than one checking method will be necessary to ensure that the appropriate piston is on its compression stroke.

   a) If the number 1 or 6 piston is being set to TDC, the simplest checking method is to watch the timing marks on the crankshaft pulley and the timing plate. When the notch in the pulley aligns with the 'O' mark on the timing plate, both the number 1 and 6 pistons are at the top of their stroke. To determine which one is on its compression stroke, use method d or e.

   b) An accurate method of locating TDC for any piston is to remove the spark plug of that cylinder and screw a dial indicator into the spark plug hole. This will tell you when the piston is at the exact top of its stroke, but method d or e should be used to determine if it's on its compression stroke.

   c) If a dial indicator is not available, a similar method can be employed using a flashlight. Remove the spark plug from the cylinder, and while an assistant turns the crankshaft, shine the flashlight through the spark plug hole to see when the piston reaches the top of its stroke. Again, use method d or e to check if it is on its compression stroke.

   d) An accurate method of determining which piston is on its compression stroke is simply to remove the distributor cap, and note which terminal in the distributor cap the rotor is pointing toward. The cylinder connected by the spark plug wire to that terminal is the one being fired.

   e) Another check for which piston is on its compression stroke can be performed with the rocker arm cover removed. Simply note the positions of the camshaft lobes for each cylinder. Only one cylinder will have both of its cam lobes pointing upwards at the same time and not in contact with the rocker arms. This means that both the intake and exhaust valves are closed, and the cylinder is under compression. This can be double-checked by lightly wiggling the rocker arms from side to side to ensure that they are loose and applying no pressure to the valves.

3 Rocker arm cover – removal and installation

1   Remove the large rubber PCV vent hose from the rocker arm cover breather fitting.

2   Disconnect the two vacuum lines running across the top of the rocker cover from their fittings on the intake manifold, and position them out of the way. Be sure to note their locations for reconnecting.

3   Disconnect the spark plug wires from the plugs. Then remove the plug wire brackets from the rocker cover complete with wires and position them out of the way. Be sure to note which plug each wire goes to.

4   Remove the auxiliary cooling disc clamp and duct.

5   Remove the eight rocker arm cover mounting bolts.

6   Remove the rocker arm cover. To break the gasket seal it may be necessary to tap the cover with your hand or a rubber mallet. Do not pry on the cover.

7   Prior to installation, clean all dirt, oil and old gasket material from the sealing surfaces of the cover and cylinder head with a degreaser.

8   Place a continuous bead of silicone sealant around the sealing lip of the cover. Be sure to apply the sealant to the inside of the mounting bolt holes.

9   Place the gasket into position on top of the cylinder head then place the rocker arm cover on the head. While the sealant is still wet, install the mounting bolts and torque them to specifications.

10 Complete the installation by reversing the sequence of the removal procedure.

Fig. 2.5 Location of mounting bolts for the auxiliary cooling fan duct and bracket (Sec 3)

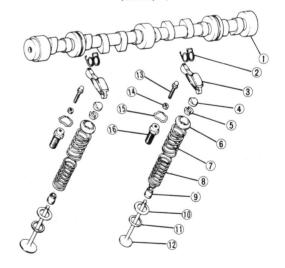

Fig. 2.6 Exploded view of the camshaft and valve train components

1	Camshaft	9	Valve oil seal
2	Valve rocker spring	10	Valve outer spring seat
3	Valve rocker	11	Valve inner spring seat
4	Valve rocker guide	12	Valve
5	Valve rocker collet	13	Valve rocker pivot
6	Valve spring retainer	14	Rocker pivot rock nut
7	Valve outer spring	15	Rocker spring retainer
8	Valve inner spring	16	Rocker pivot bushing

4 Rocker arm assembly – removal and installation

1   Remove the rocker arm cover as described in Section 3.
2   The camshaft should be rotated so that the cam lobe contacting the rocker arm to be removed is pointing upwards. This can be done either by operating the starter in short bursts (using either an assistant or a self-starter switch) or by using a ratchet wrench on the crankshaft pulley bolt to rotate the crankshaft.
3   Remove the valve rocker spring (photo).
4   Loosen the rocker pivot locknut. Then use a screwdriver, positioned as shown in Fig. 2.7, to depress the valve spring so the rocker arm can be lifted off. Do not lever the screwdriver against the machined surface of the cam lobes.
5   If more than one rocker arm is being removed, be sure to keep them in order, so that they can be reinstalled in their original positions on the cylinder head.
6   The valve rocker guides can be lifted off of the valves, but be sure to keep them with their appropriate rocker arms.
7   Inspect the contact surfaces of the rocker arm, rocker guide and rocker pivot for damage or excessive wear. Replace as necessary.
8   To replace the rocker pivot, loosen the pivot locknut and unscrew the pivot from its bushing. Do not remove the pivot bushing from the cylinder head.
9   Prior to installation, apply a dab of grease to the contact surfaces of the rocker arm, rocker guide and rocker pivot.
10 Installation is the reverse of the removal procedure.

4.3 Correct installed position of the valve rocker spring

5 Camshaft – removal and installation

1   Remove the rocker arm cover as described in Section 3.
2   Remove the rocker arms as described in Section 4.
3   Bring the number one piston to top dead center by referring to Section 2, if necessary.
4   Where the camshaft only will be removed without further disassembly of the cylinder head, it is vital that the timing sprocket position in relation to the timing chain is not altered. Make a mark on both the timing chain and the camshaft sprocket to show the correct installed position of the two. This chain must be reinstalled on the camshaft sprocket exactly as it was removed. If a major overhaul is being carried out, then the retention of the timing position is not essential as this will be reset upon installation.
5   Before removing the camshaft sprocket, cut a piece of wood 10 inches long, $\frac{3}{4}$ inch thick, $1\frac{1}{2}$ inches wide at the top and approximately 1 inch at the bottom.
6   Now remove the camshaft sprocket bolt. A rod can be positioned through the camshaft to keep it from turning while the nut is broken loose.
7   Insert the piece of wood into the timing case so that it wedges between the two runs of the chain. Be sure it is inserted securely. It is important that the timing chain should not be loosened or dropped into the inner cylinder as this would necessitate removal of the front cover in order to re-set the timing chain.
8   Carefully remove the camshaft sprocket from the camshaft and work the chain off of it until the sprocket can be removed. The chain can be left hanging on the piece of wood.
9   Lift off the camshaft thrust plate.
10 Withdraw the camshaft ensuring that the lobes do not scratch or damage the bearings as they pass through. On no account disturb the camshaft bearing cap bolts or caps as they are in-line bored after assembly.
11 Inspection of the camshaft and cam bearings is found in Section 5.
12 Prior to installing the camshaft, apply a coat of engine oil or lithium-based grease to the inner surfaces of the cam bearings. Then carefully insert the camshaft into place. The dowel located at the front of the camshaft should be in the 12 o'clock position.
13 Reinstall the thrust plate, making sure the oblong groove is toward the front.
14 With the piece of wood still in place, carefully work the timing chain over the camshaft sprocket and fit the sprocket onto the end of the camshaft, with the cam dowel located in the number 1 sprocket hole. Be sure the marks made on the chain and sprocket during removal line up.

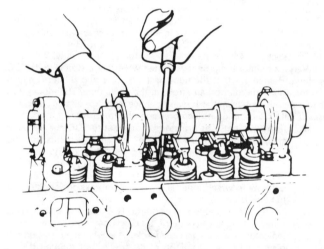

Fig. 2.7 To remove the rocker arm, positioned as shown, a screwdriver can be used to depress the valve spring (Sec 4)

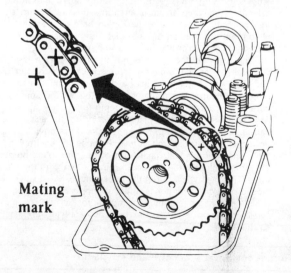

Fig. 2.8 Prior to separating the timing chain from the camshaft sprocket they should be marked for proper installation (Sec 5)

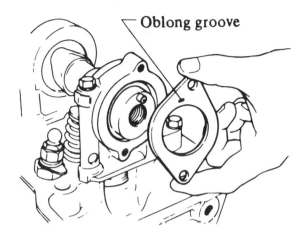

Fig. 2.9 The camshaft sprocket thrust plate must be installed with the oblong groove on top and facing outward (Sec 5)

15 Carefully remove the piece of wood, and install the camshaft sprocket bolt, torquing it to specifications.
16 Reinstall the rocker arms.
17 Adjust the valve clearance to the 'cold' specifications as described in Chapter 1.
18 Reinstall the rocker arm cover.
19 Following installation, warm up the engine and readjust the valve clearances to the 'hot' specifications as described in Chapter 1.

6 Camshaft – inspection and servicing

1 Examine the bearing surfaces and the surface of the cam lobes. Surface scratches, if very shallow, can be removed by rubbing with a fine emery cloth or an oilstone. Any deep scoring will necessitate a new camshaft.
2 Mount the camshaft on V-blocks and use a dial gauge to measure lobe lift and run-out. Reject a camshaft which does not meet the specified limits.
3 Measure the journal diameters using a micrometer. Again, reject a camshaft which does not meet the specified limits.
4 Examine the condition of the bearings in the cylinder head housings and measure their diameter at two or three points internally. Where the average of these measurement exceeds the outside diameter of the respective camshaft bearing by more than 0.0039 in (0.1 mm) then the cylinder head will have to be replaced or exchanged as the bearings can only be replaced if they can be line-bored after installation.

7 Valve springs and seals – removal and installation (cylinder head in car)

Note: *Valve mechanism components must be reinstalled in their original positions. Place all removed components in a compartmented box to aid in identification.*
1 Remove the rocker arm cover as described in Section 3.
2 Remove the camshaft as described in Section 5.
3 Remove the spark plug from the cylinder being serviced.
4 There are two methods of keeping the valve in place while the valve spring is removed. If you have access to compressed air, attach an air hose adapter to your air hose and insert it into the spark plug hole. When air pressure is applied the valves will be held in place by the pressure.
5 If you do not have access to compressed air, bring the piston of that cylinder to top dead center (TDC) on the compression stroke. Feed a long piece of ¼ in nylon cord in through the spark plug hole until it fills the combustion chamber. Be sure to leave the end of the cord hanging out of the spark plug hole so it can be removed easily.
6 Position a valve spring compressor tool over the spring. Compress

the spring just enough to allow the removal of the valve spring. Then let up on the spring.
7 Remove the collets (photo) spring retainer, inner and outer springs and oil seal. The oil seal must always be replaced whenever the spring locks have been disturbed.
8 Inspection procedures for the various valve components are detailed in Section 14.
9 Installation is the reverse of the removal procedure. **Note:** *Install the outer spring so the painted side (narrow pitch side) is toward the cylinder head. Also after installing the valve rocker assembly, adjust the valve clearances, as described in Chapter 1, to the 'cold' specifications.*
10 Following installation, warm up the engine and readjust the valve clearances to the 'hot' specifications.

7.6 With the valve spring depressed, the spring collets (arrow) can be removed

8 Intake manifold – removal and installation

Note: *If the engine has been removed from the car, proceed to paragraph 20.*
1 Eliminate the pressure in the fuel system by following the procedure described in Chapter 1.
2 Disconnect the negative battery cable.
3 Drain the cooling system.
4 Remove the upper radiator hose.
5 Remove the large rubber PCV vent hose that runs between the rocker cover and the throttle chamber.
6 Disconnect the rubber vacuum booster hose from the rear of the intake manifold.
7 Disconnect the PCV hose from the PCV valve under the intake manifold.
8 Disconnect the wiring connector from the oxygen sensor.
9 Disconnect all vacuum hoses from their fittings on the intake manifold and throttle chamber. **Note:** *Be sure to label each hose as to its location.*
10 Disconnect the throttle linkage.
11 Remove the rubber inlet duct that runs between the air flow meter and the throttle chamber.
12 Remove the entire thermostat housing assembly complete with all sensors.
13 Disconnect any remaining wires or hoses leading to the intake manifold assembly. Again, be sure they are labelled as to their location.
14 Disconnect the ignition coil wire from the distributor cap. Remove the distributor cap, complete with spark plug wires and position it out of the way on the right side of the engine.
15 Disconnect the rubber fuel hoses from the metal lines located at the front right corner of the rocker cover (photo).
16 Remove the two bolts that attach the fuel lines to the cylinder head.
17 On Turbo models, remove the bolts that attach the throttle chamber to the air inlet pipe leading from the turbocharger.

8.15 The fuel hoses connect with the metal fuel lines at the right front of the rocker cover (arrow)

18 Raise the front of the car and support it on jackstands.
19 For more clearance, remove the splash shield. Then disconnect the A/C compressor from its bracket and place it out of the way. Do not disconnect the A/C hoses from the compressor.
20 On Turbo models, remove the turbocharger and exhaust outlet referring to Chapter 4 if necessary.
21 Remove the vertical heat shield hanging from the intake manifold.
22 Remove the lower intake manifold bolts. Access is extremely limited, and they can best be removed by using a ratchet wrench with extension positioned between the intake and exhaust manifolds.
23 With the lower bolts removed, carefully remove the upper mounting bolts and lift off the intake manifold with fuel pipes, injectors and related components attached.
24 If the manifold needs to be disassembled or replaced, remove all related components from it including the EFI/ECCS components, throttle chamber, fuel pipe assembly with injectors and all sensors and switches. If a new intake manifold is being installed, transfer these components directly to the new one.
25 Before installing the manifold clean the engine cylinder head and manifold gasket surface. All gasket material and sealing compound should be removed prior to installation.
26 Place a new intake manifold gasket into position on the manifold and loosely install the lower manifold mounting bolts and washers into the cylinder head. Be sure the chamfered side of the washers is towards the engine. Place the manifold in position against the cylinder head and install the remaining mounting bolts finger tight.
27 Tighten the manifold mounting bolts and nut evenly in relation to one another. They should be tightened a little at a time until they are torqued to specifications.
28 The remainder of the installation is the reverse of the removal procedure.
29 Fill the radiator with coolant, start the engine and check for leaks. Also check and adjust the idle speed as described in Chapter 1.

9 Exhaust manifold – removal and installation

Note: *If the engine is out of the car, disregard the steps which do not apply.*
1 Because of limited access, removal of the exhaust manifold is a somewhat difficult procedure. It is somewhat easier to remove it from the underside of the engine compartment although another method is to first remove the intake manifold, and then remove the exhaust manifold from the top.
2 Raise the front of the car and support it on jackstands.
3 For more clearance, remove the splash shield and then disconnect the A/C compressor from its bracket and place it out of the way. Do not disconnect the A/C hoses from the compressor.
4 Remove the front exhaust pipe. Refer to Chapter 6, if necessary.

5 On Turbo models, remove the turbocharger and exhaust outlet referring to Chapter 4 if necessary.
6 Disconnect the wiring connector from the oxygen sensor.
7 Remove the vertical heat shield hanging from the intake manifold.
8 Remove any tubes from the exhaust manifold, such as those leading to the EGR valve or air induction valve case.
9 Remove the eight bolts and two nuts that attach the exhaust manifold to the cylinder head. **Note:** *The rear engine lift bracket is also retained by the rearmost manifold nut.*
10 Lift out the exhaust manifold.
11 Before installing the exhaust manifold clean the mating surfaces on the cylinder head and manifold. All excess gasket material should be removed.
12 Place a new exhaust manifold into position on the cylinder head then place the manifold into position and install the mounting bolts finger tight.
13 Tighten the manifold mounting bolts in the sequence shown in the accompanying figure. The bolts should be tightened a little at a time until all of the bolts are torqued to specifications.
14 Install the remaining components. The remainder of the installation is the reverse of the removal procedure.
15 Start the engine and check for exhaust leaks between the manifold and cylinder head and between the manifold and exhaust pipe.

10 Cylinder head – removal

1 Drain the cooling system.
2 Remove the rocker arm cover as described in Section 3.
3 Remove the intake manifold as described in Section 8.
4 Remove the exhaust manifold as described in Section 9.
5 Remove the upper radiator hose.
6 Disconnect the wiring connectors from the various temperature sensors attached to the thermostat housing and the cylinder head.
7 Remove the spark plugs.
8 Disconnect the water hoses from their fittings at the right rear of the cylinder head.
9 Bring the number 1 piston to TDC (refer to Section 2 if necessary) and remove the camshaft sprocket, being sure to use the procedure described in Section 5.
10 Remove the power steering pump, if equipped, from its bracket and position it out of the way. The hydraulic hoses do not need to be disconnected from the pump.
11 Remove the power steering pump bracket and idler pulley, if equipped.
12 Loosen the 14 cylinder head bolts in the sequence shown in the accompanying figure.
13 Remove the bolts that attach the cylinder head to the front cover.
14 Lift the head free of the engine. If the head is stuck to the engine block do not attempt to pry it free as this may ruin the sealing surfaces. Instead use a hammer and a block of wood, tapping on the thick part of the casting. The timing chain should be left securely in place, held by the piece of wood.
15 Remove the cylinder head gasket. Place the head on a block of wood to prevent damage.
16 Refer to the following sections for inspection and installation procedures.

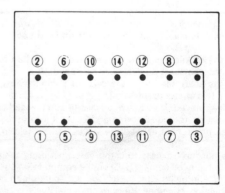

Fig. 2.10 The cylinder head bolts should be loosened evenly in the sequence shown (Sec 10)

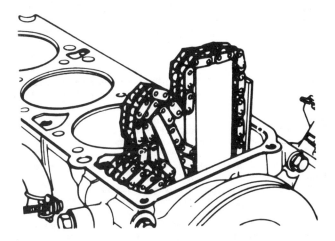

Fig. 2.11 With the cylinder head removed, a specially-cut wooden 'tool' should be used to keep the chain tight on the crankshaft sprocket (Sec 10)

11 Cylinder head – disassembly

Note: *New and rebuilt cylinder heads are commonly available for Datsun engines at dealerships and auto parts stores. Due to the fact that some specialized tools are necessary for the dismantling and inspection of the heads, and replacement parts may not be readily available, it may be more practical and economical for the home mechanic to purchase a replacement head and install it referring to Section 16.*

Another alternative is to take the cylinder head complete to a competent automotive machine shop or Datsun dealership for the overhaul process. If the complete engine is being overhauled at the same time, it may be wise to refer to Section 33 before a decision is made. If it is decided to overhaul the cylinder head, read through the following Sections first to gain an understanding of the steps involved and the tools and replacement parts necessary for the job. Proceed as follows.

1　Remove the camshaft as described in Section 5.

2　Using a valve spring compressor (available at tool or auto parts stores), compress each of the valve springs and remove the valve locking keys or collets. Work on one valve at a time, removing the keys, then releasing the spring and removing the spring retainer and inner and outer spring. Place the components from each valve in a compartmentalized box or rack. All valve mechanism components must be kept separate so they can be returned to their original positions.

3　Remove each valve oil seal and spring seams in turn, and place them in the box or rack.

4　To complete the valve mechanism removal, the rocker pivots can be removed by loosening the locknuts and unscrewing the pivots. These should also be kept separate, so they can be installed in their original positions.

5　Do not remove the rocker pivot bushings or the camshaft bearings from the cylinder head.

12 Cylinder head – cleaning

1　Clean all carbon from the combustion chambers and valve ports. Most auto parts stores will carry a cleaning attachment which is connected to a common hand drill motor.

2　Thoroughly clean the valve guides. Again, several tools available at auto parts stores are designed for this.

3　Use parts cleaner to remove all sludge and dirt from the valve rocker assembly components and valve springs. Work on one set of components at a time, returning each set to its original location on your box or rack.

4　A buffing wheel should be used to remove all carbon deposits from the valves. Do not mix up the order of the valves while cleaning them.

5　Clean all carbon deposits from the head gasket mating surface. Be careful not to scratch this sealing surface.

6　Clean the threads on all cylinder head attaching bolts thoroughly.

13 Cylinder head – inspection

1　Carefully inspect the head for cracks around the exhaust ports and combustion chambers, and for external cracks in the water chamber.

2　Check the valve stem-to-bore clearance in the following fashion. Using a micrometer, check the diameter of the valve stem in three places: top, center and bottom. Next, insert a small hole gauge in the valve guide bore to obtain the bore's diameter. The valve clearance can now be figured out from these measurements. If the valve stem clearance exceeds the Specifications, an oversize valve must be used, and the valve guide bore must be reamed. This is a job for your dealer or machine shop. Excessive clearance will cause excessive oil consumption while insufficient clearance will result in noisy operation and may cause the valve to stick, resulting in harsh engine operation.

3　Another method of checking this clearance is as follows: one at a time, place a valve in its installed position, with the valve head slightly (about $\frac{1}{16}$-in) off its seat. Now attach a dial indicator to the head with the indicator point just touching the valve stem where it exits the cylinder head. Grab the top of the valve and move it from side to side in a direction parallel to the rocker arm noting the movement of the dial indicator. If the deflection is more than about 0.008 in (0.2 mm) then the guide should be replaced by a machine shop.

4　Inspect each of the valve springs and its damper. Replace any spring which is deformed, cracked or broken.

5　Check the valve spring tension using an appropriate tool. The springs are compressed to a specified height and then the tension required for this is measured. This is done without the dampers. If not within 19lb of the specified load, the spring should be replaced with a new one.

6　The valve springs should be measured against the free lengths quoted in Specifications and replaced with new ones if they prove shorter as a result of continuous compression. In any event it is worthwhile to install new ones if they have been in use for 20 000 miles or more (32 000 km).

7　Check the cylinder head for warpage. Do this by placing a straightedge across the length of the head and measuring any gaps between the straightedge and the head surface with a feeler gauge. This should be done at three points across the head gasket surface, and also in a diagonal fashion across this surface (photo).

8　If warpage exceeds 0.004 in (0.1 mm) at any point when a straightedge which spans the entire head is used, the cylinder head should be resurfaced. Cylinder head resurfacing is a job for a professional automotive machine shop.

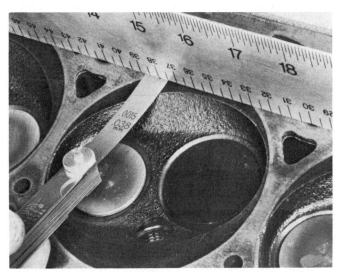

13.7 A feeler gauge and straight-edge are used to check the cylinder head for warpage

14 Valves and valve seats – inspection and servicing

1   Examine the heads of the valves for pitting and burning, especially the heads of the exhaust valves. The valve seat should be examined at the same time. If the pitting on valve and seat is very slight the marks can be removed by grinding the seats and valves together with coarse, and then fine, valve grinding paste.

2   Valve grinding is carried out as follows: smear a trace of coarse carborundum paste on the seat face and apply a suction grinder tool to the valve head. With a semi-rotary motion, grind the valve head to its seat, lifting the valve occasionally to redistribute the grinding paste. When a dull, matte even surface finish is produced on both the valve seat and the valve, wipe off the paste and repeat the process with fine carborundum paste, lifting and turning the valve to redistribute the paste as before. A light spring placed under the valve head will greatly ease this operation. When a smooth, unbroken ring of light grey matte finish is produced, on both valve and valve seat faces, the grinding operation is completed.

3   Where the valve or seat shows signs of bad pitting or burning, then the valve should be refaced by your dealer and the seat recut. If the refacing of the valve will reduce the edge of the valve head (margin width) to less than that given in the Specifications, replace the valve (photo).

4   Scrape away all carbon from the valve head and the valve stem. Carefully clean away every trace of grinding compound, taking great care to leave none in the ports or in the valve guides. Clean the valves and valve seats with a solvent-soaked rag, then with a clean rag, and finally, if an air line is available, blow the valves, valve guides and valve ports clean.

15 Cylinder head – assembly

1   Make sure all valve mechanism components are perfectly clean and free from carbon and dirt. The bare cylinder head should also be clean and free from abrasive agents which may have been used for valve grinding, reaming etc.

2   Install new oil seals and valve spring seats in the head.

3   Insert each valve in turn into its respective guide, applying a little engine oil to the stem.

4   With the aid of a spring compressor, assemble the springs (outer spring has close coils nearest cylinder head) retainers and split collets. The latter can be retained in the valve stem cut-out with a dab of thick grease.

5   Grease the camshaft bearings and insert the camshaft into position, being careful not to damage bearings. The dowel located at the front of the camshaft should be in the 12 o'clock position and the cam lobes of the number 1 cylinder should be pointing upwards.

6   Place the valve rocker guides into position.

7   Screw the rocker pivots into their pivot bushing, complete with locknuts.

8   Reinstall the rocker arms by again depressing the valve springs with a screwdriver, and install the rocker springs.

16 Cylinder head – installation

1   If not already done, thoroughly clean the gasket surface on both the cylinder head and the engine block. Do not scratch or otherwise damage these sealing areas.

2   To get the proper torque readings, the threads of the attaching bolts must be free of dirt. This also goes for the threaded holes in the engine block. Run a tap through these holes to ensure they are clean.

3   Place the gasket in place over the engine block dowel pins.

4   Be sure the number 1 piston is still at TDC and carefully lower the cylinder head onto the engine, over the dowel pins and the gaskets. Be careful not to move the gasket while doing this.

5   Install each head bolt finger-tight. Do not tighten any of the bolts at this time.

6   Tighten each of the bolts, a little at a time, in the sequence shown in the accompanying figure. Continue tightening in this sequence until the proper torque reading is obtained. As a final check, work around the head in a logical front to rear sequence to make sure none of the bolts have been left out of the sequence.

7   Reconnect the wiring connector leading to the cylinder head temperature sensor.

8   Fit the camshaft locating plate to the camshaft so that the horizontally engraved line is visible from the front and is positioned at the top of the plate.

9   With the piece of wood holding the timing chain still in place, carefully work the timing chain over the camshaft sprocket and install the sprocket onto the end of the camshaft, with the cam dowel located in the number 1 sprocket hole. **Note:** *Be sure the marks made on the chain and sprocket during removal line up.*

10 Carefully remove the piece of wood, and install the camshaft sprocket bolt, torquing it to specifications.

11 Adjust the valve clearance to the 'cold' specifications as described in Chapter 1.

12 Install the rocker arm cover, intake manifold and exhaust manifold as described in the appropriate Sections.

13 Following installation, warm up the engine and readjust the valve clearances to the 'hot' specifications as described in Chapter 1.

14 Fill the radiator with coolant, start the engine and check for leaks. Be sure to recheck the coolant level once the engine has warmed up to operating temperature. Also check and adjust the idle speed as described in Chapter 1.

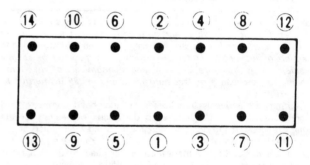

Fig. 2.12 When installing the cylinder head, the bolts should be tightened evenly in the sequence shown until they are properly torqued (Sec 16)

17 Oil pump – removal and installation

1   Set the number 1 piston at Top Dead Center (TDC). Refer to Section 2, if necessary.

2   Raise the front of the car and support it on jackstands. Then remove the front stabilizer bar. Refer to Chapter 11 if necessary.

3   After removing the distributor cap, mark the position of the rotor in relation to the distributor body.

4   Drain the engine oil from the oil pan.

5   Unscrew and remove the bolts which secure the oil pump body to the engine front cover and withdraw the oil pump/driveshaft assembly.

6   If the oil pump needs to be inspected or overhauled refer to Section 18.

7   Prior to installation, make sure that No. 1 piston is still at TDC.

8   Fill the pump body with engine oil to prime it and align the punch mark on the driveshaft with the oil hole below the drivegear.

9   Use a new flange gasket and insert the pump into its recess in the engine front cover.

10 Tighten the oil pump securing bolts and check that the rotor is still aligned with the mark made on the distributor body. If it is not, repeat the oil pump installation procedure.

11 Fill the engine with the proper quantity and grade of engine oil. (Refer to Chapter 1, if necessary).

12 Finally, check the ignition timing as described in Chapter 1.

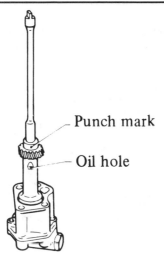

Fig. 2.13 Prior to installing the oil pump, the punch mark on the side of the drive spindle should be lined up with the pump's oil hole (Sec 17)

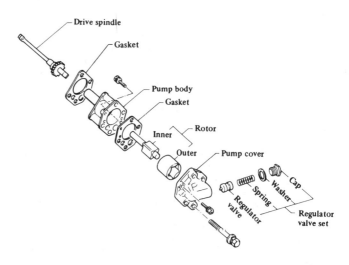

Fig. 2.14 Components of the oil pump – exploded view (Sec 18)

18 Oil pump – overhaul

1   With the oil pump removed, unbolt the cover from the oil pump and extract the inner and outer rotors.
2   Unscrew and remove the pressure regulator valve cap and washer, and extract the spring and valve.
3   Wash all components in clean solvent and allow to dry.
4   Check all components for wear or scoring. Then insert the rotors into the pump body (both the inner and outer rotors should always be assembled in the body, so the dotted marks on their end faces are not visible from the cover end) and test the rotor clearances in the following manner (Fig. 2.15).

   a)   using a straightedge, check the clearance between the rotor faces and the straightedge with a feeler gauge. Any difference between the two rotor faces-to-straight edge clearances must not exceed 0.0024 in (0.06 mm)
   b)   check the clearance between the tops (high points) of the inner and outer rotors. This should not exceed 0.0079 in (0.20 mm)
   c)   check the clearance between the outer rotor and the body. This should not exceed 0.0197 in (0.5 mm)
   d)   again using the straightedge placed across the body, check the clearance between body and straightedge, this should not exceed 0.0012 in (0.03 mm).

5   Where the specified clearances are exceeded, renew the components. The inner and outer rotors are only supplied as matched sets. If the oil pump body is worn or damaged, renew the complete pump assembly.
6   Check the condition of the pressure regulator valve and spring. The sliding surface of the valve should not be damaged or corroded. Renew if necessary.

19 Front cover and timing gear – removal and installation

Note: *If the engine has been removed from the car, proceed to paragraph 4.*
1   Open the radiator drain plug at the center underside of the radiator and drain the engine coolant.
2   Remove the fan and radiator as described in Chapter 3.
3   Drain the engine oil from the engine.
4   Remove the distributor as described in Chapter 5.
5   Remove the oil pump as described in Section 17.
6   Remove the waterpump as described in Chapter 3.
7   Remove the upper alternator adjusting bolt. Then remove the bolts that attach the alternator adjusting arm to the front cover, and remove the adjusting arm.
8   Disconnect the A/C compressor from its bracket and position it out of the way. Do not disconnect the A/C hoses from the compressor. Remove the compressor bracket and idler pulley.

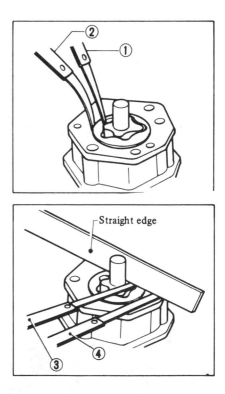

Fig. 2.15 Feeler gauges are used to check the oil pump's rotor tip clearance (1), rotor-to-body clearance (2), rotor side clearance (3) and pump body side clearance (4) (Sec 18)

9   If equipped with power steering, remove the pump from its bracket, and position it out of the way. The hydraulic hoses need not be disconnected from the pump.
10   Remove the water inlet from the right side of the front cover.
11   On Turbo models, remove the crank angle sensor from the front cover.
12   Since the front cover is sandwiched between the cylinder head and the oil pan, the oil pan must be removed in order to remove the front cover. Refer to Section 21 for this procedure.
13   With the oil pan removed, remove the crankshaft pulley bolt. There is considerable torque on this bolt and some means must be found to keep the engine from turning while the bolt is broken loose. If the engine is in the car, place the transmission in its highest forward gear and apply the parking brake. If the engine is out of the car remove the flywheel, and then reinstall the flywheel mounting bolts into the rear

end of the crankshaft. Use a long screwdriver or pry bar inserted in between these bolts to keep the crankshaft from turning.

14 Remove the crankshaft pulley.

15 Remove the mounting bolts that attach the front cover to the cylinder block and cylinder head, and lift off the front cover. If it will not come off easily, slight tapping with a soft-faced hammer will help.

16 Remove the bolts that attach the chain tensioner and chain guides to the block, and lift these components off.

17 Remove the camshaft sprocket bolt, and lift off the sprocket.

18 Remove the timing chain from both the camshaft and crankshaft sprockets.

19 From the end of the crankshaft, pull off the oil thrower, the oil pump drive gear and the chain sprocket. The latter will almost certainly require the use of an extractor. Note that three Woodruff keys are used to secure these components.

20 Examine the teeth on both the crankshaft sprocket and the camshaft sprocket for wear. Each tooth forms an inverted V with the gear periphery and, if worn, the side of each tooth under tension will be slightly concave in shape when compared with the other side of the tooth, i.e. one side of the inverted V will be concave when compared with the other. If any sign of wear is present the gears must be replaced.

21 Examine the links of the chain for side slackness and replace the chain if any slackness is noticeable when compared with a new chain. It is a sensible precaution to replace the chain at about 30 000 miles (48 000 km) and at lower mileage if the engine is stripped down for a major overhaul. The actual rollers on a very badly worn chain may be slightly grooved.

22 Rebolt the camshaft sprocket into position on the camshaft and check the endplay which should not exceed 0.004 in (0.1 mm) – otherwise replace it.

23 To avoid future difficulty, if there is any doubt at all about a worn timing chain, it is best to replace it.

24 Examine the components of the chain tensioner and guides. Replace any item which is worn or badly grooved.

25 To begin the installation, rotate the camshaft until the valves of number 1 cylinder are fully closed (equivalent to number 1 piston at TDC), then turn the crankshaft until the number 1 piston is at TDC.

26 Bolt the two timing chain guides into position.

27 To the front of the crankshaft, fit the sprocket, oil pump/distributor drivegear and the oil thrower. Make sure that the timing marks on the sprocket are visible from the front.

28 **Do not** turn the crankshaft or camshaft until the timing chain is installed, otherwise the valves will contact the piston crowns.

29 Engage the camshaft sprocket within the upper loop of the timing chain; then engage the chain with the teeth of the crankshaft sprocket and bolt the camshaft sprocket to the camshaft ensuring that the following conditions are met:

a) The keyway of the crankshaft sprocket should point vertically.

b) The timing marks (bright link plates) on the chain should align

with those on the two sprockets and be positioned on the right side when viewed from the front (photo).

c) The locating dowel on the front of the camshaft should be in the number 1 hole of the camshaft sprocket, and the timing chain should be aligned with the number 1 timing mark.

30 If reinstalling a used chain, it should be checked for excessive wear by using the following procedure. With number 1 piston at TDC (compression stroke) check whether the notch in the camshaft sprocket (with chain correctly engaged) appears to the left of the engraved line on the locating plate (photo). If this is the case disengage the camshaft sprocket from the chain and move the sprocket around so that when it is re-engaged with the chain it will locate with the camshaft flange dowel in its number 2 hole. Where this adjustment does not correct the chain slack, repeat the operation using number 3 hole of the camshaft sprocket to engage with the flange dowel. Where number 2 or 3 sprocket holes are used then number 2 or 3 timing marks must be used to position the chain. Where this adjustment procedure will not correct or compensate for the slackness in the timing chain then the chain must be replaced with a new one.

31 When the timing is satisfactory, tighten the camshaft sprocket bolt to the specified torque (photo).

32 Install the chain tensioner assembly into position on the cylinder block. Then adjust the position of the chain guide above the tensioner so there is no space between the tensioner body and the tensioner plunger unit.

33 Install a new front cover seal into the front cover by referring to Section 20.

34 Place the front cover gaskets into position on the cover then apply dabs of silicone sealant to the points shown in the accompanying figure.

35 Apply a small amount of lithium grease to the inside lip of the oil seal. Then place the front cover into position on the cylinder block and install the mounting bolts.

36 The remainder of the installation is the reverse of the removal procedure.

20 Front oil seal – replacement

1 Remove the front cover from the engine as described in Section 19.

2 Using a screwdriver, pry the old seal from the front cover. Be careful not to damage the seal mating surface in the cover.

3 Install the new seal into the front cover with the dust seal lip toward the outside. The seal can be installed by using the appropriate oil seal installing tool, or by using a flat block of wood, large enough to cover the seal. It is important that the seal be installed evenly.

4 Reinstall the front cover.

19.29 When installing the timing chain, the bright chain link should align with the number 1 sprocket mark

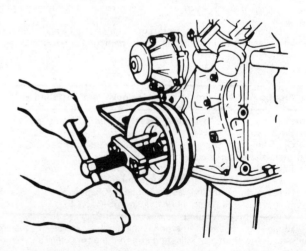

Fig. 2.16 A puller such as the one shown may have to be used to remove the crankshaft pulley (Sec 19)

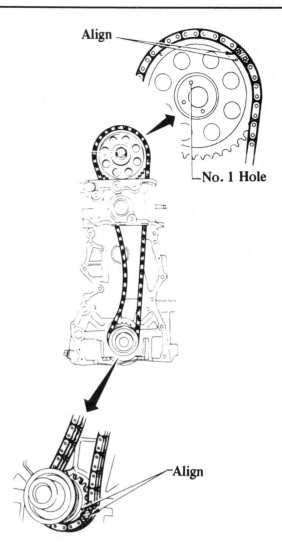

Align

No. 1 Hole

Align

Fig. 2.17 With the number 1 piston at TDC, the timing marks on chain and sprockets should align and the camshaft dowel should be in the number 1 sprocket hole (Sec 19)

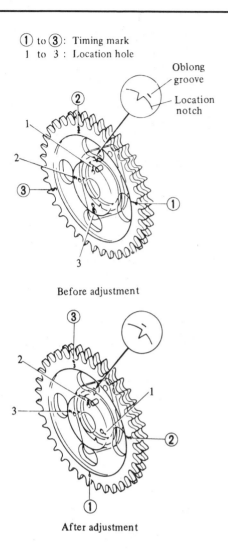

① to ③ : Timing mark
1 to 3 : Location hole

Oblong groove

Location notch

Before adjustment

After adjustment

Fig. 2.18 If the camshaft sprocket notch is to the left of the thrust plate's oblong groove, the timing chain is stretched and the next sprocket hole and timing mark combination should be used (Sec 19)

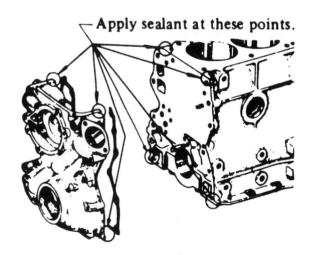

Apply sealant at these points.

Fig. 2.19 Prior to installing the front cover and gasket, silicone should be applied to the points shown (Sec 19)

21 Oil pan – removal and installation

Note: *If the engine has been removed from the car, proceed to paragraph 19.*

1   Drain the engine oil.

2   Raise the front of the car and support it on jackstands placed under the body side panels.

3   On cars equipped with rack-and-pinion, mark the relation of the steering shaft to the rack-and-pinion input shaft. Remove the bolt that secures them, and separate the shafts.

4   Remove the bolts that attach the front engine mounts to the engine.

5   In order to remove the oil pan, the engine will have to be raised slightly. Because of clearance problems when the engine is raised, some parts will have to be removed or disconnected. Among these are the fan, rubber ducts attached to the air flow meter, ignition coil wires and vacuum lines leading to the engine.

6   Remove the transmission mounting bracket.

7   Attach an engine hoist to the lifting 'eyes' mounted to the engine. These are located at the corners of the cylinder head. Make sure the chain is looped properly through the engine brackets and secured with strong nuts and bolts through the chain loops. The hook on the hoist should be over the center of the engine with the lengths of chain at equal distances so the engine can be lifted straight up.

8   Lift the engine just enough to take the weight off of the suspension crossmember, then remove the necessary bolts to lower the crossmember from the car, complete with rack-and-pinion if equipped. Refer to Chapter 11.
9   Remove the oil pan retaining bolts and lift off the oil pan.
10 Before installing the oil pan, thoroughly clean the gasket sealing surfaces on the engine block and on the oil pan with degreaser. All sealer and gasket material must be removed.
11 Before installing the oil pan, apply a $\frac{1}{8}$-in (3 mm) diameter bead of silicone sealer around the pan's sealing flange.
12 Using a new rear oil pan seal, position the oil pan against the engine block and install the mounting bolts, torquing them to specifications.
13 The remainder of the installation is the reverse of the removal procedure.
14 Fill the engine with the correct grade of oil, start the engine and check the pan for leaks.

22 Flywheel – removal and installation

1   If the engine is in the car, remove the clutch cover assembly and clutch disc as described in Chapter 8, or automatic transmission as described in Chapter 7.
2   Bend back the tabs of the lockplates and unscrew and remove the bolts which secure the flywheel to the crankshaft rear flange. If some difficulty is experienced in unscrewing the bolts due to the rotation of the crankshaft, wedge the starter ring gear by inserting a cold chisel at the starter motor opening,
3   Lift the flywheel from the crankshaft flange.
4   Unbolt and remove the engine endplate. Now is a good time to check the cylinder block rear core plug for security and leakage.
5   If the teeth on the flywheel starter ring gear are badly worn, or if some are missing then it will be necessary to remove the ring and fit a new one, or preferably exchange the flywheel for a reconditioned unit.
6   Either split the ring with a cold chisel after making a cut with a hacksaw blade between two teeth, or use a soft headed hammer (not steel) to knock the ring off, striking it evenly and alternately at equaldamage the flywheel during this process.
7   Heat the new ring in an electric oven to about 200°C (392°F).
8   Hold the ring at this temperature for five minutes and then quickly fit it to the flywheel so the chamfered portion of the teeth faces the transmission side of the flywheel.
9   The ring should be tapped gently down onto its register and left to cool naturally when the contraction of the metal on cooling will ensure that it is a secure and permanent fit. Great care must be taken not to overheat the ring, indicated by its turning light metallic blue, as if this happens, the temper of the ring will be lost.
10 Where the starter ring teeth on automatic transmission models are worn or chipped then the complete flywheel should be replaced.
11 On manual transmission flywheels, inspect the clutch friction face for scoring (photo). Light scoring may be corrected using emery cloth, but where there is deep scoring the flywheel must be replaced with a new one or clutch damage will soon occur.
12 Before installing the flywheel, clean the mating surfaces of the flywheel and the crankshaft.
13 If removed, reinstall the rear plate.
14 To install, position the flywheel in place against the crankshaft using a new spacer, if equipped, and insert the mounting bolts, securing them only fingertight. It is a good idea to use a thread sealing agent on the bolt threads.
15 Again, while preventing the flywheel from turning, tighten the bolts a little at a time until they are all torqued to specifications.
16 Complete the remainder of the installation procedure by reversing the removal steps.

23 Rear oil seal – replacement

1   Remove the flywheel from the engine as described in Section 22.
2   Using a screwdriver, pry the old seal from the rear of the cylinder block. Be careful not to damage the seal mating surface.
3   Install the new seal into the block with the dust seal lip toward the outside (photo). The seal can be installed by using the appropriate oil

22.11 The friction surface of the flywheel (arrow) should be inspected for scoring or other damage

23.3 When installed, the lip on the rear oil seal should face outward

seal installing tool, or by using a flat block of wood, large enough to cover the seal. One last method is to use a soft-face hammer to lightly tap around the seal, gradually tapping it down into its bore. It is important that the seal be installed evenly.
4   Reinstall the flywheel.

24 Engine mounts – replacement

1   Engine mounts are non-adjustable and seldom require service. Periodically, they should be inspected for hardening or cracking of the rubber, or separation of the rubber from its metal backing.
2   To replace the front engine mounts with the engine in position in the car, use the following procedure:

a)   Loosen the nuts and bolts that retain the front mounting insulator to the engine mounting bracket and suspension crossmember. Do this on both sides (photo)
b)   Next, the weight of the engine must be taken off the engine mounts. This can be done from beneath by using a jack and wooden block positioned under the oil pan, or from above by using an engine hoist attached to the two engine lifting eyes. The engine should be raised slowly and carefully, while keeping a constant check on clearances around the engine to prevent anything from binding or breaking. Play particular attention to the areas such as the fan, ignition coil wire,

vacuum lines leading to the engine and the rubber ducts attached to the air flow meter.
   c) Raise the engine just enough to provide adequate room to remove the mounting insulator.
   d) Remove the nuts and bolts retaining the insulator, and lift it out, noting its correct installed position.
   e) Installation is a reversal of removal, but be sure the insulator is installed in the same position it was in before removal.
3   To remove the rear mount, use the following procedure:
   a) Support the transmission with a jack.
   b) Remove the bolts that attach the rear insulator to the transmission.
   c) Remove the bolts that attach the rear mounting bracket to the body, and lift it out complete with insulator.
   d) Remove the nut that attaches the insulator to the mounting bracket and separate the parts.
   e) Installation is the reverse of removal.

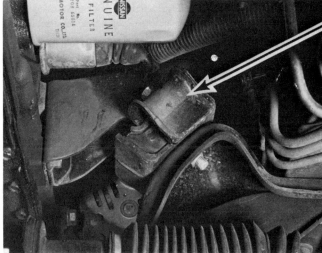

24.2 The front engine mounting insulator (arrow) is bolted in place between the crossmember and the engine mounting bracket

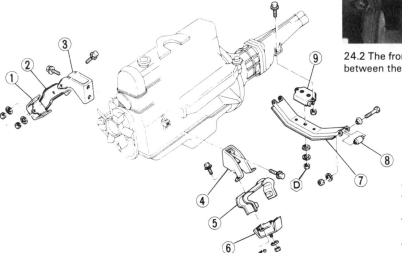

Fig. 2.20 Engine mount components (Sec 24)

1   Engine mounting front insulator, right
2   Stopper
3   Engine mounting front bracket, left
4   Engine mounting front bracket, left
5   Stopper
6   Engine mount front insulator, left
7   Engine mounting rear member
8   Engine mounting rear bushing
9   Engine mounting rear insulator

25 Engine – removal

Note: *Before disconnecting or removing any electrical wires, vacuum hoses, hydraulic hoses, etc., always mark them with pieces of tape to identify their installed locations. This will eliminate possible problems and confusion in the installation procedure.*

1   It is essential to have a good hoist, and two strong axle-stands if an inspection pit is not available. Removal will be much easier if there is someone to assist, especially during the later stages.
2   Before beginning work it is worthwhile to get all dirt cleaned off the engine at a service station equipped with steam or high pressure air and water cleaning equipment.
3   Remove the hood. Refer to Chapter 12 for the correct procedure. Set the hood in a safe place where it will not be damaged.
4   Before disconnecting any fuel lines, the pressure in the fuel system must be eliminated. This is done by following the procedure described in Chapter 1.
5   Remove the battery.
6   Drain the coolant from the radiator and engine block, referring to Chapter 1 if necessary.
7   Drain the engine oil.
8   Drain the oil from the transmission. Refer to Chapter 1, if necessary.
9   Remove the upper and lower radiator hoses.
10   Remove the radiator shroud.
11   On automatic transmission models, disconnect the oil cooler hoses from the oil cooler at the lower end of the radiator and allow the transmission fluid to drain into a pan.
12   Remove the radiator as described in Chapter 3.
13   Remove the power steering pump from its mounting bracket and secure it out of the way with wire. **Note**: *The hydraulic hoses do not need to be disconnected from the pump.*
14   Remove the splash shield on the underside of the engine compartment.

15   Remove the A/C compressor from its mounting bracket and secure it out of the way with wire. **Caution**: *Do not disconnect any of the A/C hoses from the compressor.*
16   On standard models, remove the rubber inlet duct connecting the air flow meter to the throttle chamber. On Turbo models, remove the metal inlet pipe leading from the throttle chamber to the turbocharger.
17   Disconnect the brake vacuum booster hose from its connection at the rear of the intake manifold.
18   Disconnect the throttle linkage at the points shown in Fig. 2.21.
19   Disconnect the water hoses from the water inlet on the right side of the front cover.
20   Disconnect the heater hoses from the right rear of the cylinder head.
21   Remove the ignition coil wire.
22   Disconnect the wires leading to the alternator and starter.
23   Disconnect the vacuum hoses from the top of the charcoal canister.
24   Disconnect the rubber fuel hoses from the metal lines at the right front of the rocker cover.
25   Disconnect the EFI harness connectors from the injectors and other EFI components, and position the harness out of the way (Fig. 2.22).
26   On Turbo models, remove the vacuum control modulator from its bracket and position it out of the way.
27   Disconnect the wiring connector(s) leading to the distributor.
28   On Turbo models, disconnect the oil cooler hoses at the oil filter bracket.
29   Remove the heat shield located next to the brake master cylinder.
30   Remove the front exhaust pipe, referring to Chapter 6, if necessary.
31   Remove the air flow meter.
32   Disconnect any other lines or wires running to the engine.
33   Make all necessary disconnections in preparation for removing the transmission, as described in Chapter 7. Do not yet remove the transmission mounting bracket.

34 Attach an engine hoist to the two lifting 'eyes' mounted to the engine. They are located at the corners of the cylinder head. Make sure the chain is looped properly through the engine brackets and secure with strong nuts and bolts through the chain loops. The hook on the hoist should be over the center of the engine with the lengths of chain at equal distances, so the engine can be lifted straight up.

35 Raise the hoist just until all slack is out of the chains.

36 Remove the bolts that attach the transmission mounting bracket to the body. Then remove the bolts that attach the bracket to the transmission.

37 Remove the bolts that attach the front engine mount bracket to the engine block.

38 Carefully lift the engine straight up and then forward from the engine compartment, continually checking clearances around the engine.

39 Once the engine/transmission assembly has been removed from the car, remove the starter motor. Refer to Chapter 5, if necessary.

40 To separate the engine from an automatic transmission:

   a) Unscrew and remove the dust cover from the lower half of the torque converter housing.

   b) Unscrew and remove each of the bolts which secure the torque converter to the driveplate. Access to these bolts can be gained (one at a time), by turning the engine until each bolt comes into view through the lower half of the converter housing.

   c) Withdraw the automatic transmission unit leaving the driveplate bolted to the crankshaft rear flange.

41 To separate the engine from a manual transmission:

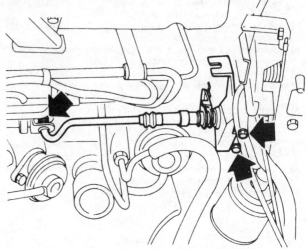

Fig. 2.21 Disengagement points for the throttle linkage, at the rear of the engine compartment (Sec 25)

   a) Unscrew and remove the bolts which secure the clutch bellhousing to the engine crankcase (photo).

   b) Withdraw the transmission in a straight line, so that its weight does not hang up on the input shaft while it is still engaged in the driven plate of the clutch mechanism.

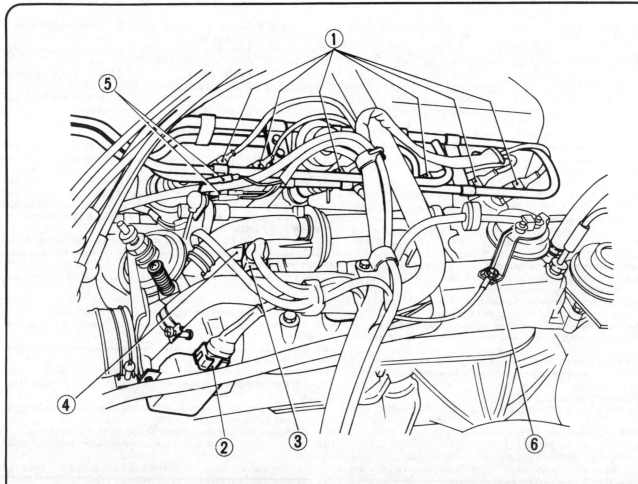

Fig. 2.22 Connection points for the EFI harness (Sec 25)

1 Injector connector	3 Cold start valve connector	5 EFL sub-harness connector
2 Throttle valve switch connector	4 Air regulator connector	6 Engine ground

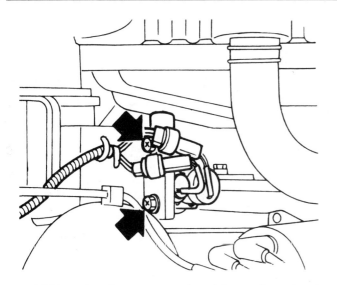

Fig. 2.23 Location of vacuum control modulator at front of engine on Turbo models (Sec 25)

26 Engine overhaul – general disassembly information

1   If the engine has been removed from the car for a major overhaul, the initial operation should be to disassemble the engine into its individual components. It is best to mount the engine on a dismantling stand but if one is not available, then stand the engine on a strong bench so that it is at a comfortable working height. Alternatively, the engine can be stripped down on the floor. Begin the disassembly operation by stripping the engine of its auxiliary accessories and related parts. This includes the following components:

Alternator and its bracket and adjusting bar
Engine mounting brackets
Clutch cover assembly and clutch disc (manual transmission) or torque converter (automatic transmission)
Drivebelt idler pulleys
Water pump
Auxiliary fan motor duct and bracket
Crankshaft pulley
Distributor
Temperature and vacuum switches and sensors
Exhaust manifold with air induction tubes, if equipped
Air conditioner compressor bracket, if equipped
Spark plugs
Engine oil dipstick and tube
PCV hose and tube
Power steering pump bracket, if equipped
Intake manifold assembly, including fuel injection components
Oil filter
Oil pressure switch
Oil pump, with drive spindle
Thermostat housing

2   With these components removed, the general engine sub-assemblies can be removed, serviced and installed by following the operations described in the other sections of this Chapter.

3   To strip the engine it is best to work from the top down. The oil pan can provide a firm base on which the engine can be supported in an upright position. When the oil pan must be removed, the engine can be turned on its side and all other work carried out with it in this position.

4   During the dismantling process the greatest care should be taken to keep the exposed parts free from dirt. As an aid to achieving this, it is a sound practice to thoroughly clean down the outside of the engine, removing all traces of oil and dirt.

5   Spray a water-soluble grease solvent onto the engine and allow it to stand for a time. Then wash it off using a vigorous jet of water. If the dirt is thick and deeply embedded, work the solvent into it with a wire brush.

6   Finally wipe down the exterior of the engine with a rag and only

then, when it is quite clean, should the dismantling process begin. As the engine is stripped, clean each part in solvent.

7   Never immerse parts which have internal oilways (such as the crankshaft) in a solvent, but wipe them carefully with a solvent-soaked rag. Probe the oilways with a length of wire and if an air line is available, blow the oilways through to clean them.

8   Be extremely careful using combustible cleaning agents near an open flame or inside an enclosed work area. Fumes can ignite from a lighted cigarette or a hot water heater pilot light. Wipe up any fuel or cleaner spills immediately, and do not store greasy or solvent-soaked rags where they can ignite.

9   Re-use of old engine gaskets is false economy and can give rise to oil and water leaks, if nothing worse. To avoid the possibility of trouble after the engine has been reassembled, *always* use new gaskets throughout.

10   Do not throw the old gaskets away, as it sometimes happens that an immediate replacement cannot be found and the old gasket is then very useful as a template. Hang up the old gaskets as they are removed on a suitable hook or nail.

11   Wherever possible, replace nuts, bolts and washers finger-tight from wherever they were removed. This helps avoid later loss and confusion. If they cannot be replaced, then lay them out in an orderly manner according to their locations.

12   If at any time during the dismantling procedure damage is found to any of the major engine components (cylinder heads, cylinder block, crankshaft, etc), consider the possibility of purchasing new or rebuilt assemblies as described in Section 33. This decision will in most cases alter your particular rebuilding sequence, as dismantling, inspection and assembly will not be required.

27 Pistons, connecting rods and bearings – removal

1   Remove the oil pan, and cylinder head as described previously in this Chapter.

2   Before the piston assemblies can be forced up through the top of the engine block, a ridge reamer should be used to remove the ridge and/or carbon deposits at the top of each cylinder. Working on one cylinder at a time, turn the engine so the piston is at the bottom of its stroke. Then place a rag on top of the piston to catch the cuttings. After the ridge is removed, crank the engine until the piston is at the top of the cylinder and remove the cloth and cuttings. Failure to remove this ridge may cause damage to the piston rings, pistons or cylinder walls.

3   While the connecting rods are still attached to the crankshaft, the connecting rod side clearance should be measured. This is done by using feeler gauges to measure the clearance between the sides of the connecting rods and the crankshaft (Fig. 2.24). Check Specifications for the proper clearance. If the measured clearance is excessive, the connecting rod should be replaced with a new one.

4   Inspect the connecting rods and connecting rod caps for cylinder identification. If these components are not plainly marked, identify each either by using a scribe to scratch the cylinder number onto it or by using a small punch to make the appropriate number of indentations to identify the cylinder it belongs to.

5   Working in sequence, remove the nuts on the connecting rod stud and lift the cap (with bearing inside) off the crankshaft. Place the connecting rod cap and bearing on a clean work surface marked cylinder number 1, 2, 3, etc.

6   Push a piece of rubber or plastic tubing over the connecting rod studs to completely cover the studs. This is important as these studs could easily damage the crankshaft or cylinder wall when the piston assembly is removed.

7   Push the piston/connecting rod assembly out through the top of the cylinder. Place the piston with its connecting rod next to its rod cap on the sequenced work area.

8   Repeat these procedures for the remaining cylinders, turning the crankshaft as necessary to gain access to the connecting rod nuts. Reuse the rubber or plastic tubing for each assembly.

9   Remove the bearings from the connecting rods and the connecting rod caps. This is easily done with a small screwdriver. If the engine has many miles on it, it is false economy to reuse the bearings, but if they are to be reinstalled, place them in a numbered rack.

10   If a piston ring expanding tool is available, use this to remove each of the rings from the piston (photo). An alternative method is to expand the ring just enough to clear the lands of the piston body. Then place

27.10 Using a piston ring compressor is the easiest method of removing and installing the piston rings

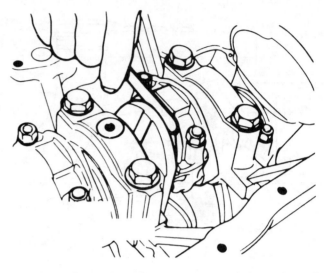

Fig. 2.24 A feeler gauge is used to measure the connecting rod side clearance (Sec 27)

strips of tin (about ¼-in wide) under the ring at equal distances around the piston. Using a slight twisting motion, 'walk' the ring up the piston and off the top.

11 Place the rings in their 'installed' order adjacent to the piston/connecting rod on your numbered work area.

12 Separating the connecting rod from the piston requires the removal of the piston pin. This job is best left to a dealer or automotive machine shop equipped with the proper support tools and an arbor press.

13 Do not take the time to clean and inspect the piston/rod assembles at this time, as they may have to be replaced with new units depending on the condition of the cylinder block and/or crankshaft.

28 Crankshaft – removal

1 Remove the engine from the car as described in Section 26 and support it on a suitable stand.

2 Remove the timing chain, oil thrower, drivegear and crankshaft sprocket from the front of the crankshaft, as described in Section 19.

3 Remove the flywheel and rear plate, as described in Section 22.

4 Remove the oil pan.

5 Remove the pistons and connecting rods from the crankshaft as described in Section 27.

6 While the crankshaft is still in the engine, the end play should be measured. This is done by first mounting a dial indicator as shown in Fig. 2.25. Then lever the crankshaft to the extreme rear position, and note the measurement on the indicator. If the endplay exceeds 0.012 in (0.3 mm) the center bearings are excessively worn and should be replaced.

7 Check that each of the main bearing caps is marked with respect to its location in the engine block. If not, use a punch to make small indentations in each cap: one indentation for the first main bearing cap, two indentations for the second cap, etc. The main bearing caps must be reinstalled in their original positions.

8 Unbolt the main bearing cap and lift each cap and its corresponding bearing off the crankshaft. A puller may be necessary to remove the center and rear main bearing cap. Place all of the main bearing caps and bearings on a work space numbered to correspond with the position of the cap in the engine block.

9 Lift the crankshaft from the engine block, being careful not to damage it in any way.

10 Remove the rear main oil seal.

11 Remove the main bearings and the main bearing caps from the block, keeping them separated as to their positions.

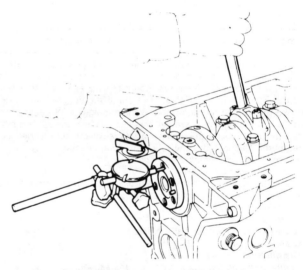

Fig. 2.25 Prior to removing the crankshaft, the end play should be measured by forcing the shaft toward the rear and measuring play with a dial indicator (Sec 28)

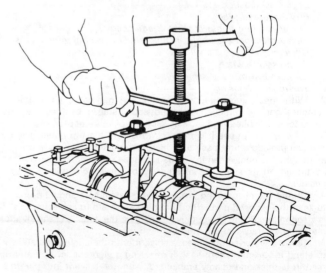

Fig. 2.26 A special puller may have to be used to remove the rear and center main bearing caps (Sec 28)

29 Cylinder block – inspection

1   It is important that the cylinder block be inspected carefully and as described. The cylinder block was designed to operate with exacting tolerances, and if the engine is reassembled without first properly inspecting the block, all work and cost involved in the rebuild may be for nothing.

2   There are two indications for excessive wear of the cylinders. First, if the vehicle was emitting blue smoke from the exhaust system before engine dismantling. This blue smoke is caused by oil seeping past the piston rings due to wear of the cylinder walls. Second, the thickness of the ridge at the top of the cylinder (which should have been removed during piston removal) can give an indication about overall cylinder wear.

3   Clean the cylinder block as necessary to remove built-up sludge and grime. Clean all excess gasket material from the sealing surfaces.

4   Inspect the cylinder block for cracks in the cylinder walls, water jacket and main bearing webs. Use a flashlight where necessary. In most cases, cracks will require that a new engine block be purchased.

5   The cylinder bores must be examined for taper, ovality, scoring and scratches. These checks are important for proper operation of the pistons and piston rings.

6   Scoring and scratches can usually be seen with the naked eye and felt with the fingers. If they are deep, the cylinder liner may have to be replaced with a new one. If the imperfections are slight, a qualified machine shop should be able to hone or bore the cylinders to a larger size. **Note:** *If the cylinder bores need servicing the pistons must be replaced with new ones.*

7   Using an internal-type dial gauge, measure each bore at three different points (photo). Take a measurement near the top of the bore and then near the bottom of the bore. Finally, measure at the center. Jot down all measurements to determine the taper of the cylinder (slightly larger at the top than the bottom or vice versa). Check these measurements with the wear limits listed in the Specifications.

8   An out-of-round condition can be found in a similar fashion, except measure the cylinder first parallel with the engine centerline and then turn the micrometers until they are perpendicular with the centerline (180 degrees from first measurement). Check these measurements with the wear limits listed in the Specifications.

9   Where the cylinder bores are worn beyond the permitted tolerances, the block will have to be honed or bored, have the cylinder liner replaced or, in extreme cases, be replaced with a new block.

10 A final check of the cylinder block would include an inspection for warpage. This is done with a straightedge and feeler gauges in the same manner as for the cylinder head. The tolerances described in Section 13 also apply to the cylinder block. If warpage is slight, a machine shop can resurface the block.

30 Pistons and connecting rods – cleaning and inspection

1   In most cases where the engine has seen high mileage, the original pistons will have to be replaced with new ones. This is because the cylinders will have to be bored to a larger size to compensate for normal wear. If, however, the cylinder walls require only a slight finish honing, the old pistons may be reused if they are in good condition.

2   Wash the connecting rods and pistons in a cleaning solvent and dry with compressed air, if available.

3   Don't use a wire brush or any abrasive cleaning tools on any part of the piston.

4   Clean the ring grooves of the piston with a groove cleaner tool and make sure the oil ring holes and slots are clean.

5   Inspect the rods for twisting, bending, nicks or cracks. If any of the above items are found, the rod must be replaced with a new one.

6   Inspect the piston for cracked ring lands, skirts or pin bosses. Check for worn or wavy ring lands, scuffed or damaged skirts and eroded areas at the top of the piston. Replace any pistons that are damaged or show signs of excessive wear.

7   Inspect the ring grooves for nicks which may cause the rings to hang up.

8   With the piston still connected to the connecting rod, swivel the rod back and forth, noting the degree of difficulty. Compare all piston/rod assemblies. If the rods seem loose on the piston pins, and move with little or no drag, the piston pins have worn and the piston pin must be replaced.

9   If the cylinder block is in need of any machine work, even finish honing, chances are good that the machinist will want the pistons on hand to check piston-to-bore clearance as the cylinder walls are cut. This measurement is critical and should be left to the machine shop.

31 Crankshaft and bearings – inspection and servicing

1   Examine the crankpin and main journal surfaces for scoring, scratches or corrosion. If evident, then the crankshaft will have to be reground professionally. Check that all oil holes in the crankshaft are clear and free of burrs (photo).

2   Using a micrometer, test each journal and crankpin at several different points for ovality. If this is found to be more than 0.0012 in (0.03 mm) then the crankshaft must be reground. Undersize bearings are available to suit the recommended reground diameter, but normally your dealer will supply the correct matching bearings with the reconditioned crankshaft.

3   After a high mileage, the main bearings and the connecting rod bearings may have worn to give an excessive running clearance. The correct running clearance for the different journals is given in the Specifications. The clearance is best checked using a product such as 'Plastigage', as described in Section 32. **Note:** *Never attempt to correct excessive running clearance by filing the caps but always fit new shell bearings, having first checked the crankshaft journals and crankpins for ovality and to establish whether their diameters are of standard or reground sizes.*

4   Checking the connecting rod bearings is carried out in a similar manner to that described for the main bearings. The correct running clearance is given in the Specifications.

5   It is good practice to check the running clearance of rod and main bearings even if new bearings are installed.

6   The crankshaft end play should also be checked, if not already done. Refer to Section 28.

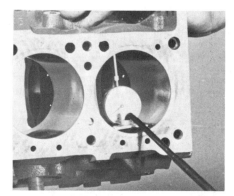

29.7 An internal-type dial gauge should be used to check for taper and out-of-round conditions in the cylinder bores

31.1 Inspect the crankshaft oil holes (arrow) to be sure they are not clogged and are free of burrs

31.2 A micrometer should be used to measure the main journals and crankpins of the crankshaft

32 Bearings (main and rod) – checking clearances

Main bearing running clearance

1   The running clearance of the main bearings should be checked anytime the crankshaft is removed from the engine. This should be to determine whether old bearings are excessively worn and if new bearings are the correct size. This clearance is best measured using a product such as Plastigage, commonly available at auto parts stores.
Note: *There are three precautions to take when working with Plastigage. These are:*

   (a) *Plastigage is soluble in oil, so all oil and grease should be removed from the crankshaft and bearing surfaces while the testing is done.*
   (b) *Do not rotate the crankshaft while the Plastigage is installed in the engine, as this may cause damage to the crankshaft or engine surfaces.*
   (c) *Remove all traces of the Plastigage when testing is complete. Be very careful not to harm the crankshaft or bearing surfaces as the Plastigage is removed. Do not use sharp tools or abrasive cleaners; remove the used Plastigage with your fingernail or a blunt wood stick.*

2   Following removal of the crankshaft and bearings, clean thoroughly with solvent, then let them dry.
3   After they are thoroughly dry, reinstall the main bearings into their respective positions in the engine block and main bearing caps. Then carefully lay the crankshaft into position in the engine block.
4   Cut a piece of Plastigage about the width of the bearing and lay it on the crank journal, in parallel with the crankshaft. Do this for each crank journal.
5   Carefully, so as not to disturb the Plastigage, install each main bearing cap and tighten the bolts to their proper torque specification. The arrow on each cap should face toward the front of the engine.
6   Now remove each bearing cap and measure the width of the Plastigage strip which will have flattened out when the caps were tightened. A scale is provided on the Plastigage envelope for measuring the width of the Plastigage strip, and thus, bearing clearance (see accompanying figure).
7   If the Plastigage is flattened more at the ends than in the middle, or vice versa, this is an indication of journal taper which can be checked in the Specifications Section.
8   To test for an out-of-round condition, remove all traces of the Plastigage (be careful not to damage the crankshaft or bearing surfaces) and rotate the crankshaft 90 degrees. With the crankshaft rotated to this point, use the Plastigage to check the clearances again. Compare these measurements with those taken previously to arrive at eccentricity or out of round.
9   If it is determined that the old bearings must be replaced, be sure to repeat the running clearance check on the new bearings before installing the crankshaft.

Connecting rod bearing running clearance

10 The running clearance of the connecting rod bearings is checked using the same method as for the main bearings. In this case, the main bearing caps should be tightened to their proper torque, and the connecting rods must be temporarily reinstalled to the crankshaft.

33 Engine – rebuilding alternatives

1   At this point in the engine rebuilding process the home mechanic is faced with a number of options for completing the overhaul. The decision to replace the cylinder block, piston/rod assemblies and crankshaft depends on a number of factors with the number one consideration being the condition of the cylinder block. Other considerations are: cost, competent machine shop facilities, parts availability, time available to complete the project and experience.
2   Some of the rebuilding alternatives are as follows:

Individual parts – *If the inspection procedures prove that the engine block and most engine components are in reusable condition, this may be the most economical alternative. The block, crankshaft and piston/rod assemblies should all be inspected carefully. Even if the block shows little wear, the camshaft bearing bores and cylinder bores should receive a finish hone; both jobs for a machine shop.*

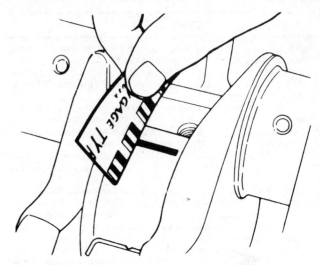

Fig. 2.27 Using Plastigage is the easiest method of measuring the main and connecting rod bearing clearances (Sec 32)

Master kit (crankshaft kit) – *This rebuild package usually consists of a reground crankshaft and a matched set of pistons and connecting rods. The pistons will come already installed with new piston pins to the connecting rods. Piston rings and the necessary bearings may or may not be included in the kit. These kits are commonly available for standard cylinder bores, as well as for engine blocks which have been bored to a regular oversize.*

Short block – *A short block consists of a cylinder block with a crankshaft and piston/rod assemblies already installed. All new bearings are incorporated and all clearances will be within tolerances. Depending on where the short block is purchased, a guarantee may be included. The existing camshaft, valve mechanism, cylinder heads and other parts can be bolted to this short block with little or no machine shop work necessary for the engine overhaul.*

Long block – *A long block consists of a short block plus oil pump, oil pan, cylinder head, valve cover, camshaft and valve mechanism, camshaft gear, timing chain and front cover. All components are installed with new bearings, seals and gaskets incorporated throughout. The installation of manifolds and external parts is all that is necessary. Some form of guarantee is usually included with purchase.*

3   Give careful thought to which method is best for your situation and discuss the alternatives with local machine shop owners, parts dealers or Datsun dealership partsmen.

34 Engine overhaul – general assembly information

1   Before assembling any parts to the engine block, the block should have all necessary machine work completed and the engine block should be thoroughly cleaned. If machine work was performed, chances are that the block was hot-tanked afterwards to remove all traces of the machine cuttings.
2   The oil galleys and water passages of the block should also be thoroughly clean and free from dirt or machining leftovers. It's good practice to install new freeze plugs in the engine whenever it is stripped for a total overhaul. These plugs are difficult to replace once the engine has been assembled and installed. If the engine was sent out for machine work and hot-tanking, it may be best to let the machine shop remove and install new plugs. If they are to be done at home, proceed as follows:

   a) Use a hammer and punch to press one side of the plug into the block.
   b) Use pliers to pry the old freeze plug out of its recess
   c) Place a suitable replacement plug into position and hammer into place until flush with the engine block. Special installation tools are available for pressing the plug into place, however a suitable sized socket will work fine.

3   Clean and examine all bolts, nuts and fasteners. Replace any that are damaged.

4 Clean and cover all engine components to keep dirt and dust away from them until they can be installed.
5 Have assembly grease and an oil can filled with engine oil handy to lubricate parts as they are installed.
6 Lay out all necessary tools and a reliable torque wrench on a clean work table for easy retrieval.
7 New gaskets and seals must be used throughout. These are commonly available together in a master rebuild gasket set.
8 In almost all cases, parts to be replaced during a major overhaul include: connecting rod bearings, main bearings, piston rings, timing chain, spark plugs and oil filter. These are in addition to any parts found damaged or excessively worn during dismantling or the various inspection processes.
9 After the crankshaft, piston/rod assemblies and the various associated bearings have been installed in the engine block, the remainder of the components (cylinder head, oil pump, camshaft, etc.,) can be installed following the installation procedures located in the various Sections of this Chapter.
10 Follow the engine disassembly sequence in the reverse order of installation, using new gaskets where necessary.

35 Pistons and piston rings – assembly

1 The piston should be attached to its appropriate connecting rod. As mentioned previously, this is a job for a professional equipped with the proper supports and an arbor press.
2 The new piston rings should be comparable in size to the piston being used.
3 The installation of the piston rings on the piston is critical to the overall performance of the rebuilt engine.
4 Measure the ring end gap of each ring before it is installed in the piston. This is done as follows:

a) Arrange the piston rings into sets for each piston. The set will contain a top ring, 2nd ring and an oil control ring.
b) Slip a top ring into the appropriate cylinder bore. Push the ring into the cylinder bore about ¼-inch below the upper limit of ring travel (a total of about 1 inch below block deck). Push the ring down into position with the top of a piston to make sure the ring is square with the cylinder wall.
c) Using a feeler gauge, measure the gap between the ends of the ring (photo). If the gap is less than specified (see Specifications), remove the ring and try another top ring for fit.
d) Check all top rings in the same manner and if necessary use a fine file to remove a slight amount of material from the ends of the ring(s). If inadequate end gap is used, the rings will break during operation.
e) Measure the end gap of each 2nd ring and oil control ring as described above.

5 Check the fit of each piston ring into its groove by holding the ring next to the piston and then placing the outer surface of the ring into its respective groove. Roll the ring entirely around the piston and check for any binding. If the binding is due to a distorted ring, replace the ring with a new one. Perform this check for the top and 2nd rings of each piston.
6 Install the piston rings as follows:

a) Study the accompanying figure thoroughly to understand exactly where each ring gap should be located in relation to the piston and other rings. The location of each ring gap is important.
b) If a piston ring expander tool is available, use this to install the rings. If not, small lengths of tin can be used to prevent the rings from entering the wrong groove (see Section 27 on piston ring removal). Be sure all rings are installed so the stamped mark on each faces up. Compare with Fig. 2.28.
c) Install the bottom oil ring in its groove positioning the gap in its proper location.
d) Install the 2nd ring and properly locate its gap.
e) Install the top ring with gap properly positioned.
f) Repeat the above procedures for all piston assemblies.

7 Proper clearance of the piston rings in their grooves is very important. Clearance between the ring and its groove is checked with a blade feeler gauge, sliding the appropriately sized feeler gauge (see Specifications) between the top of the ring and the inside of the groove. Rotate the feeler blades all the way around the piston, checking for proper clearance. Replace rings or clean and dress the groove as necessary for proper clearance.

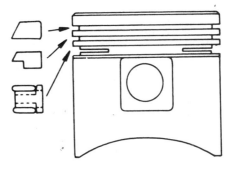
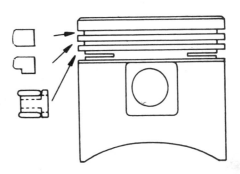

Fig. 2.28 The three piston rings should be installed on the piston as shown on non-Turbo models (above) and Turbo models (below) (Sec 35)

35.4 Prior to installing the piston rings, the ring end gap should be measured as shown

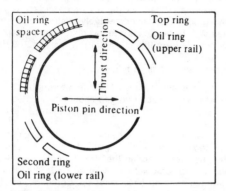

Fig. 2.29 To guard against compression leaks, the gaps of the three piston rings should be positioned as shown (Sec 35)

36.1 When installing the main bearings, be sure the oil holes (arrow) line up with those in the block

36 Crankshaft and main bearings – installation

1   Install the main bearing shells into their recesses in the crankcase, with the oil holes in correct alignment (photo). Be sure each bearing is in its proper location (see accompanying figure). Upper bearings have oil grooves, while the lower bearings are smooth. The center bearings are the only flanged ones. The number 1 and 4 bearings are the same type, as are the 2, 3 5 and 6 bearings.
2   Install the baffle plate and steel net which are components of the crankcase ventilation system (emission control).
3   Oil the main bearing shells liberally with clean engine oil and lower the crankshaft into position in the crankcase.
4   Install each of the main bearing caps, complete with shell bearings, ensuring that they are replaced in their original locations with the arrows pointing towards the front of the engine. The center shell bearing has integral thrust segments with oil grooves.
5   The corners of the rear main bearing cap should have an application of sealant at the points indicated.
6   Tighten the main bearing cap bolts progressively and in the order shown to the specified torque.
7   When installation is complete, check that the crankshaft turns smoothly and the end play is as previously established (Section 25).
8   Apply sealant to the rear main bearing cap side seals and tap them into position (photo). Also, apply sealant to the front cover and rear bearing cap-to-engine block joints.
9   Grease the crankshaft rear oil seal and tap it into position using a piece of tubing or a block of wood to install it evenly (see Section 23).
10 Bolt on the engine rear endplate.
11 Locate the flywheel on the crankshaft rear flange and tighten the bolts to the specified torque.

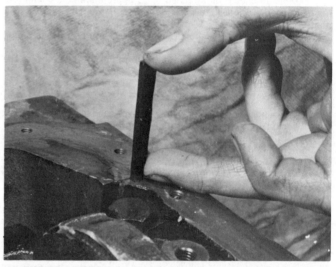

36.8 Jointing compound should be applied to the rear main bearing cap side seals prior to installing them

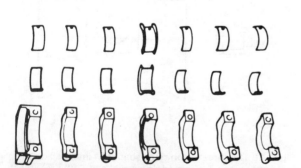

Fig. 2.30 It is important that the main bearings are installed in their proper locations, as different types are used (Sec 36)

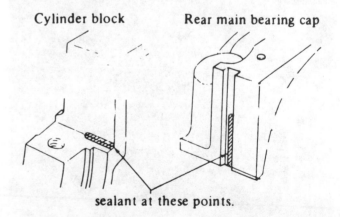

Fig. 2.31 Prior to installing the rear main bearing cap, sealant should be applied as shown (Sec 36)

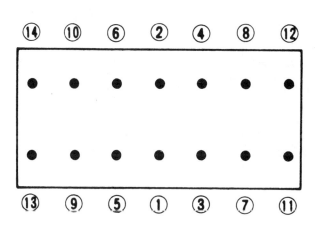

Fig. 2.32 The main bearing cap bolts should be tightened evenly in the sequence shown (Sec 36)

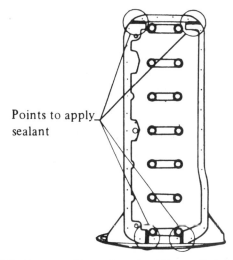

Points to apply sealant

Fig. 2.33 During assembly, sealant should be applied at the front cover and rear bearing cap as shown (Sec 36)

37 Pistons, connecting rods and bearings – installation

1   With the pistons complete with piston rings and connecting rods, they can be installed in the engine.
2   Make sure the cylinder bores are perfectly clean. Wipe the cylinder walls several times with a light engine oil and a clean, lint-free cloth.
3   Lubricate the connecting rod bearings and install them into their appropriate rod and rod cap.
4   Lightly coat the pistons, rings and cylinder walls with light engine oil.
5   Install a length of rubber or plastic tubing over the connecting rod studs on one rod assembly. This will prevent the threaded bolts from possibly damaging the cylinder wall or crankshaft journal as the piston/rod assembly is pushed into place (photo).
6   Check that all the piston ring gaps are positioned properly (see Section 35).
7   Check that the piston/rod assembly is properly positioned. Most pistons will be marked with an F or a drilled-out area indicating the piston should be installed with these marks toward the front of the engine (photo). The oil hole in the connecting rod should also be toward the right side of the engine (photo).

8   Place a piston ring compressor around the piston, with the base of the compressor flush with the cylinder block. Tighten the compressor until the rings are flush with the piston surface and then push the piston assembly into the bore. A wooden hammer handle can be used to tap the top of the piston slightly (photo). Hold the ring compressor solidly against the cylinder block until all rings are inside the bore. Continue pushing until the connecting rod is near to its installed position.
9   Ensure that all bearing surfaces and the crankshaft journal are coated with engine oil and remove the tubing protector pieces. Install the connecting rod bearing cap (with bearing) to the connecting rod. The cylinder number on the cap should be on the same side as the number on the rod (photo).
10   Torque the nuts to specifications.
11   Repeat this procedure for all cylinders, using the rubber or plastic tubing on each assembly to prevent damage as the pistons are pushed into place. Rotate the crankshaft as necessary to make the connecting rod nuts accessible for tightening.
12   If new connecting rods are being installed, following installation, recheck the connecting rod side clearances to be sure they are within Specifications. Refer to Section 27, paragraph 3.

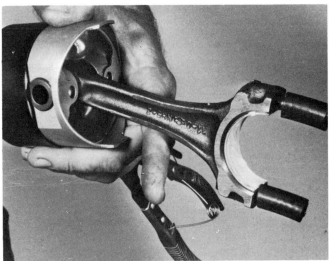

37.5 Pieces of rubber hose should be slipped over the connecting rod studs to protect the crankshaft and cylinder walls during piston/connecting rod installation

37.7a The pistons must be installed with the F mark (arrow) toward the front of the engine

37.7b The connecting rods must be installed with the oil hole (arrow) toward the right side of the engine

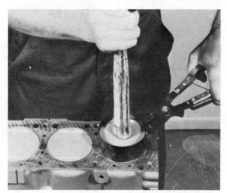

37.8 Using a piston ring compressor and tapping with a wooden hammer handle is the easiest method of installing the pistons

37.9 The connecting rod caps must be installed so the numbers on the side match up

17 See Section 39 for the starting-up procedure.

38 Engine – installation

1   If the engine has been completely stripped for overhaul, it should be assembled outside of the car so it is at the same state of assembly it was at during removal.
2   Loosely bolt the left engine mounting bracket to the cylinder block.
3   If the engine has been worked on while on an engine stand, remove it from the stand and lower it onto a wooden skid or the floor.
4   If not already done, install the rear plate and flywheel.
5   If equipped with a manual transmission, install the clutch disc and cover assembly. Be sure to use a centering tool to center the clutch disc before fully tightening the cover assembly bolts. A ratchet wrench extension and a suitable sized socket will serve as a makeshift centering tool.
6   Carefully mate the transmission with the engine by reversing the separation steps described in Section 25. This is most easily done with the transmission on a rolling-type floor jack.
7   Install the starter. Refer to Chapter 5, if necessary.
8   Install the engine gussets, if equipped to the engine and transmission.
9   Connect an engine hoist to the engine and lift it up. The chains should be positioned as during removal, with the engine/transmission sitting as level as possible. The fenders and radiator support should be covered with pads to protect them.
10 Carefully lower the rear of the transmission into the engine compartment. As you gradually lower it, also move the hoist rearward. Closely watch the clearances on all sides as the assembly is lowered.
11 When the engine/transmission assembly is in position, loosely install the transmission support bracket to the transmission and to the body.
12 Lower the engine so that the left engine mounting bracket fits over the mounting insulator stud and loosely install the mounting nut.
13 Fit the right mounting bracket into position on its mounting insulator and bolt it to the engine block. Install the nut on the mounting stud.
14 Tighten all engine and transmission mounting bolts.
15 Disconnect the engine hoist from the engine.
16 Install the remaining components and make all connections in the reverse order of the removal procedure. Do not connect the battery yet.

39 Engine start-up (following overhaul)

1   With the engine in place in the vehicle and all components connected, make a final check that all pipes and wiring have been connected and that no rags or tools have been left in the engine compartment.
2   Connect the positive battery cable, followed by the negative battery cable. If sparks or arcing occur as the negative cable is connected to the battery, check that all electrical accessories are turned off (check dome light). If arcing still occurs, check that all electrical wiring is connected properly to the engine and transmission.
3   Fill the cooling system with the proper mixture and amount of water and antifreeze.
4   Fill the engine with the proper quantity and grade of oil.
5   Fill the transmission with the proper quantity and grade of fluid.
6   Check the tension of all drivebelts.
7   Disconnect the ignition coil wire from the distributor cap and ground it on the engine.
8   Now crank the engine over for about 15 to 30 seconds. This will allow the oil pump to distribute oil and the fuel pump to start pumping fuel.
9   Now reconnect the ignition coil wire to the distributor cap and start the engine. Immediately check all gauges and warning lights for proper readings, and check for leaks of coolant or oil.
10 If the engine does not start immediately, check to make sure fuel is reaching the injectors. This may take a while.
11 After allowing the engine to run for a few minutes at low speed, turn it off and recheck the oil and coolant levels.
12 Start the engine again and check the ignition timing and idle speed. Refer to Chapter 1.
13 Finally, while the engine is thoroughly warmed up, recheck the valve clearances to make sure they correspond with the 'hot' engine specs.
14 Run the vehicle easily during the first 500 to 1000 miles (break-in period), then check the torque settings on all major engine components, particularly the cylinder head. Tighten any bolts which may have loosened.

Chapter 3 Cooling, heating and air-conditioning systems

Refer to Chapter 13 for specifications related to 1983 models

Contents

Specifications

Radiator
Cap relief pressure .... 13 psi (0.9 kg/cm²)
Leakage test pressure .... 23 psi (1.6 kg/cm²)

Thermostat
Type .... Wax pellet type
Opening temperature .... 180°F (standard type)
    190°F (frigid type)
    170°F (tropical type)

Water pump type .... Centrifugal

Air conditioner compressor
Type .... Swash plate
Model MJ167
Displacement .... 10.19 cu in (167 cm³)
Direction of rotation .... Clockwise
Drivebelt type
    1979 .... B type
    1980 thru 1982 .... A type

Refrigerant
Type R-12
Capacity
    1979 and 1980 .... 2.0 to 2.5 lb (0.9 to 1.1 kg)
    1981 and 1982 .... 1.8 to 2.2 lb (0.8 to 1.0 kg)

Lubricating oil
Type .... SUNISO 5GS
Capacity .... 5.1 fl oz (150 ml) (5.3 Imp fl oz)

Torque specifications

	ft-lbs	m-kg
Water pump mounting bolts (small)	5.0	0.7
Water pump mounting bolts (large)	10.0	1.3
A/C compressor bracket mounting bolts	37.0	5.0
A/C compressor mounting bolts	37.0	5.0

1 Cooling system – general information

1 The cooling system comprises the radiator, top and bottom water hoses, water pump, cylinder and block water jackets, radiator cap with pressure relief valve and flow and return heater hoses. The thermostat is located in a recess at the front of the cylinder head. The principle of the system is that cold water in the bottom of the radiator circulates upwards through the lower radiator hose to the water pump, where the pump impeller pushes the water round the cylinder block and head through the various cast-in passages to cool the cylinder bores, combustion surfaces and valve seats. When sufficient heat has been absorbed by the cooling water, and the engine has reached an efficient working temperature, the water moves from the cylinder head past the now open thermostat into the top radiator hose and into the radiator header tank.

2 The water then travels down the radiator tubes where it is rapidly cooled by the in-rush of air, when the vehicle is in forward motion. A multi-bladed fan, mounted on the water pump pulley, assists this cooling action. The water, now cooled, reaches the bottom of the radiator and the cycle is repeated.

3 When the engine is cold the thermostat remains closed until the coolant reaches a pre-determined temperature (see the Specifications). This assists rapid warming-up.

4 The system is pressurized by means of a spring-loaded radiator filler cap which prevents premature boiling by increasing the boiling point of the coolant. If the coolant temperature goes above this increased boiling point, the extra pressure in the system forces the radiator cap internal spring-loaded valve off its seat and exposes the overflow pipe down which displaced coolant escapes.

5 It is important to check that the radiator cap is in good condition and that the spring behind the sealing washer has not weakened or corroded. Most service stations have a machine for testing that the cap operates at the specified pressure.

6 The coolant recovery system consists of a plastic reservoir into which the overflow coolant from the radiator flows when the engine is hot. When the engine cools and the coolant contracts, coolant is drawn back into the radiator from the reservoir and thus maintains the system at full capacity.

7 The coolant level should be kept between the Min and Max marks on the recovery bottle.

8 An electrosensitive capsule located in the cylinder head measures the water temperature.

9 The cooling system also provides the heat for the car interior heater and heats the inlet manifold.

10 On vehicles equipped with automatic transmission, the transmission fluid is cooled by a cooler attached to the base of the radiator.

11 On cars equipped with air conditioning systems, a condenser is placed ahead of the radiator and is bolted in conjunction with it.

12 The radiator cooling fan incorporates either a fluid coupling or a fluid/temperature controlled coupling. The latter device comprises an oil operated clutch and is a coiled bi-metallic thermostat which functions jointly to permit the fan to slip when the engine is below normal operating temperature level and does not require the supplementary air flow provided by the fan at normal running speed.

13 At higher engine operating temperature, the fan is locked and rotates at the speed of the water pump pulley. The fan coupling is a sealed unit and requires no periodic maintenance.

14 **Note:** *If the radiator cap has to be removed when the engine is hot, rotate the cap slowly counterclockwise to the detent and allow the residual pressure to escape. Do not press the cap down until all hissing has stopped and take extreme care that the hands are not scalded.*

2 Antifreeze

1 It is recommended that the cooling system be filled with a water/ethylene glycol based antifreeze solution which will give protection down to at least –20°F at all times. This provides protection against corrosion and increases the coolant boiling point. When handling antifreeze, take care that it is not spilled on the vehicle paintwork, since it will invariably cause damage if not removed immediately.

2 The cooling system should be drained, flushed and refilled at least every alternate Fall. The use of antifreeze solutions for periods of longer than two years is likely to cause damage and encourage the formation of rust and scale due to the corrosion inhibitors gradually losing their efficiency.

3 Before adding antifreeze to the system, check all hose connections and check the tightness of the cylinder head bolts as such solutions are searching.

4 The exact mixture of antifreeze to water which you should use depends upon the relative weather conditions. The mixture should contain at least 50 percent antifreeze, offering protection to –34°F. Under no circumstances should the mixture contain more than 70 percent antifreeze.

3 Cooling system – checking and servicing

Since checking and servicing of the cooling system is included in the routine maintenance schedule for this car, these procedures are included in Chapter 1.

4   Thermostat – removal and installation

1   The thermostat is basically a restriction valve which is actuated by a heat sensitive element. It is mounted inside a housing on the right side of the engine and is designed to open and close at predetermined temperatures to allow coolant to warm up or cool the engine.

2   To remove the thermostat for replacement or testing, begin by draining the coolant until the upper level of the coolant in the radiator is below the inner grille.

3   Remove the upper radiator hose.

4   Remove the two bolts that retain the water outlet (photo).

5   Lift off the water outlet along with the gasket. Note how the thermostat is positioned in its recess, as it must be replaced in this same position (photos), then lift out the thermostat.

6   Before installation, use a gasket scraper or putty knife to carefully remove all traces of the old gasket on the thermostat housing and the cover.

7   Place the thermostat in position in its housing. Be sure that the air vent hole in the thermostat is toward the left side of the engine.

8   Place a thin bead of silicone sealant around the sealing surface on the water outlet.

9   Place a new gasket in position on the outlet.

10   Carefully install the outlet gasket onto the housing, torquing the bolts to specifications.

11   Reinstall the upper radiator hose.

12   Refill the radiator with the proper mixture of antifreeze and water. Refer to Chapter 1 if necessary.

13   With the radiator cap removed, start the engine and run it until the upper radiator hose becomes hot. At this point, the thermostat would be in the open position. Check the coolant level and add as necessary.

14   Reinstall the radiator cap.

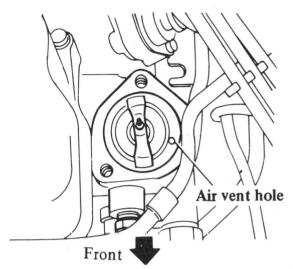

Fig. 3.2 The thermostat should be installed with the air vent hole toward the left side of the engine (Sec 4)

5   Radiator – removal and installation

1   Open the drain valve on the under side of the radiator and drain the coolant into a container.

2   Remove the upper radiator hose.

3   Remove the lower radiator hose.

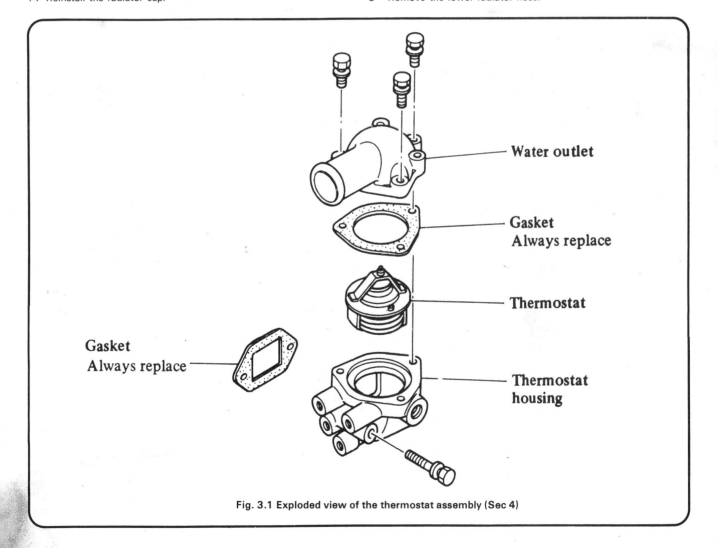

Fig. 3.1 Exploded view of the thermostat assembly (Sec 4)

4   Disconnect the reservoir bottle hose from the radiator spout.
5   Remove the screws that retain the shroud to the radiator and slide the shroud toward the engine.
6   If equipped with an automatic transmission, disconnect the cooler hoses from the radiator.
7   Remove the screws that attach the radiator to the body. The same bolts retain both the radiator and A/C condenser.
8   Lift out the radiator.
9   With the radiator removed, it can be inspected for leaks or damage. If in need of repairs, have a professional radiator shop or dealer perform the work as special welding techniques are required.
10   Bugs and dirt can be cleaned from the radiator by using compressed air and a soft brush. Do not bend the cooling fins as this is done.
11   Installation is the reverse of the removal procedure.
12   After installation, fill the cooling system with the proper mixture of antifreeze and water. Refer to Chapter 1 if necessary.
13   Start the engine and check for leaks. Allow the engine to reach normal operating temperature, indicated by the upper radiator hose becoming hot: Recheck the coolant level and add more if required.

6   Reservoir tank – removal and installation

1   Disconnect the reservoir tank hose at the radiator neck (photo).
2   Lift the reservoir tank upward and disconnect the wiring connector.
3   With your finger over the end of the hose to prevent leakage of the coolant, lift the tank from the engine compartment.
4   Drain the coolant from the tank into a container. If the tank is being replaced, disconnect the hose from the bottom of the tank.
5   Installation is the reverse of the removal procedure.
6   Refill the tank with the proper mixture of antifreeze and water. Refer to Chapter 1 if necessary.

7   Fan – removal and installation

1   Remove the radiator as described in Section 5.
2   Remove the radiator shroud.
3   Remove the four screws that retain the fan to the water pump and lift off the fan.
4   Installation is the reverse of the removal procedure.

8   Water pump – testing

1   A failure in the water pump can cause serious engine damage due to overloading. The pump will not be able to circulate cooled water through the engine.
2   There are three ways to check the operation of the water pump while it is still installed on the engine. If the pump is suspect, it should be replaced with a new or factory rebuilt unit.
3   With the engine warmed up to normal operating temperature, squeeze the upper radiator hose. If the water pump is working properly, a pressure surge should be felt as the hose is released.
4   Water pumps are equipped with weep or vent holes, if a failure occurs to the bladder of the pump, small amounts of water will leak from these weep holes. In most cases it will be necessary to use a flashlight from under the car to see evidence of leakage from this point in the pump body.
5   If the water pump shaft bearings fail there may be a squealing sound at the front of the engine while it is running. Shaft wear can be felt if the water pump pulley is forced up and down. Do not mistake drivebelt slippage, which also causes a squealing sound, for water pump failure.

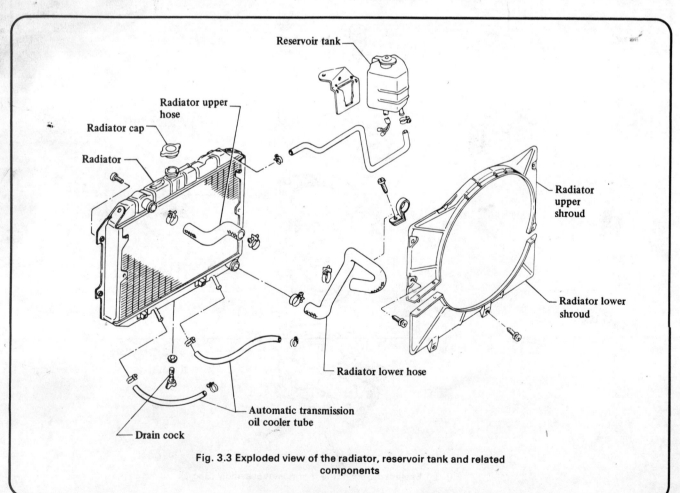

Fig. 3.3 Exploded view of the radiator, reservoir tank and related components

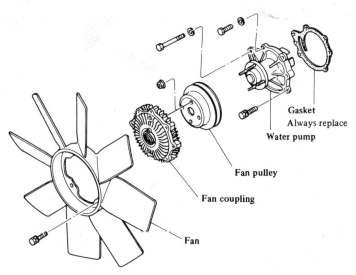

Fig. 3.4 Exploded view of the fan, fan coupling and water pump

Gasket
Always replace

Water pump

Fan pulley

Fan coupling

Fan

9 Water pump – removal and installation

1   Remove the radiator as described in Section 5.
2   Remove the fan and coupling as described in Section 7.
3   Remove the A/C compressor drivebelt.
4   Loosen the alternator adjusting bolt and remove the alternator water pump fan belt.
5   Loosen the water pump mounting bolts until the pump can be lifted off.
6   Remove the gasket.
7   This water pump fan coupling assembly is not designed to be disassembled, and if defective, should be replaced with a new or rebuilt unit.
8   Be sure the sealing surfaces of the water pump and engine front cover are clean of any dirt or gasket material. Then place a thin bead of silicone sealant on the pump sealing surface. While the sealant is still wet, install the pump and torque the mounting bolts to specs.
9   The remainder of the installation is the reverse of the removal procedure.
10 Adjust the drivebelts to the proper tension. Refer to Chapter 1 if necessary.
11 Fill the cooling system with the proper mixture of antifreeze and water, again referring to Chapter 1 if necessary. Then start the engine and allow it to idle until it reaches normal operating temperature. This is indicated by the upper radiator hose becoming hot. Check around the water pump and radiator for any leaks.
12 Recheck the coolant level and add more if necessary.

10 Heating system – general information

1   The main components of the heating system include the heater unit (which contains the heater core and cable-operated valves) the blower motor, the control assembly (mounted in the dash) and the air ducts which deliver the air to the various outlet locations.
2   Either outside air or interior (recirculated) air (depending on the settings) is drawn into the system through the blower unit. From there the blower motor forces the air into the heater unit. The lever settings on the control assembly operate the valves in the heater unit, which determines the mix of heated and ambient air by regulating how much air is passed through the heater core. The hotter the setting the more air is passed through the core.
3   The air ducts carry the heated air from the heater unit to the desired location. Again, valves within the duct system regulate where in the car the air will be delivered.
4   The heater core is heated by engine coolant passing through it. The heater hoses carry the coolant from the engine to the heater core and then back again.

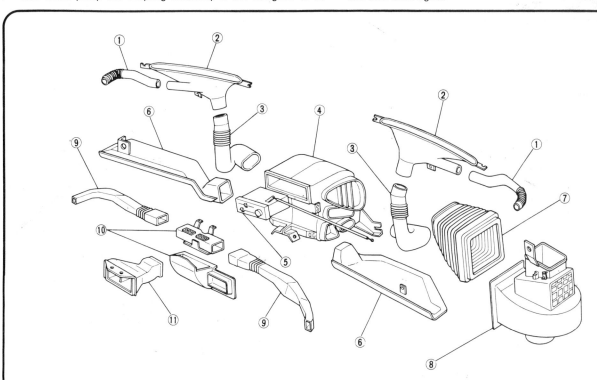

Fig. 3.5 Components of the heating system

1 Side defroster duct	4 Heater unit	7 Heater duct	10 Connector
2 Defroster nozzle	5 Heater control assembly	8 Blower unit	11 Center ventilation duct
3 Defroster duct	6 Floor nozzle	9 Side ventilation duct	

11 Heater and A/C control assembly – removal and installation

1   Refer to Chapter 10.

12 Water cock – removal and installation

1   Disconnect the negative battery cable.
2   Remove the right lower cover of the instrument panel.
3   Remove the floor nozzle and defroster duct on the right side.
4   Remove the heater duct.
5   Disconnect the heater outlet and inlet hoses.
6   Loosen the clamp of the hose connecting the water cock to the heater unit.
7   Disconnect the temperature control cable and air mix door rod from the water cock lever.
8   Remove the water cock retaining screws and lift off the water cock.
9   Installation is the reverse of the removal procedure.
10 Following installation, adjust the temperature control cable and air mix door rod as described in Chapter 10 Section 18.

13 Blower motor – removal and installation

1   Disconnect the negative battery cable from the battery.
2   Remove the right lower cover of the instrument panel.
3   Remove the floor nozzle on the right side.
4   Disconnect the wiring harness from the blower motor connector.
5   Remove the blower motor mounting screws, and lift out the motor and fan.
6   Installation is the reverse of the removal procedure.

14 Blower assembly – removal and installation

1   Disconnect the negative battery cable from the battery.
2   Remove the right lower cover of the instrument panel.
3   Remove the glove box. Refer to Chapter 10 if necessary.
4   Remove the floor nozzle, defroster duct and the right side defroster duct.
5   Remove the heater duct.
6   Disconnect the wiring harness from the blower motor.
7   If not equipped with air conditioning, remove the retaining clip from the control cable and disconnect the cable from the blower assembly.
8   If equipped with air conditioning, remove the two vacuum lines.
9   Remove the blower assembly mounting bolts, and lift out the blower assembly.
10 Installation is the reverse of the removal procedure.

15 Heater unit – removal and installation

Note: *The following procedure applies only to models without air conditioning.*
1   Disconnect the negative battery cable.
2   Set the temperature control lever to the maximum Hot position.
3   Remove the drain plug from the bottom of the radiator and drain the coolant into a suitable container.
4   Remove both lower covers from the instrument panel.
5   Remove the floor nozzles and the defroster ducts.
6   Remove the instrument console and the instrument center ventilator. Refer to Chapter 10, if necessary.
7   Remove the glove box. Again, refer to Chapter 10, if necessary.
8   Remove the heater duct.
9   Disconnect all control cables and rods from the heater unit.
10 Remove the heater control assembly mounting screws and lift out the control assembly.
11 Disconnect the heater inlet and outlet hoses from inside the car.
12 Remove the blower assembly. Refer to Section 14.
13 Remove the heater unit mounting bolts and remove the unit.
14 If the heater core needs to be removed from the heater unit use the following procedure:
    a)   Remove the water cock from the heater unit

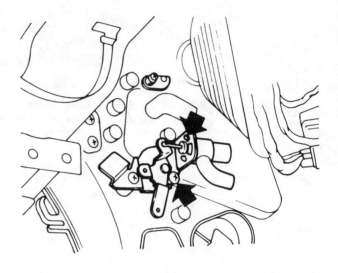

Fig. 3.6 The water cock is located on the right side of the heater unit (Sec 12)

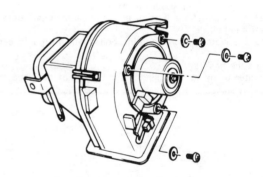

Fig. 3.7 The blower motor is attached to the underside of the blower assembly (Sec 13)

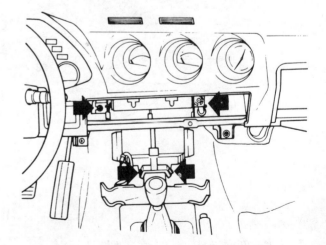

Fig. 3.8 Location of the heater unit mounting screws (Sec 15)

b) Remove the clips that attach the right and left sections of the heater case and separate the case sections
c) Remove the heater core
d) Reassemble by reversing the disassembly procedure

15 Installation of the heater unit is the reverse of the removal procedure.

16 Following installation, adjust the control cables and rods as described in Chapter 10, Section 18.

16 Air conditioning system – general information

The air conditioning system used in the Datsun 280ZX maintains proper temperature by cycling the compressor on and off according to the pressure within the system, and by maintaining a mix of cooled, ambient and heated air, using basically the same blower, heater core and outlet duct system that the heating system uses.

In addition, the system also is sensitive to the temperature of the air being taken in. If the intake air is below approximately 32°F, the compressor will not operate.

The main components of the system include a belt-driven compressor, a condensor (mounted in front of the radiator), a receiver, drier and an evaporator.

The system operates by air (outside or recirculated) entering the evaporator core by the action of the blower, where it receives maximum cooling if the controls are set for cooling. When the air leaves the evaporator, it enters the heater/air conditioner duct assembly and by means of a manually controlled deflector, it either passes through or bypasses the heater core in the correct proportions to provide the desired vehicle temperature.

Distribution of this air into the car is then regulated by a manually operated deflector, and is directed either to the floor vents, dash vents or defroster vents according to settings.

The dash-mounted control assembly used in the A/C system differs from the assembly in non-air conditioned models, in that it uses vacuum signal lines to control some of the heater A/C functions.

Beginning with the 1980 ZX models, an automatic air temperature control system was introduced, which uses a variety of electrical and vacuum linked sensors, switches and amplifiers to automatically control all the functions of the A/C and heating systems so the interior temperature is kept at a constant level. Once the control lever is set to a desired temperature range, this system automatically selects the optimum combination of air flow, air temperature and outlet location. Because of the complexity of this system, we recommend that you allow a Datsun dealer or other qualified mechanic to diagnose and repair any malfunctions of the system.

Caution: *In view of the toxic nature of the chemicals and gases employed in the system, no part of the system should be disconnected by the home mechanic. Due to the need for the specialized evacuating and charging equipment such work should be left to your dealer or a refrigeration specialist.*

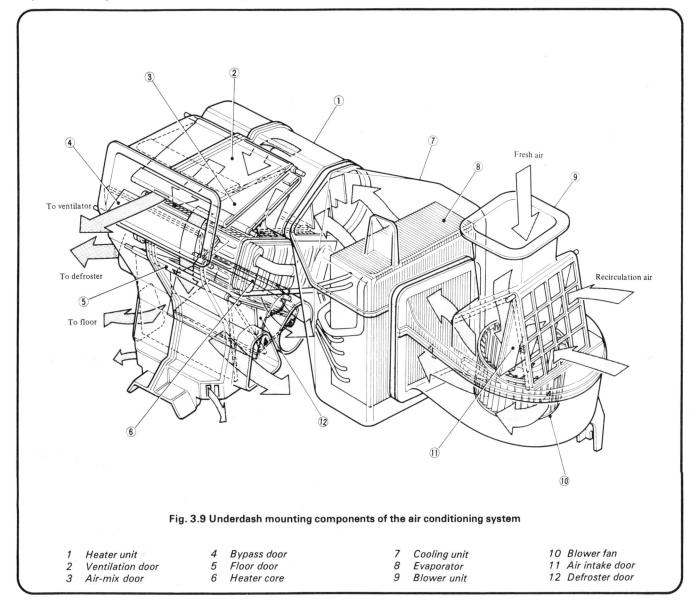

Fig. 3.9 Underdash mounting components of the air conditioning system

1 Heater unit	4 Bypass door	7 Cooling unit	10 Blower fan
2 Ventilation door	5 Floor door	8 Evaporator	11 Air intake door
3 Air-mix door	6 Heater core	9 Blower unit	12 Defroster door

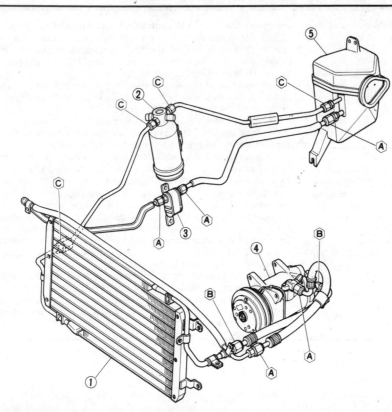

Fig. 3.10 Underhood components of the air
conditioning system

1   Condenser
2   Receiver drier
3   Accumulator
4   Compressor
5   Cooling unit

17 Air conditioning system – checks and maintenance

1   The following maintenance steps should be performed on a
regular basis to ensure that the air conditioner continues to operate at
peak efficiency.

    a)   Check the tension of the A/C compressor drivebelt and adjust
          if necessary. Refer to Chapter 1.

    b)   Visually inspect the condition of the hoses, checking for any
          cracking, hardening or other deterioration. **Note:** *Do not
          replace without first having the system discharged.*

    c)   Check that the fins of the condenser are not covered with
          foreign material, such as leaves or bugs. A soft brush and
          compressed air can be used to remove them.

2   The A/C compressor should be run for about 10 minutes at least
once every month. This is especially important to remember during the
winter months because long-term non-use can cause hardening of the
internal seals.

3   Due to the complexity of the air conditioning system and the
special equipment required to effectively work on it, accurate troubleshooting and repair of the system cannot be expected of the home
mechanic and should be left to a professional. In any case, due to the
toxic nature of the refrigerant, prior to disconnecting any part of the
system, the car should be taken to a Datsun dealer or other qualified
shop to have the system discharged. If the system should lose its
cooling action, some causes can be diagnosed by the home mechanic.
Look for other symptoms of trouble such as those in the following list.
In all cases, it's a good idea to have the system serviced by a
professional.

    a)   If bubbles appear in the sight glass (located on top of the
          receiver drier) this is an indication of either a small refrigerant
          leak or air in the refrigerant (photo). If air is in the refrigerant,
          the receiver drier is suspect and should be replaced.

    b)   If the sight glass takes on a mist-like appearance or shows
          many bubbles, this indicates a large refrigerant leak. In such
          a case, do not operate the compresser at all until the fault has
          been corrected.

    c)   Sweating or frosting of the expansion valve inlet indicates
          that the expansion valve is clogged or defective. It should be
          cleaned or replaced as necessary.

    d)   Sweating or frosting of the suction line (which runs between
          the suction throttle valve and the compressor) indicates that

the expansion valve is stuck open or defective. It should be
corrected or replaced as necessary.

    e)   Frosting on the evaporator indicates a defective suction
          throttle valve, requiring replacement of the valve.

    f)   Frosting of the high pressure liquid line (which runs between
          the condenser, receiver drier and expansion valve) indicates
          that either the drier or the high pressure line is restricted. The
          line will have to be cleared or the receiver drier replaced.

    g)   The combination of bubbles in the sight glass, a very hot
          suction line and, possibly, overheating of the engine is an
          indication that either the condenser is not operating properly
          or the refrigerant is overcharged. Check the tension of the
          drivebelt and adjust if necessary (Chapter 1). Check for
          foreign matter covering the fins of the condenser and clean if
          necessary. Also check for proper operation of the cooling
          system. If no fault can be found in these checks, the
          condenser may need to be replaced.

17.3 Location of the air conditioning system sight glass on top of the
receiver drier

18 Air conditioning compressor – removal and installation

1   Prior to disconnecting any air conditioning lines anywhere in the system the car should be taken to a Datsun dealer or other qualified automotive air conditioning repair shop to have the system depressurized. Due to the toxic nature of the chemicals and gases used in the system, this is not a job for the home mechanic.

2   Disconnect the negative battery cable.

3   Jack up the front of the car and support it on jackstands. Then remove the splash shield.

4   Loosen the bolt on the rear of the compressor idler pulley and move the pulley upward to loosen the A/C compressor drivebelt.

5   Remove the drivebelt from the compressor.

6   Disconnect both hoses leading to the compressor, and immediately plug all openings.

7   Disconnect any wires leading to the compressor.

8   Remove the four nuts and bolts that retain the compressor to its bracket and lift off the compressor.

9   Turn the compressor so the clutch is facing up and remove the compressor from the engine compartment. **Note:** *The compressor should not be left on its side or upside down for more than 10 minutes at a time, as compressor oil could enter the low pressure chambers and cause internal damage. If this should happen, the oil can be expelled from the chambers by positioning the compressor right side up and handcranking it several times.*

10   Installation is the reverse of removal with the following notes:

    a)   When reconnecting the hoses to the compressor, be sure to use new O-rings at each connection.

    b)   Check the tightness of the A/C compressor bracket bolts, while the compressor is removed, to be sure that none are loose.

    c)   After installing the compressor, turn the compressor clutch a few times by hand.

    d)   Adjust the compressor drivebelt tension. Refer to Chapter 1, if necessary.

11   Once the compressor and all A/C lines have been securely connected again, the car must once again be taken to a Datsun dealer or other qualified shop to have the system charged.

19 Condenser – removal and installation

1   Prior to disconnecting any air conditioning lines anywhere in the system the car should be taken to a Datsun dealer or other qualified automotive air conditioning repair shop to have the system depressurized. Due to the toxic nature of the chemicals and gases used in the system, this is not a job for the home mechanic.

2   Remove the air flow meter duct. Also remove the air cleaner and forward cooling fan, if equipped (photo).

3   Remove the charcoal canister.

4   Disconnect the refrigerant lines from the condenser. Be sure to use two wrenches when loosening the flare nuts, so as not to damage the lines. Immediately after disconnection, plug all openings in the lines and condenser to prevent dirt and moisture from entering.

5   Remove the condenser tube clamp.

6   Remove the air cleaner and duct.

7   Remove the four condenser mounting bolts and lift out the condenser.

8   If the condenser fins or air passages are clogged with foreign material, such as dirt, insects or leaves use compressed air or cold water and a soft brush to clean the condenser. If the condenser is in need of other repairs, have a professional radiator shop or Datsun dealer perform the work.

9   Installation is the reverse of the removal procedure. When connecting the refrigerant lines, always use new O-rings at each connection.

10   Once all A/C lines have been securely connected, the car must once again be taken to a Datsun dealer or other qualified shop to have the system charged.

20 Condenser fan (Turbo models) – removal and installation

1   Disconnect the negative battery cable.

2   Remove the right hand air cleaner duct.

3   Disconnect the condenser fan mounting nuts.

4   Disconnect the wiring connector from the condenser fan and lift it out.

5   Installation is the reverse of the removal procedure.

21 Automatic Temperature Control system – component description

The Automatic Temperature Control system works in conjunction with both the heating and air-conditioning system to maintain the interior temperature of the car at a desired level.

This section is to familiarize you with the basic function of the system and the location of its components.

Because of the complexity of the system we recommend that any malfunctioning of the system be diagnosed and repaired by a Datsun dealer or other qualified mechanic.

The Automatic Temperature Control system is divided into six subsystems which together include all of the components of the system.

System starting control
Coolant temperature switch: This switch keeps the blower unit turned off until the temperature of the engine coolant rises to normal operating temperature (about 122°F). This allows the interior air to be warmed up quickly during cold weather.

In-car switch: When the interior temperature of the car is extremely high, such as in the summer months, this switch quickly activates the starting control system, even when the coolant temperature switch is not activated.

Compressor switching control
Ambient switch: This switch turns the A/C compressor off when the outside air temperature is low.

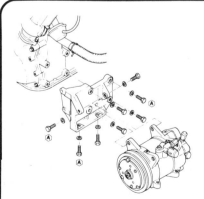

Fig. 3.11 Mounting arrangement of the A/C compressor and bracket (Sec 18)

19.2 Location of the forward cooling fan used on some models

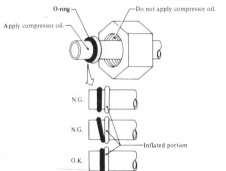

Fig. 3.12 O-rings should be properly installed in all A/C connections to prevent leaks (Sec 18 and 19)

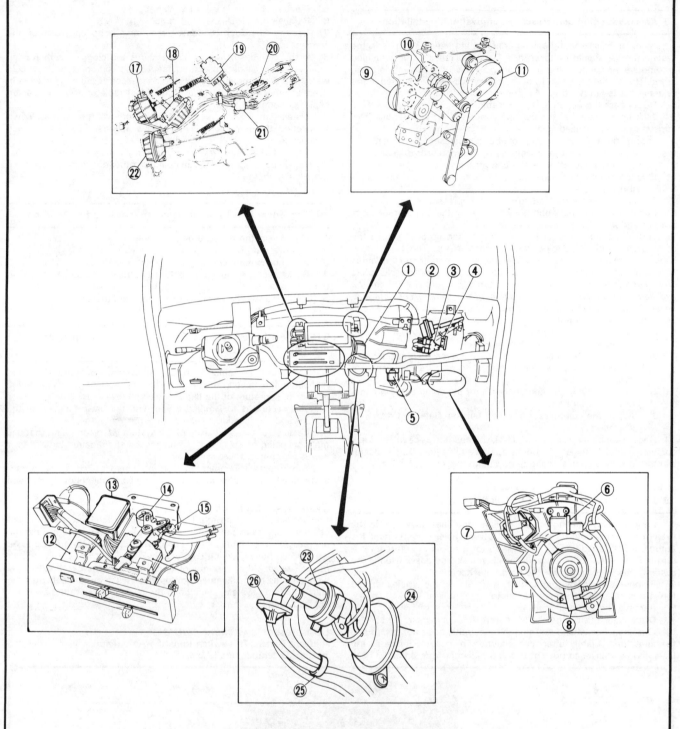

Fig. 3.13 Location of interior components of the automatic Temperature Control System (Sec 21)

1 Transducer	8 Fuse (blower motor)	14 Bypass vacuum selector	21 Air valve (Def clamp)
2 Intake door actuator	9 Blower control rheostat	15 Temperature control rheostat	22 Floor door actuator
3 Air valve (intake door)	10 Feedback rheostat	16 Program switch	23 Vacuum switch (Def clamp)
4 In-car switch	11 Vacuum program switch	17 Power servo	24 Heater cock
5 Check terminal	12 Recirculation timer	18 Ventilation door actuator	25 Vacuum divider
6 Blower relay	13 Temperature control amplifier	19 Bypass door actuator	26 Vacuum lock valve
7 Blower amplifier		20 Vacuum selector	

Fig. 3.14 Location of exterior components of the automatic Temperature Control System (Sec 21)

27 Ambient sensor
28 Ambient switch
29 Coolant temperature switch
30 In-car sensor
31 Aspirator fan

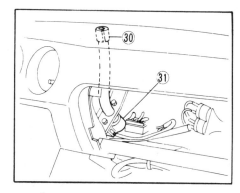

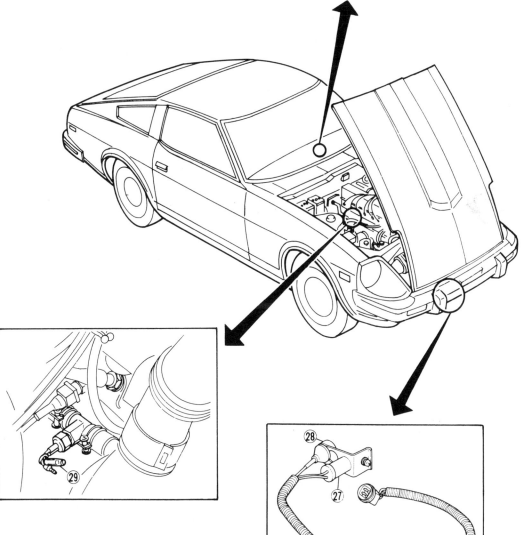

Automatic outlet air temperature control

In-car sensor: Located in the instrument panel, this switch senses the car's interior temperature.

Ambient sensor: Located behind the front bumper, this sensor senses the temperature of the outside air.

Temperature control rheostat: A variable resistor that is controlled by the position of the temperature control lever.

Feedback rheostat: This is a variable resistor which stabilizes the power servo by sending a signal which corresponds to the position of the air-mix door's position.

Temperature control amplifier: Measures the total resistance value of the in-car sensor, the ambient sensor, the temperature control rheostat and the feedback rheostat, and then sends a signal to the transducer.

Transducer: Changes the resistance signal sent from the temperature control amplifier into a vacuum signal which is sent to the power servo.

Power servo: An actuator which operates the position of the air-mix door in relation to the vacuum signal received from the transducer.

Bypass vacuum selector: When the temperature lever is set in the hottest position, this component bypasses the transducer and sends the vacuum signal directly to the power servo. When the temperature lever is set in the coldest position, the selector blocks the vacuum line completely.

Vacuum lock valve: When there is a momentary drop in vacuum at its source, this valve blocks the vacuum line.

Automatic blower speed

Blower control rheostat: A variable resistor which is activated and controlled by the position of the air-mix door.

Blower amplifier: This amplifier measures the resistance of the blower control rheostat and sends a proportional voltage signal to the blower motor.

Automatic air distribution control

Vacuum selector: Selects the appropriate vacuum lines to open and close air outlets in accordance with the position of the mode lever.

Vacuum program switch: Works in conjunction with the vacuum selector to select the appropriate vacuum lines needed to open and close air outlets in accordance with the position of the air-mix door.

Air valve and vacuum switch: Used to connect the vacuum selector and the vacuum program switch for proper operation between the two.

Recirculation control

Recirculation timer: Allows the interior air to recirculate for ten minutes, then automatically shuts it off.

Air valve: Actuates the recirculation of the interior air. When the recirculation switch is depressed, current stops flowing through the air valve, which closes and causes the actuator's vacuum line to be blocked. This automatically sets the air intake door in the recirculation position.

Chapter 4 Fuel injection and turbocharging systems

Refer to Chapter 13 for specifications and information related to 1982 and 1983 turbo models

Contents

Specifications

Fuel pressure
At idling (measured at filter) .... 30 psi
Upon initial full throttle (measured at filter) .... 37 psi
Fuel pump cut-off discharge pressure .... 43 to 64 psi
Design current .... 5.1 amps
Regulated pressure at (pressure regulator) .... 36.3 psi

Air regulator
Air flow quantity (at 68°F) (20°C) .... 971 cu ft/hr (27.5 m³)

Fuel injector
Coil resistance .... 2.35 ohms

Throttle valve switch
Idle speed when switch turns Off
    1979 models .... Approx. 1400 rpm
    1980 thru 1982 non-turbo models .... Approx. 900 rpm
    Turbo models .... Approx. 750 rpm

Thermotime switch
Temperature calibration .... On below 57° to 77°F (14° to 25°C)

Auxiliary cooling fan
Water temperature sensor switch calibration
    1979 models .... On above 230°F (110°C)
    1980 thru 1981 non-turbo models .... On above 221°F (105°C)
    1982 non-turbo models .... On above 216°F (102°C)
    Turbo models .... On above 212°F (100°C)
Fan motor timer unit operating period .... 17 minutes

Torque specifications

	ft-lb	m-kg
Throttle chamber mounting bolts	15	2.0
Exhaust gas sensor	33	4.5
Catalytic converter attaching bolts	28	3.8

	1979	1980			1981			1982	
	All	California	US Federal	Canada	All US	Canada	Turbo	All standard	Turbo
AAC valve							X		X
Air flowmeter	X	X	X	X	X	X	X	X	X
Air regulator	X	X	X	X	X	X	X	X	X
Air temperature sensor	X		X		X	X	X	X	X
Cold start valve	X	X	X	X	X	X		X	
Control unit	X	X	X	X	X	X	X	X	X
Crank angle sensor							X		X
Cylinder head temperature sensor		X	X		X		X	X	X
Dashpot	X								
Detonation sensor							X		X
Dropping resistor	X	X	X	X	X	X	X		
EGR valve							X		X
Exhaust gas sensor		X			X		X	X	X
Fuel damper	X	X	X	X	X	X	X	X	X
Injectors	X	X	X	X	X	X	X	X	X
Power transistor							X		X
Pressure regulator	X	X	X	X	X	X	X	X	X
Thermotime switch	X	X	X	X	X	X		X	
Throttle chamber	X	X	X	X	X	X	X	X	X
Throttle valve switch	X	X	X	X	X	X	X	X	X
Turbocharger							X		X
Vacuum control modulator							X		X
Water temperature sensor	X			X		X			

Fig. 4.1 Application chart for EFI and ECCS system components

103

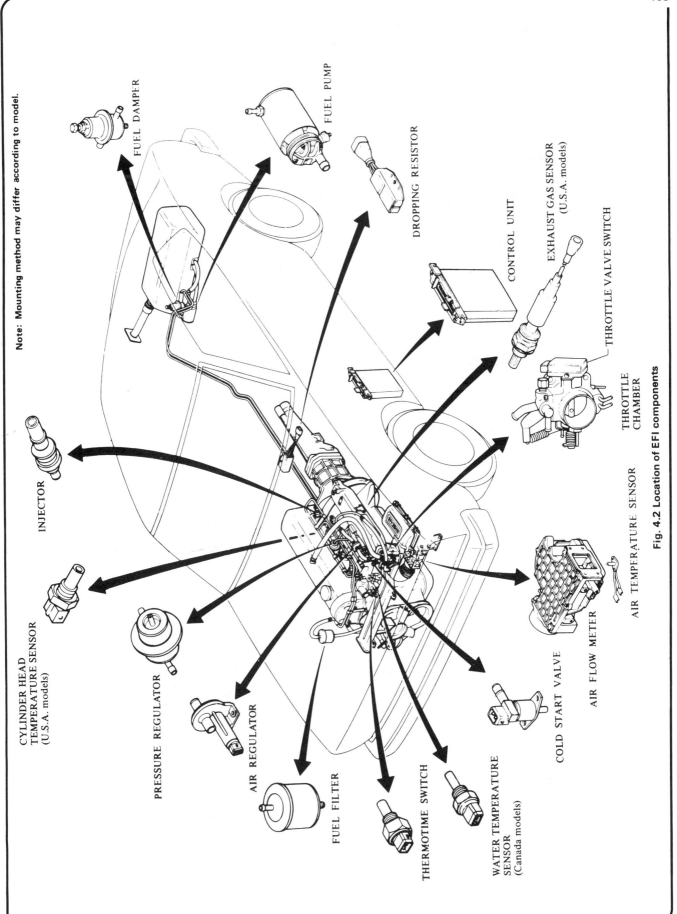

Fig. 4.2 Location of EFI components

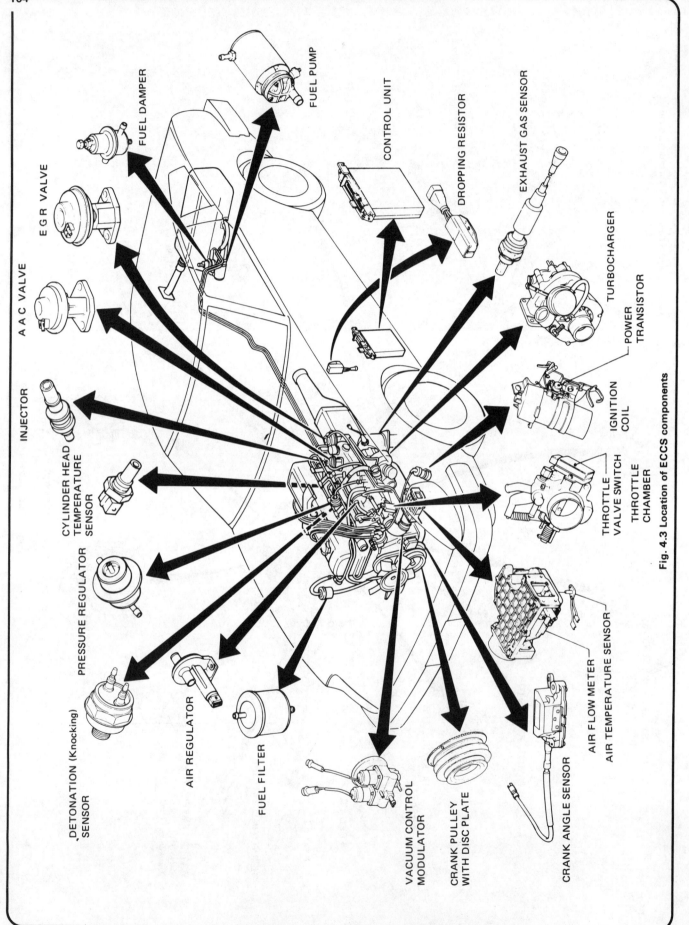

FUEL PUMP

FUEL DAMPER

CONTROL UNIT

DROPPING RESISTOR

E G R VALVE

EXHAUST GAS SENSOR

A A C VALVE

TURBOCHARGER

POWER TRANSISTOR

INJECTOR

IGNITION COIL

CYLINDER HEAD TEMPERATURE SENSOR

THROTTLE VALVE SWITCH

THROTTLE CHAMBER

PRESSURE REGULATOR

AIR FLOW METER

AIR TEMPERATURE SENSOR

DETONATION (Knocking) SENSOR

AIR REGULATOR

FUEL FILTER

VACUUM CONTROL MODULATOR

CRANK PULLEY WITH DISC PLATE

CRANK ANGLE SENSOR

Fig. 4.3 Location of ECCS components

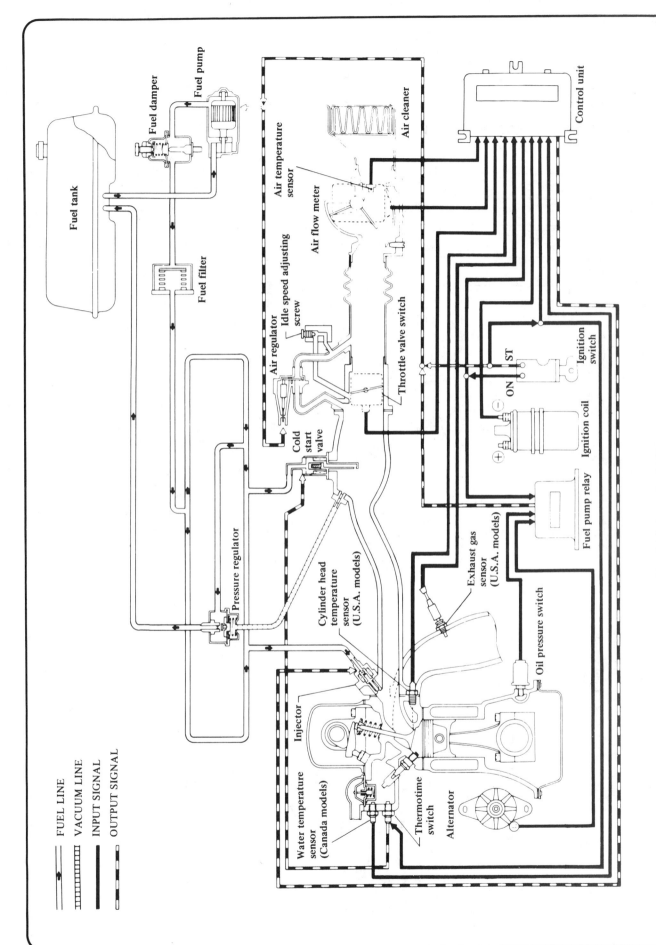

Fuel pump

Fuel damper

Fuel tank

Fuel filter

Air temperature sensor

Air flow meter

Air cleaner

Control unit

Idle speed adjusting screw

Air regulator

Throttle valve switch

ST

ON

Ignition switch

Ignition coil

Cold start valve

Fuel pump relay

Pressure regulator

Cylinder head temperature sensor (U.S.A. models)

Exhaust gas sensor (U.S.A. models)

Oil pressure switch

Injector

Water temperature sensor (Canada models)

Thermotime switch

Alternator

FUEL LINE
VACUUM LINE
INPUT SIGNAL
OUTPUT SIGNAL

Fig. 4.4 Schematic of EFI system

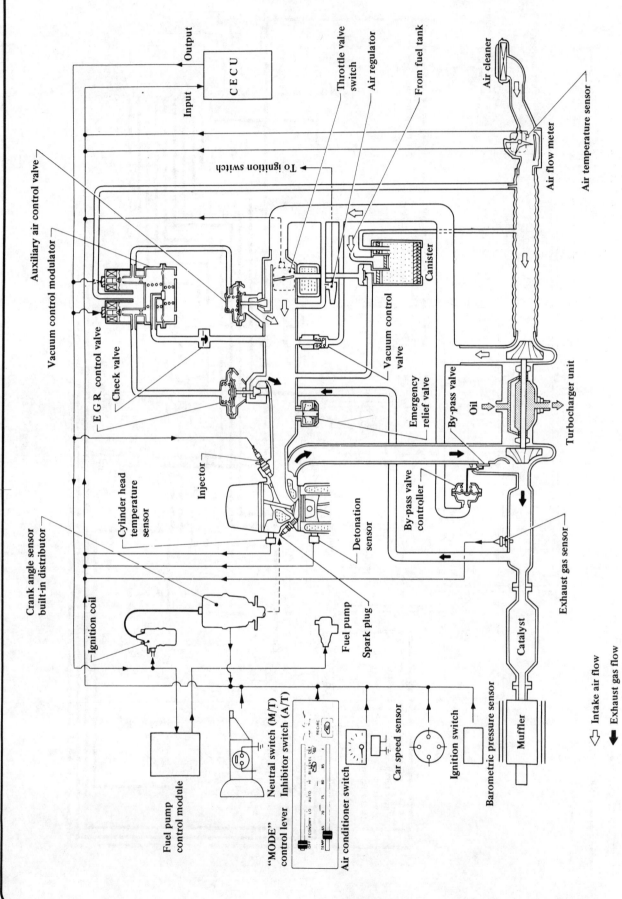

Fig. 4.5 Schematic of ECCS system

1 EFI (Electronic Fuel Injection) system – general information

The L28E engine uses an Electronic Fuel Injection (EFI) fuel system in place of the conventional carburetor-type system. Electronic fuel injection provides optimum mixture ratios at all stages of combustion, and this, together with the immediate response characteristics of the fuel injection, permits the engine to run on the weakest possible fuel/air mixture; this vastly reduces the exhaust gas toxic emission. The fuel system, is interrelated with and works in conjunction with the emissions control and exhaust systems covered in Chapter 6. Thus, some elements that relate directly to the fuel system are covered in that Chapter.

The EFI system consists of three sub-systems: The fuel flow system, the air flow system and the electrical signaling system. The various components that make up the entire EFI system are detailed in Section 2.

Fuel from the tank is delivered under pressure from the fuel pump and, to avoid pulsation, is fed through a mechanical damper. After passing through a fuel filter and a pressure regulator, it is then injected into the intake manifold. The pressure regulator is designed to maintain a constant pressure difference between the fuel line pressure and the intake manifold vacuum. Where manifold conditions are such that the fuel pressure could be beyond that specified, the pressure regulator returns surplus fuel to the tank.

An injection of fuel occurs once every rotation of the engine. Because the injection signal comes from the control unit, all six injectors operate simultaneously and independent of the engine stroke. Each injection supplies half the amount of fuel required by the cylinder, and the length of the injection period is determined by information fed to the control unit by the various sensors included in the system.

Elements affecting the injection duration include: Engine rpm, quantity and temperature of the intake air, throttle valve opening, temperature of the engine coolant, position of the ignition switch, intake manifold vacuum pressure and amount of oxygen in the exhaust gases.

Because the EFI system operates under a high fuel pressure, any slight leak can affect the system's efficiency and present a serious fire risk. Also since the intake air flow is critical to the operation of the system, even a slight air leak will cause wrong air/fuel mixtures to occur.

The electric fuel pump used in the EFI system uses three relays, located in the engine compartment relay bracket. This set-up is designed so that should the engine accidentally stop, (causing the alternator to turn off and the oil pressure to drop), the fuel pump will not operate.

Information on adjusting the idle mixture ratio is in Chapter 1.

Note: *Certain precautions should be observed when working on the EFI system, because of its critical and sensitive components.*

a) Do not disconnect either battery cable while the engine is running

b) Prior to any operation in which a fuel line will be disconnected, the high pressure in the system must first be eliminated. This procedure is described in Chapter 1. Disconnect the negative battery cable to eliminate the possibility of sparks occuring while open fuel is present.

c) Prior to removing any EFI component, be sure the ignition switch is Off and the negative battery cable is disconnected.

d) The EFI wiring harness should be kept at least four inches (10 mm) away from adjacent harnesses. This includes a CB antenna feeder cable as well. This is to prevent electrical pulses in other systems from interfering with the EFI operation.

e) Be sure all EFI wiring connections are tight, clean and secure as a poor connection can cause extremely high voltage surges in the ignition coil which could drain the IC circuit.

f) The accelerator should NOT be depressed prior to starting the engine. Immediately after starting, do not rev the engine unnecessarily.

While some basic checks of the EFI components are included in this chapter, the complexity of the system prevents many problems from being accurately diagnosed by the home mechanic. If a problem develops in the system, but cannot be pinpointed by the checks listed here, it is best to take the car to a Datsun dealer to locate the fault.

2 EFI components – general description

Control unit

The control unit is mounted under the dash on the side wall of the driver's side of the vehicle. The essential role of this unit is to generate a pulse to the injectors. Upon receiving an electrical signal from each sensor, the control unit generates a pulse whose duration (injector open time period) is controlled to provide the exact amount of fuel, according to engine characteristics at that particular time. The control unit consists mainly of three integrated circuits formed on a printed circuit board.

Airflow meter

The airflow meter measures the volume and temperature of the intake air, and sends the signal to the control unit. This is achieved by a potentiometer which is linked to the air intake flap shaft. The more air that enters the flow meter, the further the flap valve rotates, which in turn rotates the potentiometer wiper through a variable resistance coil. This increasing or decreasing resistance (dependant upon the flap angle) sends the signal to the control unit. In order to dampen any excessive movement of the flap, due to vacuum depressions in the intake manifold, a helical spring and compensating plate in a damper chamber are provided. Also built into the airflow meter is an air temperature sensor which senses air temperature and sends a signal to the control unit. This signal will define the duration of the injection time. Air that flows into the meter is first passed through the air cleaner assembly.

Air regulator

The air regulator bypasses the throttle valve, to control the quantity of air required for increasing the engine idling speed when starting the engine at an underhood temperature of below 80°C (176°F). A bi-metal spring and heater are built into the regulator. When the ignition switch is turned to the Start position, or if the engine is running, electric current flows through the heater and the bi-metal spring and, as the heater warms up, the bi-metal spring will close the air passage. The air passage will remain closed until the engine is stopped, or the underhood temperature drops below 80°C (176°F).

Injectors

An injector is mounted on each branch portion of the intake manifold. Each injector is actuated by a small solenoid valve, built into the injector body. Actuating the solenoid valve pulls the needle valve into the open position to allow the fuel to inject. The duration of the pulse sent from the control unit, defines the period of time that the solenoid valve is actuated.

Throttle chamber

The throttle chamber is mounted to the front of the intake manifold, and is equipped with a valve. This valve controls the intake airflow in response to accelerator pedal movement. The shaft of this valve is connected to the throttle valve switch. The valve remains closed during engine idling, and the air required for idling passes through a bypass port, into the intake manifold. Idle adjustment is made by the idle speed adjusting screw (refer to Chapter 1). There is also another bypass line in the throttle chamber, to pass sufficient air through the air regulator into the intake manifold, when a cold engine is started.

Fuel pump

The fuel pump is mounted near the fuel tank at the right-hand rear end of the vehicle. Built into the outlet pipe of the pump is a check valve, and at the inlet pipe, a relief valve. The relief valve is designed to open when pressure in the fuel line rises to an excessive level due to any blocking in the line. The check valve prevents any abrupt drop in pressure when the engine is stopped.

Throttle valve switch

The throttle valve switch is attached to the throttle chamber and actuates in response to accelerator pedal movement. This switch has two sets of contact points. One set monitors the idle position, and the other set monitors the full throttle position. The idle contacts close when the throttle valve is positioned at idle, and open when it is at any other position. The full throttle contacts close only when the throttle is positioned at full throttle (or more than 35° opening of the throttle valve). The contacts are open while the throttle valve is at any other position. The idle switch compensates for enrichment during idle and, after idle, sends a signal to the control unit to modify the fuel supply. The full throttle switch compensates for enrichment at the full throttle position.

Fuel filter
The fuel filter, which is mounted on the right-hand side of the engine compartment, ensures that only clean fuel reaches the injectors. A clogged fuel filter will stop the flow of fuel and cause the engine to stop. This is usually preceded by hesitation and sluggish operation.

Fuel damper
The fuel damper, which is mounted to the fuel pump at the rear of the vehicle, is designed to suppress any pulsation in fuel flow from the fuel pump.

Pressure regulator
The pressure regulator, which is mounted to the intake manifold in the fuel supply line, maintains a constant fuel pressure at all stages of acceleration and deceleration. Under extreme manifold vacuum conditions, the full pressure delivered by the fuel pump, combined with a high vacuum, could cause excessive pressure in the fuel line. Where such a condition occurs, the pressure regulator opens to return excess fuel to the fuel tank.

Water temperature sensor
This device, which is housed in the thermostat housing, monitors any changes in the engine coolant temperature. As soon as any temperature change is sensed, a signal is sent to the control unit, where a modified injector pulse duration will be computed.

Auxiliary cooling fan
The auxiliary cooling fan, mounted to the right side of the cylinder head and rocker arm cover, is designed to cool the temperature of the fuel lines atop the intake manifold after the car has been turned off. The fan begins operating when the ignition switch is turned off, and stays on for 17 minutes before automatically shutting off.

Dropping resistor
The dropping resistor, which is mounted on the left side of the engine compartment, in back of the windshield washer tank protects the injectors from alternator surges and effects of other electrical components by lowering the source voltage.

Dash pot
The dash pot is attached to the throttle chamber and prevents the throttle valve from closing abruptly, which would stall the engine.

Cold start valve
This valve is designed to improve the fuel-air mixture during cold engine operation by injecting fuel into the intake manifold, independently of the injectors. It receives its electrical signal from the thermotime switch.

Thermotime switch
The thermotime switch, mounted in the thermostat housing, uses a bi-metal contact to sense the engine coolant temperature for proper operation of the cold start valve.

Cylinder head temperature sensor
This sensor is used in place of the water temperature sensor in prior models and measures the temperature of the engine coolant. It is located on the left side of the cylinder head.

Exhaust gas sensor
The exhaust gas sensor, which works in conjunction with the EFI system and the catalytic converter, measures the amount of oxygen present in the exhaust gases. This information is fed to the control unit which adjusts the air/fuel mixture to compensate.

3   Fuel system – inspection

For inspection of the fuel system (not including the Electronic Fuel Injection), refer to Chapter 1.

4   Fuel filter – removal and installation

Because replacement of the fuel filter is part of the routine maintenance schedule, refer to Chapter 1 for this procedure.

5   Fuel line – repair and replacement

Caution: *Do not disconnect any fuel lines without first eliminating the pressure from the system, as described in Chapter 1.*
1   The fuel injection system is designed to operate at a pressure much higher than conventional fuel systems, and any slight leakage at a fuel joint can, if left, soon become a major problem. Leaving a leaking joint is a serious fire risk and the pressure loss is certain to affect the system's efficiency. From time-to-time, check the security of all the fuel joints; check also that the rigid pipes are not kinked or bent in any way. If a rubber hose shows signs of deterioration, replace it.
2   Since the electronic fuel injection system accurately meters the intake airflow through the airflow meter, even a slight air leak will cause an improper air/fuel ratio, resulting in faulty engine performance. For this reason a thorough inspection for leaks should be made at the oil filter cap, dipstick seal, blow-by hoses, airflow meter-to-throttle chamber air duct etc.
3   If a section of metal fuel line needs to be replaced only brazed seamless steel should be used, as copper or aluminum tubing does not have enough durability to withstand normal operating vibrations.
4   If only one section of a metal fuel line is damaged, it can be cut out and replaced with a piece of rubber tubing. The rubber tubing should be cut 4 inches (100 mm) longer than the section it's replacing, so that there is about 2 inches of overlap between the rubber and metal tubing at either end of the section. Hose clamps should be used to secure both ends of the repaired section.
5   If a section of metal line longer than 6 inches is being removed, use a combination of metal tubing and rubber hose so that the hose lengths will not be longer than 10 inches.
6   Never use rubber hose within 4 inches of any part of the exhaust system.

6   EFI components – testing

Note: *Most problems in the EFI system are caused by dirty or improperly connected electrical connectors. Therefore, a check should be made initially of all connections to make sure they are tight and clean. Prior to making any disconnections, always turn the ignition switch to the Off position.*

Fuel pump, damper and pressure regulator
1   The only tests that can be carried out on the fuel pump, are a basic-function test and a fuel pressure check. The discharge pressure check will involve the use of a pressure gauge capable of measuring up to 40 psi accurately, and a suitable T-piece.

Basic-function check
2   To carry out the basic-function test, first disconnect the starter motor S terminal lead.
3   Turn the ignition switch to the Start position, where an operating sound from the rear of the vehicle should be clearly audible. If no operating sound is audible, check that the electrical wiring to the fuel pump is in order. This could involve the use of special circuit testing equipment, and should be entrusted to your Datsun dealer.
4   If the fuel pump appears satisfactory in paragraph 2 proceed to check the fuel discharge pressure, as described in the following paragraphs.

Fuel pressure check
5   Release the pressure in the fuel line, as described in Chapter 1.
6   Connect the pressure gauge into the fuel hose immediately after the fuel filter, as shown in the accompanying figure. It will be helpful in the following checks if the gauge is facing toward the driver's seat.
7   Start the engine and allow it to idle. At idle, the pressure should be 30 psi (2.1 kg/cm²).
8   Next, fully depress the accelerator pedal and note the reading on the gauge at the moment the pedal is depressed. It should be 37 psi (2.6 kg/cm²).

9 If the pressure is not as specified, first check for clogged or deformed fuel lines. If the lines are alright, the pressure regulator should be tested using the following procedure:

  a) Disconnect the vacuum hose from the pressure regulator and connect a metered vacuum pump to the regulator.

  b) Fold back the carpet in the rear compartment of the car and remove the foam padding. Now disconnect the fuel pump electrical connector.

  c) Using jumper wires, connect the terminals of the fuel pump connector directly to the terminals of the battery, using Fig. 4.7 as a guide.

  d) Apply vacuum to the pressure regulator in the following increments and note the fuel pressure reading on the fuel pressure gauge at each. They should read as follows:

Vacuum	Fuel pressure
0 in Hg	36 to 37 psi
5 in Hg	33 to 35 psi
10 in Hg	31 to 32 psi
15 in Hg	29 to 30 psi
20 in Hg	26 to 28 psi

10 If the fuel pressure does not decrease as shown as vacuum increases, the pressure regulator must be replaced.

11 If the pressure regulator is functioning properly, yet the results in the original checks are not as indicated, replace the fuel pump.

Control unit

12 This check employs a miniature test lamp, to check whether the open-injector pulse for cranking the engine is actually applied to the injectors, should the engine fail to start. To carry out this check, the engine must be cranked at a speed of more than 80 rpm; also the battery must be known to be in good state of charge. The test lamp should be 12V-3W miniature type, with a suitable connection to its end.

13 Turn the igniiton switch to the Off position.

14 Disconnect the electrical connector from the cold start valve.

15 Disconnect the harness connector of number one cylinder injector.

16 Now connect the test lamp to the injector harness of the number 1 cylinder.

17 Turn the ignition switch to the Start position to crank the engine, and observe whether or not the lamp flashes. If the lamp flashes, all is well; if it does not, the control unit is faulty and must be replaced.

18 It is emphasized that this check only proves whether or not a signal pulse is reaching the injectors. If the control unit is still under suspicion, there are numerous other circuits inside the unit that could be at fault, and it is best to have it checked professionally.

Injectors

19 If more than one injector is suspect, the control unit should be checked, as previously described.

20 To trace a single faulty injector with the engine running, use a screwdriver as a stethoscope. Attach the blade of a screwdriver to the injector and hold the handle against the ear. It should be possible to hear an operational click every time the injector operates. Compare the noise of the suspect injector with the other five injectors, if the noise of the operational click is noticeably less than at the other injectors, that particular injector is faulty and should be replaced.

21 If, for any reason, the engine will not run, disconnect the electrical connector from the cold start valve and, with the assistance of a second person operating the ignition switch to crank the engine, use the screwdriver method described in paragraph 22, to trace the faulty injector or injectors.

22 Once you have traced a possibly faulty injector, this can be proved by carrying out a continuity check. To do this, first disconnect the battery ground cable.

23 Disconnect the electrical connector from the suspect injector.

24 With the probes of an ohmmeter connected to the terminals on the injector, ensure that continuity exists. If there is no continuity, the solenoid coil windings could be open-circuit, or the terminal leads supplying the coil with current may be broken inside the injector. In such cases the only remedy is to replace the faulty injector.

Air flow meter and air temperature sensor

Note: The following checks can be carried out without removing the airflow meter assembly from the vehicle.

25 Remove the air cleaner cover and element, as described in Chapter 1.

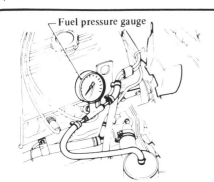

Fig. 4.6 When testing the fuel pressure, the gauge should be installed after the fuel filter as shown (Sec 6)

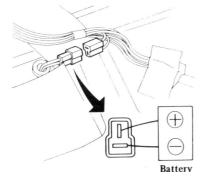

Fig. 4.7 Identification of terminals in the fuel pump wiring connector (Sec 6)

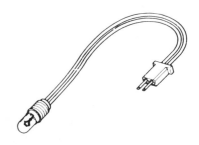

Fig. 4.8 A small 12V-3W test lamp with the proper connector is needed to test the control unit pulses going to the injectors (Sec 6)

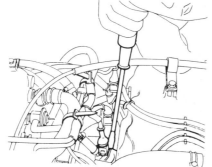

Fig. 4.9 When checking the injectors' operation, a screwdriver can be used as a stethoscope by holding it between the injector and your ear (Sec 6)

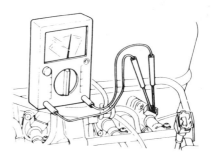

Fig. 4.10 An ohmmeter is used to check the continuity of the injectors (Sec 6)

Checking the potentiometer

26 Disconnect the battery ground cable.
27 Disconnect the harness connector from the airflow meter.
28 Now, using an ohmmeter, check the resistance between the terminals 33 and 34. The resistance should be between 100 and 400 ohms.
29 Measure the resistance between terminals 34 and 35, which should be between 200 and 500 ohms.
30 Connect the ohmmeter between terminals 32 and 34.
31 Gradually open the air intake flap by hand. If the reading is at any value other than 0 or infinite ohms, it is normal. The airflow meter should be replaced as an assembly, if any of the previously described checks are not as specified.

Checking insulation resistance of the airflow meter

32 To check the insulation resistance between the airflow meter body and the potentiometer terminals, simply hold one of the ohmmeter probes in contact with the airflow meter casing and, with the other probe, touch each of the terminals (terminals 32, 33, 34 and 35). If any continuity exists, the airflow meter is faulty, and should be replaced as an assembly.

Checking the air temperature sensor

33 Connect the ohmmeter probes to terminals 25 and 34.
34 Using a normal household thermometer, measure the air temperature as near to the sensor as possible.
35 The following table gives the resistance valve over a given temperature range. The air temperature sensor is part of the airflow meter assembly and, where the resistance readings are outside the limits listed in the chart, the airflow meter must be replaced as an assembly.

36 Finally, check the insulation resistance between terminal 25 and the airflow meter body. If continuity exists, the air temperature sensor is faulty; replace the air flow meter as an assembly.

Throttle valve switch

37 Disconnect the battery ground cable.
38 Remove the throttle valve switch connector.

Idle switch check

39 Using an ohmmeter with probes connected to terminals 29 and 30 ensure that continuity exists when the throttle valve is in the idle position. Now open the throttle valve approximately 4°, where there should be no continuity. If this is not as specified, the throttle valve switch must be replaced as an assembly.

Full throttle switch check

40 Connect the ohmmeter probes to terminals 24 and 30.
41 Gradually open the throttle valve from the fully closed position. Observe the ohmmeter reading when the valve is opened to full throttle (beyond 35°). Continuity should exist only at the full throttle position. If the throttle valve switch does not conform to the previously mentioned readings, it will have to be replaced with a new one.

Throttle valve switch insulation check

42 Connect one of the ohmmeter probes to a convenient point on the vehicle frame (ground).
43 With the other ohmmeter probe, touch terminals 24, 29 and 30 in turn, and observe that the ohmmeter reading is infinite at each terminal. If it is not, there's obviously a short-circuit somewhere, that can only be rectified by renewing the throttle valve switch as described in Section 14.

Dropping resistor

44 Disconnect the battery ground cable.
45 Disconnect the connector from the dropping resistor.
46 Carry out the following resistance checks:

Air temperature	Resistance
14°F (-10°C)	7.00 to 11.40 K ohms
68°F (20°C)	2.10 to 2.90 K ohms
122°F (50°C)	.68 to 1.00 K ohms

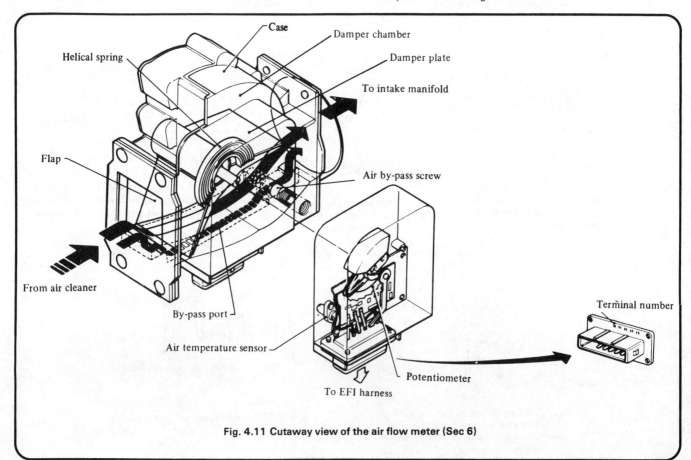

Fig. 4.11 Cutaway view of the air flow meter (Sec 6)

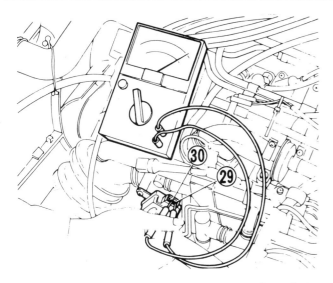

Fig. 4.12 Checking the throttle valve switch (Sec 6)

a) *Between terminal 43 and terminal 56 (number 6 cylinder resistor)*
b) *Between terminal 43 and terminal 55 (number 5 cylinder resistor)*
c) *Between terminal 43 and terminal 41 (number 4 cylinder resistor)*
d) *Between terminal 43 and terminal 40 (number 3 cylinder resistor)*
e) *Between terminal 43 and terminal 38 (number 2 cylinder resistor)*
f) *Between terminal 43 and terminal 37 (number 1 cylinder resistor)*

47 The resistance reading for all of the above mentioned checks should be approximately 6 ohms. If one particular terminal appears to differ from the others, the whole resistor should be renewed.

Water temperature sensor and cylinder head temperature sensor

Note: *The water temperature or cylinder head temperature sensor is designed to give a specific resistance reading over a given temperature range. It can be checked after removal from the engine compartment using containers of hot and cold water, but the procedure described is for one which is installed.*
48 Disconnect the battery ground cable.
49 Disconnect the sensor harness connector.
50 By placing a thermometer into the radiator filler neck, establish the temperature of the coolant, with the engine cold.
51 Connect the probes of the ohmmeter to the terminals of the sensor. Record the resistance reading obtained, and compare it with the following chart of resistance values:

Engine coolant	Resistance
−30°C (−22°F)	18.0 to 33.0 K ohms
−10°C (+14°F)	7.0 to 11.4 K ohms
20°C (68°F)	2.1 to 2.9 K ohms
50°C (122°F)	0.68 to 1.00 K ohms
80°C (176°F)	0.4 to 0.25 K ohms

52 Now reconnect the sensor harness connector and the battery ground cable. Run the engine until the normal operating temperature is reached, then repeat the operations described in the preceding paragraphs. By first carrying out a cold check, then a hot check will give a good indication of the condition of the sensor over its operating range. If the resistance readings do not come within the range specified, renew the sensor.

Air regulator
53 As an initial check, with the engine just started and running at a very cold operating temperature, grasp the hose between the air regulator and the throttle chamber, and by squeezing it with your

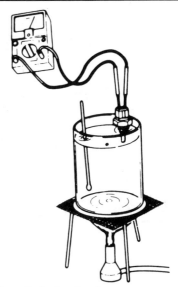

Fig. 4.13 The cylinder head and water temperature sensors are most accurately tested when removed from the car as shown (Sec 6)

fingers, cut off the airflow through the hose. The engine idle should become very erratic and be noticeably reduced in idle speed.
54 As a further speed check, allow the engine to run until the normal temperature has been reached, and the underhood temperature is above 80°C (176°F). Repeat the check described in the preceding paragraph, and, because the by-pass air passage should now be closed, the engine idle speed should remain constant.
55 If the air regulator still proves to be suspect after carrying out these checks, it is possible to visually check to observe whether the air regulator valve is working.
56 With the engine stationary and at a cold temperature, disconnect the hoses from each end of the air regulator.
57 By looking through the air regulator it is possible to see the by-pass port open. If all is well, reconnect the hoses and run the engine until normal operating temperature is reached.
58 Now disconnect the hoses again as described in paragraph 58. This time the by-pass port should be completely closed.
59 If the checks previously mentioned prove unsatisfactory, disconnect the electrical connector at the air regulator and, using an ohmmeter, check that there is continuity in the air regulator. If there is no continuity, or the air regulator is proved to be inoperative in the preceding checks, a replacement unit will have to be installed.

Cold start valve
60 At the starter motor, disconnect the S terminal lead.
61 To ensure that the fuel pump is functioning, turn the ignition switch to the *Start* position, where an operating sound should be heard from the rear end of the vehicle.
62 Disconnect the battery ground cable.
63 Unscrew and remove the two screws securing the cold start valve to the intake manifold. Remove the valve from the manifold.
64 Disconnect the electrical connector from the cold start valve.
65 Put the cold start valve into a glass container. Plug the container opening around the fuel line with a clean rag. This will help to keep the fuel in the container and minimize fire risk.
66 Disconnect either the wiring connector to the oil pressure switch, or the lead to the 'L' terminal of the alternator. Then reconnect the battery.
67 Turn the ignition switch to the *Start* position. The cold start valve should not inject fuel.
68 Turn the ignition switch to the *Off* position. Using jumper leads connected to the battery negative and positive terminals, touch the cold start valve terminals. The valve should now inject fuel into the glass container. If there is no evidence of any fuel being injected, renew the cold start valve.

Thermotime switch
Static check
69 Disconnect the battery ground cable.
70 Disconnect the electrical connector from the thermotime switch.

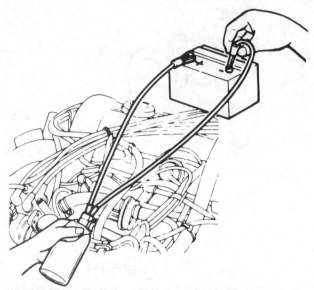

Fig. 4.14 The cold start valve is tested by connecting its terminals with the battery terminals (Sec 6)

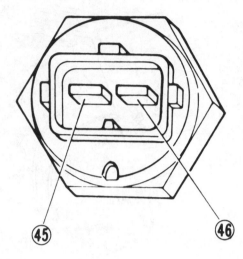

Fig. 4.15 Identification of terminals in the thermotime switch (Sec 6)

71 Using an ohmmeter, measure the resistance between terminal 46, and the switch body. The readings should be as follows:

Coolant temperature less than 14°C (57°F) ....Zero
Coolant temperature between 14 to 25°C
(57 to 77°F) ....Zero or
                                                                                                infinity
Coolant temperature more than 25°C (77°F) ....Infinity

72 Now, measure the resistance between terminal 45, and the switch, which must be between 40 to 70 ohms. If the thermotime switch does not conform to any of the previously mentioned readings, it must be renewed.

Dynamic check
73 The following dynamic check will require removal of the thermotime switch. To do this, proceed as described in the following paragraphs.
74 Disconnect the battery ground cable.
75 Drain approximately 1⅝ US quarts (1.5 liters) of coolant from the radiator. Refer to Chapter 2, if necessary.
76 For ease of access, remove the radiator top hose.
77 Disconnect the electrical connector from the thermotime switch.
78 Unscrew and remove the thermotime switch from the thermostat housing.
79 The dynamic check will involve the use of a container of water, which can be heated up very quickly.
80 Dip the heat-sensing portion of the thermotime switch into the container of water, which should be maintained at 10°C (50°F). Allow a couple of minutes to pass, in order to ensure that the thermotime switch stabilizes.
81 Measure the resistance between terminals 45 and 46. The reading should be approximately 40-70 ohms.
82 Now heat the water until the temperature is more than 30°C (86°F). Now check the continuity between terminals 45 and 46. If the reading increases to infinity, the thermotime switch is operating correctly. If the previously mentioned readings are not achieved, renew the thermotime switch.
83 To install the thermotime switch, reverse the order of removal described in paragraph 74 through 78. When topping-up the radiator coolant, always make sure that the correct antifreeze quantity is used.

7 Fuel pump – removal and installation

1 In order to prevent the fuel from being sprayed about when the fuel line is disconnected from the fuel pump, the pressure in the lines must be eliminated by using the procedure described in Chapter 1.
2 Disconnect the negative battery cable.

3 Roll back the carpet in the rear compartment of the car, and remove the foam padding. Then disconnect the fuel pump wiring connector (photo).
4 Raise the rear of the car and support it on jackstands.
5 Clamp the fuel hose that runs between the fuel tank and the fuel pump to prevent spillage when the hose is disconnected.
6 Disconnect the inlet and outlet lines from the fuel pump. Be prepared for some fuel spillage.
7 Remove the bolts that secure the fuel pump bracket to the underside of the body and lift off the bracket complete with fuel pump.
8 To remove the fuel pump from the bracket, remove the two screws that hold the pump to the bracket.
9 Installation is the reverse of the removal procedure with the following notes:

a) When reconkecting the high pressure outlet fuel line be sure to use a new hose clamp.
b) The clamp on the outlet fuel line should be approximately three mm from the end of the hose.
c) When installing the fuel lines on the fuel pump, all fuel lines after the fuel pump are considered high pressure lines. When installing these, be sure that the end of the rubber hose is butted up against the units to which they are attached.

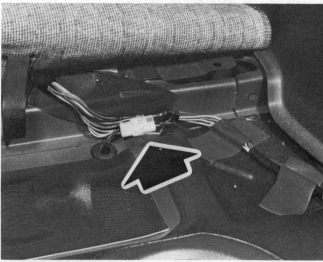

7.3 The fuel pump wiring connector (arrow) is located under the foam padding in the rear compartment

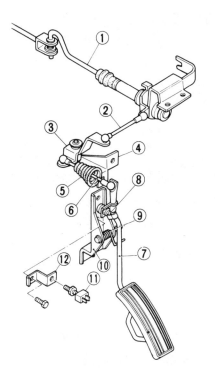

A S C D Equipped Model

1   Torsion shaft
2   Balljoint rod B
3   Bellcrank
4   Bellcrank
5   Rubber boots
6   Balljoint rod A
7   Accelerator pedal
8   Pedal stopper
9   Return spring
10 Accelerator pedal
    bracket
11 Kickdown switch
    (A/T only)
12 Kickdown switch bracket
    (A/T only)
13 ASCD cable

Fig. 4.16 Components of the accelerator linkage (Sec 9)

8   Air cleaner – removal and installation

1   Disconnect the inlet air duct leading to the air flow meter from the air cleaner.
2   Remove the air cleaner mounting screws and lift out the air cleaner.
3   Installation is the reverse of the removal procedure.

9   Accelerator linkage – removal and installation

1   Separate the balljoint rod from the pedal arm.
2   Remove the screws that retain the pedal and bracket to the floor pan and lift them out. The accelerator pedal return spring can be replaced if rusted, fatigued or damaged.
3   If equipped, disconnect the ASCD cable from the torsion shaft.
4   Separate the torsion shaft from the throttle shaft.
5   Remove the balljoint rod that connects the bellcrank with the torsion shaft.
6   Remove the screws that retain the torsion shaft and lift it out.
7   Remove the screws that retain the bellcrank bracket to the body and lift out the bracket and bellcrank.
8   Installation is the reverse of the removal procedure. **Note:** *During installation, apply a light coat of multi-purpose grease to all sliding or friction surfaces. Do NOT apply grease to the wire.*
9   Once installed, the top of the accelerator pedal should be about $5\frac{1}{2}$ in (140 mm) above the floor. If necessary, adjust the pedal height by loosening the stopper bolt locknut and turning the stopper bolt until the correct height is obtained. Retighten the locknut.

10 Fuel damper – removal and installation

1   Eliminate the pressure from the fuel system by following the procedure described in Chapter 1.
2   Raise the rear of the car and support it on jackstands.
3   Temporarily clamp the hose between the fuel tank and the fuel pump.
4   Disconnect the hoses on both sides of the fuel damper. Have a container on hand to catch the leakage.
5   Remove the nut that attaches the fuel damper to its bracket.
6   Installation is the reverse of the removal procedure. **Note:** *When*

reconnecting the fuel hoses to the damper, be sure the end of the hose is butted up against the damper and use a new hose clamp.*

11 Control unit – removal and installation

1   The control unit is mounted on the left side wall underneath the dash.
2   Turn the ignition switch to the Off position and then disconnect the negative battery cable.
3   Remove the left finisher panel that covers the lower portion of the unit. Remove the left side panel.
4   Pull the lock lever on the large 35-pin wiring harness connector back and remove the connector from the control unit.
5   Remove the bolts which secure the control unit to the side panel and lift the unit out. Installation is the reverse of the removal procedure. **Note:** *When installing the 35-pin connector into the control unit be careful not to bend or break any of the terminals.*

12 Air flow meter and air temperature sensor – removal and installation

Note: *The air temperature sensor is built into the air flow meter and is not designed to be removed. If the air temperature sensor is defective and needs replacement the entire air flow meter must be replaced as a unit.*
1   Disconnect the negative battery cable.
2   Remove the rubber boots leading from the air flow meter (photo).
3   Remove the bolts that retain the air flow meter bracket to the body.
4   Disconnect the wiring harness connector from the air flow meter.
5   Installation is the reverse of the removal procedure.

13 Dropping resistor – removal and installation

1   Disconnect the negative battery cable.
2   Disconnect the wiring harness connector from the dropping resistor (photo).
3   Remove the screws that attach the resistor to the body and lift off the resistor.
4   Installation is the reverse of the removal procedure.

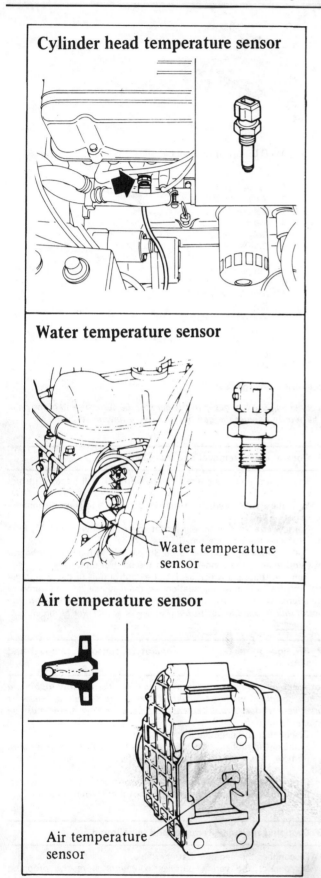

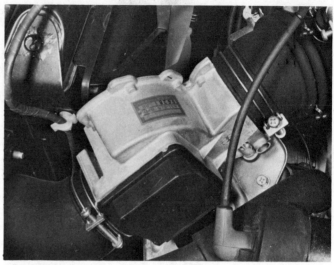

12.2 The air flow meter is located in the front left of the engine compartment

13.2 The dropping resistor is located on the left side of the engine compartment

14 Throttle valve switch – removal, installation and adjustment

1   Disconnect the negative battery cable.
2   Remove the screws that retain the throttle valve switch to the throttle chamber and pull the switch off.
3   Using a small screwdriver or other tool spread the wire clip around the wiring harness connector and disconnect it from the throttle valve switch.
4   Installation is the reverse of the removal procedure. **Note:** *After installation the throttle valve switch must be adjusted as described below.*
5   With the engine running:

   a)   Disconnect the wiring harness connector from the throttle valve switch.
   b)   Connect an ohmmeter between the number 29 and 30 terminals in the switch. The ohmmeter should show continuity.
   c)   Connect a tachometer according to the manufacturer's instructions.
   d)   With the transmission in Neutral, start the engine and check that the idle speed is correct (refer to Chapter 1, if necessary).

Fig. 4.17 Locations of the cylinder head sensor, water temperature sensor and air temperature sensor (Sec 12 and 18)

e) With the ohmmeter still connected to the throttle valve switch, have an assistant slowly depress the accelerator pedal. When the idle speed reaches about 900 rpm, the throttle valve switch should turn off, indicated by the ohmmeter showing no continuity.

f) If the switch does not turn off at the correct point, loosen the mounting screws and move the switch until it operates as described. Retighten the mounting screws.

6   With the engine not running:

g) Follow the instructions in paragraphs a and b above.

h) With the engine off, insert a feeler gauge (see chart below) between the throttle valve stopper screw and the throttle valve shaft lever (Fig. 4.18).

Model year	Gap measurement
1979	0.051 in (1.3 mm)
1980	0.020 in (0.5 mm)
1981 and 1982	0.012 in (0.3 mm)

i) With the throttle valve in this position, the throttle valve switch should turn off, indicated by the ohmmeter showing no continuity.

j) If the switch does not turn off at this point, loosen the mounting screws and move the switch until it operates as described. Retighten the mounting screws.

17 Throttle chamber – removal and installation

1   Disconnect the negative battery cable.

2   Remove the hoses and tubes from the throttle chamber. Be sure to mark them as to their location (photo).

3   Remove the screws that hold the throttle valve switch to the throttle chamber. Lift off the throttle valve switch and secure it out of the way.

4   On non-turbo models, remove the rubber air inlet boot from between the air flow meter and the throttle chamber.

5   On Turbo models, remove the metal air inlet pipe from between the throttle chamber and the turbocharger.

6   Disconnect the rod connector at the auxiliary throttle linkage shaft.

7   Remove the throttle chamber mounting bolts and lift off the chamber.

8   Installation is the reverse of the removal procedure.

17.2 Hose and throttle linkage connections at the throttle chamber

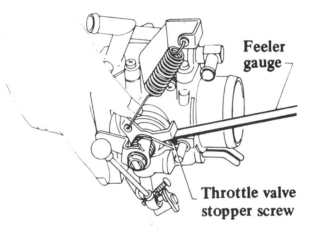

Fig. 4.18 A feeler gauge is used to adjust the throttle valve switch (be sure the engine is not running) (Sec 14)

15 Dash pot – adjustment

1   With the transmission in Neutral, set the engine speed to 2000 rpm.

2   Check that the dash pot rod end comes in contact with the throttle lever when the rod is fully extended, or when no back pressure is present at the diaphragm.

3   If necessary, turn the adjusting screw until contact is made as specified.

16 Pressure regulator – removal and installation

1   Eliminate the pressure in the fuel system by using the procedure described in Chapter 1.

2   Disconnect the vacuum hose from the pressure regulator.

3   Remove the pressure regulator mounting screws.

4   Lift the regulator up enough to place a rag underneath it. Disconnect the fuel hose from the regulator, noting its installed location.

5   Installation is the reverse of the removal procedure. Be sure the fuel hoses are installed securely in their original positions.

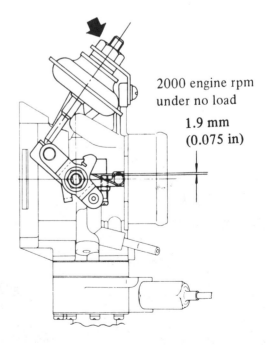

2000 engine rpm under no load

1.9 mm (0.075 in)

Fig. 4.19 A feeler gauge is used to adjust the dashpot by inserting it into the gap shown (Sec 16)

18 Cylinder head water temperature sensor – removal and installation

1   Disconnect the negative battery cable.
2   With the engine cool remove the radiator cap and drain about 1½ US qts of coolant from the radiator.
3   For clearance remove the upper radiator hose.
4   The cylinder head temperature sensor, if equipped, is located on the left side of the cylinder head. On models equipped with a water temperature sensor, this sensor is located in the thermostat housing.
5   Unscrew the sensor and remove it.
6   Prior to installing the sensor, wrap the threads with Teflon tape.
7   Installation is the reverse of the removal procedure. Be sure the copper washer is in place when installing the sensor.

19 Air regulator – removal and installation

1   Disconnect the negative battery cable.
2   Disconnect the hoses on either side of the air regulator.
3   Remove the two mounting screws.
4   Lift up on the air regulator enough to disconnect the wiring harness from it.
5   Installation is the reverse of the removal procedure.

20 Exhaust gas sensor – removal and installation

1   Disconnect the nagative battery cable.
2   The exhaust gas sensor is located in the exhaust manifold. Disconnect the wiring harness connector from the sensor.
3   Unscrew the sensor and remove it from the exhaust pipe.
4   Installation is the reverse of the removal procedure. **Note:** *Be sure the sensor is torqued to specifications and that there is no leakage of exhaust gas once installed.*

21 Cold start valve – removal and installation

1   Disconnect the battery ground cable.
2   Release the pressure in the fuel system as described in Chapter 1.
3   Undo and remove the two screws securing the cold start valve to the intake manifold. Remove the valve from the manifold
4   Unfasten the hose clip and disengage the cold start valve from the fuel hose.
5   When installing the cold start valve, reverse the procedures.

22 Injectors and fuel line assembly – removal and installation

1   In order to prevent the fuel from being sprayed about when the fuel lines are disconnected, the pressure in the lines must be eliminated by using the procedure described in Chapter 1.
2   Disconnect the negative battery cable.
3   Disconnect the electrical connectors from the injectors.
4   Disconnect the electrical connector from the cold start valve.

5   Remove the large rubber PCV vent hose that runs between the rocker arm cover and the throttle chamber (photo).
6   Disconnect the pressure regulator vacuum tube that runs to the intake manifold.
7   Remove the air regulator pipe.
8   Disconnect the rubber fuel hoses from the metal lines at the front left corner of the rocker arm cover (photo). Have a rag ready to absorb the fuel leakage.
9   Remove the bolts that hold the fuel line assembly to the intake manifold.
10 Remove the screws that secure each of the fuel injectors.
11 Lift the fuel line assembly out complete with injectors, pressure regulators and cold start valve, if equipped.
12 If the fuel injectors need to be removed from the fuel line assembly, simply loosen the clamp that retains the injector hose to the fuel line and pull the injector off (photo).
13 If the injector hoses are hardened, cracked or otherwise damaged, they should be replaced.
14 The pressure regulator and cold start valve can be removed from the fuel line assembly if necessary.
15 Also check that the lower rubber insulators on each injector are not scratched or worn.
16 Installation is the reverse of the removal procedure with the following notes:
   a)   When inserting the injectors into the intake manifold, be sure the various components shown in the accompanying figure are installed properly; the lower rubber insulator should be free of scratches or abrasion and should be installed so it is air tight.
   b)   The fuel hoses should be installed onto the line fittings so that they overlap the lines by at least 28 mm.

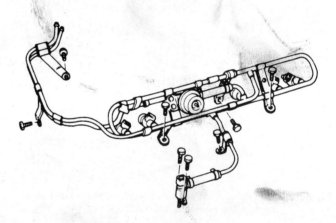

Fig. 4.20 Locations of the fuel line assembly mounting screws (Sec 22)

22.5 Proper mounting arrangements of EFI components on the intake manifold

22.8 The rubber fuel hoses connect with the metal fuel lines at the right front of the rocker cover

22.12 The injectors can be removed from the fuel line assembly after the clamp is loosened

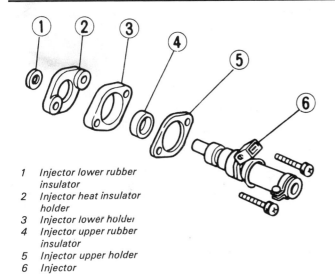

1 Injector lower rubber
  insulator
2 Injector heat insulator
  holder
3 Injector lower holder
4 Injector upper rubber
  insulator
5 Injector upper holder
6 Injector

Fig. 4.21 Components of an injector unit (Sec 22)

23 Auxiliary cooling fan – removal and installation

1 Disconnect the negative battery cable.
2 Disconnect the wiring connector leading to the fan motor.
3 Remove the bolts retaining the air duct and lift it off (photo).
4 Remove the cooling fan mounting bolts and lift it off.
5 Installation is the reverse of the removal procedure.

23.3 Location of the auxiliary cooling fan assembly

24 Auxiliary cooling fan timer unit – removal and installation

1 Disconnect the negative battery cable.
2 Remove the lower right dash panel, located under the glove box.
3 Remove the timer unit mounting screws. Then lift it off and disconnect the wiring connector.
4 Installation is the reverse of the removal procedure.

25 Electronic Concentrated Engine Control system (ECCS) – general information

The Turbo model 280ZX, equipped with the L28ET engine, uses the ECCS system to control many of the vital functions relating to engine operation. The ECCS system is very similar to the EFI system

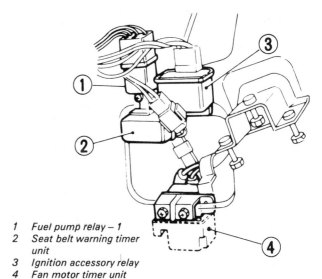

1 Fuel pump relay – 1
2 Seat belt warning timer
  unit
3 Ignition accessory relay
4 Fan motor timer unit

Fig. 4.22 Location of the auxiliary cooling fan timer unit (Sec 24)

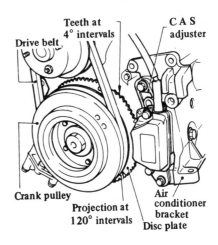

Fig. 4.23 The crank angle sensor on 1981 models is located at the crankshaft (Sec 24)

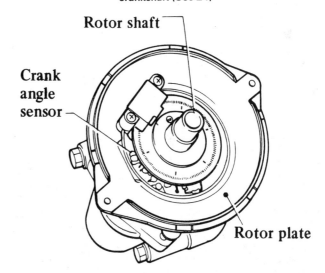

Fig. 4.24 The crank angle sensor on 1982 models is located in the distributor (Sec 24)

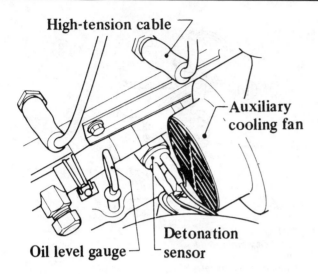

High-tension cable

Auxiliary
cooling fan

Oil level gauge

Detonation
sensor

Fig. 4.25 The detonation sensor is located on the right side of the cylinder block (Sec 24)

on non-turbo models (described in Section 1) but is more extensive in its control.

The microcomputer control unit used in the ECCS system controls the fuel injection, spark timing, idle speed, fuel pump operation, mixture ratio and exhaust gas recirculation. Therefore, on Turbo models adjustments to the idle speed, ignition timing and mixture ratio are not necessary on a regular basis.

The control unit is programmed to respond to a variety of variables within the engine operation including engine temperature, throttle valve opening, quantity and temperature of intake air, density of oxygen in the exhaust gases, engine rpm, battery voltage, altitude and the presence of detonation in the combustion chamber. Using this information, the control unit determines the optimum functioning of the various engine systems, including the EGR system, the Mixture Ratio Feedback system and the spark timing advance system all described in Chapter 6. During adverse driving conditions, such as cold engine operation, high speed driving or under a heavy load, the control unit automatically adjusts to provide good driveability. During normal driving conditions the emphasis is on low emissions levels.

Like the EFI system, the ECCS system is composed of three sub-systems, and shares many of the same components as the EFI system. Those components exclusive to the ECCS system are described in Section 26.

Because of the sophisticated and critical sensors used in the ECCS system, as well as the high fuel pressure maintained in the fuel injection system, most problems within the system arise from fuel and air leaks, and loose connections of vacuum hoses and electrical connectors. Other than regular checks of these problem areas, there is little the home mechanic can do in the way of troubleshooting and repairing the system. To accurately diagnose the ECCS system, a special analyzer is needed. For that reason, we recommend you take the car to a Datsun dealer or other mechanic suitably equipped. **Note:** *The cautionary notes at the end of Section 1 also apply to the ECCS system.*

26 ECCS components – general description

Turbocharger

The turbocharger, installed on the exhaust manifold, is designed to compress the intake air flowing from the air cleaner and thus force more air into the engine for combustion in order to increase power and torque. The turbocharger uses two turbines inside it. One turbine, integrated into the exhaust gas flow, is turned by the gases leaving the exhaust manifold. This one then turns the other turbine, which compresses the intake air and sends it into the intake manifold.

To prevent the supercharging pressure from becoming excessive, the system is equipped with an exhaust gas bypass valve which opens at a predetermined pressure to allow exhaust gases to bypass the turbocharger and go straight into the exhaust pipe. An emergency

relief valve is also incorporated into the intake manifold to relieve excessive pressure at that point.

Crank angle sensor

The crank angle sensor, mounted at the front of the crankshaft on 1981 models and in the distributor on 1982 models, is designed to detect engine rpm and pass the information along to the control unit. The sensor on 1981 models consists of a toothed sprocket mounted behind the crankshaft pulley and a 3-head pickup unit. Engine speed is measured by the teeth passing by the magnetic pickup unit. Three projections on the sprocket located 120° from each other, also indicate the position of each piston.

The sensor used on 1982 models uses a rotor plate attached to the distributor shaft and a pickup unit. This rotor has 360 slits in it at 1° intervals which transmit the rpm of the engine. In addition, six additional slits are used to transmit the piston positions. The pickup unit incorporates both a light emitting diode (LED) and a photo sensitive diode. When the slits in the rotor pass between these two diodes, they create an alternating voltage which is sent to the control unit for processing.

Exhaust Gas Recirculation (EGR) valve

The EGR valve, explained in detail in Chapter 6, is an integral part of the ECCS system on Turbo models. It is controlled directly by the control unit and receives its vacuum signal from the vacuum control modulator.

AAC valve

The AAC valve, which is attached to the intake manifold, is a vacuum-operated valve which controls the idle speed of the engine. It does this by controlling the amount of air that flows through the bypass port of the throttle chamber during idling conditions. The AAC valve is controlled by the control unit and receives its vacuum signal from the vacuum control modulator.

Vacuum control modulator

The vacuum control modulator directly controls the EGR and AAC valves by transforming the electric signal from the control unit into vacuum signals sent to the appropriate valve.

Barometric pressure sensor

This sensor is built into the control unit, and detects the altitude by sensing the density of the intake air.

Detonation sensor

The detonation sensor, located in the cylinder block just forward of the engine oil dipstick, is designed to detect any detonation (knocking) occuring in the combustion chambers.

Car speed sensor

This sensor is located in the speedometer and sends information about the speed of the car to the control unit.

Fuel pump control modulator

This modulator is mounted directly over the control unit and controls the voltage sent to the fuel pump. This is intended to reduce fuel pump noise and power consumption.

Power transistor

The power transistor is built into the ignition coil and is designed to amplify the signal from the control unit in order to create a spark at the spark plug.

27 Turbocharger – removal and installation

1   Raise the front of the car and support it on jackstands.
2   Remove the heat shield.
3   Remove the bolts that attach the air inlet pipe to the turbocharger.
4   Disconnect the air duct hose and suction air pipe from the turbocharger.
5   Disconnect the wiring connector leading to the exhaust gas sensor.
6   Disconnect the front exhaust pipe from the turbocharger.
7   Disconnect the oil delivery tube and oil drain pipe from the turbocharger (Fig. 4.27).

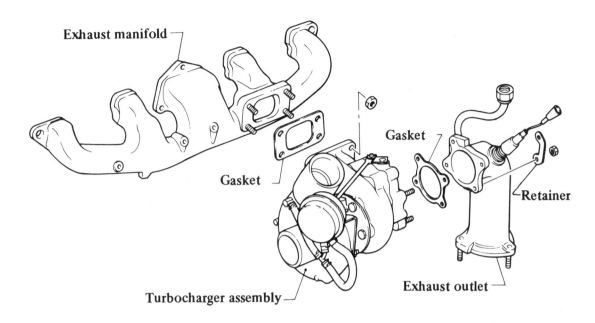

Fig. 4.26 Components of the turbocharger assembly (Sec 27)

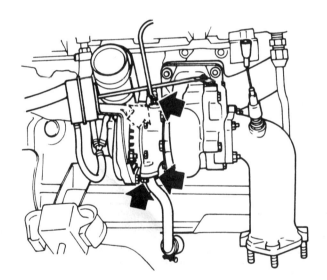

Fig. 4.27 Locations of the oil deliver tube and oil drain pipe at the turbocharger (sec 27)

8   Remove the nuts attaching the turbocharger to the exhaust manifold and carefully lower it out of the engine compartment.
9   Installation is the reverse of the removal procedure.

28 Crank angle sensor (1981 Turbo models) – replacement and adjustment

1   Disconnect the negative battery cable.
2   Disconnect the wiring connector leading to the crank angle sensor.
3   Scribe a line around the two crank angle sensor adjusting bolts. Remove the bolts and lift off the sensor and adjuster as a unit.
4   Remove the crank angle sensor from the adjuster and install the new sensor into place on the adjuster.
5   Remount the adjuster into position, making sure the adjuster bolts are aligned with the marks made during removal.
6   Following installation, use a feeler gauge to check the radial and thrust adjustments of the crank angle sensor (Fig. 4.28). Both

measurements should be 0.039 to 0.055 in (1.0 to 1,4 mm). If they are not as specified, adjust the sensor using the following procedure:
   a) To adjust the sensor in the radial direction, (dimension S in Fig. 4.28) loosen the two crank angle sensor adjuster mounting bolts. Then insert a 0.047 in (1.2 mm) feeler gauge between the sensor and the toothed sprocket and adjust the sensor to the proper gap. Retighten the bolts.
   b) To adjust the sensor in the thrust direction (dimension R in Fig. 4.28) loosen the A/C compressor mounting bolts and then loosen the compressor bracket mounting bolts. Again insert a 0.047 in (1.2 mm) feeler gauge into the gap and move the bracket until the proper gap is obtained. Retighten all bolts.
7   Also following replacement of the crank angle sensor, the ignition timing should be checked as described in Chapter 1.

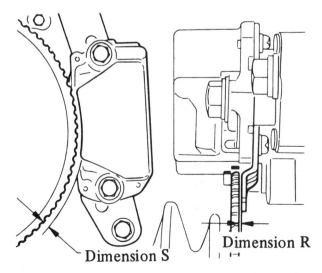

Fig. 4.28 Adjustment clearances of the crank angle sensor (1981 models) (Sec 28)

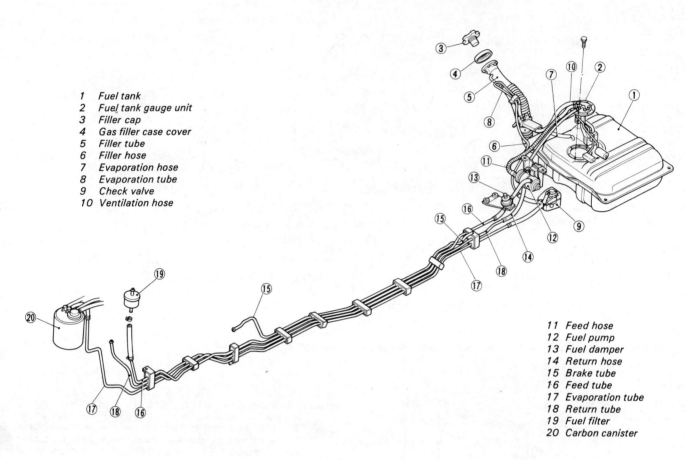

1 Fuel tank
2 Fuel tank gauge unit
3 Filler cap
4 Gas filler case cover
5 Filler tube
6 Filler hose
7 Evaporation hose
8 Evaporation tube
9 Check valve
10 Ventilation hose

11 Feed hose
12 Fuel pump
13 Fuel damper
14 Return hose
15 Brake tube
16 Feed tube
17 Evaporation tube
18 Return tube
19 Fuel filter
20 Carbon canister

Fig. 4.29 Components of the fuel delivery and vent system

29 Fuel system – cleaning

1   With time it is likely that sediment will collect in the bottom of the fuel tank. Condensation, resulting in rust and other impurities, will usually be found in the fuel tank of any car more than three or four years old. The following procedure should be performed to eliminate foreign material or contaminated fuel from the fuel system.
2   Eliminate the pressure in the fuel lines, using the procedure described in Chapter 1. Then disconnect the negative battery cable.
3   Drain and remove the fuel tank as described in Section 30.
4   Remove the fuel filter as described in Chapter 1. If the filter is clogged, replace it.
5   Remove the fuel tank gauge unit from the fuel tank as described in Section 31.
6   Purge and clean the fuel tank as necessary using one of the methods described in Section 32.
7   Disconnect the fuel inlet line at the fuel pump and clean the line out by applying air pressure through it in the direction of the fuel flow.
8   Use low air pressure to clean the lines on the tank unit.
9   Reinstall the fuel tank gauge unit.
10 Connect all wires and lines. Disconnect the fuel damper outlet line.
12 Connect a rubber hose to the damper outlet fitting.
13 Connect the negative battery cable.
14 Put about six gallons of clean fuel into the fuel tank and operate the pump by turning the engine over until about two quarts of fuel has flowed through the pump. This will clean the pump out. **Caution:** *Use a suitable container for the fuel to flow into, and be careful of fuel spray. Wear goggles.*
15 Remove the rubber hose and reconnect the damper outlet line.
16 Check all the connections to be sure they are tight.

30 Fuel tank – removal and installation

Note: *Any repairs to the fuel tank or filler neck should be carried out by a professional who has experience in this critical and potentially dangerous work.*
Caution: *While performing any work on the fuel tank, it is advisable to have a CO_2 fire extinguisher on hand and to wear safety glasses. All precautions should be taken to keep any kind of combustion (lighted cigarettes, etc.) or sparks away from the area of the tank and drained fuel.*
1   Eliminate the pressure from the fuel system by following the procedure described in Chapter 1.
2   Disconnect the negative battery cable.
3   Remove the fuel filler cap. Either siphon or pump the fuel from the tank into a suitable closed container.
4   Remove the fuel filler hose protector.
5   Disconnect the fuel filler and evaporation hoses. Plug all openings to prevent dirt from entering the lines.
6   Roll back the carpet in the rear compartment of the car and lift out the foam padding.
7   Remove the fuel tank inspection hole cover.
8   Disconnect the wiring connector leading to the fuel tank gauge unit.
9   Disconnect the fuel feed hose, fuel return hose and ventilation hoses from the top of the tank. Again, plug all hose and line openings.
10 While supporting the fuel tank either using a jack or with the help of an assistant, remove the fuel tank mounting band nuts and remove the mounting bands. The fuel tank can now be lowered and withdrawn from beneath the car.
11 It is recommended that the tank be cleaned out immediately after

removal, especially if it is to be worked on or stored. Refer to Section 32.

12 Before installing the tank make sure that all traces of dirt and corrosion are cleaned from it. A coat of rust-preventative paint is recommended. If the tank is rusted internally however, it should be replaced with a new one.

13 Installation is the reverse of the removal procedure.

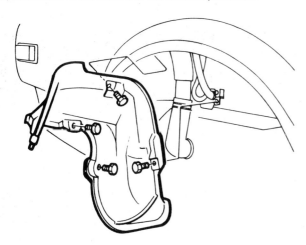

Fig. 4.30 Location of the fuel filler hose protector (Sec 30)

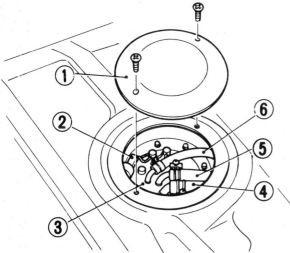

Fig. 4.31 Identification of fuel tank connections under the rear compartment of the car (Sec 30 and 31)

1	Inspection hole cover	4	Ventilation hose
2	Gauge unit harness connector	5	Fuel feed hose
3	Gauge unit	6	Fuel return hose

31 Fuel tank gauge unit – removal and installation

Caution: *While performing any work on the fuel tank, it is advisable to have a CO₂ fire extinguisher on hand and to wear safety glasses. All precautions should be taken to keep any kind of combustion (lighted cigarettes, etc.) or sparks away from the area of the tank.*

1 Disconnect the negative battery cable.

2 Roll back the carpet in the rear compartment of the car and lift out the foam padding.

3 Remove the fuel tank inspection hole cover.

4 Disconnect the wiring connector leading to the fuel tank gauge unit.

5 Disconnect the fuel feed, fuel return and ventilation hoses from the top of the fuel tank. Have a rag handy to absorb any spilled fuel. Also, immediately plug the hoses and lines to prevent the entry of dirt.

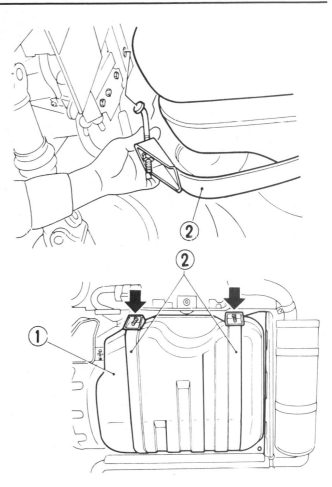

Fig. 4.32 The fuel tank is supported by mounting straps as shown above (Sec 30)

1	Fuel tank	2	Fuel tank mounting band

6 Remove the screws that retain the fuel tank gauge unit and lift it out. Cover over the opening in the tank.

7 With the gauge unit out, inspect the fuel tank filter and replace it, if necessary.

8 Installation is the reverse of the removal procedure.

32 Fuel tank – cleaning and purging

Caution: *Under no circumstancs perform repair work involving heat or flame without first carrying out the following procedure.*

1 Drain and remove the fuel tank as described in Section 30.

2 Remove the fuel tank gauge unit as described in Section 31.

3 Turn the tank over and empty out any remaining fuel.

4 If repair work needs to be done to the fuel tank that does not involve any heat or flame, the tank can be satisfactorily cleaned by running hot water into it and letting it overflow out the top for at least five minutes. **This method, however, does not remove the gas vapors.**

5 If repair work involving heat or flame is necessary, have it done by an experienced professional. The following, more thorough procedures should be used to remove all fuel and vapors from the tank.

6 Fill the tank completely with tap water, agitate vigorously and drain.

7 Add a gasoline emulsifying agent to the tank according to the manufacturer's instructions, refill with water, agitate approximately 10 minutes and drain.

8 Flush to overflowing once again with water for several minutes and drain.

9 The tank is now ready for repair work.

Chapter 5 Engine electrical systems

Contents

Specifications

Distributor

Type
1979 models	D6K8-22,-26,-02,-03,-05,-06,-07
1980 California models	D6K8-22
1980 US Federal models	D6K9-09, D6K9-10
1980 Canada models	D6K9-02
1981 models	
All US models (Non-turbo)	D6K80-03
All US models (Turbo)	D6P80-02
Canada models (Non-turbo)	D6K9-02
Canada models (Turbo)	D6P80-03
1982 models	
Non-turbo (all)	D6K81-01
Turbo (all)	D6P81-02
Air gap	0.012 to 0.020 in (0.3 to 0.5 mm)
Firing order	1 - 5 - 3 - 6 - 2 - 4
Direction of rotation	counterclockwise
Cap carbon point length	
1979 and 1982 models	0.39 in (10 mm)
1980 and 1981 models	0.47 in (12 mm)
Cap insulation resistance	over 50M ohms
Rotor head insulation resistance	over 50M ohms

Ignition coil

Type
1979 models	CIT-30 or STC-30
1980 models	CIT-43
1981 and 1982 models	
Non-turbo	CIT-43
Turbo	E12-45
Primary voltage	12 volts
Primary resistance at 68°F (20°C)	
Non-turbo models	0.84 to 1.02 ohms
Turbo models	0.63 to 0.77 ohms
Secondary resistance at 68°F (20°C)	
Non-turbo models	8.2 to 12.4K ohms
Turbo models	7.0 to 8.6K ohms

Spark plugs

All spark plug information is contained in the Chapter 1 Specifications.

Starter

Type
1979 models	S114-25B reduction gear type
1980 thru 1982 models	S114-254D reduction gear type

Terminal voltage (no load)	
1979 models	12.0 volts
1980 thru 1982 models	11.0 volts
Current (no load)	less than 100 amps
Speed (no load)	
1979 models	over 4300 rpm
1980 thru 1982 models	over 3900 rpm
Minimum brush length	0.43 in (11.0 mm)

Alternator

Type	
1979 and 1980 models	LR160-42B
1981 models	LR160-82
1982 models	
Non-turbo	LR160-82B
Turbo	LR170-02B
Nominal rating	
1982 turbo models only	12 volts/70 amps
All others	12 volts/60 amps
Hot output current	
1982 turbo models only	Over 50 amps at 2500 rpm/over 70 amps at 5000 rpm
All others	Over 50 amps at 2500 rpm/over 60 amps at 5000 rpm
Regulated output voltage	14.4 to 15.0 volts
Minimum brush length	0.28 in (7.0 mm)

1 Ignition system – general information

In order that the engine can run correctly it is necessary for an electrical spark to ignite the fuel/air mixture in the combustion chamber at exactly the right moment in relation to engine speed and load. The ignition system is based on feeding low tension (LT) voltage from the battery to the coil where it is converted to high tension (HT) voltage. The high tension voltage is powerful enough to jump the spark plug gap in the cylinders many times a second under high compression pressures, providing that the system is in good condition and that all adjustments are correct.

The ignition system is divided into two circuits; the low tension circuit and the high tension circuit.

In conventional systems, the low tension (sometimes known as the primary) circuit consists of the ignition switch, ignition and accessory relay, the primary windings of the ignition coil, the transistorized IC ignition unit, the pick-up assembly in the distributor and all connecting wires.

The high tension circuit consists of the high tension or secondary windings of the ignition coil, the heavy ignition lead from the center of the coil to the center of the distributor cap, the rotor, the spark plug leads and spark plugs.

The distributor used in Non-turbo ZX models is a pulse-triggered, transistor-controlled, inductive discharge unit in which the contact points of a conventional distributor are replaced by a control module and magnetic pick-up assembly.

The system functions in the following manner. Low tension voltage fed to the coils is changed into high tension voltage by the magnetic pick-up in the distributor. When the ignition switch is turned on, current flows through the primary circuit. A reluctor on the distributor shaft is aligned with the magnetic stator element of the pick-up assembly within the distributor housing, and as it turns it induces a low voltage in the pick-up coil. When the teeth on the reluctor and the magnets in the stator line up, a signal passes to the IC ignition unit which opens the coil's primary circuit. When the primary circuit is opened by the transistor unit, the magnetic field built up in the primary winding collapses and induces a very high voltage in the secondary winding. The high voltage current then flows from the coil, along the heavy ignition lead, to the carbon brush in the distributor cap. From the carbon brush, current flows to the distributor rotor which distributes the current to one of the terminals in the distributor cap. The spark occurs while the high tension voltage jumps across the spark plug gap. This process is repeated for each power stroke of the engine.

The system features a longer spark duration and the dwell period

automatically increases with engine speed. This is desirable for firing the leaner mixtures provided by the emissions control systems.

The distributor used on all non-turbo models is equipped with both mechanical and vacuum advanced mechanisms. The mechanical governor mechanism compresses two weights which move out from the distributor shaft due to centrifugal force as the engine speed increases. The weights are held in position by two light springs, and it is the tension of the springs which is largely responsible for the correct spark advancement.

The vacuum control consists of a diaphragm, one side of which is connected via a small-bore tube to a vacuum source, and the other side to the magnetic pick-up assembly. Vacuum in the intake manifold which varies with engine speed and throttle opening, causes the diaphragm to move, which, in turn, moves the magnetic pick-up assembly, thus advancing or retarding the spark. The distributor vacuum advance is controlled by the Spark Timing Control System, and is explained in detail in Chapter 6.

On Turbo ZX models, the primary circuit of the ignition system is integrated with the ECCS fuel injection/turbocharging system, described in detail in Chapter 4.

The engine speed and position of the pistons are monitored by a crank angle sensor, which, in this system combines with the control unit to replace the distributor pick-up assembly, mechanical and vacuum advances, and IC ignition unit. The necessary information is passed from the crank angle sensor to the control unit, which electronically determines the optimum spark timing and triggers the spark using the conventional high tension circuit (coil, rotor, distributor cap and spark plugs).

The crank angle sensor is located at the front of the crankshaft on 1981 Turbo models, and inside the distributor on 1982 models. More detailed information on the ECCS system can be found in Chapter 4.

Because of the complexity of the ECCS system, if an ignition problem develops which cannot be isolated to the high tension circuit, the car should be taken to a Datsun dealer or other ignition specialist for proper diagnosis and correction.

Caution: *Because of the higher voltage generated by these electronic ignition systems, extreme caution should be taken whenever an operation is performed involving ignition components. This not only includes the distributor, coil, control module and ignition wires, but related items which are connected to the system as well, such as the plug connections, tachometer and any testing equipment. Consequently, before any work is performed such as replacing ignition components or even connecting testing equipment, the ignition should be turned off or the battery ground cable disconnected.*

Note: *Never disconnect any of the ignition HT leads when the engine is running, or the transistor ignition unit will be permanently damaged.*

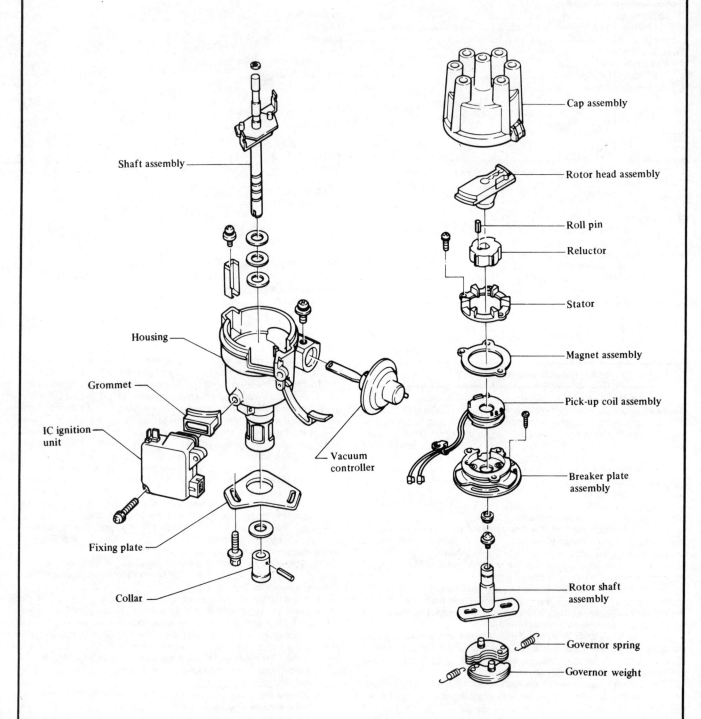

Shaft assembly

Cap assembly

Rotor head assembly

Roll pin

Reluctor

Stator

Magnet assembly

Housing

Pick-up coil assembly

Grommet

IC ignition unit

Vacuum controller

Breaker plate assembly

Fixing plate

Collar

Rotor shaft assembly

Governor spring

Governor weight

Fig. 5.1 Exploded view of the distributor (all non-turbo models)

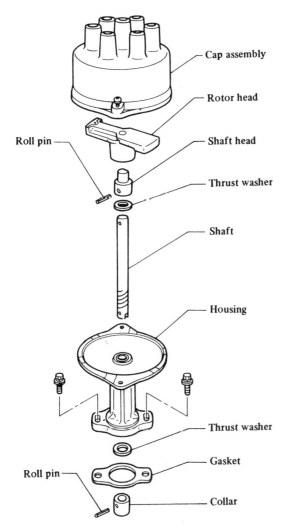

Fig. 5.2 Exploded view of the distributor (1981 Turbo models)

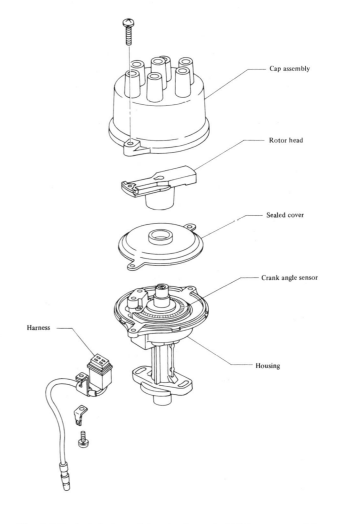

Fig. 5.3 Exploded view of the distributor (1982 Turbo models)

2 Ignition system (non-turbo models) – testing

Caution: *Never touch your bare hand to any high tension cables or parts while the engine is running or being cranked. Even insulated parts can cause a shock if they are moist. It is recommended that you wear dry, insulated gloves or wrap the part in dry cloth before handling.*

1 If the engine will turn over but will not start, the first check of the ignition system should be to visually inspect the condition of the spark plugs, spark plug wires, distributor cap and rotor as described in Chapter 1.

2 If these are all in good condition, and the plug wires are secure in their connections, the next check should be to see if current is flowing through the high tension circuit, thus sparking the plugs.

    a) Turn the ignition switch to the Off position.

    b) Disconnect the EFI fusible link connector located near the positive battery terminal (refer to Chapter 10).

    c) Disconnect the wiring connector leading to the cold start valve.

    d) Disconnect the ignition coil wire from the distributor cap and hold it approximately $\frac{3}{16}$ to $\frac{1}{4}$ inch (4 to 5 mm) from a clean metal area of the engine (note paragraph 1). Have an assistant crank the engine over and check if a spark occurs between the coil wire and the engine.

    e) If a spark occurs, the ignition system is okay, and the problem lies in another system. If no spark occurs, or occurs intermittently, proceed with further ignition system tests.

3 In order to accurately diagnose problems in the Datsun system, a voltmeter which measures in the 0 to 20 volts DC and 0 to 10 volts AC ranges, and an ohmmeter which measures in the 0 to 1000 ohms and 0 to 5000 ohms ranges are needed.

4 If it is possible to start the engine, do so and let it run about 5 to 15 minutes with the hood closed to bring all components to normal operating temperature.

5 *Checking the battery voltage with no load.*

    a) With the ignition key in the Off position, connect a voltmeter so its positive lead is on the positive battery terminal and its negative lead is on the negative battery terminal.

    b) Note the reading on the voltmeter. If the reading is between 11.5 volts and 12.5 volts, the battery is okay and you should proceed to paragraph 6.

    c) If the reading is below 11.5 volts, the battery is insufficiently charged. It should be brought to a full charge either by running the engine or by using a battery charger. If the car has been used on a regular basis and there is no obvious cause for the battery to be discharged (such as leaving the lights on), then the condition of the battery, charging system and starting system should be checked out as described in this chapter or Chapter 1.

6 *Checking the battery voltage while the engine is cranking.*

    a) Leave the voltmeter connected to the battery as in the last paragraph.

    b) Disconnect the ignition coil wire from the distributor cap and ground it to the engine.

c) Have an assistant crank the engine over for about 15 seconds and note the reading on the voltmeter.
d) If the voltage is more than 9.6 volts, the battery is okay and you should proceed to paragraph 7. If the voltage was below 9.6 volts the battery is insufficiently charged. Refer to paragraph 5.

7 *Checking the distributor cap and secondary winding.*
a) Disconnect the spark plug wires from the plugs.
b) Disconnect the ignition coil wire from the coil.
c) Remove the distributor cap, with spark plug and coil wires still attached.
d) Connect an ohmmeter so that one lead is inserted in the spark plug end of one of the plug wires and the other lead is contacting the inner distributor cap terminal that the wire is connected to.
e) If the reading on the ohmmeter is less than 30 000 ohms the cap terminal and wire are okay.
f) If the reading is more than 30 000 ohms, the resistance is too high. Check the cap and wire individually and replace the appropriate part.
g) Repeat this test on each of the spark plug and coil wires.

8 *Checking the ignition coil secondary circuit.*
a) With the ignition key in the Off position, connect the ohmmeter so that one lead is contacting the center high tension wire connector and the other lead is contacting the negative coil terminal.
b) If the reading is between 8200 and 12 400 ohms, the secondary coil windings are okay.
c) If the ohmmeter reading is not within these specs, replace the ignition coil.

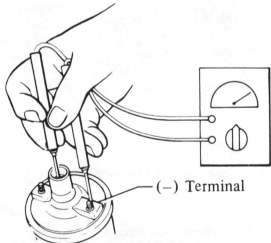

Fig. 5.4 Proper ohmmeter connections for checking the secondary circuit of the ignition coil (Sec 2)

9 *Checking the power supply circuit at the distributor*
a) Connect the positive lead of the voltmeter to the B terminal on the IC ignition unit in the distributor (when performing this or any of the following tests, it is not necessary to disconnect the wiring connector when hooking up the voltmeter or ohmmeter, providing they have probes that can be inserted into the rear of the connector).
b) Ground the negative voltmeter lead to the point shown in the accompanying illustration.
c) Turn the ignition key to the On position and note the voltmeter reading.
d) If the reading is between 11.5 and 12.5 volts, the power supply circuit is okay. If the reading is below 11.5 volts, inspect the wiring between the ignition switch and the IC unit for damage, or loose or dirty connections.

10 *Checking the power supply circuit while the engine is being cranked.*
a) Ground the coil wire to the engine.
b) Connect the voltmeter as in paragraph 19.
c) Have an assistant crank the engine over for about 15 seconds and note the reading on the voltmeter.

d) If the reading is less than 1 volt below the battery cranking voltage (measured in paragraph 6) and is greater than 8.6 volts, the circuit is okay.
e) If the reading is more than 1 volt below the battery cranking voltage and/or is below 8.6 volts, inspect the wiring between the ignition switch and the IC unit for damage, or loose or dirty connections.

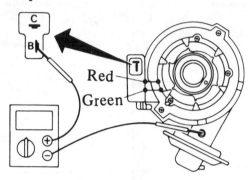

Fig. 5.5 Proper voltmeter connections for checking the power supply circuit (Sec 2)

11 *Checking the ignition primary circuit.*
a) Connect the voltmeter so the positive lead is connected to the C terminal on the IC unit, and the negative lead contacts the point shown in Fig. 5.6. Turn the ignition key to the On position and note the voltmeter reading. If between 11.5 and 12.5 volts is shown, the circuit is okay. If less than 11.5 volts is shown, proceed to paragraph 12.

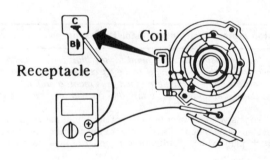

Fig. 5.6 Proper voltmeter connections for checking the ignition primary circuit (Sec 2)

12 *Checking the ignition coil primary circuit.*
a) With the ignition key in the Off position and the ignition coil wire removed from the coil, connect an ohmmeter (set in the 1x range) between the positive and negative terminals on the ignition coil.
b) If the ohmmeter reading is between 0.84 and 1.02 ohms the coil is okay, and the ignition switch and the wiring running between the ignition switch, the coil and the IC unit should be checked for damage, or loose or dirty connections.
c) If the ohmmeter reading is not within these specs, the ignition coil should be replaced.

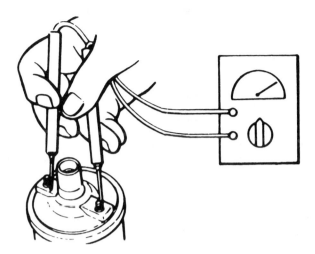

Fig. 5.7 Proper ohmmeter connections for checking the ignition coil primary circuit (Sec 2)

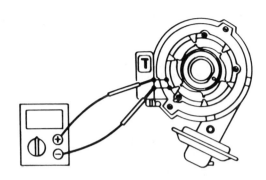

Fig. 5.9 Proper voltmeter connections for checking the pick-up coil resistance (Sec 2)

13 *Checking the IC unit ground circuit.*
   a) Remove the ignition coil wire from the distributor cap and ground it to the engine.
   b) Connect a voltmeter so its negative lead is connected to the negative battery terminal, and the positive lead is connected to the point shown in Fig. 5.8.
   c) Have an assistant crank the engine over for about 15 seconds, and note the voltmeter reading.
   d) If more than 0.5 volts is shown, check the grounding of the distributor, the wiring between the battery and the chassis ground and the negative battery cable connection.
   e) If the reading shows 0.5 volts or less further checks are still needed. Proceed to paragraph 14.

15 *Checking the pick-up coil output.*
   a) The engine should still be at normal operating temperature.
   b) Connect a voltmeter (set on the low AC volt scale) between the points shown in Fig. 5.10.
   c) Have an assistant crank the engine over for about 15 seconds, and observe the movement of the voltmeter needle.
   d) If the needle is steady, check the physical condition of the pickup coil and reluctor for damage. Also check the wiring between the pick-up coil and the IC unit for damage, or loose or dirty connections.
   e) If the needle wavers while the engine is being cranked, and there is still no spark being produced, replace the IC unit.

Ground coil secondary while cranking.

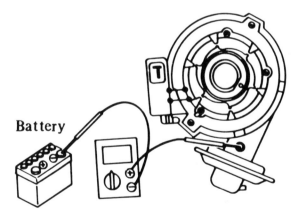

Fig. 5.8 Proper voltmeter connections for checking the IC unit ground circuit (Sec 2)

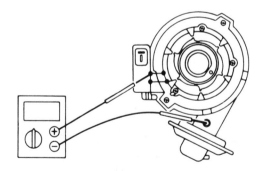

Fig. 5.10 Proper voltmeter connections for checking the pick-up coil output (Sec 2)

14 *Checking the pick-up coil resistance.*
   a) For this check the engine should be at normal operating temperature.
   b) With the ignition switch in the Off position, connect an ohmmeter (set in the 100x range) as shown in Fig. 5.9 and note the reading.
   c) If approximately 400 ohms is shown, the pickup coil resistance is okay.
   d) If the reading is substantially above or below 400 ohms, inspect the pick-up coil and its wiring for damage, or loose or dirty connections.

3 Distributor air gap – adjustment

Note: *To ensure that the ignition system functions correctly, the air-gap (distance between the pickup coil and reluctor) must be maintained as specified. To do this, proceed as follows:*

1 Disengage the two spring retaining clips and remove the cap from the distributor.
2 Remove the rotor from the end of the distributor shaft.

3   Position one of the raised segments of the reluctor directly opposite the pole piece protruding from the pickup coil. This is best carried out by removing the spark plugs (to relieve compression) and rotating the crankshaft by using a ratchet wrench on the crankshaft bolt at the front of the engine.

4   Using feeler gauges, measure the gap between the pole and the reluctor segment. If the air gap requires adjustment, loosen the pickup coil retaining screws and move the coil in the required direction.

5   When the correct air gap has been obtained, tighten the pickup coil retaining screws; install the rotor and the distributor cap, ensuring that the cap is correctly positioned.

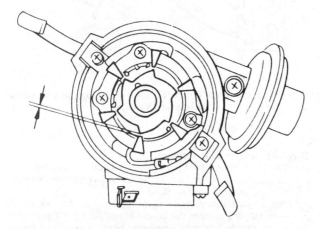

Fig. 5.11 The air gap is the distance between the reluctor teeth and the stator magnet (Sec 3)

4   IC ignition unit – removal and installation

1   The IC ignition unit is located on the outside of the distributor body, and is removed by simply disconnecting the wiring connector and removing the two mounting screws.

9   Installation is the reverse of the removal procedure.

5   Stator and magnet (pick-up assembly) – removal and installation

1   Disconnect the ignition coil wire from the top of the distributor cap.

2   Remove the distributor cap from the distributor and position it out of the way.

3   Pull off the rotor from the distributor shaft.

4   Using two screwdrivers on either side of the reluctor, carefully pry the reluctor from the distributor shaft. Be careful not to damage the teeth on the reluctor.

5   Remove the screws that retain the stator and magnet to the distributor breaker plate and lift them off.

6   Disconnect the distributor wiring harness and lift out the pickup coil assembly.

7   Installation is the reverse of the removal procedure with the following notes: When installing the reluctor, be sure the pin is lined up with the flat side of the distributor shaft. Also, before tightening the stator, check and adjust the air gap as described in Section 3.

6   Distributor – removal

1   The rubber duct between the air flow meter and throttle chamber may have to be removed for clearance.

2   Remove the ignition coil wire that leads to the distributor from the coil.

3   Remove the distributor cap from the distributor and position it out of the way.

4   Mark the rotor in relationship to the distributor housing.

5   Disconnect the wires leading to the IC ignition unit.

6   Remove the vacuum line from the vacuum advance canister.

7   Remove the two distributor mounting screws and lift out the distributor. **Note:** *Be sure not to loosen the distributor adjusting screws.*

7   Distributor – installation

Non-turbo models
If the engine was not rotated after removal

1   Position the rotor in the location it was in when the distributor was removed.

2   Lower the distributor down into the engine. To mesh the groove in the bottom of the distributor shaft with the drive spindle (which turns the distributor shaft), it may be necessary to turn the rotor slightly.

3   With the base of the distributor all the way down against the engine block and the mounting screw holes lined up, the rotor should be pointing to the mark made on the distributor housing during removal. If the rotor is not in alignment with the mark, repeat the previous steps.

4   Install the two distributor mounting screws and tighten them securely.

5   Connect the vacuum line to the vacuum advance canister.

6   Reconnect the wiring connector to the IC unit.

7   Reinstall the distributor cap and connect the ignition coil wire.

8   Check the ignition timing as described in Chapter 1.

If the engine was rotated after removal

9   Set the number 1 piston at TDC. Refer to Chapter 2, if necessary.

10 Temporarily install the distributor cap onto the distributor. Note where the number 1 spark plug terminal inside the cap is located in relation to the distributor body, and make a mark on the outside of the body at this point.

11 Remove the distributor cap again. Rotate the rotor until it is aligned with the mark. In this position it should be firing the number one spark plug.

12 Proceed with installation as detailed in paragraphs 2 through 8. Disregard the rotor mark references in paragraph 3.

1981 Turbo models

1   Set the number 1 piston at Top Dead Center (TDC) on its compression stroke as described in Chapter 2.

2   Prior to installing the distributor, pass a thin rod (approx. 0.01 in or 2.5 mm) through both the distributor cap and the rotor, as shown in Fig. 5.12 so that the rotor is kept pointing to the number 1 terminal in the distributor cap.

3   Install the distributor mounting bolts and torque them to specifications.

4   Once the distributor is securely mounted, the rod can be pulled out.

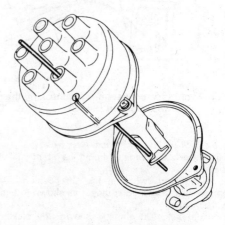

Fig. 5.12 When installing the distributor on 1981 Turbo models, a rod passed thru the cap and rotor will keep the rotor from turning (Sec 7)

8 Distributor – disassembly and reassembly

Non-turbo models

1 Remove the distributor from the car as desribed in Section 6.
2 Remove the distributor cap
3 Pull off the rotor.
4 Disconnect the wiring connector leading to the IC unit. Remove the unit's two mounting screws and lift it off.
5 Remove the stator attaching screws and lift out the stator and magnet.
6 Remove the screws that retain the vacuum canister and lift it off.
7 Using two screwdrivers placed on either side of the reluctor, carefully pry it off the distributor shaft. Be careful not to damage the reluctor teeth.
8 Drive the roll pin out of the reluctor.
9 Remove the pickup coil assembly.
10 Remove the breaker plate set screws and lift out the breaker plate assembly.
11 Using a suitable punch, drive the knock pin from the collar and pull off the collar.
12 Pull the rotor shaft assembly and driveshaft out the top of the distributor.
13 Mark the relative position of the rotor shaft and driveshaft. Then remove the packing from the top of the rotor shaft, remove the rotor shaft setscrew and separate the two shafts.
14 Mark the relationship of one of the governor springs to its bracket. Also mark the relationship of one of the governor weights to its pivot pins.
15 Carefully unhook and remove the governor springs.
16 Remove the governor weights. A small amount of grease should be applied to the weights after removal.
17 Reassembly is the reverse of the disassembly procedure with the following notes:
  a) Be sure to correctly align all positioning marks made during disassembly so that all the parts are assembled in their original position
  b) When installing the reluctor on the shaft, drive the roll pin into the reluctor so that its slit is positioned toward the outer end of the shaft. Always use a new roll pin
  c) Before installing the IC unit onto the distributor body, make sure the mating surfaces of both the IC unit and the body are clean and free from dirt or moisture. This is very important
  d) Before tightening the stator plate, adjust the air gap as described in Section 3

1981 Turbo models

18 Remove the distributor cap.
19 Pull off the rotor.
20 Using a suitable punch, drive the roll pin from the collar, then pull the shaft assembly out from the top of the distributor.
21 Again using a punch, drive the roll pin out from the shaft head, then separate the shaft head from the shaft.
22 Reassembly is the reverse of the disassembly procedure. **Note:** *When reassembling the shaft head to the shaft, be sure the shaft head is positioned exactly as shown in Fig. 5.13. Always use new roll pins during reassembly.*

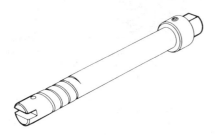

Fig. 5.13 When reassembling the 1981 Turbo distributors, this figure should be used as a guide when assembling the shaft and shaft head (Sec 8)

1982 Turbo models

23 The distributor used on these models can be disassembled only to the extent shown in Fig. 5.3. While the distributor cap, rotor, sealed cover and harness can be separated from the housing, the housing and crank angle sensor cannot be disassembled and must be replaced as one unit if defective.

9 Ignition coil – removal and installation

1 Remove the coil wire leading from the distributor.
2 Remove the dust boot.
3 Peel back the rubber dust caps from the coil terminals and remove the nuts and wires from the coil.
4 Remove the two screws that hold the coil bracket, to the body and lift off the coil.
5 If the coil needs to be removed from its bracket, loosen the bracket screws until the bracket is loose enough for the coil to be pulled out.
6 Installation is the reverse of the removal procedure.

10 Starting system – general information

The function of the starting system is to crank the engine. This system is composed of a starting motor, solenoid and battery. The battery supplies the electrical energy to the solenoid, which then completes the circuit to the starting motor which does the actual work of cranking the engine.

All ZX models use a reduction gear type of starter motor. This starter operates in a similar manner to a conventional type except that in order to combat extremely low temperatures, increased rotating torque is provided through a reduction gear located between the armature and pinion gear.

An overrunning clutch is attached to the starter motor to transmit the driving torque and to prevent the armature from overrunning when the engine fires and starts.

The solenoid and starting motor are mounted together at the rear right side of the engine. No periodic lubrication or maintenance is required for the starting system components.

The electrical circuitry of the vehicle is arranged so that the starter motor can only be operated on automatic transmission models when the lever is in Park or Neutral.

Never operate the starter motor for more than 30 seconds at a time without pausing to allow it to cool for at least two minutes. Excessive cranking can cause overheating, which can seriously damage the starter.

11 Starting system – testing

1 If the starter motor does not rotate at all when the switch is operated on an automatic transmission model, check that the shifter is in the Neutral or Park position.
2 Check that the battery is well charged and all cables, both at the battery and starter solenoid terminals, are secure.
3 If the motor can be heard spinning but the engine is not being cranked, then the overrunning clutch in the starter motor is slipping and the assembly must be removed from the engine and replaced.
4 Often when the starter fails to operate, a click can be heard coming from the starter solenoid when the ignition switch is turned to the Start position. If this is heard, proceed to paragraph 12. If even this click is not heard, disconnect the ignition wire (usually black and yellow) from the starter solenoid.
5 Connect a test light between this lead and the negative battery terminal.
6 Have an assistant turn the key, and note whether the test light comes on or not. If the light comes on, proceed to paragraph 12.
7 If the test light did not come on, connect a voltmeter (set on the low scale) between the positive battery terminal and the bayonet connector at the solenoid. The black and yellow wire should be connected.
8 Disconnect the ignition coil wire(s) from the distributor cap and ground it to the engine, so the car will not start.
9 Have an assistant attempt to crank the engine over and note the

reading on the voltmeter. If less than 1.5 volts is shown, there is an open circuit in the starter, and it should be replaced with a new or rebuilt unit.

10 If the voltmeter shows more than 1.5 volts, connect a jumper wire between the positive battery terminal and the S terminal on the solenoid.

11 Again, turn the ignition switch to the Start position and listen for a click from the solenoid. If there still is no click and the starter does not turn, both the solenoid and starter are defective and should be replaced. If a click is heard and the starter turns, then there is an open circuit in the ignition switch, inhibitor switch or relay (on automatic transmission models) or in the wires or connectors.

12 If a click was heard when the ignition switch was turned to the Start position in paragraph 4, or if the starter turned at all, then the starter current should be tested. Disconnect the positive battery cable at the starter.

13 Connect an ammeter (set in the 500A range) between this cable and its terminal on the starter.

14 Remove the ignition coil wire from the distributor cap to keep the engine from starting.

15 Have an assistant attempt to crank the engine and note the reading on the ammeter and the speed at which the starter turns.

16 If the ammeter reading was less than 150 amps and the starter speed was normal, the starter is okay and the problem lies elsewhere.

17 If the reading was less than 150 amps but the starter motor speed was slow, proceed to paragraph 22.

18 If the ammeter reading was more than 150 amps, reinstall the ignition coil wire into the distributor cap.

19 Have an assistant start the engine, but hold the key in the Start position so that the starter motor doesn't stop operating. Note the ammeter reading. (Do not allow the starter motor to turn for more than 30 seconds at a time).

20 If the ammeter reading is less than 60 amps and the starter turns fast, then the problem is a mechanical one such as a tight engine. Check that the engine oil is not too thick, and for other causes of resistance within the engine.

21 If the ammeter reading was over 60 amps, the starter is shorted and must be replaced with a new one.

22 If the ammeter reading in paragraph 15 was less than 150 amps, but the starter turned slowly, test for a voltage drop in the starter positive circuit.

23 Connect a voltmeter (set on the low scale) so the positive lead is on the positive battery post (or cable) and the negative lead is connected to the M solenoid terminal (this is the terminal with the braided copper strap leading to the starter motor).

24 Remove the ignition coil wire from the distributor cap and ground it on the engine.

25 Have an assistant attempt to crank the engine over and note the reading on the voltmeter. If less than 1 volt is shown, proceed to paragraph 28.

26 If more than 1 volt is shown, connect the negative voltmeter lead to the B solenoid terminal (this is the terminal which connects to the battery).

27 Again, have an assistant crank the engine and note the reading on the voltmeter. If more than 1 volt is shown, then the problem is a bad connection between the battery and the starter solenoid. Check the positive battery cable for looseness or corrosion. If the reading indicated less than 1 volt, then the solenoid is defective and should be replaced.

28 If the voltmeter test in paragraph 25 showed less than 1 volt, test for a voltage drop in the starter ground circuit.

29 Connect the negative lead of the voltmeter (set on the low scale) to the negative battery terminal, and hold the positive voltmeter lead to the starter housing. Be sure to make a good connection.

30 Have an assistant crank the engine and note the voltmeter reading. If the reading shows more than 0.5 volts, then there is a bad ground connection. Check the negative battery cable for looseness or corrosion. Also check the starter motor ground connections and the tightness of the starter motor mounting bolts.

31 If the voltmeter reading shows less than 0.5 volts, proceed to paragraph 7 and follow the procedure outlined there.

12 Starter motor – removal and installation

1 Disconnect the negative battery cable from the battery.

2 Remove the two wires from the starter solenoid.
3 Remove the two starter motor mounting bolts.
4 Lift out the starter motor complete with solenoid.
5 Installation is the reverse of the removal procedure.

13 Starter solenoid – removal and installation

1 Remove the starter motor as described in Section 12.
2 Remove the nut that holds the braided copper strap to the solenoid.
3 Remove the two solenoid mounting screws (photo) and lift off the solenoid from the starter motor.
4 Installation is the reverse of the removal procedure.
Note: *During installation be sure to engage the solenoid plunger with the starter motor shift lever (photo).*

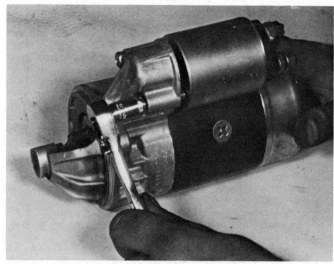

13.3 The solenoid is secured to the starter motor by two screws

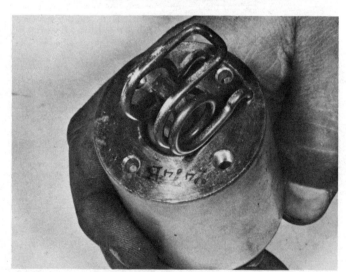

13.4 The solenoid should be assembled as shown prior to installation (during installation, the solenoid plunger should be engaged with the starter motor shift lever)

14 Starter motor – brush replacement

1 Remove the starter from the car as described in Section 12.
2 Remove the solenoid as described in Section 13.
3 Remove the through bolts by unscrewing them and drawing them out through the rear.
4 Remove the rear cover from the starter motor. Be careful not to damage the O-ring.

Measuring plug gap. A feeler gauge of the correct size (see ignition system specifications) should have a slight 'drag' when slid between the electrodes. Adjust gap if necessary

Adjusting plug gap. The plug gap is adjusted by bending the ground electrode inwards, or outwards, as necessary until the correct clearance is obtained. Note the use of the correct tool

Normal. Gray brown deposits, lightly coated core nose. Gap increasing by around 0.001 in (0.025 mm) per 1000 miles (1600 km). Plugs ideally suited to engine, and engine in good condition

Carbon fouling. Dry, black, sooty deposits. Will cause weak spark and eventually misfire. Fault: over-rich fuel mixture. Check: carburetor mixture settings, float level and jet sizes; choke operation and cleanliness of air filter. Plugs can be re-used after cleaning

Oil fouling. Wet, oily deposits. Will cause weak spark and eventually misfire. Fault: worn bores/piston rings or valve guides; sometimes occurs (temporarily) during running-in period. Plugs can be re-used after thorough cleaning

Overheating. Electrodes have glazed appearance, core nose very white – few deposits. Fault: plug overheating. Check: plug value, ignition timing, fuel octane rating (too low) and fuel mixture (too weak). Discard plugs and cure fault immediately.

Electrode damage. Electrodes burned away; core nose has burned, glazed appearance. Fault: pre-ignition. Check: as for 'Overheating' but may be more severe. Discard plugs and remedy fault before piston or valve damage occurs

Split core nose (may appear initially as a crack). Damage is self-evident, but cracks will only show after cleaning. Fault: pre-ignition or wrong gap-setting technique. Check: ignition timing, cooling system, fuel octane rating (too low) and fuel mixture (too weak). Discard plugs, rectify fault immediately

5   Remove the yoke, armature and brush holder as an assembly from the center housing. Be careful not to knock the brushes, commutator or coil against any adjacent part.

6   Lift up the brush springs and remove the brushes from the brush holder.

7   Measure the length of the brushes. If they are 11 mm (0.43 in) or shorter they should be replaced with new ones.

8   Use a soldering gun to remove the brushes from the yoke and solder new brushes on.

9   Reassembly of the starter motor is the reverse of the disassembly procedure.

15 Charging system – general information

The charging system is made up of the alternator, voltage regulator and the battery. These components work together to supply electrical power for the engine ignition, lights, radio, etc.

The alternator is turned by a drivebelt at the front of the engine. Thus, when the engine is operating, voltage is generated by the internal components of the alternator to be sent to the battery for storage.

The alternator uses a solid state regulator that is mounted inside the alternator housing. The purpose of this voltage regulator is to limit the alternator voltage to a preset value. This prevents power surges, circuit overloads, etc., during peak voltage output. The regulator voltage setting cannot be adjusted.

The charging system does not ordinarily require periodic maintenance. The drivebelts, electrical wiring and connections should, however, be inspected during normal routine maintenance (see Section 16).

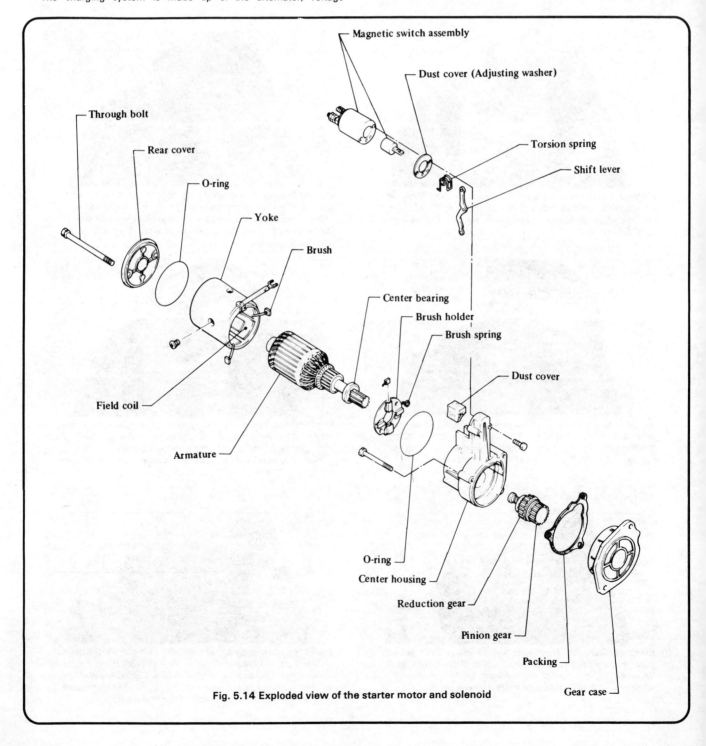

Fig. 5.14 Exploded view of the starter motor and solenoid

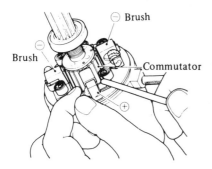

Fig. 5.15 The starter motor brushes can be removed from the brush holder by holding the brush springs aside and sliding them out one at a time (Sec 14)

16 Alternator – maintenance and special precautions

1   Alternator maintenance consists of occasionally wiping away any dirt or oil which may have collected on it.

2   Check the tension of the drivebelt (refer to Chapter 1).

3   No lubrication is required as alternator bearings are grease sealed for the life of the unit.

4   Take extreme care when making circuit connections to a vehicle equipped with an alternator and observe the following. When making connections to the alternator from a battery, always match correct polarity. Before using electric-arc welding.equipment to repair any part of the vehicle, disconnect the connector from the alternator and disconnect the positive battery terminal. Never start the car with a battery charger connected. Always disconnect both battery leads before using a charger, if boosting from another battery, always connect in parallel using heavy cable.

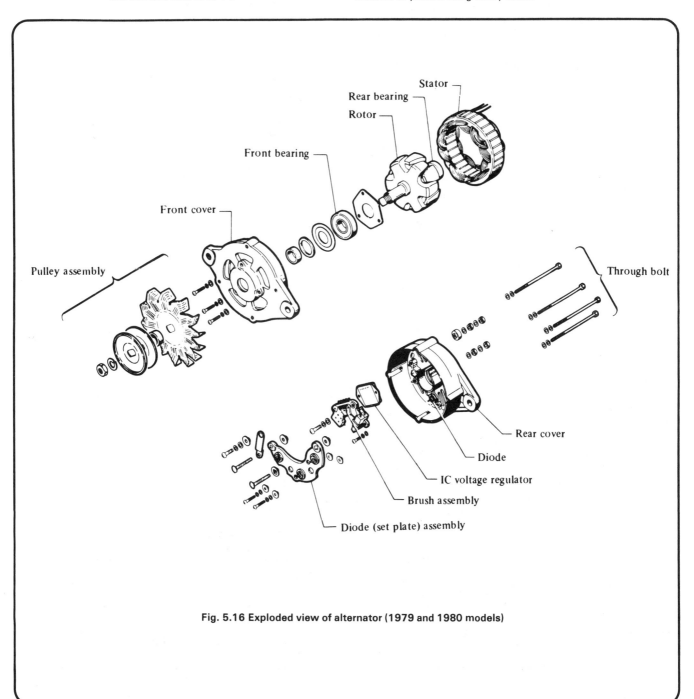

Fig. 5.16 Exploded view of alternator (1979 and 1980 models)

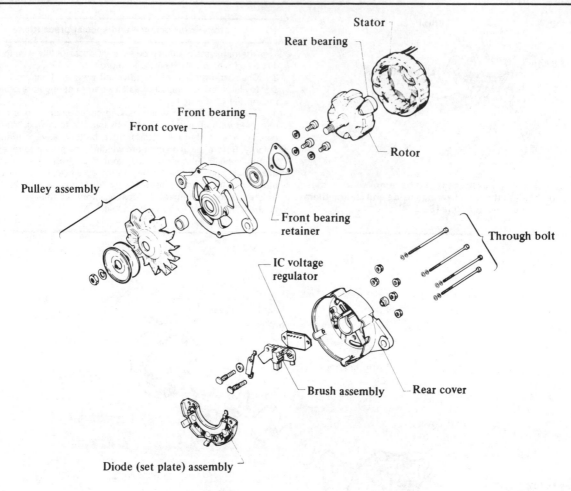

Fig. 5.17 Exploded view of alternator (1981 and 1982 models)

17 Charging system – testing

1   Where a faulty alternator is suspected, first ensure that the battery is fully charged. If necessary, have it charged from an outside source. Refer to Chapter 1.
2   Visually inspect all wires and connections to make sure they are clean, tight and in good condition.
3   A 30-volt voltmeter is necessary to accurately test the charging system.
4   Turn the ignition switch to the On position, and check that the alternator warning light in the instrument cluster illuminates. If it does, proceed to paragraph 7.
5   If the warning light did not come on, check that the warning light bulb is not burned out. To do this, disconnect the SL connector at the rear of the alternator and ground the L lead wire with a jumper wire. Again, turn the ignition switch to the On position and check the warning light. If the warning light is still off, a burned bulb or loose connection between the alternator and the warning light is indicated. Replace it by referring to Chapter 10.
6   If the warning light did come on in the previous test, the bulb is in good condition, a faulty alternator or regulator is indicated. To determine which, reconnect the SL connector, and use a jumper wire to ground the F terminal. Once again, turn the ignition switch On and check the warning light. If the light comes on, the voltage regulator is faulty. If the light remains off, the alternator is defective. Replace either component by referring to the appropriate Section of this Chapter.
7   If the warning light does come on with the ignition switch in the On position, start the engine and allow it to idle. The light should go out. If it remains on, even dimly or as a flicker, a faulty alternator is indicated. Replace it with a new or rebuilt unit.
8   Slowly increase the engine speed to 1500 rpm and maintain it at that speed.

9   Turn the headlights on and again check the alternator warning light. If it remains off, proceed to paragraph 11.
10   If the warning light comes on dimly, lower the engine speed to its normal idle speed. Connect the voltmeter between the B and L terminals and measure the voltage. If more than 0.5 volts is shown the alternator needs replacing. If less than 0.5 volts is shown, the unit is okay.
11   If the warning light remained off when the lights were turned on, maintain the engine speed at 1500 rpm and measure the voltage at the B terminal. Be sure the S terminal is correctly connected.
12   If more than 15.5 volts is shown, the IC regulator is defective. Replace the alternator.
13   If the voltage reading is between 13 and 15 volts, lower the engine speed once again to its normal level.
14   Turn the headlights on and again check the alternator warning light in the dash. It should remain off. If the light comes on, a defective alternator is indicated and it should be replaced.

18 Alternator – removal and installation

1   Disconnect the negative battery cable.
2   For clearance, raise the front of the car and support it on jackstands.
3   Remove all wires from the rear of the alternator. Be sure to label them as to their locations.
4   Loosen the upper drivebelt adjusting bolt and move the alternator toward the engine until the drivebelt can be removed from the alternator pulley.
5   Remove the adjusting bolt and the two alternator mounting bolts located at the bottom of the alternator.
6   Remove the alternator from the car.
7   Installation is the reverse of the removal procedure.

19 Alternator – voltage regulator and brush replacement

1979 and 1980 models

1 Remove the alternator from the car as described in Section 18.

2 Remove the four through-bolts from the rear cover.

3 Separate the front cover/rotor assembly from the rear cover/stator assembly by lightly tapping the front bracket with a wooden or rubber hammer.

4 Using a soldering gun, disconnect the stator coil lead wires from the diode terminals. Then remove the stator from the rear cover.

5 Again using a soldering gun, disconnect the wires at the diode terminal.

6 Remove the retaining screws and lift out the regulator and brush assembly.

7 Check for free movement of the brush and make sure the holder is clean and undamaged.

8 Check for brush wear either by noting the brush wear limiting line or by measuring the length of the brush and comparing it to the wear limit specs at the beginning of this Chapter. If the brush is worn beyond either limit, it must be replaced with a new one.

9 If the voltage regulator is defective, it and the brush assembly should be replaced as one unit.

10 Reassembly of the alternator is the reverse of the disassembly procedure, with the following notes.

a) Soldering of the stator coil lead wires to the diode assembly should be done as quickly as possible to prevent undue heat from building up around the diode assembly.

b) When installing the diode A terminal, be sure the insulating bushing is correctly installed.

c) Before joining the front and rear covers together, push the brush in the rear cover up with your fingers and hold it there as shown in Fig. 5.20 by inserting a piece of stiff wire through the brush lift hole from the outside. After the front and rear covers have been joined, the wire can be removed by pushing the outside end toward the center of the alternator and pulling it straight out. If the wire is not removed in this way, the slip-ring sliding surface can be damaged.

1981 and 1982 models

11 Remove the alternator from the car as described in Section 18.

12 Remove the four through-bolts from the rear cover.

13 Separate the front cover/rotor assembly from the rear cover/stator assembly by lightly tapping the front bracket with a soft-faced hammer.

14 From the rear of the rear cover, remove the five stator assembly retaining nuts, then lift out the stator assembly.

15 Check the length and operation of the brushes as described in paragraphs 7 and 8, and replace them if necessary. **Note:** *When soldering the brush lead wires, position the brush so that it extends about $\frac{7}{16}$ in (11 mm) from its brush holder. Then coil the lead wire $1\frac{1}{2}$ times around the terminal groove, and solder the outside of the terminal. Be careful not to let solder adhere to the insulating tube as this could weaken and crack the tube.*

16 If the IC voltage regulator needs to be replaced, use the following procedure. **Note:** *Do not remove the regulator unless it is being replaced with a new one.*

a) Disengage the regulator from the diode assembly by removing both the rivet and the solder that attaches them. This is made easier by using a soldering gun to disconnect the stator coil lead wires from the diode assembly

b) To separate the regulator from the brush holder, remove the terminal's solder and, with a pair of pliers, take out the attaching bolts

c) When installing the new regulator, place it on the brush holder and press-fit the bolts into place by either using a hand press or by carefully tapping them in.

d) Re-solder all connections and install a new rivet. Stake the rivet following installation.

17 Reassembly of the alternator is the reverse of the disassembly procedure, heeding the special notes listed in paragraph 10.

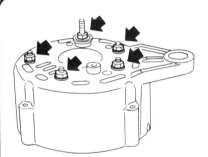

Fig. 5.18 On 1981 and 1982 models, the stator asembly is attached to the alternator rear cover by five nuts (Sec 19)

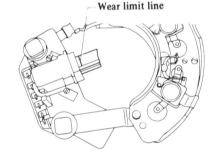

Wear limit line

Fig. 5.19 Location of the wear limit line on alternator brushes (Sec 19)

Brush lift wire

Brush lift wire

Fig. 5.20 When reassembling the alternator front and rear covers, the brushes must be retained by a stiff wire inserted thru the brush lift hole, as shown (Sec 19)

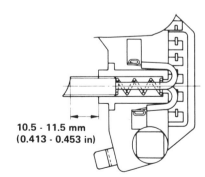

10.5 - 11.5 mm
(0.413 - 0.453 in)

Fig. 5.21 Proper soldering position for alternator brush lead wires (Sec 19)

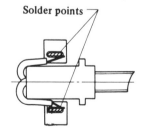

Solder points

Fig. 5.22 When installing the new alternator brush, prior to soldering, it should be positioned as shown in relationship to the brush holder (Sec 19)

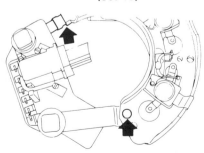

Fig. 5.23 On 1981 and 1982 models, the regulator/brush assembly is both soldered and riveted to the diode assembly (Sec 19)

Chapter 6 Emissions control and exhaust systems

Contents

Specifications

Torque specifications

	ft-lb	m-kg
Thermal vacuum valves	16 or less	2.2 or less
EAI tube attaching nuts	29	3.0
EGR tube attaching nut	29	3.0
Exhaust gas sensor	32	4.5
Catalytic converter mounting bolts	27	3.7
Front exhaust pipe-to-exhaust manifold bolts	38	5.4

1 General information

As smog standards have become more stringent, the emissions control systems developed to meet these requirements have not only become increasingly more diverse and complex, but are now designed as integral parts of the operation of the engine. Where once the anti-pollution devices used were installed as peripheral "add-on" components, the present systems work closely with such other systems as the fuel, ignition and exhaust systems, and in some cases even control vital engine operations.

Because of this close integration of systems, disconnecting or not maintaining the emissions control systems, besides being illegal, can adversely affect engine performance and life, as well as fuel economy.

This is not to say that the emissions systems are particularly difficult for the home mechanic to maintain and service. You can perform general operational checks, and do most (if not all) of the regular maintenance easily and quickly at home with common tune-up and hand tools.

While the end result from the various emissions systems is to reduce the output of pollutants into the air (namely hydrocarbons [HC], carbon monoxide [CO], and oxides of nitrogen [NOx]), the various systems function independently toward this goal. This is the way in which this Chapter is divided.

Note: *If the routing of the vacuum hoses as shown in the figures within this Chapter differs in any way from the vacuum hose routing diagram, located on the underside of the hood, the information on the diagram should take precedence over these figures.*

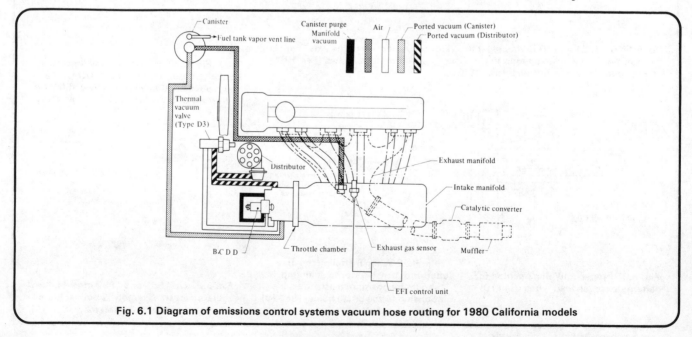

Fig. 6.1 Diagram of emissions control systems vacuum hose routing for 1980 California models

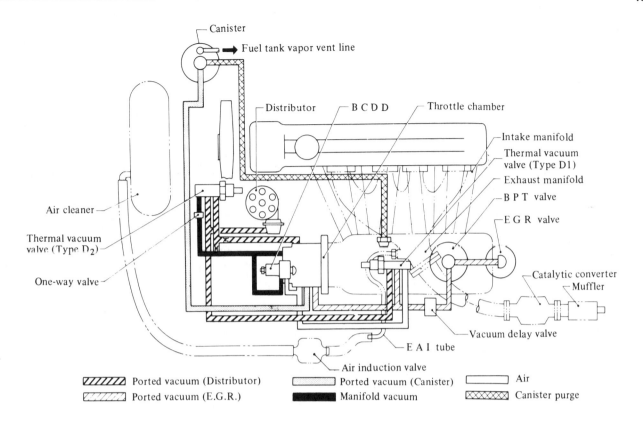

Fig. 6.2 Diagram of emissions control systems vacuum hose routing for 1980 US Federal models

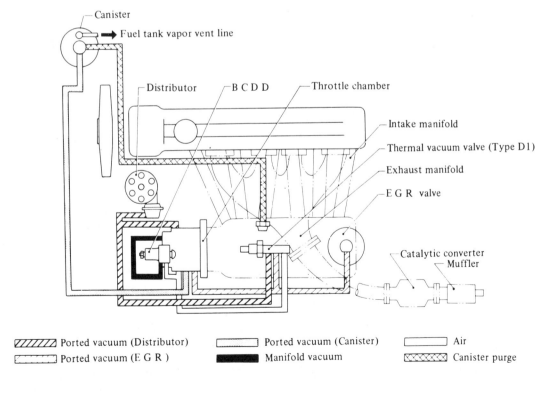

Fig. 6.3 Diagram of emissions control systems vacuum hose routing for 1980 Canada models

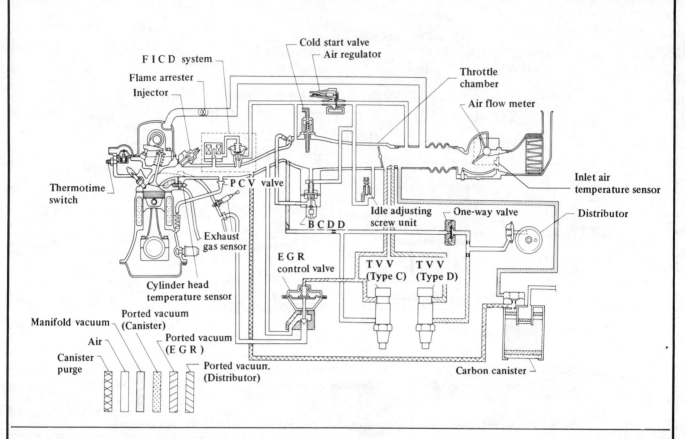

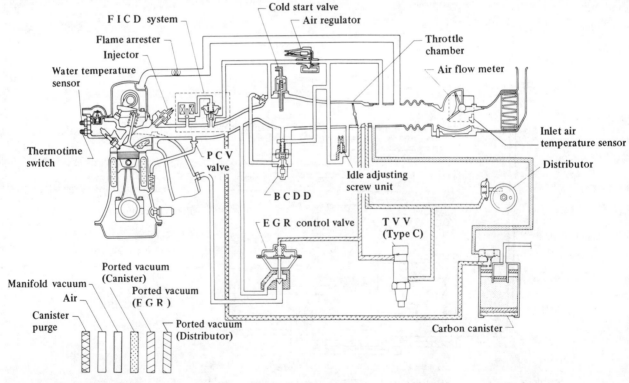

Fig. 6.4 Diagrams of emissions control systems vacuum hose routing for 1981 US (above) and Canada (below) non-turbo models

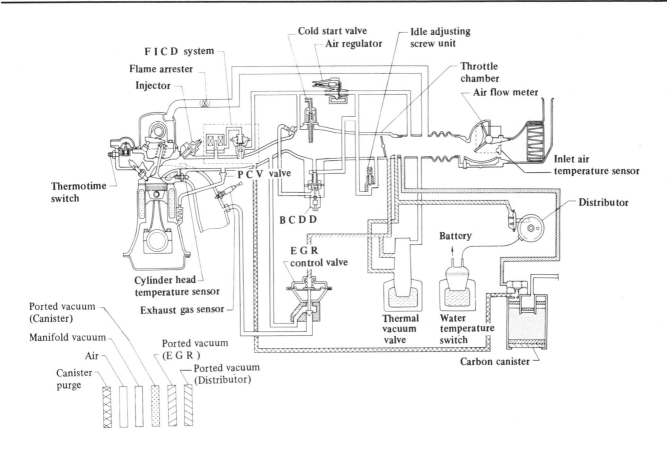

Fig. 6.5 Diagram of emissions control systems vacuum hose routing for 1982 non-turbo models

2 Positive crankcase ventilation (PCV) system

General description

The positive crankcase ventilation, or PCV, as it is more commonly called, reduces hydrocarbon emissions by circulating fresh air through the crankcase. This air combines with blow-by gases, or gases blown past the piston rings during compression, and the combination is then sucked into the intake manifold to be reburned by the engine.

This process is achieved by using one air pipe running from the air duct (suction hose on Turbo models) to the rocker arm cover, a one-way PCV valve located on the left underside of the intake manifold and a second air pipe running from the crankcase to the PCV valve.

During partial throttle operation of the engine the vacuum created in the intake manifold is great enough to suck the gases from the crankcase, through the PCV valve and into the manifold. The PCV valve allows the gases to enter the manifold, but will not allow them to pass in the other direction.

The ventilating air is drawn into the rocker arm cover from the air duct or suction hose, and then into the crankcase.

Under full-throttle operation, the vacuum in the intake manifold is not great enough to suck the gases in. Under this condition the blow-by gases flow backwards into the rocker arm cover, through the air tube and into the air duct or suction hose, where it is carried into the intake manifold in the normal air intake flow.

Positive crankcase ventilation system – checking

1   The PCV system can be checked for proper operation quickly and easily. This system should be checked regularly as carbon and gunk deposited by the blow-by gases will eventually clog the PCV valve and/or system hoses. When the flow of the PCV system is reduced or stopped, common symptoms are rough idling or a reduced engine speed at idle.

2   To check for proper vacuum in the system, disconnect the rubber air hose where it exits the air duct or suction hose.

3   With the engine idling, place your thumb lightly over the end of the hose. You should feel a slight pull of vacuum. The suction may be heard as your thumb is released. This will indicate that air is being drawn all the way through the system. If a vacuum is felt, the system is functioning properly.

4   If there is very little vacuum or none at all, at the end of the hose, the system is clogged and must be inspected further.

5   With the engine still idling, disconnect the vent tube from the PCV valve. Now place your finger over the end of the valve and feel for a suction. You should feel a relatively strong vacuum at this point. This indicates that the valve is good.

6   If no vacuum is felt at the PCV valve, remove the valve from the intake manifold. Shake it and listen for a clicking sound. That is the rattle of the valve's check needle. If the valve does not click freely, replace it.

7   If a strong vacuum is felt at the PCV valve, yet there is still no vacuum during the test described in paragraph 8, then one of the system's vent tubes is probably clogged. Both should be removed and blown out with compressed air.

8   If, after cleaning the vent tubes, there is still no suction at the air pipe, there is a blockage in an internal passage. This requires disassembly of the engine to correct.

9   When purchasing a new PCV valve, make sure it is the proper one. An incorrect PCV valve may pull too much or too little vacuum, possibly causing damage to the engine.

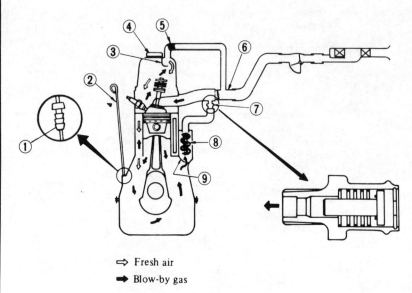

Fig. 6.6 Diagram of the PCV system (non-turbo models) (Sec 2)

1 Seal rubber
2 Oil level gauge
3 Baffle plate
4 Oil filler cap
5 Flame arrester
6 Throttle chamber
7 PCV valve
8 Steel net
9 Baffle plate

⇨ Fresh air
➡ Blow-by gas

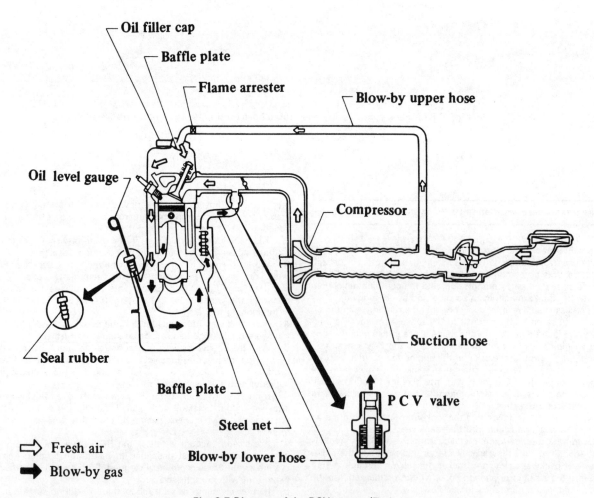

⇨ Fresh air
➡ Blow-by gas

Fig. 6.7 Diagram of the PCV system (Turbo models) (Sec 2)

3 Exhaust Gas Recirculation (EGR) system (non-turbo)

General description – overview (all models)

This system is used to reduce oxides of nitrogen (NOx) emitted from the exhaust. Formation of these pollutants takes place at very high temperatures; consequently, it occurs during the peak temperature period of the combustion process. To reduce peak temperatures, and thus the formation of NOx, a small amount of exhaust gas is taken from the exhaust system and recirculated in the combustion cycle.

Slightly different EGR systems are used in the model years 1979 thru 1982 and the differences of each are noted. There is no EGR system used on 1980 California models. Since the EGR system on Turbo models is integrated into the ECCS system, refer to Chapter 4 for these models.

In addition, within each system various EGR valves are used according to the transmission used and the altitude the car is expected to be operated at. For replacement, the EGR valve can be identified by the part number stamped on the recessed portion at the top of the valve.

Because a malfunctioning EGR system can severely affect the performance of the engine, it is important to understand how each system works in order to accurately troubleshoot it. Common engine problems associated with the EGR system are: rough idling or stalling when at an idle, rough engine performance upon light throttle application and stalling on deceleration.

General description – 1981 and 1982 models

The EGR system used in all 1981 and 1982 models is a very simple system that incorporates an EGR valve and one Thermal Vacuum Valve (TVV).

The heart of any EGR system is the EGR valve, which controls the flow of exhaust gases into the intake manifold for reburning. Under normal conditions the EGR valve is closed, which prevents the passage of exhaust gases into the intake manifold. The wax pellet type TVV is incorporated into the system to control the opening of the valve so that it will open only at the optimum time.

The direct vacuum signal that opens the valves comes from the throttle chamber venturi at the throttle valve. This vacuum signal is only great enough to open the EGR valve during mid-range throttle positions. At idle and at full throttle, the vacuum signal lessens and the EGR valve will close again.

The TVV is placed into the vacuum signal line between the throttle chamber and the EGR valve, and is designed so that it will not allow the vacuum signal to reach the EGR valve until the engine coolant temperature reaches 131°F(55°C), or normal operating temperature. This prevents the EGR system from leaning out the rich gas/air mixture needed during cold engine operation. The TVV is also designed to close again when the coolant temperature exceeds 203°F (95°C).

The EGR valve in this system, then, will operate only when the coolant is within 131° to 203°F, and then only at mid-range throttle positions.

General description – 1979 and 1980 Canada models

The EGR system used on these models operates in the same way as the system described above except that the TVV allows vacuum between the temperatures 122° to 203°F (50° to 95°C).

General description – 1979 and 1980 US models

The system used in all 1979 and 1980 US models is similar to the system just described but also incorporates a Back-Pressure Transducer (BPT) valve and a vacuum delay valve as additional controls for the opening of the EGR valve.

The Thermal Vacuum Valve (TVV) used in this system is a similar design and only allows the vacuum signal to pass when the coolant temperature is between 131° to 203°F (55° to 95°C).

The BPT valve is tapped into the vacuum signal line after the TVV, and allows an air bleed to take place in the line until it is closed. This air bleed, when present, keeps the vacuum pressure low, thus preventing the EGR valve from opening.

The BPT valve is also connected to the exhaust line running between the exhaust manifold and the EGR valve. This opens the BPT valve up to the exhaust pressure coming from the exhaust manifold. When this pressure reaches a pre-determined point, it will overcome the spring-loaded diaphragm in the BPT valve, and close off the valve.

The closing of the valve stops the air bleed in the signal line, and thus allows the vacuum signal to reach and open the EGR valve.

The vacuum delay valve is a one-way valve designed to prevent an abrupt escape of vacuum from the vacuum signal line to the EGR valve, thus increasing the length of the EGR valve operation. It allows air to pass freely toward the intake manifold, but severely limits the amount allowed to pass toward the EGR valve. **Note:** *1979 US Federal models without a catalytic converter do not utilize a vacuum delay valve.*

The conditions, then, for the EGR valve to open in this system are: 1) the engine coolant must be between 131° and 203°F, 2) the gas pressure in the exhaust manifold must be great enough to close the BPT valve, and 3) the throttle must be in a mid-range position.

EGR valve – checking

1 Locate the EGR valve at the rear of the intake manifold.
2 Place your finger under the EGR valve and push upward on the diaphragm plate. The diaphragm should move freely from the closed to the open position. If it doesn't, replace the EGR valve.
3 Now start the engine and run at idle speed. While the engine is still just beginning to warm up, with your finger, again push upward on the EGR diaphragm. If the valve or adjacent accessories are hot, wear gloves to prevent burning your fingers. When the diaphragm is pressed (valve open to recirculate exhaust), the engine should lose speed, stumble or even stall. If the engine did not change speed, the exhaust gas pipe leading to the EGR valve should be checked for blockage.
4 If equipped with a BPT valve, bypass it by connecting a hose directly between the vacuum delay valve (or TVV) and the EGR valve.
5 Now allow the engine to reach normal operating temperature. Have an assistant depress the accelerator slightly and hold the engine speed constant above idle at about 3000 rpm.
6 Pull off the vacuum signal line at the EGR valve and check that the diaphragm plate moves downward, accompanied by an increase in engine speed.
7 Reinstall the vacuum signal line to the valve and the diaphragm plate should move upward with a decrease in engine speed.
8 If the diaphragm did not move, make sure the engine was at operating temperature. Repeat the test if in doubt.
9 If the diaphragm still does not move, your next check would be that the vacuum is reaching the EGR valve. Pull off the vacuum hose at the valve, and with the engine running and accelerator slightly pressed, check for vacuum at the end of the hose with your thumb. If there is vacuum, replace the EGR valve with a new one. If there is no vacuum signal, follow the vacuum hose to its source, inspecting for any cracks, breaks or blockage in the lines. Also check that the TVV and vacuum delay valve are working properly.

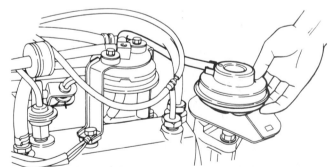

Fig. 6.8 To test the EGR valve, place your fingers under the valve and check for free movement of the diaphragm by pressing upwards on it (Sec 3)

BPT valve – checking

10 Disconnect all hoses from the BPT valve. Plug one of the upper fittings and connect a hose to the other.
11 Attempt to suck air through the hose. If air cannot be sucked through the hose, the valve is stuck closed and should be replaced.
12 Next connect a hand air pump to the fitting at the bottom of the valve.
13 While applying air pressure to the valve, again attempt to suck through the vacuum signal hose. This time you should not be able to suck air through. If you can, the valve is stuck open and should be replaced. If an air pump is not available, the same effect can be

achieved by attaching a hose, the same diameter as the one removed, to the fitting and have an assistant blow air into the valve in order to close it.

14 Before reconnecting the exhaust pressure hose to the bottom of the valve, make sure the line is not clogged by blowing air into it.

Thermal vacuum valve (TVV) – checking

15 To check for proper functioning of the thermal vacuum valve start with a cold engine. Disconnect the vacuum signal hose from the EGR valve or BPT valve, if equipped. Now start the engine and, with your thumb, feel if any vacuum is coming through the line. If vacuum is reaching the valve immediately after starting the engine, the TVV should be replaced.

16 Now wait for the engine to reach normal operating temperature (above 122°F for 1979 and 1980 models, or above 131°F for 1981 and 1982 models) and, again, feel for vacuum at the end of the hose. If no vacuum is reaching the EGR valve, first check that the hoses are not clogged. Then, if all lines are clear, replace the TVV.

17 The easiest method of testing the thermal vacuum valve is off the car. Allow the car to cool down enough so the lower TVV can be removed from the car, complete with the hoses attached to it. Once removed, attempt to suck air through the vacuum signal hose leading from the middle fitting (3-fitting type) or lower fitting (2-fitting type except 1981 models where you should use the upper fitting). While the valve is cold, the TVV on 1979 models should be closed, preventing you from drawing air through it. On all other model years, it should be open, allowing air to be drawn through. If this is not the case, replace the valve.

18 Plug the hose leading from the lower fitting on 3-fitting types and 1981 TWs. Now put the valve in a pan and submerge it in water. **Note:** *Do not submerge the top of 1981 TVVs.* Do not let the water get into the hoses or the inside of the valve. Heat the water until its temperature is above 122°F or 131°F as appropriate. Now attempt to suck air through the hose leading from the same fitting. At this point the valve should be open on 1979 TVVs or closed on all others. If the valve does not function in this manner, and the hose is not clogged or split, replace the valve. Continue to heat the water until it is over 203°F. At this temperature, the valve should return to its original operation.

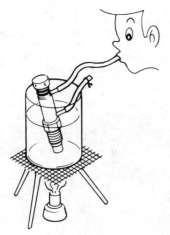

Fig. 6.9 When testing a 1981 model TVV, do not submerge the top of it in water, as it draws air in through the top (Sec 3)

EGR valve – removal and installation

19 For clearance, reposition any hoses that will be in the way of working on and removing the EGR valve. If hoses are disconnected, be sure to label them and their fittings for proper reconnection.

20 Remove the vacuum signal hose from the top of the EGR valve.

21 Remove the EGR valve heat shield, if equipped.

22 Remove the two EGR valve mounting nuts and lift off the valve.

23 Clean the mating surfaces of the EGR valve and the intake manifold, removing all traces of old gasket material.

24 Installation is the reverse of the removal procedure. **Note:** *Be sure to use a new gasket when installing the EGR valve.*

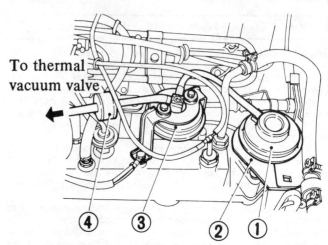

To thermal vacuum valve

Fig. 6.10 Typical components of the EGR system (1979 and 1980 models) (Sec 3)

1	EGR control valve	4	Vacuum delay valve
2	Heat shield plate		(California models)
3	BPT valve (For USA)		

BPT valve – removal and installation

25 Disconnect the vacuum signal hoses from the top of the BPT valve.

26 Remove the screws that hold the valve to its bracket, and lift off the valve.

27 Disconnect the exhaust back-pressure hose from the bottom of the valve, and remove the valve from the engine compartment.

28 Installation is the reverse of the removal procedure. **Note:** *If replacing the valve, be sure the new valve has the same type number stamped on it as the old one.*

Thermal vacuum switch – replacement

29 Drain about one liter of the engine coolant.

30 Disconnect the vacuum hoses from the switch, noting their positions for reassembly.

31 Using a suitable wrench, remove the switch.

32 When installing the switch, apply thread sealer to the threads, being careful not to allow the sealant to touch the bottom sensor.

33 Install the switch and tighten it to specifications.

---

4 Evaporative Emission Control System (EEC)

General description

The evaporative emissions control system (EEC) is designed to prevent the release of hydrocarbons in the form of fuel vapor to the outside air.

This is achieved by venting the vapor in the fuel tank to a canister filled with activated charcoal, where the vapor is stored when the engine isn't running.

On top of this canister is a purge control valve with two hoses leading from it. The thicker hose is the purge hose, and runs directly to the intake manifold while the smaller hose is the vacuum signal line. Inside the purge control valve, are two holes. One, a very small hole, is called the constant purge orifice and is always open to the intake manifold. The second hole, a larger one directly in the center of the valve, is the main purge orifice and is normally covered by the valve's diaphragm.

When the engine is started fresh air is drawn into the canister through an opening in the bottom. This fresh air picks up the stored vapors and carries them to the intake manifold. At idle, there is enough vacuum coming through the constant purge line to draw in a small amount of this air/vapor mixture through the constant purge orifice. The purge control valve, however, remains closed. As the engine speed increases, the manifold vacuum becomes great enough to open the diaphragm of the purge control valve, which allows the air/vapor mixture to be drawn in greater quantity to the intake manifold. The system used on Turbo models operates in the same manner, except that the constant purge orifice uses a separate hose which leads to the suction hose, instead of the intake manifold.

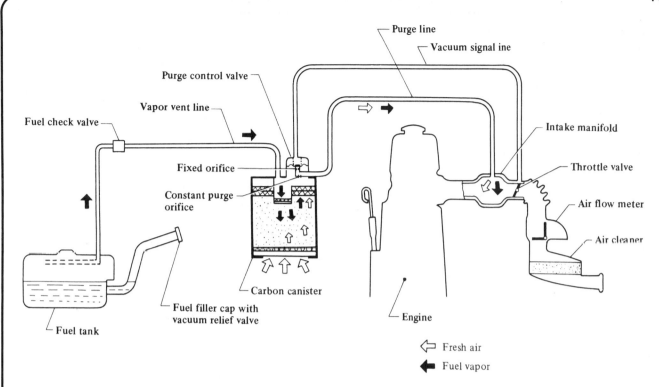

Fig. 6.11 Diagram of the evaporative emission control system (non-turbo) models (Sec 4)

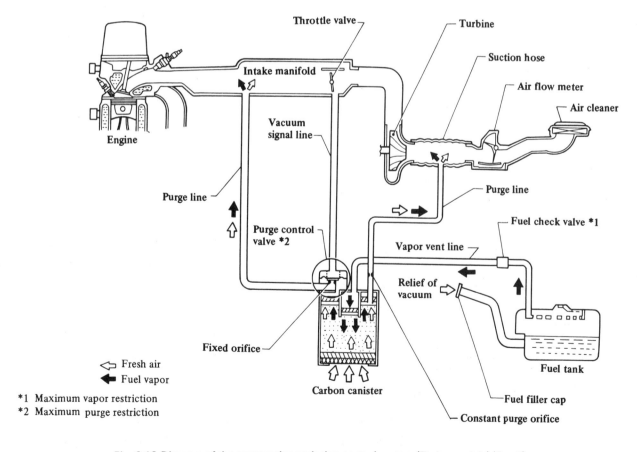

*1 Maximum vapor restriction
*2 Maximum purge restriction

Fig. 6.12 Diagram of the evaporative emission control system (Turbo models) (Sec 4)

The operation of this system depends on maintaining a sealed fuel system. Therefore, a positive sealing gas cap is used which, under normal conditions, provides only a small vent to the outside air, and will open fully only if vacuum within the fuel tank becomes too great.

A fuel check valve is located in the vent line between the fuel tank and the canister. When the engine is off, this valve allows the fuel vapor to bleed off into the canister when the pressure in the fuel tank reaches a certain level. When the engine is running, this valve allows outside air to be drawn into the tank from the canister. This effectively vents the tank so the fuel being drawn out for burning doesn't eventually cause a vacuum in the tank which restricts fuel flow.

Other than the periodic replacement of the canister air filter detailed in Chapter 1, the EEC system normally requires no periodic attention.

Checking
1   One symptom that the EEC system is not operating properly is an abnormally strong smell of gasoline around the car. Another symptom is if a vapor lock condition should occur while the engine is operating, causing the engine to stop running.
2   Begin the inspection of the system by checking the vent and vacuum lines for leaks or deterioration. Also check that the air filter in the bottom of the canister is clean. If not, replace it as described in Chapter 1.
3   To check for fuel vapor leakage at the purge control valve, follow the rubber hose leading from the valve outlet fitting to its other end and disconnect it. Attempt to lightly suck air through the hose. If you are able to suck air through the hose, then remove the top cover from the purge control valve and check for a dislocated or cracked diaphragm. If the valve is defective, a diaphragm kit can be bought and installed to correct the problem.
4   To check the constant purge orifice, follow the constant purge line down to its other end and disconnect it. Blow or inhale air through the hose to ensure that the hose and orifice are clear. If air cannot be blown through, remove the purge control valve and clear the constant purge orifice and hose if necessary.
5   Inspect the fuel tank filler cap. Wipe the valve housing clean on the underside of the cap. Suck the valve gently and a slight resistance should be felt. Suck harder and note that as the valve clicks, any resistance should disappear. Failure to operate in this way will mean a new cap must be installed.
6   Finally test the fuel check valve. Disconnect the valve and blow into the valve from the fuel tank side. A severe resistance should be felt with a proportion of air passing out of the opposite side. Now blow into the valve from the engine side. No resistance should be felt.

Purge control valve – diaphragm replacement
7   Purchase a diaphragm kit.
8   Remove the hoses from their fittings on top of the canister.
9   Release the retaining strap around the body of the canister and lift the canister out of the engine compartment.
10 Pry off the top cover of the purge control valve and lift out the spring and retainer.
11 Remove the diaphragm from the canister.
12 Install a new diaphragm making sure it is sealed correctly.
13 Replace the diaphragm spring and retainer with new ones supplied with the diaphragm kit.
14 With the new spring and retainer in place, snap the valve cover back onto the canister.
15 Reinstall the canister.
16 Reconnect the hoses, making sure they are in the proper locations.

---

5   Spark timing control system (non-turbo)

General information
The spark timing control system is designed to control the distributor vacuum advance under varying conditions, in order to help reduce HC and NOx emissions, as well as to assure stable idling and good fuel economy.

Although the basic function of the system is the same in all models, the design of the system has continually changed from one year to the next. These differences are noted in the following sub-sections.

Because the spark timing control system used in Turbo models is

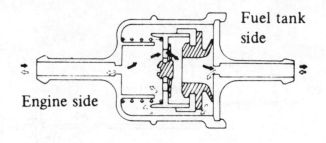

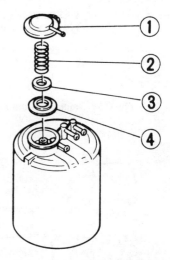

⇦ Evaporative fuel flow
⬅ Fresh air flow

Fig. 6.13 When testing the fuel check valve, blowing air through from the fuel tank side should be difficult, while from the engine side it should be easier (Sec 4)

Fig. 6.14 Components of the charcoal canister's purge control valve (Sec 4)

1 Cover	3 Retainer
2 Diaphragm spring	4 Diaphragm

integrated into the ECCS system, information for these models is included in Chapter 4.

1979
The spark timing control system used in 1979 models is an extremely simple one that uses a vacuum delay in the vacuum signal line running between the throttle chamber and the distributor's vacuum advance canister. **Note:** *This system is only used on models equipped with a catalytic converter.*

The in-line vacuum delay valve is essentially a one-way valve that restricts the flow of air toward the throttle chamber. This reduces the rate of the vacuum change reaching the distributor when the throttle valve moves to the mid-range position, thus providing the vacuum advance unit some delay time in responding.

Because of the one-way design of the valve, a decrease in vacuum at the throttle valve (at idle or full throttle) is passed along in a normal manner to the distributor, thus de-activating the advance mechanism.

1980
The system used in 1980 models uses a thermal vacuum valve (TVV) to control the actuation of the advance mechanism in relation to engine temperature. This TVV is tapped into the vacuum signal line running between the throttle valve and the distributor. When the TVV is open it allows an air bleed in the vacuum signal line which prevents

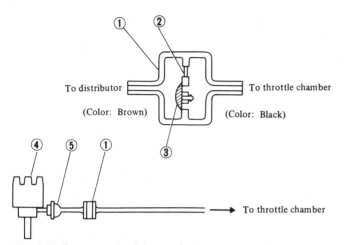

Fig. 6.15 Components of the spark timing control system (1979 models) (Sec 5)

1   Vacuum delay valve
2   Sintered metal disc
3   One-way umbrella
4   Distributor
5   Vacuum advance unit

the vacuum from advancing the timing. Only when the TVV is closed, can the vacuum reach the advance mechanism.

The opening and closing of the valve is determined by the temperature of the engine coolant. The TVV used on California models is calibrated to be closed until the coolant temperature reaches 59°F (15°C). At this point it will stay open between 59° and 140°F (60°C). Above 140°F it will close again. Therefore, the distributor is advanced while the engine is cold, in order to quickly warm up the engine. As the engine warms up, the vacuum signal is cut off, and the timing is retarded until the engine reaches its normal operating temperature, when it advances again.

In addition, since the vacuum signal is taken from the throttle valve, at idle the vacuum is not great enough to advance the distributor, so the spark timing control system does not operate at all at idle.

The system used on Canada models is basically the same as the one used on California models, except for the TVV temperature calibrations. The TVV stays closed until the coolant temperature reaches 95°F (35°C). Then it opens between 95° and 131°F (55°C). Above 131°F, the TVV will close again.

The system used on US Federal models used two TVV's and a one-way valve to regulate the advance. One TVV (type D1) as in the other systems, acts as an air bleed in the vacuum signal line and is calibrated to the same temperature as in the Canada system. The other, (type D2) is mounted in-line in the main vacuum signal line, between the distributor and the throttle chamber. A second vacuum signal line runs between the intake manifold and the D2 TVV, and has a one-way valve mounted in-line. This second line with its one-way valve assures good driveability during cold engine conditions by accumulating manifold vacuum in the line and advancing the distributor. When the coolant reaches a pre-determined temperature the D2 TVV cuts off the secondary vacuum line and opens up the main vacuum line, which operates in the same manner as the Canada system.

1981

The system used in 1981 US models is similar to the 1980 US Federal model system in that it uses two TVVs (type-C and type-D), a one-way valve and two separate vacuum signal lines, (the main one leading to the throttle chamber and the secondary one leading to the intake manifold). The type D-TVV is tapped into the secondary vacuum line, which also contains the one-way valve.

When the engine coolant temperature is below 95°F (35°C), both TVVs are closed, allowing only manifold vacuum, passing through the secondary line to reach the distributor. The one-way valve accumulates the vacuum in the line, causing the distributor to advance (even during idling). As the coolant temperature rises to between 95° and 131°F (55°C), the type-C TVV opens allowing an air bleed in the

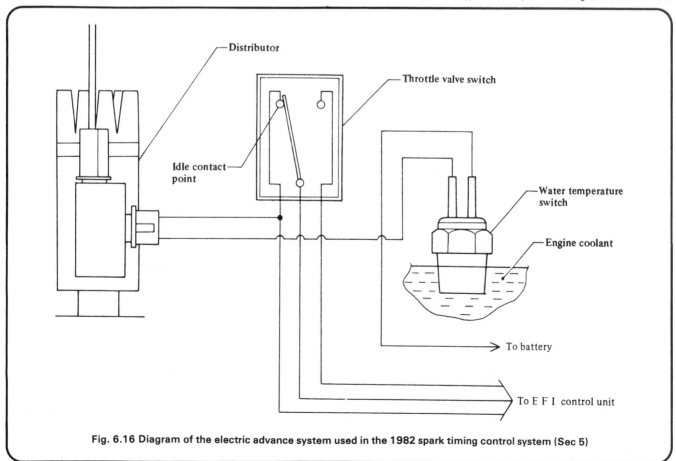

Fig. 6.16 Diagram of the electric advance system used in the 1982 spark timing control system (Sec 5)

secondary line, which cuts off any vacuum signal to the distributor. When the temperature rises above 131°F (normal operating temperature), the type-D TVV opens the main vacuum line, allowing the distributor to advance during mid-range throttle application. At the same time, the type-C TVV closes again allowing the secondary line to pass manifold vacuum during the idling conditions.

The system used in 1981 Canada models is virtually the same as that used in 1980 Canada models.

1982

On 1982 models, two separate systems are used to control the distributor's advance. One is a normal vacuum operated system, and the other is an electric advance system.

The vacuum advance system uses one thermal vacuum valve (TVV) which is tapped into the vacuum signal line running between the distributor and throttle chamber. When the engine coolant is below 131°F (55°C) the TVV remains open, allowing an air bleed in the vacuum signal line and, thus, preventing the vacuum from reaching the distributor. When the engine warms up to over 131°F, the TVV closes off the air bleed, and allows the vacuum signal to reach the distributor.

The electric advance, although working in conjunction with the vacuum system, is totally separate. This system incorporates a water temperature switch which senses engine coolant and an idle contact point switch located in the throttle valve switch, which turns on only when the throttle valve is in the idle position.

This system electrically advances the ignition timing whenever either one or both of these switches are turned on. Since the water temperature switch is only on when the engine coolant is below 95°F (35°C), the timing is, therefore, electrically advanced both during cold engine operation and whenever the car is idling. When the car is being driven at normal operating temperature, the vacuum system takes over control of the ignition timing.

Checking
1979

1 Remove the vacuum delay valve from the vacuum signal line leading to the distributor.
2 Blow air through the valve from the throttle chamber (black) side. If the air flows through without restriction, the valve is normal. If not, it needs to be replaced.
3 Next, attempt to blow air through it from the distributor (brown) side. If there is greater resistance than in the previous step (some air should escape the opposite side), the valve is in good condition. If not, replace it. **Note:** *When installing the valve into the vacuum line, be sure the brown side is toward the distributor.*

1980 and 1981

4 Begin any check of this system by inspecting all lines and hoses, making sure they are properly connected and there are no leaks or cracks.
5 Next the advance mechanism inside the distributor should be checked to be sure it is operating correctly. To do this, first remove the distributor cap so that the rotation of the timing plate can be observed. Next disconnect the vacuum line from the distributor, and connect a vacuum pump to the fitting. Apply vacuum to the distributor and watch that the timing plate rotates inside. If the timing plate does not rotate, then there is a fault with the advance mechanism which must be corrected (refer to Chapter 5). If a vacuum pump is not handy, the same effect can be achieved by attaching a long rubber hose (the same diameter as the vacuum hose removed) to the fitting and sucking through it.
6 Reconnect the vacuum line to the distributor and reinstall the distributor cap.
7 Hook up a timing light according to the manufacturer's instructions. With the engine cold, start the engine and have an assistant apply throttle to keep the engine running at about 2000 rpm (1981 US models can be left at idle). Immediately check the spark timing with the timing light. The needle in the coolant temperature gauge should be on the C. The system should be actuated and the timing should be advanced from its normal setting (Chapter 1 Specifications).
8 Continue to run the engine at around 2000 rpm and observe the spark timing while the engine warms up. You may wish to adjust the idle speed screw to maintain this engine speed. The timing should retard as the engine begins to warm up.
9 By the time the engine approaches normal operating temperature (the needle in the middle of the gauge), the spark timing should have

advanced again. If this sequence does not take place, the TVVs are suspect and should be replaced.
10 The procedure for removing and installing TVVs is described in Section 3.

1982

11 When checking the spark timing advance system on 1982 models, the vacuum and electric actuating systems should be tested individually.
12 To test the vacuum advance system use the following procedure:

   a) Begin any check of this system by inspecting all lines and hoses, making sure they are properly connected and there are no leaks or cracks.
   b) Next the advance mechanism inside the distributor should be checked to be sure it is operating correctly. To do this, first remove the distributor cap so that the rotation of the timing plate can be observed. Next disconnect the vacuum line from the distributor, and connect a vacuum pump to the fitting. Apply vacuum to the distributor and watch that the timing plate rotates inside. If the timing plate does not rotate, then there is a fault with the advance mechanism which must be corrected (refer to Chapter 5). If a vacuum pump is not handy, the same effect can be achieved by attaching a long rubber hose (the same diameter as the vacuum hose removed) to the fitting and sucking through it.
   c) Reconnect the vacuum line to the distributor and reinstall the distributor cap.
   d) Disconnect the wiring connector (grey) from the distributor IC unit.
   e) Hook up a timing light according to the manufacturer's instructions. With the engine cold, start the engine and have an assistant apply throttle to keep the engine running at about 2000 rpm. Immediately check the spark timing with the timing light. The needle in the coolant temperature should be on the C. The system should not be actuated and the timing should be at its normal setting (Chapter 1 Specifications).
   f) By the time the engine approaches normal operating temperature (the needle in the middle of the gauge), the spark timing should have advanced from its normal setting. If this does not take place, the TVV is suspect and should be replaced.

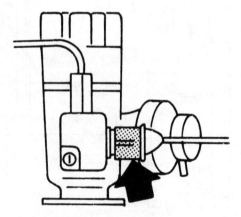

Fig. 6.17 Location of the electric advance system wiring connector at the distributor IC unit (Sec 5)

13 To test the electric advance system, use the following procedure:
   a) Disconnect the vacuum hose from the distributor vacuum advance canister and plug it.
   b) Check that all wiring connectors are clean and securely connected to their proper connectors.
   c) With the engine cold, connect a timing light according to the manufacturer's instructions.
   d) Disconnect the wiring connector from the throttle valve

switch and using a lead (jumper) wire with male spade terminals at both ends, connect the number 24 and 30 terminals of the throttle valve switch connector (Fig. 6.18).

e) Start the engine, and immediately note the location of the timing marks. Then shut off the engine again.

f) Remove the lead wire from the throttle valve switch connector. Then start the engine again and recheck the timing. The timing marks should not have changed from their positions in the last step.

g) Allow the engine to reach normal operating temperature (the needle in the middle of the temperature gauge), and recheck the timing. Now it should be retarded from its previous position.

h) Stop the engine once more and reconnect the throttle valve wiring connector. Again, start the engine and check the timing. Now it should be advanced once again to its original position.

i) If the electric timing system does not react in the manner described above, the throttle valve switch and water temperature switch should be tested individually to determine where the fault lies. Refer to Chapter 4 for testing of the throttle valve switch.

Water temperature switch – testing (1982)

14 Drain about one liter of coolant from the radiator.

15 Disconnect the wiring leading to the water temperature switch.

16 Using an appropriate wrench, remove the switch from the engine.

17 With a continuity tester connected to the switch terminals, dip the sensor portion of the switch into a pan of water at a temperature below 95°F (35°C). The switch should show continuity.

18 Heat the water until its temperature is above 95°F and again test the switch. This time there should be no continuity through it.

19 If the switch does not respond as described above, it must be replaced.

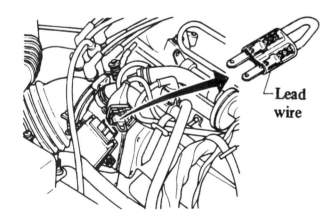

Fig. 6.18 When testing the electric advance system, a jumper lead wire must be used to connect the number 24 and number 30 terminals of the throttle valve switch connector (Sec 5)

6 Boost controlled deceleration device (BCDD)

This device is designed to reduce emission of hydrocarbons during periods when the car is coasting. The unit is installed under the intake manifold and supplies extra air to the intake manifold in order to maintain the manifold vacuum at its correct operating pressure.

The unit incorporates two diaphragms, one to monitor the manifold vacuum and open the vacuum control valve, and the second to operate the air control valve according to the degree of vacuum transmitted through the vacuum control valve.

Operating pressure variations due to differences in operating altitudes are taken into account. The system used in 1979 models incorporates a vacuum control solenoid valve, which is linked to the transmission inhibitor switch on automatic transmission models, and to a speed detecting switch in the speedometer on manual transmission models.

The BCDD is easily removed by unscrewing the three mounting screws (marked '1' in Fig. 6.19), and lifting it off. The BCDD is not designed to be disassembled. If defective it must be replaced as a unit.

Although the BCDD is designed to be adjusted, this is not a routine operation and normally will be required only when a new unit is being installed. Because of the critical nature of this operation, this should be performed by a Datsun dealer or other qualified mechanic. separate them.

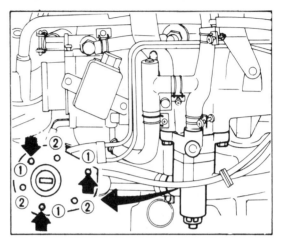

Fig. 6.19 Location of the three BCDD mounting screws (labelled 'I') (Sec 6)

7 Mixture ratio feedback system – general description

The mixture ratio feedback system is designed to increase the efficiency of the catalytic converter, by monitoring and adjusting the fuel/air mixture ratio being burned.

The principal components of this system are an exhaust gas sensor located in the exhaust manifold and an electronic control unit which is tied into the fuel injection system.

The operation of the catalytic converter is most efficient at a specific mixture ratio. The exhaust gas sensor measures the amount of oxygen present in the exhaust and relays this information to the electronic control unit. The control unit then adjusts the injection pulse width to obtain the optimum mixture ratio.

Due to the complexity of this system and its relationship with the fuel injection system, it is difficult for the home mechanic to properly diagnose and troubleshoot it. One simple check of proper functioning of the system is the one used to check the exhaust gas sensor, described in Chapter 1. If this check shows a fault or if there are other indications that the system is malfunctioning, take the car to a Datsun dealer or other qualified mechanic to have the system checked out.

8 Air induction system (AIS) (1980 US Federal only)

General description

The purpose of the AIS system is to reduce hydrocarbons in the exhaust by drawing fresh air directly into the exhaust manifold. The fresh, oxygen-rich air helps burn the remaining hydrocarbons burn before they are expelled as exhaust.

The components of this simple system include an air filter and a one-way reed valve, both of which are located in a case located near the ignition coil, a metal EAI pipe running between the valve case and the exhaust manifold, and rubber hoses connecting the valve case with the EAI pipe and air cleaner.

The opening and closing of the exhaust valves creates vacuum pulses which draw in fresh air through the filter and valve assembly. The reed valve only admits air to be drawn into the manifold, and prevents exhaust back-pressure from forcing the gases back out.

Checking

1 The simplicity of the system makes it a very reliable one which seldom causes problems. Periodic checks should be made, however, of the condition of the components to be sure there are no leaks or cracks in the system.

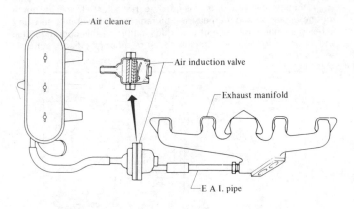

Fig. 6.20 Components of the air induction system (Sec 8)

2   Two simple functional tests can be performed to ensure that the system is operating properly. Disconnect the rubber hose from the metal EAI tube. For the first test, attempt to suck air through the rubber hose, and then attempt to blow air through the hose. The reed valve should allow you to suck air through the hose but prevent you from blowing it back through. If you are able to blow air through the hose then the valve is defective and should be replaced. If you are not able to suck air in, then check for a clogged air filter or hose. If this is not the case, then replace the valve.
3   For the second test, start the engine and allow it to idle. With the engine idling hold your hand over the open end of the metal EAI tube. There should be a steady stream of air being sucked into it. Have an assistant apply throttle and as the engine gains speed the suction should increase. If this does not happen, either there are leaks or blockage in the tube.

Air induction valve and valve case filter – removal and installation
4   Refer to Chapter 1.

EAI tubes – removal and installation
5   Disconnect the rubber hose from the EAI tube.
6   Unscrew the nut that attaches each tube to the exhaust manifold. Due to the high temperature in this area, these nuts may be difficult to loosen. Penetrating oil applied to the threads of these nuts may help.
7   Remove the screw that attaches the EAI tube brackets to the engine and lift the tube off.
8   Before installing, apply a coat of anti-seize compound to the threads of the large end nuts.
9   Installation is the reverse of the removal procedure.

9   Deceleration control system (1981 Turbo only)

General description
The deceleration control system is designed to prevent backfiring in the exhaust system and excessive oil consumption during deceleration.
The only operating component in the system is a vacuum control valve (VCV) attached to the intake manifold. When, during deceleration, the vacuum in the intake manifold reaches a specified value, the VCV will open, admitting outside air to the intake manifold, thus reducing the vacuum.

Vacuum control valve (VCV) – checking
1   To check the operation of the vacuum control valve. Disconnect the opposite ends of the rubber hose running from the VCV, from its fitting at the air regulator.
2   Allow the engine to idle and/or place your finger over the end of the hose. There should be no air being drawn in through the hose at this time. If there is, then the valve is stuck open and should be replaced.
3   Next have an assistant rev the engine to about 4000 rpm for a few moments, and then quickly let off the throttle. You should feel air being drawn into the hose immediately following the let-up on the throttle.
4   If no air was being drawn in during the moments of deceleration, check that the hose is not clogged or leaking. If the hose is okay, then the VCV should be replaced.
5   **Note:** *This method of testing the VCV is not accurate at an altitude of 2300 to 4000 feet (700 to 1200 meters) and above, due to the fact that intake manifold vacuum often will not reach the value necessary to open the VCV.*

Vacuum control valve (VCV) – removal and installation
6   Disconnect the rubber hose from the VCV.
7   Unscrew the VCV from the intake manifold.
8   Prior to installation, wrap the threads of the VCV with teflon tape.
9   Screw the VCV into the intake manifold and reconnect the rubber hose to it.

10   Catalytic converter and exhaust system

General information
The exhaust system consists of the muffler, catalytic converter and exhaust pipes and includes three main pieces: the front exhaust pipe which attaches to the exhaust manifold, the catalytic converter and the intermediate pipe-muffler-tailpipe assembly.
The catalytic converter is attached to both the front exhaust pipe and the intermediate pipe by mounting bolts. The muffler, on the other hand, is welded to the intermediate pipe and the tailpipe.
The interior of the catalytic converter is a honeycomb-like design that is coated with platinum and rhomium. When these elements interact with the hydrocarbon (HC), carbon monoxide (CO) and oxides of nitrogen (NOx) in the exhaust, it causes reactions to occur that convert the CO to CO_2 (carbon dioxide), the HC to H_2O (water), and reduces the NOx.
The mixture ratio feedback system aids the converter by keeping the fuel/air mixture at the optimum ratio for the conversions to take place.
Since lead and phosphorus additives in gasoline can poison the converter's catalytic elements, thus rendering it ineffective in altering the gases' toxic elements, only unleaded fuel should be used in the vehicle.
Periodic maintenance of the converter is not required but it has limited working life after which it must be replaced. This is usually intervals of around 30 000 miles (48 000 km).
In order to accurately test the functioning of the converter, a CO tester is needed. For this reason, we recommend you take the car to a Datsun dealer or other qualified shop to have the converter tested.
If, through physical damage, the use of leaded fuels or because its active elements have been depleted, the catalytic concerter is rendered ineffective, it must be replaced as a unit.
Caution: *It should be noted that since the internal chemical conversions occur between 600° and 1200°F, the converter operates at a very high temperature. Before performing any work on or near the converter, be sure it has cooled sufficiently to avoid serious burns.*
When replacing any exhaust system parts, be sure you allow enough clearance from all points on the underbody to avoid overheating the floor pan and possibly damaging the interior carpet and insulation.
The entire exhaust system is attached to the body with mounting brackets and mounting rubbers. If any one of the parts are improperly installed, excessive noise and vibration will be transmitted to the body.
Regular inspection of the exhaust system should be made to keep it at maximum efficiency. Look for any damage or mispositioned parts, open seams, holes, loose connections, excessive corrosion or other defects which could allow exhaust fumes to seep into the car.

Exhaust system inspection
1   Because inspection of the exhaust system is part of the *Routine maintenance* schedule, refer to Chapter 1 for this procedure.

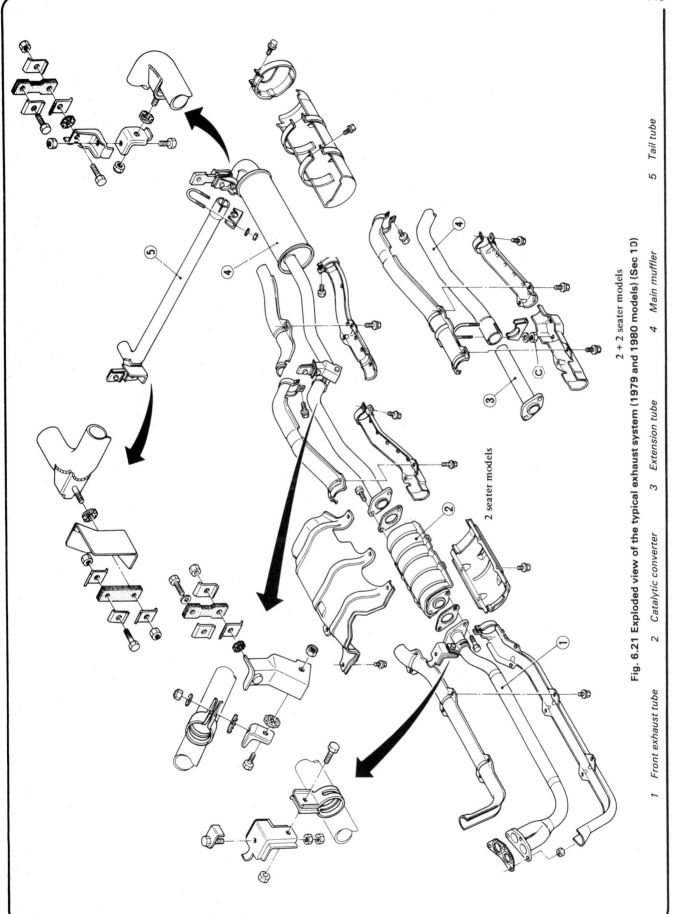

Fig. 6.21 Exploded view of the typical exhaust system (1979 and 1980 models) (Sec 10)

2 + 2 seater models

2 seater models

1   Front exhaust tube
2   Catalytic converter
3   Extension tube
4   Main muffler
5   Tail tube

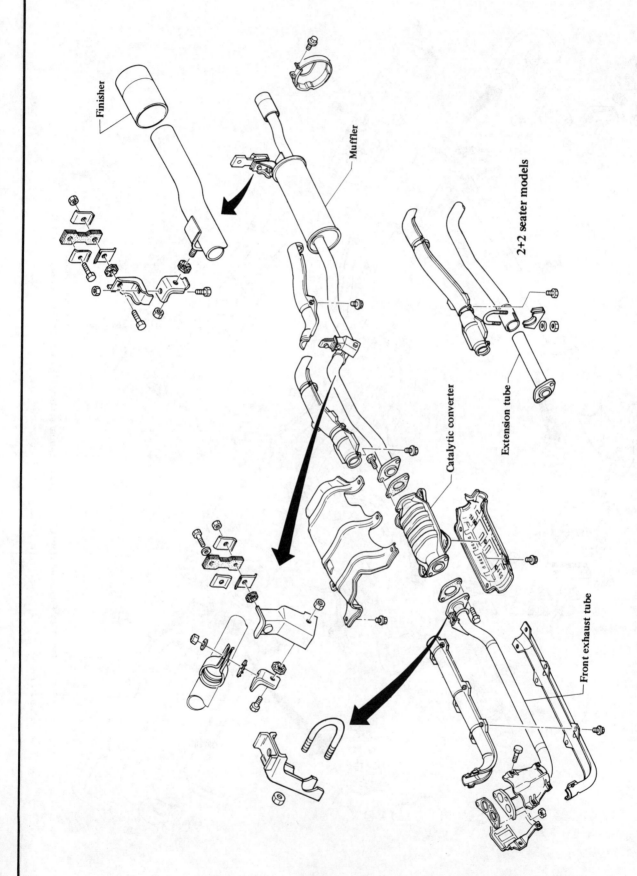

Finisher

Muffler

2+2 seater models

Catalytic converter

Extension tube

Front exhaust tube

Fig. 6.22 Exploded view of the typical exhaust system (1981 and 1982 non-turbo models) (Sec 10)

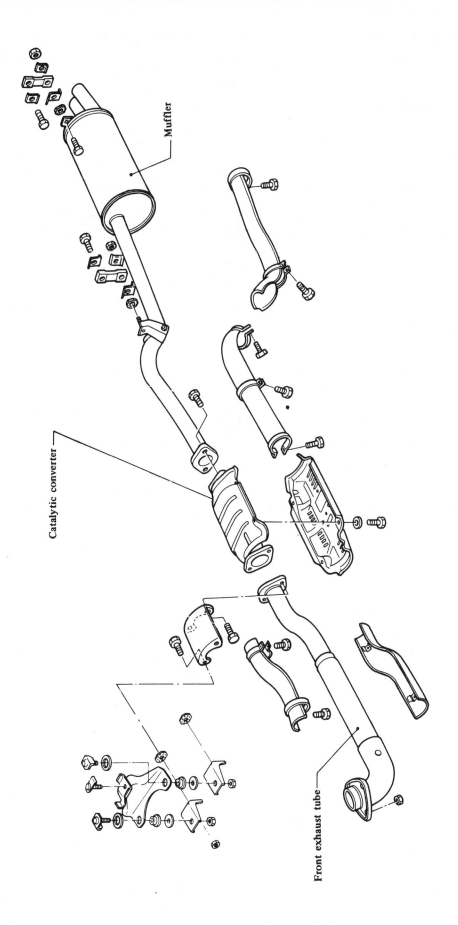

Muffler

Catalytic converter

Front exhaust tube

Fig. 6.23 Exploded view of the typical exhaust system (Turbo models) (Sec 10)

Front exhaust pipe – removal and installation

2 Raise the front of the car and support it on jackstands.
3 Remove the lower catalytic converter shield.
4 Using a piece of thick wire, secure the catalytic converter to the underside of the car.
5 If equipped, remove the lower exhaust pipe shield. Also disconnect any brackets that attach the front exhaust pipe to the transmission or body.
6 Loosen, but do not remove the two bolts attaching the front exhaust pipe to the catalytic converter. If the bolts are corroded and cannot be easily broken loose, penetrating oil and tapping with a plastic-head hammer may help.
7 Remove the bolts that attach the front exhaust pipe to the exhaust manifold. Again, penetrating oil and tapping may be necessary.
8 Now, while supporting the front exhaust pipe, remove the two bolts holding the pipe to the converter and lift out the pipe.
9 Installation is the reverse of the removal procedure. **Note**: *Be sure to use new gaskets between the front exhaust pipe and the exhaust manifold, and the front exhaust pipe and the catalytic converter. Also, before installing the bolts that attach these parts, apply an anti-sieze compound to the threads.*

Catalytic converter – removal and installation

10 Raise the front of the car and support it on jackstands.
11 Remove the lower catalytic converter shield.
12 Using a piece of strong wire, secure the intermediate exhaust pipe to the driveshaft.
13 While supporting the catalytic converter, break loose, but do not yet remove the four converter mounting bolts that attach the converter to the front and intermediate exhaust pipes. If the bolts are corroded and cannot be easily broken loose, penetrating oil and tapping with a plastic headed hammer may help.
14 While supporting the catalytic converter, remove all four mounting bolts, and remove the converter from the car.
15 Installation is the reverse of the removal procedure. **Note**: *Be sure to use new gaskets during installation. Also, before installing the mounting bolts, apply an anti-seize compound to the threads.*

Pre-muffler – removal and installation

16 A pre-muffler is used on certain 1979 models that are not equipped with a catalytic converter. It is mounted in the same place as the converter.
17 To remove, first raise the front of the car and support it on jackstands.
18 Using a piece of strong wire, secure the front exhaust pipe to the underside of the car.
19 Remove the bolts attaching the pre-muffler to the front pipe. If these are difficult to break loose, refer to the above sub-section.
20 Remove the U-bolt and clamp attaching the pre-muffler to the intermediate pipe.
21 Tap the pre-muffler forward with a rubber hammer, and remove it.
22 Installation is the reverse of the removal procedure, using new gaskets and an anti-seize compound on the mounting bolt threads.

Muffler assembly – removal and installation

23 On 1979 and 1980 models, remove the tailpipe.
24 On 1981 and 1982 models, the muffler is welded onto both the rear intermediate pipe and the tailpipe, and the entire assembly is designed to be replaced as a unit. However, if the muffler needs replacing but the tail or intermediate pipe is in good condition, a muffler shop will be able to cut off the old muffler and weld on a new one without having to replace the pipes as well. If you wish to replace the entire section as one piece, access to a hydraulic lift is needed for clearance reasons. If a hydraulic lift is not available and the assembly is to be replaced, the intermediate pipe can be cut just behind the suspension member.
25 Raise the car as needed and securely support it.
26 Remove the rear crossmember.
27 Wire the catalytic converter (or pre-muffler) to the underside of the car. Then remove the bolts attaching it to the intermediate pipe.
28 On 2 + 2 models, if the extension tube is not to be replaced, it should be removed at this time.
29 Remove any heat shields around the muffler and rear pipe assembly.
30 Remove the nuts attaching the assembly to the mounting brackets, then lower it from the car and remove it.
31 Installation is the reverse of the removal procedure. **Note**: *Before installing the bolts that attach the converter to the intermediate pipe, apply an anti-seize compound to the threads.*

Extension tube removal and installation

32 An extension tube is used to connect the catalytic converter with the rear intermediate pipe on 2 + 2 models.
33 To remove it, first raise the rear of the car and support it on jackstands.
34 Remove the catalytic converter.
35 If equipped, remove the heat shields from around the intermediate pipe.
36 Remove the U-bolt and clamp that attaches the extension tube to the intermediate pipe.
37 Lightly tap around the connection with a hammer to break it loose.
38 The extension tube can now be removed by twisting it and pulling it outward.
39 Installation is the reverse of the removal procedure. **Note**: *Before installing the bolts that attach the extension tube to the converter, apply an anti-seize compound to the threads.*

Tailpipe – removal and installation

40 Raise the rear of the car and support it on jackstands.
41 Remove the nut attaching the tailpipe to the mounting bracket.
42 Remove the U-bolt and clamp that secures the tailpipe to the muffler assembly.
43 Lightly tap around the connection with a hammer to break it loose.
44 The tailpipe can now be removed by twisting and pulling outward.
45 Installation is the reverse of the removal procedure.

Chapter 7 Part A: Manual transmission

Contents

Specifications

Model
5-speed FS5W17B
4-speed (1979 only) F4W71B

Synchromesh type
5-speed .... Warner (1st to 4th) Servo (5th)
4-speed .... Warner

Gear ratios

	1979	1980	1981 and 1982
5-speed			
1st	3.321	3.062	3.062
2nd	2.077	1.858	1.858
3rd	1.308	1.308	1.308
4th	1.000	1.000	1.000
5th	0.864	0.773	0.745
Reverse	3.382	3.026	3.026
4-speed			
1st	3.321		
2nd	2.077		
3rd	1.308		
4th	1.000		
Reverse	3.382		

Final gear ratio
1979 models
  2-seater GL models 3.700
  All other models 3.364
1980 thru 1982 models
  2-seater GL and all 2 + 2 models 3.900
  2-seater Deluxe models 3.545

Speedometer gear ratio
1979 models
  2-seater GL models 18/6
  All other models 16/6
1980 thru 1982 models
  2-seater GL and all 2 + 2 models 19/6
  2-seater Deluxe models 17/6

Gear end play

	in	(mm)
1st main gear	0.0106 to 0.0134	(0.27 to 0.34)
2nd main gear	0.0047 to 0.0075	(0.12 to 0.19)
3rd main gear	0.0051 to 0.0146	(0.13 to 0.37)
5th main gear (5-speed only)	0.0039 to 0.0067	(0.10 to 0.17)
Reverse idler gear (5-speed only)	0.0020 to 0.0197	(0.05 to 0.50)
Reverse counter gear (4-speed only)	less than 0.0079	(0.20)

Baulk ring/gear clearance

	in	(mm)
Standard	0.0472 to 0.0630	(1.20 to 1.60)
Wear limit	0.031	(0.08)

Snap-ring sizes

	in	(mm)
Main drive gear bearing	0.0681	(1.73)
	0.0709	(1.80)
	0.0736	(1.87)
	0.0764	(1.94)
	0.0792	(2.01)
	0.0819	(2.08)
Mainshaft front	0.055	(1.4)
	0.059	(1.5)
	0.063	(1.6)
Mainshaft rear end bearing (5-speed only)	0.043	(1.1)
	0.047	(1.2)
	0.051	(1.3)
	0.055	(1.4)
Counter drive gear	0.055	(1.4)
	0.059	(1.5)
	0.063	(1.6)
Counter reverse gear (4-speed only)	0.055	(1.4)
	0.059	(1.5)
	0.063	(1.6)

Oil capacity

5-speed	$4\frac{1}{4}$ pt (2.0 liters) ($3\frac{1}{2}$ Imp pt)
4-speed	$3\frac{5}{8}$ pt (1.7 liters) (3 Imp pt)

Torque specifications

	ft-lb	m-kg
Transmission-to-engine bolts	37	5.2
Clutch operating cylinder mounting bolts	26	3.6
Transmission mounting bracket-to-body bolts	27	3.7
Rear mounting insulator attaching bolts	27	3.7
Gusset attaching bolts	22	3.1
Rear extension attaching bolts	131.8	18.5
Starter motor mounting bolts	25	3.5
Bearing retainer-to-adapter plate bolts	15	2.0
Mainshaft locknut	112	15.5
Counter gear locknut	83	11.5
Front cover attaching bolts	14	1.9
Filler plug	22	3.0
Drain plug	22	3.0
Ball pin	20	2.8
Striking lever locknut	7.6	1.0
Check ball plug	16	2.2
Electrical switches	18	2.5

1 General information

The 5-speed manual transmission offered with the ZX models 1979 through 1982 is of the five forward speed and one reverse type. A 4-speed manual transmission was also available only in 1979, and had four forward and one reverse gear. Both types of transmissions have synchromesh on all forward gears. The forward gears are of a helical formation, and the reverse gear a sliding mesh type using spur gears.

The main driveshaft gear is meshed with the counter drivegear. The forward speed gears on the countershaft are in constant mesh with the main gears. Each of the main gears rides on the mainshaft on needle roller bearings, rotating freely.

When the shift lever is operated, the relevant coupling sleeve is caused to slide on the synchronizer hub and engages its inner teeth with the outer teeth formed on the mainshaft gear. The synchronizer hub is splined to the mainshaft so enabling the parts to rotate in unison. Moving the gearchange lever to the Reverse gear position moves the mainshaft reverse gear into engagement with the reverse idler gear.

The gear selector mechanism is controlled from a floor-mounted lever. Movement of the lever is transferred through a striking rod to dogs on the ends of the selector rods, and then through the medium of shift forks which are permanently engaged in the grooves of the synchro unit sleeves.

The 5-speed transmission used in the 1979/1980 models and the 1981/1982 models are identical with the exception of the design of the overdrive/reverse gear synchronizer assembly. Refer to the appropriate exploded diagram for your model.

2 Rear oil seal – replacement

1   Remove the driveshaft as described in Chapter 8.
2   Being careful not to damage the output shaft of the transmission housing, use a screwdriver to pry out the old seal (photo).
3   Apply a coat of gear oil to the lips of the new seal and drive it into place using an appropriate sized socket.
4   Reinstall the driveshaft.

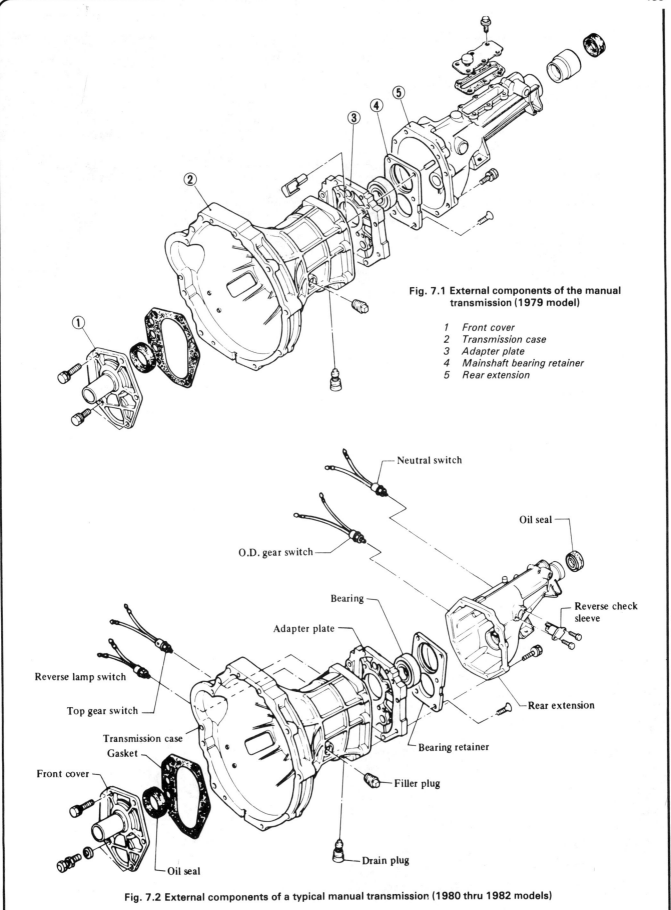

Fig. 7.1 External components of the manual transmission (1979 model)

1   Front cover
2   Transmission case
3   Adapter plate
4   Mainshaft bearing retainer
5   Rear extension

Neutral switch

Oil seal

O.D. gear switch

Reverse check sleeve

Bearing

Adapter plate

Reverse lamp switch

Rear extension

Top gear switch

Bearing retainer

Transmission case

Gasket

Filler plug

Front cover

Drain plug

Oil seal

Fig. 7.2 External components of a typical manual transmission (1980 thru 1982 models)

2.2 The rear oil seal can be removed with the transmission still in the vehicle

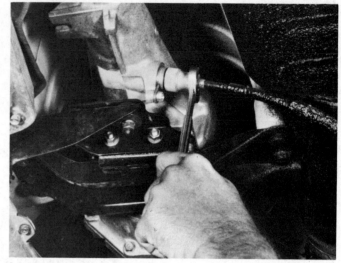

3.9 Disconnecting the speedometer cable from the manual transmission

3 Removal and installation

1   Disconnect the negative battery cable.
2   Working inside the car, disconnect the accelerator linkage
3   Remove the console as described in Chapter 12.
4   Remove the rubber boot from the shift lever
5   Place the shifter in the Neutral position. Then remove the E-ring and pin and lift out the shifter.
6   Jack up the car and safely support its weight on suitable blocks or stands. Be sure the car is high enough that the transmission can be slid out from underneath when removed.
7   Remove the front exhaust pipe.
8   Disconnect the wires from the back-up light switch, the top gear switch, the neutral switch and/or the overdrive switch, as equipped.
9   Disconnect the speedometer cable (photo).
10   Drain the oil from the transmission.
11   Remove the heat shield plate.
12   Remove the driveshaft, as described in Chapter 8. As this is done, plug up or cover over the opening at the rear of the transmission to prevent leakage of oil.
13   Unbolt and remove the clutch operating cylinder and tie it back out of the way. There is no need to disconnect the hydraulic line. (Further information can be found in Chapter 8).

14   Remove the exhaust pipe support bracket from the transmission mount.
15   Support the engine under the oil pan using a suitable jack and a block of wood as an insulator.
16   Place a second jack under the transmission.
17   Undo and remove the transmission mounting insulator securing nuts and the mounting-to-frame bolts.
18   Remove the starter motor from the bellhousing.
19   Unscrew and remove the bolts which secure the clutch bellhousing to the engine crankcase (photo).
20   Lower each of the two jacks simultaneously, until the transmission can be withdrawn to the rear and removed from beneath the vehicle. Do not allow the weight of the transmission to hang upon the input shaft while it is engaged with the splines of the clutch driven plate.
21   For details on repairing or overhauling a manual transmission, refer to Section 4 or 5, as appropriate.
22   Installation is a reversal of removal but smear a trace of grease on the input shaft splines and check if the clutch mechanism has been aligned as described in Chapter 8.
23   Check the clutch pedal free-travel and adjust if necessary (Chapter 1) and remember to fill the transmission with the correct grade and quantity of oil.

3.18 The transmission should be well supported prior to removing the clutch housing-to-engine bolts

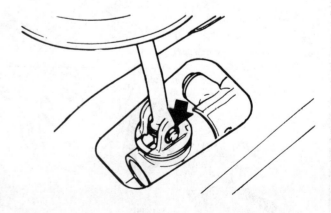

Fig. 7.3 Location of the shift lever retaining pin (arrow) (Sec 3)

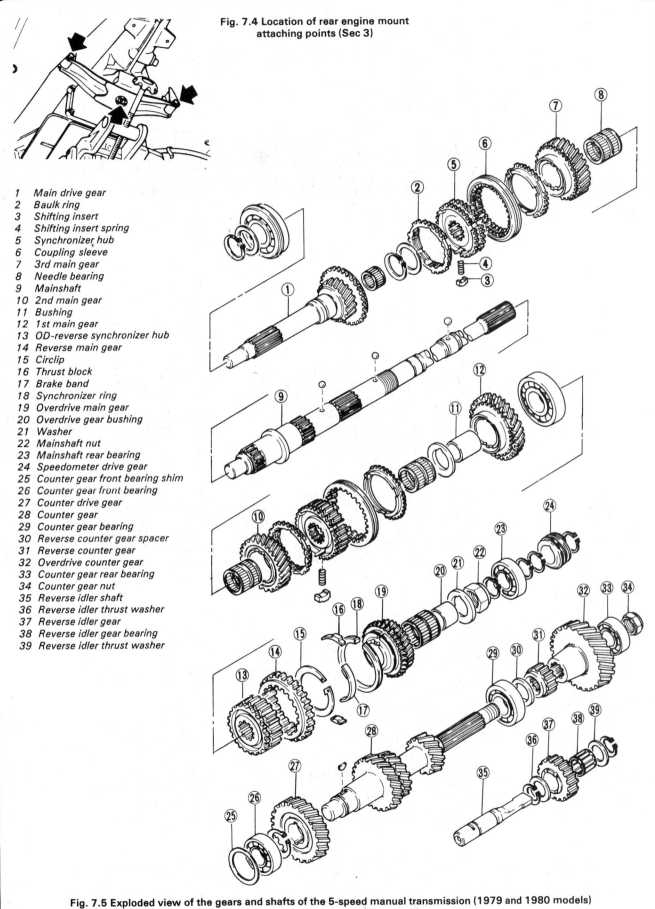

Fig. 7.4 Location of rear engine mount
attaching points (Sec 3)

1 Main drive gear
2 Baulk ring
3 Shifting insert
4 Shifting insert spring
5 Synchronizer hub
6 Coupling sleeve
7 3rd main gear
8 Needle bearing
9 Mainshaft
10 2nd main gear
11 Bushing
12 1st main gear
13 OD-reverse synchronizer hub
14 Reverse main gear
15 Circlip
16 Thrust block
17 Brake band
18 Synchronizer ring
19 Overdrive main gear
20 Overdrive gear bushing
21 Washer
22 Mainshaft nut
23 Mainshaft rear bearing
24 Speedometer drive gear
25 Counter gear front bearing shim
26 Counter gear front bearing
27 Counter drive gear
28 Counter gear
29 Counter gear bearing
30 Reverse counter gear spacer
31 Reverse counter gear
32 Overdrive counter gear
33 Counter gear rear bearing
34 Counter gear nut
35 Reverse idler shaft
36 Reverse idler thrust washer
37 Reverse idler gear
38 Reverse idler gear bearing
39 Reverse idler thrust washer

Fig. 7.5 Exploded view of the gears and shafts of the 5-speed manual transmission (1979 and 1980 models)

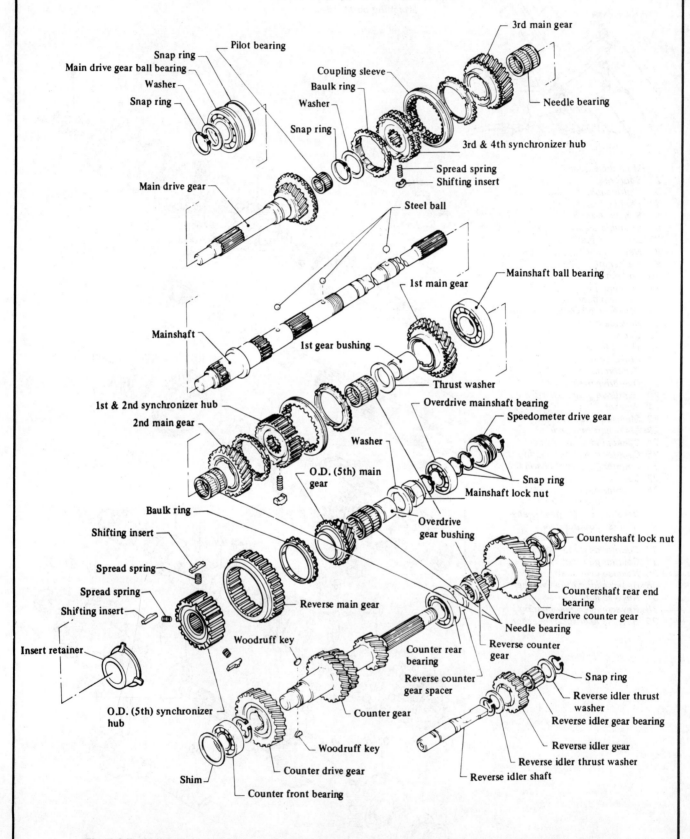

Fig. 7.6 Exploded view of the gears and shafts of the 5-speed manual transmission (1981 and 1982 models)

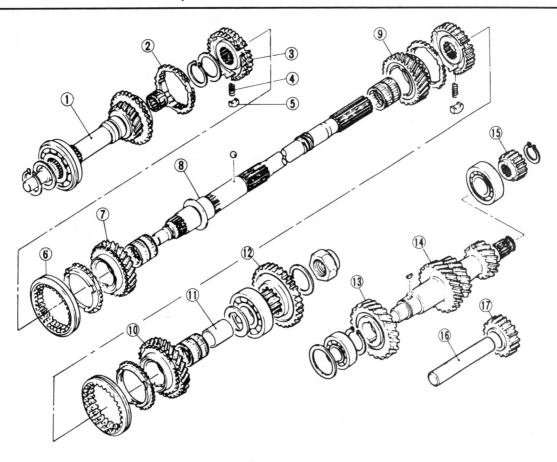

Fig. 7.7 Exploded view of the gears and shafts of the 4-speed manual transmission

1	Main drive gear shaft	6	Coupling sleeve
2	Baulk ring	7	3rd main gear
3	Synchronizer hub, 3rd & 4th	8	Mainshaft
4	Shifting insert spring	9	2nd main gear
5	Shifting insert		

10	1st main gear	14	Counter gear
11	1st gear spacer	15	Reverse counter gear
12	Reverse main gear	16	Reverse idler shaft
13	Counter drive gear	17	Reverse idler gear

---

4   Overhaul (5-speed)

Initial disassembly

1   With the transmission removed, thoroughly clean the external faces.

2   Remove the rubber dust boot from the withdrawal lever opening in the clutch bellhousing.

3   Remove the release bearing and hub together with the withdrawal lever (Chapter 8).

4   Remove the reverse lamp switch, neutral switch, top gear switch, and/or overdrive gear switch, as equipped.

5   Remove the screw that retains the speedometer gear to the rear extension housing and lift out the gear (photo).

6   Pry off the E-ring from the stopper guide pin and drive out the pin (photo).

7   Remove the return spring plug, and lift out the return spring and plunger (photo).

8   Remove the two screws that retain the reverse check cover to the housing and lift out the reverse check sleeve (photo).

9   Unscrew the securing bolts, and drive the rear extension housing from the main transmission casing, using a soft mallet.

10   Unscrew and remove the front cover retaining bolts: remove the front cover and extract the countershaft bearing shim and the input shaft bearing snap-ring.

11   Drive off the one-piece bellhousing/transmission casing from the adapter plate.

12   Make up a suitable plate and bolt it to the transmission adapter plate and then secure the support plate in a vise.

13   Drive out the securing pins from each of the shift forks, using a suitable thin drift (photo).

14   Unscrew and remove the three detent ballplugs.

15   Withdraw the selector rods from the adapter plate.

16   Catch the shift forks, and extract the balls and springs as the selector rods are withdrawn. The four smaller balls are the interlock balls.

17   At this point, inspect the gears and shafts for any wear, chipping or cracking.

18   Also, use a feeler gauge between each mainshaft gear to determine the amount of gear end play that exists. Compare the results to the Specifications.

19   If the gear end play is not within specifications, or if the gears or shafts show signs of wear or damage, the gear assemblies should be disassembled and the defective parts replaced.

20   Lock the gears and using a suitable two legged puller, draw the front bearing from the countershaft.

21   Extract the now exposed snap-ring from the countershaft.

22   Withdraw the countershaft gear together with the input shaft. Take care not to drop the needle roller bearing which is located on the front of the mainshaft.

23   Extract the snap-ring from the front end of the mainshaft, followed by the thrust washer.

24   Withdraw 3rd/4th synchronizer unit, followed by 3rd gear.

25   Both the mainshaft nut and the countershaft nut are staked to prevent them from loosening. Use a hammer and punch to drive out the staking.

4.5 The O-ring on the speedometer pinion should be replaced during reassembly

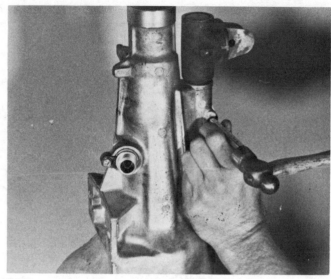

4.6 The stopper guide pin can be driven out with a punch

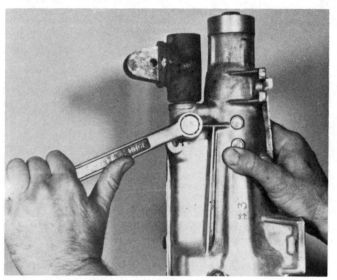

4.7 Removing the return spring plug

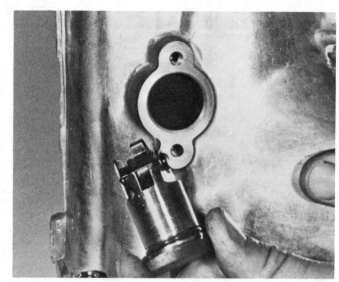

4.8 The reverse check sleeve is retained by two screws

4.11a Internal components of the manual transmission (side view)

4.11b Internal components of the manual transmission (front view)

4.11c Internal components of the manual transmission (rear view)

4.13 Installed positions of the shift rods and forks

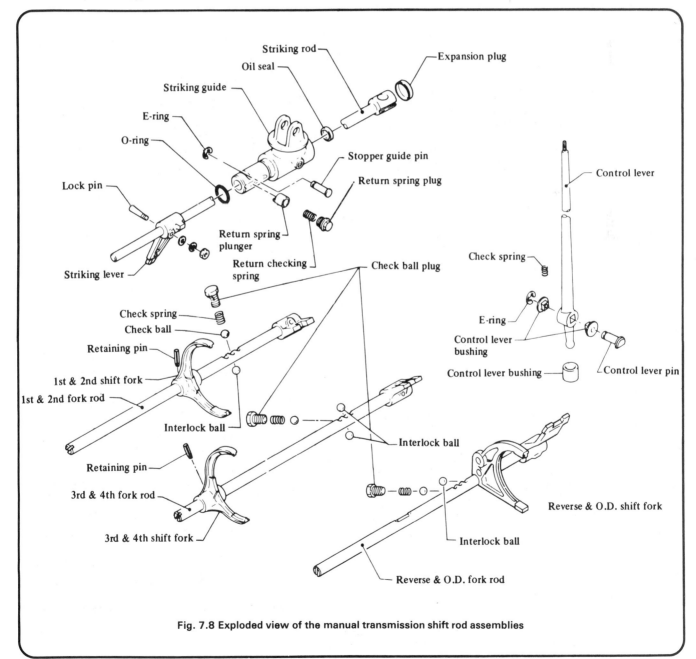

Fig. 7.8 Exploded view of the manual transmission shift rod assemblies

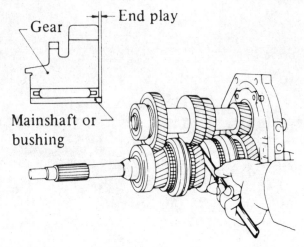

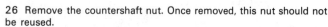

Fig. 7.9 Gear end play should be measured both before and after disassembling the transmission to check for wear and proper installation (Sec 4)

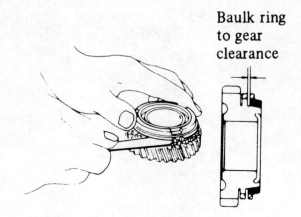

Fig. 7.10 The baulk ring should be checked for wear by mating it with its gear and measuring the gap with a feeler gauge (the proper clearance is shown in the Specifications) (Sec 4)

26 Remove the countershaft nut. Once removed, this nut should not be reused.
27 Use a gear puller to remove the countershaft overdrive gear and bearing.
28 Remove the reverse counter gear and spacer.
29 Remove the snap-ring from the reverse idler shaft and remove the reverse idler gear.
30 Remove the snap-ring that retains the speedometer gear to the mainshaft, and remove the speedometer gear and steel ball.
31 Remove the other two snap-rings from behind the speedometer gear and withdraw the overdrive mainshaft bearing.
32 Drive out the staking on the mainshaft nut and remove it. Once removed, this nut should not be reused.
33 Remove the thrust washer, overdrive gear bushing, needle bearing, overdrive gear, reverse main gear, overdrive synchronizer assembly and insert retainer.
34 Drive the mainshaft and countershaft assemblies simultaneously from the adapter plate, using a soft-faced hammer.

Mainshaft
35 Carefully examine the gears and shaft splines for chipping of the teeth or wear and then dismantle the gear train into its component parts, replacing any worn or damaged items.
36 Examine the shaft itself for scoring or grooving, also the splines for twist, taper or general wear.
37 Examine the synchromesh units for cracks or wear or general looseness in the assembly and replace them if evident, particularly if there has been a history of noisy gearchange or where the syncromesh can be easily 'beaten'.
38 Press the baulk ring tight against the synchromesh cone and measure the gap between the two components. If it is less than specified, replace the components (refer to Specifications and accompanying figure).
39 When reassembling the synchromesh unit ensure that the ends of the snap-ring on opposite sides of the units do not engage in the same slot.
40 Begin assembly of the mainshaft by installing the 2nd gear needle bearing, 2nd gear, the baulk ring followed by the 1st/2nd synchromesh unit, noting carefully the direction of installing the latter.
41 Now install the 1st gear baulk ring, needle bearing, steel ball, thrust washer, bushing and 1st gear. Be sure the steel ball is well greased when installed.

Countershaft
42 The countershaft front bearing was removed at the time of dismantling the transmission into major units.
43 The countershaft rear bearing was left in position in the adapter plate.
44 Withdraw the countershaft drive gear and extract the two Woodruff keys.
45 Check all components for wear, especially the gear teeth and shaft

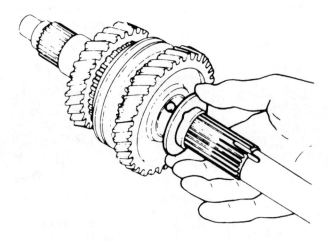

Fig. 7.11 The steel balls should be well greased before installing them onto their shafts (Sec 4)

splines for chipping. Reinstall the Woodruff keys and the snap-ring.
46 Reassembly is a reversal of dismantling.

Input shaft (main drive gear)
47 Remove the snap-ring and spacer.
48 Withdraw the bearing using a two-legged puller or a press. Once removed (by means of its outer race), discard the bearing.
49 Press the new bearing onto the shaft, applying pressure to the center race only.
50 Reinstall the washer.
51 Several thicknesses of snap-rings are available for the main input shaft bearing, as listed in the Specifications. Choose a size that will eliminate bearing end play.

Oil seals
52 Pry out the oil seal from the rear extension and drive in a new one, with the seal lips facing inwards.
53 Reinstall the speedometer pinion sleeve O-ring seal.
54 Reinstall the oil seal in the front cover by prying out the old one and driving in a new one, with an appropriate sized socket (photo).

Rear extension housing
55 Loosen the nut on the end of the striking rod lock pin, until it is half off the threads.
56 Using the nut as a guide, drive the lock pin from the striking rod with a punch (photo).

4.54 The front oil seal is located in the front cover and can be pryed out with a screwdriver

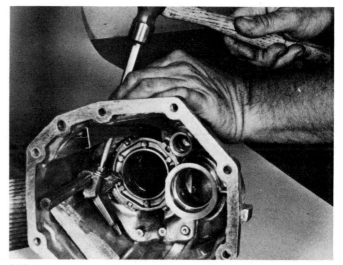

4.56 Use a punch to drive the striking rod lock pin from the striking lever

57 Slide the striking lever from the striking rod, and withdraw the rod from the rear of the housing.
58 Check the rod and lever for wear or damage and replace if necessary. Replace the O-ring on the striking rod.
59 Inspect the bushing in the rear of the extension housing. If this bushing is worn or cracked, the entire rear extension housing must be replaced.
60 Reinstall the striking rod assembly by reversing the removal procedure.

Reassembly

61 Before beginning to reassemble the transmission, the mainshaft and countershaft adapter plate bearings should be removed, examined and replaced if worn. To do this, unscrew the six screws which retain the bearing retainer plate to the adapter plate. The use of an impact driver will probably be required for this operation.
62 With the bearing retainer plate removed, press the mainshaft and countershaft bearings from the adapter plate. Apply pressure only to the outer races of the bearings.
63 Check the bearings for wear by first washing them in clean solvent and drying in air from a tire pump. Spin them with the fingers, and if they are noisy or loose in operation, reinstall them.
64 Check that the dowel pin and oil trough are correctly positioned on the adapter plate.
65 Tap the mainshaft bearing lightly and squarely into position in the adapter plate.
66 Drive the reverse idler shaft into the adapter plate so that $\frac{2}{3}$rds of its length is projecting rearwards. Ensure that the cutout in the shaft is positioned to receive the edge of the bearing retainer plate.
67 Install the bearing retainer plate and tighten the screws to the specified torque.
68 Stake each screw in two places to prevent them from loosening.
69 Tap the countershaft rear bearing into position in the adapter plate.
70 Press the mainshaft assembly into position in the bearing in the adapter plate. Support the rear of the bearing center track during this operation.
71 Press the countershaft assembly into position in the bearing in the adapter plate. Again support the rear of the bearing center race during this operation.
72 Install the needle bearing, 3rd gear, baulk ring and the 3rd/4th synchromesh unit to the front of the mainshaft.
73 Install the thrust washer, and then choose a snap-ring from the sizes listed in the Specifications that will minimize end play.
74 Insert the needle pilot bearing in its recess at the end of the input shaft.
75 Mesh the countershaft drive-gear with the 4th gear on the input shaft. Push the drive gear and input shaft onto the countershaft and mainshaft simultaneously, but a piece of tubing will be needed to drive the countershaft gear into position while supporting the rear end of the countershaft.

76 Select a countershaft drive gear snap-ring from the sizes listed in the Specifications, so that the gear end play will be minimized.
77 Using an appropriate sized socket, drive the front bearing onto the countershaft.
78 Install the reverse counter gear spacer onto the rear of the countershaft.
79 Install the snap-ring, thrust washer, needle bearing, reverse idler gear, reverse idler thrust washer and rear snap-ring onto the reverse idler shaft.
80 Onto the rear side of the mainshaft, install the insert retainer (1981 models only), synchronizer assembly, reverse gear, overdrive gear bushing, needle bearing and baulk ring.
81 Install the reverse counter gear on the countershaft.
82 Mesh the overdrive gear with the overdrive counter gear and install them on their respective shafts with the overdrive gear on the mainshaft and the overdrive counter gear on the countershaft.
83 Apply grease to the steel ball and install it and the thrust washer onto the rear of the mainshaft.
84 Install a new locknut onto the rear of the mainshaft and torque it to specs. **Note:** *In order to accurately tighten the nut to its torque specifications, a wrench adapter should be used as shown in the accompanying figure. Used with the adapter, the torque reading on the wrench will not be accurate and should be converted to the correct torque by referring to the chart shown.*
85 Install the countershaft rear end bearing onto the countershaft.
86 Install the countershaft locknut and torque it to specs.
87 Use a hammer and punch to stake both the mainshaft and countershaft locknuts so they engage the grooves in their respective shafts.
88 Once again measure the gear end play, as described in paragraph 18.
89 Fit a snap-ring onto the mainshaft and then install the overdrive mainshaft bearing.
90 Choose a snap-ring from the sizes listed in the Specifications to eliminate end play of the mainshaft rear bearing.
91 Install the next snap-ring, then grease the steel ball and install the ball and the speedometer drive gear onto the mainshaft. Finally install the last snap-ring.
92 Locate the 1st/2nd shift fork onto the 1st/2nd synchronizer unit, (the long end of the shift fork must be towards the countershaft). Now locate the 3rd/4th shift fork onto the 3rd/4th synchronizer unit, (the long end of the shift fork must be the opposite side to the 1st/2nd shift fork).
93 Locate the overdrive reverse shift fork onto the overdrive synchronizer so that the upper rod hole is in line with the 3rd/4th shift fork.
94 Slide the 1st/2nd selector rod through the adapter plate and into the 1st/2nd shift fork; align the hole in the rod with the hole in the fork and drive in a new retaining pin.
95 Align the notch in the 1st/2nd selector rod with the detent (check) ball bore, then install the detent (check) ball, spring and screw in the detent ball plug. Apply a little thread sealant to the detent ball plug.

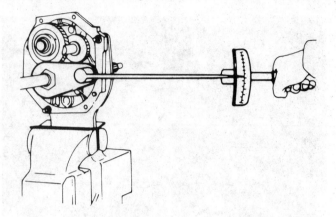

Fig. 7.12 The mainshaft locknut should be tightened using a torque wrench and adapter as shown (Sec 4)

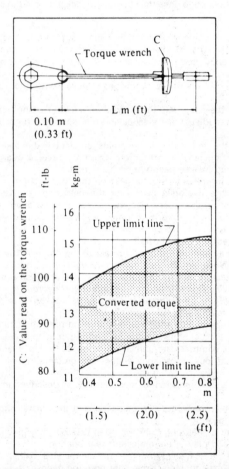

Fig. 7.13 When tightening the mainshaft locknut, the true torque can be found by matching the torque reading on the wrench with the chart above (Sec 4)

96 Now invert the adapter plate assembly (hold the 3rd/4th and OD/reverse shift forks in position) so that the check ball plug assembled at paragraph 95, is lowermost. Drop two interlock balls into the 3rd/4th detent ball plug hole and, using a suitable thin probe, push them up against the 1st/2nd selector rod (if the adapter plate is correctly positioned, the interlock balls will drop into position). Slide the 3rd/4th selector rod through the upper hole of the OD/reverse shift fork and the adapter plate, ensuring that the interlock balls are held between this selector rod and the 1st/2nd selector rod, and into the

3rd/4th shift fork. Align the holes in the shift fork and selector rod, and drive in a new retaining pin. Now install a detent ball, spring and detent ball plug (with thread sealant applied) to the 3rd/4th detent ball plug bore. Ensure that the notch in the 3rd/4th selector rod is aligned with the detent ball plug bore before assembling the detent ball.
97 Drop two interlock balls into the remaining detent ball plug bore, ensuring that they locate against the 3rd/4th selector rod. Slide the overdrive/reverse selector rod through the overdrive reverse shift fork and into the adapter plate. Ensure that the two interlock balls are held in position between the 3rd/4th selector rod and the overdrive/reverse selector rod, sliding the overdrive/reverse selector rod into the adapter plate until the notch in the selector rod aligns with the detent ball plug bore. Insert the detent ball, spring and detent ball plug as before. Drive in a new retaining pin to retain the overdrive/reverse shift fork to the overdrive/reverse selector rod.
98 Finally, tighten the three detent ball plugs to the specified torque.
99 Thoroughly oil the entire assembly and check to see that the selector rods operate correctly and smoothly.
100 Clean the mating faces of the adapter plate and the transmission casing and apply gasket sealant to both surfaces.
101 Tap the transmission casing into position on the adapter plate using a soft-faced hammer, taking particular care that it engages correctly with the input shaft bearing and countershaft front bearing.
102 Fit the outer snap-ring to the input shaft bearing.
103 Clean the mating faces of the adapter plate and rear extension housing and apply gasket sealant.
104 Arrange the shift forks in their neutral mode and then lower the rear extension housing onto the adapter plate so that the striking lever engages correctly with the selector rods.
105 Fit the bolts which secure the sections of the transmission together and tighten them to the specified torque.
106 Measure the amount by which the countershaft front bearing protrudes from the transmission casing front face. Use feeler blades for this and then select the appropriate shims after reference to the following table:

Measurement	Shim (thickness)
0.1150/0.1185 in (2.92/3.01 mm)	0.0236 in (0.6 mm)
0.1189/0.1124 in (3.02/3.11 mm)	0.0197 in (0.5 mm)
0.1228/0.1264 in (3.12/3.21 mm)	0.0157 in (0.4 mm)
0.1268/0.1303 in (3.22/3.31 mm)	0.0118 in (0.3 mm)
0.1307/0.1343 in (3.32/3.41 mm)	0.0079 in (0.2 mm)
0.1346/0.1382 in (3.42/3.51 mm)	0.0039 in (0.1 mm)

107 Stick the shim in position using a dab of thick grease, then fit the front cover to the transmission casing (within the clutch bellhousing) complete with a new gasket and taking care not to damage the oil seal as it passes over the input shaft splines.
108 Tighten the securing bolts to the specified torque, making sure that the bolt threads are coated with gasket sealant to prevent oil seepage.
109 Complete the reassembly by reversing the steps described in paragraphs 1 through 8 of this Section.

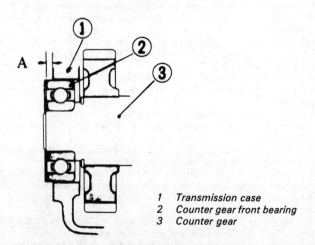

1 Transmission case
2 Counter gear front bearing
3 Counter gear

Fig. 7.14 Measurement for selection of countershaft front bearing shim (Sec 4)

5 Overhaul (4-speed)

1 The overhaul procedure for the 4-speed transmission is basically the same as for the 5-speed transmission. The only differences are those noted below.

2 The procedure in the following section should be used in place of steps 17 through 34 of Section 4.

   a) Inspect the gears and shafts for any wear, chipping or cracking.

   b) Use a feeler gauge between each mainshaft gear to determine the amount of gear end play that exists. The standard end play for each gear is listed in the Specifications.

   c) If the gear end play is not within Specifications, or if the gears or shafts show signs of wear or damage, the gear assemblies should be disassembled and the defective parts replaced.

   d) Lock the gears and using a suitable two-legged extractor, draw the front bearing from the countershaft.

   e) Extract the now exposed snap-ring from the countershaft.

   f) Withdraw the countershaft gear together with the input shaft. Take care not to drop the needle roller bearing which is located on the front of the mainshaft.

   g) Extract the snap-ring from the front end of the mainshaft, followed by the thrust washer.

   h) Withdraw the 3rd/4th synchronizer unit, followed by 3rd gear.

   i) Release the staked portion of the mainshaft nut and then loosen it.

   j) Remove the mainshaft nut, the thrust washer and reverse gear.

   k) Extract the snap-ring from the rear end of the countershaft and remove the reverse idler gear.

   l) Drive the mainshaft and countershaft assemblies simultaneously from the adapter plate, using a soft-faced hammer.

3 The procedure in the following Section should be used in place of steps 78 through 91 of Section 4.

   a) To the rear of the mainshaft, install the reverse gear and the plain washer and screw on the nut, finger-tight.

   b) Install the counter reverse gear on the countershaft and use a snap-ring from the thickness listed to give minimum end play.

   c) Install the reverse idler gear on the reverse idler shaft

   d) Tighten the mainshaft nut (after locking the gears) to the specified torque.

   e) Stake the collar of the nut into the groove of the mainshaft.

   f) Once again measure the gear end play, as described in paragraph 2.

Chapter 7 Part B: Automatic transmission

Contents

Specifications

Model 3N71B

Code number
Non-turbo X2707
Turbo X2770

Torque converter code
Non-turbo .... G
Turbo .... A

Small torque ratio 2.0:1

Gear ratios
1st 2.458
2nd 1.458
3rd 1.000
Reverse 2.182

Recommended fluid .... Dexron-type automatic transmission fluid

Fluid capacity .... $5\frac{7}{8}$ qt (5.5 liters)

Torque specifications

	ft-lb	m-kg
Torque converter-to-flywheel bolts	33	4.5
Converter housing-to-engine-bolts	33	4.5
Oil pan mounting bolts	4.3	0.6
Inhibitor switch mounting bolts	4.3	0.6
Shift linkage locknut	25	3.5
Oil cooler pipe-to-connections	29	4.0

6 General information

The automatic transmission unit is the type JATCO 3N71B.

The unit provides three forward ratios and one reverse. Changing of the forward gear ratios is completely automatic in relation to the vehicle speed and engine torque output and is dependent upon the vacuum pressure in the manifold and the vehicle speed to actuate the gear change mechanism at the precise time.

The transmission has six selector positions:

P – Parking position which locks the output shaft to the interior wall of the transmission housing. This is a safety device for use when the vehicle is parked on an incline. The engine may be started with Park selected and this position should always be selected when adjusting the engine while it is running. Never attempt to select Park when the vehicle is in motion.

R – Reverse gear.

N – Neutral. Select this position to start the engine or when idling in traffic for long periods.

D – Drive, for all normal motoring conditions.

2 – Locks the transmission in second gear for wet road conditions or steep hill climbing or descents. The engine can be over-revved in this position.

1 – The selection of this ratio above speeds of approximately 25 mph (40 kph) will engage second gear and as the speed drops below 25 mph (40 kph) the transmission will lock into first gear. Provides maximum retardation on steep descents.

Due to the complexity of the automatic transmission unit, any internal adjustment or servicing should be left to a Datsun dealer, or other qualified transmission specialist. The information given in this Chapter is therefore confined to those operations which are considered within the scope of the home mechanic. An automatic transmission should give many tens of thousands of miles service provided normal maintenance and adjustment is carried out. When the unit finally requires major overhaul, consideration should be given to exchanging the old transmission for a factory reconditioned one, the removal and installation being well within the capabilities of the home mechanic as described later in this Chapter.

The routine maintenance chart in Chapter 1 calls for an automatic transmission fluid change once every 30 000 miles. This interval should be shortened to every 15 000 miles if the car is normally driven under one or more of the following conditions: heavy city traffic, where the outside temperature normally reaches 90°F or higher; in very hilly or mountainous areas; or if a trailer is frequently pulled. Refer to Chapter 1 for the proper procedures for checking and changing the automatic transmission fluid and filter.

The automatic transmission uses an oil cooler, located at the radiator, to prevent excessive temperatures from developing inside the transmission. Should the oil cooler need flushing or other servicing, take it to a dealer or other radiator specialist.

If rough shifting or other malfunctions occur in the automatic transmission, check the following items first before assuming the fault lies within the transmission itself: the fluid level, the kickdown switch adjustment, manual shift linkage adjustment and engine tune. All of these elements can adversely affect the performance of the transmission.

Periodically clean the outside of the transmission housing as the accumulation of dirt and oil is liable to cause overheating of the unit under extreme conditions.

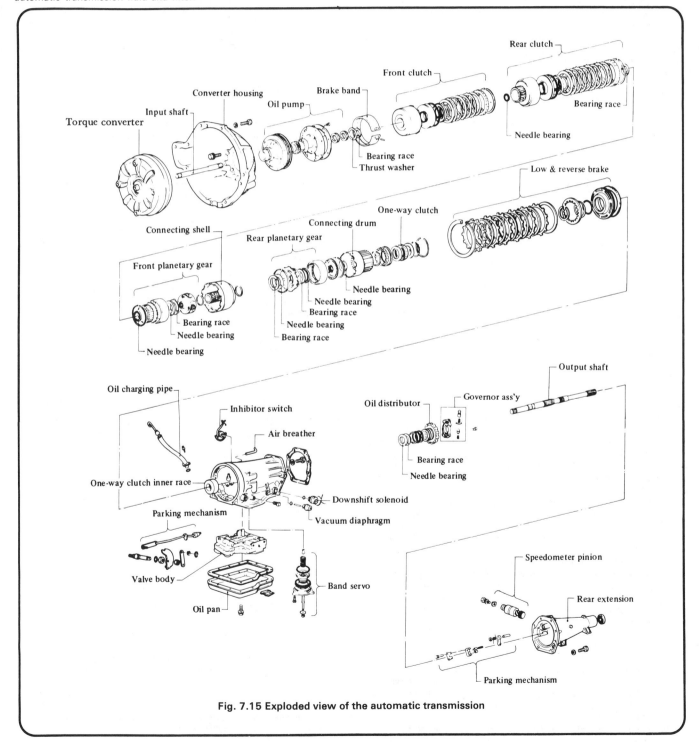

Fig. 7.15 Exploded view of the automatic transmission

7 Shift linkage – adjustment

1   To check the manual shift linkage adjustment, move the shifter through the entire range of gears. You should be able to feel the detents in each gear. If these detents are not felt or if the pointer is not properly aligned with the correct gear selection, the shift linkage should be adjusted in the following manner.
2   With the engine off, place the shift lever in Drive gear.
3   Working underneath the car, loosen the locknuts shown in Fig. 7.16.
4   Move the shift lever so that it is correctly aligned with the D position.
5   Move the selector lever on the transmission so that it is also correctly aligned in the Drive position.
6   Tighten the locknuts and recheck the levers. There should be no tendency for the selector rod to push or pull one rod against the other.
7   Again run the shifter through the entire range of gear positions. If there are still problems, the grommets that connect the selector rod with the levers may be worn or damaged and should be replaced.

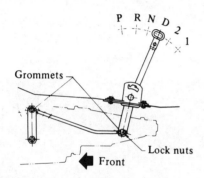

Fig. 7.16 Location of the selector rod locknut (Sec 7)

8 Inhibitor switch – adjustment

1   The inhibitor switch peforms two functions. It provides current to the back-up lights when the transmission is in the Reverse position. It also prevents the car from being started in any gear position except Park or Neutral. If the back-up lights fail to operate, or if the car will not start when the shifter is in the middle of the Park or Neutral positions, the inhibitor switch should be checked and, if necessary, adjusted.
2   Locate the inhibitor switch on the right side of the transmission and connect a continuity tester to the black and yellow wires.
3   With the engine off, but the ignition switch on, have an assistant run the gear shifter through the entire range of gear positions. The tester should show current passing through the switch only when the shifter is in the Park or Neutral positions.
4   Now connect the continuity tester to the red and black wires. With this arrangement the tester should show current passing through the switch only when the shifter is in the Reverse position.
5   If the continuity tests did not give the results described above, the switch should be adjusted as follows:
   a)   Place the selector lever on the transmission in the neutral (vertical) position.
   b)   Remove the screw shown in Fig. 7.17.
   c)   Loosen the inhibitor switch attaching bolts.
   d)   Using a thin rod or piece of wire, align the screw hole with the hole in the rotor behind the switch, by moving the switch. Holding this alignment, retighten the inhibitor switch attaching bolts.
   e)   Remove the alignment rod or wire and install the screw.

6   With the switch adjusted, recheck it for continuity by repeating steps 3 and 4. If the switch still does not function properly, replace it with a new one.

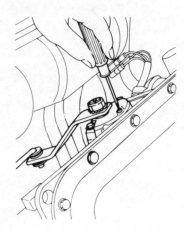

Fig. 7.17 The inhibitor switch is adjusted by removing the screw shown and aligning the screw hole with the rotor hole underneath it (Sec 8)

9 Kickdown switch – adjustment

1   The kickdown switch, coupled with the downshift solenoid, causes the transmission to downshift when the accelerator pedal is fully depressed. This is to provide extra power when passing. If the transmission is not downshifting upon full throttle, the system should be inspected.
2   With the engine off, but the ignition on, depress the accelerator pedal all the way and listen for a click just before the pedal bottoms.
3   If no click is heard, locate the kickdown switch at the upper post of the accelerator pedal. Loosen the locknut and with the pedal still depressed, extend the switch until it makes contact with the post and clicks. The switch should click only as the pedal bottoms. If it clicks too soon, it will cause the transmission to downshift on part throttle.
4   Tighten the locknut, and recheck the adjustment.
5   If the kickdown switch adjustment is correct but the transmission still will not downshift check that current is reaching the switch, and, with a continuity tester, check that the switch is passing current through it.
6   If the switch checks out okay, but the problem persists, have the downshift solenoid tested and replace it if necessary.

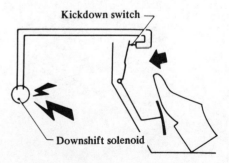

Fig. 7.18 The kickdown switch is located at the upper post of the accelerator pedal (Sec 9)

10 Vacuum diaphragm rod – adjustment

1   The vacuum diaphragm and the length of its rod affect the shift patterns of the transmission. If the transmission is not shifting at precisely the right points, a different vacuum diaphragm rod may have to be installed.

2   Disconnect the vacuum hose from the vacuum diaphragm on the left side of the transmission.

3   Remove the vacuum diaphragm.

4   Be sure the vacuum throttle valve is pushed into the valve body as far as possible, and measure the distance L in Fig. 7.19 with a depth gauge.

5   Once this measurement is taken, use the chart below to determine the correct vacuum diaphragm rod length.

Measured depth L in (mm)	Rod length in (mm)
Under 1.0059 (25.55)	1.42 (29.0)
1.0098 to 1.0256 (25.65 to 26.05)	1.161 (29.5)
1.0295 to 1.0453 (26.15 to 26.55)	1.181 (30.0)
1.0492 to 1.0650 (26.65 to 27.05)	1.201 (30.5)
Over 1.0689 (27.15)	1.220 (31.0)

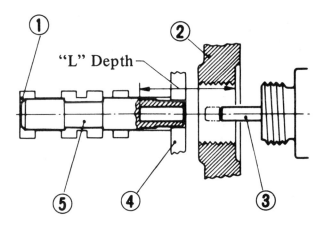

Fig. 7.19 Measurement of vacuum diaphragm rod (Sec 10)

1   Note sealed valve body
2   Transmission case wall
3   Diaphragm rod
4   Valve body side plate
5   Vacuum throttle valve

11 Rear oil seal – replacement

1   Remove the driveshaft as described in Chapter 8.

2   Being careful not to damage the output shaft or transmission housing, use a screwdriver to pry out the old seal.

3   Apply a coat of gear oil to the lips of the new seal and drive it into place using an appropriate sized socket.

4   Reinstall the driveshaft.

12 Removal and installation

Note: *Due to the complexity of the automatic transmission and the special equipment needed to service it, an automatic transmission overhaul is not practical for the home mechanic to perform. Considerable money can be saved however, by removing and installing the transmission yourself. Read through this Section to become familiar with the procedure and the tools needed for the job. The car must be raised high enough so the transmission can be lowered from the car and slid out from underneath.*

1   Prior to removal of the transmission, have the car test driven and diagnosed by a qualified transmission specialist, so that he may determine the nature and cause of the problem.

2   Removal of the engine and automatic transmission as a combined unit is described in Chapter 2 of this manual. Where it is decided to remove the transmission leaving the engine in position in the vehicle proceed as follows:

3   Disconnect the battery ground cable.

4   Drain the fluid from the transmission unit, retaining it in a clean container if required for further use.

5   Disengage the torsion shaft from the accelerator linkage. Then jack the car to an adequate working height and support on stands or blocks.

6   Remove the driveshaft as described in Chapter 8. As this is done, plug or cover the opening at the rear of the transmission to prevent oil leakage.

7   Disconnect the exhaust downpipe from the engine and wire it out of the way.

8   Disconnect the wires from the starter inhibitor switch.

9   Disconnect the wire from the downshift solenoid.

10   Disconnect the vacuum pipe from the vacuum capsule which is located just forward of the downshift solenoid.

11   Separate the selector lever from the selector linkage.

12   Disconnect the speedometer drive cable from the rear extension housing.

13   Disconnect the fluid filler tube. Plug the opening.

14   Disconnect the fluid cooler tubes from the transmission casing and plug the openings.

15   Support the engine oil pan with a jack and use a block of wood to prevent damage to the surface of the oil pan.

16   Remove the cover from the lower half of the torque converter housing, then mark the torque converter and drive plate in relation to each other for exact replacement.

17   Unscrew and remove the four bolts which secure the torque converter to the drive plate. Access to each of these bolts in turn is obtained by rotating the engine slowly, using a wrench on the crankshaft pulley bolt.

18   Unbolt and withdraw the starter motor.

19   Support the transmission with a jack (preferably a floor type).

20   Remove the bolts that secure the transmission mounting bracket to the transmission.

Fig. 7.20 When installing the torque converter, the notch in the converter should be aligned with the notch in the oil pump (Sec 12)

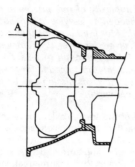

Fig. 7.21 Following torque converter installation, distance A should be measured to check for proper installation (Sec 12)

21 Remove the transmission mounting bracket from the body.
22 Unscrew and remove the transmission-to-engine securing bolts.
23 Lower the two jacks sufficiently to allow the transmission unit to be withdrawn from below and to the rear of the vehicle. The help of an assistant will probably be required due to the weight of the unit. If an automatic transmission is in need of minor repair, take it to a Datsun dealer or other qualified transmission specialist. If an automatic transmission is in need of a complete overhaul, it may be more economical to replace the old transmission with a rebuilt one.
25 Installation is a reversal of removal but should the torque converter have been separated from the main assembly, ensure that the notch on the converter is correctly aligned with the corresponding one on the oil pump. To check that the torque converter has been correctly installed, the dimension A should exceed 0.846 in (21.5 mm) (Figs. 7.20 and 7.21).
26 When bolting the torque converter to the driveplate, be sure the marks made during removal are aligned. Once the converter is installed, rotate the crankshaft several times to make sure the transmission turns freely with no binding.
27 Tighten all bolts to the specified torque settings and refill the unit with the correct grade and quantity of fluid.
28 Check the operation of the inhibitor switch and the selector linkage and adjust if necessary as described in this Chapter.

Chapter 8 Clutch and driveline

Contents

Specifications

Clutch

Type	Single plate, diaphragm spring with hydraulic actuation
Disc type	
2-seater non-turbo models	225CBL
2 + 2 and Turbo models	240TBL
Number of torsion springs	6
Wear limit of lining surface to rivet head	0.012 in (0.3 mm)
Runout limit	
All 2-seater and 1982 2 + 2 models	0.020 in (0.5 mm)
1979 thru 1981 2 + 2 and 1982 Turbo models	0.028 in (0.7 mm)
Distance of runout checking point from hub center	
2-seater non-turbo models	4.23 in (107.5 mm)
2 + 2 and Turbo models	4.35 in (115 mm)
Disc diameter	
2-seater non-turbo models	8.86 in (225 mm)
2 + 2 and Turbo models	9.45 in (240 mm)
Cover/pressure plate assembly type	
2-seater standard models	C225S
1979 thru 1981 2 + 2 models	D240K
1982 2 + 2 and Turbo models	C240S
Diaphragm spring height	
2-seater non-turbo models	1.299 to 1.378 in (33 to 35 mm)
2 + 2 and Turbo models	1.476 to 1.555 in (37.5 to 39.5 mm)
Maximum unevenness of spring toe height	0.020 in (0.5 mm)
Pedal	
Height	7.99 in (203 mm)
Free play	0.04 to 0.20 in (1 to 5 mm)

Driveshaft

Type	
Non-turbo models	2S63A
Turbo models	2S71A
Number of universal joints	2
Outer diameter	
Non-turbo models	2.5 in (63.5 mm)
Turbo models	2.95 in (75 mm)
Length (spider to spider)	
Non-turbo 2-seater models	22.83 in (580 mm)
Non-turbo 2 + 2 models	30.71 in (780 mm)
Turbo 2-seater models	22.64 in (575 mm)
Turbo 2 + 2 models	30.51 in (775 mm)

Rear axle stub and wheel bearing
Wheel bearing preload torque .... Less than 6.1 in-lb (7.0 kg-cm)
Axle stub endplay .... Less than 0.012 in (0.3 mm)

Drive axles (standard models)
Ball spline radial play .... Less than 0.008 in (0.2 mm)
Spider journal axial play .... Less than 0.0008 in (0.02 mm)
Journal swinging torque .... Less than 8.7 in-lb (10.0 kg-cm)
Spider journal snap-ring selection

Thickness	Identification color
0.0587 in (1.49 mm)	White
0.0598 in (1.52 mm)	Yellow
0.0610 in (1.55 mm)	Red
0.0622 in (1.58 mm)	Green
0.0634 in (1.61 mm)	Blue
0.0646 in (1.64 mm)	Light brown
0.0657 in (1.67 mm)	Black

Differential
Type
    Turbo models R200
    Non-turbo 2-seater models, 2 + 2 models with automatic
        transmission and Deluxe models with manual transmission ... R180
    Non-turbo GL models with automatic transmission and 2+ 2
        models with manual transmission R200
Gear ratio (1979 models)
    R180 differential
        Automatic transmission .... 3.545 : 1
        Manual transmission .... 3.364 : 1
    R200 differential
        Deluxe models .... 3.364 : 1
        GL models .... 3.700 : 1
Gear ratio (1980 thru 1982 models)
    R180 differential .... 3.545 : 1
    R200 differential
        Non-turbo models .... 3.900 : 1
        Turbo models .... 3.545 : 1
Drive pinion bearing preload
    1979 thru 1981 models .... 9.5 to 14.8 in-lb (11 to 17 kg-cm)
    1982 models
        R180 differential .... 7.8 to 14.8 in-lb (9 to 17 kg-cm)
        R200 differential .... 10.0 to 15.2 in-lb (11.5 to 17.5 kg-cm)
Oil capacity
    R180 differential .... $2\frac{1}{8}$ pt (1.0L) ($1\frac{3}{4}$ Imp pt)
    R200 differential .... $2\frac{3}{4}$ pt (1.3L) ($2\frac{1}{4}$ Imp pt)

Torque specifications

	ft-lb	m-kg
Clutch		
Master cylinder mounting nuts	7	1.0
Tube flare nut	12	1.6
Operating cylinder mounting bolts	26	3.6
Cover mounting bolts	14	1.9
Driveshaft mounting bolts	29	4.0
R180 differential		
Drive pinion nut	134	18.0
Drain and filler plugs	36	5.0
Driveshaft-to-differential bolts	29	4.0
Differential-to-suspension member bolts	50	7.0
Rear cover-to-mounting insulator nuts	50	7.0
Side yoke fitting bolt	27	3.2
Rear cover mounting bolts	32	4.5
R200 differential		
Drive pinion nut	149	20.5
Drain and filler plugs	36	5.0
Driveshaft-to-differential bolts	29	4.0
Differential-to-suspension member bolts	50	7.0
Rear cover-to-mounting insulator nuts	76	10.5
Rear cover mounting bolts	15	2.0
Side flange-to-drive axle mounting nut	40	5.5
Side bearing cap bolt	68	9.5
Drive axles, rear axle stubs and wheel bearings		
Wheel bearing locknut	210	29.0
Drive axle-to-differential mounting bolts (R180)	27	3.7
Drive axle-to-differential bolts (R200)	40	5.5
Drive axle-to-hub rear wheel hub bolts	40	5.5
Wheel nuts	65	9.0

1 Clutch – general information

The clutch is located between the engine and the transmission and its main components are the clutch disc, the pressure plate assembly and the release bearing. Other components which make up the hydraulically operated clutch system are the clutch pedal, clutch master cylinder, operating cylinder and release lever.

The clutch disc, pressure plate assembly and release bearing are mounted on the transmission input shaft. The clutch disc is sandwiched between the flywheel and the pressure plate and has a splined hub which engages and turns the input shaft. When engaged, the pressure plate is held against the clutch disc by the spring pressure of its metal fingers, and the clutch disc, in turn, is held against the engine's flywheel. The spinning of the engine is thus transmitted from the flywheel to the clutch disc and into the input shaft.

The clutch pedal is connected to the clutch master cylinder by a short pushrod. The master cylinder and hydraulic reservoir are mounted on the engine side of the bulkhead in front of the driver.

Depressing the clutch pedal moves the piston in the master cylinder forward and forces hydraulic fluid through the clutch hydraulic pipe to the operating cylinder.

The piston in the operating cylinder moves forward on the entry of the fluid and actuates the clutch release lever by means of a short pushrod.

The other end of the release lever, located inside the clutch housing is fork-shaped. This fork engages the clutch release bearing and forces the bearing against the pressure plate assembly's release fingers. When the fingers receive pressure from the release bearing they withdraw the mating surface of the pressure plate from the clutch disc which disengages the clutch assembly from the engine's flywheel.

As the friction linings on the clutch disc wear, the pressure plate automatically moves closer to the disc to compensate and eliminates the necessity for adjustment.

Because access to the clutch components is difficult, any time either the engine or the transmission is removed, the clutch disc, pressure plate assembly and release bearing should be carefully inspected and, if necessary, replaced. Since the clutch disc is the highest wear item, it should be replaced as a matter of course if there is any question as to its quality.

2 Bleeding the clutch hydraulic system

1   Bleeding will be required whenever the hydraulic system has been dismantled and reassembled and air has entered the system.
2   First fill the fluid reservoir with clean brake fluid which has been stored in an airtight container. Never use fluid which has drained from the system or has been bled out on a previous occasion, it may contain grit.
3   Fit a rubber or plastic bleed tube to the bleed screw on the operating cylinder and immerse the open end of the tube in a glass jar containing an inch or two of fluid.
4   Open the bleed screw about half a turn and have an assistant quickly depress the clutch pedal fully. Tighten the bleed screw and then have the clutch pedal slowly released with the foot completely removed. Repeat this sequence of operations until air bubbles are no longer seen to be ejected from the open end of the tube beneath the fluid in the jar.
5   After two or three strokes of the pedal, check that the fluid level in the reservoir has not fallen too low. Keep it well topped-up with fresh fluid otherwise air will again be drawn into the system.
6   Tighten the bleed nipple finally on a down stroke, do not overtighten it, remove the bleed tube and jar, top-up the reservoir and refit the cap.
7   If the help of an assistant is not readily available, alternative 'one-man' bleeding operations can be carried out using a bleed tube fitted with a one way valve or a pressure bleed kit both of which should be used in accordance with the manufacturer's instructions.

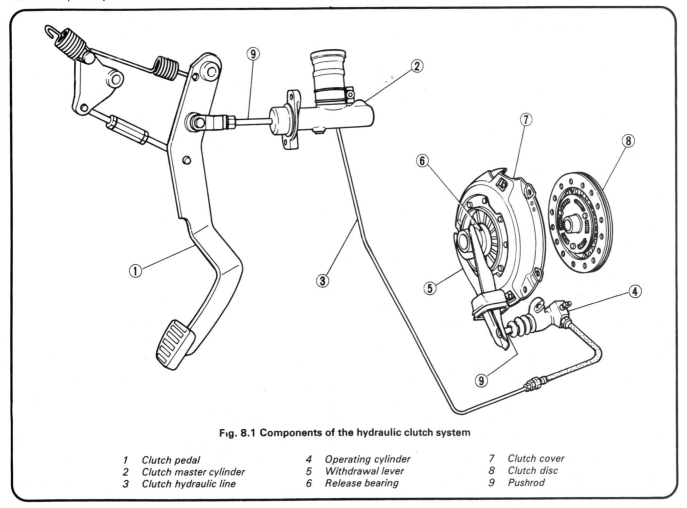

Fig. 8.1 Components of the hydraulic clutch system

1	Clutch pedal	4	Operating cylinder	7	Clutch cover
2	Clutch master cylinder	5	Withdrawal lever	8	Clutch disc
3	Clutch hydraulic line	6	Release bearing	9	Pushrod

3 Clutch pedal adjustments

Because the height and free play adjustments for the clutch pedal are included in the car's *Routine maintenance* schedule, these procedures are described in Chapter 1.

4 Clutch pedal – removal and installation

1 Remove the lower instrument cover, located directly below the steering column and the air nozzle behind it.
2 Disconnect the master cylinder pushrod from the pedal by prying off the snap-ring and withdrawing the clevis pin.
3 Pry off the E-ring from the adjusting rod and disengage the rod from the pedal.
4 Remove the fulcrum bolt.
5 Disengage and remove the return spring and assist return spring.
6 Remove the assist spring clutch lever.
7 Clean the parts in solvent and replace any that are damaged or excessively worn.
8 Installation is the reverse of the removal procedure. **Note:** *During installation, apply multi-purpose grease to all friction surfaces.*
9 Following installation, check the height and free play of the clutch pedal, and make adjustments as necessary as described in Chapter 1.

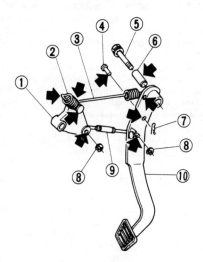

◄ : greasing point

Fig. 8.2 Components of the clutch pedal assembly; grease should be applied to the points shown (arrows) during installation (Sec 4)

1	Assist spring clutch lever	6	Collar
2	Return spring	7	Snap pin
3	Assist return spring	8	E-ring
4	Clevis pin	9	Adjusting rod
5	Fulcrum bolt	10	Pedal

5 Clutch master cylinder – removal and installation

Caution: *Hydraulic fluid can damage paint, so take care not to spill any on any painted surfaces of the car.*
1 Disconnect the master cylinder pushrod from the pedal arm.
2 Disconnect the fluid line from the master cylinder and drain the fluid into a suitable container.
3 For clearance, remove the windshield washer tank and the EFI dropping resistor from the body, and position them so they will not interfere with the removal of the master cylinder.
4 Remove the master cylinder flange mounting bolts and withdraw the unit from the engine compartment rear bulkhead.
5 Installation is the reverse of removal, but check the pedal height and free play as described in Chapter 1 and bleed the hydraulic system (Sec 2).

6 Clutch master cylinder – overhaul

1 Drain any fluid from the reservoir and clean away all external dirt from the cylinder.
2 Peel back the flexible rubber boot at the end of the cylinder and pry out the stopper ring.
3 Remove the pushrod and stopper from the cylinder.
4 Use a rod to depress the piston into the cylinder and hold it depressed while you unscrew and remove the supply valve stopper bolt from the bottom of the cylinder.
5 With the supply valve stopper removed, the piston and spring assembly can be removed.
6 Do not detach the reservoir from the cylinder body, as a new one will have to be installed if the old one is removed.
7 Always use brake fluid to clean or wash parts. Never use mineral-based solvents, such as gasoline or kerosene as these will ruin the rubber parts of the system.
8 Examine the inner surface of the cylinder bore. If it is scored or exhibits "bright" wear areas, the entire master cylinder should be replaced.
9 If the cylinder bore is in good condition, obtain a clutch master cylinder rebuild kit, which will contain all of the necessary replacement parts.
10 Prior to installing any parts, first dip them in brake fluid to lubricate them. **Note:** *Do not use other solvents or lubricants.*
11 If the piston seals are not already mounted on the new piston supplied in the rebuild kit, use your fingers to manipulate them into their grooves. Be sure the lips face in the proper directions (photo).
12 The installation of the parts into the cylinder is the reverse of the removal procedure.

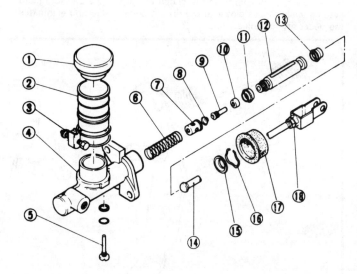

Fig. 8.3 Components of the clutch master cylinder (Sec 6)

1	Reservoir cap	10	Supply valve
2	Reservoir	11	Primary cup
3	Reservoir band	12	Piston
4	Cylinder body	13	Secondary cup
5	Supply valve stopper	14	Push rod
6	Return spring	15	Stopper
7	Spring seat	16	Stopper ring
8	Valve spring	17	Dust cover
9	Supply valve rod	18	Locknut

7 Clutch operating cylinder – removal and installation

1 In order to prevent excessive loss of hydraulic fluid, when the operating cylinder hose is disconnected, remove the master cylinder reservoir cap and place a piece of polyethylene sheeting over the open reservoir. Screw on the cap and thus create a vacuum which will stop the fluid running out of the open hose.

2   Loosen the clutch line flare nut at the bracket mounted on the body sidemember.
3   Remove the locking clip from the bracket, and disengage the hose.
4   Remove the clutch hose from the operating cylinder.
5   Unscrew and remove the two bolts which secure the operating cylinder to the clutch housing (photo). The operating cylinder can now be removed.
6   Installation is a reversal of removal but bleed the hydraulic system as described in Section 2.

7.5 The clutch operating cylinder is located on the right side of the clutch housing

8   Clutch operating cylinder – overhaul

1   Pull off the dust boot complete with pushrod and then tap the cylinder gently on a block of wood to extract the piston and spring.
2   Unscrew and remove the bleeder screw.
3   Examine the surfaces of the piston and cylinder bore for scoring or 'bright' wear areas. If any are found, discard the complete cylinder and purchase a new one.
4   If the components are in good condition, wash them in clean brake fluid, remove the seal and discard it noting carefully which way the seal lips face.
5   Obtain a repair kit which will contain all the necessary new items.
6   Fit the new seal using the fingers only to manipulate it into position. Be sure the lips face in the proper direction.
7   Dip the piston assembly in clean brake fluid before installing it and the spring into the cylinder.
8   Reinstall the bleeder valve.
9   Complete the reassembly by installing the pushrod and the dust cover. Be sure the dust cover is secure on the cylinder housing.

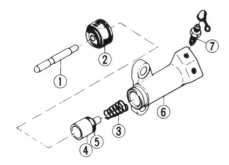

Fig. 8.4 Components of the clutch operating cylinder (Sec 8)

1 Pushrod	5 Piston cup
2 Dust cover	6 Operating cylinder
3 Piston spring	7 Bleeder screw
4 Piston	

9   Clutch disc and pressure plate assembly – removal, inspection and installation

1   Due to the slow-wearing qualities of the clutch, it is not easy to decide when to go to the trouble of removing the transmission in order to check the wear on the friction lining. The only positive indication that something needs doing is when it starts to slip or when squealing noises on engagement indicate that the friction lining has worn down to the rivets. In such instances it can only be hoped that the friction surfaces on the flywheel and pressure plate have not been badly worn or scored.
2   A clutch will wear according to the way in which it is used. Much intentional slipping of the clutch while driving – rather than the correct selection of gears – will accelerate wear. It is best to assume, however, that the friction disc will need renewal at about 40 000 miles (64 000 km).
3   Because of the clutch's location between the engine and transmission the clutch cannot be worked on without removing either the engine or transmission. If repairs which would require removal of the engine are not needed, the quickest way to gain access to the clutch is by removing the transmission, as described in Chapter 7.
4   With the transmission removed, but before removing the pressure plate assembly from the flywheel, check that none of the metal fingers on the pressure plate are distorted or bent. If any damage is evident the pressure plate will need to be replaced.
5   The pressure plate need not be marked in relation to the flywheel as it can only be fitted one way due to the positioning dowels.
6   In a diagonal pattern to keep from distorting the pressure plate, loosen the attaching bolts a little at a time until the spring pressure is relieved (photo). If the flywheel begins to turn, insert a screwdriver through the starter motor opening and engage it in the teeth of the flywheel.
7   While supporting the pressure plate assembly, remove the bolts. Then remove the pressure plate and clutch disc.
8   Clean the pressure plate, flywheel mating surfaces and the bearing retainer outer surfaces of any oil and grease.
9   Examine the pressure plate surface where it contacts the clutch disc. This surface should be smooth, with no scoring, gouging or warping. Check the pressure plate cover and fingers for damage. Use a feeler gauge to measure the unevenness of the diaphragm spring toe height and check that it is within the specified limit as shown in the Specifications. If any fault is found with the pressure plate assembly it must be replaced as an entire unit.
10   Inspect the clutch disc for lining wear. Check for loose or broken rivets or springs. Because of the difficulty in gaining access to the clutch disc, if the lining surface is not at least $\frac{1}{32}$ (0.8 mm) above the rivets, even though it is not down to the lining wear limit, it is a good idea to replace the disc. If the lining material shows signs of breaking up or black areas where oil contamination has occurred it should also be renewed.
11   Inspect the surface of the flywheel for rivet grooves, burnt areas or scoring. If the damage is slight, the flywheel can be removed and reconditioned using a lathe. If the damage is deep, the flywheel should be replaced. Check that the ring gear teeth are not broken, cracked or seriously burned. Refer to Chapter 2 for the flywheel removal procedure.
12   If any traces of oil are detected on the clutch components the source should be found and eliminated. If oil is coming from the center of the flywheel, this indicates a failure of the rear oil seal (Chapter 2). Oil at the rear of the clutch assembly may indicate the need to replace the transmission input shaft seal (Chapter 7).
13   While servicing these clutch components, it's also a good idea to replace the release bearing at the same time. Refer to Section 10.
14   Prior to installation, apply a light coat of molybdenum disulphide grease to the splines of the transmission main drive gear. Wipe off any excessive grease.
15   To install, hold the clutch disc and pressure plate together against the flywheel and insert a centering tool through the center of them. Since the transmission input shaft must pass through the center of these components, they must be properly aligned to ease the installation of the transmission. If a centering tool is not available, a ratchet extension and an appropriate sized socket can be made to work (photo). The clutch disc must be installed with the damper springs offset toward the transmission. The flywheel side should be identified as such by stamped letters in the disc.

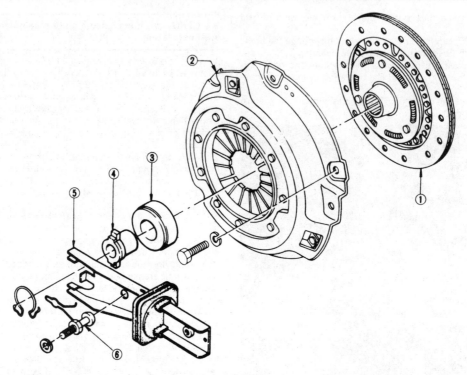

Fig. 8.5 Exploded view of the clutch disc, cover assembly and release bearing assembly (Sec 9)

1 Clutch disc assembly
2 Clutch cover assembly
3 Release bearing
4 Release sleeve
5 Withdrawal lever
6 Withdrawal lever ball pin

9.6 The clutch cover mounting bolts should be unscrewed in a diagonal pattern one turn at a time

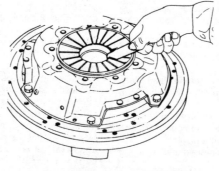

Fig. 8.6 Use a feeler gauge to measure the unevenness of the clutch cover's diaphragm spring toe height (Sec 9)

9.15 Before tightening the clutch cover mounting bolts, it should be centered using either a centering tool or ratchet extension and socket as shown

16 Locate the clutch pressure plate so that the cover engages with the dowels and install the mounting bolts. Tighten them in steps and in a diagonal cross-pattern until they are torqued to specs.
17 Install the transmission.

10 Release bearing – replacement

1 The sealed release bearing, although designed for long life, is worth replacing at the same time as the other clutch components are being replaced or serviced.
2 Deterioration of the release bearing should be suspected when there are signs of grease leakage or if the unit is noisy when spun with the fingers.
3 Remove the rubber dust boot which surrounds the withdrawal lever at the bellhousing opening.
4 Using a screwdriver, unhook and detach the retainer spring from the ball-pin in the front transmission cover (photo).
5 Remove the withdrawal lever (photo).

6 The clutch release bearing and sleeve assembly can now be removed.
7 If necessary, remove the release bearing from its sleeve using a two or three legged puller (photo).
8 Press on the new bearing but apply pressure only to the center track.
9 Reassembly is a reversal of dismantling but apply multi-purpose grease to the internal recess of the release bearing sleeve.
10 Also apply similar grease to the pivot points of the clutch withdrawal lever, the sliding surface of the bearing sleeve and the splines on the transmission main drive gear. **Note**: *Apply only a thin coat of grease to these points, as too much grease will run onto the friction plates when hot, causing damage to the clutch disc surfaces.*

11 Pilot bushing – replacement

1 Remove the clutch disc and cover assembly as described in Section 9.

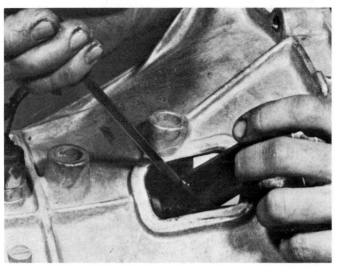

10.4 A screwdriver can be used to disengage the spring from the ball pivot

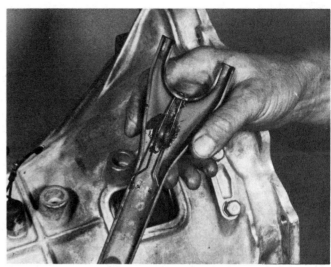

10.5 The spring is attached to the backside of the withdraw lever

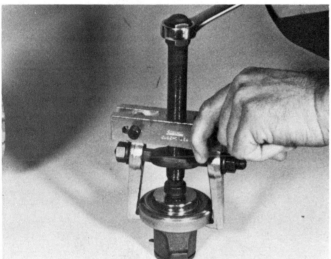

10.7 A puller can be used to separate the release bearing from its hub

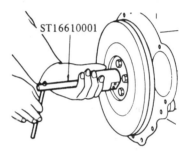

Fig. 8.7 A pilot bushing puller, such as the Datsun tool shown, is needed to remove the pilot bushing (Sec 11)

2   A special tool is needed to remove the pilot bushing (Fig. 8.7). This tool can be obtained from a Datsun dealer or from a well-stocked auto parts store.

3   Before installing the new bushing, thoroughly clean the bushing hole.

4   Using an appropriate sized socket or piece of tubing, insert the new bushing into the hole until the outer end of the bushing is 0.157 in (4.0 mm) from the outside surface of the crankshaft flange. When installing the bushing, be careful not to damage its outer end.

5   Reinstall the clutch assembly and transmission.

12 Drivetrain – general information

A single-piece driveshaft is installed on all models. The driveshaft is supported at the rear by the pinion flange of the differential, and at the front by the transmission rear extension housing. It incorporates two universal joints, one at either end of the shaft. These universal joints are of the sealed type; therefore no maintenance can be carried out on them.

The driveshaft is finely balanced during manufacture and, in the case of worn universal joints, a replacement driveshaft will have to be purchased. When removing the driveshaft for other than replacement reasons, the yoke-to-companion flange relationships must be marked so the driveshaft can be reinstalled in the exact position it was prior to removal.

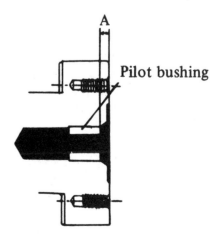

Fig. 8.8 The pilot bushing should be installed so that the distance A is as specified in the text (Sec 11)

The main rear axle component is the hypoid final drive and differential unit, which is fixed to the body at the rear using a cross-bracket located in rubber mountings. The front of the differential is mounted to the suspension crossmember.

Two differential types are used on ZX models, which require slightly different service procedures. The models equipped with each differential type are listed in Specifications.

Because of the complexity and critical nature of the differential adjustments, as well as the special equipment needed to perform the operations, we recommend any disassembly of the differential be done by a Datsun dealer or other qualified mechanic.

The power is transferred from the differential to the rear wheels by rear drive axles, which rotate through two universal joints, one attached to the differential and the other to the rear hub. The type of drive axle used on non-turbo ZX models is of the Cardan universal joint type, while the axle used on Turbo models is of the tripod universal joint type.

The rear hub/axle stub assemblies incorporate two rear wheel bearings, and are mounted on the trailing ends of the suspension arms.

13 Drivetrain – inspection

Refer to Chapter 1 for drivetrain inspection procedures.

14 Rear axle stub, bearings and oil seal – removal and installation

1   Jack up the rear of the vehicle and remove the wheel. Support the frame and the suspension securely.
2   Unscrew and remove the four bolts which secure the drive axle flange at the wheel hub; move the drive axle to one side out of the way.
3   Temporarily install the wheel and tyre and lower the jacks. Apply the parking brake fully and then unscrew the wheel bearing locknut. This nut is very tight and will require leverage from a socket having an operating arm extension of from two to three feet (0.60 to 0.90 meters).
4   Jack up the vehicle again, remove the brake caliper and rotor, and using a slide hammer extract the rear axle shaft stub. This will come out complete with outer bearing.
5   Remove the inner flange, distance piece and the bearing washer.
6   Using a tubular drift, drive out the inner bearing and oil seal.
7   Examine the condition of the outer bearing/oil seal. If the seal face is cracked or the bearing is rough or noisy in operation, it must be pressed off and a new one installed so that the side of the bearing with the seal will be facing the wheel and tire.
8   Drive in the inner bearing and new oil seal. Be sure the sealed side of the inner bearing is toward the differential.
9   Pack general purpose grease into the bearing and into the space between them, and then install the distance piece. Should the ends of the distance piece be deformed it should be installed after reference to the grading mark stamped on it (this is repeated on the bearing housing).
10 Insert the axle stub and the inner flange, taking care not to damage the oil seal.
11 Fit the thrust washer and bearing locknut. Tighten the locknut to specification after having temporarily installed the wheel and brake drum and lowered the car to the ground. Raise the car again and remove the wheel. Attach a spring balance to a wheel stud and check the point at which the hub will rotate. This should be at a reading on the spring balance of 2.6 lb (1.2 kg) or less. Where this condition is not met, tighten the locknut progressively up to 240 ft-lb (33 kg/m) testing each increase in torque tightening until the preload is correct. When the preload is correctly set, the endplay of the rear axleshaft stub should not exceed 0.012 in (0.3 mm).
12 Securely stake the bearing locknut, install the drive axle, brake caliper and rotor and wheel and tire, and lower the vehicle.

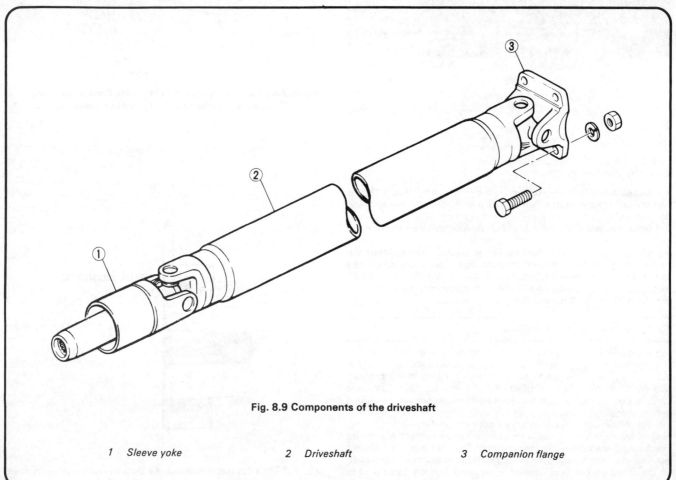

Fig. 8.9 Components of the driveshaft

1   Sleeve yoke   *2   Driveshaft*   *3   Companion flange*

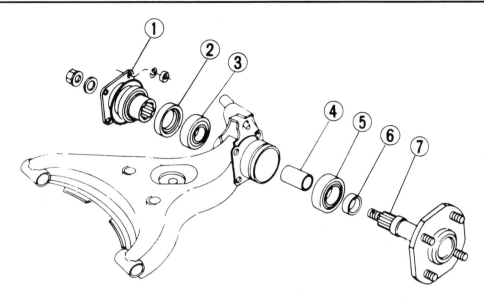

Fig. 8.10 Exploded view of the rear axle stub and wheel bearing assembly (Sec 14)

1 *Companion flange*
2 *Grease seal*
3 *Inner wheel bearing*

4 *Distance piece*
5 *Outer wheel bearing*

6 *Bearing spacer*
7 *Rear axle shaft assembly*

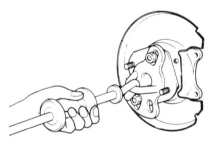

Fig. 8.11 A rear axle adapter plate and slide hammer may be needed to remove the rear axle assembly (Sec 14)

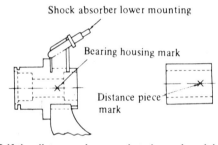

Fig. 8.12 If the distance piece needs to be replaced, be sure the new piece has a code letter matching that of the bearing housing (Sec 14)

15 Driveshaft – removal and installation

1   Raise the rear of the car and support it on jackstands.
2   Remove the front exhaust pipe, catalytic converter and necessary heatshields for access to the driveshaft. Refer to Chapter 6 if necessary.
3   Mark the edges of the driveshaft rear flange and the differential pinion flange so that they can be realigned upon installation.
4   Using a screwdriver placed through the rear universal joint to keep the shaft from turning, remove the four bolts that connect the rear flange with the pinion flange.
5   Push the shaft forward slightly to disconnect the rear flanges. Then lower the shaft and carefully pull it rearward until the forward end is withdrawn from the rear of the transmission.
6   While the driveshaft is removed, the rear of the transmission should be covered or plugged to prevent loss of oil.
7   The universal joints cannot be disassembled and, if defective, the entire section of the driveshaft that it is attached to must be replaced.
8   Installation is the reverse of the removal procedure. **Note:** *During installation make sure the marks on the rear flanges line up.*

16 Rear drive axle – removal and installation

Cardan universal joint type
1   Raise the rear end of the car and support it on jackstands.
2   On R180 differentials, remove the bolts that attach the drive axle flange to the rear hub and separate the axle from the hub.

3   Hold the drive axle at the maximum angle the universal joint will allow, and remove the side yoke fitting bolt. Then disengage the drive axle from the differential. Take care that the differential side oil seal is not damaged when the shaft is pulled out.
3   On R200 differentials, remove the bolts and nuts that attach the drive axle flange to both the differential flange and the rear wheel hub, and remove the drive axle.
4   Visually inspect the assembly for any signs of wear or damage. Slide the driveshaft in and out of the sleeve yoke and ensure that it operates smoothly. When the splines are fully compressed into each other try rocking the driveshaft inside the sleeve yoke to detect any side play. If any of the previously mentioned checks are not as specified, the driveshaft will have to be replaced as an assembly.
5   Operate the two universal joints and check for a smooth action. If the axial play in the spiders exceeds 0.0008 in (0.2 mm), or the operation is not smooth, the universal joints can be replaced as described in Section 17.
7   Installation of the driveshaft is a reversal of removal but ensure that the bolts are tightened to the specified torque. When installing the yoke retaining bolt always use a new O-ring.

Tripod universal joint type
7   Raise the rear of the car and support it with jackstands.
8   Remove the bolts that attach the drive axle to the rear hub and separate the two.
9   Using a suitable steel bar, pry the drive axle from the differential, and lift the axle out.
10 Installation is the reverse of the removal procedure. Be careful not to damage the differential side oil seal when installing the axle shaft.

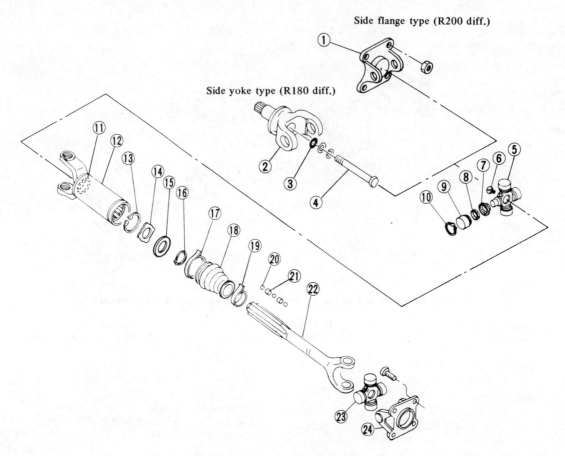

Fig. 8.13 Components of the rear drive axle assembly

1	Yoke flange	7	Dust cover	13	Snap-ring	19	Boot band (short)
2	Side yoke	8	Oil seal	14	Driveshaft stopper	20	Ball
3	O-ring	9	Bearing race assembly	15	Sleeve yoke stopper	21	Ball spacer
4	Side yoke bolt	10	Bearing race snap-ring	16	Snap-ring	22	Driveshaft
5	Spider journal	11	Sleeve yoke plug	17	Boot band (long)	23	Spider assembly
6	Filler plug	12	Sleeve yoke	18	Rubber boot	24	Flange yoke

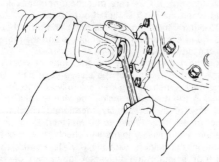

Fig. 8.14 On models with the R180 differential, the side yoke
fitting bolt must be removed in order to remove the drive axle
(Sec 16)

17 Rear drive axle – servicing

Cardan universal joint type

1   If only the spider assemblies need to be disassembled, extract the
snap-rings from the four journals of the spider, then, using a soft-faced
mallet, tap the yoke to remove the bearing races. With the bearing
races removed, it is quite simple to remove the spider from the yoke.
To reassemble the universal joints, reverse the dismantling procedure.

2   If the driveshaft assembly has to be dismantled (to renew a rubber
boot) remove the two boot retainers, peel back the larger diameter of
the boot and extract the snap-ring from the sleeve yoke. Remove the
stoppers and carefully draw out the driveshaft from the sleeve yoke
taking care not to lose the balls and spacers.

3   Before commencing reassembly, thoroughly clean all the parts in
solvent then slide the new rubber boot over the driveshaft and align
the two yokes so that they are on the same center line. Assemble the
snap-ring to the driveshaft. Fit the steel balls and spacers after
greasing their running groove and the area inside the sleeve yoke and
slide the driveshaft into the sleeve yoke. Now locate the stoppers into
the sleeve yoke and install the snap-ring.

4   Adjust the distance between the spider journals so that they are at
their standard length of 13.54 in (344 mm), then manipulate the
rubber boot into its correct position and secure with the boot retainers.

5   The axial play of the universal joint must be adjusted so that it is
not greater than 0.0008 in (0.02 mm). This is done by selecting a
suitable snap-ring from the seven different thicknesses listed in the
Specifications. Be sure that snap-rings positioned opposite one
another are of equal thickness.

Turbo models

6   Servicing the drive axles used on Turbo models is a critical and
complicated procedure, requiring the use of a press. Because of this it
is not a suitable job for the home mechanic and should be taken to a
Datsun dealer or other qualified mechanic.

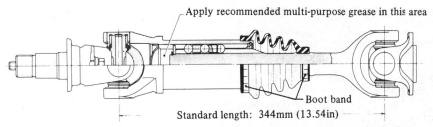

Apply recommended multi-purpose grease in this area

Boot band

Standard length: 344mm (13.54in)

Fig. 8.15 Correct distance between the spider journals of the drive axle (Sec 17)

18 Differential front oil (pinion) seal – replacement

1   Place a suitable container beneath the differential, then remove the drain plug and allow the oil to drain from the unit. Install the drain plug.
2   Raise the rear of the vehicle to obtain access to the unit, and support the frame and differential housing securely on suitable stands or blocks.
3   On R200 type differentials, remove the insulator and muffler/exhaust pipe mounting bolt to free them from the body.
4   Disconnect the rear end of the driveshaft as described in Section 15 and move the shaft to one side.
5   Hold the pinion (companion) flange by placing two 2 in (50 mm) long bolts through two opposite holes. Bolting them up tight, undo the self-locking nut while holding a large screwdriver or tire lever between the two bolts as a lever.
6   Using a suitable puller, withdraw the pinion flange from the differential unit.
7   Remove the defective oil seal by driving in one side of it and levering it out.
8   Install the new oil seal first having greased the mating surfaces of the seal and the axle housing. The lips of the oil seal must face inwards. Using a suitable socket carefully drive the new oil seal into the axle housing recess until the face of the seal is flush with the housing. Make sure that the end of the pinion is not knocked during this operation.
9   Install the pinion flange and thrust washer onto the drive pinion and screw on the pinion nut.
10   Again holding the pinion flange still with the screwdriver or tire lever, tighten the pinion nut to specs.
11   Once the pinion nut is torqued, use the wrench to turn the pinion shaft in both directions several times to settle the bearing rollers. Then fit an inch-pound torque wrench over the pinion nut and slowly turn the pinion shaft, noting the amount of torque needed to begin the shaft rotating. This is the drive pinion preload, and should be as shown in the Specifications. If the preload is below these specs, tighten the pinion nut a little at a time until the proper preload setting is obtained.
12   The remainder of the installation is the reverse of the removal procedure.
13   Following installation, refill the differential with the proper grade and quantity of oil.

19 Differential side oil seal – replacement

R180 differential
1   Detach the rear drive axle from the differential as described in Section 16.
2   Using a suitable screwdriver, pry out the oil seal. Be careful not to scratch or damage the mating surface of the seal bore.
3   Drive in a new seal using a suitable tubular drift or socket.
4   Apply grease to the cavity between the oil seal lips.
5   Reinstall the drive axle.

R200 differential
6   Raise the rear of the car and support it on jackstands.
7   Disconnect the drive axle from the differential as described in Section 16.
8   Using a suitable pry bar, pry the side flange out from the differential. While prying, keep one hand on the flange to keep it from dropping out and possibly being damaged.

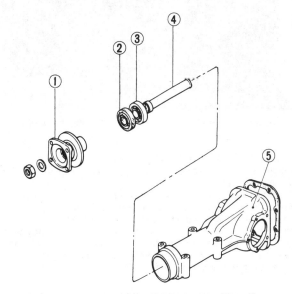

Fig. 8.16 Typical location of the front oil (pinion) seal at the front of the differential (Sec 18)

1   Companion flange   4   Pilot bearing spacer
2   Front oil seal   5   Gear carrier
3   Front pilot bearing

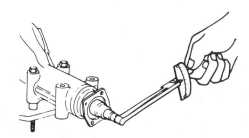

Fig. 8.17 An in-lb torque wrench is used on the pinion nut as shown to adjust the pinion bearing preload (Sec 18)

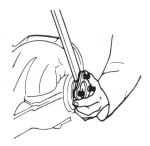

Fig. 8.18 To replace the side oil seal on R200 differentials, the side flange must be pryed out using a suitable bar (Sec 19)

20.7 The differential is attached to the rear mounting insulator by two nuts (arrow)

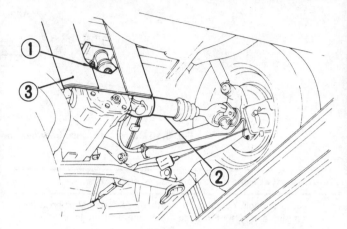

Fig. 8.19 Mounting arrangement of the differential rear cover (Sec 20)

1	Mounting nut	3	Mounting plate
2	Drive axle		

9   Pry the oil seal out with a screwdriver, being careful not to scratch or damage the surface of the bore.
10   Drive in a new seal using a suitable tubular drift or socket.
11   Apply grease to the cavity between the oil seal lips.
12   To reinstall the side flange, insert the shaft of the side flange into the differential until the splines engage, and then apply light hammer blows to the flange until the clip slips into its groove. Be careful not to damage the lips of the oil seal when installing the flange.
13   Reinstall the drive axle and lower the car.

20 Differential – removal and installation

1   Jack up the rear of the vehicle, support the frame on suitable stands or blocks and drain the differential oil.

2   Place a jack (preferably a trolley type) beneath the differential unit.
3   Disconnect the driveshaft from the differential pinion drive flange (Chapter 7).
4   Disconnect the drive axles and remove them from the vehicle, as described in Section 2.
5   Remove the rear mounting plate (number 3 in Fig. 8.19).
6   Raise the jack beneath the differential unit to take its weight.
7   Unscrew and remove the two nuts which hold the differential mounting insulator (photo).
8   Unscrew and remove the four bolts that secure the front of the differential unit to the suspension crossmember. The differential unit can now be carefully lowered and removed from the underside of the vehicle.
9   Installation is the reverse of removal but ensure that all nuts and bolts are tightened to the specified torque.

Chapter 9 Braking system

Refer to Chapter 13 for specifications related to 1983 models

Contents

Specifications

Front disc brake

Type	Disc-CL28V
Cylinder inner diameter	2.386 in (60.6 mm)
Pad dimensions (width x thickness x length)	1.93 x 0.43 x 4.65 in (49 x 11 x 118 mm)
Rotor outer diameter	9.92 in (252 mm)

Rear disc brake

	1979 thru 1981	1982
Type	Disc-AN14H	Disc-CL14H
Cylinder inner diameter	1.685 in (42.8 mm)	1.685 in (42.8 mm)
Pad dimensions (width x thickness x length)	1.65 x 0.41 x 2.24 in (42.0 x 10.3 x 56.8 mm)	1.57 x 0.31 x 2.95 in (40 x 8 x 75 mm)
Rotor outer diameter	10.59 in (269 mm)	10.16 in (258 mm)

Pad wear limit (minimum thickness)

0.079 in (2.0 mm)

Rotor

Maximum runout	
Front	0.0039 in (0.10 mm)
Rear	0.0059 in (0.15 mm)
Maximum parallelism (both types)	0.0012 in (0.03 mm)
Minimum thickness	
Front	0.709 in (18.0 mm)
Rear	0.339 in (8.6 mm)

Master cylinder

Inner diameter	0.9375 in (23.81 mm)
Allowable clearance between cylinder and piston (maximum)	0.0059 in (0.15 mm)

Booster (vacuum servo unit)

Type	M90
Pushrod length	
1979 thru 1981 models	0.374 to 0.413 in (9.5 to 10.5 mm)
1982 models	0.384 to 0.394 in (9.75 to 10.0 mm)
Operating rod length	5.63 in (143 mm)

Parking brake

Correct adjustment (number of notches)	4 to 6
Stroke	3.39 to 4.29 in (86 to 109 mm)

Brake pedal

Free play	0.04 to 0.20 in (1 to 5 mm)
Height	
Manual transmission	7.13 to 7.36 in (181 to 187 mm)
Automatic transmission	7.48 to 7.72 in (190 to 196 mm)
Depressed height (minimum)	
Manual transmission	3.15 in (80 mm)
Automatic transmission	3.54 in (90 mm)

Torque specifications

	ft-lb	m-kg
Brake tube flare nut	12	1.7
Brake hose connector	13	1.8
Air bleeder valve	6	0.8
Booster mounting nuts	7	1.0
Booster input rod locknut	14	2.0
Master cylinder mounting bolts	7	1.0
Front disc caliper mounting bolts	62	8.5
Front disc rotor mounting bolts	47	6.5
Rear disc caliper mounting bolts	33	4.6
NP valve mounting bolts	5	0.6
Brake pedal fulcrum bolt	27	3.7
Lower cylinder pin bolt	20	2.7

1 General information

1   The braking system in the 280ZX is a split system design. It incorporates two separate circuits; one for the front brakes and one for the rear brakes. With this system if one circuit fails, the other circuit will still function.

2   The master cylinder is designed for the split system and incorporates a primary piston for one circuit and a secondary system for the other.

3   A vacuum servo unit is used which draws vacuum from the intake manifold to add power assistance to the normal brake pressure.

4   An NP (Neutral Pressure) valve regulates the fluid pressure in the brake lines so that all wheels receive equal pressure.

5   All four wheels are equipped with disc brakes. These consist of a flat, disc-like rotor which is attached to the axle and wheel. Around one section of the rotor is mounted a stationary caliper assembly which houses two hydraulically-operated disc brake pads. The inner pad is mounted to a piston facing the inner surface of the rotor, while the outer pad is mounted either to a moveable yoke or to the cylinder body so that it faces the outer surface of the rotor. When the brake pedal is applied, brake fluid pressure forces both pads against the rotor. The pressure and resultant friction on the rotor is what slows the wheel.

6   The rear brakes are also equipped with cable-operated parking brake mechanisms, which lock the rear pads against their rotors.

7   All four brakes adjust automatically to lining wear.

8   After completing any operation involving the dismantling of any part of the brake system always test drive the car to check for proper braking performance before resuming normal driving. When testing the brakes, perform the tests on a clean, dry, flat surface. Conditions other than these can lead to inaccurate test results. Test the brakes at various speeds with both light and heavy pedal pressure. The car should brake evenly without pulling to one side or the other. Avoid locking the brakes, as this slides the tires and diminishes braking efficiency and control.

9   Tires, car load and front end alignment are factors which also affect braking performance.

2 Brakes – inspection

Since inspection of the braking system is included in the *Routine Maintenance* schedule, this procedure is described in Chapter 1.

3 Bleeding the brake system

Caution: *Spilled brake fluid can damage the car's paint. Therefore, when using it cover the fenders to protect the paint, clean up any spilled fluid immediately and wash with plenty of water.*

1   Anytime any part of the brake system is disassembled or develops a leak, or when the fluid in the master cylinder reservoir runs low, air will enter the system and cause a decrease in braking performance. To eliminate this air the brakes must be bled using the procedure described in this Section.

2   If air has entered the system because the master cylinder has been disconnected, or the master cylinder reservoir has been low or empty of fluid, or if a complete flushing of the system is needed, all four brakes should be bled. If a brake line serving only one brake is disconnected then only that brake need be bled. Likewise, if any line is disconnected anywhere in the system, the brakes served by that line must be bled.

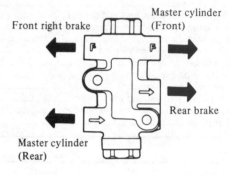

Fig. 9.1 NP valve outlet identification (Sec 1)

3   Before beginning, have an assistant on hand, as well as a good supply of new brake fluid, an empty clear container such as a glass jar, a length of $\frac{3}{16}$-inch plastic, rubber or vinyl tubing to fit over the bleeder valve and a wrench to open and close the bleeder valve. The car may have to be raised and placed on jackstands for clearance.

4   If the car is equipped with power brakes, remove the vacuum reserve in the system by applying the brakes several times.

5   Check that the master cylinder reservoir is full of fluid and be sure to keep it at least half full during the entire operation. If, at any point the reservoir runs low of fluid the entire bleeding procedure must be repeated.**Note**: *Do not mix different types of brake fluid, and do not re-use any old fluid, as this could could deteriorate brake system components.*

6   On 1979 through 1981 models, begin at one of the bleeder valves located on the engine side of the master cylinder. Since the master cylinder in 1982 models has no bleeder valves, begin with the right rear wheel. Loosen the bleeder valve slightly to break it loose then tighten it to a point where it is snug but can still be loosened quickly and easily.

7   Place one end of the tubing over the bleeder valve and submerge the other end in brake fluid in the container (photo).

3.7 Recommended set-up for bleeding brakes

8   With your assistant sitting in the driver's seat, have him pump the brakes a few times to get pressure in the system. On the last pump have him hold the pedal firmly depressed.

9   While the pedal is held depressed, open the breather valve just enough to allow a flow of fluid to leave the valve. Watch for air bubbles to exit the submerged end of the tube. When the fluid flow slows after a couple of seconds, close the valve again and have your assistant release the pedal. If he releases the pedal before the valve is closed again air can be drawn back into the system.

10 Repeat paragraphs 8 and 9 until no more air is seen in the fluid leaving the tube. Then fully tighten the bleeder valve and proceed to the other master cylinder valve, the right rear wheel (as needed), the left rear wheel, the left front wheel, and the right front wheel, in that order, and perform the same operation. Be sure to check the fluid in the master cylinder reservoir frequently.

11 Refill the master cylinder with fluid at the end of the operation.

4   Brake lines – general inspection and replacement

1   About every six months the flexible hoses which connect the steel brake lines should be inspected for cracks, chafing of the outer cover, leaks, blisters, and other damage. These are important and vulnerable parts of the brake system and inspection should be complete. A light and mirror will prove helpful for a thorough check. If a hose exhibits any of the above conditions, replace it with a new one.

2   Prefabricated brake lines are available from dealer parts departments and auto parts stores. **Note:** *Do not, under any circumstances, use lines that have been formed from copper or other soft metals.*

3   When installing the brake line, leave at least 0.75 in (19 mm) clearance between the line and any moving or vibrating parts. Be sure to bleed the brakes after the line is installed.

5   Front disc brake – pad replacement

1   Remove the wheel and tire.
2   Remove the lower pin bolt from the brake caliper.
3   Lift the cylinder body upward to allow access to the brake pads.
4   Remove the upper and lower pad retainers.
5   Remove the inner and outer shims.
6   Lift out the brake pads (photo). **Note:** *After removing the pads, do not depress the brake pedal, as this will force the pistons out of the cylinder.*

7   If the pads are glazed, damaged, fouled with oil or grease or worn beyond their limit (see Specifications or Chapter 1), they should be replaced. **Note:** *Always replace all four pads on the axle (two in each brake assembly) at the same time, and do not mix different pad materials.*

8   Prior to installation, use brake fluid to clean the end of the piston and the pin bolts. Do not use a mineral based solvent.

9   Install the new inner pad into position.

10 Insert a long lever or screwdriver into the cylinder body opening so it is resting on the torque member as shown in Fig. 9.5, and apply outward pressure to depress the inner piston.

11 Raise the cylinder body once more and apply a silicone-based grease to the contact surfaces between the torque member and the pads. Be careful not to get grease on the friction surfaces of the pads.

12 Install the new outer pad, and then the inner and outer shims.

13 Reinstall the pad retainers, making sure they are positioned correctly.

14 Lower the cylinder body and install the lower pin bolt, torquing it to specifications.

15 Depress the brake pedal several times to settle the pads into their proper positions.

16 Reinstall the wheels and tires.

5.6 With the caliper raised, the front pads can be lifted from the torque member

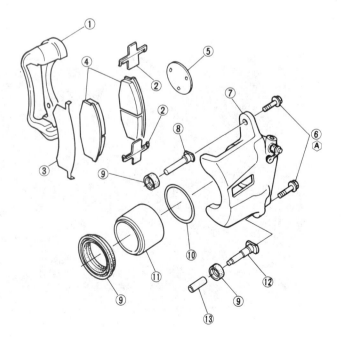

Fig. 9.2 Exploded view of the front disc brake assembly (Sec 5)

1   Torque member
2   Pad retainer
3   Outer shim
4   Pad
5   Inner shim
6   Pin bolt
7   Cylinder body
8   Main pin
9   Dust seal
10 Piston seal
11 Piston
12 Sub pin
13 Rubber seal

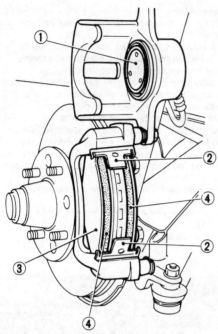

Fig. 9.3 The cylinder body of the front caliper must be lifted upward to gain access to the brake pads (Sec 5)

1	Inner shim	3	Outer shim
2	Pad retainer	4	Pads

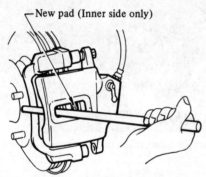

Fig. 9.5 After installing the inner pad, the cylinder body must be levered over to center it (Sec 5)

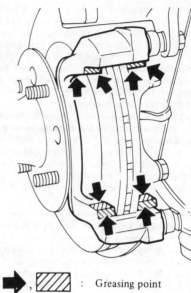

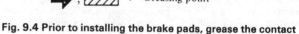

Fig. 9.4 Prior to installing the brake pads, grease the contact surface between the pads and the torque member (Sec 5)

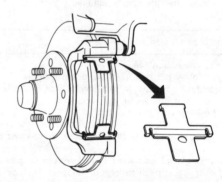

Fig. 9.6 Proper installed position of front brake pad retainers (Sec 5)

6 Front disc caliper – removal and installation

1   Remove the wheel and tire.
2   Remove the brake line and immediately plug the opening to prevent leakage of fluid and to keep foreign matter from entering the line.
3   Remove the two caliper mounting bolts and lift the caliper off the rotor (photo).
4   Installation is the reverse of the removal procedure.
5   Bleed the brakes as described in Section 3.

7 Front disc caliper – overhaul

Note: *Prior to overhauling the brake caliper, purchase a front disc brake overhaul kit for your appropriate model.*
1   Remove the caliper as described in Section 6.
2   Drain any remaining brake fluid from the cylinder body.
3   Clean the outside of the caliper thoroughly.
4   Remove the two pin bolts, and separate the cylinder body from the torque member.
5   Remove the upper and lower pad retainers, and inner and outer shims.

6.3 The caliper mounting bolts are located on the backside

6   Lift out both brake pads.
7   Use clean rags to pad the inside of the caliper. If you have access to compressed air, place an air nozzle into the caliper inlet hole and slowly apply air until the piston is forced out of its bore. **Caution:** *Do not use your fingers to try and catch the piston as serious injury could result.* If you do not have access to compressed air, hold the caliper with the inlet hole up and carefully bang the caliper down on a block of wood to force the piston out. As a last resort, temporarily re-install the brakeline to the caliper and have an assistant depress the brake pedal. The fluid pressure will force the piston out.
8   Using a wooden or plastic dowel, pry the piston seal from the cylinder body, being careful not to scratch the bore.
9   Remove the sub pin and main pin, along with their dust seals.
10 Clean all of the metal parts in brake fluid or denatured alcohol. **Note:** *Never use mineral-based solvents as this can cause the rubber seals to swell and possibly fail.*
11 Check the inside surface of the cylinder bore for any scoring, rust, nicks or other damage. If light scoring or rust is present it can be removed by polishing the bore with a fine 600 grade emery cloth. If the damage is deep the entire body will have to be replaced.
12 Check the torque member for cracks, excessive wear or other damage and replace it if necessary.
13 Inspect the piston for scoring, rust, nicks or other damage. The sliding surface of the piston is plated and cannot be polished with emery paper. If any defects are found, the piston must be replaced. If rubber grease is supplied with the overhaul kit use it to lubricate the cylinder bore. Brake fluid can also be used for this purpose.
14 All rubber seals should be replaced during the overhaul process.
15 Prior to reassembly the cylinder bore should be lubricated with either rubber grease or brake fluid.
16 Install the piston seal into the cylinder body, taking care not to damage it.
17 Apply brake fluid to the sliding surface of the piston. Then apply rubber grease to the inside of the dust seal.
18 Fit the dust seal to the non-grooved end of the piston (photo).
19 Install the seal into the cylinder bore groove and carefully slide the piston into the cylinder bore until the dust seal can also be inserted into the piston groove. Correct engagement of the dust seal in both the piston and cylinder is shown in Fig. 9.7.
20 Apply a coat of multi-purpose grease to the main pin rubber bushing and to the sub pin, and then install them into the cylinder body.
21 The remainder of the assembly procedure is the reverse of the disassembly procedure.

8   Front disc rotor – removal and installation

1   Remove the caliper assembly as described in Section 6.
2   Use a screwdriver to pry off the hub dust cap (photo).
3   Remove the cotter pin.

4   Remove the adjusting cap.
5   Remove the wheel bearing nut and washer.
6   Remove the outer wheel bearing.
7   Remove the hub and rotor assembly.
8   If the rotor needs machining, remove only the inner wheel bearing and grease seal.
9   If the rotor needs replacing it must be separated from the hub. First, remove the bolts (photo) that secure the rotor to the hub. Then use a plastic hammer to tap along the outer edge of the hub until the hub can be removed from the rotor. Once the hub has been separated slightly, two flathead screwdrivers (one on each side) can be used to pry the two pieces apart. If the hub and rotor do not separate easily, apply penetrating oil where the two meet.
10 When installing the rotor to the hub fit it into position on the hub and loosely install the bolts.
11 Tighten the bolts in a crisscross pattern a little at a time until they are torqued to specs.
12 To complete the installation procedure, refer to Chapter 11 for re-packing the wheel bearings and installing the hub and rotor assembly onto the shaft.

9   Rear disc brake – pad replacement

1979 thru 1981 models

1   Remove the wheel and tire.
2   Remove the pad clip (photo).
3   While holding the anti-squeal springs in position, remove the two pad pins. Lift off the springs (photo).
4   Pull out both the inner and outer pads, along with their shims (photo).
5   Using a flat-head screwdriver, rotate the outer piston clockwise, to retract the piston slightly into the caliper (photo). Be careful not to damage the dust seal.
6   Prior to installing the pads, use a large screwdriver or similar lever to slide the yoke outward until there is equal clearance on both sides of the rotor to install the pads.
7   Apply a light coat of an aerosol Teflon coating (disc brake anti-squeak coating) to the back of both pad shims.
8   Position the outer piston so that one of its notches is positioned as shown in Fig. 9.10. Then install the inner pad and shim so that the protrusion on the back of the pad engages with the piston notch.
9   Install the outer pad.
10 Apply a light coat of grease to the pad pins.
11 While holding the anti-squeal springs in place, install the pad pins. Be careful you do not get grease on the friction side of the pads.
12 Install the pad clip.
13 Reinstall the wheel and tire.
14 Following installation, depress the brake pedal a few times to automatically adjust the clearance between the brake pads and the rotor.

7.18 Prior to installation, the dust seal should be positioned on the non-grooved side of the piston

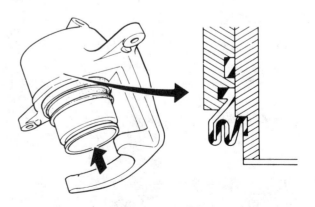

Fig. 9.7 The piston dust seal should be engaged in the grooves of both the piston and cylinder body (Sec 7)

8.2 Use a screwdriver to pry off the hub dust cap

8.9 Location of the hub-to-rotor mounting bolts

9.2 Removing the rear brake pad pin retaining clip

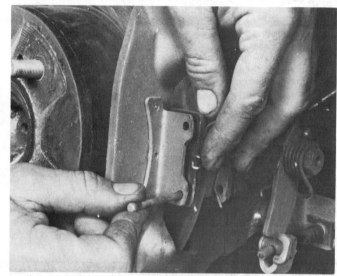

9.3 Hold the springs in place while removing the pad pins

9.4 Removing the rear pads and shims

9.5 Use a screwdriver to rotate the outer piston clockwise to retract it into the caliper

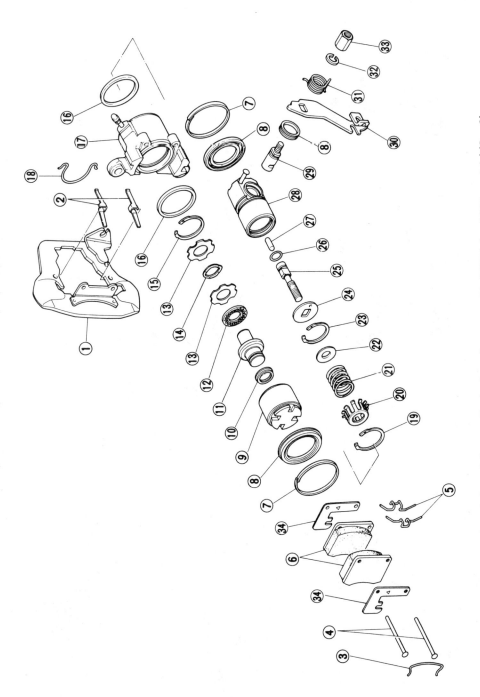

Fig. 9.8 Exploded view of the rear disc brake caliper assembly (1977 thru 1981 models) (Sec 9)

1 Yoke
2 Yoke spring
3 Clip
4 Pad pin
5 Anti-squeal spring
6 Pad
7 Retaining ring
8 Dust seal
9 Outer piston
10 Oil seal
11 Adjusting nut
12 Bearing
13 Spacer
14 Wave washer
15 Snap ring B
16 Piston seal
17 Cylinder body
18 Retainer
19 Snap ring A
20 Spring cover
21 Spring
22 Spring seat
23 Snap ring C
24 Key plate
25 Push rod
26 O-ring
27 Strut
28 Inner piston
29 Cam
30 Toggle lever
31 Spring
32 Washer
33 Nut
34 Anti-squeal shim

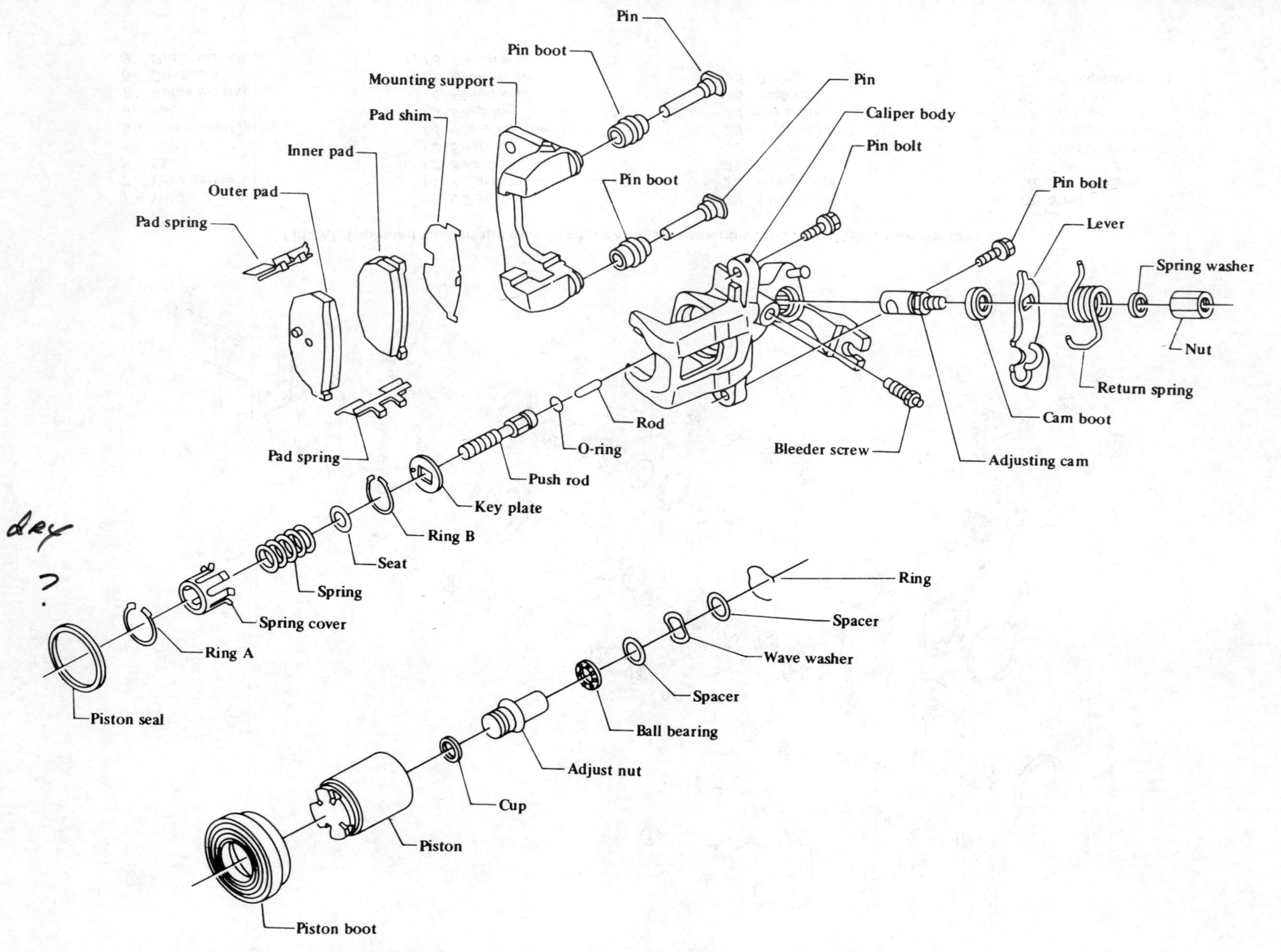

190

Fig. 9.9 Exploded view of the rear disc brake caliper assembly (1982 models) (Sec 9)

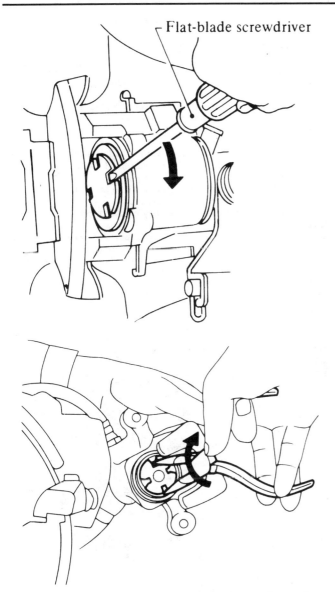

Fig. 9.10 Needle-nosed pliers or a screwdriver can be used to retract or remove the piston by rotating it clockwise or counterclockwise (Sec 9)

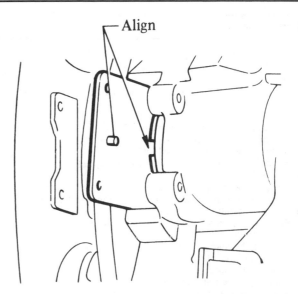

Fig. 9.11 When installing the inner rear disc pad, be sure the locating pin engages with the outer piston's notch (Sec 9)

10 Rear disc caliper – removal and installation

1   Remove the wheel and tire. On 1979 through 1981 models, also remove the brake pads as described in Section 9.
2   Disconnect the brake tube from the caliper. Immediately plug the opening to prevent leakage of fluid, and to keep foreign material from entering the line.
3   Remove the retaining clip that secures the parking brake cable casing to the caliper (photo).
4   Remove the cotter pin from the cable end pin and disconnect the cable from the parking brake toggle lever.
5   Withdraw the parking brake cable housing out of the bracket.
6   Remove the two caliper mounting bolts located on the rear of the caliper assembly.
7   Remove the caliper assembly.
8   Installation is the reverse of the removal procedure.
9   Bleed the brakes as described in Section 3.
10 Following installation, depress the brake pedal a few times to adjust the clearance between the brake pads and the rotor. Also check for any leakage of oil. Pressing on the brake pedal will automatically adjust this clearance.

1982 models
15 Remove the wheel and tire.
16 Remove the pin bolts.
17 Remove the pad springs.
18 Lift out the brake pads and shim.
19 If the pads are glazed, damaged, fouled with oil or grease or worn beyond their specified limit (see Specifications or Chapter 1), they should be replaced. **Note:** *Always replace all four pads on the axle (two in each brake assembly) at the same time, and do not mix different pad materials.*
20 Prior to installation, use brake fluid to clean the end of the piston and the area around the pin bolts. Be careful not to get fluid on the rotor.
21 Using a pair of needle-nosed pliers as shown in Fig. 9.11, rotate the piston clockwise to retract it into the cylinder body.
22 Apply a small amount of silicone-based grease to the contact area between the pads and the mounting support.
23 Install the new pads, shim and pad springs into position.
24 Reinstall the cylinder body on the mounting support, and torque the pin bolts to 20 ft-lb (2.7 m-kg).
25 Depress the brake pedal several times to settle the pads into their proper positions.
26 Reinstall the wheel and tire.

10.3 Removing the locking clip that retains the rear parking brake cable to the caliper assembly

11 Rear disc caliper – overhaul

1979 through 1981 models
1   Unclip the two anti-squeal clamps and remove them from the yoke (photo).
2   Separate the caliper from the yoke by pushing it outward and remove it (photo).
3   Remove the yoke springs (photo).
4   Remove the caliper retainer clip (photo).
5   Remove the inner and outer seal retainer clips (photo).
6   Remove the outer dust seal (photo).
7   Remove the pistons from the caliper by pushing on the outer piston (photo).
8   Using a wooden or plastic dowel remove the two piston seals from the caliper bore. A metal tool is not recommended for this as it could easily scratch the bore surface.
9   Remove the outer piston assembly by unscrewing it counter-clockwise (photo).
10 Remove the snap-ring from the outer piston (photo), and lift out the piston components for inspection.
11 Remove the dust seal from the inner piston (photo).
12 Remove the outer snap-ring from the inner piston. Lift off the spring cover and spring.
13 Remove the inner snap-ring from the inner piston.

14 Turn the inner piston upside down and remove the spring seat and key plate.
15 Pull the push rod out of the piston and remove the strut and O-ring.
16 Disengage the return spring from the toggle lever (photo).
17 Remove the toggle lever and cam assembly by pulling it out of the inner piston.
18 Remove the toggle lever lip seal from the inner piston.
19 Use a screwdriver to carefully pry out the seal and bearing retainer from the inner piston.
20 Check the outer surfaces of the inner and outer pistons for scoring, nicks, rust or other damage. If light rust or scoring is present it can be removed by using No. 600 grid emery cloth. If damage is deep the piston must be replaced.
21 Check the threads on the push rod. Make sure they are in good condition and replace the rod if necessary.
22 Inspect the push rod spring for any cracks or other damage and replace it if necessary.
23 Inspect the inner surface of the caliper bore for any nicks, scoring, rust or other damage. Again, if light rust or scoring is present it can be removed by using No. 600 grit emery cloth. If damage is more serious the caliper housing will have to be replaced.
24 Inspect the needle bearing inside the outer piston for freedom of movement. If any of the rollers are binding the bearing will have to be replaced by prying it out.

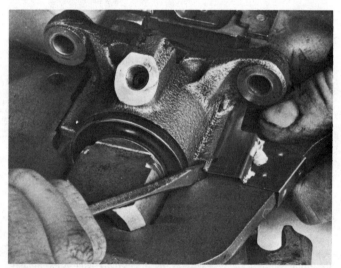

11.1 Removing the anti-squeak clamps from the yoke

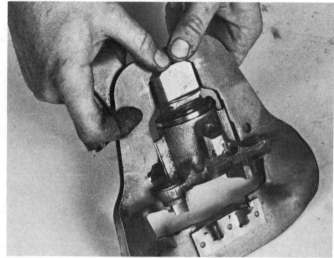

11.2 Separate the caliper from the yoke by pushing outward on the inner piston

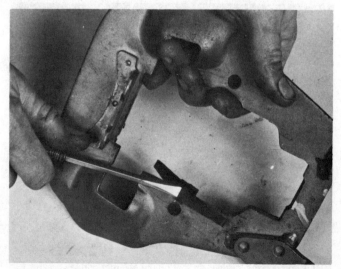

11.3 Removing the yoke springs

11.4 Removing the caliper retainer clip

11.5 Remove the retaining rings from both piston dust seals

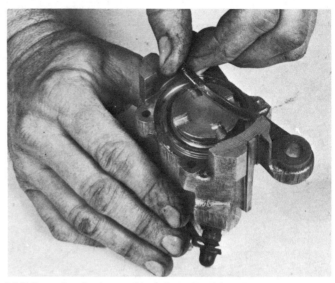

11.6 Removing the dust seal from the outer piston

11.7 Both pistons are removed from the caliper by pushing on the outer piston

11.9 The pistons are separated by turning the outer piston counterclockwise

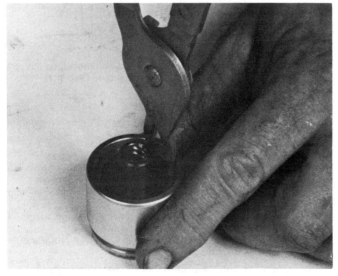

11.10 Removing the snap-ring from the outer piston

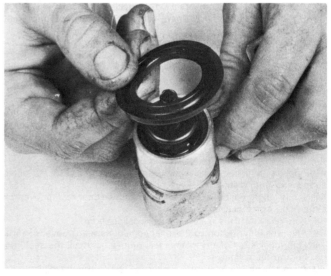

11.11 Removing the dust seal from the inner piston

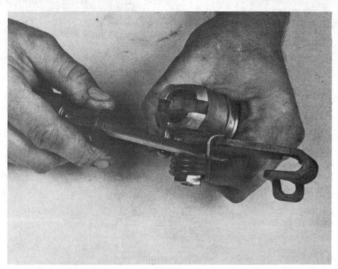

11.16 Use a screwdriver to remove the return spring from the toggle lever

25 Apply a coat of silicone-based grease to the needle bearings.
26 Install the seal and bearing retainer by gently tapping it into place with a plastic-head hammer.
27 Install a new lip seal onto the retainer.
28 Carefully insert the toggle lever and cam assembly into the outer piston.
29 Lubricate both ends of the strut with silicone-based rubber grease and insert it in the push rod.
30 Lightly lubricate the push rod O-ring with silicone-based grease and install it into its groove on the push rod.
31 Insert the strut and push rod into the piston.
32 Install the key plate over the push rod. Be sure that the push rod is aligned so that the locating pin in the key plate is properly fitted into its hole in the piston.
33 Install the inner snap-ring into its groove in the piston.
34 Install the spring seat, spring and spring cover over the push rod.
35 Place the outer snap-ring into position over the spring cover then place an appropriately sized socket over the push rod so that it sits on the spring cover. Place the assembly in a vise and tighten the vise until the spring is compressed enough for the outer snap-ring to be installed in its groove. Be careful that the spring cover is properly centered in the bore so that the tangs do not get damaged.
36 Install a new lip seal onto the adjusting nut. Be sure the lip is facing in the direction shown in Fig. 9.12. Lubricate the lip seal lightly with rubber grease.
37 Place the adjusting screw into the outer piston bore.
38 Place the bearing spacer, wave washer and spacer, in that order, over the adjusting nut.
39 Install the snap-ring into the outer piston.
40 Install the outer piston onto the push rod.
41 Apply a light coat of silicone-based rubber grease to the cylinder bore.
42 Install the new pistons seals into their grooves inside the bore. Lightly lubricate the seals with rubber grease.
43 Apply a light coat of sealing grease into the seal groove on the inner piston. Wipe off any residual grease that may have gotten onto the exterior surface of the piston.
44 Install a new dust seal into position on the inner piston.
45 Install the dust seal retaining ring on the inner piston.
46 Apply a light coat of silicone-based rubber grease to the outer surfaces of both pistons.
47 Apply a light coat of seal grease into the two dust seal grooves on either side of the caliper housing.
48 Carefully insert the pistons into the caliper bore.
49 Align the inner piston so the inner edge of its seal groove is in line with the inner edge of the caliper seal groove, and pull the seal into position on the caliper.
50 Align the outer piston in a similar fashion to the inner piston so that the inner edge of the seal groove is in line with the inner edge of the caliper seal groove.

51 Install the outer piston dust seal.
52 Install the dust seal retaining ring onto the outer piston.
53 Place the caliper retainer in its groove.
54 Install the yoke springs into position on the yoke (photo).
55 Apply a light coat of grease to the surfaces shown in Fig. 9.13.
56 Install the caliper into the yoke.
57 Install the anti-squeak clamps onto the yoke.

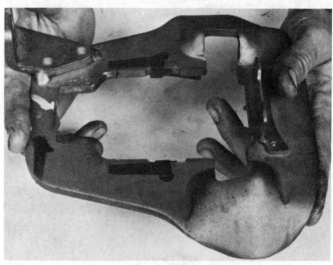

11.54 The yoke springs should be installed prior to attaching the caliper to the yoke

Fig. 9.12 The rubber cup should be installed on the adjust nut so the seal lip points in the direction shown (Sec 11)

1982 models
Note: *Prior to overhauling the brake caliper, purchase the appropriate rear brake overhaul kit for your particular model.*
58 Remove the caliper as described in Section 10.
59 Drain any remaining brake fluid from the cylinder body.
60 Remove the two pin bolts, and separate the cylinder body from the mounting support.
61 Remove the brake pad springs, pads and shim from the mounting support.
62 Remove the piston from the cylinder body by using a pair of needle-nosed pliers to rotate the piston counterclockwise.
63 Once the piston is removed, use the following procedure to disassemble it:

a) Use a thin flat-blade screwdriver to pry out the ring.
b) Remove the spacers, wave washer, ball bearing and adjust nut from the piston.

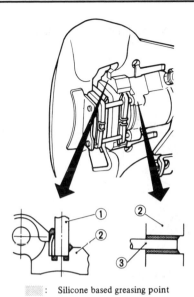

: Silicone based greasing point

Fig. 9.13 During reassembly of the rear caliper, silicone grease should be applied to the points shown (Sec 11)

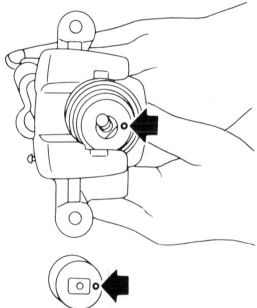

Fig. 9.14 When assembling the cylinder components, the convex point of the key plate must fit together with the concave point of the cylinder (Sec 11)

c)   Remove the rubber cup from the adjust nut.
d)   Remove the piston boot from the piston.

64 Disassemble the cylinder body by using the following procedure:

a)   Using suitable pliers, pry out ring A, and then remove the spring cover, spring and seat.
b)   Pry out ring B, and then remove the key plate, push rod and rod.
c)   Remove the O-ring from the push rod.

65 Using a wooden, plastic dowel, pry out the piston seal from the cylinder body, being careful not to scratch the bore.
66 Disengage and remove the return spring from the lever, then remove the nut, spring washer, adjusting cam and cam boot.
67 Remove the pins and pin boots from the mounting support.
68 Clean all of the metal parts in brake fluid or denatured alcohol.
Note: *Never use mineral-based solvents as this can cause the rubber seals to swell and possibly fail.*
69 Check the inside surface of the cylinder bore for any scoring, rust,

nicks or other damage. If light scoring or rust is present it can be removed by polishing the bore with a fine 600 grit emery cloth. If the damage is deep the entire body will have to be replaced.
70 Check the yoke for cracks, excessive wear or other damage and replace it if necessary.
71 Inspect the piston for scoring, rust, nicks or other damage. The sliding surface of the piston is plated and cannot be polished with emery paper. If any defects are found, the piston must be replaced.
72 All rubber seals should be replaced during the overhaul process.
73 Prior to reassembly, apply a thin coat of rubber grease to the push rod groove and O-ring, the adjust nut groove and rubber cup, the piston seal, the inside of the piston boot and the sliding surfaces of the piston and pins.
74 Install the rubber cup on the adjust nut so the lip faces in the direction shown in Fig. 9.12.
75 Installation is the reverse of the removal procedure with the following note: when assembling the cylinder body components, fit the push rod into the square hole of the key plate, and fit the convex point of the key plate so it engages with the concave point of the cylinder.

12 Rear disc rotor – removal and installation

1   Remove the rear disc caliper as described in Section 10.
2   Remove the rotor by sliding it off the hub and wheel studs. If the rotor will not separate easily from the hub, apply penetrating oil where the hub and rotor meet, and tap on the rotor with a soft-faced hammer.
3   Installation is the reverse of the removal procedure.

13 Master cylinder – removal and installation

1   Disconnect the negative battery cable.
2   Place newspaper or rags under the master cylinder to catch any leaking brake fluid. **Note:** *Be sure not to let brake fluid touch the painted surfaces of the car.*
3   Disconnect the electrical lead(s) going to the reservoir caps.
4   Loosen the nuts securing the two brake lines to the master cylinder.
5   Remove the two nuts that secure the master cylinder to the vacuum servo unit (photo).
6   Carefully lift the cylinder off its mounting studs, remove the brake lines from the cylinder, and immediately place your fingers over the holes to prevent leakage of fluid. Then lift the cylinder out of the engine compartment.
7   Plug the fluid lines to prevent further leakage of fluid. If the master cylinder needs to be disassembled, refer to Section 14.
8   Installation is the reverse of the removal procedure.
9   Bleed the entire brake system as described in Section 3.

13.5 To remove the master cylinder, remove the nuts at the 12 and 6 o'clock positions attaching it to the brake booster

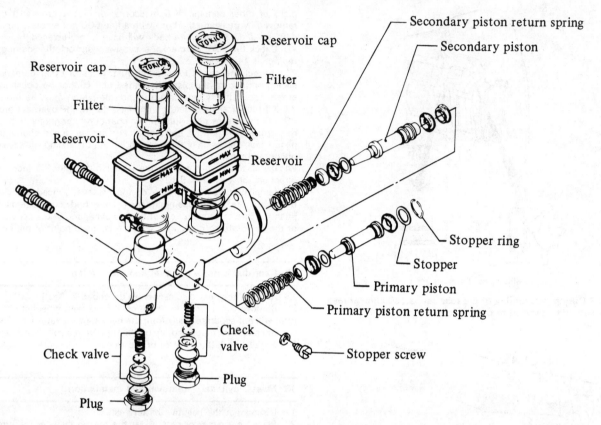

Fig. 9.15 Exploded view of a typical master cylinder (1970 thru 1981 models)

14 Master cylinder – overhaul

1   Obtain a master cylinder rebuild kit. **Note:** *280ZX models use one of two different makes of master cylinder, either a Nabco or a Tokico. As there is no interchangeability of parts between the two models, be sure you get the appropriate rebuild kit for your car.*
2   Clean away external dirt and then remove the reservoir caps and filters and empty out the fluid.
3   From the end of the master cylinder pry out the snap-ring or stopper ring. Then remove the stop washer (if equipped), the primary piston and the spring.
4   Insert a rod to depress the secondary piston and then unscrew the stop screw from the master cylinder. Release the rod and withdraw the secondary piston.
5   The check valve assemblies can be removed by unscrewing the check valve plugs.
6   At this stage, inspect the surfaces of the pistons and cylinder bores for scoring or 'bright' wear areas. If these are evident, replace the complete master cylinder.
7   Wash all components in clean hydraulic fluid or alcohol – nothing else.
8   Do not detach the reservoirs unless absolutely necessary.
9   Commence reassembly by manipulating the new seals into position using the fingers only. Be sure the seal lips are facing in the proper directions.
10 Dip all internal components in clean hydraulic fluid before reassembly.
11 Install the secondary spring and piston assembly. Hold it depressed and screw in the stop screw.
12 Install the primary spring and the primary piston assembly. Fit the stop washer (if equipped) and the snap-ring, or stopper ring.

15 Vacuum servo (booster) unit – general information and testing

1   A vacuum servo unit is fitted into the brake hydraulic circuit in series with the master cylinder, to provide assistance to the driver

when the brake pedal is depressed. This reduces the effort required by the driver to operate the brakes under all braking conditions.
2   The unit operates by vacuum obtained from the intake manifold and comprises basically a booster diaphragm and check valve. The servo unit and hydraulic master cylinder are connected together so that the servo unit piston rod acts as the master cylinder pushrod. The driver's braking effort is transmitted through another pushrod in the servo unit piston and its built-in control system. The servo unit piston does not fit tightly into the cylinder, but has a strong diaphragm to keep its edges in constant contact with the cylinder wall, so assuring an air tight seal between the two parts. The forward chamber is held under vacuum conditions created in the intake manifold of the engine and, during periods when the brake pedal is not in use, the controls open a passage to the rear chamber so placing it under the vacuum conditions as well. When the brake pedal is depressed, the vacuum passage to the rear chamber is cut off and the chamber opened to atmospheric pressure. The consequent rush of air pushes the servo piston forward in the vacuum chamber and operates the main pushrod to the master cylinder.
3   The controls are designed so that assistance is given under all conditions and, when the brakes are not required, vacuum in the rear chamber is established when the brake pedal is released. All air from the atmosphere entering the rear chamber is passed through a small air filter.
4   Under normal operating conditions the vacuum servo unit is very reliable and does not require overhaul except at very high mileage. In this case it is far better to obtain a service exchange unit, rather than repair the original unit.
5   It is emphasised, that the servo unit assists in reducing the braking effort required at the foot pedal and in the event of its failure, the hydraulic braking system is in no way affected except that the need for higher pedal pressures will be noticed.
6   To check for a satisfactory vacuum servo unit, depress the brake pedal several times. The distance which the pedal travels on each depression should not vary.
7   Now hold the pedal fully depressed and start the engine. The pedal should be felt to move down slightly when the engine starts.
8   Depress the brake pedal, switch off the engine holding the pedal

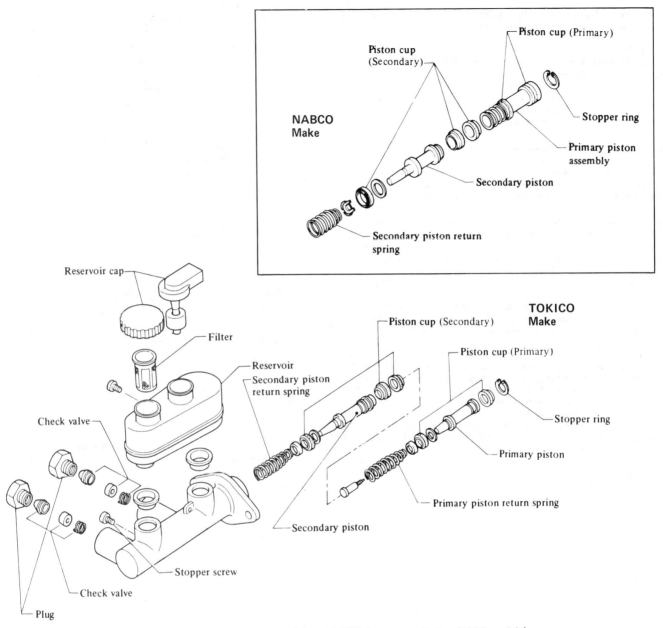

Fig. 9.16 Exploded view of NABCO and TOKICO master cylinders (1982 models)

down for about 30 seconds. The position of the pedal should not alter.
9   Restart the engine, run it for a minute or two and then turn it off. Depress the brake pedal firmly several times. The pedal travel should decrease with each application.
10 If the unit does not perform as indicated locate the source of the problem by performing the following tests:

    a)   First, carefully inspect the condition of the vacuum hoses connecting the servo unit with the check valve, the check valve with the intake manifold, and the check valve with its other connections. If any holes, cracking or other damage is found replace the defective hoses.

    b)   Next, remove the check valve from the vacuum line. If a vacuum pump is available, apply 7.87 inHg (26.7 kPa) of vacuum to the valve opening that leads to the servo unit. If a vacuum pump is not available, put your mouth to the opening and attempt to suck air through the valve. If the pressure on the pump drops more than 0.39 inHg (1.3 kPa) in 15 seconds, or if you are able to suck air through the valve, the valve is defective and should be replaced.

    c)   Now blow air into the valve through the same opening as

before. If the valve does not allow you to blow air into it, it is defective and should be replaced.

    d)   To test the servo unit, connect a vacuum gauge between the unit and the check valve. Start the engine and slowly increase the engine speed. Shut off the engine when the vacuum reading reaches 19.69 inHg (66.7 kPa) and observe the gauge. If the reading drops more than 0.98 inHg (3.3 kPa) within 15 seconds after the engine has been shut off, the servo unit is defective and should be replaced.

    e)   One final test is to repeat the previous test with the brake pedal fully depressed. Again, if the vacuum leakage is greater than specified, replace the servo unit.

16 Vacuum servo (booster) unit – removal and installation

1   Remove the master cylinder as described in Section 13.
2   Disconnect the vacuum line from the servo unit.
3   Working under the dash, disconnect the servo pushrod from the brake pedal by removing the clevis pin.

4　Remove the four retaining nuts from the servo unit's mounting studs. Return to the engine compartment and withdraw the unit from the car.

5　Installation is the reverse of the removal procedure. **Note**: *Following installation, measure the length of the unit's pushrod and operating rod by referring to Fig. 9.17. before installing the master cylinder. If they are not as specified, adjust them.*

6　Bleed the entire brake system as described in Section 3.

7　Check the brake pedal height and free play and adjust them if necessary as described in Chapter 1.

17　Parking brake – adjustment

As adjustment of the parking brake is a part of the routine maintenance schedule, this procedure is described in Chapter 1.

18　Parking brake lever and front cable – removal and installaion

1　Working first inside the car, remove the passenger seat, referring to Chapter 12, is necessary.

2　Disconnect the wiring connector leading to the parking brake warning switch.

3　Remove the bolts that secure the parking brake lever to the floor.

4　Now raise the rear of the car and support it on jackstands.

5　Remove the locknut and adjusting nut from the end of the front cable at the equalizer.

6　Remove the lock plate that secures the front cable to the body.

7　Moving back to the car's interior, pull the front cable into the interior and remove it from the car, complete with the lever assembly.

8　The front cable can be separated from the lever by breaking or cutting the retaining pin. A replacement clevis pin and cotter pin are available for mounting the new front cable to the lever.

9　Installation is the reverse of the removal procedure, with the following note: during installation, apply a coating of multi-purpose grease to all sliding surfaces.

10　Following installation, adjust the parking brake as described in Chapter 1.

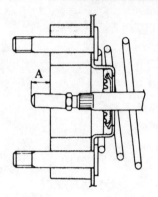

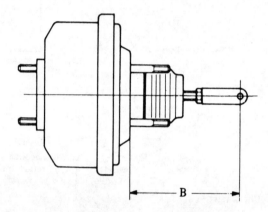

Fig. 9.17 The pushrod A and operating rod B of the brake booster should be adjusted to the measurements shown in the Specifications (Sec 16)

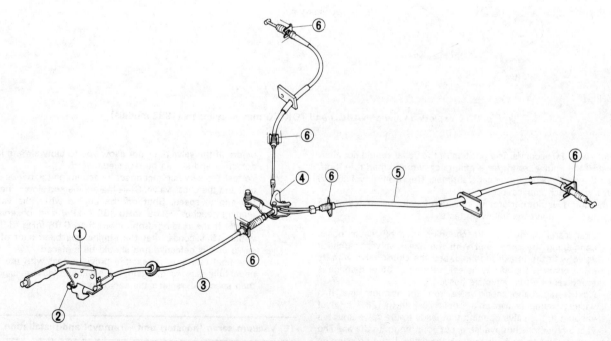

Fig. 9.18 Components of the parking brake system

1	Control lever	3	Front cable	5	Rear cable
2	Brake warning switch	4	Equalizer	6	Lock plate

19 Parking brake rear cable – removal and installation

1   Raise the rear of the car and support it on jackstands.
2   Remove the locknut and adjusting nut from the end of the front cable at the equalizer.
3   Remove the cotter pin and clevis pin that attaches the equalizer to the return lever, and remove the equalizer.
4   Remove the locking clips that attach the rear cable to the rear suspension and rear brakes on both sides.
5   Remove the cotter pins and clevis pins that attach the rear cable to the rear brakes on both sides (photo).
6   Remove the bolts that attach the rear cable mounting plates to the suspension arms, and lift out the rear cable.
7   Installation is the reverse of the removal procedure, with the following note: during installation, apply a thin coat of multi-purpose grease to all sliding surfaces.
8   Following installation, adjust the parking brake as described in Chapter 1.

20 Brake light switch – removal and installation

1   The brake light switch is mounted to the brake pedal bracket just to the rear of the brake pedal.
2   Disconnect the wires leading to the switch.
3   Loosen the locknut.
4   Unscrew the switch from the bracket.
5   Installation is the reverse of the removal procedure. Note that the brake light switch controls the height of the brake pedal. Install the switch so that the brake pedal height is within the specs given at the beginning of this Chapter. For more detailed information on brake pedal adjustments, refer to Chapter 1.

21 Brake pedal adjustments

Because brake pedal adjustments are a part of the car's routine maintenance schedule, this procedure is included in Chapter 1.

22 Brake pedal – removal and installation

1   Remove the left lower instrument cover, located blow the steering column, and also the floor assist nozzle of the heating system.
2   Remove the snap pin and clevis pin that attach the brake booster operating rod to the brake pedal.
3   Remove the fulcrum bolt, disengage the return spring from the pedal and lift the pedal out.
4   Check the pedal bushing for wear or damage, and replace it with a new one if necessary.
5   Installation is the reverse of the removal procedure with the following notes: during installation, apply a small amount of multi-purpose grease to the sliding surfaces of the return spring, fulcrum bolt and clevis pin.
6   Following installation, check and adjust the brake pedal as described in Chapter 1.

19.5 The rear parking brake cables are retained to the rear brakes with cotter pins and locking clips (arrow)

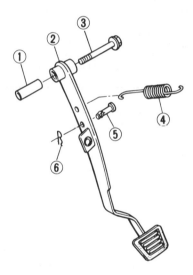

Fig. 9.19 Components of the brake pedal assembly

1   Collar   4   Return spring
2   Brake pedal   5   Clevis pin
3   Fulcrum bolt   6   Snap pin

Chapter 10 Chassis electrical system

Refer to Chapter 13 for information related to 1983 models

Contents

Specifications

Bulbs

Application	Wattage	Type
Headlight (high/low)		
Sealed beam	50/40	6012
Halogen	60/50	
Front combination light		
Turn signal/clearance	27/8	1157
Front side marker light	3.4	158
Rear side marker light	3.4	158
Rear combination light		
Stop/tail	27/8	1157
Turn signal	27	1156
Backup	27	1156
License plate light	10	89
Interior light	10	–
Spot light	8	–
Step light	3.4	158
Rear compartment light	5	–
Door edge light	3	–
Vanity mirror light	5	–
Combination meter		
Illumination light	3.4	158
Combination warning light	3.4	158
Warning gauge light	3.4	158
Illumination light	2.7	161
Cruise control switch		
Illumination/indicator light	1.4	–
Heater (A/C) control panel		
Illumination/A/C indicator light	1.7	–
Glove box light	3.4	158
A/T selector lever illumination light	2.7	161
Cigarette lighter/ashtray illumination light	1.7	–
Ignition switch illumination light	1.4	–
Radio illumination light	2.5	–
Rear defroster indicator light	1.4	–
Instrument console illumination light	1.4	–
Inspection light	8	–

Fuses

1979 thru 1981 models

Circuit	Amperes
Headlight (R)	10
Headlight (L)	10
Horn, stop	20
Clearance, tail	15
Interior	10
Hazard	20
Air conditioner	20
Radio	10
Wiper	15
Flasher	10
Meter, gauge	10
Rear defroster	20

1982 models

Circuit	Amperes
Headlight (R)	10
Headlight (L)	10
Horn, power door lock	15
Stop	15
Clearance, tail	15
Interior, clock	10
Hazard	10
Heater, air conditioner	20
Radio	10
Rear wiper, washer	10
Front wiper, washer, headlight cleaner	15
Flasher, reverse, ASCD	10
Meter, gauge	10
Rear defroster	20
Cigarette lighter	15
Radiator fan motor	15

Fusible links

Circuit	Color
Ignition switch	Brown
Power supply to the fuse box	Black
Electronic Fuel Injection circuit	Green
Electronic Fuel Injection circuit	Brown
Headlight circuit	Brown

Wiring harness color coding

Circuit	Base color
Starting and ignition systems	Black (B)
Charging system	White (W)
Lighting system	Red (R)
Turn signal and horn	Green (G)
Instrument system	Yellow (Y)
Others	Blue (L), Brown (Br) and Light Green (Lg)
Ground	Black (B)

1 General information

This Chapter covers the repair and service procedures for the various lighting and electrical components not associated with the engine, as well as general information on troubleshooting the car's various electrical circuits. Information on the battery, generator, distributor and starter motor can be found in Chapter 5.

The electrical system is of the 12-volt, negative ground type with power supplied by a lead/acid-type battery which is charged by the alternator.

Electrical components located in the dashboard do not use ground wires or straps, but rather use grounding provisions which are integrated in the printed circuit mounted behind the instrument cluster.

It should be noted that whenever portions of the electrical system are worked on, the negative battery cable should be disconnected to prevent electrical shorts and/or fires.

2 Electrical troubleshooting – general information

A typical electrical circuit consists of an electrical component, any switches, relays, motors, etc. relevant to that component and the wiring and connectors that connect the component to both the battery and the chassis. To aid in locating a problem in any electrical circuit, complete wiring diagrams of each model are included at the end of this Chapter.

Before tackling any troublesome electrical circuit, first thoroughly study the appropriate diagrams to get a complete understanding of what makes up that individual circuit. Trouble spots, for instance, can often be narrowed down by noting if other components related to that circuit are operating properly or not. If several components or circuits fail at one time, chances are the fault lies in the fuse or ground connection, as several circuits often are routed through the same fuse and ground connections. This can be confirmed by referring to the fuse box and ground distribution diagrams in this Chapter.

Often, electrical problems stem from simple causes, such as loose or corroded connections, a blown fuse or melted fusible link. Prior to any electrical troubleshooting, always visually check the condition of the fuse, wires and connections of the problem circuit.

If testing instruments are going to be utilized, use the diagrams to plan ahead of time where you will make the necessary connections in order to accurately pinpoint the trouble spot.

The basic tools needed for electrical troubleshooting include a circuit tester or voltmeter (a 12 volt bulb with a set of test leads can also be used), a continuity tester (which includes a bulb, battery and set of test leads) and a jumper wire, preferably with a circuit breaker incorporated, which can be used to bypass electrical components.

Voltage checks should be performed if a circuit is not functioning properly. Connect one lead of a circuit tester to either the negative battery terminal or a known good ground. Connect the other lead to a connector in the circuit being tested, preferably nearest to the battery or fuse. If the bulb of the tester goes on, voltage is reaching that point, which means the part of the circuit between that connector and the battery is problem-free. Continue checking along the circuit in the same fashion. When you reach a point where no voltage is present, the problem lies between there and the last good test point. Most of the time the problem is due to a loose connection. *Keep in mind that some circuits only receive voltage when the ignition key is in the Accessory or Run position.*

A method of finding shorts in a circuit is to remove the fuse and connect a test light or voltmeter in its place to the fuse terminals. There should be no load in the circuit. Move the wiring harness from side to side while watching the test light. If the bulb goes on, there is a short to ground somewhere in that area, probably where insulation has rubbed off of a wire. The same test can be performed on other components of the circuit, including the switch.

A ground check should be done to see if a component is grounded properly. Disconnect the battery and connect one lead of a self-powered test light such as a continuity tester to a known good ground. Connect the other lead to the wire or ground connection being tested. If the bulb goes on, the ground is good. If the bulb does not go on, the ground is not good.

A continuity check is performed to see if a circuit, section of circuit or individual component is passing electricity through it properly. Disconnect the battery, and connect one lead of a self-powered test light such as a continuity tester to one end of the circuit being tested and the other lead to the other end of the circuit. If the bulb goes on, there is continuity, which means the circuit is passing electricity through it properly. Switches can be checked in the same way.

Remember that all electrical circuits are composed basically of electricity running from the battery, through the wires, switches, relays, etc. to the electrical component (light bulb, motor, etc). From there it is run to the car body (ground) where it is passed back to the battery. Any electrical problem is basically an interruption in the flow of electricity from the battery and back.

3   Fuses – general information

The electrical circuits of the car are protected by a combination of fuses and fusible links.

The fuse box is located in the side panel underneath the dash on the right side of the car.

Each of the fuses is designed to protect a specific circuit, as identified on the fuse cover.

If an electrical component has failed, your first check should be the fuse. A fuse which has "blown" can be readily identified by inspecting the curved metal element inside the plastic housing. If this element is broken the fuse is inoperable and should be replaced with a new one.

Fuses are replaced by simply pulling out the old one and pushing in the new one.

It is important that the correct fuse be installed. The different electrical circuits need varying amounts of protection, indicated by the amperage rating on the fuse. A fuse with too low a rating will blow prematurely, while a fuse with too high a rating may not blow soon enough to avoid serious damage.

At no time should the fuse be bypassed by using metal or foil. Serious damage to the electrical system could result.

If the replacement fuse immediately fails, do not replace it with another until the cause of the problem is isolated and corrected. In most cases this will be a short circuit in the wiring system caused by a broken or deteriorated wire.

4   Fusible links – general information

In addition to fuses, the wiring system incorporates fusible links for overload protection. These links are used in circuits which are not ordinarily fused, such as the ignition circuit and the Electronic Fuel Injection circuit.

The fusible links are located near the positive battery terminal, and are easily removed by unplugging the connectors at either end.

If an electrical failure occurs in one of the circuits covered by a fusible link, these should be the first check. If the link is melted, the

entire fusible link harness should be replaced, but only after checking and correcting the electrical fault that caused it.

5   Relays – general information

The various electrical relays are grouped together either in the engine compartment or under the dash for convenience in the event of needed replacement (Fig. 10.3).

The main relay bracket in the engine compartment is located on the right side, just forward of the right shock well.

If a faulty relay is suspected, it can be removed and tested by a Datsun dealer or other qualified shop. Defective relays must be replaced as a unit.

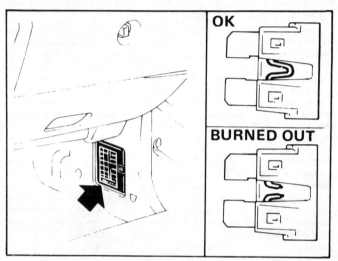

Fig. 10.1 Location of fuse box and reading of fuse condition (Sec 3)

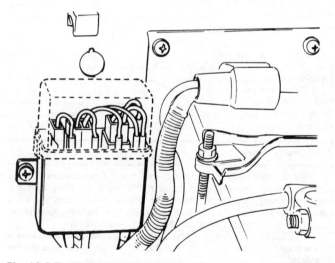

Fig. 10.2 The fusible links are contained in a compartment located just forward of the battery (Sec 4)

6   Turn signals and hazard flashers – general information

Small canister-shaped flasher units are incorporated into the electrical circuits for the directional signals and hazard warning lights; these are located under the dash and just above the steering column. **Note:** *In 1982 models, these two flasher canisters have been combined into one unit.*

When the units are functioning properly an audible click can be heard with the circuit in operation. If the turn signals fail on one side only and the flasher unit cannot be heard, a faulty bulb is indicated. If the flasher unit can be heard, a short in the wiring is indicated.

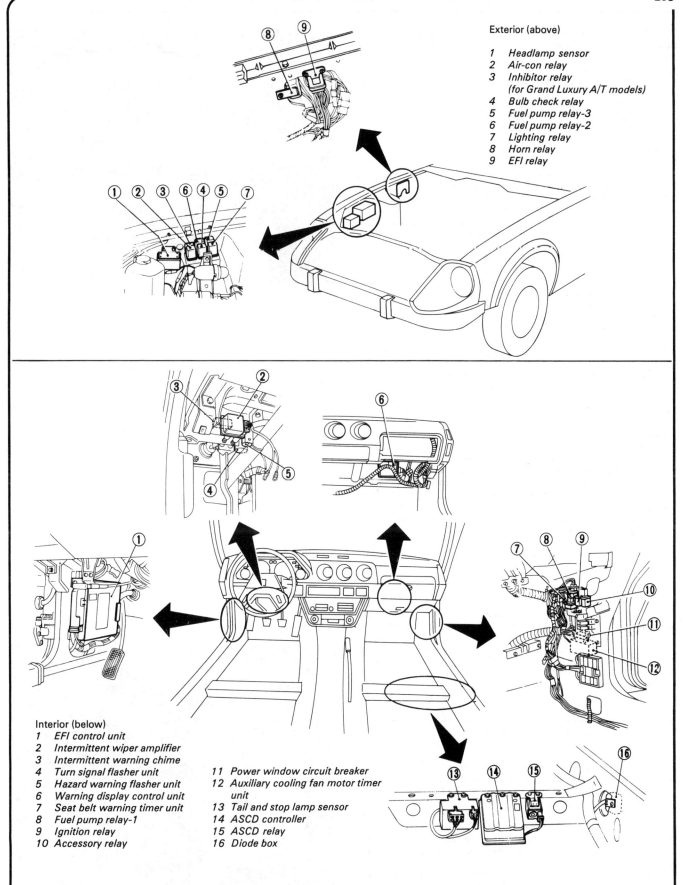

Exterior (above)

1 Headlamp sensor
2 Air-con relay
3 Inhibitor relay
  (for Grand Luxury A/T models)
4 Bulb check relay
5 Fuel pump relay-3
6 Fuel pump relay-2
7 Lighting relay
8 Horn relay
9 EFI relay

Interior (below)
1 EFI control unit
2 Intermittent wiper amplifier
3 Intermittent warning chime
4 Turn signal flasher unit
5 Hazard warning flasher unit
6 Warning display control unit
7 Seat belt warning timer unit
8 Fuel pump relay-1
9 Ignition relay
10 Accessory relay
11 Power window circuit breaker
12 Auxiliary cooling fan motor timer
   unit
13 Tail and stop lamp sensor
14 ASCD controller
15 ASCD relay
16 Diode box

Fig. 10.3 Locations of relays and other accessory electrical components (Sec 5)

If the turn signal fails on both sides, the fault may be due to a blown fuse, faulty flasher unit or switch, or a broken or loose connection. If the fuse has blown, check the wiring for a short before installing a new fuse.

The hazard warning lamps are checked in the same manner as paragraph 3 above.

When replacing either of these flasher units it is important to buy a replacement of the same capacity. Check the new flasher against the old one to be assured of the proper replacement.

7 Horn – checking

1 Two horns are used, one with a low tone and the other with a high tone. They are both mounted behind the front bumper. The horn switch is located in the steering wheel, and can be activated by pressing the center pad or one of the side buttons. The pressing of one of the horn buttons grounds it against the metal frame of the steering wheel, which completes the electrical circuit and sounds the horns. The horn relay is located on the right side of the engine compartment (see accompanying figure).
2 If the horn proves inoperable, your first check should be the fuse. A blown fuse can be readily identified at the fuse box under the lower right side of the dashboard.
3 If the fuse is in good condition, disconnect the electrical lead at one of the horns. Run a jumper wire from the positive battery terminal to the wiring terminal on the horn. If the horn does not blow, the fault lies in the grounding of the horn or the horn itself. Test the other horn also.
4 If the horn did sound in the previous test, this indicates that no current is reaching the horn. In most cases the problem will be in the horn relay. Other checks should include bent metal contacts in the horn switch assembly, or loose or broken wires in the system.

8 Headlight – adjustment

1 The headlight adjustment screws are located to the side and top of each light. The top screw adjusts the beam vertically and the side screw adjusts the beam horizontally. Although due to legal specifications, proper adjustment of the headlights should be done using appropriate beam setting equipment, the following procedure will get them very close. Final adjustment should be done by a qualified mechanic with the proper equipment.
2 Position the car on level ground, facing and at right angles to a wall, and at a distance of approximately 30 feet.
3 Measure the height of the centers of the headlights from the ground and mark these measurements on the wall.
4 Measure the distance from the centerline of the car and the center of each headlight and mark these measurements on the wall, so that you have intersecting lines even with the center of each headlight.
5 Turn on the regular beam of the headlights and turn the horizontal adjusting screws until each beam is centered with their corresponding marks on the wall. Then, turn the vertical adjusting screw until the top of each beam is level with the horizontal centerline mark on the wall.
6 Bounce the car on its suspension and check that the beams return to their correct positions.

9 Headlight – removal and installation

1 Open the hood.
2 If removing the right side headlight, first remove the charcoal canister from its bracket and position it out of the way. Lift the coolant reservoir out from its bracket and position it out of the way. Remove the reservoir bracket from the body.
3 If removing the left side headlight, first remove the headlight cleaner tank and pump, if equipped.
4 Disconnect the wiring connector from the rear of the bulb.
5 Remove the screws that retain the headlight mounting bracket (photo) and lift out the bracket.
6 Remove the screws that secure the headlight retaining ring, and lift the ring and headlight out of the housing.
7 Installation is the reverse of removal, but be sure that the bulb is positioned correctly in the housing, by noting the word TOP in raised letters.

9.5 The headlight mounting bracket is held to the body by three screws

10 Taillight – bulb and lens replacement

Bulb replacement
1 Remove the rear finisher panel from the rear compartment of the car. To gain access to the right side taillight, the right finisher panel must also be removed.
2 Replace bulbs as required by unscrewing their sockets from the taillight housing (photo).
3 Reinstall the finisher panels.

Lens replacement
4 Remove the rear finisher panel from the rear compartment of the car. To gain access to the right side taillight, the right finisher panel must also be removed.
5 Unscrew and remove the bulb sockets from the rear of the taillight housing.
6 Disconnect the wiring connectors from the taillight.
7 Remove the nuts that retain the taillight bracket to the housing and lift the bracket out.
8 Remove the taillight housing by pulling it out from the outside of the car. The housing should break free of the molding without undue force.

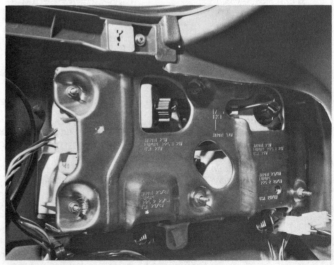

10.2 Once the rear flasher panel is removed, the taillight assembly is exposed

9   Remove the screws that retain the lens to the housing and lift it off.

10 Inspect the gaskets for tears, cracking, hardness or other damage and replace it if necessary. A defective gasket will allow moisture to get inside the taillight, which will result in corrosion.

11 Installation is the reverse of the removal procedure.

11 Lights (exterior and interior) – bulb and lens replacement

1   The lenses of most lights used in the car are held on by a couple of screws, which makes it a simple procedure to gain access to the bulbs.

2   A few lights have their lenses held in by clips. On these the lens can either be removed by unsnapping it by hand or, as with the interior overhead light, using a small screwdriver, inserted in the rear, to pry it off.

3   Three different types of bulbs are used. Type A is removed by depressing it into its socket and turning it counterclockwise. Type B simply unclips from its terminals, and Type C simply pulls out of its socket.

12 Ignition switch – removal and installation

Refer to the steering lock removal and installation procedure described in Chapter 11.

13 Steering column combination switch – removal and installation

1   Disconnect the negative battery cable.

2   Remove the steering wheel as described in Chapter 11.

3   Remove the steering column cover.

4   Disconnect the wiring harness connectors leading to the combination switch.

5   Loosen the retaining screw and slide the combination switch off the front of the steering column.

6   Installation is the reverse of the removal procedure.

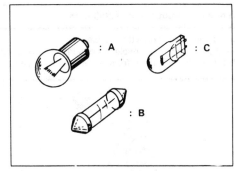

Fig. 10.4 The three types of bulbs used in most of the car's lighting accessories (Sec 11)

14 Wiper switch (1979 and 1980 models) – removal and installation

1   Disconnect the negative battery cable.

2   Remove the steering column cover.

3   Disconnect the wiring connector leading to the wiper switch.

4   Remove the screws that retain the wiper switch to the combination switch and lift it off.

5   Installation is the reverse of the removal procedure.

15 Instrument console – removal and installation

1   Disconnect the negative battery cable.

2   Remove the instrument console bracket covers.

3   Remove the lower instrument covers on both sides. Disconnect any wiring connectors, vacuum lines or heating ducts attached to them.

4   Remove the instrument console mounting screws (Fig. 10.6), and lower the console from the dash until the wiring connectors can be disconnected from the rear.

5   Installation is the reverse of the removal procedure.

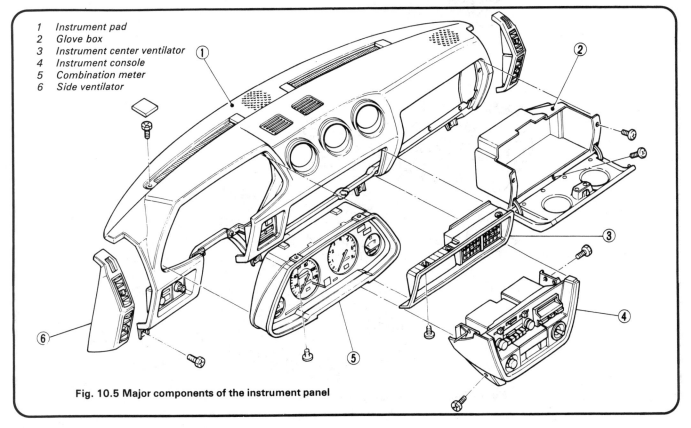

1   Instrument pad
2   Glove box
3   Instrument center ventilator
4   Instrument console
5   Combination meter
6   Side ventilator

Fig. 10.5 Major components of the instrument panel

16 Radio/stereo – removal and installation

1   Disconnect the negative battery cable.
2   Remove the instrument console, as described in Section 15.
3   Pull off the knobs and dials from the front of the radio.

4   Remove the nuts from the radio shafts.
5   Loosen the radio retaining screws, and lift the radio out.
6   If equipped with a stereo, remove the stereo mounting screws and lift out the stereo.
7   Installation is the reverse of the removal procedure.

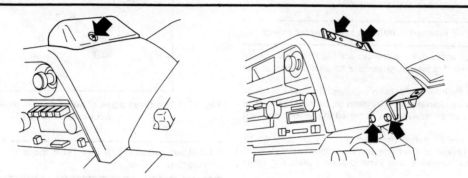

Fig. 10.6 Mounting screw locations for the instrument console (bottom) and bracket cover (top) (Sec 15)

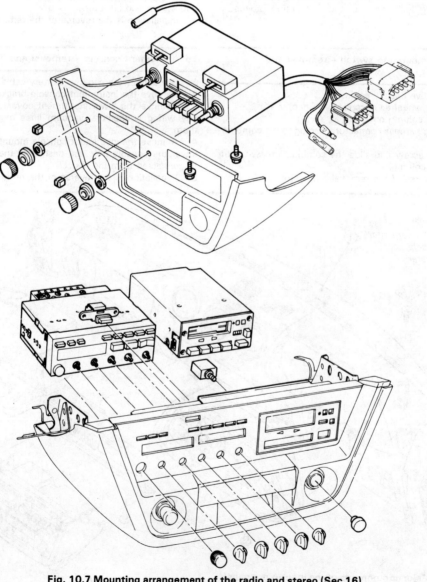

Fig. 10.7 Mounting arrangement of the radio and stereo (Sec 16)

17 Speakers – removal and installation

1 Depending on the type of grille, remove it either by removing the mounting screws or by carefully prying on it with a small screwdriver.
2 Remove the speaker mounting screws.
3 Lift the speaker out of its mounting hole enough to disconnect the wires from the rear.
4 Installation is the reverse of the removal procedure.

18 Heater/A/C control assembly – removal and installation

1 Disconnect the negative battery cable.
2 Remove the instrument console, as described in Section 15.
3 Remove the screws that attach the instrument center ventilator to the dash and lift it off.
4 Disconnect the control cables and rod from the doors of the heater assembly.
5 Remove the screws that attach the heater/A/C control assembly to the dash and lift it out.
6 Installation is the reverse of the removal procedure. **Note:** *After installing the control assembly into the dash the control cables and rod must be adjusted in the following manner:*
Air intake door cable
   a) Set the control lever in the Off position. While pushing the intake door lever toward the front of the car, pull the outer case of the intake door control cable toward the rear and then secure the cable casing with the securing clip.
Temperature control cable
   b) Set the temperature control lever in the maximum cold position. Tighten the control rod mounting screw temporarily. While pushing the water cock lever in the direction shown in Fig. 10.10, pull the outer casing of the temperature control cable away from the lever, and secure the outer casing with the retaining clip.
   c) Set the temperature lever in the maximum hot position, push the air-mix door lever downward and securely tighten the control rod to air-mix door lever.
Air, ventilation door, floor door, and defroster door control rods
   d) Set the control lever in the Vent position. Position the link so it contacts stoppers A and B (Fig. 10.12), and secure the air control rod.
   e) With the link maintained in the same position, push up on the ventilation door lever and secure the ventilation floor rod. Push the floor door lever downward and secure the floor door rod.
   f) If equipped with a defroster door rod, set the control lever in the Def position. Then fully open the defroster door and secure the defroster door rod.

Fig. 10.9 Procedure for adjusting the air intake door cable (Sec 18)

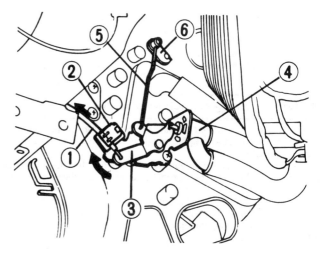

Fig. 10.10 Procedure for adjusting the temperature control cable (Sec 18)

1 Temperature control cable outer cable	4 Water cock
2 Clip	5 Rod
3 Water cock lever	6 Air-mix door lever

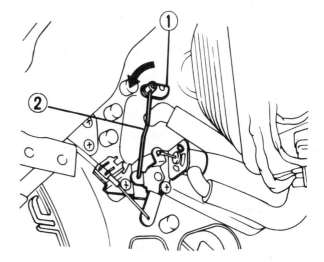

Fig. 10.11 Procedure for adjusting the air mix door control rod (Sec 18)

1 Air-mix door lever	2 Rod

Fig. 10.8 Locations of the instrument center ventilator mounting screws (Sec 18)

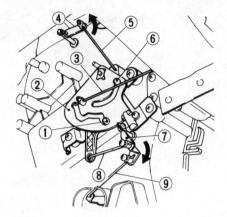

Fig. 10.12 Procedure for adjusting the heater system control rods
(Sec 18)

1	Stopper A	6	Stopper B
2	Link	7	Floor door lever
3	Air control rod	8	Floor door rod
4	Ventilation door lever	9	Defroster door rod
5	Ventilation door rod		

Fig. 10.13 Exploded view of the cigarette lighter assembly
(Sec 19)

1	Lighter	3	Housing cover
2	Housing	4	Retaining nut

19 Cigarette lighter – removal and installation

1 Remove the instrument console as described in Section 15.
2 Remove the cigarette lighter retaining nut from the back of the lighter assembly.
3 Pull the lighter assembly out from the front of the cluster. As this is done, the light bulb housing will also come off the back of the cluster.
4 Installation is the reverse of the removal procedure. When installing the cigarette lighter components, be sure all the components are lined up properly by engaging the locating tabs in their respective slots.

20 Combination meter – removal and installation

1 Disconnect the negative battery cable.
2 Remove the steering wheel as described in Chapter 11.
3 Remove the screws that retain the steering column cover to the column and lift it off.
4 Remove the lower left instrument cover, located directly under the steering column.
5 Disconnect the speedometer at its intermediate connection.
6 Remove the combination switch from the steering column as described in Section 13.
7 Remove the combination meter mounting screws (Fig. 10.4).
8 Carefully pull the combination meter out from the dash far enough to disconnect the wiring connectors from its rear. Lift the combination meter out from the dash.
9 The combination meter housing can be disassembled to allow access to the enclosed gauges and indicators by removing the retaining screws. The printed circuit board can be removed by removing the bulb sockets from the rear of the housing and then removing the retaining screws or clips. Be careful that you do not tear or damage the printed circuit board.
10 Installation is the reverse of the removal procedure.

21 Combination gauge assembly – removal and installation

1 Disconnect the negative battery cable.
2 Remove the screws that retain the glove box and lift the glove box out of the dash.
3 Disconnect the wiring connector from the rear of the combination gauge.
4 Remove the screw that retains the right-end of the gauge assembly to the dash.

Fig. 10.14 Locations of the combination meter mounting screws
(Sec 20)

5 Pull the combination gauge toward the glove box compartment, while simultaneously pushing it toward the front of the car. Then lift it out of the dash.
6 The combination meter housing can be disassembled and the oil temperature gauge, clock, voltmeter and/or boost meter, as well as the printed circuit board can be removed by removing the bulbs from the rear of the housing and removing the retaining screws.
7 Installation is the reverse of the removal procedure.

22 Speedometer cable – inspection and replacement

1 If the speedometer is noisy during operation or if the indicator needle wavers, the speedometer should be inspected for damage and alignment.
2 Visually inspect the length of the speedometer cable, checking that there are no sharp bends or other damage to the outer casing. Also check that the cable is properly installed in the speedometer.
3 If the initial inspection reveals no damage, disconnect the cable from the speedometer and pull the inner cable from the casing.
4 Inspect the cable for worn spots, breaks or kinks. Any of these conditions necessitates replacement of the cable.
5 Prior to installing an inner cable, lubricate it with a suitable speedometer cable lubricant, to prevent rusting.

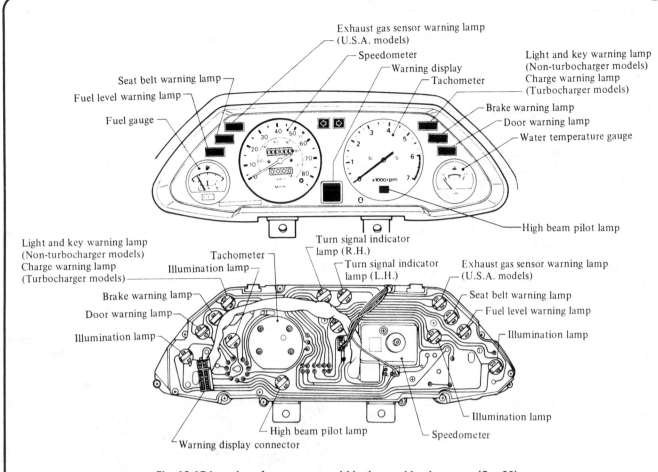

Fig. 10.15 Location of components within the combination meter (Sec 20)

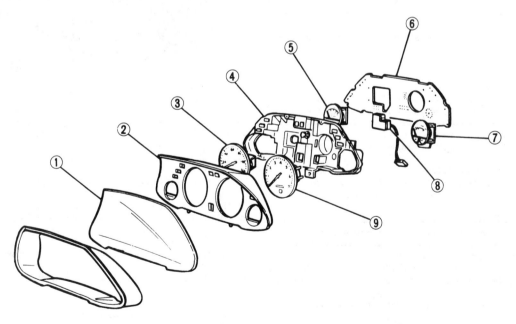

Fig. 10.16 Exploded view of the combination meter (Sec 20)

1	Front cover	4	Lower housing	7	Water temperature gauge
2	Upper housing	5	Fuel gauge	8	Warning display
3	Speedometer	6	Printed circuit board	9	Tachometer

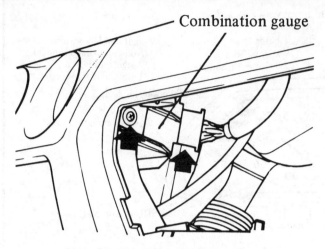

Combination gauge

Fig. 10.17 Location of the combination gauge assembly wiring connector and mounting screw, looking through glove box opening (Sec 21)

23 Warning display control unit – removal and installation

1   Disconnect the negative battery cable.
2   Remove the lower right instrument cover, located under the glove box.
3   Remove the glove box.
4   Disconnect the wiring connectors from the display control unit.
5   Remove the display control unit mounting screws and lift the unit out.
6   Installation is the reverse of the removal procedure.

24 Remote control door mirror switches – removal and installation

1   Disconnect the negative battery cable.
2   Remove the console box mounting screws, referring to Chapter 12 if necessary.
3   Disconnect the wiring connectors leading to the mirror switches.
4   Remove the ring nuts that retain the switches to the console box, and lift the switches out from the rear of the console box.
5   Installation is the reverse of the removal procedure.

25 Door mirror (remote control type) – removal and installation

1   Disconnect the negative battery cable.
2   Remove the door trim panel and sealing screen as described in Chapter 12.
3   Disconnect the wiring connector leading to the mirror.
4   Remove the mirror mounting nuts and lift out the mirror.
5   Installation is the reverse of the removal procedure.

26 Power window switches and motor – replacement

1   Disconnect the negative battery cable.
2   Remove the lower instrument cover on the appropriate side of the dash. If removing the switch on the passenger door, also remove the glove box.
3   Remove the door glass and power window regulator as described in Chapter 12.
4   If the motor is to be replaced, it can be separated from the regulator.
5   If removing a switch, disconnect all necessary wiring connectors both inside the door and under the dash.
6   Remove the switch mounting screws and lift it out.
7   Installation is the reverse of the removal procedure. During installation, be sure to adjust the door glass as described in Chapter 12.

27 Windshield wiper system – general information

1   The windshield wiper consists of a wiper motor unit, link mechanism, wiper arms, blades and an intermittent amplifier.
2   The motor incorporates an auto-stop device and operates the wipers in three different stages: intermittent, low speed, and high speed.
3   The electrically operated windshield washer consists of a reservoir tank (with built-in motor and pump), washer nozzles and vinyl tubes used to connect the components.
4   Models equipped with a rear windshield wiper have a similar wiper motor mounted to the inside of the rear door. The rear wiper motor is a one-speed unit.

28 Wiper motor – removal and installation

1   Remove the brake booster vacuum hose clamp from the wiper motor bracket (photo).
2   Disconnect the wiring connector from the wiper motor.
3   Remove the screws that attach the motor to the body.
4   Lift the motor from the body enough so that the nut that attaches the linkage to the motor can be removed. Separate the components and lift the motor off.
5   Installation is the reverse of the removal procedure.

28.1 Mounting arrangement of the wiper motor at the rear of the engine compartment

29 Windshield wiper linkage assembly – removal and installation

1   If the wiper blades strike or ride over the windshield frame this is an indication that the bushings in the linkage are worn and need replacing.
2   Remove the wiper arms from the pivots. Refer to Chapter 1 if necessary.
3   Remove the screws that retain the cowl grille and lift the grille off.
4   Remove the wiper motor as described in Section 28.
5   Remove the nuts that retain the pivots to the cowl. The wiper linkage assembly can now be lifted out.
6   Once removed, the linkage can be disassembled as required.
7   Installation is the reverse of the removal procedure. Prior to installation, apply a little grease to the pivots and moving parts of the assembly.

30 Windshield washer – servicing

1   The washer fluid reservoir is located on the left side of the engine compartment. The washer pump is mounted under the fluid reservoir.
2   Normally the windshield washer requires no maintenance other than keeping the reservoir topped-up with water to which a little windshield cleaning fluid has been added.
3   If the washer reservoir or electric pump have to be replaced

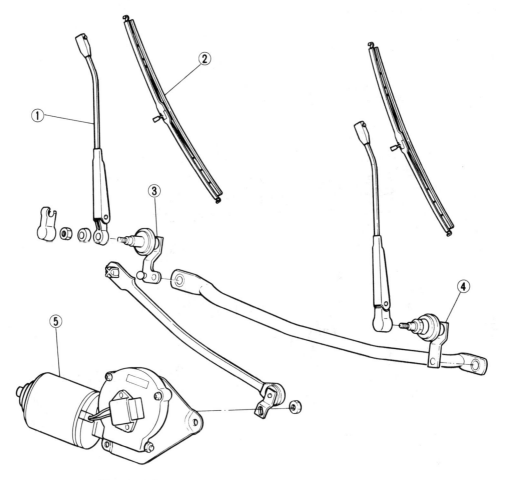

Fig. 10.18 Components of the windshield wiper system (Sec 27)

1	Windshield wiper arm	4	Pivot (left)
2	Windshield wiper blade	5	Windshield wiper
3	Pivot (right)		motor assembly

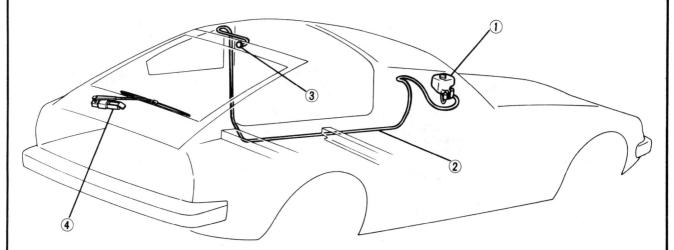

Fig. 10.19 Location of the rear door wiper motor and routing of the washer tube (Sec 27)

1	Washer tank	3	Washer nozzle
2	Washer tube	4	Wiper motor

Speed sensor is incorporated in speedometer.

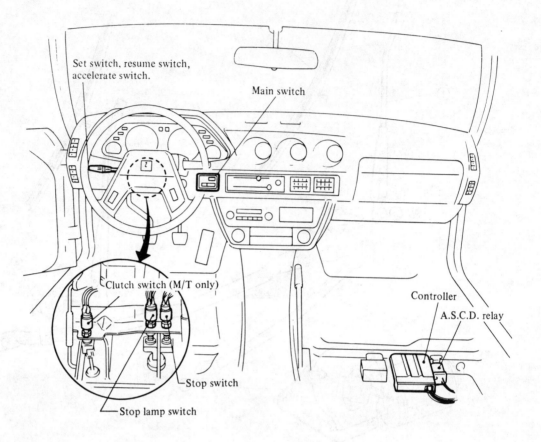

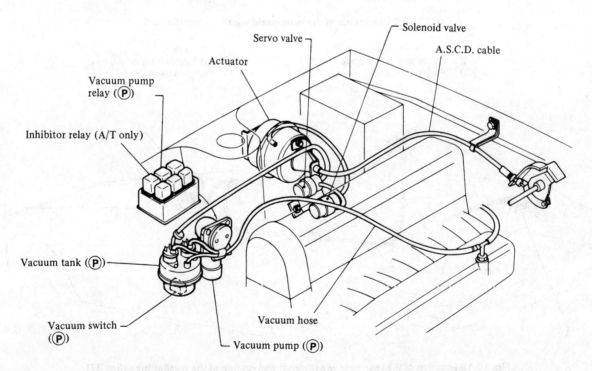

P : Turbocharger models

Fig. 10.20 Components of the Automatic Speed Control Device (ASCD) (Sec 30)

individually, they may be separated after disconnecting the lines and electrical leads.

4   When reconnecting the pump to the base of the reservoir, warm the reservoir by immersing it in hot water and use a solution of soapy water to lubricate the neck of the pump opening in the reservoir.

31 Rear wiper motor – removal and installation

1   Disconnect the battery ground cable.
2   Remove the wiper blade arm.
3   Open the rear door and carefully remove the trim panel.
4   Disconnect the wiper motor wire connectors.
5   Loosen and remove the motor attaching bolts and lift away the motor.
6   Installation is the reverse of removal.

32 Intermittent amplifier – general information

1   The intermittent amplifier, which is located on the engine compartment relay mounting bracket, controls the intermittent operation of the wipers.
2   In the unlikely event of its failure, it is not possible to repair the amplifier and it must be replaced as an assembly.

33 Rear window defogger – testing and repair

1   This option consists of a rear window with a number of horizontal elements that are baked into the glass surface during the glass forming operation.
2   Small breaks in the element system can be successfully repaired without removing the rear window.
3   To test the grids for proper operation, start the engine and turn on the system.
4   Ground one lead of a test lamp and lightly touch the other lead to each grid line.
5   The brilliance of the test lamp should increase as the lead is moved across the element from right to left. If the test lamp glows brightly at both ends of the grid lines, check for a loose ground wire for the system. All of the grid lines should be checked in at least two places.
6   The materials needed to repair a break in a grid line include a conductive silver composition (available specifically for this purpose), a drawing pen, electrical tape, alcohol and cloth. Complete repair kits can also be obtained.
7   To repair a break, first turn off the system and allow it to de-energise for a few minutes.
8   Lightly buff the grid line area with fine steel wool and then thoroughly clean the area with alcohol.
9   Use electrician's tape above and below the area to be repaired. The space between the pieces of tape should be the same as existing grid lines. This can be checked from outside the car. Press the tape tightly against the glass to prevent seepage.
10 Dip the pen in the silver and apply it at the break between the pieces of tape, overlapping the damaged area slightly on either end.
12 Carefully remove the tape. If a hot air gun is available, apply a constant stream of hot air directly to the repaired area. A heat gun set at 500 to 700 degrees Fahrenheit is recommended. Hold the gun about one inch from the glass for one to two minutes.
13 If the new grid line appears off color, tincture of iodine can be used to clean the repair and bring it back to the proper color. This mixture should not remain on the repair for more than 30 seconds.
14 Although the defogger is now fully operational, the repaired area should not be disturbed for at least 24 hours.

34 Power radio antenna – removal and installation

1   Lower the antenna mast fully by turning off the radio or ignition key switch. If the unit has failed with the antenna mast in the Up position, it may be advisable to cut off the mast portion to make replacement easier.
2   Disconnect the negative battery cable.
3   Raise the rear door.
4   Remove the rear and left trim panels to gain access to the power antenna motor.
5   Disconnect the wiring harness and the antenna lead.
6   Remove the screws that hold the motor to the body and lift the motor out.
7   When installing a new unit, be sure the mast is fully retracted and that both ground screws are tight.

35 Automatic Speed Control Device (ASCD) – general information

1   The ASCD is a cruise control system that allows the driver to maintain a constant highway speed without the necessity of continually applying foot pressure to the accelerator pedal.
2   The system utilizes a combination of electronic and vacuum controls. Basically, the ASCD controller senses the difference between the preset speed and the actual speed picked up by the speed sensor in the speedometer, and transmits an electrical signal to the servo valve. The servo valve then adjusts the vacuum which operates the actuator, which, in turn, adjusts the throttle valve opening to maintain the speed at the desired setting.
3   See the accompanying figures for the components that comprise the ASCD system. They are:

a) **Main switch:** When the main switch is turned on (with the ignition switched on, also), the ASCD relay will become energized and will supply current to the system. The relay will turn off when the ignition switch is turned off, and will stay off until both the ignition switch and the main switch are once again turned on.

b) **Set switch:** When the set switch is depressed, the "cruise" light will illuminate and the controller will cancel the preset car speed. When the set switch is released, the controller will set the speed setting to the speed at which the car is running.

c) **Speed sensor:** The speed sensor is located in the speedometer, and signals the speed of the car by sending out two electrical pulses per revolution of the meter cable.

d) **Servo valve:** The servo valve controls the opening and closing of the vacuum valve and atmospheric valve according to the current received from the controller, and makes appropriate adjustments to the vacuum line from the intake manifold.

e) **Controller:** The controller compares the preset speed with the actual speed, and maintains the preset speed by increasing or decreasing the current flowing through the servo valve.

f) **Solenoid valve:** This is the safety valve which shuts off the air bleed to the vacuum line when the system is activated.

g) **Actuator:** The actuator controls the opening and closing of the throttle valve, and is vacuum controlled by the servo valve.

h) **Stop switch:** When the brake pedal is depressed, the stop switch cuts off the power to the ASCD circuit and deactivates the system.

i) **Inhibitor relay (automatic transmission models only):** The inhibitor relay releases the ASCD system when the gear selector is set to the N or P position.

j) **Clutch switch (manual transmission models only):** The clutch switch releases the ASCD system when the clutch pedal is depressed.

h) **Accelerate/resume switch:** Located on the steering column combination switch, this switch allows the set speed to be increased without touching the accelerator pedal (Accel), or returns the car to the set speed it was at prior to being released by application of the brake pedal, clutch pedal, etc. (Resume).

4   Due to the complexity and critical nature of the ASCD system, if it begins to operate improperly, take the car to a Datsun dealer or other qualified shop to have it diagnosed and corrected.

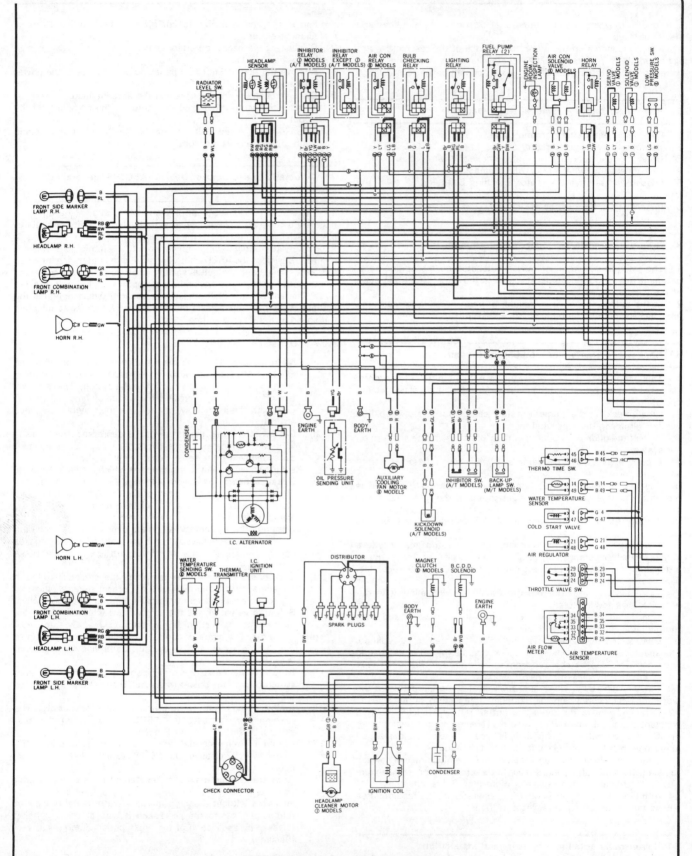

Fig. 10.21 Wiring diagram for 1979 280ZX

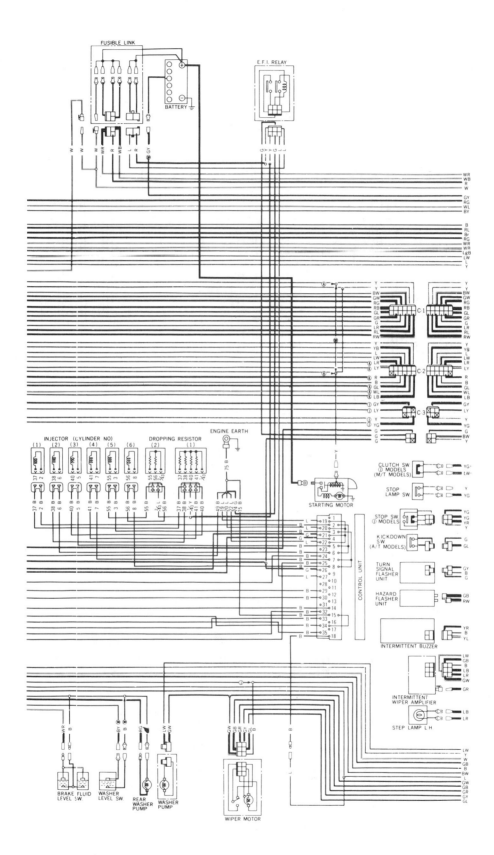

Fig. 10.22 Wiring diagram for 1979 280ZX (continued)

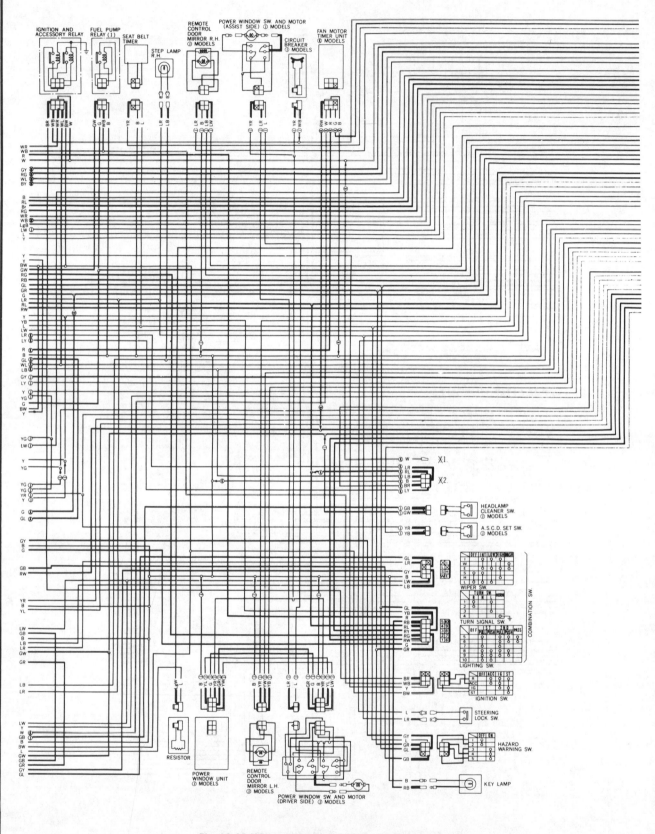

Fig. 10.23 Wiring diagram for 1979 280ZX (continued)

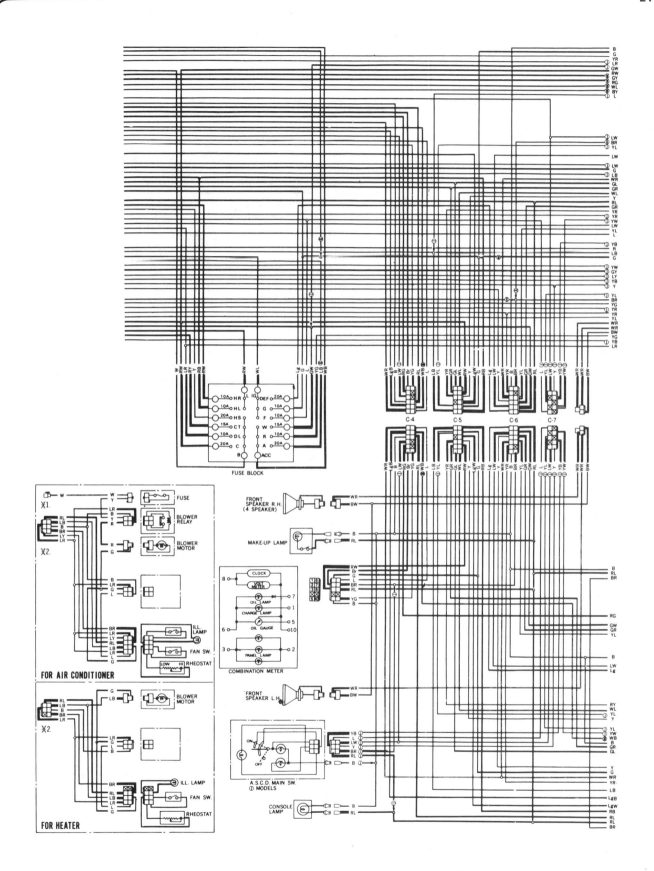

Fig. 10.24 Wiring diagram for 1979 280ZX (continued)

218

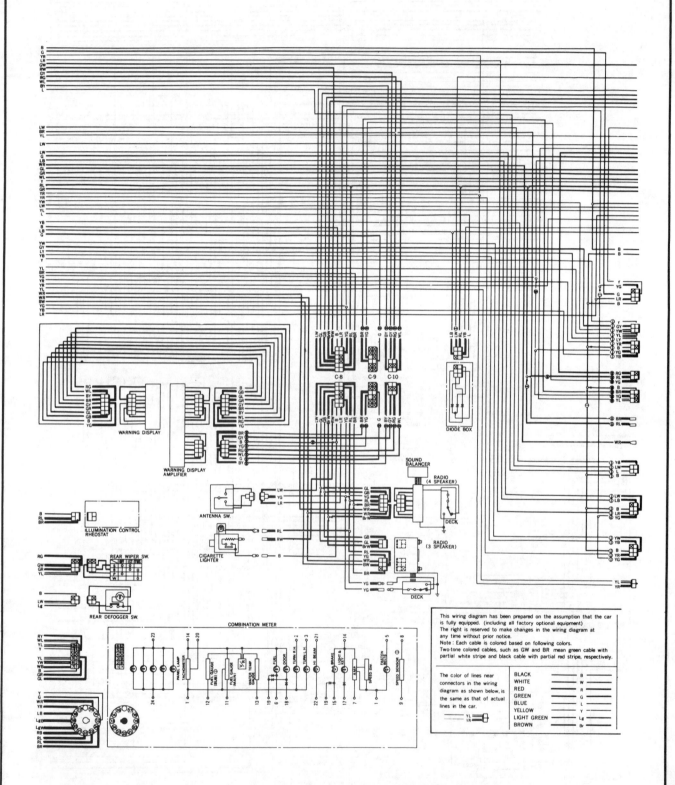

Fig. 10.25 Wiring diagram for 1979 280ZX (continued)

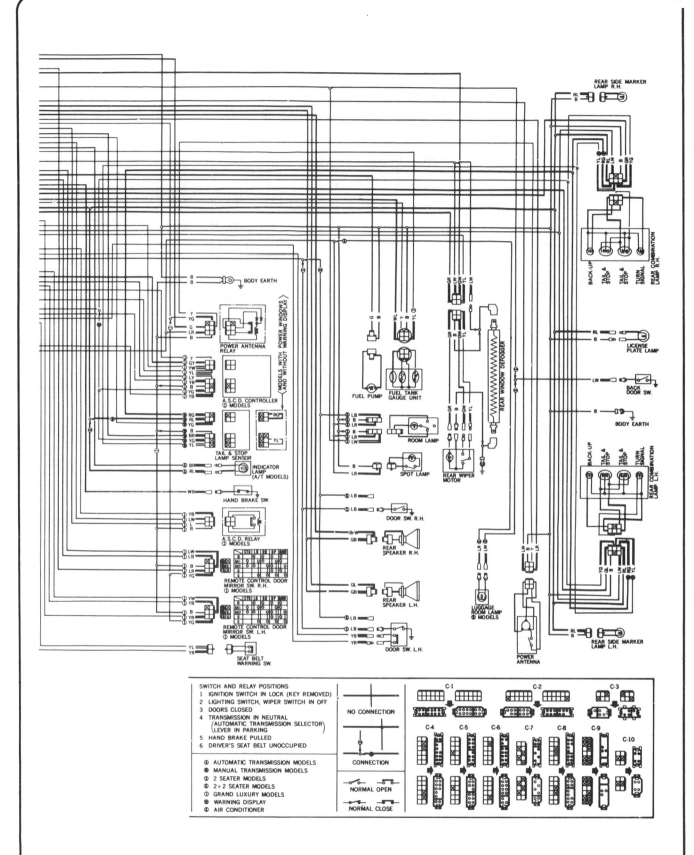

Fig. 10.26 Wiring diagram for 1979 280ZX (continued)

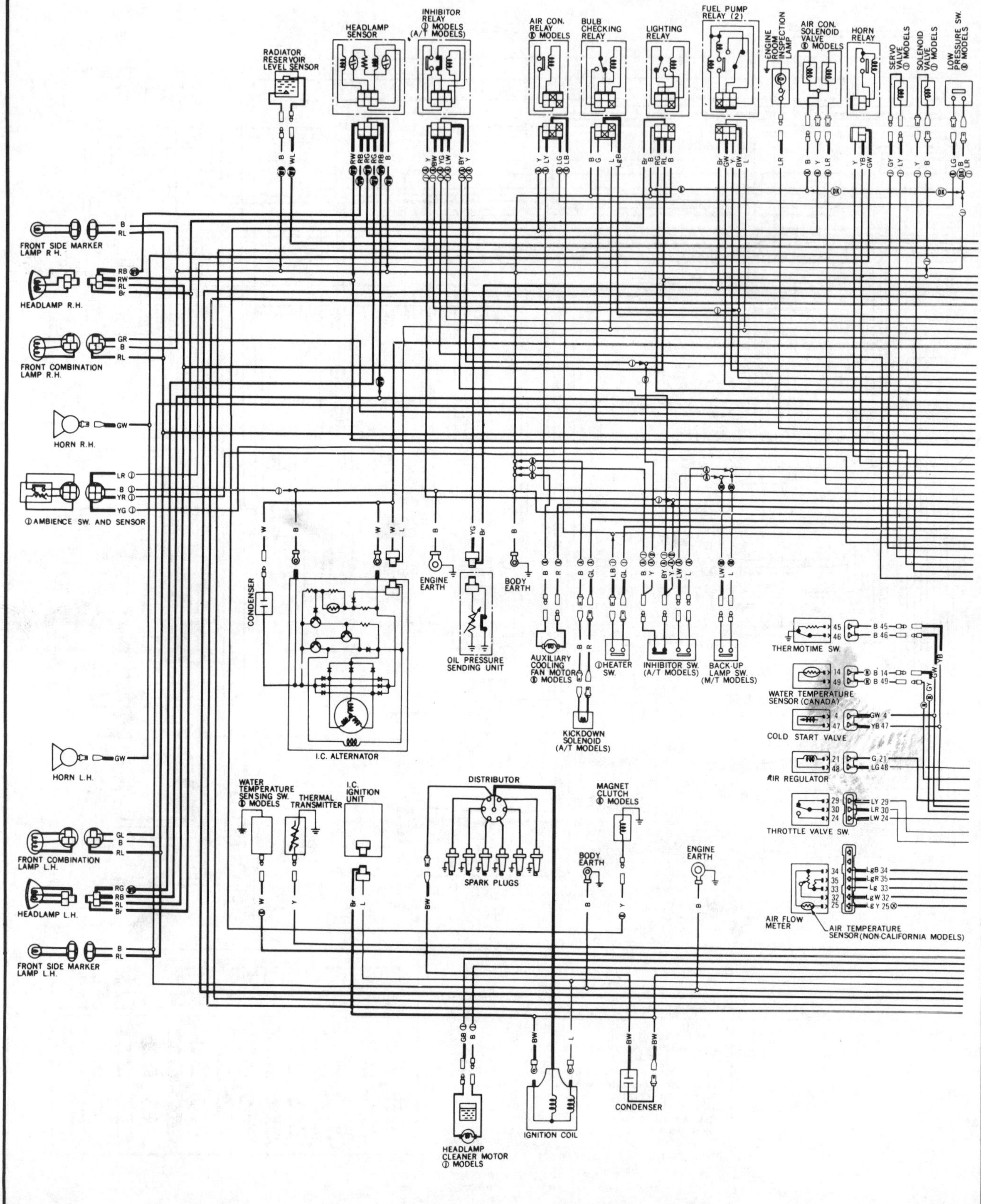

Fig. 10.27 Wiring diagram for 1980 280ZX

221

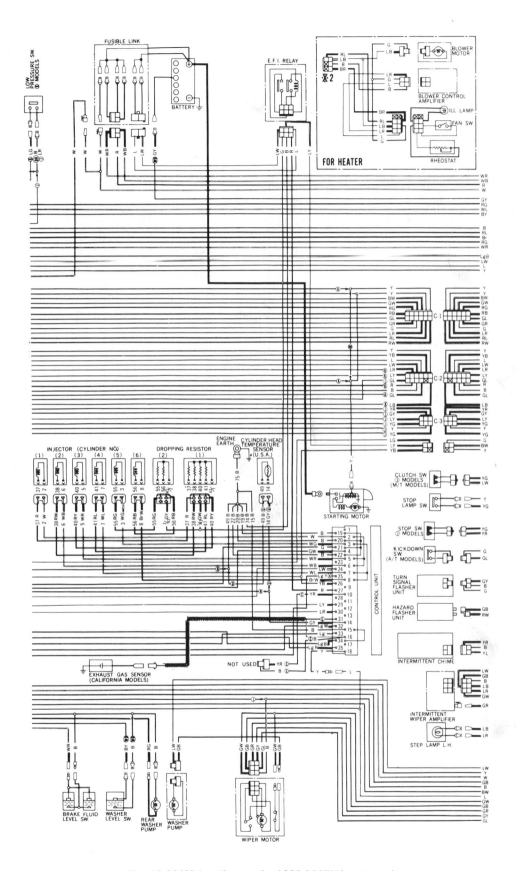

Fig. 10.28 Wiring diagram for 1980 280ZX (continued)

222

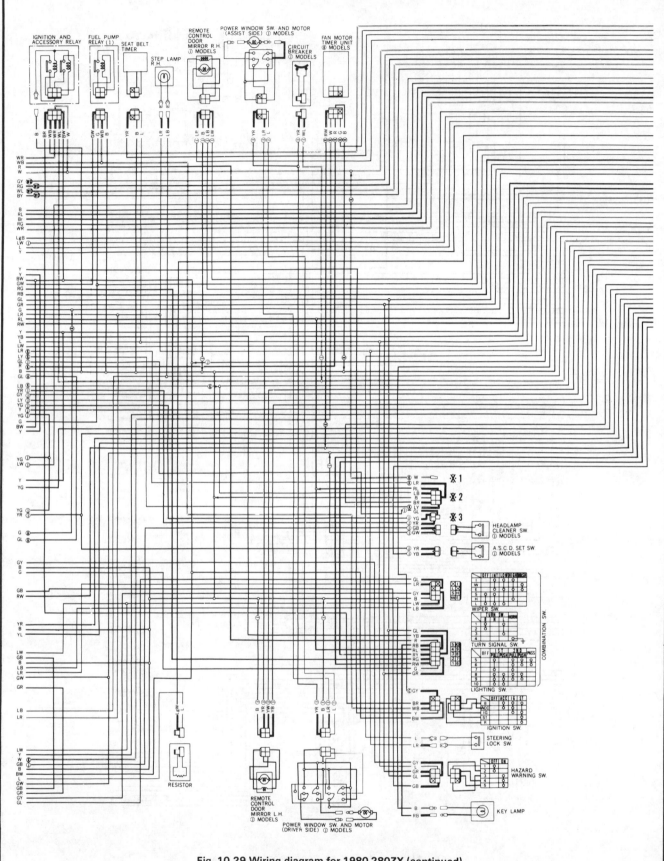

Fig. 10.29 Wiring diagram for 1980 280ZX (continued)

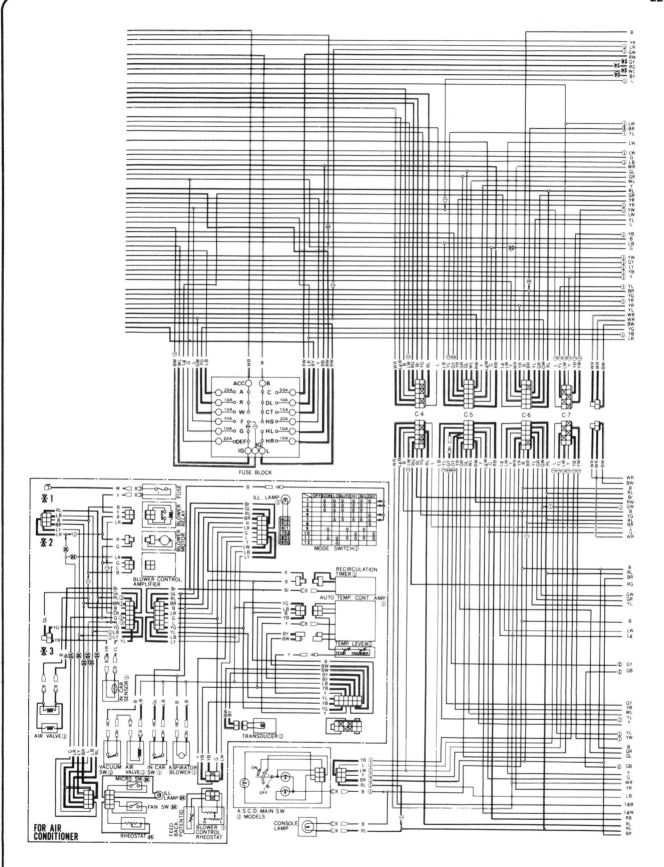

Fig. 10.30 Wiring diagram for 1980 280ZX (continued)

224

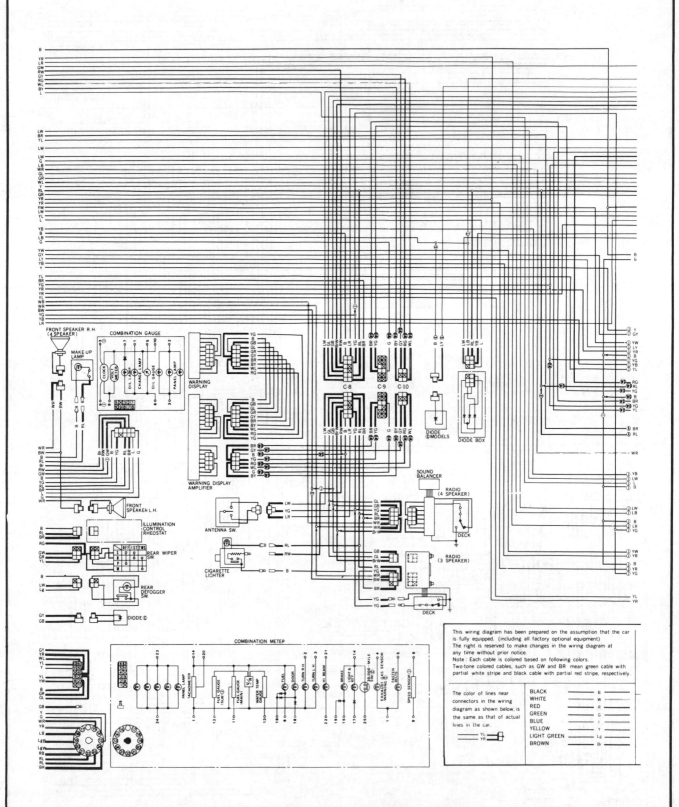

Fig. 10.31 Wiring diagram for 1980 280ZX (continued)

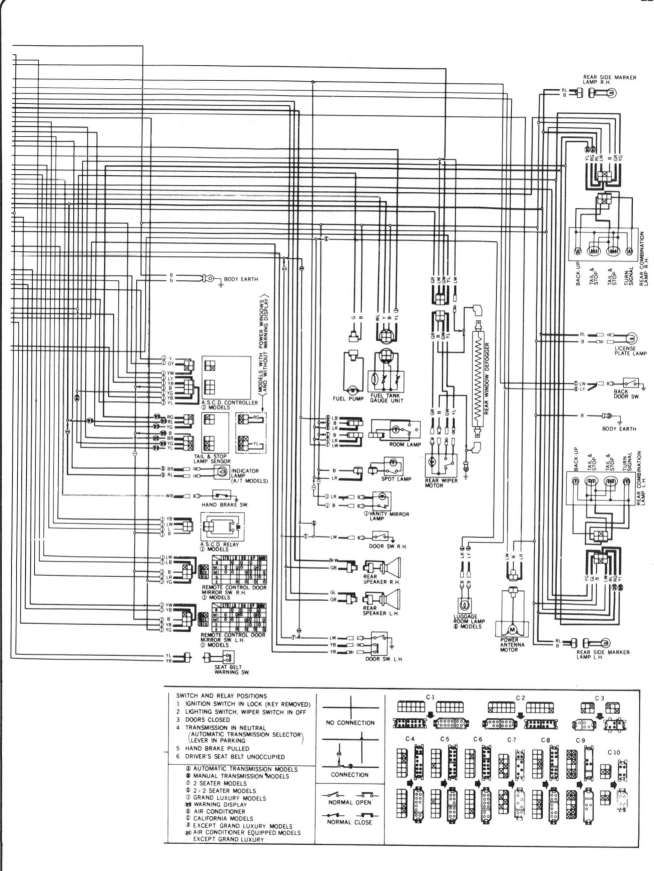

Fig. 10.32 Wiring diagram for 1980 280ZX (continued)

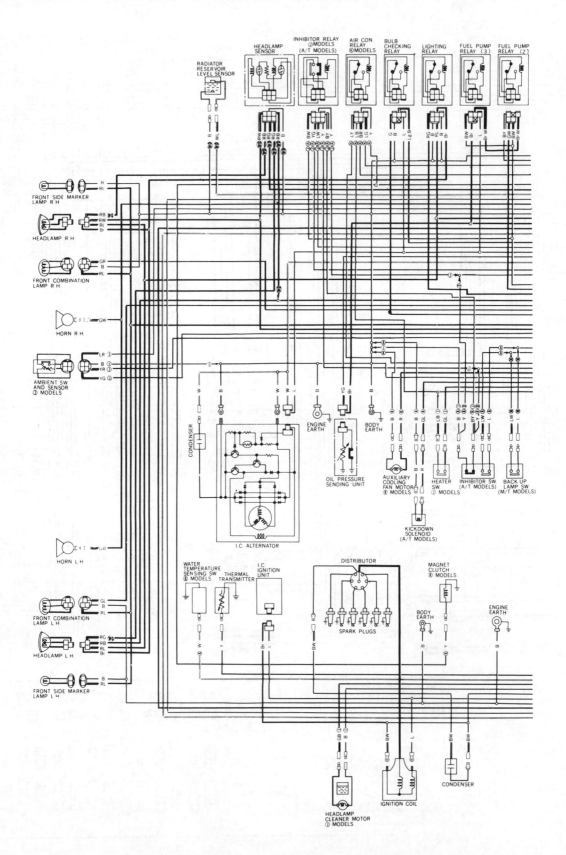

Fig. 10.33 Wiring diagram for 1981 280ZX (GL and Deluxe models)

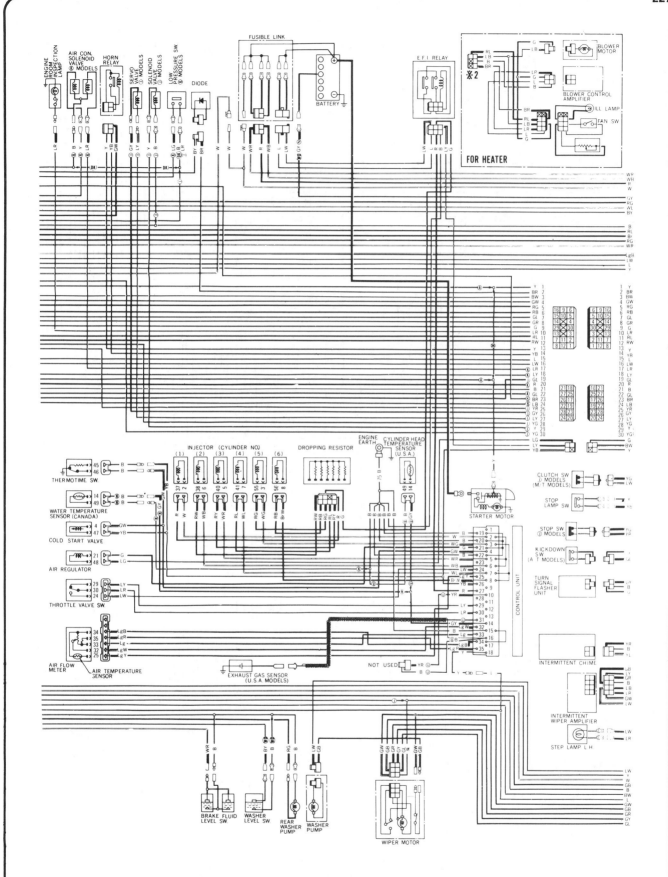

Fig. 10.34 Wiring diagram for 1981 280ZX (GL and Deluxe models) (continued)

228

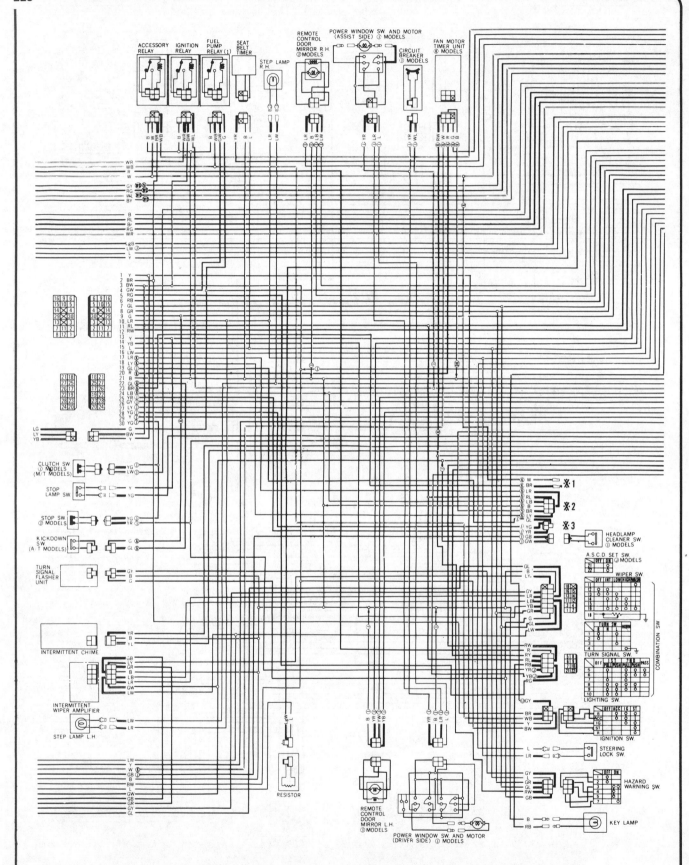

Fig. 10.35 Wiring diagram for 1981 280ZX (GL and Deluxe models) (continued)

229

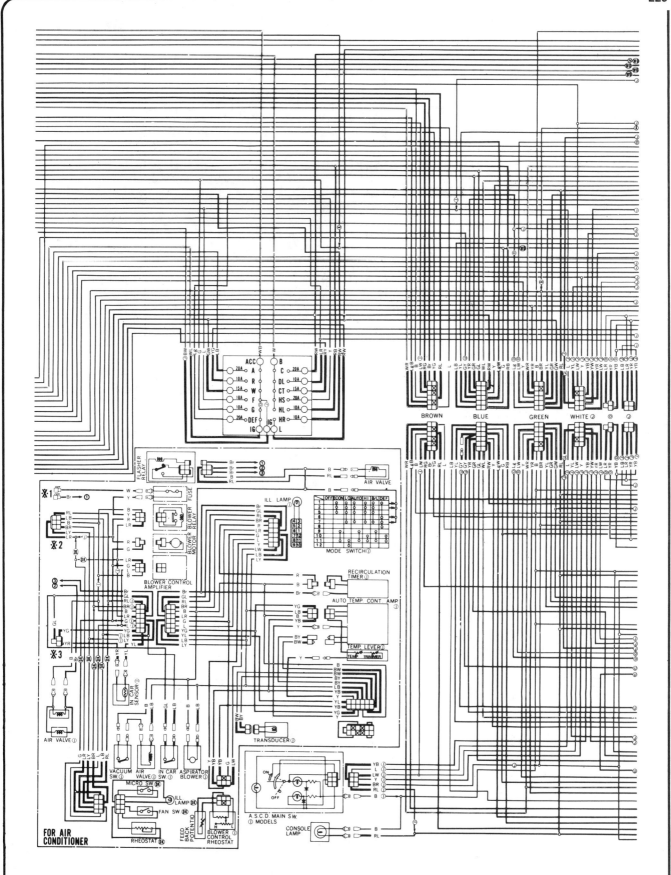

Fig. 10.36 Wiring diagram for 1981 280ZX (GL and Deluxe models) (continued) (refer to Figs. 10.41 and 10.44)

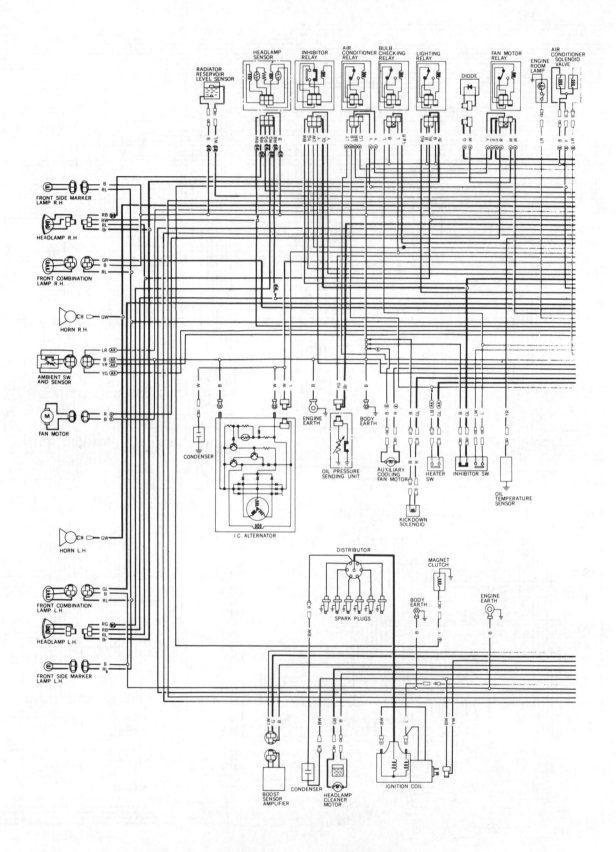

Fig. 10.37 Wiring diagram for 1981 280ZX (Turbo models)

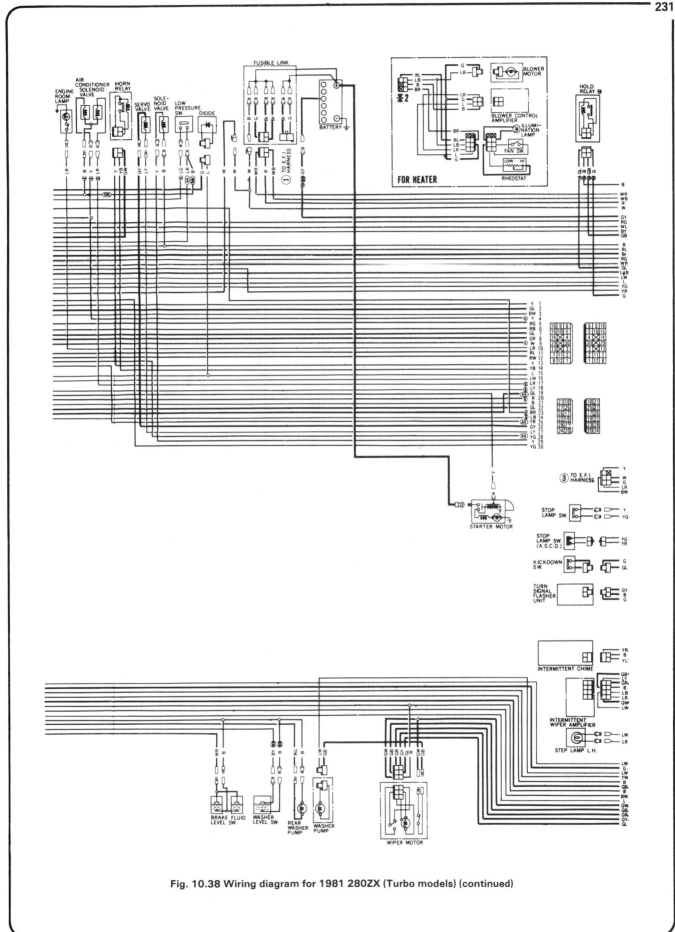

Fig. 10.38 Wiring diagram for 1981 280ZX (Turbo models) (continued)

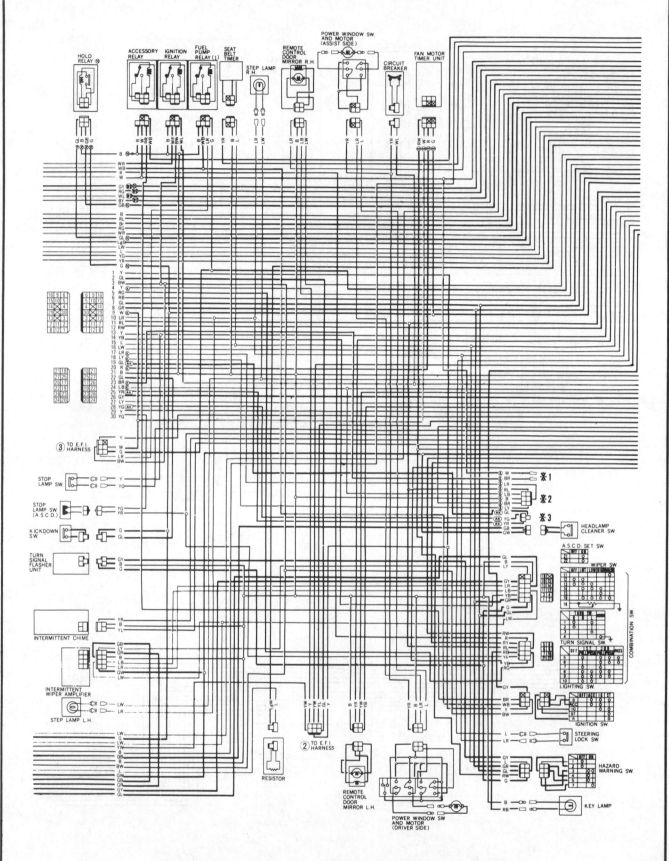

Fig. 10.39 Wiring diagram for 1981 280ZX (Turbo models) (continued)

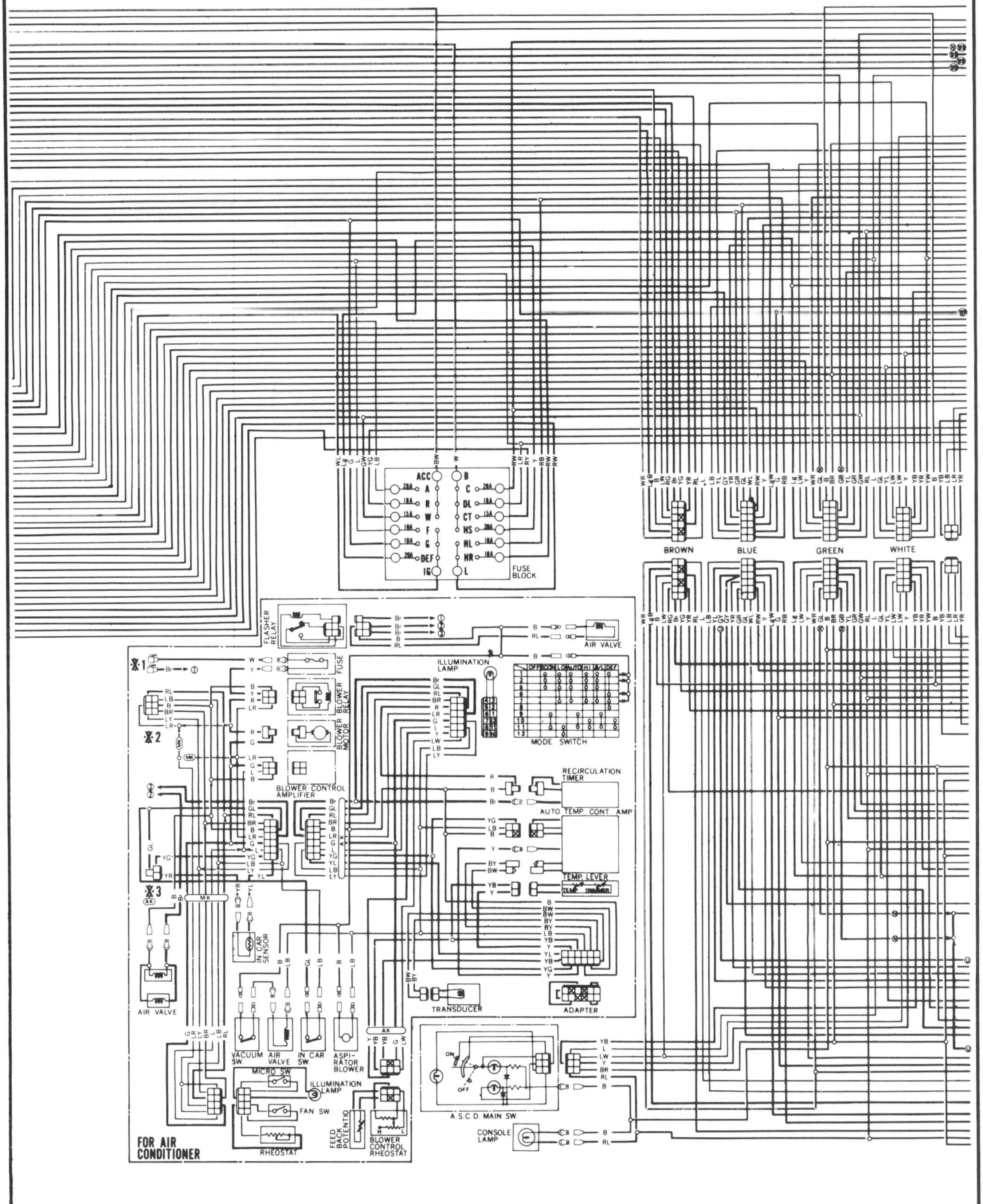

Fig. 10.40 Wiring diagram for 1981 280ZX (Turbo models) (continued)

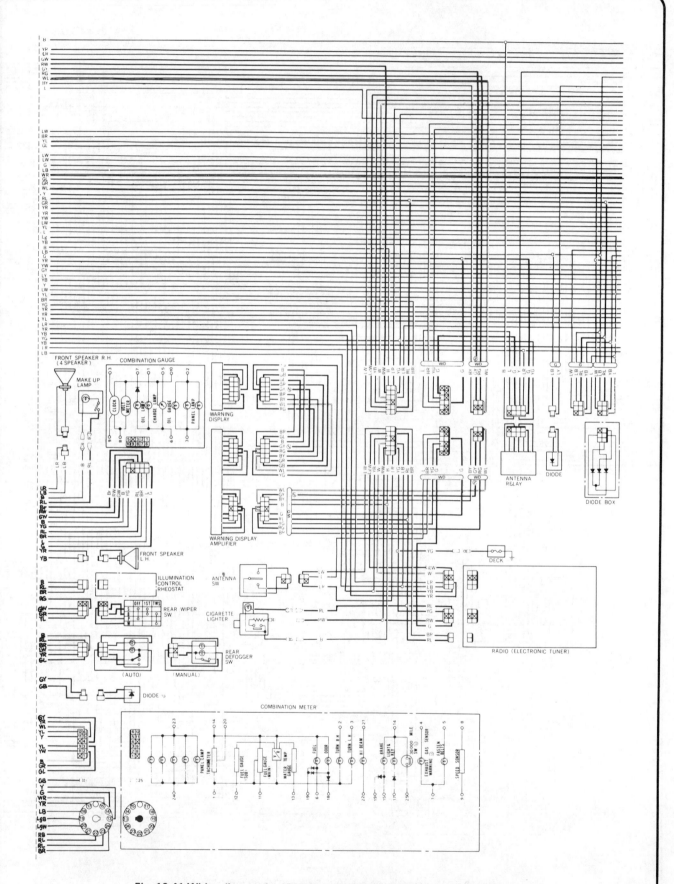

Fig. 10.41 Wiring diagram for 1981 280ZX (GL and Turbo models) (continued)

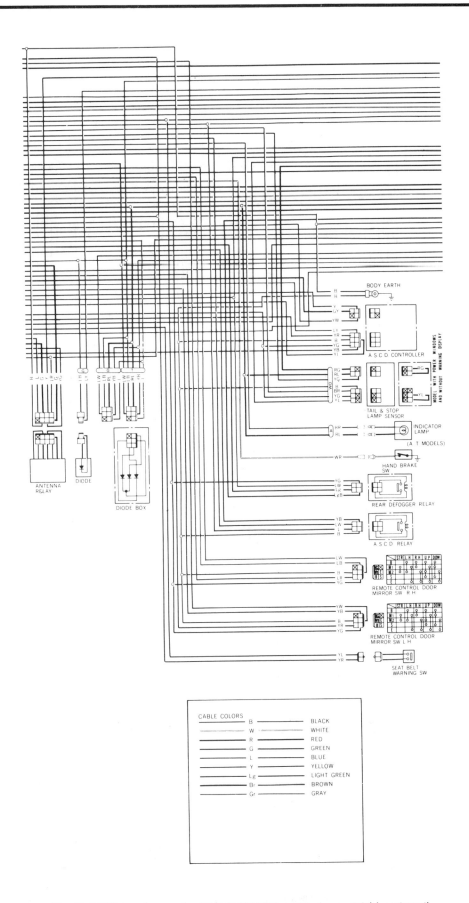

Fig. 10.42 Wiring diagram for 1981 280ZX (GL and Turbo models) (continued)

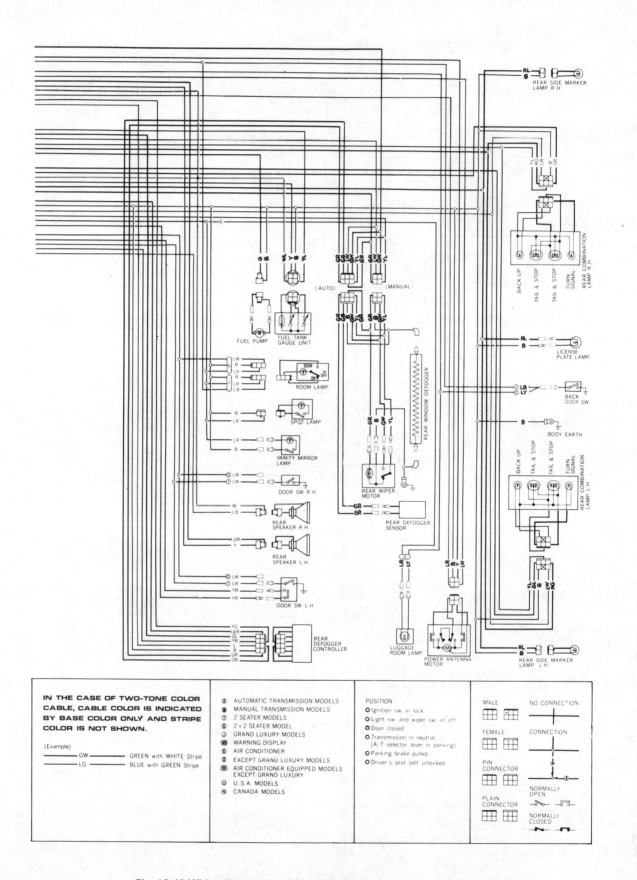

Fig. 10.43 Wiring diagram for 1981 280ZX (GL and Turbo models) (continued)

237

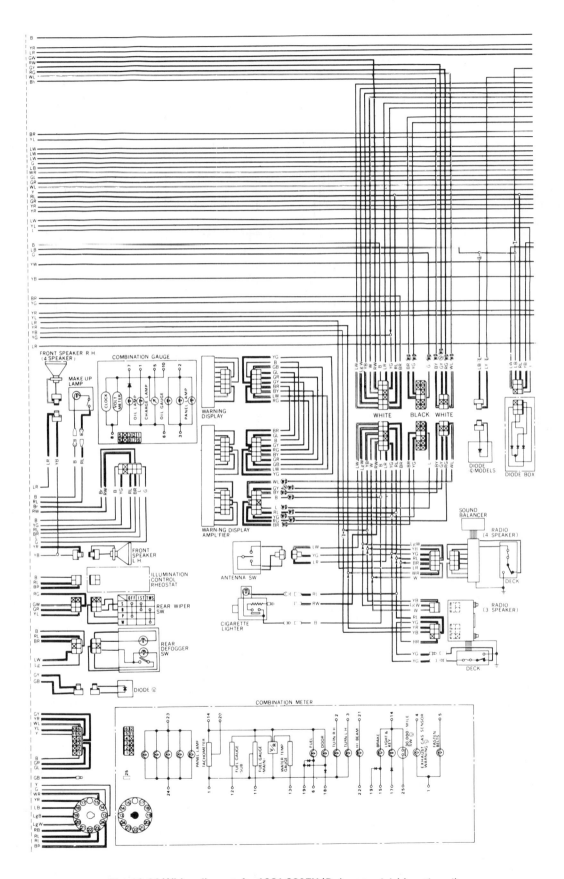

Fig. 10.44 Wiring diagram for 1981 280ZX (Deluxe models) (continued)

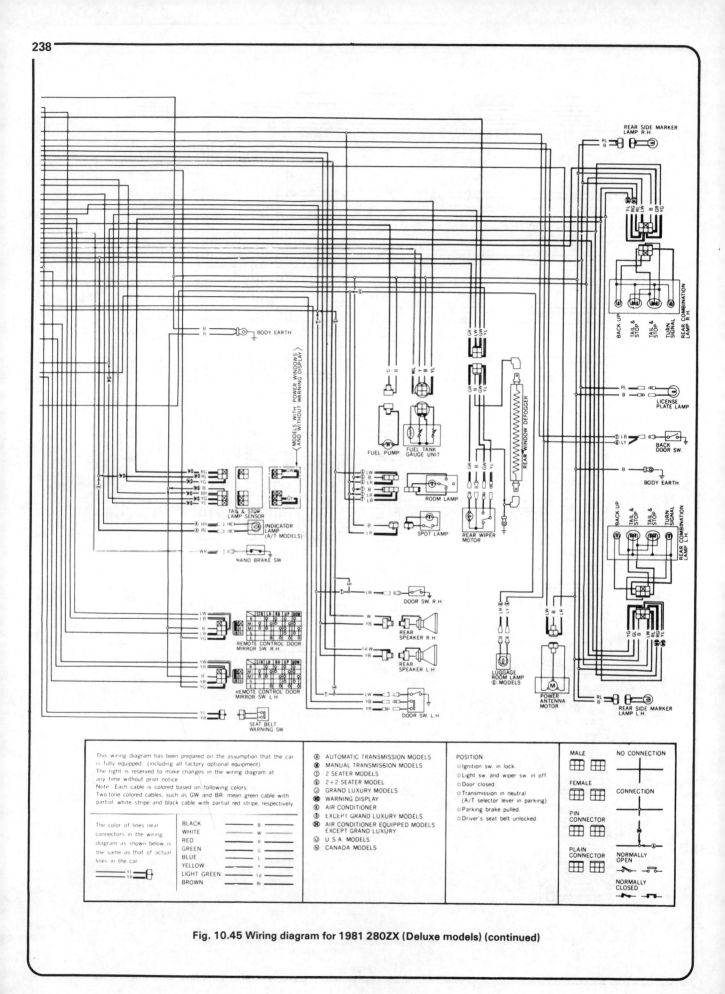

Fig. 10.45 Wiring diagram for 1981 280ZX (Deluxe models) (continued)

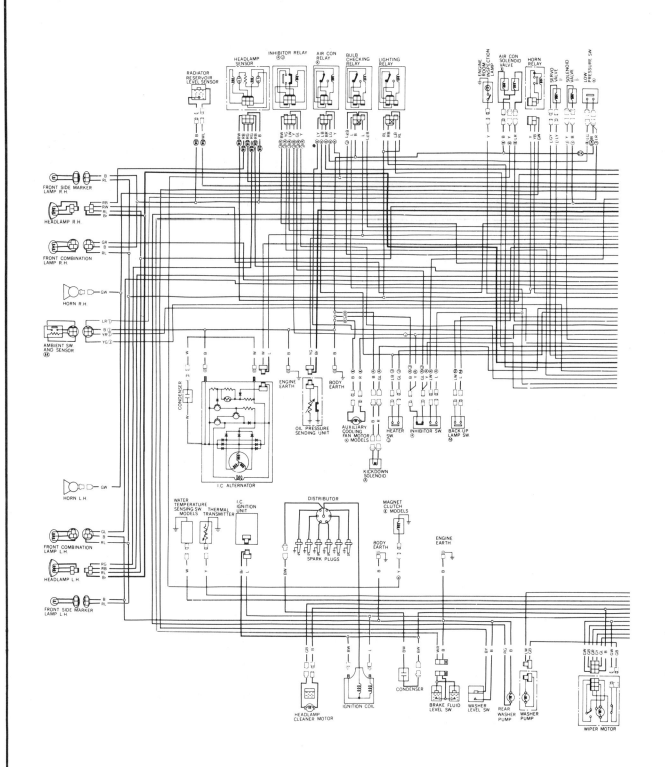

Fig. 10.46 Wiring diagram for 1982 280ZX (GL and Deluxe models)

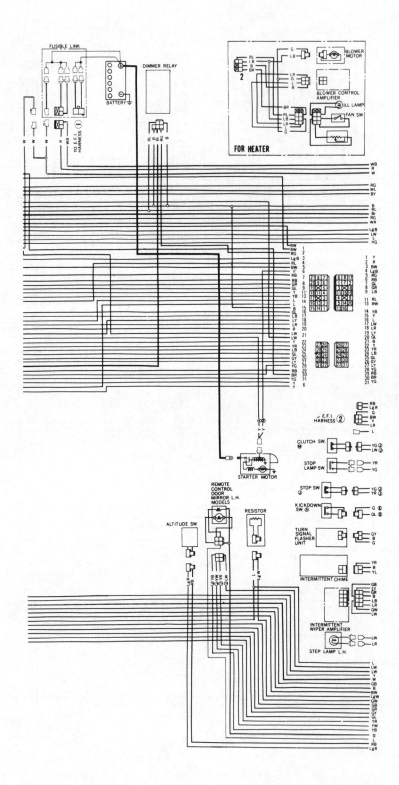

Fig. 10.47 Wiring diagram for 1982 280ZX (GL and Deluxe models) (continued)

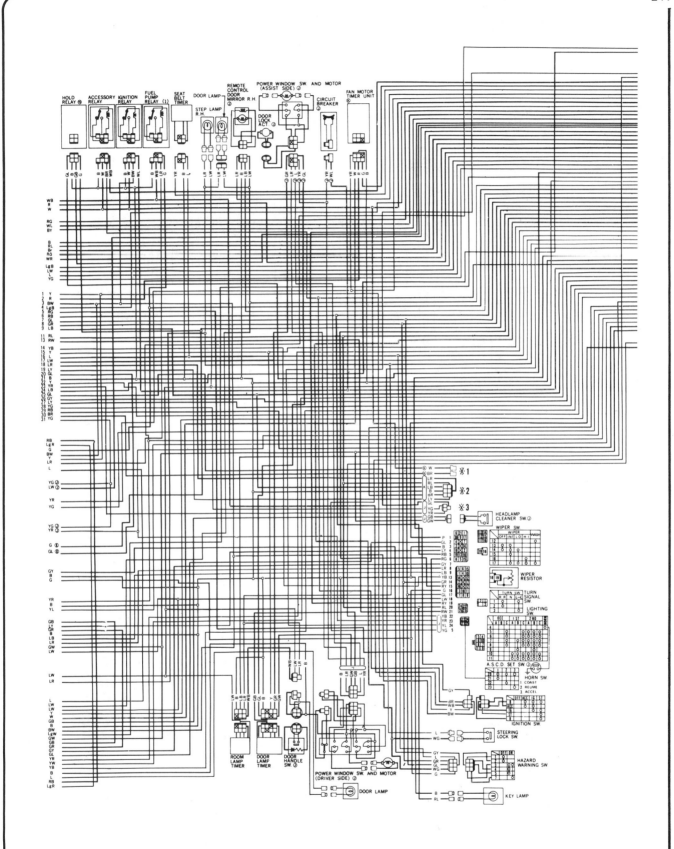

Fig. 10.48 Wiring diagram for 1982 280ZX (GL and Deluxe models) (continued)

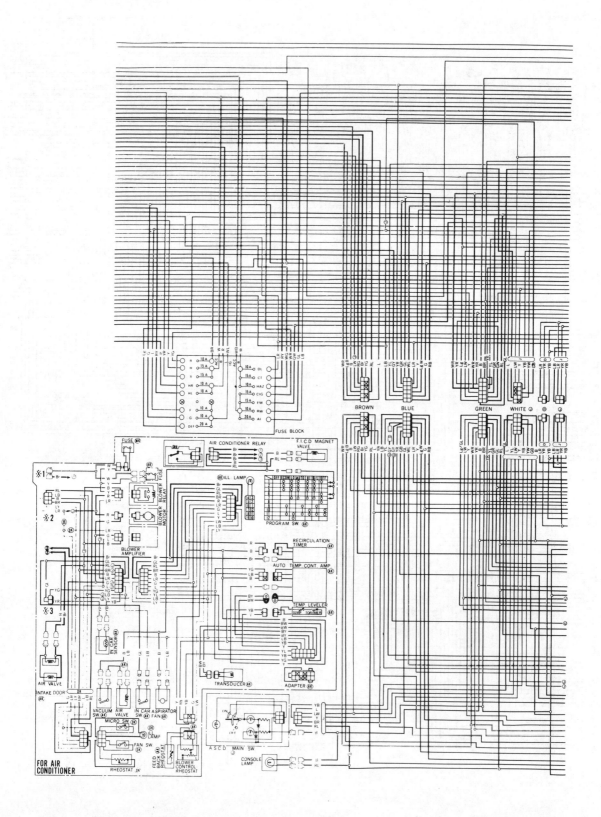

Fig. 10.49 Wiring diagram for 1982 280ZX (GL and Deluxe models) (continued) (refer to Figs. 10.54 and 10.56)

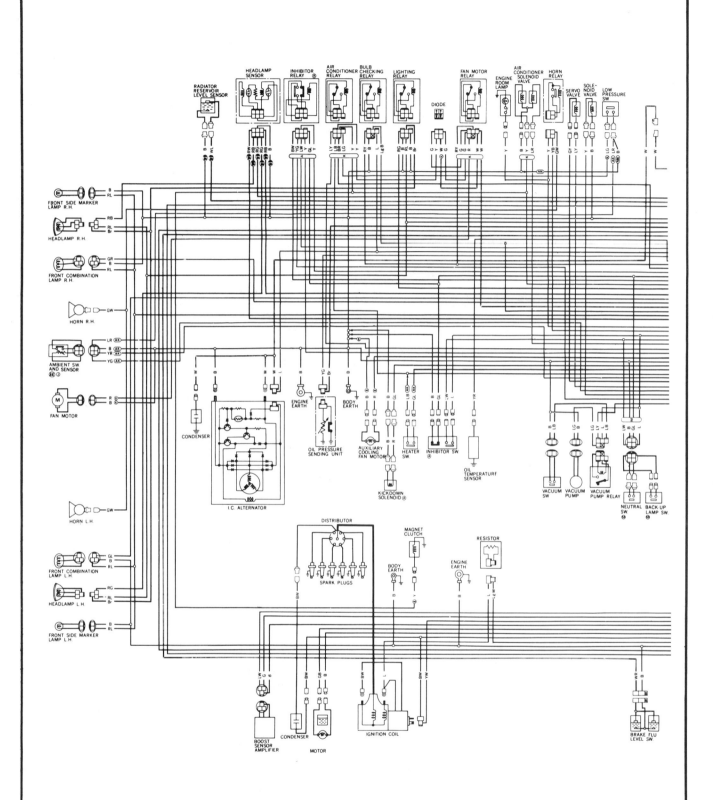

Fig. 10.50 Wiring diagram for 1982 280ZX (Turbo models)

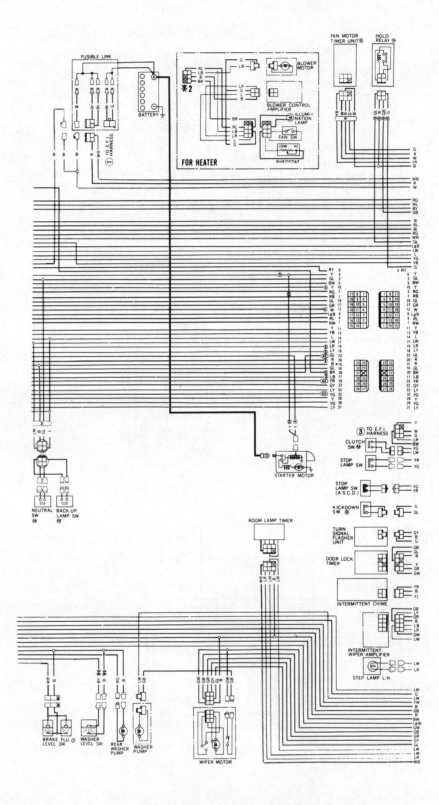

Fig. 10.51 Wiring diagram for 1981 280ZX (Turbo models) (continued)

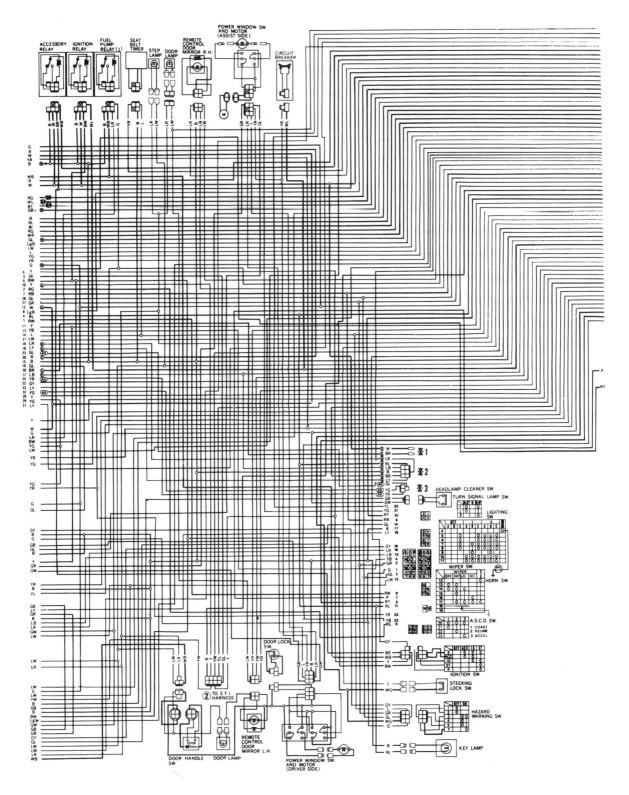

Fig. 10.52 Wiring diagram for 1982 280ZX (Turbo models) (continued)

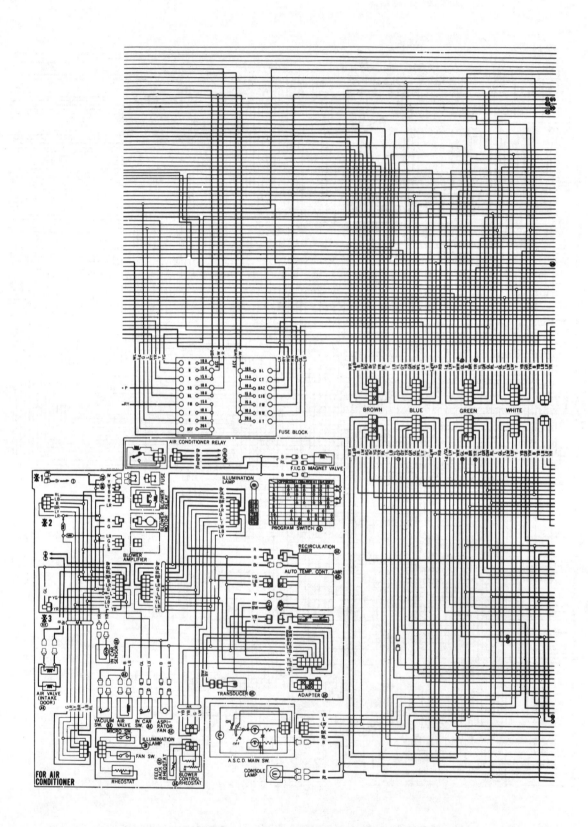

Fig. 10.53 Wiring diagram for 1982 280ZX (Turbo models) (continued)

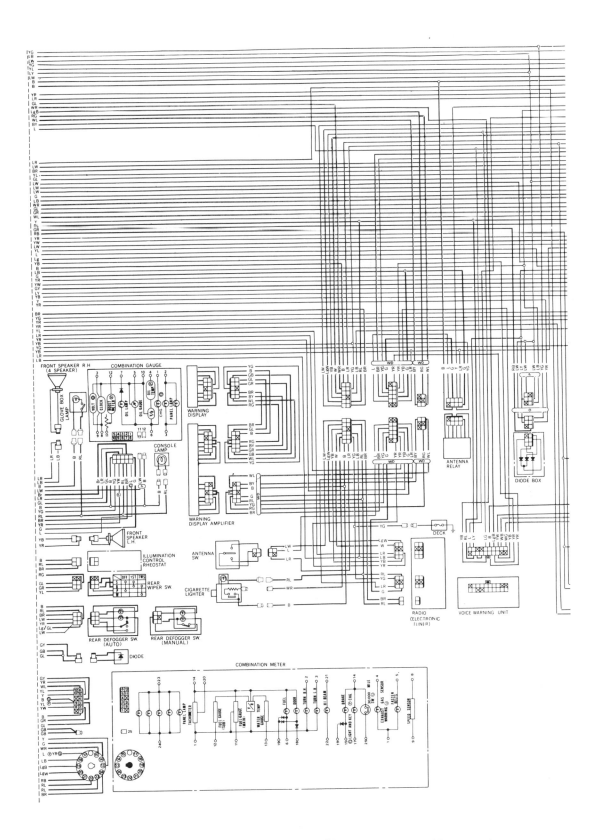

Fig. 10.54 Wiring diagram for 1982 280ZX (GL and Turbo models) (continued)

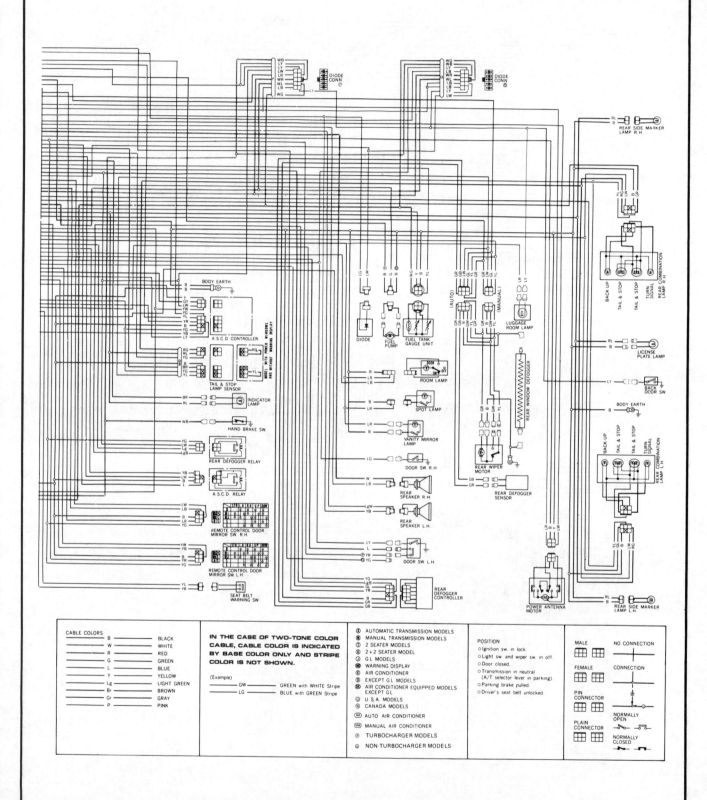

Fig. 10.55 Wiring diagram for 1982 280ZX (GL and Turbo models) (continued)

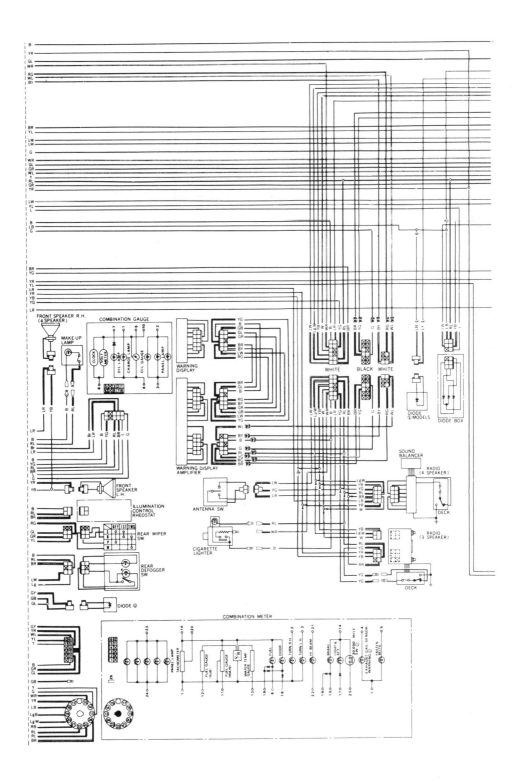

Fig. 10.56 Wiring diagram for 1982 280ZX (Deluxe models) (continued)

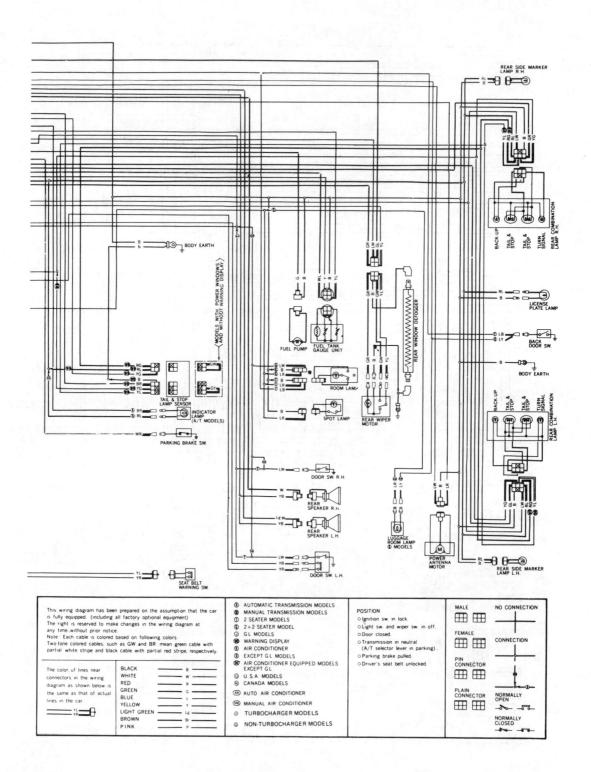

Fig. 10.57 Wiring diagram for 1982 280ZX (Deluxe models) (continued)

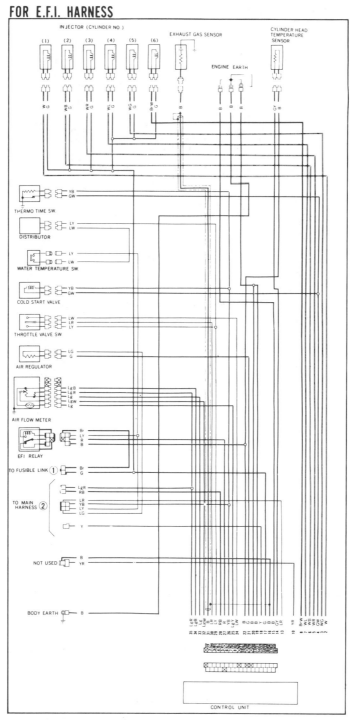

1982 DATSUN 280ZX (NON-TURBO)
FOR E.F.I. HARNESS

Fig. 10.58 Wiring diagram for EFI system (1982 non-Turbo models)

1982 DATSUN 280ZX (Turbo)
FOR E.F.I. HARNESS

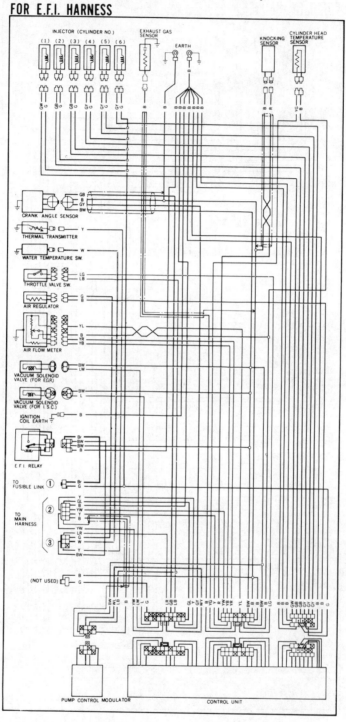

Fig. 10.59 Wiring diagram for EFI system (1982 Turbo models)

Chapter 11 Suspension and steering systems

Contents

Specifications

Front suspension

Shock absorber fluid capacity	9.3 fl oz (275 ml/9.7 Imp fl oz)
Spring color identification	
2-seater Deluxe models	White and yellow
2-seater GL and 2 + 2 Deluxe models	White and white
2 + 2 GL models	Red and blue

Rear suspension

Shock absorber maximum length (from center of lower eye to bottom of upper bushing	21.15 in (537.3 mm)
Rear spring identification color	
2-seater Deluxe models	Orange 1 and orange 2
2-seater GL and all 2 + 2 models	Pink 1 and orange 2

Steering system

Manual system type	RP 15L (rack and pinion)
Power system type	
1979 thru 1981 non-turbo models	ISP 56L (steering gear)
1981 Turbo and all 1982 models	IPRP 15L (rack and pinion)
Turns of steering wheel (lock-to-lock)	
Manual system	3.5
Power system	
ISP 56L	2.7
IPRP 15L	3.2
Steering wheel play	
Manual systems	0.79 to 1.18 in (20 to 30 mm)
Power system	Less than 1.38 in (35 mm)
Steering wheel axial play	0
Standard side rod length	
Manual system	1.161 in (29.5 mm)
Power system	
IPS 56L	14.42 in (366.3 mm)
IPRP 15L	1.323 in (33.6 mm)

Torque specifications

	ft-lb	m-kg
Wheel lugs	65	9.0
Front wheel bearing nut	20	2.8
Rotor-to-hub bolts	45	6.5
Upper strut mounting nuts	25	3.5
Gland packing	84	11.0
Strut-to-knuckle arm bolts	63	8.5
Piston rod self-locking nut	48	6.8
Caliper-to-strut bolts	63	8.5
Knuckle arm-to-side rod nut	55	7.5
Balljoint-to-knuckle arm bolts	82	11.0
Balljoint-to-transverse link bolts	36	5.0
Transverse link-to-crossmember bolts	70	9.5
Crossmember mounting bolt	58	8.0
Rear wheel bearing locknut	210	29.0
Engine mount-to-crossmember nuts	27	3.7
Tension rod-to-tension bracket nut	36	5.0
Tension rod-to-transverse link bolts	37	4.7
Tension rod bracket-to-body bolts	27	3.7
Front stabilizer bar link nut	14	1.9
Front stabilizer bar bracket bolts and nuts	24	3.2
Suspension arm pin nut	65	9.0
Suspension member mounting locknuts	65	9.0
Rear shock absorber piston rod nut	16	2.2
Rear shock absorber upper mounting nut	25	3.5
Rear shock absorber lower mounting bolt	50	7.0
Steering wheel nut	32	4.4
Jacket tube bracket-to-dash bolts	2.9	0.4
Steering column mounting bracket bolts	11	1.6
Idler arm mounting bolts	27	3.7
Idler arm nut	56	7.7
All ball stud and swivel pin retaining nuts	56	7.7
Side rod locknut (rack and pinion)	65	9.0
Side rod locknut (steering gear)	11	1.5
Stub shaft-to-coupling bolt (steering gear)	26	3.6
Steering gear mounting bolts	42	5.8
Sector shaft-to-gear arm nut (steering gear)	100	14
Rack and pinion mounting bolts	38	5.3
Lower joint-to-rubber coupling bolt (rack and pinion)	18	2.5
Lower joint-to-pinion gear bolt (manual)	32	4.5
Lower joint-to-pinion gear bolt (power)	26	3.6
Bleeder screw (steering gear)	6.0	0.8
Oil pump-to-bracket bolts	20	2.7
Oil pump pulley nut	38	5.3
Fluid hoses-to-oil pump nuts	29	4.0
Fluid hoses-to-steering gear	44	6.0

1 Suspension system – general information

This car features an independent front suspension of the Mac-Pherson strut design. This design uses a combination shock absorber and spring assembly which is mounted to the steering knuckle. The front axle spindles, on which the front hubs are mounted, are also part of the strut assembly.

A lower control arm (transverse link) which pivots on the front axle crossmember is also attached to the steering knuckle by way of a balljoint. The balljoint allows for free movement between the transverse link and the front wheel when the strut compresses during normal driving.

Front and rear forces are controlled by tension rods, and a front stabilizer bar is installed to control body roll in corners.

The rear suspension is also of independent type, the layout comprising a crossmember assembly, suspension arm assemblies, and coil springs through which are passed the shock absorbers.

The suspension member is bolted directly to the body, and supports the front of the differential. The wheel and lower mount of the shock absorber are both mounted to the suspension arm, which pivots on the suspension member. A rear stabilizer bar is mounted to the body and the suspension member to control body lean.

The shock absorbers are conventional sealed hydraulic units. They are non-adjustable, non-refillable and cannot be disassembled. They are mounted at the bottom to a bracket on the axle housing and at the top to the body.

Never attempt to heat or straighten any suspension part, as this can weaken the metal or in other ways damage the part.

2 Suspension system – inspection

Since regular inspection of the suspension system is part of the routine maintenance of the car, these procedures are described in Chapter 1.

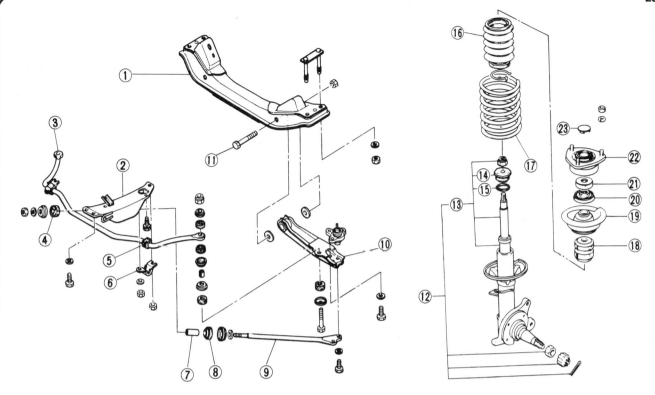

Fig. 11.1 Components of the front suspension system

1 Suspension crossmember	8 Tension rod mounting bushing	15 O-ring
2 Tension rod bracket	9 Tension rod	16 Dust cover
3 Stabilizer bar	10 Transverse link	17 Front spring
4 Tension rod mounting bushing	11 Transverse link mounting bolt	18 Bound bumper
5 Stabilizer bushing	12 Strut assembly	19 Front spring upper seat
6 Stabilizer bracket	13 Shock absorber	20 Dust seal
7 Tension rod collar	14 Gland packing	21 Strut mounting bearing
		22 Strut mounting insulator
		23 Cap

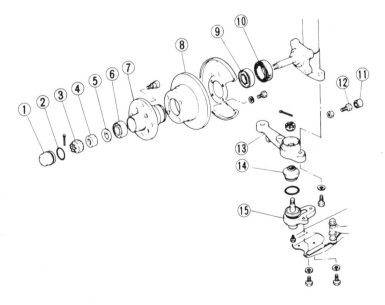

Fig. 11.2 Components of the front hub, steering knuckle and balljoint assemblies

1 Hub cap
2 O-ring
3 Adjusting cap
4 Wheel bearing nut
5 Wheel bearing washer
6 Outer wheel bearing
7 Wheel hub
8 Disc brake rotor
9 Inner wheel bearing
10 Grease seal
11 Stopper bolt cap
12 Stopper bolt
13 Knuckle arm
14 Dust cover
15 Lower ball joint

3 Front hub and wheel bearings – removal and installation

1 Raise the front of the car and support it on jackstands.
2 Remove the wheel and tire.
3 Remove the brake caliper as described in Chapter 9.
4 Pry off the hub dust cap using a screwdriver.
5 Remove the cotter pin and discard it.
6 Remove the adjusting cap from over the wheel bearing nut.
7 Remove the wheel bearing nut and its washer from the end of the spindle.
8 Remove the hub and rotor components from the spindle, catching the outer bearing as it comes out.
9 On the rear side of the hub, use a screwdriver to pry out the inner bearing grease. As this is done, note the direction in which the seal is installed.
10 The inner bearing can now be removed from the hub, again noting how it is installed.
11 Use clean parts solvent to remove all traces of the old grease from the bearings, hub and spindle. A small brush may prove useful; however, make sure no bristles from the brush embed themselves inside the bearing rollers. Allow the parts to air dry.
12 Carefully inspect the bearings for cracks, heat discoloration, bent rollers etc. Check the bearing race inside the hub for cracks, scoring or uneven surfaces. If the bearing races are in need of replacement, use a drift or brass bar to carefully drive them out of the hub, as shown in the accompanying illustration. To install the new races, use an approved installing tool. These can usually be rented. If a large enough socket is available, that can also be used.

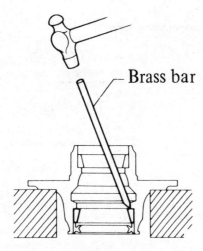

Fig. 11.3 The bearing races inside the front hub can be removed by tapping them with a brass bar or drift (Sec 3)

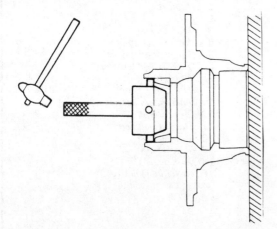

Fig. 11.4 A special tool or large socket can be used to install the bearing races into the front hub (Sec 3)

13 Use an approved high temperature front wheel bearing grease to pack the bearings. Work the grease fully into the bearings, forcing the grease between the rollers, and cage.
14 Apply a thin coat of grease to the spindle at the outer bearing seat, inner bearing seat, shoulder and seal seat.
15 Put a small quantity of grease inboard of each bearing race inside the hub. Using your finger, form a dam at these points to provide extra grease availability and to keep thinned grease from flowing out of the bearing.
16 Place the grease-packed inner bearing into the rear of the hub and put a little more grease outboard of the bearing.
17 Place a new seal over the inner bearing and tap the seal with a flat plate or socket and a hammer until it is flush with the hub.
18 Carefully place the hub assembly onto the spindle and push the grease-packed outer bearing into position.
19 Install the washer and spindle nut. Tighten the nut to 20 ft-lb (2.8 m-kg).
20 In a forward direction, spin the hub to seat the bearings and remove any grease or burrs which could cause excessive bearing play later.
21 Again, tighten the nut to the specified torque; then turn it counterclockwise about 60°.
22 At this point the wheel bearing preload must be checked. Place a torque wrench over the wheel bearing nut and slowly begin to rotate the hub in the forward direction, taking note of how much torque is needed to start the hub turning. With new parts installed, the torque should be 3.5 to 7.4 in-lb (4.0 to 8.5 cm-kg), while with old parts installed, the torque should be 0.9 to 3.9 in-lb (1.0 to 4.5 cm-kg). If the measured torque is not within these specifications, tighten or loosen the wheel bearing nut until the proper bearing preload is obtained.
23 Place the adjusting cap over the nut and check that the cotter pin hole in the spindle lines up with the slot in the cap. If it does not, turn the nut clockwise *only* until this alignment is obtained. Then, with the adjusting cap in place, insert a new cotter pin through the spindle hole, and bend the ends of the cotter pin so they do not interfere with the dust cap.
24 Install the dust cap complete with new O-ring, tapping it into place with a rubber mallet.
25 The remainder of the installation is the reverse of the removal procedure.
26 If the brake line was disconnected, bleed the brake system as described in Chapter 9.

4 Wheel stud – replacement

1 Jack up the wheel to be worked on and support it on jackstands.
2 Remove the wheel and tire.
3 Remove the brake caliper as described in Chapter 9.
4 Remove the rotor as decribed in Chapter 9.
5 On front wheels, the hub will have to be separated from the rotor as described in Chapter 9.
6 Position the stud to be replaced at either the 5 or 7 o'clock position. Install a lug nut onto the end of the stud and, using an appropriate wheel stud puller, press the stud from its seat.
7 Remove the lug nut, and then the stud.
8 With the stud hole at either the 5 or 7o'clock position, insert the new stud in the hole, making sure the serrations are aligned with those made by the original bolt.
9 Place four flat washers over the outside end of the stud, and then thread a lug onto the stud.
10 Tighten the lug nut until the stud head seats against the rear of the hub. Then remove the lug nut and washers.
11 Reinstall the components in the reverse order in which they were removed.
12 Mount the wheel and lower the car to the ground.

5 Front spring and strut components – removal and installation

1 Raise the front of the car and support it on jackstands.
2 Remove the wheel and tire.
3 Disconnect the brake line from the brake caliper, and plug the line to prevent fluid leaking.
4 Remove the caliper as described in Chapter 9.
5 Remove the hub and rotor components as described in Section 1.

6   Remove the deflector plate (photo).
7   Remove the two bolts that hold the strut components to the steering knuckle arm (photo).
8   Remove the three upper strut mounting nuts, located in the shock well under the hood.
9   While supporting the strut, use a lever or large screwdriver to separate the steering knuckle arm from the base of the strut, (photo), and lift out the strut components.
10 If the strut components need to be disassembled, refer to Section 8.
11 Installation is the reverse of the removal procedure. **Note:** *Prior to installing the strut components, apply a bead of silicone sealant to the steering knuckle mating surface as shown in the accompanying illustration. Also be sure the brake hose is not twisted and will not rub on any other parts.*
12 Bleed the brake system as described in Chapter 9.

6   Front spring and strut components – disassembly and reassembly

1   The spring on the front shock absorber is under considerable pressure, requiring a special spring compressor to be used to safely

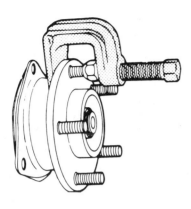

Fig. 11.5 A wheel stud removing tool can be used to press the studs from the hub (Sec 4)

5.6 Removing the deflector shield (it is mounted to the front hub with four screws)

5.7 Removing the two bolts that retain the steering knuckle to the strut

5.9 A screwdriver can be used to pry the steering knuckle down to separate it from the strut

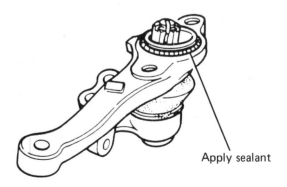

Apply sealant

Fig. 11.6 Prior to installing the front strut assembly, sealant should be applied to the steering knuckle as shown (Sec 5)

compress the spring and disengage its components. Do not attempt to disassemble the spring without the proper compressor, as serious injury can occur.

2   A strut spring compressor can be purchased through Datsun dealers or through most auto parts stores. Compressors can also be rented on a daily basis from rental agencies and some auto parts stores.

3   Hold the shock absorber in a vise using wood blocks to cushion the jaws to prevent damage to the shock.

4   Following the manufacturer's instructions for the particular spring compressor being used, slightly compress the spring, making sure that the jaws of the compressor are firmly seated around the coils and cannot slip off.

5   Tighten the compressor from side to side, a little at a time, until the spring seat is clear of the uppermost coil.

6   With the spring firmly compressed and clear of its seat, reinstall the nuts onto the upper studs to protect the threads. Hold the mounting insulator stationary by placing a bar between the mounting studs, and remove the top locknut and washer.

7   Pull the mounting insulator off the top of the shock absorber assembly.

8   Remove the bearing, dust seal, spring seat, bumper and dust cover.

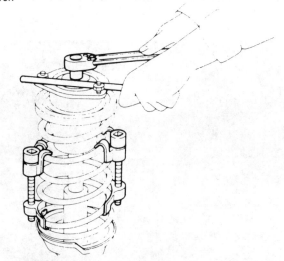

Fig. 11.7 When removing the upper retaining nut from the strut assembly, use a bar to keep the mounting insulator from turning (Sec 6)

9   It is wise at this time to relieve all tension on the spring and remove it from the shock absorber. Loosen the compressor a little at a time until it is free to be lifted off the shock absorber body. Although some compressors would allow you to lift the spring off the shock absorber in its compressed state, this could prove dangerous should the compressor and spring be jostled and accidentally disengaged from each other.

10 The spring should be checked for cracking or deformation of any kind. If the vehicle was sagging in the front, this is an indication that the springs are in need of replacement.

11 To test the shock absorber, hold it in an upright position and work the piston rod up and down its full length of travel, four or five times. If you can feel a strong resistance because of hydraulic pressure, the shock absorber is functioning properly. If you feel no marked resistance or if there is a sudden free movement in travel, the shock absorber should be repaired or replaced.

12 If there are excessive amounts of fluid evident on the outside of the shock absorber, the shock absorber should be repaired or replaced.

13 If the shock absorber is defective, a new sealed cartridge-type unit can be obtained from a Datsun dealer, or, the shock absorber can be overhauled. If oil is leaking from the gland packing, replacement of that component may be all that's required. If an overhaul is to be done, first obtain a cylinder and piston rebuild kit from a Datsun dealer. One special tool will also be needed as described in the following procedure.

14 Push the piston rod in until it bottoms, then remove the gland packing.

15 Remove the O-ring from the top of the outer casing and draw out the guide bushing.

16 Lift out the piston rod together with the inner cylinder.

17 Drain the fluid from the inner cylinder and the outer casing.

18 Wash all of the metal parts in solvent.

19 Prior to reassembly, make sure that all parts are completely free of dirt.

20 If a cartridge-type unit is being installed, simply insert it in the outer casing. Then gently shake the strut components to center the cartridge. Proceed to paragraph 25.

21 If a cylinder and piston rebuild kit is being installed, support the outer casing in a vise between wood blocks, and then insert the complete shock absorber kit into the casing.

22 Pour in exactly 9.3 fl. oz. (275 ml) of Nissan strut fluid or equivalent shock fluid.

23 Install the guide bushing over the piston rod and into the outer casing.

24 Install a new O-ring into the top of the outer casing.

25 Lubricate the inner sealing lip of the gland packing with multi-purpose grease.

26 Wrap the threads on the end of the piston rod with electrical tape, and carefully slide the gland packing over the top of the piston rod.

27 Thread the gland packing into the outer casing and, using a special torque wrench adapter as shown in the accompanying illustration, tighten it to the specified torque.

28 Remove the shock from the vise, hold it in an upright position and stroke the piston out its full length. Then invert the shock absorber and push the piston in until it bottoms. Do this several times to remove all air from the shock absorber.

29 Using the spring compressor, compress the spring approximately 2 in (50.7 mm). Then with the shock absorber main body mounted in a vise with protective wood blocks, install the spring over the shock absorber body. Make sure the lower coil conforms to the spring seat.

30 Install the dust cover and bumper to the shock body.

31 Install the spring seat, dust seal and mounting bearing.

32 Install the mounting insulator.

33 Install the lock washer and locknut to the top of the piston rod. Tighten this nut to its proper torque setting.

34 Carefully relieve tension on the coil spring by loosening the compressor from side to side, a little at a time. Check to be sure the top of the spring is raised properly into its seat.

7   Front stabilizer bar – removal and installation

1   Raise the front of the car and support it on jackstands.

2   Remove the splash shield.

3   Remove the lower nuts from both of the stabilizer links located at each end of the stabilizer bar.

4   Remove the stabilizer links from the transverse links. Remove the bushings, washers and spacers being sure to keep them in their installed order, and then remove the stabilizer links from the stabilizer bar.

5   Remove the bolts and nuts that mount the stabilizer support brackets to the body and lift off the stabilizer bar.

6   If the stabilizer bar bushings need to be replaced simply spread them apart and slide them off the bar.

7   Inspect the stabilizer link bolts and bushings for any cracking or other damage and replace them as necessary.

8   Fit the stabilizer support brackets onto the stabilizer bar. If marked, the bracket marked with an L goes on the left side of the bar.

9   Raise the stabilizer bar into position and loosely tighten both nuts and both mounting bolts.

10 Install the links through the transverse link and stabilizer bar, arranging the components in the same order they were originally.

11 Install the stabilizer link nuts and torque them to specifications.

12 Lower the car to the ground so that the full weight of the car is on the wheels and then torque the stabilizer bar mounting bolts and nuts to specifications.

13 Reinstall the splash shield.

8   Tension rod – removal and installation

1   Raise the front of the car and support it on jackstands for clearance, then remove the splash shield.

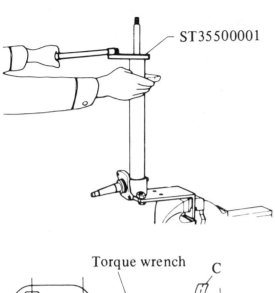

ST35500001

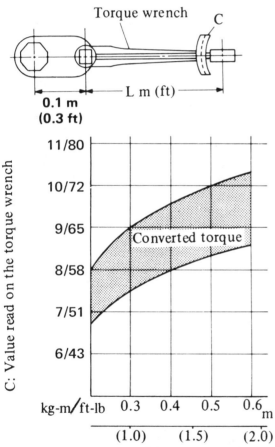

Torque wrench

0.1 m
(0.3 ft)

L m (ft)

C: Value read on the torque wrench

11/80

10/72

9/65

Converted torque

8/58

7/51

6/43

kg-m/ft-lb   0.3   0.4   0.5   0.6
                                      m
              (1.0)   (1.5)   (2.0)

L: Effective length of torque wrench (ft)

Fig. 11.8 To properly torque the gland packing, a special adapter must be used with a torque wrench and the torque indicated on the wrench must be converted using the chart above (Sec 6)

2   Remove the nut from the forward end of the tension rod (photo) and lift off the bushings and washer plates.
3   Remove both the bolts at the rear end of the tension rod and remove the tension rod from the car.
4   If both tension rods are being removed at once, be sure to note the marks referring to left and right for installation.
5   Installation is the reverse of the removal procedure. **Note:** *Do not torque tighten the mounting bolts until the car has been lowered to the ground and the full weight is on the wheels.*

8.2 Removing the nut from the front end of the tension rod

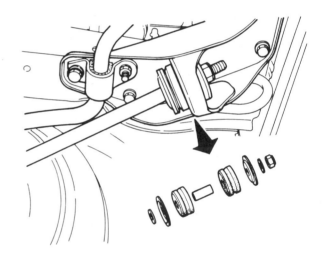

Fig. 11.9 Correct arrangement of the tension rod front mounting components (Sec 8)

---

9   Balljoint and transverse link – removal and installation

1   Raise the front of the car and support it on jackstands.
2   Remove the wheel and tire. Remove the splash shield.
3   Remove the stabilizer bar link.
4   Remove the bolts that attach the tension rod to the transverse link.
5   Remove the cotter pin and nut that attaches the side rod to the steering knuckle, and use a suitable tool to separate the two. Then remove the bolts that attach the steering knuckle to the strut components.
6   Remove the pivot bolt that holds the inner end of the transverse link to the crossmember.
7   If necessary, turn the wheel outward for clearance, and remove the transverse link.
8   Place the transverse link in a vise, and remove the bolt that attaches the steering knuckle and balljoint to the transverse link. To replace the balljoint, press the balljoint from the knuckles, using a hydraulic press. Then press the new balljoint into the knuckle.
9   If the transverse link bushing needs to be replaced, it must be pressed out and a new bushing pressed in. Be sure that the outer end of the new bushing is flush with the end of the transverse link.
10 Installation is the reverse of the removal procedure. **Note:** *Do not tigten the pivot bolt at the inner end of the transverse link until the car has been lowered to the ground.*

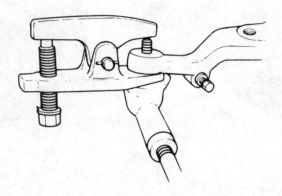

Fig. 11.10 A special tool must be used to separate the ballstud and swivel joints used in the steering linkage (Sec 9)

10 Crossmember – removal and installation

1   Raise the front of the car and support it safely on stands placed under the body side members. The car should be high enough for the front wheels to hang free.
2   Remove the engine splash shield.
3   If equipped with a rack-and-pinion, make all necessary disconnections in preparation for removal, as described in Section 27.
4   Remove the transverse link as described in the preceding Section.
5   Support the weight of the engine either on a jack and wooden insulating block placed under the oil pan or by attaching an overhead hoist to it.
6   Disconnect the engine mountings from the crossmember.
7   Support the crossmember on a jack and unbolt it from the body sidemembers.
8   Separate the rack-and-pinion from the crossmember, if so equipped.
9   Installation is a reversal of removal, tighten all nuts and bolts to the specified torque.

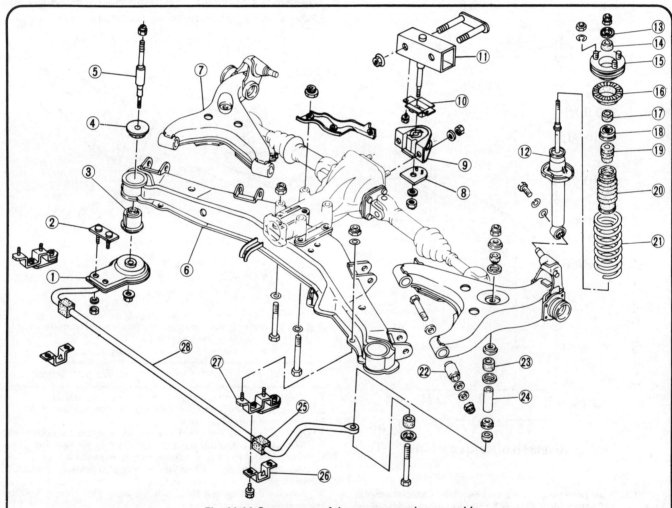

Fig. 11.11 Components of the rear suspension assembly

1	Suspension member mounting stay	10	Differential mounting adapter plate	19 Bound bumper
2	Suspension member mounting bolt	11	Differential mounting bracket	20 Dust cover
3	Member mounting insulator	12	Shock absorber assembly	21 Coil spring
4	Member mounting upper stopper	13	Special washer	22 Suspension arm bushing
5	Suspension mounting bolt	14	Shock absorber mounting bushing A	23 Stabilizer bushing
6	Suspension member assembly	15	Shock absorber mounting insulator	24 Stabilizer collar
7	Suspension arm assembly	16	Spring seat rubber	25 Stabilizer mounting bushing
8	Differential mounting plate	17	Shock absorber mounting bushing B	26 Stabilizer mounting clip
9	Differential mounting insulator	18	Bound bumper cover	27 Stabilizer mounting bracket
				28 Rear stabilizer

11 Front axle – removal and installation

The front axle, which consists of the crossmember and the two transverse links can be removed as one piece by following the crossmember removal procedure described in Section 10, but without disconnecting the transverse links from the crossmember.

12 Rear stabilizer bar – removal and installation

1 Jack up the rear of the car and support it on jackstands.
2 Remove the stabilizer bar link bolts that pass through the suspension arms and attach to the body.
3 Remove the bolts that attach the stabilizer bar mounting brackets to the suspension member and remove the bar.
4 If the bushings exhibit any hardening or cracking, they should be replaced.
5 Installation is the reverse of the removal procedure, with the following notes:

    a) Be sure to install the stabilizer bar bushings with the locating mark on the bar just to the outside of the bushing.
    b) The stabilizer bar mounting brackets should be installed so the arrow is pointing toward the front of the car.

13 Rear shock absorber and spring components – removal and installation

1 Jack up the rear of the vehicle and support the frame side-members securely on suitable stands. The front wheels should also be chocked.
2 Working inside the rear compartment, unscrew the cap and remove the three nuts securing the shock absorber upper mounting to the body (photo).
3 Working beneath the vehicle, disconnect the bottom of the shock absorber from the suspension arm (one bolt).
4 Remove the shock absorber and coil spring assembly from beneath the vehicle.
5 When installing the assembly to the vehicle, the upper end of the assembly should be installed first. Tighten all nuts and bolts to the specified torque.

14 Rear shock absorber and spring components – disassembly and reassembly

1 The spring on the rear shock absorber is under considerable pressure, requiring a special spring compressor to be used to safely compress the spring and disengage its components. Do not attempt to disassemble the spring without the proper compressor, as serious injury can occur.
2 A strut spring compressor can be purchased through Datsun dealers or through most auto parts stores. Compressors can also be rented on a daily basis from rental agencies and some auto parts stores.
3 Hold the shock absorber in a vise using wood blocks to cushion the jaws to prevent damage to thr shock.
4 Mark the relative positions of the upper shock absorber mounting and the lower end pin to ensure correct reassembly.
5 Following the manufacturer's instructions for the particular spring compressor being used, slightly compress the spring, making sure that the jaws of the compressor are firmly seated around the coils and cannot slip off.
6 Tighten the compressor from side to side, a little at a time, until the spring seat is clear of the uppermost coil.
7 With the spring firmly compressed and clear of its seat, reinstall the nuts onto the upper studs to protect the threads. Hold the mounting insulator stationary by placing a bar between the mounting studs, and remove the top lock nut.
8 Withdraw the top mounting insulator together with the bushings and washer. Remove the spring seat rubber. The compressor and coil spring can now be removed from the assembly.
9 Remove the inner bushing, bumper and dust cover assembly, and the bumper stop from the assembly.

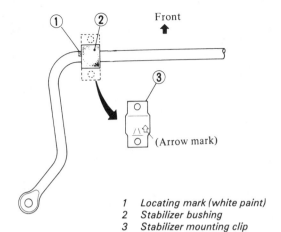

1 Locating mark (white paint)
2 Stabilizer bushing
3 Stabilizer mounting clip

Fig. 11.12 Correct mounting position of the rear stabilizer bar bushings and brackets (Sec 12)

13.2 The upper mounting bolts of the rear shock are accessible through the rear compartment of the car

10 With the coil spring removed from the spring compressor, visually check the coil for any cracks or deformation. Measure the free length and compare the measurement with that given in the specifications.
11 Inspect the shock absorber for oil leakage. Hold the assembly vertically, and fully extend and depress the piston rod several times. Unless there is a definite resistance with smooth operation in both directions, the unit must be renewed.
12 Check all rubber components for wear, cracks, damage or deformation, renewing where necessary.
13 Reassembly of the coil spring and shock absorber assembly is a reversal of removal but ensure that the coil spring is correctly located in the lower spring seat.

15 Rear axle and suspension components – removal and installation

1 Jack up the rear end of the vehicle and support it on jackstands placed under the body side panels. Chock the front wheels. Remove the rear wheels.
2 Refer to Chapter 6, and remove the rear exhaust pipe and muffler.
3 Remove the driveshaft as described in Chapter 8.
4 Disconnect the brake flexible hoses from the rigid hydraulic lines on both sides of the vehicle. Before disconnecting the hoses, place a sheet of polyethylene over the mouth of the hydraulic master cylinder, to create a vacuum and prevent excessive loss of the hydraulic fluid. Ensure that the disconnected hoses and pipes are suitably covered to

prevent dirt from entering the system. Disconnect the parking brake linkage by removing the locknut and clevis pin at the adjuster.

5   Remove the heat shield in front of the fuel tank.

6   Using a floor jack, support the differential housing in such a manner that when the assembly is lowered it will not tilt to one side or slip off the jack.

7   Disconnect each shock absorber from its lower suspension arm mounting point.

8   Loosen and remove the nut at each side of the suspension member.

9   Loosen and remove the rear differential mounting nut, and note the exact position the rear mounting insulator is installed in. This insulator must be installed in the same position.

10 Very carefully lower the jack, ensuring that the assembly does not tilt to one side or slip off. Once the assembly has been lowered enough to clear the frame it can be withdrawn from beneath the vehicle.

11 With the rear suspension removed, examine all parts for wear or damage. Particular attention should be given to the bushings in the suspension arms. Also check the condition of the rubber bushings in the suspension member and the differential mounting member. Any of these components, if worn, can result in noise and vibration.

12 Replacement of the suspension member bushings, will require the use of a suitable bushing extractor. The old bushing is simply forced out and a new one installed in the same way. Ensure that the bushings are correctly installed, and inserted from the underside of the member.

13 Begin installation by jacking the assembly up into position to locate on the three mounting studs (two suspension member studs and differential mounting member studs). Secure the assembly by installing the securing nuts and tightening them to the specified torque.

14 Once the shock absorbers have been connected, the jack can be removed. The rest of the installation procedure is a reversal of removal but the rear brake hydraulic lines should be bled as described in Chapter 9.

16 Suspension member – removal and installation

1   Replacement of the suspension member bushings is described in Section 15. This can be carried out without removing the suspension member from the front of the differential case and the suspension arms. However, if the suspension member is to be replaced proceed as described in the following paragraphs.

2   Remove the rear stabilizer bar, as described in Section 12.

3   Place a jack under the differential to support its weight.

4   Disconnect the parking brake rear cable from the adjuster and suspension components. Refer to Chapter 9, if necessary.

5   Disconnect the brake lines from the suspension arms.

6   Disconnect the front end of the differential case from the suspension member by removing the four securing bolts.

7   Disconnect each suspension arm by removing the nuts and driving out the two pivot pins.

8   Remove the bolts attaching the suspension member to the body and carefully lower it.

9   Installation of the suspension member is a reversal of removal, but before tightening the suspension arm pivot pins the vehicle must be lowered to the ground. This will ensure that the rubber bushings are clamped in a neutral or unloaded position.

17 Suspension arm – removal and installation

1   Jack up the rear of the vehicle and support it firmly on suitable stands. Chock the front wheels.

2   Remove the appropriate wheel and tire.

3   Remove the rear stabilizer bar.

4   Disconnect the hydraulic brake line from the rear wheel cylinder and the flexible hose. Remove the line from the suspension arm. Before dismantling the pipe, place a sheet of polyethylene over the

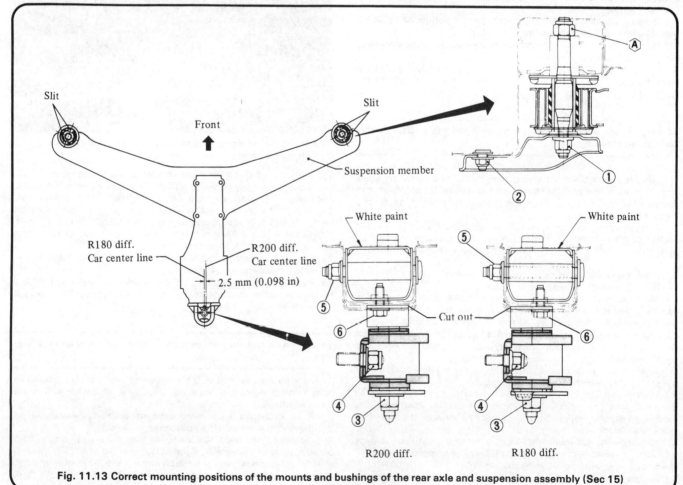

Fig. 11.13 Correct mounting positions of the mounts and bushings of the rear axle and suspension assembly (Sec 15)

mouth of the rear reservoir of the master cylinder. This will create a vacuum in the hydraulic system and prevent excessive fluid loss. Be sure to plug the open end of the disconnected hose.

5   Disconnect the parking brake cable from the operating lever on the caliper. Remove the cable assembly from the suspension arm.

6   Refer to Chapter 8 and remove the rear axle stub, wheel bearings and oil seal.

7   Disconnect the shock absorber at its lower mounting.

8   Remove the suspension arm by loosening the two pivot pin nuts, removing them, and driving out the pivot pins with a suitable drift.

9   Replacement of the pivot pin bushings will require the use of a bushing extractor. The old ones are drawn out and new ones are installed using the same tool.

10 Installation of the suspension arm is a reversal of removal but ensure that all nuts and bolts are tightened to the specified torque. The weight of the vehicle must be on the rear wheels before the suspension arm pivot pins are tightened.

11 Ensure that the brake system is bled and that all relevant adjustments are carried out before driving the vehicle.

18 Steering system – general information

Prior to 1982, all 280 ZX cars with power steering systems used a steering gear of the worm-and-nut recirculating-ball type with hydraulic pressure to boost the manual steering force. The power steering system in 1982 models and all turbo models uses a rack-and-pinion in place of the steering gear and linkage. In addition, all manual steering systems are also of the rack-and-pinion type.

The components that make up the steering gear system are the steering wheel, steering column, steering gear (steering box), and steering linkage assembly. In addition the system also uses a belt-driven pump with integrated reservoir tank to provide hydraulic pressure.

The components that make up the rack-and-pinion system are the steering wheel, steering column, intermediate shaft, rack and pinion assembly and side rods. In addition, the power steering system also uses a belt-driven pump to provide hydraulic pressure in the same manner as the above system.

If the power steering system loses its hydraulic pressure it will still function manually, though with increased effort.

The steering column is of the collapsible, energy-absorbing type, designed to compress in the event of a front end collision to minimize injury to the driver. The column also houses the ignition switch, steering column lock, headlight switch, turn signal control, headlight dimmer switch, windshield wiper and washer control and, on GL models, the cruise control switch. The ignition and steering wheel can both be locked while the car is parked to inhibit theft.

Due to the column's collapsible design, it is important that only specified screws, bolts and nuts be used as designated and that they be tightened to the specified torque. Other precautions particular to this design are noted in appropriate Sections.

19 Steering system – inspection

Since periodic inspection of the steering system is part of the routine maintenance of the car, these procedures are described in Chapter 1.

20 Steering wheel – removal and installation

1   Disconnect the negative battery cable.

2   Grab the top of the center steering wheel pad and pull it off the steering wheel.

3   Be sure the steering wheel is in the unlocked position, and then remove the steering wheel nut.

4   Be sure the wheels are in the straight-ahead position and then mark the position of the steering wheel in relation to the steering shaft.

5   Note the two threaded holes in the steering wheel on either side of the shaft. Install an appropriate steering wheel puller in these holes, and remove the steering wheel. **Note:** *Because of the collapsible design of this steering column, under no circumstances should the end of the shaft be hammered on as this could weaken the column's rigidity.*

6   Prior to installation, apply a light coat of grease to the sliding portion of the rear of the steering wheel.

7   Installation is the reverse of the removal procedure with the following note: when installing the steering wheel on the shaft be sure the front wheels are still pointing straight ahead and that the alignment marks on the wheel and shaft match. Tighten the steering wheel nut to the proper torque and turn the wheel to check for drag.

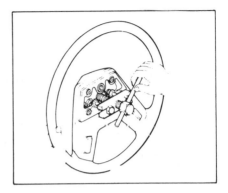

Fig. 11.14 To remove the steering wheel, a puller should be installed as shown (Sec 20)

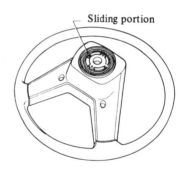

Sliding portion

Fig. 11.15 Prior to reinstalling the steering wheel, grease should be applied to the sliding portion of the rear (Sec 20)

21 Steering lock – removal and installation

1   Obtain two self-shear screws from your Datsun dealer, needed to reinstall the steering lock.

2   Remove the steering wheel as described in Section 20.

3   Remove the steering column cover.

4   The steering lock is secured to the steering shaft with two regular screws and two self-shear screws. Removing the shear screws will involve very careful drilling of the screws. Start by center punching a dot in the center of the screw. Select a drill that is about the diameter of the root of the thread. Very carefully ensuring that the drill is square to the screw, drill out the center of the screw until a screw extractor can be used to remove the screw.

5   Remove the two regular attaching screws and disengage the steering lock from the shaft. Disconnect the ignition switch wires.

6   To install, align the mating surface of the steering lock with the hole in the steering column tube. Then loosely install the two regular attaching screws. Once the operation of the lock is checked using the key, these screws can be tightened.

7   Install the two self-shearing screws in their appropriate holes, making sure the tops snap off as shown in the accompanying illustration.

8   The remainder of the installation is the reverse of the removal procedure.

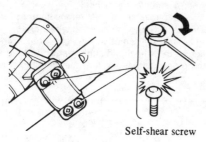

Self-shear screw

Fig. 11.16 Two self-shear screws are used in the positions shown to retain the steering lock to the column (Sec 21)

22 Steering column – removal and installation

1   For clearance, remove the front seat as described in Chapter 12.
2   Open the hood and locate the end of the steering column. Remove the bolt that secures the rubber coupling on the column to either the stub shaft (steering gear systems) or lower joint (rack-and-pinion systems).
3   Disconnect the negative battery cable.
4   Remove the steering wheel as described in Section 20.
5   Remove the steering column combination switch assembly as described in Chapter 10.
6   Remove the lower shaft instrument cover, located directly below the steering column.
7   Remove the heater duct located below the steering column.

8   Remove the screws that attach the jacket tube bracket to the firewall.
9   While supporting the column, remove the two bolts that secure the column mounting bracket to the dash and lift out the column. **Note:** *Because of its collapsible design, the steering column is very susceptible to damage when removed from the car. Be careful not to lean on or drop the column, as this could weaken the column's structure and impair its performance.*
10   If the car has been in an accident which resulted in frame damage, major body damage or steering column impact, the column could be damaged or misaligned and should be checked by a qualified mechanic.
11   If the steering wheel has not been turning smoothly, check the column bearings for wear or damage, the jacket tube for breakage or deformation and the column spring for damage or weakening. Replace any of these components as necessary.
12   Prior to installing the column, measure the dimension L, as shown in the accompanying illustration. The measurement should be $15\frac{3}{4}$ in (400 mm).
13   Prior to installation be sure the wheels are set in a straight-ahead position.
14   Lower the end of the column through the firewall and install it onto the stub shaft or lower joint. Be sure the punch mark at the top end of the column shaft is in the 12 o'clock position.
15   Loosely install the bolts that secure the mounting bracket to the dash.
16   Loosely install the bolt that secures the column to the stub shaft or lower joint.
17   Install the nuts that retain the jacket to the firewall and torque them to specifications.
18   Torque the remaining mounting bolts to specifications.
19   The remainder of the installation is the reverse of the removal procedure.

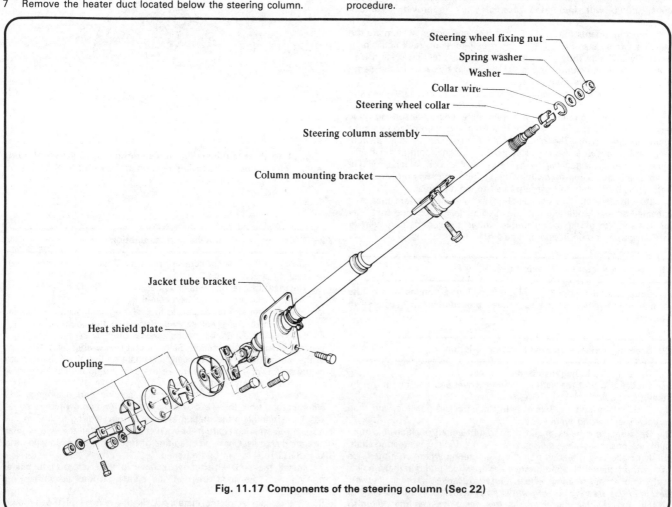

Fig. 11.17 Components of the steering column (Sec 22)

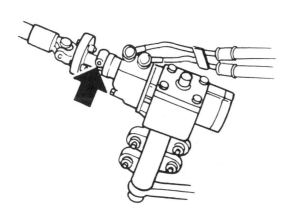

Fig. 11.18 Location of the rubber coupler-to-stub shaft bolt (steering gear systems) (Sec 22)

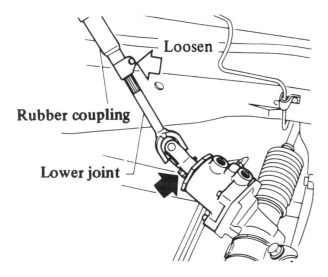

Fig. 11.19 Locations of the bolts attaching the lower joint to the steering column coupler and rack-and-pinion (Sec 22)

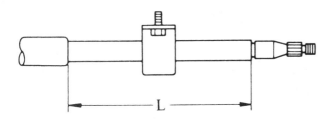

Fig. 11.20 Prior to installing the steering column, the dimension L (above) should be measured to check for column compression (Sec 22)

23 Power steering system – maintenance and adjustment

1　The hydraulic components used in the power steering system include a belt-driven oil pump with integrated reservoir tank, power steering gear or rack-and-pinion assembly and connecting hoses and lines.

2　Normal maintenance of the power steering system consists mainly of periodically checking the fluid level in the reservoir, keeping the pump drivebelt tension correct and visually checking the hoses for any evidence of fluid leakage. It will also be necessary, after a system component has been removed, to bleed the system as described in Section 24.

3　If the operational characteristics of the system appear to be suspect, and the maintenance and adjustment mentioned in this Section is in order, the vehicle should be taken to a Datsun dealer, who will have the necessary equipment to check the pressure in the system and the operational torque needed to turn the steering wheel. These two operations are considered beyond the scope of the home mechanic, in view of the high working pressure of the system and the special tools required.

4　If the checks mentioned in paragraph 2 prove that either the oil pump assembly or the steering gear or rack-and-pinion components are at fault, a new component will have to be purchased as it is not possible to overhaul them.

5　If there are oil leaks from the power steering gear or rack-and-pinion assembly, individual oil seals can be replaced without replacing the entire assembly. But, once again, due to the critical nature of the assembly, this job should be done by a Datsun dealer or other qualified repair shop.

6　The oil pump drivebelt tension is adjusted by loosening the idler pulley locknut and turning the adjustment bolt as necessary. Refer to Chapter 1, for the proper procedure.

7　Excluding the oil pump, power steering gear and its associated pressure hoses, the rest of the steering system components are identical to those used on the manual steering models. Servicing these components can be carried out by following the operations described in the relevant Sections of this Chapter.

24 Power steering system – bleeding

Note: *Whenever a hose in the power steering hydraulic system has been disconnected, it is quite probable, no matter how much care was taken to prevent air entering the system, that the system will need bleeding. To do this, proceed as described in the following paragraphs.*

1　First, ensure that the reservoir level is correct; if necessary, add fluid to bring the level to the mark on the dipstick. If necessary, refer to Chapter 1. If the car has not just been driven, the power steering oil should be brought up to operating temperature. This can be done either by idling the engine and turning the steering wheel from left to right for about two minutes, or by driving the car for several miles.

2　Raise the front end of the vehicle until the front wheels are just clear of the ground.

3　Quickly turn the steering wheel all the way to the right lock and then the left lock. Do not allow the lock stoppers to be struck with a bang. Try to gauge the end of the lock and only lightly touch the lock stoppers. This operation should be repeated about ten times.

4　Now check the reservoir fluid lever again, as detailed in paragraph 1.

5　Start the engine and allow it to idle. On rack-and-pinion systems, shut the engine off again after a few seconds, and recheck the fluid level. Repeat paragraphs 3 through 5 several times, if necessary, to purge the system of air. Note paragraphs 7 and 8.

6　On steering gear systems only, repeat the operations described in paragraph 3. With the steering wheel in full lock position, quickly open the bleed nipple at the oil pump and allow a little fluid to escape. **Caution:** *Do not hold steering at lock position for more than fifteen seconds at a time.* This operation should be repeated several times on both locks, until the fluid escaping from the bleed nipple is free from air bubbles. The bleed nipple should only be opened for a few seconds and then shut again. Check the oil in the reservoir frequently to make sure it stays at the correct level.

7　If the air bleeding is insufficient, the oil reservoir will be extremely foamy and the pump will be noisy. In this case, allow the foam in the reservoir to disperse, recheck the level again and repeat the entire bleeding process.

8   If it becomes obvious, after several attempts, that the system cannot be satisfactorily bled, there is quite probably a leak in the system. Visually check the hoses and their connections for leaks. If no leaks are evident, the problem could be in the steering box itself and the only solution is to have the entire system checked by a Datsun dealer.

25 Power steering pump – removal and installation

1   Loosen the locknut on the idler pulley and turn the drivebelt adjusting bolt counterclockwise to loosen the bolt.
2   Remove the drivebelt from the power steering pump.
3   Loosen, but do not remove the hoses where they attach to the pump.
4   Remove the pump mounting bolts and lift it up as much as the hoses will allow. Place it in a shallow drain pan and disconnect the hoses, allowing the oil to drain into the pan.
5   Securely plug the ends of the hoses to prevent oil loss or dirt from entering the hose system.
6   If necessary, the drive pulley can be removed by unscrewing the retaining nut and using a standard puller to withdraw the pulley from the shaft.
7   Installation of the oil pump assembly is a reversal of removal but before tightening the mounting bolts ensure that the correct drivebelt tension exists, as described in Chapter 1.
8   Once installation is complete, refill the pump reservoir with the correct grade and quantity of fluid. If necessary, bleed the system as described in Section 24.

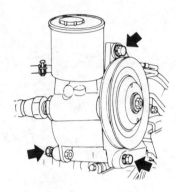

Fig. 11.21 Location of the power steering pump mounting bolts (Sec 25)

26 Side rod and rubber boot (rack and pinion models) – removal and installation

1   Raise the front of the car and support it on jackstands.
2   Remove the cotter pin and nut that secures the side rod to the steering knuckle.

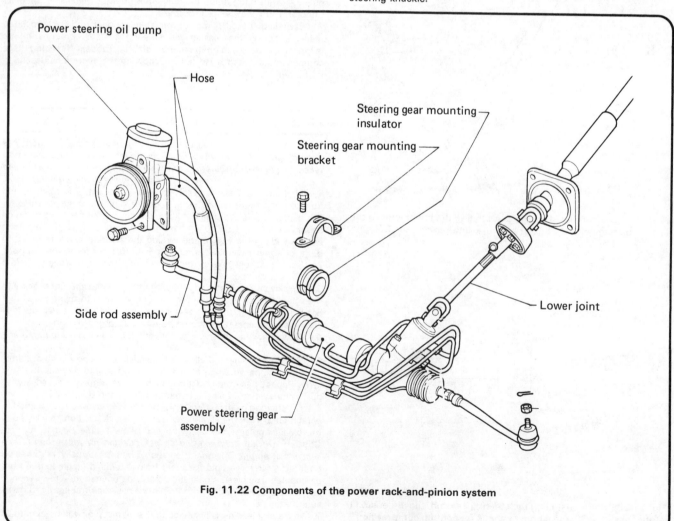

Fig. 11.22 Components of the power rack-and-pinion system

3   Use an appropriate separating tool to separate the side rod from the steering knuckle.
4   Remove the clamps that secure the rubber boot to the rack and pinion.
5   Loosen the side rod locknut and remove the side rod.
6   Slide the boot off the rack and pinion.
7   Installation is the reverse of the removal procedure.

27 Rack and pinion – removal and installaion

1   Raise the front of the car and support it on jackstands.
2   Remove the splash shield.
3   On power steering models, remove the bolts that attach the hydraulic lines to the crossmember.
4   Place a drain pan under the rack and pinion and disconnect the flare nuts where the hydraulic lines enter the rack and pinion. Allow the fluid to drain into the pan. Immediately plug all the openings to prevent the entry of foreign matter into the system.
5   Loosen the bolt securing the lower joint shaft to the rubber coupling of the steering column.
6   Disconnect the bolt securing the lower joint to the rack and pinion pinion gear and separate the two pieces.
7   Remove the cotter pins and nuts securing the side rods to the

steering knuckles. Then using a suitable separating tool, separate the side rods from the knuckles.
8   Loosen, but do not remove the bolts securing the rack-and-pinion to the crossmember.
9   Remove the nuts that attach the front engine mounting insulators to the crossmember.
10 Securely connect an engine hoist to the lifting 'eyes' on the engine, and lift the engine slightly until the weight is taken off the engine mounts.
11 One of two methods must be employed to remove the rack and pinion from the engine compartment. Either the engine can be lifted enough so the rack and pinion can be removed from the crossmember or the crossmember and related front suspension components can be lowered. If the engine is lifted, do it slowly and keep a careful check on clearances around the engine while it is being lifted. Check especially the fan shroud, vacuum lines leading to the engine and the rubber ducts connected to the air flow meter.
12 If it is decided to lower the crossmember, support it securely with a garage jack, and remove the bolts shown in Fig. 11.25. Carefully lower the components until the rack and pinion can be removed.
13 Remove the rack and pinion mounting bolts and lift the unit from the crossmember.
14 If the rack and pinion unit needs to be overhauled, this should be done by a Datson dealer or other qualified mechanic.
15 Installation is the reverse of the removal procedure.

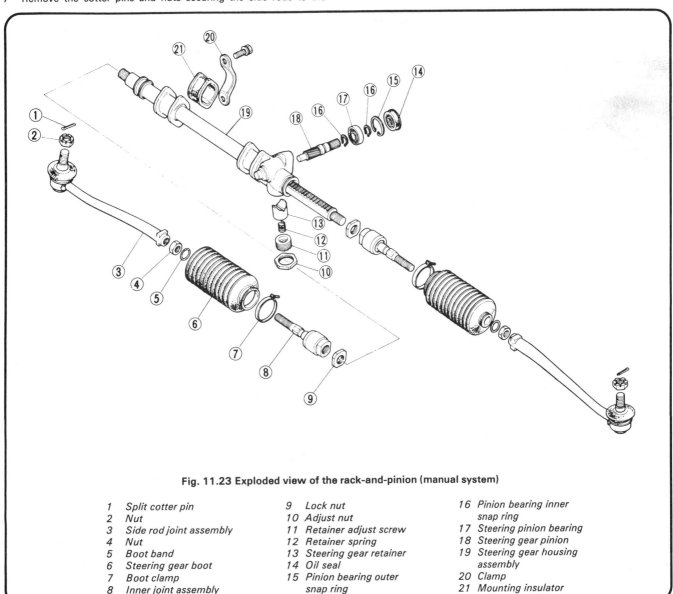

Fig. 11.23 Exploded view of the rack-and-pinion (manual system)

1 Split cotter pin	9 Lock nut	16 Pinion bearing inner
2 Nut	10 Adjust nut	snap ring
3 Side rod joint assembly	11 Retainer adjust screw	17 Steering pinion bearing
4 Nut	12 Retainer spring	18 Steering gear pinion
5 Boot band	13 Steering gear retainer	19 Steering gear housing
6 Steering gear boot	14 Oil seal	assembly
7 Boot clamp	15 Pinion bearing outer	20 Clamp
8 Inner joint assembly	snap ring	21 Mounting insulator

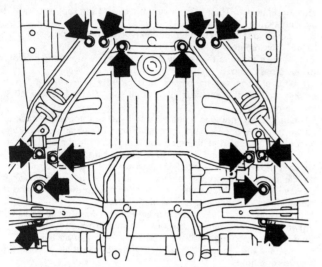

Fig. 11.24 The bolts shown above must be removed to lower the crossmember and related parts (Sec 27)

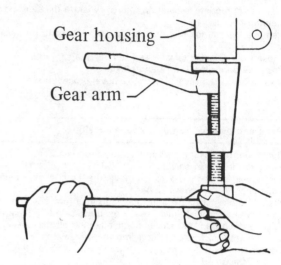

Fig. 11.26 To separate the gear arm from the steering gear's sector shaft, a puller must be used (Sec 28)

28 Steering gear (1979 thru 1981 non-turbo models) – removal and installation

1   To aid reassembly, place the front wheels in the straight-ahead position. Loosen and remove the bolt securing the coupler to the stub shaft at the steering box.
2   Place a suitable drain pan beneath the steering box hose connections, disconnect the hoses and allow the oil to drain from the hoses and the steering box into the pan. Plug the ends of the hoses and the open ports at the steering box.
3   Unscrew the nut and remove the washer securing the gear arm to the sector shaft.
4   Scribe a line across the sector shaft and the gear arm to ensure correct installation.
5   Withdraw the gear arm from the sector shaft using an appropriate puller.
6   Loosen and remove the bolts securing the steering box to the frame and remove the unit from the vehicle.

7   Installation of the steering box assembly is a reversal of removal but observe the alignment marks on the sector shaft and gear arm. Screw in the coupler-to-stub shaft bolt finger-tight. Tighten the steering box-to-frame bolts to the specified torque, then tighten the bolt to its proper torque.
8   When installation is complete, refill the oil pump reservoir with new oil of the correct grade and quantity. Bleed the air from the system, as described in Section 24.

29 Steering linkage (steering gear models) – removal and installation

1   The steering linkage is basically a system of rods that is designed to transmit the steering motion in the steering gear to the front wheels.
2   Included in this system is a cross rod, two side rods, (tie-rods), an idler arm and a gear arm. The gear arm connects the steering gear to

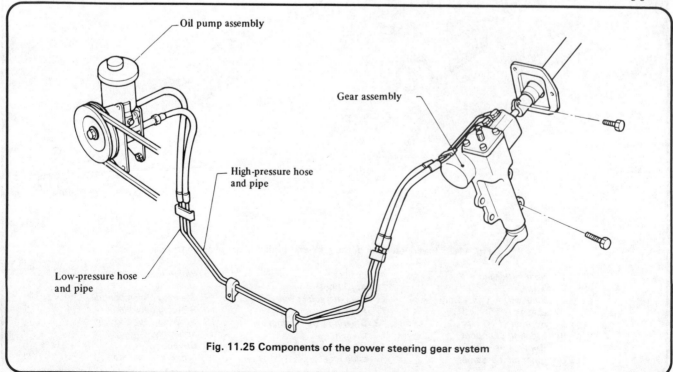

Fig. 11.25 Components of the power steering gear system

one end of the cross rod. The other end of the cross rod is connected to the idler arm, which is in turn bolted directly to the body. Each end of the cross rod is also connected to the front wheels by way of the side rods.

3 The individual components of the steering linkage can be removed as a whole. Following any dismantling of the steering linkage, the front end alignment should be checked and adjusted, if necessary. **Note:** *For each of the following procedures, the front of the car should be raised and supported on jackstands. Following reinstallation of the component all nuts that are coupled with bushings should be left only finger tight until after the car has been lowered to the ground. Only when the full weight of the car is on wheels should these nuts be tightened to their specified torque.*

Side rod

4 Remove the cotter pins and locknuts at both ends of the side rod.

5 Using a special separator tool, as illustrated in Fig. 11.10, disengage the side rod from the knuckle arm and cross rod and lift it out.

6 Inspect the bushings and if they are hardened or cracked, replace them with new ones.

7 If the side rod needs to be disassembled, first mark the points of adjustment by applying a dab of white paint on the rod clamps and threads. Then loosen the clamp bolts, and unscrew the ends from the center rod.

8 Reassembly and installation is the reverse of the removal procedure. If the old side rod has been disassembled, be sure the adjustment is reset at the marks made during disassembly. If a new side rod is being installed, prior to installation, set the adjustment so the distance between the ballstud centers is 14.42 in (366.3 mm). Torque the securing nuts at either end of the rod to specs.

Idler arm

9 Play in the idler arm assembly can be remedied by replacing the bushings with new ones.

10 Remove the two nuts and bolts that secure the idler arm to the body.

11 Swing the idler arm around into an accessible position. If the idler arm needs to be removed, remove the cotter pin and locknut that retain it to the cross rod. Then using an appropriate separating tool, disengage the idler arm from the cross rod.

12 If only the bushings in the idler arm have to be replaced, first remove the upper nut and washer (photo). Then lift the idler arm bracket off and remove the two bushings from it. Install new ones. Reassemble the idler arm.

13 Installation is the reverse of the removal procedure. Be sure to torque all attaching nuts to specs.

Cross rod

14 Remove the four sets of cotter pins and locknuts that retain the cross rod to the idler arm, gear arm and both side rods.

15 Using an appropriate separating tool, disengage the cross rod from each of these other components, and lift out the cross rod.

16 Inspect the bushings at each end of the rod for hardening or cracking and replace them if necessary.

17 Installation is the reverse of the removal procedure.

Complete linkage

18 To remove the steering linkage as a complete assembly, first remove the nut that retains the gear arm to the steering gear. Then using an appropriate puller as shown in the accompanying illustration, disengage the gear arm from the steering gear shaft.

19 Remove the two nuts and bolts that retain the idler arm to the body and lift the idler arm off.

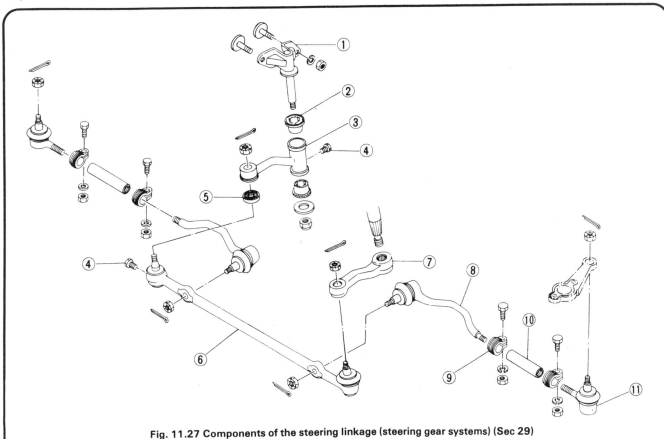

Fig. 11.27 Components of the steering linkage (steering gear systems) (Sec 29)

1	Idler bracket	5	Dust cover	9	Side rod clamp
2	Idler bushing	6	Cross rod	10	Adjusting tube
3	Idler arm	7	Gear arm	11	Outer side rod assembly
4	Filler plug	8	Inner side rod assembly		

20 Remove the cotter pins and locking nuts that retain the side rods to the steering knuckle arms. Then using an appropriate separating tool, disengage the side rods from the knuckle arms.

21 The entire steering linkage assembly can now be lowered from the car.

22 Installation is the reverse of the removal procedure.

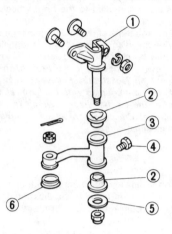

Fig. 11.28 Components of the idler arm assembly (Sec 29)

1	Idler bracket	4	Filler plug
2	Idler arm bushing	5	Plain washer
3	Idler arm	6	Dust cover

29.12 After removal from the body, the idler arm can be swung into an accessible position for disassembly

Chapter 12 Bodywork

Contents

Specifications

	2-seater	2+2
Overall length	174.0 in	181.9 in
Overall width	66.5 in	66.5 in
Overall height	51.0 in	51.4 in
Wheelbase	91.3 in	99.2 in
Curb weight (approx)	2800 lb	2900 lb
Torque specifications	**ft-lb**	**kg-m**
Bumper-to-energy absorber nuts	14	1.8
Energy absorber mounting bolts	27	3.7
Hood-to-hinge bolts	7	1.0
Seat belt anchor bolts	20	2.8
Rear door stay retaining bolts	16	2.2

1 General information

During the years covered by this manual, the 280ZX was available in two basic body styles: the 2-seater Coupe and the 2+2 model. In addition, each was offered with either the Deluxe, GL (Grand Luxury) or Turbo (1981 and 1982 only) package, which included various convenience and trim items. Differences between the various styles are noted when appropriate in the service procedures within this Chapter.

The 280ZX used a unitized body construction in which the body is designed to provide vehicle rigidity so that a separate frame is not necessary.

Certain body panels which are particularly vulnerable to accident damage can be replaced by unbolting them and installing replacement items. These panels include the fenders, inner fender skirts, grille, front apron, headlamp case, bumpers, hood and trunk.

2 Body – general maintenance

1 The condition of your vehicle's bodywork is of considerable importance as it is on this that the resale value will mainly depend. It is much more difficult to repair neglected bodywork than mechanical components. The hidden portions of the body, such as the wheel arches, fender skirts, the underframe and the engine compartment, are equally important, although obviously not requiring such frequent attention as the immediately visible paint.

2 Once a year or every 12 000 miles it is a good idea to visit your local dealer and have the underside of the body steam cleaned. All traces of dirt and oil will be removed and the underside can then be

inspected carefully for rust, damaged hydraulic lines, frayed electrical wiring and similar trouble areas. The front suspension should be greased on completion of this job.

3   At the same time, clean the engine and the engine compartment either using a steam cleaner or a water-soluble cleaner.

4   The wheel arches and fender skirts should be given particular attention as undercoating can easily come away here and stones and dirt thrown up from the wheels can soon cause the paint to chip and flake, and so allow rust to set in. If rust is found, clean down to the bare metal and apply an anti-rust paint.

5   Use a mild detergent and soft sponge to wash the exterior of the car and rinse immediately with clear water. Owners who live in coastal regions and where salt or chemicals are used on the roads should wash the finish religiously to prevent damage to the finish. Do not wash the car in direct sunlight or when the metal is warm. To remove road tar, insects or tree sap use a tar remover rather than a knife or sharp object which could scratch the surface.

6   A good coat of wax or polish may be your best protection against the elements. Use a good grade of polish or wax suitable for a high-quality synthetic finish. Do not use a wax or polish which contains large amounts of abrasives as these will scratch the finish.

7   Bright metal parts can be protected with wax or a chrome preservative. During winter months or in coastal regions apply a heavier coating or, if necessary, use a non-corrosive compound like petroleum jelly for protection. Do not use abrasive cleaners, strong detergents or materials like steel wool on chrome or anodized aluminium parts as these may damage the protective coating and cause discoloration or deterioration.

8   Interior surfaces can be wiped clean with a damp cloth or with cleaners specifically designed for car interior fabrics. Carefully read the manufacturer's instructions and test any commercial cleaners on an inconspicuous area first. The carpet should be vacuumed regularly and can be covered with mats.

9   Cleaning the mechanical parts of the car serves two useful functions. First it focuses your attention on parts which may be starting to fail, allowing you to fix or replace them before they cause problems. Second, it is much more pleasant to work on parts which are relatively clean. You will still get dirty on major repair jobs, but it will be less extreme. Large areas like the firewall and inner fender panels should be brushed with detergent, allowed to soak for about 15 minutes and then carefully rinsed clean. Cover ignition and carburetor parts with plastic to prevent moisture from penetrating these critical components.

---

3   Body damage – minor repair

See color photo sequence on pages 278 and 279.

Repair of minor scratches

If the scratch is very superficial, and does not penetrate to the metal of the body, repair is very simple. Lightly rub the area of the scratch with a fine rubbing compound to remove loose paint from scratch and to clear the surrounding paint of wax buildup. Rinse the area with clean water.

Apply touch-up paint to the scratch, using a small brush. Continue to apply thin layers of paint until the surface of the paint in the scratch is level with the surrounding paint. Allow the new paint at least two weeks to harden, then blend it into the surrounding paint by rubbing with a very fine rubbing compound. Finally, apply a coat of wax to the scratch area.

Where the scratch has penetrated the paint and exposed the metal of the body, causing the metal to rust, a different repair technique is required. Remove any loose rust from the bottom of the scratch with a pocket knife, then apply rust inhibiting paint to prevent the formation of rust in the future. Using a rubber or nylon applicator, coat the scratched area with glaze type filler. If required, this filler can be mixed with thinner to provide a very thin paste, which is ideal for filling narrow scratches. Before the glaze filler in the scratch hardens, wrap a piece of smooth cotton cloth around the top of a finger. Dip the cloth in thinner and then quickly wipe it along the surface of the scratch. This will ensure that the surface of the filler is slightly hollowed. The scratch can now be painted over as described earlier in this section.

Repair of dents

When denting of the vehicle's body has taken place, the first task is to pull the dent out until the affected area nearly attains its original shape. There is little point in trying to restore the original shape completely as the metal in the damaged area will have stretched on impact and cannot be reshaped fully to its original contours. It is better to bring the level of the dent up to a point which is about $\frac{1}{8}$ in below the level of the surrounding metal. In cases where the dent is very shallow, it is not worth trying to pull it out at all.

If the underside of the dent is accessible, it can be hammered out gently from behind using a mallet with a wooden or plastic head. While doing this, hold a suitable block of wood firmly against the metal to absorb the hammer blows and thus prevent a large area of the metal from being stretched out.

If the dent is in a section of the body which has double layers, or some other factor making it inaccessible from behind, a different technique is in order. Drill several small holes through the metal inside the damaged area, particularly in the deeper sections. Screw long self-tapping screws into the holes just enough for them to get a good grip in the metal. Now the dent can be pulled out by pulling on the protruding head of the screws with a pair of locking pliers.

The next stage of repair is the removal of paint from the damaged area and from an inch or so of the surrounding 'sound' metal. This is accomplished most easily by using a wire brush or sanding disk in a drill motor, although it can be done just as effectively by hand with sandpaper. To complete the preparation for filling, score the surface of the bare metal with a screwdriver or the tang of a file (or drill small holes in the affected area). This will provide a very good grip for the filler material. To complete the repair, see the Section on filling and painting.

Repair of rust holes or gashes

Remove all paint from the affected area and from an inch or so of the surrounding 'sound' metal using a sanding disk or wire brush mounted in a drill motor. If these are not available, a few sheets of sandpaper will do the job as effectively. With the paint removed, you will be able to determine the severity of the corrosion and therefore decide whether to replace the whole panel if possible, or repair the affected area. New body panels are not as expensive as most people think and it is often quicker to install a new panel than to attempt to repair large pieces of rust.

Remove all trim pieces from the affected area (except those which will act as a guide to the original shape of the damaged body i.e. headlamp shells etc). Then, using metal snips or a hacksaw blade, remove all loose metal and any other metal that is badly affected by rust. Hammer the edges of the hole inwards to create a slight depression for the filler material.

Wire brush the affected area to remove the powdery rust from the surface of the metal. If the back of the rusted area is accessible, treat it with rust-inhibiting paint.

Before filling can be done it will be necessary to block the hole in some way. This can be accomplished with sheet metal riveted or screwed into place, or by stuffing the hole with wire mesh.

Once the hole is blocked off the affected area can be filled and painted (see the following section on filling and painting).

Filling and painting

Many types of body fillers are available, but generally speaking, body repair kits which contain filler paste and a tube of resin hardener are best suited for this type of repair work. A wide, flexible plastic or nylon applicator will be necessary for imparting a smooth and contoured finish to the surface of the filler material.

Mix up a small amount of filler on a clean piece of wood or cardboard (use the hardener sparingly). Follow the maker's instructions on the package, otherwise the filler will set incorrectly.

Using the applicator, apply the filler paste to the prepared area. Draw the applicator across the surface of the filler to achieve the desired contour and to level the filler surface. As soon as a contour that approximates the original one is achieved, stop working the paste. If you continue, the paste will begin to stick to the applicator. Continue to add thin layers of filler paste at 20-minute intervals until the level of the filler is just above the surrounding metal.

Once the filler has hardened the excess can be removed using a body file. From then on, progressively finer grades of sandpaper should be used, starting with a 180-grit paper and finishing with 600-grit wet-or-dry paper. Always wrap the sandpaper around a flat rubber or wooden block, otherwise the surface of the filler will not be completely flat. During the sanding of the filler surface, the wet-or-dry paper should be periodically rinsed in water. This will ensure that a very smooth finish is produced in the final stage.

At this point, the repair area should be surrounded by a ring of bare metal, which in turn should be encircled by the finely feathered edge of the good paint. Rinse the repair area with clean water until all of the dust produced by the sand operation is gone.

Spray the entire area with a light coat of primer. This will reveal any imperfections in the surface of the filler. Repair these imperfections with fresh filler paste or glaze filler and once more smooth the surface with sandpaper. Repeat this spray-and-repair procedure until you are satisfied that the surface of the filler and the feathered edge of the paint are perfect. Rinse the area with clean water and allow it to dry completely.

The repair area is now ready for painting. Paint spraying must be carried out in a warm, dry, windless and dustfree atmosphere. These conditions can be created if you have access to a large indoor working area, but if you are forced to work in the open, you will have to pick the day very carefully. If you are working indoors, dousing the floor in the work area with water will help to settle the dust which would otherwise be in the air. If the repair area is confined to one body panel mask off the surrounding panels. This will help to minimize the effects of a slight mismatch in paint color. Trim pieces such as chome strips, door handles, etc., will also need to be masked off or removed. Use masking tape and several thicknesses of newspaper for the masking operations.

Before spraying, shake the paint can thoroughly, then spray a test area until the spray painting technique is mastered. Cover the repair area with a thick coat of primer. The thickness should be built up using several thin layers of primer rather than one thick one. Using 600-grit wet-or-dry sandpaper, rub down the surface of the primer until it is very smooth. While doing this, the work area should be thoroughly rinsed with water and the wet-or-dry sandpaper periodically rinsed as well. Allow the primer to dry before spraying additional coats.

Spray on the top coat, again building up the thickness by using several thin layers of paint. Begin spraying in the center of the repair area and then, using a circular motion, work out until the whole repair area and about two inches of the surrounding original paint is covered. Remove all masking material 10 to 15 minutes after spraying on the final coat of paint. Allow the new paint at least two weeks to harden, then using a very fine rubbing compound, blend the edges of the new paint into the existing paint. Finally, apply a coat of wax.

4   Body damage – major repair

1   Major damage must be repaired by an auto body/frame repair shop with the necessary welding and hydraulic straightening equipment.
2   If the damage has been serious, it is vital that the frame be checked for correct alignment, as the handling of the vehicle will be affected. Other problems, such as excessive tire wear and wear in the transmission and steering may also occur.

5   Grille – removal and installation

1   Remove the screws that retain the grille (Fig. 12.1) and carefully lift it off the car.
2   To install, simply hold the grille in place and reinstall the screws.

6   Front apron – removal and installation

1979 thru 1981 models

1   Remove the grille as described in Section 5.
2   Remove the screws that retain the front apron and lift it from the car.
3   Remove the screws that attach the side apron to the front fender.
4   Remove the front bumper as described in Section 9.
5   Remove the screws retaining the side apron and lift it off.
6   Installation is the reverse of the removal procedure.

1982 models

7   Remove the bumper as described in Section 9.
8   Remove the grille as described in Section 5.

9   Remove the screws that retain the front apron and lift it off.
10   Installation is the reverse of the removal procedure.

7   Headlight case – removal and installation

1   Remove the front apron as described in Section 6.
2   Remove the headlight. Refer to Chapter 10, if necessary.
3   Remove the screws that retain the inner fender protector and remove the protector.
4   Remove the screws that attach the headlight case to the front fender and lift off the case.
5   Installation is the reverse of the removal procedure.

8   Bumpers and energy absorbers – general information

1   Both the front and rear bumpers are equipped with gas/hydraulic energy absorbers designed to withstand a collision into a fixed barrier at up to five mph without damage. The combination of the inert gas and the hydraulic fluid allows the energy absorber unit to compress upon impact, thus absorbing the shock, and then return to its original position.
2   After any collision, the energy absorbers should be inspected. If obvious physical damage or leaking oil is evident, the unit should be replaced. These absorbers are not designed to be disassembled and, if defective, should be replaced as a unit.
3   Due to the gas contained in the units, never apply heat to an absorber or weld in its vicinity.
4   A method of testing the condition of the energy absorbers is as follows:

a)   Position the vehicle in front of a solid, fixed barrier such as a wall, post, etc. The ignition should be off, the shifter should be in Park or 1st gear (depending upon the transmission) and the parking brake should be on.
b)   Position a hydraulic or mechanical jack between the barrier and the bumper, so that the jack is in direct line with the absorber being checked. A folded rag between the jack and the bumper is recommended to protect the bumper's finish.
c)   Operate the jack so that it applies pressure to and compresses the bumper at least $\frac{3}{8}$-in.
d)   Release the pressure and the bumper should return to its original position. If it doesn't, the absorber needs replacing.

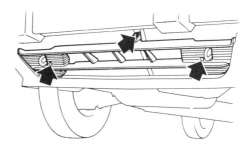

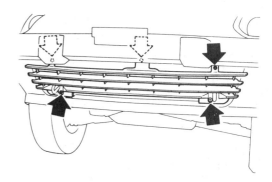

Fig. 12.1 Location of mounting screws for both grille styles (Sec 5)

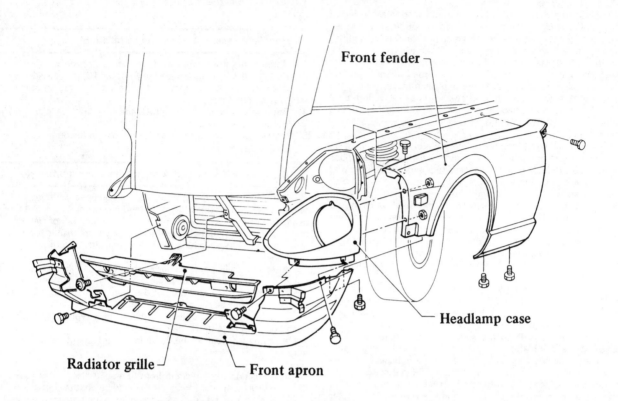

Fig. 12.2 Mounting arrangement of the front end components

e)   Repeat the same procedure on all absorbers to be checked. If, following a collision, the absorbers seize in their compressed position and the bumper does not return to its original position, care must be taken in replacing the absorbers. An unexpected spring-back while they're being repaired could cause serious injury. Due to this, it is recommended that a Datsun dealer or other qualified mechanic perform these repairs.

9   Bumpers and energy absorbers – removal and installation

1979 thru 1981 models

1   Remove the nuts that attach the bumper sides to the fenders.
2   Remove the grille as described in Section 5 (front bumpers only). Then disconnect the wiring connectors leading to the front combination lamps.
3   Remove the bolts that attach the energy absorbers to the body (photos) and lift off the bumper and energy absorbers as one assembly. **Note:** *In order to reach the upper mounting bolts of the rear energy absorbers, the rear carpet and padding must be lifted up.*
4   If necessary, remove the nuts that attach the energy absorbers to the bumper and lift them off.
5   Installation is the reverse of the removal procedure.

1982 models

6   Disconnect the wiring connectors leading to the front combination lamps (front bumpers only). Then open the hood.
7   Remove the nuts that attach the bumper to the energy absorbers and lift off the bumper.

8   Remove the screws that attach the side bumper to the body and lift it off.
9   If necessary, the energy absorber can be removed by removing the bolts that attach it to the body. **Note:** *The rear carpet and padding must be lifted up in order to reach the upper mounting bolts of the rear energy absorbers.*
10 Installation is the reverse of the removal procedure.

9.3a The front energy absorbers on some models as shown above

9.3b Location of rear energy absorber mounting bolts (shown from exterior)

9.3c The upper mounting bolts of the rear energy absorbers are located under the rear compartment foam padding

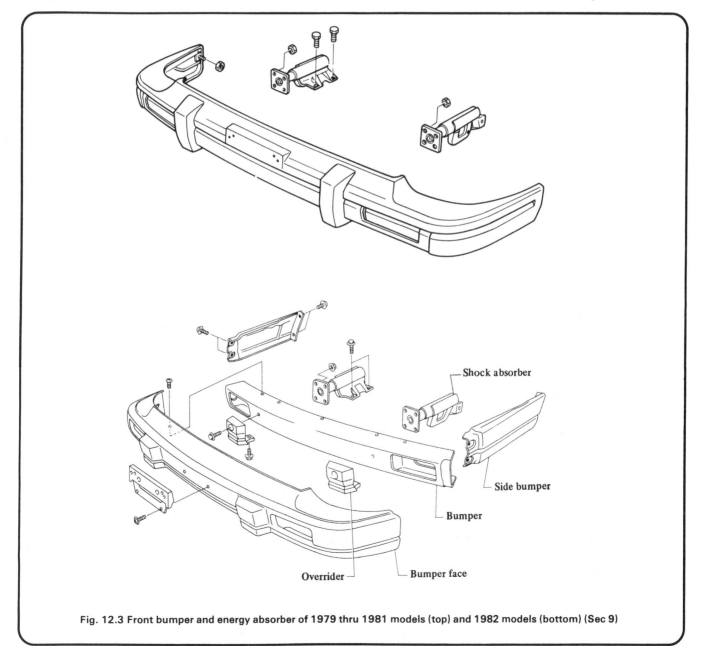

Shock absorber

Side bumper

Bumper

Overrider — — Bumper face

Fig. 12.3 Front bumper and energy absorber of 1979 thru 1981 models (top) and 1982 models (bottom) (Sec 9)

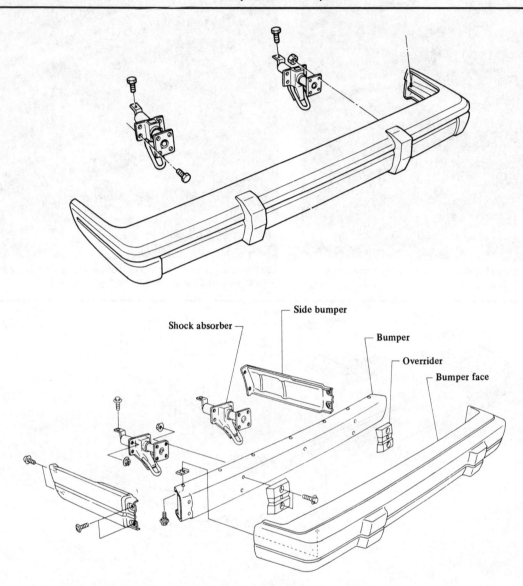

Fig. 12.4 Rear bumper and energy absorber assemblies of 1979 thru 1981 models (top) and 1982 models (bottom) (Sec 9)

10 Front fender – removal and installation

1   Remove the headlight case, as described in Section 7.
2   Disconnect the wiring connector leading to the side marker lamp.
3   Remove the screws that retain the front fender and lift off the fender.
4   Installation is the reverse of the removal procedure.

11 Hood – removal and installation

1   Raise the hood.
2   Use blankets or cloths to cover the cowl area of the body and the fenders. This will protect the body and paint as the hood is lifted free of the car.
3   Mark the position of the hood on its hinges by outlining the hinges. This will greatly aid alignment when reinstalling.
4   While an assistant supports the hood, remove the hinge-to-hood screws on both sides.
5   Lift off the hood.
6   Installation is the reverse of the removal procedure.

7   Check the hood alignment and adjust if necessary as described in Section 12.

12 Hood – alignment

1   To prevent engine compartment fuses from being pulled into the car interior through the cowl vent it is important that the hood be properly adjusted and sealed at the cowl area. Fore-and-aft and side-to-side adjustments of the hood are made by moving the hood-to-hinge bolts in their slots. Up-and-down adjustments are made by moving the hinge-to-body bolts in their slots.
2   Fore-and-aft and side-to-side adjustments are made as follows: Scribe a line around the entire hinge plate where it contacts the hood. Do this on both sides. This will enable you to judge the amount of movement.
3   Loosen the hood-to-hinge bolts slightly and move the hood into correct alignment. Move the hood only a little at a time. Tighten the hinge bolts and carefully lower the hood to check the position.
4   Once the position is correct, check that the hood latch engages securely in the hood lock. If not, loosen the hood latch screws slightly and move it left or right until it engages correctly. Retighten the mounting bolts.
5   If up-and-down adjustments are necessary, loosen the locknuts on the rubber bumpers (located at the rear corners of the engine

5   If up-and-down adjustments are necessary, loosen the locknuts on the rubber bumpers (located at the rear corners of the engine compartment) and turn the bumpers clockwise to lower them so they will not make contact with the closed hood.

6   Scribe a line around the hinges where they contact the body on both sides as mentioned above. Then loosen the mounting bolts slightly and move the hinges up or down as necessary, to adjust the front of the hood. The same should be done to the hood latch in order to adjust the rear of the hood. Retighten all mounting bolts after adjustment.

7   Once adjusted, turn the rubber bumpers counterclockwise to raise them so they firmly contact the hood when it is closed. Retighten the locknuts.

13 Hood latches – general information

1   The primary and secondary hood latches are both incorporated in one assembly attached to the firewall at the rear of the engine compartment. This assembly has widened mounting bolt holes which allow it to be repositioned for alignment purposes.

2   To remove the hood latch assembly, first mark the position of the mounting bolts by scribing a circle around them. This will simplify alignment during installation. Then simply remove the three mounting bolts and disconnect the hood release cable from the latch.

3   To install the assembly, reverse the removal procedure, being sure to match the mounting screws up with their original positions.

4   The hood latch assembly should be lubricated periodically, especially the catch lever, return spring, lift spring and hood catch.

14 Hood latch release cable – removal and installation

1   The hood latch cable is a one-piece assembly that includes the pull handle, control cable and housing.

2   To remove, raise the hood, disengage the cable from the hood latch and remove the clip that secures it to the assembly. Take precautions to keep the hood from closing and locking while the cable is disconnected.

3   To the side of the hood latch assembly, the cable is held to the body by a screw and clamp arrangement. Loosen the screw and remove the cable from under the clamp.

4   Moving to the car's interior, remove the lower left instrument cover.

5   Carefully withdraw the cable through the firewall.

6   Installation is the reverse of the removal procedure. When installing, check that the sealing grommet located where the cable passes through the firewall is in place.

15 Rear door lock and cylinder – removal and installation

1   Open the rear door.

2   Remove the rear interior trim panel to expose the rear door lock.

3   If equipped with a cable release lock set-up, disconnect the cable from the lock.

4   Using a marker, mark the position of the lock on the body by outlining the lock.

5   Remove the four door lock mounting bolts.

6   If the lock cylinder needs to be removed, first remove the license lamp housing. Then remove the two lock cylinder mounting screws and remove the cylinder.

7   Installation is the reverse of the removal procedure. **Note:** *Before reinstalling the rear trim panel, close the hatchback door and check the engagement of the lock with its striker. If any adjustment is necessary, loosen the four door lock mounting bolts and reposition the lock as necessary. The lock should be aligned with the mark made during removal.*

16 Rear door release cable – removal and installation

1   Working along the right side of the car's interior, loosen the lap-shoulder harness securing bolt and remove the seat belt plate.

2   Remove the left lower instrument cover.

3   Remove the side dash trims, then remove the kick plate and turn up the carpet to expose the release cable.

4   Remove the rear seat as described in Section 24.

5   Remove the front side body trim and the wheel house trim.

6   Remove the rear panel finisher, the body side rear finisher and the padding.

7   Remove the rear door lock from the body.

8   Disconnect the release cable from the lock assembly.

9   Detach the release cable from the opener lever by the front seat and lift out the cable.

10 Installation is the reverse of the removal procedure. **Note:** *When reinstalling the cable to the rear door lock, it should be adjusted so the clearance between the end of the cable and the locking lever is less then 1 mm. This is done by positioning the cable as stated and tightening the clamp securing bolt.*

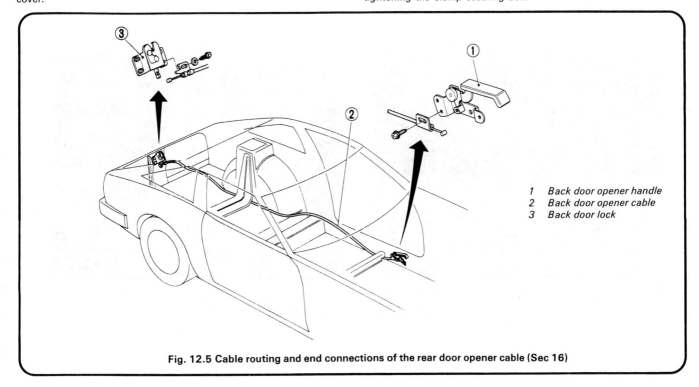

1   Back door opener handle
2   Back door opener cable
3   Back door lock

Fig. 12.5 Cable routing and end connections of the rear door opener cable (Sec 16)

This photo sequence illustrates the repair of a dent and damaged paintwork. The procedure for the repair of a hole is similar. Refer to the text for more complete instructions

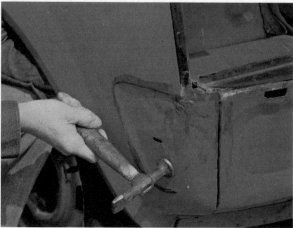

After removing any adjacent body trim, hammer the dent out. The damaged area should then be made slightly concave

Use coarse sandpaper or a sanding disc on a drill motor to remove all paint from the damaged area. Feather the sanded area into the edges of the surrounding paint, using progressively finer grades of sandpaper

The damaged area should be treated with rust remover prior to application of the body filler. In the case of a rust hole, all rusted sheet metal should be cut away

Carefully follow manufacturer's instructions when mixing the body filler so as to have the longest possible working time during application. Rust holes should be covered with fiberglass screen held in place with dabs of body filler prior to repair

Apply the filler with a flexible applicator in thin layers at 20 minute intervals. Use an applicator such as a wood spatula for confined areas. The filler should protrude slightly above the surrounding area

Shape the filler with a surform-type plane. Then, use water and progressively finer grades of sandpaper and a sanding block to wet-sand the area until it is smooth. Feather the edges of the repair area into the surrounding paint.

Use spray or brush applied primer to cover the entire repair area so that slight imperfections in the surface will be filled in. Prime at least one inch into the area surrounding the repair. Be careful of over-spray when using spray-type primer

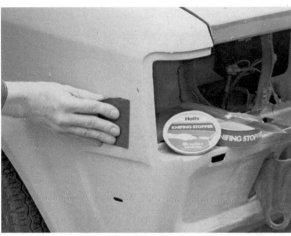

Wet-sand the primer with fine (approximately 400 grade) sandpaper until the area is smooth to the touch and blended into the surrounding paint. Use filler paste on minor imperfections

After the filler paste has dried, use rubbing compound to ensure that the surface of the primer is smooth. Prior to painting, the surface should be wiped down with a tack rag or lint-free cloth soaked in lacquer thinner

Choose a dry, warm, breeze-free area in which to paint and make sure that adjacent areas are protected from over-spray. Shake the spray paint can thoroughly and apply the top coat to the repair area, building it up by applying several coats, working from the center

After allowing at least two weeks for the paint to harden, use fine rubbing compound to blend the area into the original paint. Wax can now be applied

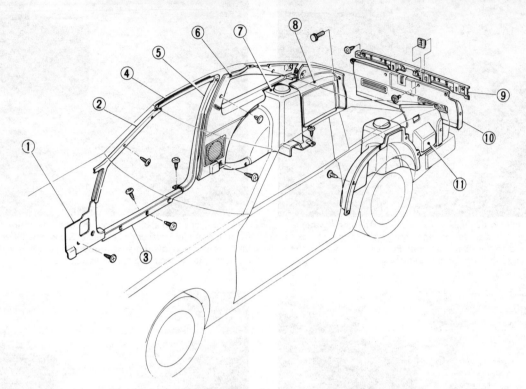

Fig. 12.6 Identification of interior trim components (Sec 16)

1 Dash side trim
2 Front pillar garnish
3 Kicking plate
4 Side body welt

5 Lock pillar garnish
6 Front body side trim
7 Wheel house trim
8 Space saver spare tire cover

9 Rear finisher support
10 Rear panel finisher
11 Rear body side trim

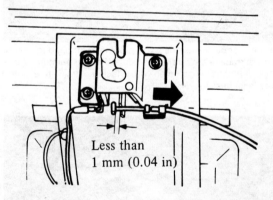

Less than
1 mm (0.04 in)

Fig. 12.7 The gap between the rear door opener cable end and the
locking lever should be adjusted as shown (Sec 16)

17 Rear door – removal and installation

1 Open the rear door.
2 Cover the edges around the rear door with cloths or pads to
protect the painted surfaces when the door is lifted free.
3 Mark the location of the rear door hinges by circling them with a
marker.
4 While an assistant supports the door, remove the bolts that retain
the gas spring stays to the rear door.
5 If equipped with rear defogger or rear window wiper, disconnect
the wiring harness and/or hose leading to the rear door.
6 Remove the hinge bolts and lift the door off the car.
7 Installation is the reverse of the removal procedure. **Note**: *Be sure
the rear door stay bolts are assembled as shown in the accompanying
illustration*

8 When installation is completed, close the lid and check that the
door is in proper alignment with the surrounding panels. Adjustments
of the rear door are controlled by the position of the hinge bolts in their
slots. To adjust, loosen the hinge bolts and reposition the door either
side-to-side or fore-and-aft the desired amount and retighten the bolts.
9 Check also the engagement of the door lock with its striker. If any
adjustment is necessary, refer to Section 15.

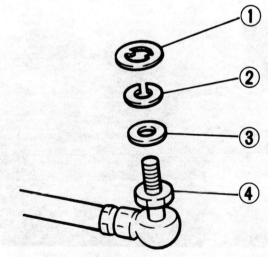

Fig. 12.8 Correct mounting arrangement of the rear door stay bolt
components (Sec 17)

1 Stopper ring
2 Spring washer

3 Spacer rubber
4 Stay stud

18 Front door trim panel – removal and installation

1   Pry out the plastic plugs and remove the two screws that retain the arm rest to the trim panel.
2   Remove the window crank handle. The crank handle is held onto its shaft by a spring clip, requiring the use of a small hooked tool to remove it. One can be fabricated out of a piece of coat hanger. With one hand, press the trim panel inward slightly to expose the shaft and clip, and with the other hand insert the tool behind the crank handle until you can hook the spring clip. Then pull the clip toward the handle knob and remove it. Lift off the crank handle and plastic washer.
3   If equipped, remove the power window escutcheon.
4   Remove the door handle escutcheon.
5   The trim panel is attached to the door with plastic retaining clips. To disengage these clips, insert a flat, blunt tool (like a screwdriver wrapped with tape) between the metal door skin and the trim panel. Carefully pry the door panel away from the door, keeping the tool close to the clips to prevent damage to the panel. Start at the bottom and work around the door toward the top. The top section is secured at the window channel. Once the retaining clips are pried free, lift the trim panel upward and away from the door.
6   Before installing the trim panel, check that all the trim retaining clips are in good condition and the sealing screen is correctly applied to the door.

7   Engage the top of the trim panel first and then position the panel correctly on the door. The shaft for the window winder can be used as a rough guide.
8   Press the retaining clips into their respective cups or holes in the door. Pressure can be applied with the palm of your hand or with a clean rubber mallet.
9   Complete the installation by reversing the removal procedure. To install the crank handle, first install the spring clip into its groove on the handle with the closed end facing the handle knob, align the handle with the one on the opposite door and push it onto its shaft until the spring clip clicks into place.

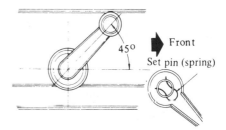

Fig. 12.9 Mounting position of front door window crank handle clip (Sec 18)

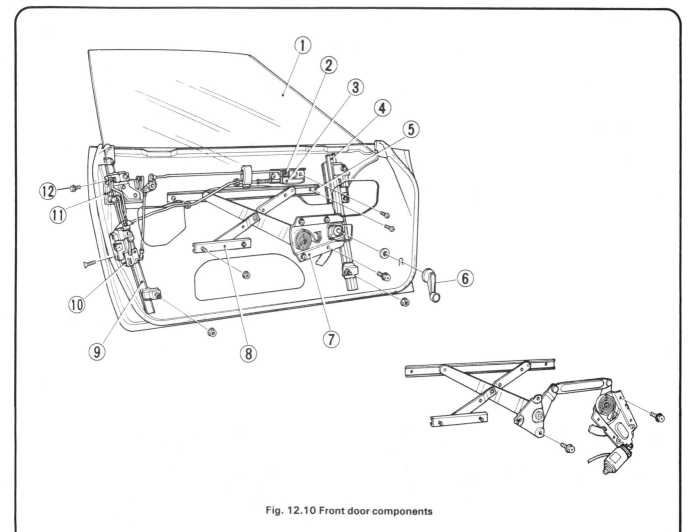

Fig. 12.10 Front door components

1 Door glass	4 Front guide rail assembly	7 Regulator assembly	10 Door lock assembly
2 Door lock knob	5 Guide channel A	8 Guide channel B	11 Door outside handle
3 Door inside handle	6 Regulator handle	9 Rear guide channel B	12 Rear guide rail upper Securing bolt

19 Front door window – removal and installation

1   Remove the front door trim panel as described in Section 18.
2   Temporarily install the window crank handle without its clip onto the shaft and lower the window as far as possible.
3   Using a flathead screwdriver, rotate the exterior door molding retaining clips 90 degrees and remove the molding.
4   Remove the inner sealing screen.
5   Raise the window just until the regulator-to-glass attaching screws become accessible. Then remove the front and rear upper stopper bolts.
6   While holding the glass by hand, remove the regulator-to-glass attaching screws. Then remove the glass from the door by drawing it upwards and away from the door.
7   If necessary remove the regulator by using the following procedure:

a)   Remove the two attaching screws, then remove the front guide rail assembly through the large access hole at the bottom of the door panel.
b)   Remove the mounting screws, then remove the regulator assembly, including the motor (if equipped), through the access hole. If equipped with power windows, the wiring connector must be disconnected.
c)   Remove the two mounting screws and then remove the rear guide rail assembly.

8   Prior to installing the regulator and guide channels, apply a light coat of lithium grease to all their sliding surfaces.
9   Installation is the reverse of the removal procedure. Following installation of the window, but before the sealing screen and trim panel are installed, roll the window up completely and use the following procedure to bring it into correct alignment.

a)   Loosen the nuts that secure the upper ends of both the front and rear guide rails. Then raise the window completely and turn the upper adjusting bolts so the glass pushes the upper lip of the door waist molding just 1 mm, as shown in Fig. 12.14.
b)   Loosen the nuts securing the lower ends of both guide rails and turn the adjusting bolts until the glass is positioned as shown in Fig. 12.15.
c)   With the front and rear guide rails securing nuts already loosened, now loosen the front and rear upper stopper securing bolts. Adjust the door regulator so that the upper side of the glass is parallel with the body side weatherstrip. Refer to Fig. 12.16. Following adjustment, retighten all of the loosened nuts and bolts.
d)   Loosen the nut that secures the upper rear stopper and adjust the rear height of the glass to the proper specs by sliding the stopper up or down (Fig. 12.17). Retighten the nut.
e)   Loosen the nut that secures the upper front stopper and adjust the front height of the glass to the proper specs by sliding the stopper up or down (Fig. 12.17). Retighten the nut.

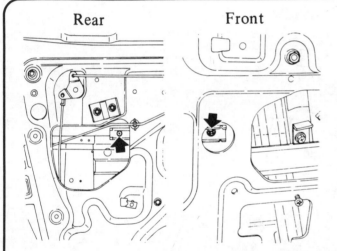

Fig. 12.11 Location of regulator-to-glass attaching screws (Sec 19)

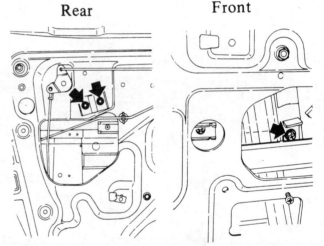

Fig. 12.12 Location of front and rear upper stopper bolts (Sec 19)

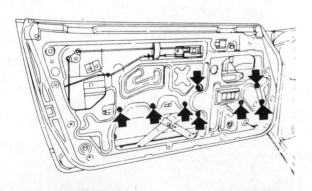

Fig. 12.13 Location of regulator assembly mounting screws (Sec 19)

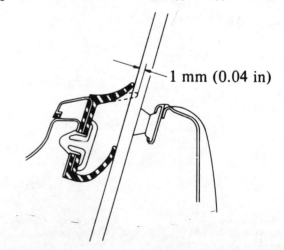

1 mm (0.04 in)

Fig. 12.14 Proper pressure between the window and the door waist molding rubber seal (Sec 19)

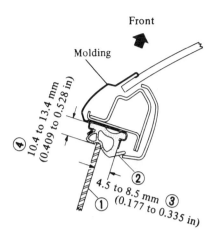

Fig. 12.15 Proper adjustment of upper edge of front door window glass (viewed from top) (Sec 19)

1 Door glass
2 Body side
    weatherstrip
3 In-out adjustment
    (upper side of glass)
4 Fore-and-aft adjustment

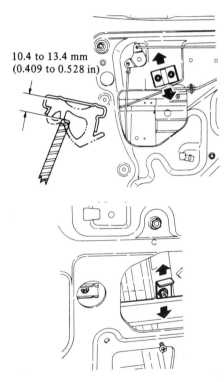

Fig. 12.17 The height of the front door window should be adjusted as shown by moving the front (bottom) and the rear (top) upper stoppers up or down as required (Sec 19)

20 Front door lock and lock control – removal and installation

1 Remove the front door glass as described in Section 19.
2 Remove the screws that retain the interior door handle.
3 Disengage the knob rods from the rod holders on the bellcrank and door lock. Then remove the interior door handle assembly.
4 Loosen the bellcrank mounting screws, and disconnect the key rod from the door lock. Then remove the door lock assembly together with the bellcrank.
5 The exterior door handle can be removed by removing the mounting nuts.
6 Installation is the reverse of the removal procedure. **Note:** *Apply a light coat of multi-purpose grease to all sliding surfaces of levers and springs.*

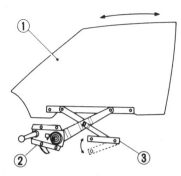

Fig. 12.16 The regulator must be adjusted as shown to ensure that the front door window is parallel with the body side weatherstrip (Sec 19)

1 Door glass
2 Regulator
3 Guide channel

21 Front door – removal and installation

1 Remove the lower cover from the appropriate side of the instrument panel.
2 Remove the side dash trim, and then disconnect the wiring connectors leading to the power windows and remote electric door mirror.
3 Open the door and either place a jack or stand under the door or have an assistant on hand to support it when the hinge bolts are removed. **Note:** *To protect the door's painted surfaces, place a rag between the door and stand or jack, if used.*
4 Remove the hinge-to-door bolts and lift off the door.
5 Installation is the reverse of the removal procedure.
6 Following installation of the door, check that it is in proper alignment and adjust if necessary as follows:

a) Up-and-down and forward-and-backward adjustments are made by loosening the hinge-to-body bolts and moving the door as necessary.
b) Side-to-side adjustments are made by loosening the hinge-to-door bolts and moving the door as necessary.
c) The door lock striker can be adjusted so it engages properly with the door lock by loosening its mounting bolts and repositioning it as necessary. **Note:** *The front fender may have to be removed to gain access to certain door hinge bolts for adjustment. If necessary, refer to Section 10.*

22 Side window – removal and installation

2-seater models

1 Remove the center piller finisher.
2 Remove the front body side trim.
3 Remove the two side window retaining bolts.
4 The side window is butyl-sealed all around its edge. Pull the glass out slightly, then insert a knife into the butyl sealant at the front edge of the glass. Carefully cut the sealant around the entire periphery of the glass.
5 Cut out the glass.
6 The sealant should be thoroughly cleaned from the car body by using a rag dampened with unleaded gasoline.
7 Prior to installation, the sealing surfaces of the glass should also be thoroughly cleaned using a rag dampened with unleaded gasoline. After cleaning, do not allow any oil, grease or water to get on the cleaned surfaces of the glass or body.
8 Apply butyl sealant around the entire periphery of the glass, overlapping the edges at least $\frac{3}{8}$ in (10 mm) to ensure against possible water leaks. Use Fig. 12.21 as a guide for applying the sealant.
9 Install the four side window spacers on the body opening, using Fig. 12.22 as a guide for positioning.
10 Position the side window glass in its opening flange. Then, while

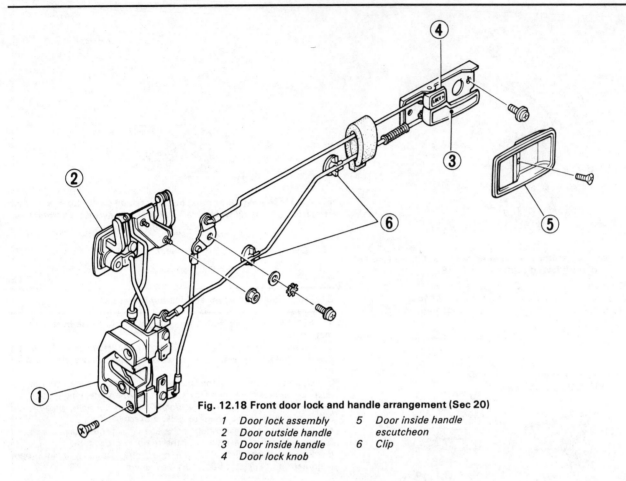

Fig. 12.18 Front door lock and handle arrangement (Sec 20)

1 Door lock assembly
2 Door outside handle
3 Door inside handle
4 Door lock knob

5 Door inside handle
   escutcheon
6 Clip

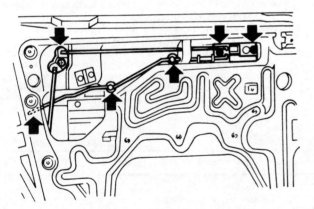

Fig. 12.19 Disengagement points for removing the interior door handle assembly (Sec 20)

an assistant wearing gloves applies hand pressure to the outside of the glass, use a hot air gun to heat the butyl sealant along the inside of the glass.
11 When the sealant adheres sufficiently, install the screws and nuts to secure the glass.
12 The remainder of the installation is the reverse of the removal procedure.

1979 thru 1981 2+2 models
13 Remove the center piller finisher.
14 Remove the screws that attach the side window to the body.
15 Remove the side window handle cover.

16 Remove the screws that attach the side window handle to the body.
17 Lift out the window, complete with handle.
18 The handle can be detached from the glass by removing the retaining screw.
19 Installation is the reverse of the removal procedure.

1982 2+2 models
20 Remove the screw that attaches the side window opener cable to the window.
21 Remove the center piller finisher.
22 Remove the screws that attach the window hinges to the body, and lift out the window.
23 Installation is the reverse of the removal procedure.

23 Front seat – removal and installation

1 Slide the seat all the way forward and remove the plastic trim covers over the two rear seat mounts.
2 Remove the two rear mounting bolts.
3 Slide the seat all the way to the rear and remove the two forward mounting bolts.
4 Lift out the seat.
5 Installation is the reverse of the removal procedure.

24 Rear seat – removal and installation

1 Remove the two screws that secure the rear seat cushion. Then pull the cushion forward and simultaneously guide the center seat belts through the holes in the seat cushion. Remove the cushion.
2 Remove the rear seat backs by removing the mounting bolts and releasing the lock knob.
3 Installation is the reverse of the removal procedure.

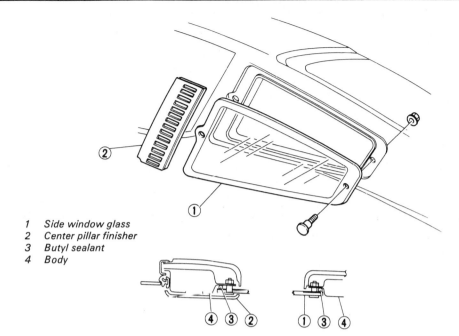

1 Side window glass
2 Center pillar finisher
3 Butyl sealant
4 Body

Fig. 12.20 Mounting arrangement of the side window (2-seater models) (Sec 22)

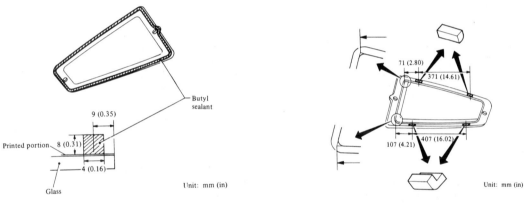

9 (0.35)

Butyl sealant

Printed portion 8 (0.31)

4 (0.16)

Glass

Unit: mm (in)

71 (2.80)

371 (14.61)

107 (4.21)

407 (16.02)

Unit: mm (in)

Fig. 12.21 Proper application of butyl sealant on side window (Sec 22)

Fig. 12.22 Prior to side window installation, spacers must be placed along the window opening at the locations shown (Sec 22)

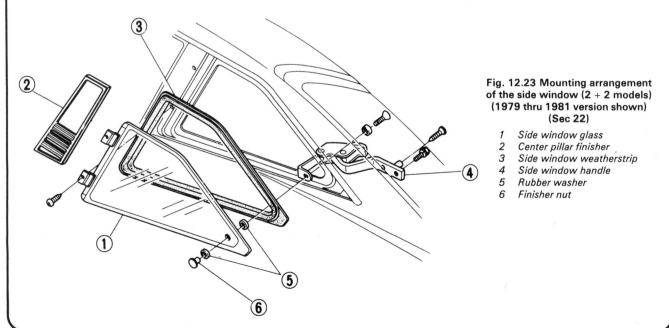

Fig. 12.23 Mounting arrangement of the side window (2 + 2 models) (1979 thru 1981 version shown) (Sec 22)

1 Side window glass
2 Center pillar finisher
3 Side window weatherstrip
4 Side window handle
5 Rubber washer
6 Finisher nut

25 Seat belts – removal and installation

Front seat belts

1   Disconnect the negative battery cable.
2   If working on the driver's side, disconnect the wiring connector leading to the seat belt warning device.
3   Remove the inner lap belt or latch mechanism, bolted to the base of the seat.
4   Remove the front side body trim panel.
5   Remove the three bolts that retain the lap-shoulder harness assembly to the body.
6   Installation is the reverse of the removal procedure.

Rear seat belts

7   To remove the rear seat belts, simply remove the rear seat cushion

(referring to Section 24, if necessary), then remove the bolts that retain the belts to the body.

26 Console box – removal and installation

1   If equipped with a remote side window opener, remove the knobs from the opener levers.
2   Remove the console box mounting screws.
3   Disconnect the wiring connector leading to the outside mirror switch.
4   Lift out the console box.
5   If necessary, remove the shift lever rubber boot.
6   Installation is the reverse of the removal procedure.

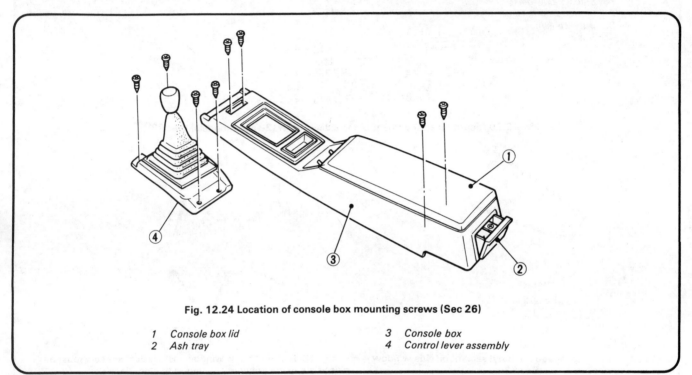

Fig. 12.24 Location of console box mounting screws (Sec 26)

1   Console box lid
2   Ash tray

3   Console box
4   Control lever assembly

Chapter 13 Supplement:
Revisions and information on later models

Contents

1 Introduction

1   This Supplement contains specification and service procedure changes that apply to all Datsun 280ZX models produced in 1983.
2   Where no differences (or very minor differences) exist between 1982 models and 1983 models, no information is given. In those instances, the original material included in Chapters 1 through 12 pertaining to 1982 models should be used.

2 Specifications

Turbocharger

Axial play .... 0.0005 to 0.0036 in
(0.013 to 0.091 mm)
By-pass valve controller stroke .... 0.0150 in (0.38 mm)

Torque specifications	Ft-lbs	M-kg
Exhaust manifold to turbocharger	38	5.2
Turbocharger to exhaust outlet pipe	19	2.6

Cooling system

Torque specifications	Ft-lbs	M-kg
Water pump mounting bolts (small)	5.5	0.75
Water pump mounting bolts (large)	14	1.9

Braking system
Booster (vacuum servo unit)
  Pushrod length .... 0.4045 to 0.4144 in
(10.275 to 10.525 mm)

3 Fuel injection and turbocharging system

Disassembly and assembly
Due to the precise tolorances required in the turbocharging assembly, disassembly is not recomended. If the turbocharger is found defective, it should be exchanged for a new or remanufactured unit.

Inspection
2   For an accurate inspection of the turbocharger the following tools will be needed:
  a) A dial indicator accurate to 0.0001 in.
  b) Compressed air regulated to 6 to 6.8 psi.
3   Inspect the turbocharger for any cracks, deformity or other damage in the housing or the turbine.
4   Inspect the inlet and outlet passages for signs of clogging by oil or carbon.
5   Rotate the turbine to make sure it spins freely without any unusual noise.
6   Measure the axial play of the turbine by mounting a dial indicator on the turbine shaft (Fig. 13.1). Do not allow the turbine to rotate when

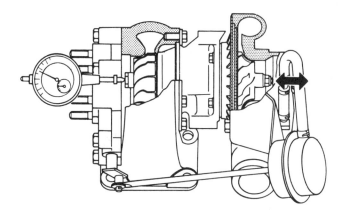

Fig. 13.1 An accurate dial indicator must be used to measure axial play of the turbine shaft (Sec 3)

checking axial play. The reading should be within specifications.

7   To check operation of the by-pass valve controller, mount a dial indicator at the end of the by-pass control rod and connect a compressed air source to the by-pass valve controller (Fig. 13.2).

8   Apply between 6.0 and 6.8 psi to the by-pass valve controller and measure the distance travelled on the dial indicator. See the specifications for the correct distance.

9   Move the by-pass valve back and forth to make sure it is not stuck or restricted.

10   If the turbocharger fails any one of these tests, it must be replaced as an assembly.

4 Electrical System

General description

1   A digital combination meter has been added to the list of options available on the 1983 280ZX. This combination meter is removed and disassembled in the same manner as the standard meter, so the procedure in Chapter 10 (Section 20) should be followed. Due to the complexity of the digital gauges any testing and/or repairing should be left to a qualified technician.

Wiring diagrams

2   Note that the updated wiring diagrams for the later model years have been included at the end of this chapter. Due to space limitations we are not able to provide every diagram; however, a representative sampling is included.

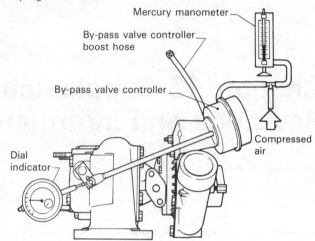

Fig. 13.2 When checking the operation of the by-pass valve controller, take care not to use too much air pressure or the controller could be damaged (Sec 3)

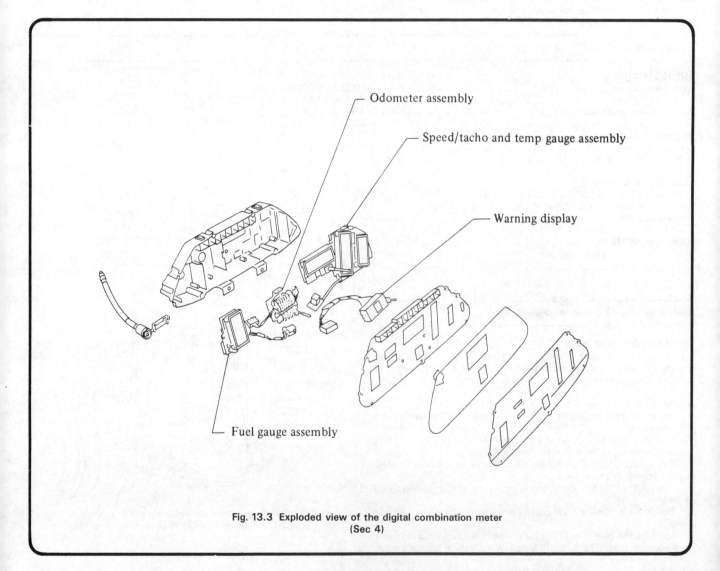

Fig. 13.3 Exploded view of the digital combination meter
(Sec 4)

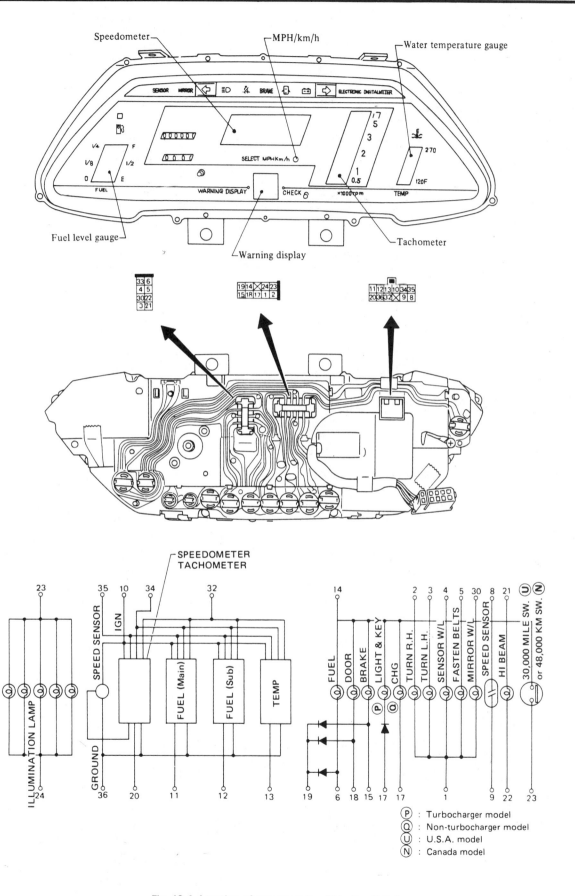

Fig. 13.4 Location of components within the digital combination meter (Sec 4)

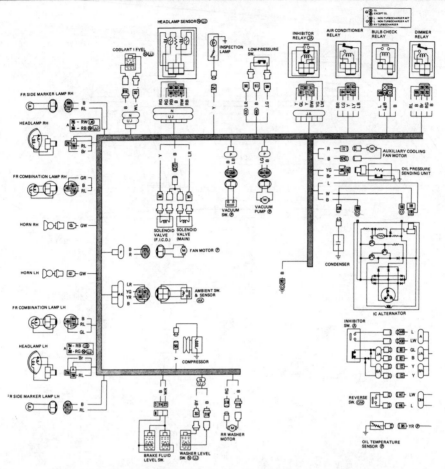

Fig. 13.5 Wiring diagram for the standard 1983 model (1 of 4)

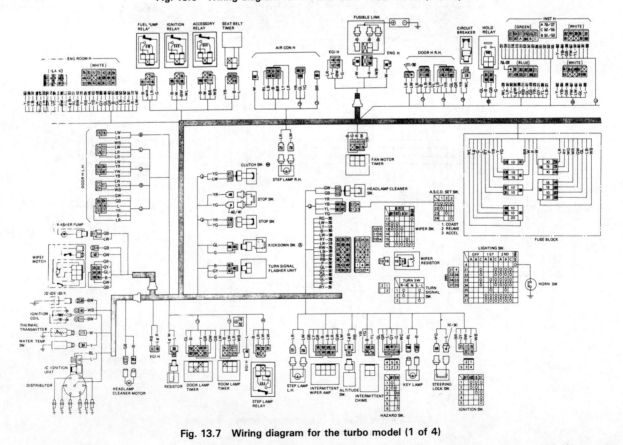

Fig. 13.7 Wiring diagram for the turbo model (1 of 4)

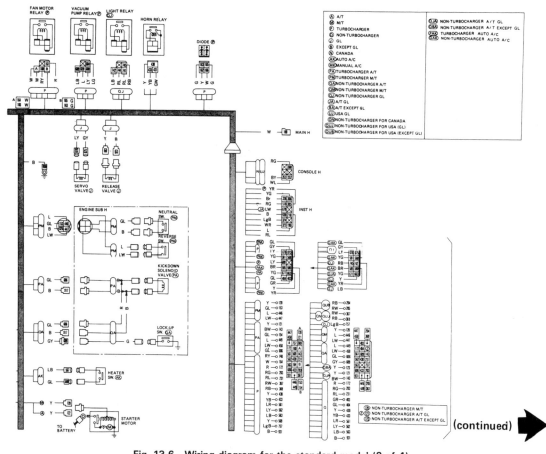

Fig. 13.6 Wiring diagram for the standard model (2 of 4)

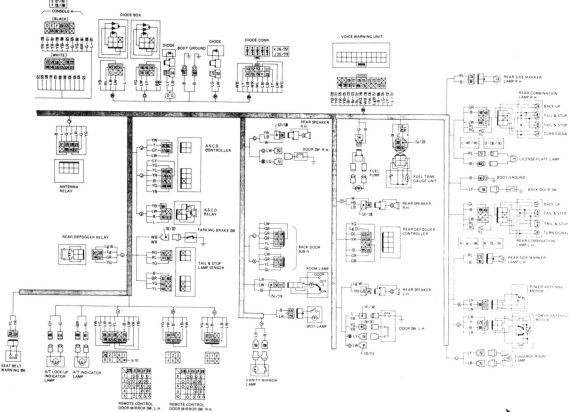

(continued)

Fig. 13.8 Wiring diagram for the turbo model (2 of 4) (continued)

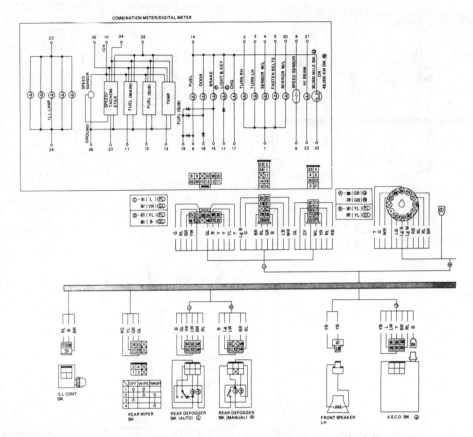

Fig. 13.9 Wiring diagram for the standard model (3 of 4)

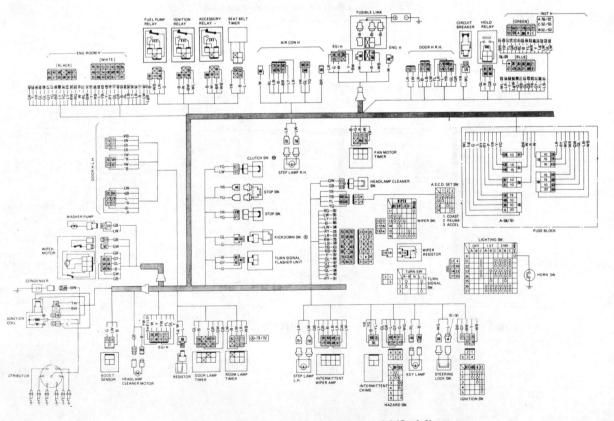

Fig. 13.11 Wiring diagram for the turbo model (3 of 4)

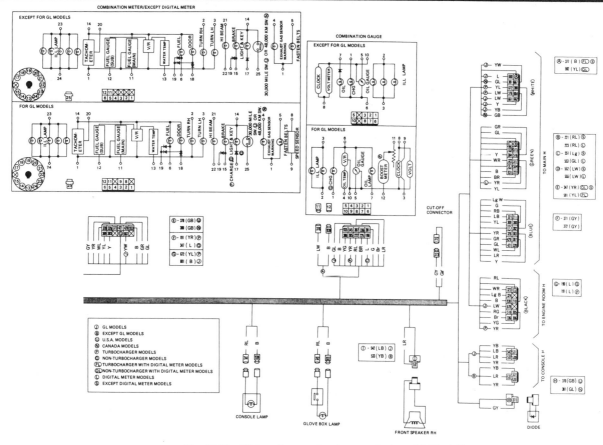

Fig. 13.10 Wiring diagram for the standard model (4 of 4)

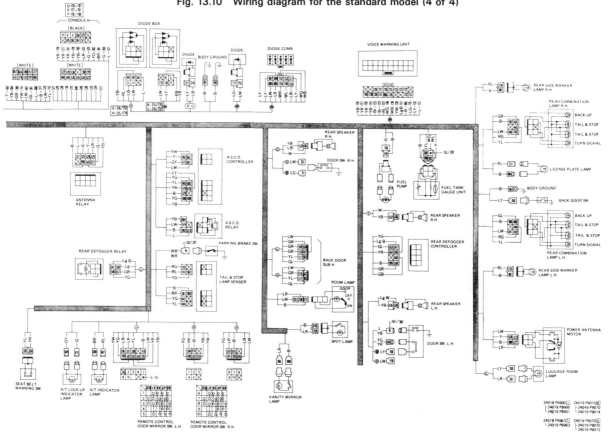

Fig. 13.12 Wiring diagram for the turbo model (4 of 4)

294

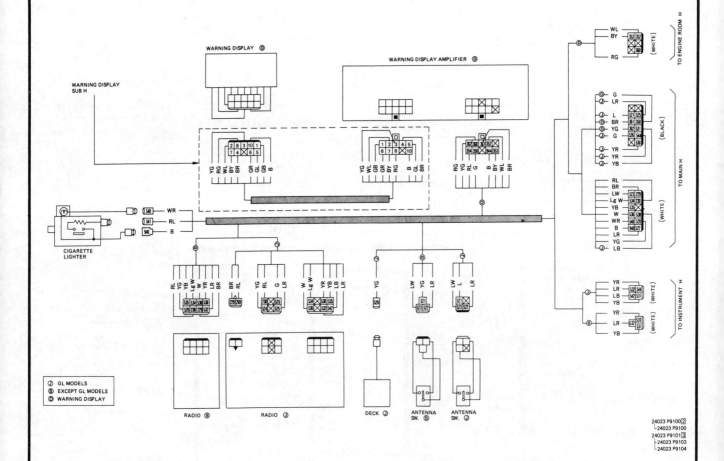

Fig. 13.13 Wiring diagram for the console (all models)

Conversion factors

Length (distance)
Inches (in)	X	25.4	= Millimetres (mm)	X 0.0394	= Inches (in)
Feet (ft)	X	0.305	= Metres (m)	X 3.281	= Feet (ft)
Miles	X	1.609	= Kilometres (km)	X 0.621	= Miles

Volume (capacity)
Cubic inches (cu in; in³)	X	16.387	= Cubic centimetres (cc; cm³)	X 0.061	= Cubic inches (cu in; in³)
Imperial pints (Imp pt)	X	0.568	= Litres (l)	X 1.76	= Imperial pints (Imp pt)
Imperial quarts (Imp qt)	X	1.137	= Litres (l)	X 0.88	= Imperial quarts (Imp qt)
Imperial quarts (Imp qt)	X	1.201	= US quarts (US qt)	X 0.833	= Imperial quarts (Imp qt)
US quarts (US qt)	X	0.946	= Litres (l)	X 1.057	= US quarts (US qt)
Imperial gallons (Imp gal)	X	4.546	= Litres (l)	X 0.22	= Imperial gallons (Imp gal)
Imperial gallons (Imp gal)	X	1.201	= US gallons (US gal)	X 0.833	= Imperial gallons (Imp gal)
US gallons (US gal)	X	3.785	= Litres (l)	X 0.264	= US gallons (US gal)

Mass (weight)
Ounces (oz)	X	28.35	= Grams (g)	X 0.035	= Ounces (oz)
Pounds (lb)	X	0.454	= Kilograms (kg)	X 2.205	= Pounds (lb)

Force
Ounces-force (ozf; oz)	X	0.278	= Newtons (N)	X 3.6	= Ounces-force (ozf; oz)
Pounds-force (lbf; lb)	X	4.448	= Newtons (N)	X 0.225	= Pounds-force (lbf; lb)
Newtons (N)	X	0.1	= Kilograms-force (kgf; kg)	X 9.81	= Newtons (N)

Pressure
Pounds-force per square inch (psi; lbf/in²; lb/in²)	X	0.070	= Kilograms-force per square centimetre (kgf/cm²; kg/cm²)	X 14.223	= Pounds-force per square inch (psi; lbf/in²; lb/in²)
Pounds-force per square inch (psi; lbf/in²; lb/in²)	X	0.068	= Atmospheres (atm)	X 14.696	= Pounds-force per square inch (psi; lbf/in²; lb/in²)
Pounds-force per square inch (psi; lbf/in²; lb/in²)	X	0.069	= Bars	X 14.5	= Pounds-force per square inch (psi; lbf/in²; lb/in²)
Pounds-force per square inch (psi; lbf/in²; lb/in²)	X	6.895	= Kilopascals (kPa)	X 0.145	= Pounds-force per square inch (psi; lbf/in²; lb/in²)
Kilopascals (kPa)	X	0.01	= Kilograms-force per square centimetre (kgf/cm²; kg/cm²)	X 98.1	= Kilopascals (kPa)
Millibar (mbar)	X	100	= Pascals (Pa)	X 0.01	= Millibar (mbar)
Millibar (mbar)	X	0.0145	= Pounds-force per square inch (psi; lbf/in²; lb/in²)	X 68.947	= Millibar (mbar)
Millibar (mbar)	X	0.75	= Millimetres of mercury (mmHg)	X 1.333	= Millibar (mbar)
Millibar (mbar)	X	0.401	= Inches of water (inH₂O)	X 2.491	= Millibar (mbar)
Millimetres of mercury (mmHg)	X	0.535	= Inches of water (inH₂O)	X 1.868	= Millimetres of mercury (mmHg)
Inches of water (inH₂O)	X	0.036	= Pounds-force per square inch (psi; lbf/in²; lb/in²)	X 27.68	= Inches of water (inH₂O)

Torque (moment of force)
Pounds-force inches (lbf in; lb in)	X	1.152	= Kilograms-force centimetre (kgf cm; kg cm)	X 0.868	= Pounds-force inches (lbf in; lb in)
Pounds-force inches (lbf in; lb in)	X	0.113	= Newton metres (Nm)	X 8.85	= Pounds-force inches (lbf in; lb in)
Pounds-force inches (lbf in; lb in)	X	0.083	= Pounds-force feet (lbf ft; lb ft)	X 12	= Pounds-force inches (lbf in; lb in)
Pounds-force feet (lbf ft; lb ft)	X	0.138	= Kilograms-force metres (kgf m; kg m)	X 7.233	= Pounds-force feet (lbf ft; lb ft)
Pounds-force feet (lbf ft; lb ft)	X	1.356	= Newton metres (Nm)	X 0.738	= Pounds-force feet (lbf ft; lb ft)
Newton metres (Nm)	X	0.102	= Kilograms-force metres (kgf m; kg m)	X 9.804	= Newton metres (Nm)

Power
Horsepower (hp)	X	745.7	= Watts (W)	X 0.0013	= Horsepower (hp)

Velocity (speed)
Miles per hour (miles/hr; mph)	X	1.609	= Kilometres per hour (km/hr; kph)	X 0.621	= Miles per hour (miles/hr; mph)

Fuel consumption*
Miles per gallon, Imperial (mpg)	X	0.354	= Kilometres per litre (km/l)	X 2.825	= Miles per gallon, Imperial (mpg)
Miles per gallon, US (mpg)	X	0.425	= Kilometres per litre (km/l)	X 2.352	= Miles per gallon, US (mpg)

Temperature
Degrees Fahrenheit = (°C x 1.8) + 32

Degrees Celsius (Degrees Centigrade; °C) = (°F - 32) x 0.56

*It is common practice to convert from miles per gallon (mpg) to litres/100 kilometres (l/100km), where mpg (Imperial) x l/100 km = 282 and mpg (US) x l/100 km = 235

Index

HAYNES AUTOMOTIVE MANUALS

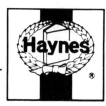

NOTE: New manuals are added to this list on a periodic basis. If you do not see a listing for your vehicle, consult your local Haynes dealer for the latest product information.

ALFA-ROMEO
531 **Alfa Romeo Sedan & Coupe** '73 thru '80

AMC
Jeep CJ – *see JEEP (412)*
694 **Mid-size models,** Concord, Hornet, Gremlin & Spirit '70 thru '83
934 **(Renault) Alliance & Encore** all models '83 thru '87

AUDI
615 **4000** all models '80 thru '87
428 **5000** all models '77 thru '83
1117 **5000** all models '84 thru '88
207 **Fox** all models '73 thru '79

AUSTIN
049 **Healey 100/6 & 3000** Roadster '56 thru '68
Healey Sprite – *see MG Midget Roadster (265)*

BLMC
260 **1100, 1300 & Austin America** '62 thru '74
527 **Mini** all models '59 thru '69
*646 **Mini** all models '69 thru '88

BMW
276 **320i** all 4 cyl models '75 thru '83
632 **528i & 530i** all models '75 thru '80
240 **1500 thru 2002** all models except Turbo '59 thru '77
348 **2500, 2800, 3.0 & Bavaria** '69 thru '76

BUICK
Century (front wheel drive) – *see GENERAL MOTORS A-Cars (829)*
*1627 **Buick, Oldsmobile & Pontiac Full-size (Front wheel drive)** all models '85 thru '90
Buick Electra, LeSabre and Park Avenue; **Oldsmobile** Delta 88 Royale, Ninety Eight and Regency; **Pontiac** Bonneville
*1551 **Buick Oldsmobile & Pontiac Full-size (Rear wheel drive)**
Buick Electra '70 thru '84, Estate '70 thru '90, LeSabre '70 thru '79
Oldsmobile Custom Cruiser '70 thru '90, Delta 88 '70 thru '85, Ninety-eight '70 thru '84
Pontiac Bonneville '70 thru '86, Catalina '70 thru '81, Grandville '70 thru '75, Parisienne '84 thu '86
627 **Mid-size** all rear-drive **Regal & Century** models with V6, V8 and Turbo '74 thru '87
Regal – *see GENERAL MOTORS (1671)*
Skyhawk – *see GENERAL MOTORS J-Cars (766)*
552 **Skylark** all X-car models '80 thru '85

CADILLAC
*751 **Cadillac Rear Wheel Drive** all gasoline models '70 thru '90
Cimarron – *see GENERAL MOTORS J-Cars (766)*

CAPRI
296 **2000 MK I Coupe** all models '71 thru '75
283 **2300 MK II Coupe** all models '74 thru '78
205 **2600 & 2800** V6 Coupe '71 thru '75
375 **2800 Mk II** V6 Coupe '75 thru '78
Mercury Capri – *see FORD Mustang (654)*

CHEVROLET
*1477 **Astro & GMC Safari Mini-vans** all models '85 thru '90
554 **Camaro** V8 all models '70 thru '81
*866 **Camaro** all models '82 thru '90
Cavalier – *see GENERAL MOTORS J-Cars (766)*
Celebrity – *see GENERAL MOTORS A-Cars (829)*
625 **Chevelle, Malibu & El Camino** all V6 & V8 models '69 thru '87

449 **Chevette & Pontiac T1000** all models '76 thru '87
550 **Citation** all models '80 thru '85
*1628 **Corsica/Beretta** all models '87 thru '90
274 **Corvette** all V8 models '68 thru '82
*1336 **Corvette** all models '84 thru '89
704 **Full-size Sedans** Caprice, Impala, Biscayne, Bel Air & Wagons, all V6 & V8 models '69 thru '90
Lumina – *see GENERAL MOTORS (1671)*
319 **Luv Pick-up** all 2WD & 4WD models '72 thru '82
626 **Monte Carlo** all V6, V8 & Turbo models '70 thru '88
241 **Nova** all V8 models '69 thru '79
*1642 **Nova and Geo Prizm** all front wheel drive models, '85 thru '90
*420 **Pick-ups '67 thru '87 – Chevrolet & GMC,** all V8 & in-line 6 cyl 2WD & 4WD models '67 thru '87
*1664 **Pick-ups '88 thru '90 – Chevrolet & GMC** all full-size (C and K) models, '88 thru '90
*1727 **Sprint & Geo Metro** '85 thru '91
*831 **S-10 & GMC S-15 Pick-ups** all models '82 thru '90
*345 **Vans – Chevrolet & GMC,** V8 & in-line 6 cyl models '68 thru '89
208 **Vega** all models except Cosworth '70 thru '77

CHRYSLER
*1337 **Chrysler & Plymouth Mid-size** front wheel drive '82 thru '89
K-Cars – *see DODGE Aries (723)*
Laser – *see DODGE Daytona (1140)*

DATSUN
402 **200SX** all models '77 thru '79
647 **200SX** all models '80 thru '83
228 **B-210** all models '73 thru '78
525 **210** all models '78 thru '82
206 **240Z, 260Z & 280Z** Coupe & 2+2 '70 thru '78
563 **280ZX** Coupe & 2+2 '79 thru '83
300ZX – *see NISSAN (1137)*
679 **310** all models '78 thru '82
123 **510 & PL521 Pick-up** '68 thru '73
430 **510** all models '78 thru '81
372 **610** all models '72 thru '76
277 **620 Series Pick-up** all models '73 thru '79
720 Series Pick-up – *see NISSAN Pick-ups (771)*
376 **810/Maxima** all gasoline models '77 thru '84
124 **1200** all models '70 thru '73
368 **F10** all models '76 thru '79
Pulsar – *see NISSAN (876)*
Sentra – *see NISSAN (982)*
Stanza – *see NISSAN (981)*

DODGE
*723 **Aries & Plymouth Reliant** all models '81 thru '89
*1231 **Caravan & Plymouth Voyager Mini-Vans** all models '84 thru '89
699 **Challenger & Plymouth Saporro** all models '78 thru '83
236 **Colt** all models '71 thru '77
419 **Colt (rear wheel drive)** all models '77 thru '80
610 **Colt & Plymouth Champ (front wheel drive)** all models '78 thru '87
*556 **D50 & Plymouth Arrow Pick-ups** '79 thru '88
*1668 **Dakota Pick-up** all models '87 thru '90
234 **Dart & Plymouth Valiant** all 6 cyl models '67 thru '76
*1140 **Daytona & Chrysler Laser** all models '84 thru '89
*545 **Omni & Plymouth Horizon** all models '78 thru '90
*912 **Pick-ups** all full-size models '74 thru '90
*349 **Vans – Dodge & Plymouth** V8 & 6 cyl models '71 thru '89

FIAT
080 **124 Sedan & Wagon** all ohv & dohc models '66 thru '75
094 **124 Sport Coupe & Spider** '68 thru '78
310 **131 & Brava** all models '75 thru '81
479 **Strada** all models '79 thru '82
273 **X1/9** all models '74 thru '80

FORD
*1476 **Aerostar Mini-vans** all models '86 thru '90
788 **Bronco and Pick-ups** '73 thru '79
*880 **Bronco and Pick-ups** '80 thru '90
014 **Cortina MK II** all models except Lotus '66 thru '70
295 **Cortina MK III** 1600 & 2000 ohc '70 thru '76
268 **Courier Pick-up** all models '72 thru '82
780 **Escort & Mercury Lynx** all models '81 thru '90
560 **Fairmont & Mercury Zephyr** all in-line & V8 models '78 thru '83
334 **Fiesta** all models '77 thru '80
754 **Ford & Mercury Full-size,** Ford LTD & Mercury Marquis ('75 thru '82); Ford Custom 500, Country Squire, Crown Victoria & Mercury Colony Park ('75 thru '87); Ford LTD Crown Victoria & Mercury Gran Marquis ('83 thru '87)
359 **Granada & Mercury Monarch** all in-line, 6 cyl & V8 models '75 thru '80
773 **Ford & Mercury Mid-size,** Ford Thunderbird & Mercury Cougar ('75 thru '82); Ford LTD & Mercury Marquis ('83 thru '86); Ford Torino, Gran Torino, Elite, Ranchero pick-up, LTD II, Mercury Montego, Comet, XR-7 & Lincoln Versailles ('75 thru '86)
*654 **Mustang & Mercury Capri** all models including Turbo '79 thru '90
357 **Mustang V8** all models '64-1/2 thru '73
231 **Mustang II** all 4 cyl, V6 & V8 models '74 thru '78
204 **Pinto** all models '70 thru '74
649 **Pinto & Mercury Bobcat** all models '75 thru '80
*1026 **Ranger & Bronco II** all gasoline models '83 thru '89
*1421 **Taurus & Mercury Sable** '86 thru '90
*1418 **Tempo & Mercury Topaz** all gasoline models '84 thru '89
1338 **Thunderbird & Mercury Cougar/XR7** '83 thru '88
*1725 **Thunderbird & Mercury Cougar** '89 and '90
*344 **Vans** all V8 Econoline models '69 thru '90

GENERAL MOTORS
*829 **A-Cars** – Chevrolet Celebrity, Buick Century, Pontiac 6000 & Oldsmobile Cutlass Ciera all models '82 thru '89
*766 **J-Cars** – Chevrolet Cavalier, Pontiac J-2000, Oldsmobile Firenza, Buick Skyhawk & Cadillac Cimarron all models '82 thru '90
*1420 **N-Cars** – Buick Somerset '85 thru '87; Pontiac Grand Am and Oldsmobile Calais '85 thru '90; Buick Skylark '86 thru '90
*1671 **GM: Buick** Regal, **Chevrolet** Lumina, **Oldsmobile** Cutlass Supreme, **Pontiac** Grand Prix, all front wheel drive models '88 thru '90

GEO
Metro – *see CHEVROLET Sprint (1727)*
Tracker – *see SUZUKI Samurai (1626)*
Prizm – *see CHEVROLET Nova (1642)*

GMC
Safari – *see CHEVROLET ASTRO (1477)*
Vans & Pick-ups – *see CHEVROLET (420, 831, 345, 1664)*

(continued on next page)

---

* Listings shown with an asterisk (*) indicate model coverage as of this printing. These titles will be periodically updated to include later model years — consult your Haynes dealer for more information.

Haynes Publications Inc., P.O. Box 978, Newbury Park, CA 91320 ● (818) 889-5400 ● (805) 498-6703

HAYNES AUTOMOTIVE MANUALS
(continued from previous page)

NOTE: New manuals are added to this list on a periodic basis. If you do not see a listing for your vehicle, consult your local Haynes dealer for the latest product information.

HONDA
- 138   **360, 600 & Z** Coupe all models '67 thru '75
- 351   **Accord CVCC** all models '76 thru '83
- *1221   **Accord** all models '84 thru '89
- 160   **Civic 1200** all models '73 thru '79
- 633   **Civic 1300 & 1500 CVCC** all models '80 thru '83
- 297   **Civic 1500 CVCC** all models '75 thru '79
- *1227   **Civic** all models '84 thru '90
- *601   **Prelude CVCC** all models '79 thru '89

HYUNDAI
- *1552   **Excel** all models '86 thru '89

ISUZU
- *1641   **Trooper & Pick-up**, all gasoline models '81 thru '90

JAGUAR
- 098   **MK I & II**, 240 & 340 Sedans '55 thru '69
- *242   **XJ6** all 6 cyl models '68 thru '86
- *478   **XJ12 & XJS** all 12 cyl models '72 thru '85
- 140   **XK-E** 3.8 & 4.2 all 6 cyl models '61 thru '72

JEEP
- *1553   **Cherokee, Comanche & Wagoneer Limited** all models '84 thru '89
- 412   **CJ** all models '49 thru '86

LADA
- *413   **1200, 1300. 1500 & 1600** all models including Riva '74 thru '86

LAND ROVER
- 314   **Series II, IIA, & III** all 4 cyl gasoline models '58 thru '86
- 529   **Diesel** all models '58 thru '80

MAZDA
- 648   **626** Sedan & Coupe (rear wheel drive) all models '79 thru '82
- *1082   **626 & MX-6 (front wheel drive)** all models '83 thru '90
- *267   **B1600, B1800 & B2000 Pick-ups** '72 thru '90
- 370   **GLC Hatchback (rear wheel drive)** all models '77 thru '83
- 757   **GLC (front wheel drive)** all models '81 thru '86
- 109   **RX2** all models '71 thru '75
- 096   **RX3** all models '72 thru '76
- 460   **RX-7** all models '79 thru '85
- *1419   **RX-7** all models '86 thru '89

MERCEDES-BENZ
- *1643   **190 Series** all four-cylinder gasoline models, '84 thru '88
- 346   **230, 250 & 280** Sedan, Coupe & Roadster all 6 cyl sohc models '68 thru '72
- 983   **280 123 Series** all gasoline models '77 thru '81
- 698   **350 & 450** Sedan, Coupe & Roadster all models '71 thru '80
- 697   **Diesel 123 Series** 200D, 220D, 240D, 240TD, 300D, 300CD, 300TD, 4- & 5-cyl incl. Turbo '76 thru '85

MERCURY
See FORD Listing

MG
- 475   **MGA** all models '56 thru '62
- 111   **MGB** Roadster & GT Coupe all models '62 thru '80
- 265   **MG Midget & Austin Healey Sprite** Roadster '58 thru '80

MITSUBISHI
- *1669   **Cordia, Tredia, Galant, Precis & Mirage** '83 thru '90
       Pick-up – *see Dodge D-50 (556)*

MORRIS
- 074   **(Austin) Marina 1.8** all models '71 thru '80
- 024   **Minor 1000** sedan & wagon '56 thru '71

NISSAN
- 1137   **300ZX** all Turbo & non-Turbo models '84 thru '89
- *1341   **Maxima** all models '85 thru '89
- *771   **Pick-ups/Pathfinder** gas models '80 thru '88
- *876   **Pulsar** all models '83 thru '86
- *982   **Sentra** all models '82 thru '90
- *981   **Stanza** all models '82 thru '90

OLDSMOBILE
-      **Custom Cruiser** – *see BUICK Full-size (1551)*
- 658   **Cutlass** all standard gasoline V6 & V8 models '74 thru '88
-      **Cutlass Ciera** – *see GENERAL MOTORS A-Cars (829)*
-      **Cutlass Supreme** – *see GENERAL MOTORS (1671)*
-      **Firenza** – *see GENERAL MOTORS J-Cars (766)*
-      **Ninety-eight** – *see BUICK Full-size (1551)*
-      **Omega** – *see PONTIAC Phoenix & Omega (551)*

PEUGEOT
- 161   **504** all gasoline models '68 thru '79
- 663   **504** all diesel models '74 thru '83

PLYMOUTH
- 425   **Arrow** all models '76 thru '80
       For all other PLYMOUTH titles, see DODGE listing.

PONTIAC
-      **T1000** – *see CHEVROLET Chevette (449)*
-      **J-2000** – *see GENERAL MOTORS J-Cars (766)*
-      **6000** – *see GENERAL MOTORS A-Cars (829)*
- 1232   **Fiero** all models '84 thru '88
- 555   **Firebird** all V8 models except Turbo '70 thru '81
- *867   **Firebird** all models '82 thru '89
-      **Full-size Rear Wheel Drive** – *see Buick, Oldsmobile, Pontiac Full-size (1551)*
-      **Grand Prix** – *see GENERAL MOTORS (1671)*
- 551   **Phoenix & Oldsmobile Omega** all X-car models '80 thru '84

PORSCHE
- *264   **911** all Coupe & Targa models except Turbo & Carrera 4 '65 thru '89
- 239   **914** all 4 cyl models '69 thru '76
- 397   **924** all models including Turbo '76 thru '82
- *1027   **944** all models including Turbo '83 thru '89

RENAULT
- 141   **5 Le Car** all models '76 thru '83
- 079   **8 & 10** all models with 58.4 cu in engines '62 thru '72
- 097   **12 Saloon & Estate** all models 1289 cc engines '70 thru '80
- 768   **15 & 17** all models '73 thru '79
- 081   **16** all models 89.7 cu in & 95.5 cu in engines '65 thru '72
- 598   **18i & Sportwagon** all models '81 thru '86
       Alliance & Encore – *see AMC (934)*
- 984   **Fuego** all models '82 thru '85

ROVER
- 085   **3500 & 3500S Sedan** 215 cu in engines '68 thru '76
- *365   **3500 SDI V8** all models '76 thru '85

SAAB
- 198   **95 & 96** V4 all models '66 thru '75
- 247   **99** all models including Turbo '69 thru '80
- *980   **900** all models including Turbo '79 thru '88

SUBARU
- 237   **1100, 1300, 1400 & 1600** all models '71 thru '79
- *681   **1600 & 1800** 2WD & 4WD all models '80 thru '89

SUZUKI
- *1626   **Samurai/Sidekick and Geo Tracker** all models '86 thru '89

TOYOTA
- *1023   **Camry** all models '83 thru '90
- 150   **Carina Sedan** all models '71 thru '74
- 229   **Celica ST, GT & liftback** all models '71 thru '77
- 437   **Celica** all models '78 thru '81
- *935   **Celica** all models except front-wheel drive and Supra '82 thru '85
- 680   **Celica Supra** all models '79 thru '81
- 1139   **Celica Supra** all in-line 6-cylinder models '82 thru '86
- 361   **Corolla** all models '75 thru '79
- 961   **Corolla** all models (rear wheel drive) '80 thru '87
- *1025   **Corolla** all models (front wheel drive) '84 thru '91
- *636   **Corolla Tercel** all models '80 thru '82
- 230   **Corona & MK II** all 4 cyl sohc models '69 thru '74
- 360   **Corona** all models '74 thru '82
- *532   **Cressida** all models '78 thru '82
- 313   **Land Cruiser** all models '68 thru '82
- 200   **MK II** all 6 cyl models '72 thru '76
- *1339   **MR2** all models '85 thru '87
- 304   **Pick-up** all models '69 thru '78
- *656   **Pick-up** all models '79 thru '90

TRIUMPH
- 112   **GT6 & Vitesse** all models '62 thru '74
- 113   **Spitfire** all models '62 thru '81
- 028   **TR2, 3, 3A, & 4A** Roadsters '52 thru '67
- 031   **TR250 & 6** Roadsters '67 thru '76
- 322   **TR7** all models '75 thru '81

VW
- 091   **411 & 412** all 103 cu in models '68 thru '73
- 159   **Beetle & Karmann Ghia** all models '54 thru '79
- 238   **Dasher** all gasoline models '74 thru '81
- *884   **Rabbit, Jetta, Scirocco, & Pick-up** all gasoline models '74 thru '89 & **Convertible** '80 thru '89
- 451   **Rabbit, Jetta & Pick-up** all diesel models '77 thru '84
- 082   **Transporter 1600** all models '68 thru '79
- 226   **Transporter 1700, 1800 & 2000** all models '72 thru '79
- 084   **Type 3 1500 & 1600** all models '63 thru '73
- 1029   **Vanagon** all air-cooled models '80 thru '83

VOLVO
- 203   **120, 130 Series & 1800 Sports** '61 thru '73
- 129   **140 Series** all models '66 thru '74
- 244   **164** all models '68 thru '75
- *270   **240 Series** all models '74 thru '90
- 400   **260 Series** all models '75 thru '82
- *1550   **740 & 760 Series** all models '82 thru '88

SPECIAL MANUALS
- 1479   **Automotive Body Repair & Painting Manual**
- 1654   **Automotive Electrical Manual**
- 1480   **Automotive Heating & Air Conditioning Manual**
- 1763   **Ford Engine Overhaul Manual**
- 482   **Fuel Injection Manual**
- 1666   **Small Engine Repair Manual**
- 299   **SU Carburetors** thru '88
- 393   **Weber Carburetors** thru '79
- 300   **Zenith/Stromberg CD Carburetors** thru '76

See your dealer for other available titles

4-1-91

---

* Listings shown with an asterisk (*) indicate model coverage as of this printing. These titles will be periodically updated to include later model years — consult your Haynes dealer for more information.

Over 100 Haynes motorcycle manuals also available

Haynes Publications Inc., P.O. Box 978, Newbury Park, CA 91320 ● (818) 889-5400 ● (805) 498-6703

Printed by
J H Haynes & Co Ltd
Sparkford Nr Yeovil
Somerset BA22 7JJ England